Internа̲...

Third edition

Providing an introduction to and detailed examination of substantive, enforcement and procedural aspects of international criminal law, this book's examination of international and transnational crimes under treaty and customary law has been fully updated and revised.

The book explores the discipline of international criminal law from the perspective of domestic tribunals engaged with transnational/international offences, cross-border cooperation in criminal matters with particular emphasis on recent EU initiatives, as well as the practice of the Security Council-based tribunals for Yugoslavia and Rwanda, the International Criminal Court and other hybrid tribunals, such as those for Cambodia, Sierra Leone, Lockerbie and truth commissions. The authors analyse in detail substantive crimes, such as terrorism, offences against the person, criminal law of the sea, jurisdiction and immunities amongst a variety of other topics.

In order to reflect developments in the field of international and transnational criminal law, the third edition contains new chapters on:

- Various forms of liability and participation in international crime
- War crimes
- Crimes against humanity
- Genocide
- Abduction and extraordinary rendition.

Topics introduced in the first and second editions have been expanded upon, including enforced disappearances, transnational criminal offences, police co-operation and mutual legal assistance mechanisms.

This book continues to draw together a wide variety of different topics that are not usually found under the same cover to provide a book that gives both students and practitioners a sound theoretical and practical understanding of international and transnational criminal law. It is an ideal text for undergraduate and postgraduate students of law or international relations, practitioners and those interested in gaining an insight into international and transnational criminal law.

Ilias Bantekas is Professor of International Law and Deputy Head of the Law School at Brunel University. He has published widely in leading international journals. Books authored or edited by him include: *International and European Financial Criminal*

Law (Butterworths, 2006) and *Principles of Direct and Superior Responsibility in International Humanitarian Law* (Manchester University Press, 2002).

Susan Nash is Professor of Law at the University of Westminster and Head of Department of Postgraduate Legal Studies. She is a barrister and a door tenant in Tooks Chambers. Her research interests include criminal procedure and evidence, human rights and mutual legal assistance. She has published widely in both national and international journals and is the co-author of several books including *The Cartel Offence* (Hart, 2004) and *Essential Human Rights Cases* (Jordans, 2002).

International Criminal Law

Third edition

Ilias Bantekas and Susan Nash

Routledge·Cavendish
Taylor & Francis Group
LONDON AND NEW YORK

First published 2007
by Routledge-Cavendish
2 Park Square, Milton Park, Abingdon, Oxon OX14 4RN, UK

Simultaneously published in the USA and Canada
by Routledge-Cavendish
270 Madison Ave, New York, NY 10016

*Routledge-Cavendish is an imprint of the Taylor & Francis Group, an
informa business*

© 2001, 2007 Ilias Bantekas and Susan Nash

Previous editions published by Cavendish Publishing Limited

First edition   2001
Second edition   2003

Typeset in Times and Gill Sans by
RefineCatch Limited, Bungay, Suffolk
Printed and bound in Great Britain by
MPG Books Ltd, Bodmin, Cornwall

British Library Cataloguing in Publication Data
A catalogue record for this book is available from the British Library

Library of Congress Cataloging-in-Publication Data
A catalog record for this book has been requested

ISBN10: 0–415–41845–3
ISBN13: 978–0–415–41845–4

Contents – Summary

1 Theory of International Criminal Law 1

2 Principles of Liability and Participation in International Criminal Law 21

3 Defences in International Criminal Law 51

4 State Jurisdiction and Immunities 71

5 War Crimes and Grave Breaches 113

6 Crimes Against Humanity 125

7 Genocide 139

8 Offences Against the Person 151

9 International Criminal Law of the Sea 173

10 Terrorism 195

11 Transnational Offences 1 233

12 Transnational Offences 2 265

13 Extradition 293

14 Abduction 343

15 Mutual Legal Assistance 357

16 Mutual Legal Assistance: National Perspectives 387

17 International Police Co-operation 407

18 Evidence before the Ad Hoc Tribunals 437

19 Nuremberg, Tokyo and the Birth of Modern
International Criminal Law 495

20 The International Criminal Tribunals for Yugoslavia
and Rwanda 513

21 The Permanent International Criminal Court 535

22 Internationalised Domestic Criminal Tribunals 557

Contents

Preface		xiii
Table of cases		xv
Table of legislation		xxvii

1 Theory of International Criminal Law   **1**

  1.1   *Introduction 1*
  1.2   *Sources of International Law and Individual Legal Personality 2*
  1.3   *The International Criminalisation Process 6*
  1.4   *Enforcement of International Criminal Law 10*
  1.5   *State 'Criminality' 15*
  1.6   *International Criminal Law and Human Rights 18*

2 Principles of Liability and Participation in International Criminal Law   **21**

  2.1   *Aiding and Abetting 21*
  2.2   *Ordering 24*
  2.3   *Planning/Preparation 26*
  2.4   *Instigation 28*
  2.5   *Joint Criminal Enterprise 29*
  2.6   *Conspiracy 34*
  2.7   *Commission Through Another Person 36*
  2.8   *Command/Superior Responsibility 37*
  2.9   *International Corporate Criminal Liability 47*

3 Defences in International Criminal Law   **51**

  3.1   *Theoretical Underpinnings of Criminal Defences 51*
  3.2   *Superior Orders 56*

3.3   *Duress and Necessity 61*
3.4   *Self-defence 65*
3.5   *Intoxication 67*
3.6   *Mistake of Fact or Mistake of Law 68*
3.7   *Mental Incapacity 69*

4   State Jurisdiction and Immunities   **71**

4.1   *Criminal Jurisdiction: An Introduction 71*
4.2   *Territorial Jurisdiction 73*
4.3   *The Active Personality Principle 79*
4.4   *The Passive Personality Principle 81*
4.5   *The Protective Principle 83*
4.6   *Universal Jurisdiction 85*
4.7   Aut Dedere Aut Judicare *Principle 91*
4.8   *Jurisdiction with Respect to Crimes against Civil Aviation 92*
4.9   *International Criminal Jurisdiction 93*
4.10 *Immunities from Criminal Jurisdiction 96*
4.11 *Immunity under Domestic Law and* Jus Cogens *Norms 103*
4.12 *Foreign and Multinational Armed Forces Abroad 106*
4.13 *Diplomatic and Consular Immunities 108*
4.14 *Immunity from International Criminal Jurisdiction 110*

5   War Crimes and Grave Breaches   **113**

5.1   *Grave Breaches of the 1949 Geneva Conventions 113*
5.2   *Classification of Armed Conflicts 115*
5.3   *Types of International Armed Conflict War Crimes 117*
5.4   *Violations of the Laws or Customs of War in Internal Conflicts 120*
5.5   *Specific Internal Armed Conflict War Crimes 123*

6   Crimes Against Humanity   **125**

6.1   *Origins of the Concept 125*
6.2   *The Fundamental Elements of the Offence 127*
6.3   *Crimes Against Humanity in the ICC Statute 134*

7   Genocide   **139**

7.1   *Historical Origins and Legal Status 139*
7.2   *Destruction of the Group 'in Whole or in Part' 140*

7.3   The Specific Intent (Dolus Specialis) *Required for Genocide 143*
7.4   Membership of the Targeted Group 145

8   Offences Against the Person   151

8.1   Introduction 151
8.2   Slavery and Related Practices 151
8.3   Torture as a Crime under International Law 161
8.4   Apartheid 166
8.5   Enforced or Involuntary Disappearances 168

9   International Criminal Law of the Sea   173

9.1   Introduction: The Law of the Sea 173
9.2   Piracy Jure Gentium *174*
9.3   Offences Against Submarine Cables and Pipelines 185
9.4   Unauthorised Broadcasting from the High Seas 188
9.5   The Right of Hot Pursuit 189

10   Terrorism   195

10.1   Introduction 195
10.2   The Thematic Approach in International Law 197
10.3   The Specialised Anti-Terrorist Conventions 199
10.4   State-sponsored Terrorism 218
10.5   Terrorism and National Liberation Movements 222
10.6   Organised Crime and its Relation to Terrorism 225
10.7   Terrorist Acts as Political Offences 227
10.8   Terrorism and Human Rights 229

11   Transnational Offences   233

11.1   Transnational Organised Crime 233
11.2   Drug Trafficking 239
11.3   Money Laundering 247

12   Other Transnational Offences   265

12.1   Cybercrime 265
12.2   Bribery of Foreign Public Officials 280
12.3   International Postal Offences 285
12.4   Circulation and Trafficking in Obscene Publications 288

13   Extradition   293

13.1   Introduction 293
13.2   The Extradition Process: General Principles 294
13.3   International Initiatives 310
13.4   The UK Extradition Act 2003 325
13.5   Extradition and International Human Rights Instruments 326
13.6   Extradition and the Case of Senator Pinochet 336

14   Abduction   343

14.1   Introduction 343
14.2   The Male Captus, Bene Detentus *Rule 343*
14.3   Approach Taken by Courts in the US 345
*14.4   Approach Taken by the European Court of
          Human Rights 347*
14.5   The Doctrine of Abuse of Process 348
14.6   Collusion by Law Enforcement Agencies 349
14.7   Seriousness of the Crime 351
14.8   Extraordinary Rendition 352

15   Mutual Legal Assistance   357

15.1   Introduction 357
15.2   UN Initiatives 359
*15.3   1959 European Convention on Mutual Assistance in
          Criminal Matters 360*
15.4   EU Initiatives 362
15.5   Mutual Recognition Programme 376

16   Mutual Legal Assistance: National Perspectives   387

16.1   Crime (International Co-operation) Act 2003 387
16.2   The Use of Evidence Obtained Abroad 390
16.3   Admissibility of Foreign Evidence: Fair Trial Issues 398
*16.4   Evidence Obtained in Breach of International Human
          Rights Standards 399*
16.5   Failure to Use Mutual Legal Assistance Provisions 401
16.6   Mutual Legal Assistance Treaties and Individual Rights 403
16.7   Informal Methods of Mutual Assistance 405

17 International Police Co-operation — 407

17.1 *Introduction 407*
17.2 *Interpol 407*
17.3 *EU Initiatives 414*

18 Evidence before the Ad Hoc Tribunals by Caroline Buisman — 437

18.1 *Introduction 437*
18.2 *General Evidentiary Principles 440*
18.3 *Admissibility 444*
18.4 *Documentary Evidence 457*
18.5 *Hearsay Evidence 460*
18.6 *Deposition Evidence 463*
18.7 *Character Evidence 465*
18.8 *Investigator's Report 468*
18.9 *Expert Evidence 471*
18.10 *Exclusion of Improperly Obtained Evidence 476*
18.11 *Determination of Weight of Evidence 479*

19 Nuremberg, Tokyo and the Birth of Modern International Criminal Law — 495

19.1 *Introduction 495*
19.2 *Efforts to Try International Crimes Prior to the Second World War 495*
19.3 *The Background to the Establishment of the International Military Tribunals 497*
19.4 *The International Military Tribunal for the Far East 507*
19.5 *The International Law Commission's Role in the Post-Nuremberg Era 509*

20 The International Criminal Tribunals for Yugoslavia and Rwanda — 513

20.1 *Introduction 513*
20.2 *Formative Years of the Ad Hoc Tribunals 517*
20.3 *Enforcement Capacity of the Tribunals 528*
20.4 *Rights of the Accused 531*

21 The Permanent International Criminal Court — 535

21.1 *The Historical Origins of the International Criminal Court 535*
21.2 *Jurisdiction and Admissibility 538*

21.3   Subject Matter Jurisdiction 544

21.4   General Principles of Criminal Law 547

21.5   International Cooperation and Judicial Assistance 549

21.6   Reservations and Amendments to the Statute 552

21.7   Reparation to Victims 554

22   Internationalised Domestic Criminal Tribunals   **557**

22.1   Introduction 557

22.2   The Sierra Leone Special Court 558

22.3   The East Timor Special Panels 564

22.4   UNMIK and the Kosovar Judicial System 568

22.5   The Cambodian Extraordinary Chambers 570

22.6   The Iraqi Special Tribunal for Crimes Against Humanity 573

22.7   The Lockerbie Trial 577

22.8   National Truth Commissions and Amnesties 580

Index   585

Preface

Although the third edition of this book has been significantly expanded, our aim remains to provide a book that gives both students and practitioners a sound theoretical and practical understanding of international and transnational criminal law. It explores and links together a range of topics which until recently could only be found in separate texts. Until the 1990s, international criminal law was not generally considered to be a discrete topic for inclusion in either the undergraduate or postgraduate law curricula. However, the need to study certain particularities of the international criminal justice process has been highlighted by lawyers and non-lawyers working for intergovernmental organisations and academic institutions not only in the field of human rights and criminal justice, but also in diverse fields, such as commerce, energy and the environment. Furthermore, the continued growth in both the volume and diversity of transnational crime, and the increased mobility of suspects and witnesses, continues to result in international criminal law and procedure assuming critical importance for domestic lawyers and law enforcement agencies. In order to reflect recent developments we have added chapters on a greater range of transnational offences and abduction, and have expanded the chapters dealing with mutual legal assistance mechanisms and international police co-operation. We have also included new chapters on general principles of criminal liability and participation in crime, war crimes, genocide and crimes against humanity. We have also developed several topics introduced in the first two editions, including the work of hybrid tribunals, truth commissions, international law of the sea, transnational criminal offences and mutual legal assistance mechanisms. While the limitations of this broad categorisation in the horizontal law-making framework of international law are self-evident, the gradual evolution of international criminal justice into a coherent system cannot be underestimated. As demonstrated throughout the book, the international criminal process is shaped not only by traditional participants, but also by non-traditional actors, including organisations such as the Organisation for Economic Co-operation and Development, the European Union, as well as by non-state actors, such as private financial institutions in the fields of money laundering and terrorist financing.

In the preparation of this edition the authors are both jointly responsible for the content and any errors are ours alone. Ilias Bantekas is primarily responsible for chapters 1–10 and 19–21 and Susan Nash is responsible for chapters 13–17. Chapters 11 and 12 are a joint effort. While we have made changes to material included in the first edition, where it has been retained we remain grateful to Mark Mackarel for his work on the first edition, and to Caroline Buisman for revising her chapter on evidence before the ad hoc tribunals. We would also like to express our thanks to Dr Adam Lazowski for his helpful comments with regard to some EU developments. In the preparation of this new edition the production team at Routledge-Cavendish have done an excellent job in dealing with a significant number of changes, and we are grateful to them for their patience and professionalism.

The date of completion of this edition was 26 December 2006.

Ilias Bantekas, Susan Nash
January 2007

Table of cases

A and others v Secretary of State for the Home Department
[2004] UKHL 56; [2005] UKHL 71; [2005] 3 WLR 1249 . . . . 332, 400
A v UK (1998) 27 EHRR 112 165
Abbott v R [1977] AC 755 62
AG of the Government of Israel v Eichmann (1961) 36 ILR 5;
(1962) 36 ILR 277 . . . . 84, 90, 147, 344–5
AG's Reference (No 5 of 1980) [1985] 3 All ER 816 290
Ahlstrom v Commission (Wood Pulp case) [1988] 4 CMLR 901 76
Ahmad v Wigen 910 F 2d 1063 (1990) 309
Ahmed v Austria (1996) 24 EHRR 278 . . . . 328, 333
Al-Adsani v UK (2001) 34 EHRR 11 104
Alejandre v Republic of Cuba 996 F Supp 1239 (1997) 221
Al-Fawwaz v Governor of Brixton Prison and Another [2001] UKHL 69 . . . 297, 299
Allan v UK App No 48539/99 352
Al-Meghrahi v HM Advocate 580
Alves v DPP [1992] 4 All ER 787 299
Ambrose Light (1885) 25 Fed 408 177–8
AMCO v Republic of Indonesia (1990) 89 ILR 366 4
Anglo-Norwegian Fisheries (UK v Norway) (1951) ICJ Reports 116 72
The Antelope 23 US 66 (1825) 152
Araunah case (1888) 193, 194
Argentina v de Blake 507 US 1017 161
Arizona v Willoughby (1995) 114 ILR 586 74
Arton, Re [1896] 1 QB 108 295
Athens Maritime Enterprises Corp v Hellenic Mutual War Risks Association
Ltd [1983] 1 All ER 590 178
Atkinson v US Government [1971] AC 197 307
Atta, Re Extradition of 104 ILR 52 . . . . 82, 228
Austrian Universal Jurisdiction case 28 ILR 341 89–90
Aydin v Turkey (1998) 25 EHRR 251 164
Azanian Peoples Organisation v President of the Republic of South Africa
91 AJIL (1997) 360; (1996) 4 SA 671 . . . . 105, 584

Baader-Meinhof Group Terrorist case (1977) 74 ILR 493 228
Banco Nacional de Cuba v Sabbatino 376 US 398 (1964) 102
Bankovic and others v Belgium and Sixteen Others ECHR App 52207/99 73
Barayagwiza v Prosecutor 98–34-S 52
Beckford v R [1988] AC 130 69

Belgium v Spain (Barcelona Traction case) (1970) ICJR 3 . . . . .11, 139, 153
Bennett, Petitioner [1994] SCCR 902 351
Bennett v Horseferry Road Magistrates' Court [1993] 3 All ER 138 . . . . .347, 348–51
Berrehab v Netherlands (1988) 11 EHRR 322 333
Blackmer v USA 284 US 421 (1932) 79
Blockburger v USA 52 S Ct 180 (1932) 307
Bolivia v Indemnity Mutual Marine Insurance Co Ltd [1909] 1 KB 785 177
Border Guards Prosecution case 100 ILR 364 102
Bosnia v Federal Republic of Yugoslavia (1993) ICJ Reports 3 140
Bouzari v Islamic Republic of Iran (2004) 124 ILR 427 .105
Bozano v France (1986) 9 EHRR 297 301
Brugge (Klaus) Case No C-385/01 419
Brulay v USA 383 F 2d 345 (1967) 397
Buck v AG [1965] Ch 745; 42 ILR 11 97
Burgos v Urugua (1981) HRC 400

C v Australia HRC Com No 900/1999 162
Calfa (Donatella), Criminal Proceedings against Case C-348/96
    [1999] ECR I-11 420
Canada v USA (I'm Alone case) (1935) III UNRIAA 1609 191
Castioni, Re [1891] 1 QB 149 . . . . .227–8, 303
Chahal v UK (1996) ECHR SerA 22; (1996) 23 EHRR 413 . . . . .162, 331
Chaudhary v State of Madhya Pradesh (1948) 3 SCC 243 154
Chinoy v UK App No 15199/89 391
Chow Hung Ching v R (1948) 77 CLR 449; 15 AD 47 106
Chung Chi Cheung v R [1939] AC 160 78
Cicippio v Islamic Republic of Iran 18 F Supp 2d 62 (1998) 221
Commission v Council Case C-176/03 ECR I-7879 . . . . .418, 420
Commission v Council Case C-444/05 422
Compania Naviera Vascogando v SS Cristina [1938] AC 485 73
Conegate Ltd v HM Customs and Excise [1986] ECR 1007 289
Connelly v Director of Public Prosecutions [1964] AC 1254 348
Costello-Roberts v UK (1993) 19 EHRR 112 165
The Creole (1853) 152, 179
Croissant, Re (1978) 74 ILR 505 . . . . .208, 228
Cruz Varas v Sweden (1991) 14 EHRR 1 328
Cuba Sumbarine Co Ltd Claim (1923–24) 2 AD 419 187
Cutting case 81

D v UK (1997) 24 EHRR 423 332
Delta v France 460
Demjanjuk, In re 457 US 1016 (1986) 90
Democratic Republic of Congo v Belgium
    (Belgian Arrest Warrant case) 87–8, 97, 100, 101, 105
Denmark, Norway, Sweden and Netherlands v Greece (1969)
    12 ECHR Yearbook 134 14
The Diana (1813) 165 ER 1245 152
Dickinson v Del Solar [1930] 1 KB 376 . . . . .100, 108
Doe v Unocal 963 F Supp 880 (1997) 103, 159
Dole v New England Mutual Marine Insurance Co (1864) 7 F Cas 838 177
Dombo Beheer BV v Netherlands (1993) 18 EHRR 213 .399
Dover Castle case 16 AJIL (1921) 704 . . . . .57, 496

DPP v Doot [1973] 1 All ER 940 76–7
DPP v P [1991] 2 AC 447 465
Driver, Ex P [1986] QB 95 344
Dunhill (Alfred) of London Inc v Republic of Cuba 425 US 682 (1976) 102
Dunlayici, Ex p (1996) *The Times* 22 August 303

Eastern Extension, Australasia and China Telegraph Co Ltd Claims
    (1923–24) 2 AD 415 187
Eck and others, Re (The Peleus) (1945) 13 AD 248 59
Empson v Smith [1966] 1 QB 426 108
Engelke v Musmann [1928] AC 433 108
Estate of Marcos, Re 25 F 3d 1745 169

FDR v Denmark; FDR v Netherlands (North Sea Shelf cases) (1969) ICJR 3 3
Fédération Nationale de Déportés et Internés Résistants et Patriotes and
    Others v Barbie 78 ILR 125 ....85, 127
Flatow v Islamic Republic of Iran 999 F Supp 1 (1998) 221
Folkerts v Prosecutor (1978) 74 ILR 498 228
Ford v USA 273 US 593 (1927) 75
Former Syrian Ambassador to the German Democratic Republic case (1996)
    115 ILR 597 ....78–9, 108
Forti v Suarez-Mason 672 F Supp 1531 (1987) 105, 169
The Fortuna (1811) 165 ER 1240 152
France v Turkey (Lotus case) (1927) PCIJ Reports Ser A No 10 ...72, 75, 78, 81, 176
Frisbie v Collins 342 US 519 (1952); L ED 541 345
Funke v France (1993) 16 EHRR 297 399

Galdeano case (1984) 111 ILR 505 228
Germany v Poland (1928) PCIJ Reports SerA 15 145
Gherebi v Rumsfeld (2003) 225
Gil v Canada (1994) 107 ILR 168 228
Giles v Tumminello 38 ILR 120 ....84, 90
Gozutok (Huseyin) Case No C-187/01 419
Grace and Ruby 283 F 475 (1922) 193
Greek case (1969) ECHR Yearbook 134 163
Gulay Asliturk v Government of Turkey [2002] EWHC 559 293
Gutierez, Re [1957] 24 ILR 265 80

Hajrizi and Others v Yugoslavia 165
Hamdan v Rumsfeld 548 US (2006) 225
Hamdi v Rumsfeld 542 US 507 (2004) 224, 225
Handyside case (1976) 58 ILR 150 289
Hartford Fire Insurance Co v California 113 S Ct 2891 (1993) 76
Hatch v Baez 7 Hun 596 (1876) 102
Healy, Ex P [1983] 1 WLR 108 344
Hilal v UK (2001) 33 EHRR 2 ....306, 330, 333
Hirsch v State of Israel and State of Germany 113 ILR 543 100
HLR v France (1997) 26 EHRR 29 ....165, 332–3
HM Advocate v McKay (1961) SLT 176 394–5
Honecker Prosecution case 100 ILR 393 104
Honorary Consul of X v Austria 86 ILR 553 109
Hoogmans v High Authority [1962] ECR 253 44

I Congresso del Partido [1981] 2 All ER 1064 99
ICI v Commission (Dyestuff case) [1972] ECR 619 76
IG Farben case 10 LRTWC 1 ....34, 48
Iran v USA (1989) 203
Ireland v UK (1978) 2 EHRR 25; (1978) ECHR SerA 25 .... 163, 164, 230, 333, 516
Ismail, Re [1999] AC 320 295

Jabari v Turkey (2000) 9 BHRC 1 330
Javar and Munyeshyaka, Re 83 AJIL (1999) 525 90–1
Jhirad v Ferrandina 536 f 2d 478 (1976) 309
Jimenez v Aristeguieta 311 F 2d 547 (1962) 102–3
Johnson v Jamaica (1997) 41 HRR 21 400
Jones and Others v Kingdom of Saudi Arabia [2006] UKHL 26 ....88, 105
Jorgic case 3 StR 215/98 (1999) 141
Joyce v DPP [1946] AC 347 ....79, 83, 84

Kahan v Pakistan Federation [1951] 2 KB 1003 100
Kanana v Zaire 164
Kasper-Ansermet, Re Request from 132 FRD 622 (1990) 358
Ker v Illinois 119 US 436 (1886) 345
Kindler v Canada (1991) 84 DLR (4th) 438 ....293, 334
Kirkpatrick v Environmental Tectonics 493 US 403 (1990) 102
Kostovski v Netherlands 461
Krupp case 10 LRTWC (1949) 34, 48, 62
Kurt v Turkey 170
Kuwait Airways Corp v Iraqi Airways Co [1995] 1 WLR 1147 97

Lafontant v Aristide (1994) 103 ILR 581 103
Levinge v Director of Custodial Services, Department of Corrective Services
    and Others (1987) 9 NSWLR 546 349
Libman v R (1986) 21 DLR 174 74
Libya v UK; Libya v USA (1992) ICJ Reports 3 114 ....204, 578
Llandovery Castle case 16 AJIL (1922) 708 ....57, 496
Lockerbie case 16, 78, 91–2, 204–5, 220–1, 577–80
Lodhi v Governor of Brixton Prison; Government of the UAE
    [2002] EWHC 2029 349
Lome Amnesty case 584
Le Louis (1817) 2 Dods 213 152
Lovelace v Canada UNHRC (1981) 68 ILR 17 145
Lüdi v Switzerland 460

McAliskey, Re (1997) *The Times* 22 January 308
McBoyle v USA 43 F 2d 273 (1930) 75
McCann v UK (1996) 21 EHRR 97 208
Mackeson, Ex p (1982) 75 Cr App R 24 344
Macleod v AG for New South Wales [1891] AC 455 71
McMullen, Re 668 F 2d 122 (1981) 303–4
McMullen v INS 788 F 2d 91 (1986) 228
Magellan Pirates (1853) 1 A&E 81 177
Makin v AG for New South Wales [1894] AC 57 465
Mamatkulov and Abdurasulovic v Turkey App Nos 468279/99 and 46951/99 330
Mannington Mills Inc v Congoleu Corp 55 F 2d 1287 (1979) 76

Marsoner v USA 40 F 3d 959 (1994) 401–2
Martin (Howard) v Jamaica App No 317/1988 334
Maryland v Craig 497 US 836 (1990) 534
Mejia (Fernando and Raquel) v Peru 164
Meunier, Re [1894] 2 QB 415 303
Miango Muiyo v Zaire 164
Miller v California 413 US 15 (1973) 290
Molyneaux, Ex p [1986] 1 WLR 331 97
Mueller (Emil), Trial of 16 AJIL (1922) 684 496
Murray v UK (1996) 22 EHRR 29 399

The Newton Bay case 36 F 2d 729 (1929) 193
Nicaragua v USA (1986) ICJ Reports 14 . . . . .121, 209, 219
Nielsen, Re [1984] AC 606 . . . . .296, 298, 299
The North case 11 Ex Rep (1905) 141 . . . . .190, 192
Nottebohm case (Guatemala v Liechtenstein) (1955) ICJ Reports 4 . . . . . .72, 79, 145
Nulyarimma v Thompson [1999] FCA 1192; 39 ILM (2000) 20 91
Nunez Chipana v Venezuela Case No 110/1998; CAT/C/21/D/110/1998 335–6
Nyiramasuhuko v Prosecutor 457

Öcalan v Turkey App No 46221/99 347
Oppenheim v Cattermole [1976] AC 249 98
Osborne v Ohio 495 US 103 (1990) 291

Palar v Court of First Instance of Brussels BLD 184051604 323
Parada Cea (Lucio) and Others 583
Pepper v Hart [1993] AC 593 290
Phillips v UK (2002) 11 BHRC 280 261
Pinochet, Re 93 AJIL (1999) 690; 93 AJIL (1999) 700 . . . . .85, 90
Piracy Jure Gentium, Re [1934] AC 856 177
Prefecture of Voiota and Others v Federal Republic of Germany
    92 AJIL (1998) 765 97
Propend Finance Pty Ltd and Others v Sing and Others (1998) 111 ILR 611 101
Prosecutor v Akayesu 26, 28, 122, 130–1, 132, 143, 144, 145, 147,
                          148, 149, 443, 444–5, 472, 478, 479, 480, 482,
                          484, 486, 487, 488, 490, 492, 493, 525, 526
Prosecutor v Aleksovski .22, 38, 117, 441, 446, 456, 460, 461,
                          462, 483, 484, 492, 517, 527, 531, 548
Prosecutor v Bagilishema 142, 489
Prosecutor v Bagosora et al 442, 446, 447, 448, 449, 457, 458, 459,
                          463, 464, 467, 468, 472, 473, 476, 478, 479, 484
Prosecutor v Bizimungu et al 470, 472, 473, 481, 491, 492
Prosecutor v Blagojevic and Jokic 443, 458, 492
Prosecutor v Blaskic 21, 22, 24, 25, 26, 27, 28, 38, 43, 47, 96,
                          114, 117, 128, 130, 131, 132, 133, 458,
                          460, 462, 469, 484, 529, 548, 551
Prosecutor v Brdjanin and Talic 22, 24, 27, 28, 33, 439, 441, 442, 445,
                          454, 455, 456, 458, 481, 482, 484
Prosecutor v Delalic et al (Celebici case) 39, 41, 43, 45, 52, 69–70, 129, 163, 439,
                          443, 449, 456, 457, 459, 460, 461, 464,
                          477, 478, 481, 484, 485, 487, 493, 548
Prosecutor v Elastic 461

Prosecutor v Erdemovic 44, 62, 63–4, 531–2, 548
Prosecutor v Furundzija 30, 54, 161, 162, 163, 164, 166, 486, 492, 493, 525,
526, 527, 583
Prosecutor v Gacumbitsi 480
Prosecutor v Galic 26, 28, 448
Prosecutor v Hadzihasanovic & Kubura 458
Prosecutor v Halilovic 37, 43, 443
Prosecutor v Haradinaj et al 442
Prosecutor v Jelisic 131, 134, 143, 144, 146
Prosecutor v Joni Marques and Others (Los Palos case)
(East Timor Special Panels) 567
Prosecutor v Joseph Leki (East Timor Special Panels) 568
Prosecutor v Kajelijeli 480, 533
Prosecutor v Kallon (SLSC) 563
Prosecutor v Kambanda 522
Prosecutor v Kamdzic 525
Prosecutor v Kamuhanda 483
Prosecutor v Kanyabashi 94
Prosecutor v Karadzic and Mladic .18, 131, 143, 518, 520
Prosecutor v Karemera et al 449, 456, 457
Prosecutor v Kayishema and Ruzindana 18, 122, 131, 142, 144, 146, 147,
443, 479, 480, 485, 486, 488, 489, 492
Prosecutor v Kondewa (SLSC) 562
Prosecutor v Kordic and Cerkez 25, 27, 28, 46, 47, 65, 130, 131, 441, 459,
461, 463, 468, 473, 474, 477, 483, 517
Prosecutor v Kovac et al 115
Prosecutor v Kovacevic 473
Prosecutor v Krajisnik 23, 30, 142, 143, 147
Prosecutor v Krnojelac 22, 23, 30, 43, 129, 163, 164,
165, 443, 466, 480, 481, 483, 485
Prosecutor v Krstic 23, 141, 142, 144, 145, 146, 147, 148
Prosecutor v Kunarac, Kovac and Vukovic 128, 129, 130, 131, 132, 133–4, 134,
163, 164, 443, 486, 487, 492, 526, 527, 528
Prosecutor v Kupreskic and others 130, 131, 132, 134, 463, 467
Prosecutor v Kvocka and others 23, 31, 32, 164, 165, 463, 527
Prosecutor v Limaj et al 31, 443, 479, 483, 485, 487, 488, 489, 491
Prosecutor v Martic 447, 472
Prosecutor v Milosevic 94, 446, 447, 462, 470, 482, 483, 492, 520, 529
Prosecutor v Milutinovic et al 33
Prosecutor v Mrksic (Vukovar Hospital) 128, 133
Prosecutor v Muhimana 447
Prosecutor v Musema 35, 36, 147, 442, 445, 456, 457, 458, 459, 462,
480, 481, 482, 487, 488, 489, 490, 492, 493, 525
Prosecutor v Muvunyi 449, 457, 459, 463
Prosecutor v Nahimana et al 35, 448, 457, 472, 484
Prosecutor v Naletilic 483
Prosecutor v Natelic & Martinovic 27, 462, 464–5, 483
Prosecutor v Ndayambaje, Kamyabashi and others 448
Prosecutor v Ndlindliyamana et al 466
Prosecutor v Nikolic 42, 128, 131, 143, 519
Prosecutor v Niyitegeka 36, 464, 465
Prosecutor v Norman et al (SLSC) 561, 563, 582

Prosecutor v Ntagenra and others 446
Prosecutor v Ntagerura 484
Prosecutor v Ntahobali and others 462
Prosecutor v Ntakirutimana 129, 484
Prosecutor v Nyiramasuhuko et al 448, 472, 478
Prosecutor v Plavsic 13
Prosecutor v Ruggiu 149
Prosecutor v Rutaganda 144, 146, 445, 454, 459, 480, 488, 490
Prosecutor v Rwamakuba 449, 462
Prosecutor v Saric 519
Prosecutor v Semanza 23, 463, 480
Prosecutor v Serushago 532
Prosecutor v Sikirica and others 142, 143
Prosecutor v Simba 448, 457, 458, 463, 464, 467, 483
Prosecutor v Simic 22, 483, 484, 487, 530
Prosecutor v Stakic 33, 129, 146, 472
Prosecutor v Strugar 39, 43, 46, 47
Prosecutor v Tadic 3, 9, 29–30, 31, 32, 33, 94, 114, 115, 116, 117, 120, 121,
                      128, 182, 209, 439, 443, 445, 448, 450, 455, 456, 457, 461,
                      462, 467, 479, 480, 481, 483, 492, 515, 516, 519, 527, 531
Prosecutor v Taylor (SLSC) 562
Prosecutor v Todorovic 534
Prosecutor v Vasiljevic 8, 21, 30
Prosecutor v Zigiranyirazo 449
Public Prosecutor v Antoni (1960) 32 ILR 140 80
Public Prosecutor v Ashby 93 AJIL (1999) 219 107
Public Prosecutor v Djajic 92 AJIL (1998) 528 ....90, 141, 519
Public Prosecutor v Grabec 92 AJIL (1998) 78 ....90, 519
Public Prosecutor v SHT 74 ILR 162 ....93, 200
Pupino (Maria), Criminal Proceedings against Case C105/03
    ECR [2005] I-5285 ....258, 417

Quirin, Ex p 317 US 27 (1942) 503

R (Kashanu) v Governor of Brixton Prison [2002] QB 887 326
R (on the application of Abbasi and Another) v FCO Secretary of State and
    Others [2002] EWCA Civ 1598 98
R v Anderson (1868) 11 Cox Crim Cases 198 77
R v Aujla [1998] 2 Cr App R 16 396
R v Benjafield and Rezvi [2001] 3 WLR 75 261
R v Bow Street Metropolitan Stipendiary Magistrates and others
    ex p Pinochet Ugarte (No 1) [1998] 3 WLR 1456 338
R v Bow Street Metropolitan Stipendiary Magistrates and others
    ex p Pinochet Ugarte (No 3) [1999] 2 All ER 97;
    [1999] 2 WLR 827 ....86, 97, 103–4, 105, 106, 298, 336, 338–41
R v Byrne [1960] 3 All ER 1 69
R v Caldwell [1982] AC 341 33
R v Casement [1917] 1 KB 98 79
R v Chalkley [1988] 2 Cr App R 79 477
R v Cloutier [1979] 2 SCR 709; 99 DLR (3d) 577 456
R v Dawson (1696) 13 St Tr 451 176
R v Donyadideh and Others 101 ILR 259 207

R v Dudley and Stephens (1884) 14 QBD 273 64
R v Earl Russell [1901] AC 446 79
R v Finta (1994) 104 ILR 284 . . . . .60, 127
R v G [2004] 1 AC 1034 33
R v Governor of Ashford ex p Postlethwaite [1988] AC 924 294–5
R v Governor of Belmarsh Prison ex p Martin [1995] 1 WLR 412 395–6
R v Governor of Brixton Prison ex p Kolczynski [1955] 1 QB 540 303
R v Governor of Brixton Prison ex p Osman (No 3) [1992] 1 All ER 122 300–1
R v Governor of Brixton Prison ex p Schtraks [1964] AC 556 . . . . .228, 303
R v Governor of Pentonville Prison and Another ex p Lee
   [1993] 3 All ER 504 . . . . .298, 301
R v Governor of Pentonville Prison ex p Cheng [1973] AC 931 303
R v Governor of Pentonville Prison ex p Chinoy [1992] 1 All ER 317 . . . .390–2, 393
R v Graham (2000) LTL 6 April 291
R v Harrer [1995] 3 SCR 562 477
R v Hartley [1978] 2 NZLR 199 349
R v Hennand Derby [1979] ECR 3795 289
R v Howe and Others [1987] 1 AC 417 . . . . .57, 62
R v Jameson [1896] 2 QB 425 89
R v Kelly [1981] 2 All ER 1098 80
R v Konscol [1993] Crim LR 950 395
R v Land (1998) 1 CAR 301 290
R v Madan [1961] 2 QB 1 108
R v Mills (unreported) 192, 193, 194
R v Mullen [1999] 2 Cr App R 143 . . . . .343, 351
R v Nekuda (1989) 39A Crim R 5 NSW 74
R v Neumann (1949) 3 SA 1238 84
R v O/C Depot Battalion, RASC, Colchester ex p Elliot
   [1949] 1 All ER 138 344
R v Quinn [1990] Crim LR 581 . . . . .393–4, 395
R v Radak [1999] 1 Cr App R 187 402
R v Robb (1991) 93 Cr App R 161 471
R v Sang [1980] AC 402 477
R v Sawoniuk (1999) 79
R v Secretary of State ex p Johnson [1999] 2 WLR 932 301–2
R v Secretary of State ex p Peter Elliott [2001] EWHC 559 293
R v Secretary of State for the Home Department ex p (1) Mohammed
   Sani Abacha (2) Abubakar Baguda & Federal Republic of Nigeria
   [2001] EWHC 787 358
R v Secretary of State for the Home Department ex p Rachid Ramda
   [2002] EWHC 1278; [2001] 4 All ER 168 310
R v Silver Lock [1894] 2 QB 766 471
R v Stockwell (1993) 97 Cr App R 260 471
R v Sunila and Soleyman (1986) 28 DLR 450 193
R v Turner [1975] QB 834 471
R v Williams (1984) 78 Cr App R 276 69
R v Wray [1971] SCR 272 477
Rahimtoola v Nizam of Hyderabad [1958] 3 All ER 961 .97
Rasul v Bush 542 US 466 (2004) 225
The Red Crusader case (1962) 35 ILR 485 191
Rees v Secretary of State for the Home Department [1986] 2 All ER 321 . . . . .82, 307
Rein v Socialist People's Libyan Arab Jamahiriya 162 F 3d 748 (1998) 221

Rey v Government of Switzerland [1998] 3 WLR 1 295
Rivard v USA 375 2d 882 (1967) 84
Rocha v USA 288 F 2D 545 (1961) 84
Rohrig, Re (1950) 17 ILR 393 86
Rubio v Colombia 164
Ruiz Torija v Spain 493
Rutaganda v Prosecutor 457

Saadi, Ex p [2002] UKHL 41 332
Saifi, Re [2001] 4 All ER 168 ....293, 309–10
St John v Governor of HM Prison Brixton [2001] EWHC 543 294
Saint Vincent and the Grenadines v Guinea (M/V Saiga (No 2) case)
    38 ILM (1999) 1323 ....191, 193
San Juan Nepomuceno (1824) 166 ER 94 152
Sanchez Ramirez v France App No 28780/95 328
Saunders v UK (1994) 18 EHRR CD 23 399
Saunders v UK (1997) 23 EHRR 313 352
Schenk v Switzerland (1988) 13 EHRR 242 400
Schooner Exchange v MacFaddon (1812) 7 Cranch 116 ....78, 97, 106
Scott, Ex p (1829) 9 B&C 446 343–4
Sealed Case, Re 832 F 2d 1268 (1987) 401
Semanza v Prosecutor 473
Sharon v Time Inc 599 F Supp 538 (1984) 103
Siderman de Blake v Argentina 965 F 2d 699 (1992) 161
Sinclair v HM Advocate (1890) 17 R(J) 38 ....344, 351
Smith v Socialist People's Libyan Arab Jamahiriya (1997)
    113 ILR 534 ....78, 100
Soering v UK (1989) ECHR SerA 161; (1989) 11 EHRR 439 ....162, 305, 328,
                                                329, 330, 332, 348, 400
Special Court for Sierra Leone Prosecutory v Taylor 94
Staatsanwaltschaft Augsburg v Jurgen Kretzinger Case C-288/05 419–20
State v Brown 543A 2d 750 (1988) 477
Stocke v Germany SerA 199 347
Stonehll v USA 405 F 2d 738 (1968) 397

T v Australia Case No 706/1996 334–5
T v Immigration Officer [1996] AC 742 304–5
T v Secretary of State for the Home Department 107 ILR 552;
    [1996] 2 All ER 865 ....91, 228, 303
Talbot v Jansen 3 US 153 (1795) 176, 178
Teixera v Portugal (1998) 28 EHRR 101 352
Tel-Oren v Libyan Arab Republic 726 F 2d 795 (1984) 196
Teper v R [1952] AC 480 460
Timberlane Lumber Co v Bank of America (1976) 66 LUR 270 76
Touvier case (1992) 100 ILR 337 127
Trendtex Trading Corp v Central Bank of Nigeria [1977] 1 All ER 881 99
Tyrer case (1978) ECHR SerA 26 516

Underhill v Hernandez 168 US 250 (1897) 102
United Brands Co v Commission [1978] ECR 207; 1 CMLR 429 77
Universal Jurisdiction over Drug Offences case 28 ILR 166 90
Unterpertinger v Austria 460

Urios, Re (1920) 1 AD 107 83
USA v Aluminium Co of America 148 F 2d 416 (1945) 76, 77
USA v Alvarez-Machain 112 S Ct 2188 (1992) 346, 402
USA v Artt 38 ILM (1999) 100 229
USA v Baker (1955) 22 ILR 203 89
USA v Bank of Nova Scotia 740 F 2d 817 402
USA v Bermingham and others [2006] EWHC 200 326
USA v Bright-Barker 784 F 2d 161 (1986) 84
USA v Burns and Rafay QL (2001) SCJ 8 306
USA v Busic 587 F 2d 577 (1978) 397
USA v Calley 46 CMR 1131 (1973) 59
USA v Cargo of the Brig Malek Adhel 43 US 210 (1844) 176
USA v Columba-Colella 604 F 2d 356 (1979) 79
USA v Cotroni 527 F 2d (1975) 397
USA v Flick 6 Trials (1948) 1217 48
USA v Garcia 37 F 3d (1994) 404
USA v George D Davis 767 F 2d 1025 (1985) 404
USA v Groner 494 F 2d 499 290
USA v Iran (1980) ICJ Reports 3 ....108, 207
USA v Johnpoll 739 F 2d 702 (1984) 359
USA v Keller 451 F Supp 631 (1978) 84
USA v Kinder 14 CMR 742 (1954) 59
USA v Leon 468 US 897 (1984) 477
USA v List et al (Hostages case) (1949) 8 LRTWC 34 ....4, 45, 206
USA v Mackin Case No 3–78–1899 MG (ND Cal 11 May 1979) 303
USA v Marino-Garcia 679 F 2d 1373 (1982) 90
USA v Marzano 537 F 2d 257 (1975) 397, 398
USA v Noriega 99 ILR 143 ....103, 104
USA v Ohlendorf and Others (Einsatzgruppen case) 15 ILR 656;
    15 ILR 376 ....57, 59
USA v Palmer 16 US 610 (1818) 179
USA v Pizzarusso 388 F 2d 8 (1968) 84
USA v Postal 589 F 2d 862 (1979) 193
USA v Rancher 119 US 407 (1886) 300
USA v Smith 18 US 153 (1820) 176
USA v Sturman and others 951 F 2d 1466 (1991) 404–5
USA v The Public Service Alliance of Canada 32 ILM (1993) 99
USA v Thomas 726 F 2d 1191 (1982) 290
USA v Toscanino 500 F 2d 267 (1974) 345–6, 397
USA v Verdugo-Urquidez 939 F 2d 1341 (1990) 346, 392–3, 402
USA v von Leeb and Others (High Command case) [TWC] 510;
    (1949) 1 ILR 376 ....24, 57
USA v von Weizsaecker (Mininstries case) 14 Trials 684 42
USA v Yunis (1991) 88 ILR 176 ....82, 84, 87

Van den Plas, Re 22 ILR 205 84
Van Droogenbroeck v Belgium (1982) EHRR 443 157
Van Mechelen and Others v Netherlands 460, 468
Velasquez v Rodriguez (1994) 95 ILR 232 ....136, 169
Victory Transport Inc v Comisaria General de Abastecimientos y
    Transpertos 35 ILR 110 99
Visser v Netherlands 468

Walker (Neil) v Governor of HM Prison Nottingham [2002] EWHC 39 296
Waltier v Thomson 189 F Supp 319 (1960) 109
Wei Ye v Jiang Zemin and Falun Gong Control Office 383 F 3d 620
   (7th Circuit 2004) 103
Wildenhus case 120 US 1 (1887) 77
Wright v Cantrell (1943–45) 12 AD 37 106

Xuncax and Others v Gramajo 886 F Supp 162 (1995) 161

Yamashita case 327 US 1 (1946) 45–6, 503, 508
Yugoslav Terrorism case (1978) 74 ILR 509 228

Zelaya Blanco v Nicaragua (1995) 2 IHRR 123 400

Table of legislation

Australian legislation
Criminal Code
  s 218A 279
Cybercrime Act 2001 278
Internationally Protected Persons Act
  1976
  s 8(2)–(3) 207

Austrian legislation
Criminal Code
  Art 40 90

Belgian legislation
Code d'Instruction Criminelle
  Art 342 450
Law Relative to the Repression of
    Grave Breaches 1993 87
Loi du 13 Octobre 1930
  Art 17 397

Cambodian legislation
Law on the Establishment of
    Extraordinary Chambers
    2001 . . . . .571, 572, 573
  Art 3–Art 8 572
  Art 11(2)–(3) 571
  Art 14 573
  Art 29(4) 572
  Art 40 573
  Art 46 573

Canadian legislation
Canadian Charter 477
  Art 7 306
  Art 24(2) 477

European Union legislation
Convention on the Establishment of a

European Police Office 1995
  (Europol Convention) 422
Annex 272
Art 2 424
Art 2(1)–(2) 424
Art 2(3) 425
Art 3 424
Art 8 425
Art 10 425
Art 14 425
Art 43(1) 260
Art 43(3) 424
Protocol .422–3
Directive 91/308 . . . .235, 248, 258, 259,
                261, 263
Directive 95/46 271
Directive 2001/97 . . . . . .235, 248, 258–9
Directive 2005/60 . . . . .248, 257, 259–60
EU Convention on Mutual Assistance
  in Criminal Matters
  2000 . . . . . .367–70, 378, 388, 390
  Art 3 369
  Art 4 369
  Art 5–Art 6 368
  Art 6(7) 368
  Art 7 369
  Art 9–Art 12 369
  Art 13 . . . . .369, 375
  Art 14 369
  Art 15–Art 18 370
  Protocol 2001 . . . . .368, 370, 378,
                388, 389
EU Convention on Simplified
  Extradition Procedure Between
  Member States of the EU
  1995 . . . . .313, 314–15, 318
Art 16(2) 317
Art 16(3) 318

EU Convention Relating to Extradition
   Between Member States of the
   EU 1996 . . . . . .313, 315–19, 324
   Art 2(1) 316
   Art 3 316
   Art 3(1)(a)–(b) 316
   Art 5(1)–(2) 317
   Art 5(4) 317
   Art 6 317
   Art 6(3) 317
   Art 7 317
   Art 7(2) 317
   Art 10 317
   Art 10(3) 317
   Art 18(3) 317
   Art 18(4) 318
Regulation 881/2002 215
Regulation 1889/2005 260
Regulation 1986/2006 432
Regulation 1987/2006 432
Regulation 2424/2001 432
Regulation 2580/2001 215
Schengen Agreement 1985 428–31
Schengen Implementing Convention
   1990 . . . . .236, 245, 313, 322,
    366–7, 378, 387, 388, 417,
    419, 428, 429–30, 431, 434
   Art 39 .429, 431
   Art 46 431
   Art 53 358
   Art 54 . . . . .381, 419, 420
   Art 55–Art 58 419
   Art 63 317
   Art 93 431
   Art 96 315
Treaty of Amsterdam 1998 . . . . .72, 217,
    313, 363, 364, 414, 415, 418
   Art 30 426
Treaty of Nice 373, 384
Treaty of Rome 1957
   (EC Treaty) 289, 418
Treaty on European Union . . .271, 363,
    365, 415, 423, 432
   Art 6 . . . . .271, 319, 321
   Art 29 .363, 418
   Art 30 .363, 415
   Art 31 363
   Art 31(1) 384
   Art 34 .363, 367
   Art 34(2)(b) 364
   Art 42 418
   Art K1–Art K3 217

Art K3(d) 72
Art K4 . . . . .217, 363
Art K5–Art K9 217
Schengen Protocol
   Art 4 . . . . .366, 432
   Art 5 . . . . .430, 432

French legislation
Criminal Procedure Code
   Art 427 450
   Art 430 468
   Art 537 468
   Art 689(1) .82
Penal Code
   Art 122–Art 127 64
   Art 689 90

German legislation
Allied Control Council Law for
   Germany No 10 . . . . .58, 127,
    497, 502
   Art II(1)(c) 524
   Art II(4)(a) 110
   Art II(4)(b) 57, 58
Criminal Code
   Art 6(5) 90
Criminal Procedure Code 449
German Military Penal Code 1872
   Art 47 57
Prussian Military Code 1845 57

Greek legislation
Constitution 1975/86
   Art 93(4) .229
Hellenic Criminal Code 1985
   Art 5 80

Indian legislation
Bonded Labour System (Abolition)
   Act 1976 (No 19) 154

International Conventions and Treaties
Agreement for the Suppression of the
   Circulation of Obscene
   Publications 1910 288
   Protocol 1949 289
Benelux Convention on Extradition
   and Mutual Assistance in
   Criminal Matters 1962 313
Brussels General Act Relative to the
   African Slave Trade 1890 152

Charter of the International Military
   Tribunal for the Far East 508
   Art 6 110
Conakry Convention on Sub-regional
   Co-operation in the Exercise
   of Hot Pursuit 189
Convention Against Corruption
   2003 253
   Art 26 49
   Art 26(3) 49
Convention Against Illicit Traffic in
   Narcotic Drugs and
   Psychotropic Substances 1988
   (Vienna Convention) . . . 235, 238,
      241, 243–4, 248, 251, 252, 357
   Art 2(1) 243
   Art 3(1)(a)(iv) 244
   Art 3(1)(a)(v) 235
   Art 3(1)(b) 247
   Art 3(1)(c)(iv) 235
   Art 3(5) 235
   Art 5(3) 252
   Art 12 244
   Art 14(4) 244
   Art 17 . . . . 190, 245
   Art 19 287
Convention Against Torture and Other
   Cruel Inhuman or Degrading
   Treatment or Punishment
   1984 . . . . . . 106, 162, 163, 335–6,
      352, 354, 567
   Art 1 . . . . 165, 335, 337
   Art 1(1) 104, 162
   Art 3 . . . . 104, 162, 335, 336
   Art 5 88
   Art 5(1)(a) 88
   Art 5(1)(b) 81, 88
   Art 5(1)(c) 82, 88
   Art 5(2)–(3) 88
   Art 8(4) 89
   Art 16 165
   Art 17 335
   Art 22 336
Convention Against Transnational
   Organised Crime (CATOC)
   2000 . . . . . 159, 211–12, 226, 227,
      234, 235, 236, 237, 253, 283
   Art 1 253
   Art 2(a) 226, 235
   Art 2(b) 234
   Art 3 . . . . 227, 234
   Art 3(2) 234

Art 5 . . . . 234, 236
Art 6 234
Art 7 237
Art 7(1)(a)–(b) 253
Art 7(2)–(3) 253
Art 8 . . . . 234, 283
Art 12(6) 237
Art 16 236
Art 18 236
Art 23 . . . . 234, 236
Art 27–Art 28 236
Art 30(2)(b)–(c) 236
Art 37(2) 237
Art 40–Art 41 236
Protocol Against the Illicit
   Manufacturing and Trafficking
   in Firearms, their Parts and
   Components, and
   Ammunition 234, 238
   Art 2 238
   Art 5 238
   Art 7–Art 12 238
Protocol Against the Smuggling of
   Migrants by Land, Sea and
   Air 234, 237, 238
   Art 8(2) 238
   Art 8(5) 238
   Art 12–Art 13 237
   Art 16 237
   Art 18 237
Protocol to Prevent, Suppress and
   Punish Trafficking in Persons,
   Especially Women and Children
   2000 . . . . 158, 159, 234, 237
   Art 3(a) 158–9
   Art 4–Art 6 237
Convention for Limiting the
   Manufacture and Regulating
   the Distribution of Narcotic
   Drugs 1931 240
Convention for the Prevention of
   Illicit Drug Traffic 1936 74
Convention for the Protection of
   Cultural Property in the Event
   of Armed Conflict 1954 572
Convention for the Protection of
   Submarine Cables 1884 186
   Art 2(1)–(2) 186
   Art 4 186
   Art 8 186
   Art 10(2) 187
   Art 15 187

Convention for the Suppression of
  Acts of Nuclear Terrorism
  2005 .210
Art 2 211
Art 2(1) 210
Art 2(2)–(4) 211
Art 2(4)(c) 34, 182
Art 3–Art 4 211
Art 4(3) 211
Art 9(2)(b) 211
Convention for the Suppression of
  Counterfeiting Currency
  1929 .74, 91
Convention for the Suppression
  of Terrorist Bombings
  1998 . . . . .196, 209
Art 2(1)–(2) 209
Art 2(3)(a)–(c) 209
Art 3 209
Art 5 . . . . .12, 209, 228
Art 7(3) 230
Art 8(2) 92
Art 9 .12, 228
Art 11 228
Art 12 230
Art 14 230
Convention for the Suppression of the
  Circulation of and Traffic in
  Obscene Publications 1923
Art 1 288–9
Art 2 291
Convention for the Suppression of
  the Financing of Terrorism
  1999 . . . . .196, 212, 213, 254, 255
Art 2(1) 212
Art 2(4)–(5) 212
Art 2(d) 212
Art 6–Art 7 228
Art 7(5) 72
Art 8(1) 213
Art 9(3) 230
Art 10(2) 92
Art 11 228
Art 13–Art 14 228
Art 15 230
Art 18(1)(b)(ii) 213
Art 18(1)(b)(iv) 213
Convention for the Suppression of the
  Traffic in Persons and of the
  Exploitation of the
  Prostitution of Others
  1949 . . . . .7, 8, 153, 158

Art 1–Art 2 157
Convention for the Suppression of
  Unlawful Acts Against the
  Safety of Civil Aviation
  1971 . . . . .93, 180, 196, 200, 202,
                        203, 205, 221
Art 1 202
Art 2(a) 202
Art 2(b) 93
Art 5(1)(a) .93
Art 5(2)–(3) 204
Art 5(3) 81
Art 6(3) 230
Art 7 . . . . .92, 204, 578
Art 8 12
Art 11(1) .204
Protocol 203
  Art II(1) .203
Convention for the Suppression of
  Unlawful Acts Against the
  Safety of Maritime Navigation
  1988 . . . . .180, 181
Art 3(1) 180
Art 3*bis* 181, 182
Art 3*quater* 182
Art 5*bis* 183
Art 6(1)(c) .81
Art 6(2)(b) .81
Art 7 181
Art 8*bis* 182
Art 8*bis*(5)(d) 182
Art 8*bis*(5)(e) 183
Art 11 180
Fixed Platforms Protocol 181
Protocol I 181, 182
  Art 4(5) .181
Convention of the Organisation of the
  Islamic Conference on
  Combating International
  Terrorism 1999
Art 2(1)(a)–(b) 212
Convention on Consent to Marriage,
  Minimum Age for Marriage
  and Registration of
  Marriages 1962 155
Art 1 155
Convention on Prohibitions on the
  Use of Certain Conventional
  Weapons
Protocol II on Prohibitions or
  Restrictions on the Use of
  Mines 1980 119

Protocol IV on Blinding Laser
    Weapons 1995 119
Convention on Psychotropic
    Substances 1971 . . . . . . .241, 243
    Art 2 243
    Art 22 243
Convention on the Elimination of All
    Forms of Discrimination Against
    Women
    Art 6 158
Convention on the Elimination of
    All Forms of Racial
    Discrimination 1965 166
    Art 3–Art 4 166
Convention on the Law of the Sea 1982
    (UNCLOS) 1, 2, 5, 87, 173,
            183, 185, 186, 189, 192,
            193, 194, 201, 238
    Art 3 77
    Art 8 77
    Art 27 . . . . .75, 77, 183
    Art 27(1)–(2) 78
    Art 30 78
    Art 33 . . . . .78, 190
    Art 33(1)(a)–(b) 78
    Art 51 186
    Art 56 190
    Art 58 185
    Art 58(2) 179
    Art 87(1)(c) 185
    Art 97(1) 78
    Art 99 . . . . .86–7, 160, 238
    Art 100 183
    Art 101 . . . . .178, 179, 201
    Art 102 179
    Art 105 . . . . .86, 87, 183
    Art 107 183
    Art 109 . . . . .188, 189
    Art 109(1) .189
    Art 109(4) .189
    Art 110 . . . . .183, 189
    Art 110(1)(b) 160
    Art 111 . . . . .189, 190, 192, 194
    Art 111(4) 193, 194
    Art 112 185
    Art 113 . . . . .186, 187
    Art 114 186
Convention on the Marking of Plastic
    Explosives for the Purpose of
    Detection 1991 203
Convention on the Non-Applicability of
    Statutory Limitations to War

Crimes and Crimes Against
    Humanity 1968 . . . . .52, 127
    Art 1 544
    Art 1(b) 136
Convention on the Physical
    Protection of Nuclear Material
    1979 209
    Art 7–Art 11 210
Convention on the Prevention and
    Punishment of Crimes
    Against Internationally
    Protected Persons, Including
    Diplomatic Agents
    1973 . . . . . . .206–7, 208, 213, 572
    Art 1 207
    Art 1(a) 207
    Art 2 207
    Art 3(1)(c) .82
    Art 6(2) 230
    Art 9 230
Convention on the Prevention and
    Punishment of the Crime of
    Genocide 1948 . . . . . . .6, 58, 127,
            139, 145, 146, 147, 506,
            524, 535, 567, 572, 575
    Art 2 . . . . .141, 547
    Art 3 . . . . .35, 141, 148
    Art 3(b) 35
    Art 3(c) 28
    Art 4 106
    Art 6 .11, 535
Convention on the Prevention and
    Suppression of Apartheid 1973
    Art I 136
    Art V 11
Convention on the Privileges and
    Immunities of the United
    Nations 1946
    Art VI
        s 22(b) 110
Convention on the Prohibition of the
    Development, Production,
    Stockpiling and Use of
    Chemical Weapons and on
    their Destruction 1993
    Art 1 123
    Art 22 . . . . .12, 552
Convention on the Prohibition of the
    Development, Production and
    Stockpiling of Bacteriological
    and Toxic Weapons and on
    their Destruction 1972 118

Convention on the Prohibition of the
    Use, Stockpiling, Production
    and Transfer of Anti-Personnel
    Mines and on their
    Destruction 1997 119
    Art 19 ....12, 552
Convention on the Rights of the
    Child 1989 156
    Art 34–Art 36 156
    Art 38(2) 119
    Art 38(3) 119, 563
    Option Protocol II on the Sale of
    Children, Child Prostitution
    and Child Pornography
    2000 156
        Art 2(b)–(c) 156
        Art 3 156
        Art 3(1)(c) 291
        Art 4 291
Convention on the Safety of UN
    and Associated Personnel
    1999 544
Convention on the Status of Refugees
    1951 331
    Art 33 328
Convention Relating to the Suppression
    of the Abuse of Opium and
    Other Drugs 1912 240
European Agreement for the Prevention
    of Broadcasts Transmitted from
    Stations Outside National
    Territories 1965 188
    Art 2 188
    Art 2(2)(e) 188
    Art 3 188
European Convention for the
    Protection of Human Rights
    and Fundamental Freedoms
    1950 .....261, 306, 326, 327–32,
        347, 383, 391, 397, 460, 477
    Art 1 305
    Art 2(1) 329
    Art 3 ....165, 230, 305, 328, 329, 330,
        331, 332, 333, 400, 401
    Art 5 ....301, 347
    Art 5(1)(c) 347, 348
    Art 5(1)(f) 328
    Art 6 ....229, 259, 331, 352, 399,
        401, 433
    Art 6(3) 403, 477
    Art 6(3)(d) 403, 461, 468
    Art 8 ....273, 326, 391, 396, 401

    Art 10(2) 289
    Art 15 230
    Art 52 353
European Convention of State
    Immunity 1972 100
European Convention on
    Cybercrime 267–9
    Art 27 268
    Protocol 268
European Convention on Extradition
    1957 ....301, 304, 305, 308, 310,
        311, 312–13, 314, 315,
        316, 327, 339
    Art 2 312
    Art 2(1) 316
    Art 2(3)–(4) 316
    Art 3 312
    Art 3(3) 307
    Art 4 ....306, 312
    Art 5 312
    Art 6 ....308, 312, 317
    Art 9 307
    Art 10 307
    Art 11 312
    Art 14 ....300, 302, 312
    Art 14(1)(a) 317
    Art 15 ....301, 302, 312
    Art 17 312
    Art 27(4) 302
    Art 28(3)(d) 302
    Protocol 1975 ....304, 307, 314
    Second Protocol 1991 ..306, 307, 314
European Convention on Laundering,
    Search, Seizure and
    Confiscation of the Proceeds
    from Crime 1990 ......235, 248,
        256, 257, 260, 357, 358
    Art 2–Art 4 256
    Art 6 256
    Art 39 257
European Convention on Laundering,
    Search, Seizure and
    Confiscation of the Proceeds
    from Crime and on the
    Financing of Terrorism
    2005 257–8
    Art 52(4) 258
European Convention on Mutual
    Assistance in Criminal Matters
    1959 ......256, 357, 360–2, 367,
        378, 435–6
    Art 1(2) 358

Art 2 361
Art 3 . . . . 361, 362
Art 5 362
Art 6 . . . . 361, 362
Art 7–Art 8 362
Art 12 362
Art 14 362
Protocol I 1978 . . . . 361, 378
   Art 1 361
Protocol II 2001 . . . . 361, 378
European Convention on the Fight
   Against Corruption Involving
   Officials of the EC or Officials
   of Member States of the
   EU 282–3
Art 2–Art 3 283
Art 6 283
Art 8 283
European Convention on the
   Non-Applicability of
   Statutory Limitations to Crimes
   Against Humanity and War
   Crimes 1974 127
European Convention on the
   Suppression of Terrorism
   1976 . . . . 198, 230, 304, 340
Art 1 . . . . 198, 316, 317
Art 1(c) 207
Art 1(d) 206
Art 2 . . . . 316, 317
Art 5 230
Art 13 317
European Convention on the Transfer
   of Proceedings in Criminal
   Matters 1972 256
European Criminal Law Convention
   on Corruption 1999 283
General Act of the Conference of
   Berlin Concerning the
   Congo 1885 152
General Treaty for the Renunciation
   of War as an Instrument of
   National Policy 1928
   (Kellogg-Briand Treaty/Pact
   of Paris) 500, 545
Geneva Convention for the Amelioration
   of the Condition of the
   Wounded in Armies in the
   Field 1864 503
Geneva Convention on the High
   Seas 1958 . . . . 173, 176, 178, 185,
   186, 189, 190, 192, 194

Art 2(3) 185
Art 14 178
Art 15 201
Art 23 . . . . 189, 192
Art 26(1) 185
Art 27–Art 28 186
Geneva Conventions 1949 . . . 58, 85, 87,
   90, 113, 120, 121, 164, 165,
   206, 506–7, 524, 572
Additional Protocol I 1977 . . . . 85, 87,
   113, 116, 118, 122, 164, 165, 524
Art 1(1) 122
Art 1(4) 116, 222, 223, 224
Art 4 223
Art 4(d) 223
Art 11 119
Art 13(3) 122
Art 35 119
Art 37 . . . . 115, 119
Art 39–Art 40 119
Art 41(2)(b) 119
Art 48 223
Art 49(1) 128
Art 50 . . . . 122, 133
Art 51 118
Art 51(4)–(6) 66
Art 52 118
Art 54 119
Art 55 118
Art 75 . . . . 164, 224
Art 76(1) 119, 524
Art 77(2) 119, 563
Art 85(4)(c) 524
Art 86 45
Art 86(2) 41
Art 87 . . . . 41, 45
Art 90 513
Additional Protocol II 1977 . . . . 9, 85,
   87, 121, 165, 523, 524
Art 4 . . . . 164, 523
Art 4(1) 524
Art 4(2)(a) 524
Art 4(2)(c) 524
Art 4(3)(c) 563
Art 6(5) 583
Convention I 523
Art 2 . . . . 115, 568
Art 3 . . . . . . 120, 121, 122, 164, 177,
   208, 224, 225, 523, 524
Art 12 164
Art 13 114
Art 50 . . . . 113, 164

Convention II 523
    Art 2 ....115, 568
    Art 3 ......120, 121, 122, 164, 177,
                208, 224, 225, 523, 524
    Art 12 164
    Art 13 114
    Art 51 ....113, 164
Convention III 123, 523
    Art 2 ....115, 568
    Art 3 ......120, 121, 122, 164, 177,
                208, 224, 225, 523, 524
    Art 4 ....114, 123
    Art 4(2) 115
    Art 4A 133
    Art 5 225
    Art 13–Art 14 164
    Art 130 ....113, 164
Convention IV 114, 121, 523, 563
    Art 2 ....115, 568
    Art 3 ......120, 121, 122, 164, 177,
                208, 224, 225, 523, 524
    Art 4 114
    Art 4(2) 114
    Art 27 ....164, 524
    Art 28 119
    Art 32 ....119, 164
    Art 49 ....120, 124
    Art 55 119
    Art 66 573
    Art 147 ....113, 164, 524
Hague Convention for the
    Suppression of Unlawful Seizure
    of Aircraft 1970 ...180, 196, 200,
                201, 202, 203
    Art 1 200
    Art 3(1) 200
    Art 4(1)–(2) 93
    Art 6(3) 230
    Art 8 12
    Art 8(1) 201
Hague Convention on Certain
    Questions Relating to the
    Conflict of Nationality Laws
    Art 1 79
Hague Convention on Protection of
    Children and Co-operation in
    Respect of Inter-Country
    Adoptions 1993
    Art 1 156
    Art 21 156
Hague Conventions 1907 ......500, 503
    Convention IV 120, 125, 503, 546

Regulations 120, 500
    Art 1(2) 116
    Art 2(3) 118
    Art 23(h) 120
    Art 28 119
    Art 46 524
    Art 47 119
    Art 54 187
Hague Declaration No III
    Concerning Expanding
    Bullets 1899 118
ILO Convention for the Prohibition
    and Immediate Action for the
    Elimination of the Worst
    Forms of Child Labour
    (No 182) 1999 ....154–5, 156
    Art 3(a) 155, 156
    Art 3(b) 156
    Art 7 155
ILO Forced Labour Convention
    (No 29) 1930
    Art 2(1) 152, 159
    Art 2(2) 159
    Art 25 159
Inter-American Convention Against
    Corruption 1996 282
    Art 11 283
Inter-American Convention on
    Extradition 1981 310
Inter-American Convention on
    Human Rights 1969
    Art 4 169
    Art 5 ....169, 400
    Art 7 169
    Art 13(4) 162
Inter-American Convention on the
    Forced Disappearance of
    Persons 1994 ....136, 171
    Art II 169
Inter-American Torture Convention
    1985
    Art 3 162–3
International Convention Against
    the Taking of Hostages
    1979 ....205, 206
    Art 1(1) 205–6
    Art 2 206
    Art 3(1)–(2) 206
    Art 6(3)–(4) 230
    Art 9(1) 230
    Art 10(1) 206
    Art 13 206

International Convention on the
    Suppression and Punishment
    of the Crime of Apartheid
    1974 167
Art II–Art III 167
International Covenant on Civil and
    Political Rights (ICCPR)
    1966 . . . . 14, 333–5, 400
Art 1 222
Art 4 230
Art 6 334
Art 7 . . . . 105, 136, 161, 165, 333,
                             334, 400
Art 8(1)–(3) 152
Art 14 . . . . 229, 399
Art 14(4)(e) 461
Art 14(7) 333
Art 28 334
Optional Protocol 1 400
International Criminal Police
    Organisation (Interpol)
    Constitution
Art 2 408
Art 3 409
Lausanne Treaty 1923 126
League of Nations Convention
    for the Prevention and
    Suppression of Terrorism
    1937 195
Art 1(2) 195
Art 9–Art 10 91
League of Nations Covenant 500
London Charter for the Nuremberg
    International Military Tribunal
    (Nuremberg Tribunal) 35,
              127, 497, 498, 505
Art 1 497
Art 3(b) 26
Art 6 . . . . 498–9, 504, 505, 506
Art 6(a) 26, 34, 36, 501, 544, 545
Art 6(b) 502
Art 6(c) 125, 127, 502, 503, 506
Art 7 . . . . 110, 504
Art 8 . . . . 57, 504
Art 9 . . . . 48, 576
Art 10 . . . . 48, 576
Art 16(d) 506
Art 17–Art 25 506
Nuclear Non-Proliferation Treaty . . 182
OAS Convention Against the Illicit
    Manufacturing of and Trafficking
    in Firearms, Ammunition,

Explosives and Other Related
    Materials 238
OAS Convention to Prevent and Punish
    the Acts of Terrorism Taking the
    Form of Crimes Against Persons
    and Related Extortion that are
    of International Significance
    1971
Art 2 207
OECD Convention on Combating
    Bribery of Foreign Officials in
    International Business
    Transactions 1997 . . . 8, 235, 282,
                          283, 284
Art 1 282
Art 1(1)–(2) 282
Art 2 49
Art 3(1)–(2) 49
Art 4(1) 282
Art 10 283
Protocol for the Prohibition of the
    Use in War of Asphyxiating,
    Poisonous or Other Gases and
    of Bacteriological Methods
    of Warfare 1925 118
Sèvres Treaty (1920) 126
Art 226 126
Art 230 126
Sierra Leone Special Court
    Statute/Agreement 2002 559
Art 2 . . . . 560, 562
Art 2(g) 560
Art 3 . . . . 560, 562
Art 4 . . . . 560, 562, 563–4
Art 5 560
Art 6 561
Art 8 559
Art 10 562
Art 12(1) 560
Art 14(1)–(2) 561
Art 15(3)–(4) 560
Art 15(5) 564
Art 16 560
Art 20(3) 561
Single Convention on Narcotic
    Drugs 1961 . . . . 241, 242
Art 30(2)(a) 242
Art 36 . . . . 90, 242
Protocol 1972 . . . . 241, 242
Art 2 242
Art 12 242
Art 18 242

Slavery Convention 1927
  Art 1(1) 153
  Art 1(2) 153, 154
  Art 2(b) 152
  Art 5 152
  Protocol 1953 152
Statute of the International Court of
    Justice 4
  Art 38 54
  Art 38(1) 2
Statute of the International Criminal
    Court 1998 .... 26, 36, 46, 51, 53,
      59, 65, 70, 107, 118, 122, 137,
      246, 501, 510, 536, 538, 567
  Art 1 .... 536, 541
  Art 2 537
  Art 4(1) 537
  Art 5 .... 538, 544, 553
  Art 5(2) 65, 545
  Art 6 .... 547, 553, 575
  Art 7 .... 133, 134, 136, 137, 553, 575
  Art 7(1) 134
  Art 7(1)(g)–(h) 137
  Art 7(1)(j) 168
  Art 7(1)(k) 136
  Art 7(2)(a) 134
  Art 7(2)(b) 285
  Art 7(2)(e) 137, 165
  Art 7(2)(f) 137
  Art 7(2)(g) 136
  Art 7(2)(h) 134–5, 168
  Art 7(2)(i) 136, 169
  Art 7(3) 137
  Art 8 .... 553, 575
  Art 8(2)(b) 118, 119, 120
  Art 8(2)(b)(xxvi) 563
  Art 8(2)(c) 122, 124
  Art 8(2)(e) 122, 124
  Art 12 .... 95, 538, 542
  Art 12(1) 95, 538
  Art 12(2) 11, 95, 538, 539,
                540, 541, 542, 553
  Art 12(3) 95, 539
  Art 13 542
  Art 13(a) 543
  Art 13(b) 538, 543, 553
  Art 14(1) 538, 543
  Art 15 542
  Art 15(1) 543
  Art 15(2) 550
  Art 16 .... 540, 543
  Art 17 .... 541, 543
  Art 17(1) 541
  Art 17(1)(a)–(b) 95
  Art 17(2) 541
  Art 17(2)(a) 95
  Art 17(6) 543
  Art 18 543
  Art 18(3) 543
  Art 18(5) 543
  Art 19 543
  Art 19(2) 541
  Art 19(8) 543
  Art 20 52
  Art 21 .... 53, 54
  Art 21(1)(c) 51, 55, 64, 67
  Art 22 52
  Art 22(2) 576
  Art 23–Art 24 52
  Art 25(3) 548
  Art 25(3)(a)–(b) 29, 36
  Art 25(3)(d) ... 26, 29, 33, 34, 36, 182
  Art 25(3)(e) 28, 149
  Art 26 .... 544, 548
  Art 27(1)–(2) 111
  Art 28 .... 38, 42, 44, 45
  Art 28(a) 41
  Art 28(a)(i) 548
  Art 28(b)(i) 44
  Art 29 .... 52, 544
  Art 30(2)(b) 285
  Art 31(1)(a) 70, 548
  Art 31(1)(b) 67, 68, 70, 548
  Art 31(1)(c) 65, 66, 548
  Art 31(1)(d) 61, 62, 548
  Art 31(3) 51, 53, 54, 56, 67
  Art 32 .... 68, 549
  Art 32(2) 68
  Art 33 .... 59, 60, 61, 505
  Art 33(1) 549
  Art 35–Art 36 537
  Art 42 537
  Art 43(4) 537
  Art 59 550
  Art 66 .... 52, 53
  Art 67(1)(i) 52, 53
  Art 72(5) 551
  Art 72(7)(a)(i)–(iii) 551
  Art 72(7)(b)(i) 551
  Art 75 554
  Art 75(4) 554
  Art 79 555
  Art 85 555
  Art 86 .... 107, 540, 549

Art 87(4) 549
Art 87(5) 549
Art 87(5)(b) 552
Art 87(7) 15, 552
Art 88 552
Art 90 551
Art 93(1)(k) 554, 555
Art 93(4) 551
Art 98 .539, 541
Art 98(1) 541
Art 98(2) 540
Art 101 551
Art 112 553
Art 112(3) .553
Art 112(7) .553
Art 115(1)–(2) 554
Art 115(b) .537
Art 116 . . . . .537, 554
Art 117 554
Art 120 552
Art 121 . . . . .544, 553
Art 123 544
Art 123(1) .553
Art 124 .95, 553
Rules of Procedure and
    Evidence 53, 56
    r 80(1)–(3) 56
    r 121(9) 53
    r 135(1) 70
    r 135(3) 70
Statute of the International Criminal
    Tribunal for Rwanda 60, 127,
        129, 134, 399, 516, 525, 572
Art 2 . . . . .140, 523
Art 2(2)(a)–(c) 147
Art 2(3) 150
Art 3 . . . . .128, 134, 523
Art 3(g) 525
Art 4 . . . . .120, 122, 140
Art 4(e) 525
Art 6(1) 523
Art 6(2) 110
Art 6(3) 523
Art 6(4) 57
Art 8 522
Art 12(2) 515
Art 14 .437, 439
Art 15(3) 515
Art 19 442
Art 20 441
Art 20(3) 443
Art 20(4) 442

Art 20(4)(e) 442, 461
Art 21 527
Art 21(2) 492
Rules of Procedure and
    Evidence 439, 440, 561
    r 6 440
    r 54 448
    r 70 527
    r 70(F) .445
    r 71 . . . . .445, 449, 463, 465
    r 87 443
    r 87(A) .443
    r 88(C) .492
    r 89 . . . . .440, 444
    r 89(A) .445
    r 89(B) 445, 446
    r 89(C) .445, 446, 447, 470, 478, 479
    r 90(A) 445, 447, 461
    r 90(C) .480
    r 92*bis* 446, 447, 448
    r 92*bis*(A) 447
    r 93 . . . . .448, 466, 467
    r 93(C) .467
    r 95 . . . . .440, 448, 477, 478
    r 96 480
    r 96(i) 440
    r 97 450
Statute of the International Criminal
    Tribunal for the Former
    Yugoslavia 37, 60, 69, 128,
        129, 134, 148, 399, 400,
        514, 516, 525, 530
Art 1 523
Art 2 . . . . .117, 140, 523, 527
Art 3 . . . . .117, 120, 165, 523
Art 4 .140, 523
Art 5 . . . . .127, 128, 134, 165, 523
Art 5(g) 525
Art 7 36
Art 7(1) 24, 25, 26, 29, 30, 523
Art 7(2) 110
Art 7(3) 37, 41, 42, 523
Art 7(4) 57
Art 9 522
Art 9(1) 94–5
Art 9(2) 95
Art 15 .437, 518
Art 20 .442, 531
Art 21 .441, 531
Art 21(1) 531
Art 21(2) 442, 531
Art 21(3) 443

Art 21(4) .442
Art 21(4)(b) 531
Art 21(4)(d) 531
Art 21(4)(e) 442, 461, 469, 531
Art 21(4)(g) 531
Art 21(d) .518
Art 22 527
Art 22(2) .492
Art 24(1) 4, 55
Art 29 . . . . .95, 518, 528, 529, 530
Art 29(2) .518
Art 30(1)(b) 25
Art 33 24
Rules of Procedure and
    Evidence 437, 438, 439,
                    440, 518, 530
  r 6 440
  r 34(A)(i)–(ii) 528
  r 39(ii) .521
  r 40 532
  r 61 . . . . .518, 520
  r 61(C)–(E) 518
  r 69(A) .534
  r 70 527
  r 71 . . . . .463, 465
  r 71*bis* .448
  r 71(D) .534
  r 75(B)(i)–(ii) 534
  r 79 534
  r 87 443
  r 87(A) .443
  r 88(C) .492
  r 89 . . . . .440, 444, 457
  r 89(A) .445
  r 89(B) 445, 446
  r 89(C) 445, 446, 447, 454–7,
                    459, 469, 478, 479, 518
  r 89(D) 440, 444
  r 89(F) 445, 447, 461, 463
  r 90(A) 445, 447, 463
  r 90(B) .480
  r 92*bis* 446, 447, 451–3
  r 92*bis*(A) 447
  r 92*quater* 454
  r 92*ter* .453
  r 93 . . . . .448, 466, 467
  r 93(A) .466
  r 93(C) .467
  r 95 . . . . .440, 448, 455, 477, 478
  r 96 . . . . .480, 528
  r 96(1) .527
  r 96(i) .440

  r 97 450
  r 98*ter*(c) 492
Statute of the Sierra Leone Special
    Court 2002 13
Supplementary Convention on the
    Abolition of Slavery, the Slave
    Trade, and Institutions Similar
    to Slavery 1956 . . . . .154, 155
  Art 1 154
  Art 1(a) .154
  Art 1(b) .156
  Art 1(c)–(d) 155
  Art 3(1) .154
Tokyo Convention on Offences and
    Certain Other Acts Committed
    on Board Aircraft 1963 93,
                    196, 199, 200, 203
  Art 1(1)–(4) 199
  Art 4 93
  Art 11 199
  Art 16(2) 199
United Nations Charter 1945 . . .65, 95,
                    204, 206, 223, 227,
                    514, 529, 531, 538,
                    542, 545, 578
  Art 1(2) .222
  Art 2(4) 65, 221, 545, 546
  Art 2(7) .103
  Art 6 547
  Art 25 . . . . .11, 204, 514, 529
  Art 29 514
  Art 39 545
  Art 41 . . . . .11, 514
  Art 42 . . . . .14, 65, 66, 546
  Art 51 . . . . .65, 66, 220, 545, 546
  Art 55 222
  Art 103 . . . . .204, 543, 578
Universal Declaration on Human
    Rights
  Art 4 152
Universal Postal Union Constitution
    Final Protocol 286, 287
Universal Postal Union Convention
    1878 .286
  Art 11 286
Universal Postal Union Convention
    1905
  Art 16(3) 286
  Art 18 286
Universal Postal Union Convention
    1906
  Art 16(3)(2)(d) 288

Universal Postal Union Convention
  1920
  Art 18(1) 286
  Art 18(2)(d) 288
  Art 18(5) 286
  Art 20 286
Universal Postal Union Convention
  1924
  Art 41 286
  Art 79 286
Universal Postal Union Convention
  1929
  Art 45 286
  Art 80 286
Universal Postal Union Convention
  1939
  Art 46 286
  Art 81 286
Versailles Treaty 1919 . . . . 126, 496
  Art 227 545
Vienna Convention on Consular
  Relations 1963
  Art 41 109
  Art 43 109
Vienna Convention on Diplomatic
  Relations 1961 572
  Art 29 . . . . 108, 109, 207
  Art 30 207
  Art 31(1) 109
  Art 32 108
  Art 32(2) 108
  Art 37 109
  Art 39(1)–(2) 108
Vienna Convention on the Law of
  Treaties 1969
  Art 2(a) 516
  Art 5 516
  Art 19(c) 158
  Art 31(1) 516
  Art 32 516
  Art 34 538
  Art 53 . . . . 3, 87
  Art 65 318
World Trade Organisation
  Agreement on Government
  Procurement 161

Iraqi legislation
Criminal Code 576
Special Tribunal Statute 574, 576
  Art 1 575
  Art 1(b) 575

Art 4(d) 577
Art 6(b) 577
Art 7(n) 577
Art 8(j) 577
Art 10 577
Art 11–Art 13 575
Art 14 . . . . 574, 575
Art 17(b) 575, 577
Art 24(e) 577
Art 29(a) 574
Art 29(b) 574
Art 33 576
Transitional Administrative Law
  2004 . . . . 574, 576
  Art 15(I) 574
  Art 31 576
  Art 48(A) 574
  Art 48(B) 574

Israeli legislation
Nazi and Nazi Collaborators Law
  1951 84
Penal Code
  s 7(a) 82

Italian legislation
Penal Code 1930
  Art 54(1) 64

Netherlands legislation
Code of Criminal Procedure
  Art 339(1) 450
  Art 341(4) 468
  Art 342(3) 468
  Art 359(a) 450
Penal Code 1971
  Art 385(a) 200

Polish legislation
Constitution
  Art 55 324

Sierra Leone legislation
Constitution 97
Malicious Damage Act 1861 560
Prevention of Cruelty to Children
  Act 1926 560

South African legislation
Constitution (interim) 1993 581
Promotion of National Unity and
  Reconciliation Act 1995 581

Spanish legislation
Judicial Branch Act 1985
  Art 23(4) 90

United Kingdom legislation
Abolition of Slavery Act 1833 152
Anti-Terrorism, Crime and Security
  Act 2001 .... 318, 332
Aviation Security Act 1982 577
Computer Misuse Act 1990 279
Crime (International Co-operation)
  Act 2003 .... 387–9, 390
  s 7–s 8 389
  s 8(3) 389
  s 9 390
  s 16 389
  s 19 389
  s 81–s 85 388
Criminal Damage Act 1971 80
Criminal Justice Act 1988 261
  s 134 .... 337–8, 340
Criminal Justice Act 1993 261
  s 1–s 2 77
  s 134 88
Criminal Justice Act 2003 387
Criminal Justice and Public Order Act
  1994
  s 84(3)(b) 290
Criminal Justice (International
  Co-operation) Act 1990 387
  s 3 403
Criminal Procedures and Investigations
  Act 1996
  s 31(3) 396
  s 35(1) 396
  Sched 1
    para 26 391
Diplomatic Privileges Act 1964
  s 2(3) 108
Drug Trafficking Act 1986 261
Drug Trafficking Act 1994 261
EU Extradition Regulations 2002 ... 319
European Communities Act 1972
  s 2(2) 263
Extradition Act 1989 .... 295, 297, 298,
               337, 338, 339
  s 1(1)(a) 295
  s 2 296
  s 6 360
  s 6(1) 309
  s 6(1)(c)–(d) 309
  s 8 337

  s 11(3) 309
  Sched 1 .... 297, 339
Extradition Act 2003 ...... 305, 325–6
  s 87 325
  s 94 306
  Sched 2 321
Geneva Conventions Act 1957 90
Geneva Conventions (Amendment)
  Act 1995 90
Human Rights Act 1998 .. 351, 352, 477
Immigration Act 1971
  s 3(5)(b) 331
Interception of Communications
  Act 1985 395–6
Internationally Protected Persons Act
  1978
  s 1 207
  s 1(3) 297
Merchant Shipping Act 1995
  s 281 80
  s 686(1) 80
Money Laundering Regulations
  1993 .... 263, 264
  reg 2 264
  reg 14 262
Northern Ireland (Emergency
  Provisions) Act 1978 229
Obscene Publications Act 1857 288
Obscene Publications Act 1959 289
  s 1(1)–(3) 290
  s 2(1) 290
  s 2(5) 290
Obscene Publications Act 1964
  s 1(3) 290
Offences Against the Person
  Act 1861
  s 9 79
  s 57 79
Offences at Sea Act 1537 (Statute of
  Henry VIII) 176
Official Secrets Act 1989
  s 15(1) 79
Police and Criminal Evidence
  Act 1984
  s 28(3) 389
  s 76 395
  s 78 .... 391, 477
  s 78(1) 391, 394
  s 78(3) 391
Police and Justice Act 1996
  s 35–s 37 279
Police and Justice Act 2006 279

Postal Services Act 2000
  s 85(3)–(5) 287
Prevention of Terrorism Act 2005
  s 16(2) 332
Prevention of Terrorism (Temporary
    Provisions) Act 1984 331
Proceeds of Crime Act 2002 ... 262, 263
  s 6 263
  s 327–s 331 262
  s 333 262
  s 340 262
  s 340(11) 264
  s 377 263
  Sched 9 262
Protection of Trading Interests Act
    1980 76
Regulation of Investigatory Powers Act
    2000
  s 76 388
  s 76A 388
Serious and Organised Crime Act
    2005 263
Sexual Offences Act 1956 80
Sexual Offences Act 2003 279
  s 15 279
Sexual Offences (Conspiracy and
    Incitement) Act 1996 ..... 80, 81
State Immunity Act 1978 ...... 99, 100,
                              104, 340
  s 3 99–100
  s 14(1) 101
  s 20(1) 101
Submarine Telegraph Act 1885 187
Suppression of Terrorism Act
    1978 340
  s 4 340
Taking of Hostages Act 1982 340
  s 3(4) 82
Terrorism Act 2000
  s 18 264
Treason Act 1351 79
USA (Extradition Amendment)
    Order 1986 329
USA (Extradition) Order 1976 329
War Crimes Act 1991
  s 1(2) 79

United States legislation
Aliens Tort Claims Act 1789 105,
                              159, 168
Anti-Hijacking Act 1974 82
Anti-Terrorism and Effective Death
    Penalty Act 1996 ...... 197, 221
Anti-Trust Act 1890
    (Sherman Act) 76
Constitution
  4th Amendment 392, 397
  6th Amendment 404
  14th Amendment 345, 397
Export Administration Act 1979 ... 221
Federal Rules of Evidence
  r 402 450
  r 404(a) 465
  r 404(b) 466
  r 405(a) 466
  r 703 471
  r 705 471
Foreign Assistance Act 1961 221
Foreign Corrupt Practices Act
    1977 .... 280, 282, 283
Foreign Sovereign Immunities Act
    1976 .... 100, 103, 221
  §1605 100
Hostage Taking Act 1984 82
International Anti-Bribery and Fair
    Competition Act 1998 282
Mail Fraud Act 1948 287
Military Commissions Act 2006 225
Obscenity Act 1948 .... 287, 290
Omnibus Diplomatic Security and
    Anti-Terrorism Act
    1986 .... 82, 84
Piracy and Privateering Act 1948 ... 176
Racketeering act 1951 233
Restatement (Third) of the Foreign
    Relations Law of the USA
    1986 .... 76, 84
  §443 89
Submarine Cable Act 1888 187
Uniform Code of Military Justice .. 225
US Cuban Liberty and Democratic
    Solidarity Act (Helms Burton
    Act) 1996 76

Chapter 1

Theory of international criminal law

1.1 INTRODUCTION

International criminal law (ICL) constitutes the fusion of two legal disciplines: international law and domestic criminal law. While it is true that one may discern certain criminal law elements in the science of international law, it is certainly not the totality of these elements that make up the discipline of ICL. Its existence is dependent on the sources and processes of international law, as it is these sources and processes that initially create it and ultimately define it. This can be illustrated by examining any one of the acknowledged international offences. Piracy *jure gentium*, for example, exists simultaneously as a crime under customary international law, as well as treaty law, specifically the 1982 United Nations Convention on the Law of the Sea (UNCLOS).[1] In examining its status and nature, whether as a treaty or customary rule, recourse is to be made not only to the relevant sources and norms of international law, but also to the non-piracy clauses of UNCLOS itself. The concept of piracy cannot be fully realised unless other concepts are first explored, such as the freedom to navigate on the high seas, delimitation of maritime zones, Flag State jurisdiction and many others. Similarly, one cannot examine an international offence, such as piracy, without recourse to those rules which delineate the legal standing of natural persons in the international legal system and their capacity to enjoy rights directly from this system, as well as to suffer lawful consequences for any violations (international legal personality). Undoubtedly, it does not suffice simply to discern and extrapolate mechanically all those criminal elements that are abundant in general international law and then combine them to establish a new discipline, as this does not help explain the binding nature of rules, nor their role in any given normative system.

The criminal laws of nations, expressed both through legislative action and the common law, constitute a vital component of ICL. International rules are

---

1 Reprinted in 21 ILM (1982), 1261.

generally imperfect and imprecise, not least because of the political difficulties in their drafting and in reaching agreement among competing national interests. With few exceptions, and in correlation to the preceding argument, international treaties rely on signatory States to further implement their provisions with precision at the domestic level, not necessarily in identical manner, but with a certain degree of consistency and uniformity based on the object and purpose of each particular treaty. In the case of piracy *jure gentium*, for example, the national legislation implementing the piracy provisions of UNCLOS into domestic criminal law will have to address the question of the material and mental attributes of the offence. UNCLOS is largely silent on the *mens rea* of piracy and so a myriad of mental components has to be prescribed at the domestic level, including whether or not the offence is one of strict liability. Some States may further posit that, according to general principles of their own criminal law, the perpetrator of an offence is relieved from criminal culpability if the act was based on political or other ideological motivation (the so called 'political offence exception') – in those instances where a convention is unclear or silent on the issue. Similarly, the imposition of penalties, at the discretion of parliament or the national judiciary, as well as the judicial determination of the extent of the various maritime zones, serve to indicate that certain elements of even a very old and reasonably well established international offence, such as piracy, may vary from country to country. But, this is an unavoidable occurrence, since criminal law is above all a practical discipline, and so ICL cannot operate in a theoretical vacuum, but in strict accordance with its objectives, that is to prevent the commission of offences, to prosecute and ultimately to punish offenders. In the absence of an all-embracing international criminal authority, these functions have been bestowed to national authorities, whose conformity to international law generally passes through domestic channels, such as national law and the dictates of the executive. As will be demonstrated below, however, the discretion of States to define international offences in their domestic law is not unlimited, but circumscribed by general international law and certain ICL principles.

1.2 SOURCES OF INTERNATIONAL LAW AND INDIVIDUAL LEGAL PERSONALITY

Article 38(1) of the 1945 Statute of the International Court of Justice recognises two types of sources: primary and secondary. The primary sources of international law are treaties, international custom and general principles of law, all being independent and capable of producing binding rules. The secondary sources of international law, namely the writings of renowned publicists and the decisions of international courts, simply serve to ascertain, and perhaps interpret, the primary sources. Treaties are agreements between sovereign nations, governed by international law and generally binding only upon parties to each particular agreement. Customary law is composed of two elements, an objective and a subjective.[2] The objective element is made up of the uniform and continuous practice of States with regard to a specific issue and, depending on its adherents, this may take the form of a universal or a local custom. The subjective element comprises a State's conviction that its practice on a particular issue emanates from a legal obligation, which it feels bound to respect. It has been reasonably argued that the objective element is not always required in the formation of a customary rule. This is predicated on the notion that, although every sovereign State has an interest in the development of international norms, not all States have the capacity to demonstrate some kind of material action. For example, the utilisation of outer space has been possible only by certain developed nations, as has the exploration of the natural resources lying beneath the seabed of the high seas. This, it is argued, should not prevent less developed States from having a voice in the regulation of these areas. It is for this reason that General Assembly resolutions, which are not otherwise binding, may be declaratory of customary law where they evince universal consensus through the unanimity of participating States.[3] But, even where State practice may be deemed to be required, physical action is not necessarily the best determinant. In the field of international humanitarian law, for example, it would be impracticable to ascertain State practice with regard to the behaviour of troops on the battlefield, and recourse should be made to military manuals and decrees, ratification of relevant instruments and other similar official pronouncements indicating a legal commitment.[4]

International customary rules bind all States, except for those States that have consistently and openly objected to the formation of a rule from its inception.[5] This general framework is subject to one exception; where there exists consistent objection to a customary rule in cases where the said rule is also a peremptory norm of international law (that is, a *jus cogens* norm) any objection is unacceptable.[6] No derogation is allowed from *jus cogens* norms, which generally comprise fundamental human rights and rules of international humanitarian law, as well as the prohibition of the use of unlawful

2 *FDR v Denmark; FDR v The Netherlands* (*North Sea Continental Shelf* cases) (Merits) (1969) ICJ Reports 3, paras 73–81; see generally M Akehurst, 'Custom as a Source of International Law', 47 BYIL (1974–75), 1.

3 R Sloan, 'General Assembly Resolutions Revisited (Forty Years After)', 58 BYIL (1987), 39.

4 *ICTY Prosecutor v Tadic*, Appeals Chamber Decision on the Defence Motion for Interlocutory Appeal on Jurisdiction (2 October 1995), para 99; see T Meron, The Continuing Role of Custom in the Formation of International Humanitarian Law', 90 AJIL (1996), 238, pp 239–40, who states that due to the scarcity of supporting practice in both human rights and humanitarian law, evidence of *opinio juris* is compensated through official statements.

5 J Charney, 'The Persistent Objector Rule and the Development of Customary International Law', 56 BYIL (1985), 1.

6 1969 Vienna Convention on the Law of Treaties, 1155 UNTS 331, Art 53.

armed force. Similarly, treaty provisions reflecting peremptory norms of international law are binding upon third parties to such treaties by virtue of their peremptory nature.

General principles of law can be found both in international law itself, as well as in the domestic legal systems of States.[7] General principles of international law, such as *pacta sunt servanda*, constitute *a priori* principles that underlie both customary and treaty law. On the other hand, general principles of municipal law are practices or legal principles common to a substantial number of nations.[8] It has been accepted by post-Second World War military tribunals,[9] as well as by contemporary international judicial bodies such as the European Court of Justice (ECJ),[10] that for a domestic principle to be regarded as generally accepted it must be recognised by most legal systems, not all. Under customary international law, reliance upon principles deriving from national legal systems is justified either when rules make explicit reference to national laws,[11] or when such reference is 'necessarily implied by the very content and nature of the concept'.[12] This suggests that the practice of international tribunals has been to explore all the means available at the international level before turning to national law. It is instructive to note that the 1998 International Criminal Court (ICC) Statute places general principles of law derived from legal systems of the world in a position of last resort and only then to be utilised if they are consistent with international law.[13] To a very large degree, these propositions reflect the fact that the vast

---

7 B Cheng, *General Principles of Law as Applied by International Courts and Tribunals*, 1987, Cambridge: Grotius; A D McNair, 'The General Principles of Law Recognised by Civilised Nations', 33 BYIL (1957), 1.

8 *AMCO v Republic of Indonesia*, Decision of the Arbitration Tribunal of the International Centre for the Settlement of Investment Disputes, reprinted in (1990) 89 ILR 366, 461.

9 The tribunal in the *Hostages* case noted that if a principle is found to have been accepted generally as a fundamental rule of justice by most nations in their municipal law, its declaration as a rule of international law would seem to be fully justified: *USA v List* (*Hostages* case) (1949) 8 LRTWC 34, 49.

10 In the words of Advocate General Lagrange in *Hoogovens v High Authority* [1962] ECR 253, pp 283–84: 'The Court is not content to draw on more or less arithmetical common denominators between different national solutions, but chooses from each of the Member States those solutions which, having regard to the objects of the Treaty, appear to be the best or . . . the most progressive.'

11 As does, eg, International Criminal Tribunal for the Former Yugoslavia (ICTY) Statute, Art 24(1) which states that, in determining the terms of imprisonment, the Trial Chambers shall have recourse to the general practice regarding prison sentences in the courts of the former Yugoslavia.

12 *Advisory Opinion Concerning Exchange of Greek and Turkish Populations* (1925) PCIJ Reports, Ser B, No 10, 19–20, cited by Judges McDonald and Vohrah in *ICTY Prosecutor v Erdemovic*, Appeals Chamber Judgment (7 Oct 1997).

13 This formulation was consistent with the Report of the Preparatory Committee on the International Criminal Court at the Diplomatic Conference held in Rome (15 June–17 July 1998), UN Doc A/CONF 183/2/Add 1 (14 April 1998), 46–47.

majority of fundamental general principles of national laws, such as the principle of legality and the prohibition of retroactive laws, have matured into customary and treaty norms. The fundamental problem with general principles, however, is their identification by international criminal tribunals without having set forth in advance a clear and consistent methodology. In practice, judges at the International Criminal Tribunal for the former Yugoslavia (ICTY) and International Criminal Tribunal for Rwanda (ICTR) have referred to principles encountered in legal systems with which they, or their assistants, were familiar with, but: (a) omitted significant references to legal systems that would better represent a global consensus, such as that of Muslim, former communist or African States; and (b) did not provide the legal context in which a particular concept is framed, thus failing to clearly demonstrate whether a particular concept is identical only in name or essence in two or more nations.

States have been the traditional subjects of international law, the entities primarily endowed with international legal personality, that is, the ability to enjoy and enforce rights and duties directly under international law.[14] From the latter part of the 19th century, a certain amount of international legal competence was granted to international intergovernmental organisations. Natural persons, it has been advocated, became subjects, and not merely objects, of the international legal system at the end of the Second World War, at which time they assumed personal liability under the 1945 London Agreement for the Prosecution and Punishment of the Major War Criminals of the European Axis.[15] This is not true, as a substantial number of international offences were recognised by the international community prior to the dawn of the 20th century, such as piracy *jure gentium*, war crimes, injuries to submarine cables, postal offences and others. This personality, however, was limited strictly to these instruments and relevant customary law. At present, natural persons are endowed with legal personality in a plethora of international fields, such as human rights and humanitarian law, international financial transactions, European Community law and others. For the purposes of ICL, the fundamental question is whether the attribution of legal personality to natural persons in relation to a treaty crime necessarily entails, as a direct correlation, individual criminal liability under international law. To put it simply, where the United Nations Convention on the Law of the Sea (UNCLOS) defines piracy as an act that may be perpetrated only by natural persons, does it establish an offence under international law or an offence under domestic law, and what is the difference between the two in practical terms?

14 See generally R Higgins, *Problems and Process: International Law and How We Use It*, 1994, Oxford: OUP, 48–55.
15 59 Stat 1544.

1.3 THE INTERNATIONAL CRIMINALISATION PROCESS

An international offence is any act entailing the criminal liability of the perpetrator, and emanating from treaty or custom. The heinous nature of an act, such as the extermination of an identified group, is not the sole determinant for elevating such behaviour to the status of an international offence, although this may serve as a good incentive to do so. Rather, as Dinstein correctly points out, 'the practice of States is the conclusive determinant in the creation of international law (including international criminal law), and not the desirability of stamping out obnoxious patterns of human behaviour'.[16] Simply put, the establishment of international offences is the direct result of interstate consensus, all other considerations bearing a distinct subordinate character.

The legal basis for considering an offence to be of international import is where existing treaties or customs consider the act as being an international crime.[17] Since every international offence is now codified in multilateral agreements, we shall continue our analysis on the basis of treaty law. Although international treaties define or prescribe offences by employing inconsistent terminology, it is possible to discern two broad categories where they purport to so criminalise specific conduct. The first category comprises those treaties, such as the 1948 Convention on the Prevention and Punishment of the Crime of Genocide,[18] which contain a categorical provision that the forbidden behaviour constitutes a crime under international law (usually termed 'universal' crimes). A second category of treaties may or may not describe the forbidden conduct as a crime, but clearly imposes a duty on contracting parties to prosecute or extradite the alleged offender, or simply render the said conduct an offence under their national law. The different variants of this latter category have attracted wide application in the international criminalisation process and have been the major vehicle for the anti-terrorist treaties. The fact that a treaty defines certain conduct simply as an offence, or imposes a duty on States to take action at the domestic criminal level without, however, describing the conduct as an international crime, in no way detracts from the international nature of the offence prescribed by the treaty. Treaties of this nature usually point out that they are not applicable to acts perpetrated solely within a single country – although this may be subject to change in the post-11 September 2001 era.

---

16 Y Dinstein, 'International Criminal Law', 20 *Israel Law Review* (1985), 206, 221.
17 The authors have not found an international offence emanating independently from general principles of international law or the criminal laws of nations. For a contrary view, see CM Bassiouni (ed), *International Criminal Law*, 1986, Dobbs Ferry, New York: Transnational, 2.
18 78 UNTS 277.

Bassiouni's analysis of 22 categories of international crimes revealed that the conventions in which they were contained demonstrated the following 10 penal characteristics:

1 explicit recognition of proscribed conduct as constituting an international crime, or a crime under international law, or as a crime;
2 implicit recognition of the penal nature of the act by establishing a duty to prohibit, prevent, prosecute, punish, or the like;
3 criminalisation of the proscribed conduct;
4 duty or right to prosecute;
5 duty or right to punish the proscribed conduct;
6 duty or right to extradite;
7 duty or right to cooperate in prosecution, punishment (including judicial assistance in penal proceedings);
8 establishment of a criminal jurisdictional basis (or theory of criminal jurisdiction or priority in criminal jurisdiction);
9 reference to the establishment of an international criminal court or international tribunal with penal characteristics (or prerogatives); and
10 elimination of the defence of superior orders.[19]

No ICL convention embodies all 10 of these characteristics. Bassiouni discovered that crimes with a significant ideological or political component, such as aggression, contain the least number of these characteristics in contrast to those offences devoid of political considerations, such as drug offences. He concluded that, due to the decidedly penal nature of these treaties, or their provisions, the existence of any one of the 10 aforementioned characteristics in a convention makes it part of ICL.[20]

When examining the general effect of treaties and their passing into the realm of customary law, one automatically looks at the status of ratifications. This does not necessarily paint a true picture. Treaties that encompass a wide variety of topics and, at the same time, expressly exclude reservations, or where certain reservations would be deemed to conflict with the object and purpose of a treaty will, in most cases, attract few parties, not because other States fundamentally disagree with the entire convention, but simply particular aspects of it. A good example is the 1949 Convention for the Suppression of the Traffic in Persons and of the Exploitation of the Prostitution of Others.[21] This instrument, which penalises the procurement and enticement to prostitution as well as the maintenance of brothels, has received a marginal number of ratifications, simply because a large number of States possess

---

19 Op cit, Bassiouni, note 17, 3.
20 Ibid, note 17, 4.
21 96 UNTS 271.

legislation legalising voluntary prostitution. From a number of sources, such as the *travaux preparatoires* of the Convention, in addition to the global uniformity ascertained in national legislations, as well as from official pronouncements in international fora and other relevant treaties, it is beyond doubt that the enticement to and maintenance of all forms of involuntary prostitution constitute international offences under customary law. Thus, even though the Convention is not widely ratified, one of the conducts it criminalises is clearly an offence under customary law.

Where international custom criminalises certain conduct, the incumbent court must also satisfy itself that the particular offence is 'defined with sufficient clarity under customary international law for its general nature, its criminal character and its approximate gravity to have been sufficiently foreseeable and accessible'.[22] In the *Vasiljevic* judgment, the Prosecution charged the accused, *inter alia*, with the offence of 'violence to life and person'. The Trial Chamber was faced with the decision whether the definition of the offence was of sufficient clarity in order to satisfy the requirements of the principle *nullum crimen sine lege*. Despite the existence of the offence in the ICTY Statute, the Trial Chamber very boldly stated that in the absence of any clear indication in the practice of States as to what the definition of the offence of 'violence to life and person' may be under customary law, it was not satisfied that such an offence giving rise to individual criminal responsibility exists under that body of law.[23]

Every offence prescribed in treaties or custom must ultimately be implemented into national law through an act of legislation. This process is followed not only where the offence is not precisely defined in the treaty, but also where it is set out in detail in its constitutive instrument. The national legislator might wish further to elaborate the substantive or procedural elements of the offence, and/or adapt it to domestic exigencies, but should be guided in this respect by the framework established in the relevant treaty. In practice, contemporary ICL treaties dealing with a particular offence leave other aspects of implementation, such as the form of liability of legal persons, domestic investigations, etc, to be adapted in accordance with their Member State's domestic legislation, in accordance with the 'functional equivalence' doctrine. For example, the 1997 OECD Bribery Convention simply provides that States parties must adopt 'effective, proportionate and dissuasive sanctions' against legal persons, recognising that legal persons do not incur criminal liability in all States. Thus, functional equivalence is a result-based method, rather than a form-based method, but should not be considered generally applicable to definitions of crimes found in ICL treaties. A State violating its treaty obligations by either failing to incorporate a treaty into its

---

22 *ICTY Prosecutor v Vasiljevic*, Trial Chamber Judgment (29 November 2002), para 201.
23 Ibid, para 203.

domestic legal system, or by omitting fundamental aspects of the treaty from its implementing statute, will generally be held liable vis-à-vis other contracting parties. In the field of ICL there may be great divergence in the views of States during the negotiation of a treaty. Where the treaty is finally adopted through a compromise the divergence remains, and in the absence of a contrary provision there is no reason why a State party cannot adopt implementing legislation that helps to supplement or fortify the provisions of a weak treaty. A State may decide, for example, that the 1977 Protocol II Additional to the 1949 Geneva Conventions and Relating to the Protection of Victims of Non-International Armed Conflicts[24] does not cover enough offences, nor does it establish a high enough gravity, nor sufficient jurisdictional bases. Such fortifications to ICL treaties should be accepted with extreme caution however, as long as they: (a) are not expressly or tacitly prohibited; (b) do not conflict with the object or purpose or other obligations under that treaty; and (c) they, moreover, do not violate the rights of the accused.

The practical difference between offences clearly specified under international law, and those whose further elaboration is left to the discretion of contracting States, relates primarily to the removal of perplexities associated with the negotiation and drafting of definitions at preparatory conferences. If it is felt that, in order to get more States on board, a well-signed convention is more important than a 'strong' convention; in this sense, specificity, depth, or other elements that were initially envisaged to be included in the convention may have to be sacrificed. Ultimately, the gravity of an offence as a universal crime is devoid of significance if political or other considerations prevent prosecution or other criminal enforcement action. Thus, while several instances of genocide have occurred since 1948 no action was taken at either national or international level until the creation of the ad hoc tribunals for Yugoslavia and Rwanda in 1993 and 1994, respectively.

Although the majority of international penal proscriptions require that each crime have an international or transnational element, which itself is based on the nature of the violative conduct, the nationality of the offender or the victim, or its impact, these two elements (the international or transnational) are no longer required in the international criminalisation process.[25] This was clearly demonstrated by the elevation of breaches of humanitarian law, applicable in non-international armed conflicts, to the status of international offences entailing the individual responsibility of the offenders.[26] Non-international armed conflict violations do not by their nature possess international or transnational elements and are confined to a single territory, unless other States decide to intervene. This development further shows the

---

24 1125 UNTS 609.
25 For a contrary view, see op cit, Bassiouni, note 17, 24.
26 *Tadic* Appeals jurisdiction decision, op cit, note 4, para 134.

evolution of the international society in regulating areas otherwise falling within the exclusive domain of States, thus eroding the principle of domestic jurisdiction.

In conclusion, the prohibition of certain conduct by treaty or custom always entails the criminal liability under international law of the offender, irrespective of whether the prohibited conduct is defined as a universal crime or an offence to be further elaborated through domestic law. This represents the first step in the criminalisation process. In the dawn of the 21st century, one should dismiss the notion espoused in 1950 by Schwarzenberger that ICL is 'merely a loose and misleading label for topics which comprise anything but international criminal law'; he argued further that whatever the content of these rules, there is no evidence that they are endowed with a prohibitive character and specific penal sanctions.[27] Schwarzenberger grounded his argument on the fact that, in the absence of international enforcement mechanisms, the concept of offences against the law of nations was redundant, unless regulated and enforced before a domestic setting, believing that ICL could not function outside each individual State. This led him to believe that ICL was, in fact, domestic criminal law. He also argued that sovereign States could not and would not agree to being held liable for State crimes, a notion that now seems to be settled within the ranks of the International Law Commission and general *opinio juris*.[28] Next, we will examine the final step of the international criminal process, which comprises the enforcement of substantive ICL.

1.4 ENFORCEMENT OF INTERNATIONAL CRIMINAL LAW

Unlike national legal systems, the international community predicates its rules not upon a preconceived hierarchical ladder, but on the basis of the principle of juridical equality among States. It is, therefore, a horizontal system of law making. Since it does not possess a legislative body, a law enforcement agency, or a compulsory judicial jurisdiction, its primary subjects must necessarily premise their relations on a framework of mutual interdependence. International enforcement action against natural persons for violations of ICL takes two general forms: direct and indirect.

Direct enforcement implies prosecutorial and judicial action against persons suspected of having committed an international offence. Although, in the

27 G Schwarzenberger, 'The Problem of an International Criminal Law', 3 CLP (1950), 263, 274.
28 The much contested draft Art 19 of the ILC's Draft Articles on State Responsibility, which made reference to international offences giving rising to State responsibility, was removed from the ILC's finalised Articles. See UN Doc A/CN4/L600 (21 August 2000).

past a substantial number of quasi-judicial commissions were set up to investigate breaches of the laws of war alleged to have taken place in various armed conflicts, it was not until the establishment of the Nuremberg and Tokyo tribunals at the close of the Second World War that enforcement took place before an international forum and on the basis of international law. Two later conventions, Art VI of the 1948 Convention on the Prevention and Punishment of the Crime of Genocide (Genocide Convention) and Art V of the 1973 Convention on the Prevention and Suppression of Apartheid,[29] called for the creation of an international penal tribunal with authority to adjudicate violations of these Conventions. Similarly, on the basis of contractual obligations stemming from Art 25 of the 1945 United Nations (UN) Charter, which renders Security Council resolutions binding on UN Member States, the ad hoc tribunals for Yugoslavia[30] and Rwanda[31] were established under the process of Art 41 of the 1945 UN Charter (that is, measures authorised by the UN Security Council not involving the use of armed force). Unlike the two ad hoc tribunals, the ICC, whose Statute was adopted in 1998,[32] is not endowed with compulsory jurisdiction. Subject to an exception under Art 12(2) of its Statute, whereby the ICC may assume jurisdiction where either the territorial State or the State of nationality of the accused submits to its jurisdiction, the ICC is generally empowered to adjudicate a case only after the concerned State has given its unequivocal consent.

It is not only international tribunals that possess the capacity to take direct enforcement action, but also domestic criminal courts. When domestic courts exercise wide-ranging extraterritorial jurisdiction, especially universal jurisdiction over piracy *jure gentium*, war crimes and crimes against humanity, they, too, are acting as international tribunals, since they are directly enforcing international law. The prosecution of cases subject to universal jurisdiction in particular, where the forum State does not have any connection to the elements of the offence, necessarily implies that domestic courts assume more than an international character; they are discharging that State's obligation to the whole of the international community, in protecting and enforcing fundamental human rights (*erga omnes* obligations). As the International Court of Justice (ICJ) pointed out in the *Barcelona Traction* case, all States have a legal interest in the protection of fundamental rights worldwide.[33] This would render the exercise of extra-territorial jurisdiction, particularly of the universal nature, not only a right but an obligation. The non-contractual character of the 1948 Genocide Convention, for example, is premised on its

---

29 1015 UNTS 243.
30 SC Res 827 (25 May 1993).
31 SC Res 955 (8 November 1994).
32 37 ILM (1998), 999.
33 *Belgium v Spain (Barcelona Traction Light and Power House Co Ltd)* (1970) ICJ Reports 3, Second Phase, 32.

capacity to create obligations, even vis-à-vis non-affected States, on the basis of its compelling humanitarian nature.

In the absence of international tribunals and general reluctance in the exercise of universal jurisdiction, States have found themselves compelled to reach minimum agreement on international co-operation in criminal matters. The various facets of this co-operation extend not only to purely domestic offences, but, more importantly, to international crimes with a view to preventing impunity. Most prominent among these measures is the insertion of a provision in ICL treaties obligating parties either to prosecute or extradite persons accused of having committed an offence stipulated by the relevant convention (*aut dedere aut judicare*). This clause, whose origin can be traced in the work of Hugo de Groot (Grotius), does not constitute an independent basis for extradition, but requires an additional agreement between the requesting and requested States. It does, nonetheless, serve as a deterrent to establishing safe havens for alleged criminals and forces parties to a convention to take responsible enforcement action. The mechanism of extradition itself also supplements indirect enforcement processes by enabling a more willing and better-equipped (in terms of evidence and proximity to the facts of the case) jurisdiction to investigate a particular case. Another complementary safeguard is the inclusion of broad jurisdictional competence in most international criminal treaties, thereby enabling national prosecutorial authorities to assume direct action. Similarly, contemporary treaties have allowed few or no reservations[34] and have refused contracting States the ability to characterise offences within the framework of a convention as politically or ideologically motivated.[35] This has deprived States of the ability to otherwise refuse extradition and has created a large degree of uniformity as regards the *mens rea* of international offences. Finally, through bilateral and multilateral mutual legal assistance agreements, it has become possible to communicate evidence and other documentation facilitating criminal prosecution between two or more States, as has the process of transferring judicial proceedings across two jurisdictions.

The threefold objective of ICL, that is, to prevent, prosecute and punish offenders, must ultimately be beneficial to all people. If international criminal justice does not serve this purpose, it will have failed. Although the UN has

---

34 1993 Convention on the Prohibition of the Development, Production, Stockpiling and Use of Chemical Weapons and on Their Destruction, Art 22, 32 ILM (1993), 804; 1997 Convention on the Prohibition of the Use, Stockpiling, Production and Transfer of Anti-Personnel Mines and on their Destruction, Art 19, 320 IRRC (1997), 563; 1998 ICC Statute, Art 120.

35 See, eg, 1970 Convention for the Suppression of Unlawful Seizure of Aircraft, Art 8, 860 UNTS 105; 1971 Convention for the Suppression of Unlawful Acts against the Safety of Civil Aviation, Art 8, 974 UNTS 177; 1998 UN Convention for the Suppression of Terrorist Bombings, Arts 5 and 9, 37 ILM (1998), 249.

persistently taken a contrary view,[36] should an independent and impartial Truth and Reconciliation Commission that has the potential to restore trust and facilitate redevelopment in a shattered community be used as an alternative to criminal prosecutions? If there is even one such instance available, it must not be denied to fulfil that perspective. Since the aim of criminal justice is not only to punish the culprit, but to restore law and order, other supplementary mechanisms should be allowed to function alongside. In the *Plavsic* case, the accused was co-President of the Serbian Republic of Bosnia and Herzegovina between February and May 1992, occupying thereafter other significant posts within the Bosnian Serb leadership. Having been informed of an indictment against her, she surrendered to the ICTY and entered a guilty plea with regard to a wide range of crimes against humanity. A number of mitigating factors were set out by Plavsic, among which was that her unequivocal guilty plea, surrender and acceptance of responsibility contributed to the establishment of truth and was a significant effort towards the advancement of reconciliation. The Trial Chamber went to great pains to demonstrate that the process of reconciliation was one of its primary aims, besides retribution, and that the accused's full disclosure and acceptance of responsibility facilitated the purpose and processes of reconciliation, thus indeed constituting a mitigating factor.[37]

As will become evident in other chapters, the UN is opposed to blanket immunities and not to truth commissions in general. Moreover, the aforementioned threefold objective of ICL is served not only through State action, but also through the efforts of private organisations. These efforts relate solely to preventive action, since prosecution and punishment constitute exclusively public functions. Private organisations such as the International Committee of the Red Cross (ICRC), the Piracy Reporting Centre, established by the International Chamber of Commerce, and the International Cable Protection Committee, established by corporations active in that industry, undertake a range of preventive measures to minimise the risk of offences associated with their field of interest. This is welcome and unavoidable to a large extent, as in the case of piracy, for example, most developing States do not have the resources to patrol their coastlines, let alone the adjacent high seas. Moreover, these organisations have, in the past, been the protagonist instigators for the evolution of international norms in a certain field, such as the development of international humanitarian law through the efforts of the ICRC.

---

36 The negotiations leading to the adoption of the Statute of the 2002 Sierra Leone Special Court, after agreement between the UN and the Government of Sierra Leone, vigorously reflected the position of the Secretary General that the granting of amnesties would not bar prosecutions. Report of the Secretary General on the Establishment of a Special Court for Sierra Leone, UN Doc S/2000/915 (4 October 2000), para 22. See Chapter 22, section 22.2.

37 *ICTY Prosecutor v Plavsic*, Sentencing Judgment (27 February 2003), paras 79–81.

The process of ICL enforcement, however, may also involve State entities, in the sense that they may be responsible for the perpetration of an international offence, or because they have transgressed their international obligations by failing to co-operate with other States or international organisations in the suppression of particular criminal activity. A State that breaches any of its international obligations commits an internationally wrongful act and bears responsibility vis-à-vis injured States. Some wrongful acts, however, especially those relating to gross violations of human rights within one country and against that country's nationals, do not produce harm to any particular State. They do, nonetheless, breach obligations owed to the international community as a whole and, as such, every country possesses a legal interest in their termination and satisfaction of the victims. In both aforementioned cases (that is, direct injury and obligations *erga omnes*) recourse is available to the ICJ or other interstate judicial bodies, although no case has so far been entertained by the ICJ on account of a non-injured party alleging breach of a *jus cogens* norm.[38] Increasingly, natural persons have been granted legal standing before international judicial bodies with compulsory jurisdiction, capable of rendering binding judgments, such as the European Court of Human Rights. Judgments and non-binding rulings emanating from other quasi-judicial bodies, such as the UN Human Rights Committee, have in recent years been respected and complied with by a large number of States that have been found to breach particular human rights provisions in the 1966 International Covenant on Civil and Political Rights (ICCPR), although levels of compliance are far from perfect.[39] Moreover, Security Council resolutions are binding upon all States, thus rendering any recalcitrant State subject to possible Council countermeasures on account of its refusal to comply. The Security Council may even authorise the use of armed force in accordance with Art 42 of the 1945 UN Charter, where it is convinced, and its members are capable of deciding, that such action would best counter a particular breach or threat to the peace, or an act of aggression.[40] This was amply exemplified in the case of Iraqi aggression against Kuwait in 1990, where the Council authorised a coalition of allied States to use force in order to restore not only Kuwaiti independence, but also international peace and security in the region.[41] Sanctions can also be imposed by regional organisations and this is usually decided and executed in co-operation, or in execution of, relevant Security Council

---

38 The European Court and Commission of Human Rights has had a chance to examine interstate complaints alleging human rights violations taking place solely on the territory and against the nationals of a single State. See *Denmark, Norway, Sweden and The Netherlands v Greece* (*Greek* case) (1969) 12 ECHR Yearbook 134.

39 D McGoldrick, *The Human Rights Committee*, 1994, Oxford: Clarendon, 202–04.

40 See C Gray, *International Law and the Use of Force*, 2000, Oxford: OUP.

41 SC Res 678 (29 November 1990).

resolutions.[42] Finally, recalcitrant States may also suffer adverse consequences on the basis of particular treaty regimes and the obligations contained therein.[43] Inevitably, all the aforementioned means relating to measures against States, as part of the ICL process, are premised on political considerations as to whether a judicial or other confrontational avenue should be followed, except where this involves individual claimants.

1.5 STATE 'CRIMINALITY'

The notion of 'criminality' essentially refers to liability of a criminal nature. Liability itself is based on the attribution of a criminal offence to a particular individual. Criminal liability in both national and international law is generally attributed to natural persons and, exceptionally, also to other legal entities, as was the case with several Nazi-related organisations after the Second World War. Even so, it was not the legal person that was deemed to be liable; rather, it was individual membership that constituted the particular criminal offence. It is, therefore, evident that any discussion of liability that does not involve any natural persons as perpetrators – or in some specific instances of private legal persons – is devoid of a criminal nature, but not necessarily a civil one.

Equally, it has become common for associations of the private sector to self-regulate themselves in order to avoid the intrusion of criminal legislation. This is particularly common with regard to the banking and financial services industry in relation to money laundering and terrorist financing and not simply financial crime that causes economic loss to such institutions. The European Banking Federation (EFB), for example, tabled seven recommendations aiming to improve the implementation of the EU anti-terrorist financing sanctions regime.[44] The EFB Recommendations clearly suggest that its member institutions are only bound to adhere to EU legislation. Hence, EFB members support the application only of that portion of international law that has been transposed into EU law and not of all relevant Security Council resolutions. Additionally, on 30 October 2000, eleven of the world's largest banks, later followed by two others, established anti-money laundering guidelines applicable to private international banks. The Group adopted a set of principles guiding its members how to better conduct their business

---

42 European Union implementation of petroleum embargo, 1999 OJ L108/1; freezing of Yugoslav funds abroad and bar of future investment in Serbia, Council Regulation 1294/ 1999, 1999 OJ L153/63 and Council Decision 1999/424/CFSP, 1999 OJ L163/86, 26 June 1999.
43 See ICC Statute, Art 87(7).
44 EFB Recommendations for Drafting, Interpreting and Implementing Financial Sanctions Regulations (21 Dec. 2001).

and avoid the circulation of illegitimate funds. On this basis, the members unanimously adopted the so-called Wolfsberg Principles.[45] As a result of the 11 September events, the group met again in January 2002 to discuss terrorist financing, and updated its Principles to make reference to the role of financial institutions. Additional measures were adopted by the Basel Committee, which was established by the central-bank governors of the Group of Ten (G10) Countries in 1974. It is composed of about 30 technical working groups and task forces, and its conclusions or recommendations do not have the force of law, but are intended to formulate broad supervisory standards and guidelines, while recommending statements of best practice in the expectation that individual authorities will implement them based on their own particular needs. The Committee's Secretariat is provided for by the Bank for International Business Settlements (BIS).[46]

All crimes are committed by natural persons and it seems self-evident that personal culpability should somehow follow. Personal attribution, however, that will eventually materialise into criminal liability is a complex exercise in the international legal system. The majority of international offences are committed by individuals acting under the guise of, or on behalf of, State orchestrated policies, whether overtly or clandestinely. The policy of apartheid in South Africa, the genocides against Jews, Armenians and Tutsi, as well as cases of State-sponsored terrorism (for example, Libyan involvement in the *Lockerbie* case)[47] are just some instances where an international offence originates from the highest echelons of a State apparatus and is, subsequently, executed by its subordinate organs or agents. Leaving aside the issue of personal immunity for acts perpetrated by or on behalf of the State,[48] is there any room for the State itself to be viewed as having committed a criminal act, and if so, is this a worthwhile exercise? Until August 2000, this notion, even though progressive, was entertained although not wholly accepted by the international community. Then draft Art 19 of the International Law Commission's (ILC) Draft Articles on State Responsibility distinguished between international 'crimes' and 'delicts'. In accordance with Art 19(2), an international crime resulted 'from the breach by a State of an international obligation so essential for the protection of fundamental interests of the international community that its breach is recognised as a crime by that community as a whole'. Any other breach falling below this standard was classified as an international delict. The formulation found in draft Art 19, however, was not universally acceptable and was possibly unnecessary. Nonetheless, the idea that there do exist obligations owed to the international

---

45 Available at <http://www.wolfsberg-principles.com>.
46 Available at <http://www.bis.org/bcbs/aboutbcbs.htm>.
47 See Chapter 10, section 10.3.1 and Chapter 22, section 22.7.
48 See Chapter 4, section 4.10.

community as a whole and that serious breaches should attract special consequences was never doubted.[49]

In August 2000, the ILC, prompted also by its new rapporteur, James Crawford, decided to delete draft Art 19, as well as any reference to the word 'crime', from the text. The Articles no longer differentiate between criminal and delictual responsibility, viewing, instead, a State's internationally wrongful acts as forming a single category of violations. While, as explained, the problematic notion of 'international State crime' was deleted, it was recognised that a State may be liable for acts breaching peremptory norms (*jus cogens*), as well as obligations owed to the international community as a whole (*erga omnes*).

State responsibility in no way precludes individual responsibility, but if the ILC Articles are to have any real significance it is imperative that additional consequences flow from the serious breach of community obligations. In its last reading, the Commission favoured the idea of proportionate damages in accordance with the gravity of the offence. Such damages would be sought by the victim State, or in the absence of such a State, by any other State acting on behalf of, and in the interests of, the individual victims of the breach.[50] Moreover, the Commission's draft endorses, under strict circumstances, the possibility of countermeasures. Article 54 constitutes a compromise balance between the reservations about collective countermeasures and the revulsion against turning a blind eye to gross breaches, especially human rights breaches.[51] This provision limits such countermeasures to those which are taken in response to serious and manifest breaches of obligations to the international community, and obliges participating States to co-operate in order to ensure that the principle of proportionality is observed.[52]

Although the debate on the international criminality of States seems to have ended as far as the ILC is concerned, many still argue that the regime contained in former draft Art 19 answers an indisputable need, pointing out, however, that it was the legal regimes of the envisaged crimes that were debatable.[53] The new regime contained in the adopted Articles strikes a right balance between the need to formulate a realistic framework for enforcement of *jus cogens* and *erga omnes* obligations, while at the same time rendering the text more accessible to States that would otherwise have objections to the definitional uncertainty and scope of draft Art 19.

---

49 J Crawford, 'Revising the Draft Articles on State Responsibility', 10 EJIL (1999), 435.
50 J Crawford *et al*, 'The ILC's Draft Articles on State Responsibility: Toward Completion of a Second Reading', 94 AJIL (2000), 660, 673.
51 See C Antonopoulos, *The Unilateral Use of Force by States in International Law*, 1997, Athens: Sakkoulas.
52 Op cit, Crawford *et al*, note 50, 674.
53 A Pellet, 'Can a State Commit a Crime? Definitely, Yes!', 10 EJIL (1999), 425.

1.6 INTERNATIONAL CRIMINAL LAW AND HUMAN RIGHTS

Bassiouni convincingly argues that the last stage in the development of a rights regime is the 'criminalisation' stage.[54] It is there that the shared values contained in that particular right are further protected by the promulgation of penal proscriptions. This is true of all rights. The whole concept of human rights was premised on the notion that the State is the violator, although it is not infrequent for private individuals to commit depredations. The prohibitions contained in human rights treaties are addressed to States and are of two types: the first involves a negative obligation, requiring that State officials or agents thereof be prevented from violating human rights (such as torture and apartheid); the second type involves a negative obligation, requiring States to ensure that the rights guaranteed are not violated, or in any other way suppressed by entities beyond the public domain (such as slavery and terrorist offences against the person). On this basis, it may reasonably be argued that the promulgation of a right at the international level entails the obligation to criminalise at the domestic level. For example, the right to be free from involuntary servitude[55] would be meaningless unless implementing legislation, among other measures, effectively penalised and suppressed all forms of slavery – although slavery is explicitly criminalised by a plethora of international conventions. Many offences that were traditionally attributable to State agents, such as crimes against humanity and war crimes, are at present also attributable to non-State entities, in particular paramilitary organisations,[56] while other international offences that can only be perpetrated by private actors, such as organised crime, have not subsided. Although private individuals bear criminal liability for committing international offences, they cannot assume international responsibility for violating international human rights, as the obligations arising from this legal regime are addressed exclusively to States. Despite this observation, a number of States have been supporting the idea that non-State entities are responsible for the 'destruction' of human rights, especially where acts of terrorism are attributed to national liberation or other guerilla movements.[57] Such a discourse can only have adverse effects on the human

54 CM Bassiouni, 'International Criminal Law and Human Rights', 9 *Yale Journal of World Public Order* (1982), 193.
55 International Covenant on Civil and Political Rights, Art 8(1), (2), 999 UNTS 171.
56 ILC report, Draft Code of Crimes Against the Peace and Security of Mankind, UN Doc A/51/10 (1996) Supp No 10, p 94; in *ICTR Prosecutor v Kayishema and Ruzindana*, Judgment (21 May 1999), para 125, the ICTR convicted the accused Ruzindana, a local businessman, of crimes against humanity because he partook in the overall Hutu extremist policy to exterminate the minority Tutsis; see also *ICTY Prosecutor v Karadzic and Mladic*, r 61 Decision (11 July 1996), paras 60–64.
57 GA Res 48/122 (20 December 1993); GA Res 49/185 (23 December 1994); GA Res 50/186 (22 December 1995); GA Res 51/210 (17 December 1996); GA Res 52/133 (27 February 1997).

rights movement, since it helps certain States that frequently violate human rights to shift global attention from their obligations and legitimately deny the enjoyment of rights, especially the right to self-determination.[58]

Selectivity in international criminal law is undeniable. The great powers of our times praise or are silent about atrocious regimes that suffocate and exterminate their people, simply because it suits their geopolitical agenda. On the other hand, they are willing to go to great lengths to invade a nation, willingly accept the loss of many thousand civilian lives – most of which inflicted directly by the acts of the occupying power – when their interests are no longer entertained by the incumbent regime, which they had helped install in the first place. The same great powers openly abuse fundamental human rights and have no hesitation to abduct and torture persons over whom they may only have a suspicion of criminal conduct, or secretly transfer them to undemocratic regimes that routinely torture their political opponents. Moreover, under the pretext of sanctions the aim of which is to topple a 'brutal' regime the great powers accept that many innocent civilians will go unnourished and that thousands will die due to lack of medicines. When a government does the same to its people by denying it food and medicines it is branded as authoritarian and brutal. We are not for one minute advocating that those denying their people of fundamental rights should not be brought to justice, we are simply highlighting the fact that there exist others, particularly heading the great powers, that are responsible for the deaths and hardship of hundreds of thousands of civilians. They proclaim themselves as liberators and few dare discuss their criminal liability which is a disgrace for the modern world.

Finally, as will be evident throughout this book, the rights of the accused should prevail above all other considerations. Fundamental procedural and judicial guarantees, such as the right to a fair trial within a reasonable time, the prohibition of retroactive legislation, the observation of the doctrine *ne bis in idem*, and others, have matured as general principles of law, or generally accepted custom and have found their way into the Statutes of all contemporary international criminal tribunals. The same set of principles should also guide domestic criminal proceedings on the basis at least of their customary force, which are not to be dismissed lightly under the guise of emergency measures, as occurs all too often with terrorist-related offences. In many countries, so called domestic terrorism constitutes a pretext for suspending democracy and civil liberties and is a solid excuse for engaging in widespread curtailment and violation of fundamental freedoms. On the basis of the aforementioned, the reader will come to realise that the international criminal process is inextricably linked with the development and application of human rights.

---

58 See Chapter 10, sections 10.5 and 10.8.

Chapter 2

Principles of liability and participation in international criminal law

In this chapter we seek to explore the various forms of participation in international crime, particularly as an accomplice and liability thereof. This task is not undertaken through comparative criminal law but solely on the basis of international law sources, particularly treaties, custom and judgments of international tribunals. The latter have relied to a very large degree on comparative methods in order to demonstrate the existence of a general principle of criminal law. Our selection of International Criminal Tribunal for the former Yugoslavia (ICTY) and International Criminal Tribunal for Rwanda (ICTR) judgments is not meant to convey the impression that we consider these as binding statements of the law generally, but that they represent authoritative statements of the relevant law, or of the direction the law may be taking. We should always keep in mind, however, that the law and jurisprudence of international criminal tribunals is context-specific and not of general application.

2.1 AIDING AND ABETTING

Aiding and abetting consists of all acts that are 'specifically directed to assist, encourage or lend moral support to the perpetration of a specific crime (a single crime, such as murder or rape and not a criminal design) and where, moreover, this support has a substantial effect upon the perpetration of the crime.'[1] The *Blaskic* appeal judgment, while noting that the *actus reus* of aiding and abetting requires a substantial effect upon the crime committed by the principal, stated that no proof of a cause-effect relationship between the aider and the commission of the crime is required, nor proof that such conduct 'served as a condition precedent to the commission of the

---

1 *Prosecutor v Vasiljevic*, Appeals Chamber Judgment (25 Feb 2004), para 102; *Prosecutor v Blaskic*, Appeals Chamber Judgment (29 July 2004), para 45.

crime'.[2] The acts of aiding and abetting, while mostly tangible in practice, may be perpetrated through an omission where a duty to act exists and the omission itself had a substantial effect on the commission of the crime, provided that the accused possessed the appropriate *mens rea*.[3] The *actus reus* of aiding and abetting does not require the presence of the aider at the location where the crime was perpetrated, nor proof of a plan or agreement. Equally, the mere presence of a person with superior authority at the crime scene is insufficient to determine whether that person in fact encouraged or supported the principal. A combination of the following elements: superior authority and presence that may be deemed to have a significant legitimising or encouraging effect on the principal, may be taken as weighty circumstantial evidence of substantial encouragement and support.[4] The participation of the aider may occur before, during, or after the act is committed by the principal.[5]

As far as the *mens rea* for aiding and abetting is concerned, while it is not required that the aider shared the *mens rea* of the principal, it must be demonstrated that the aider 'was aware of the essential elements of the crime which was ultimately committed by the principal'.[6] In other words, the law is interested in ascertaining the particular intent of the aider as to the act of the principal and his participation therein, and in this sense it is not necessary for the aider to know the precise crime that was intended and ultimately committed, as long as he is aware that one of a number of crimes will probably be, and are in fact, committed and has intended to facilitate the commission of anyone of those crimes.[7] If, however, the aider facilitates only a single crime of the principal, he must be aware of the essential elements of the principal's crime, including his relevant *mens rea*.[8] Unlike other forms of participation in crime, the *mens rea* for aiding and abetting requires only direct intent as to the act of the principal and awareness as to the significance of one's contribution and is thus not satisfied with the demonstration of foreseeability as to the result or the effect of the contribution (*dolus eventualis* or recklessness). With regard to persecution, a specific intent crime, the *mens rea* for aiding and abetting requires not only awareness of the facilitated crime, but also of the discriminatory intent of the principal. The aider need not share the intent of

---

2 *Blaskic* Appeals Judgment, ibid, para 1, 48; *Prosecutor v Brdjanin*, Trial Chamber Judgment (1 Sept 2004), para 271.

3 Op cit, *Blaskic* Appeals Judgment, note 1, para 47; *Prosecutor v Simic*, Trial Chamber Judgment (17 Oct 2003), para 162.

4 Op cit, *Brdjanin* Trial Judgment, note 2, para 271; *Simic* Trial Judgment, ibid note 3, para 165.

5 Op cit, *Blaskic* Appeals Judgment, note 1, para 48; *Simic* Trial Judgment, ibid, para 162.

6 *Prosecutor v Aleksovski*, Appeals Chamber Judgment (24 March 2000), para 162; *Prosecutor v Krnojelac*, Appeals Chamber Judgment (17 Sept 2003), para 51.

7 Op cit, *Blaskic* Appeals Judgment, note 1, para 50.

8 Op cit, *Krnojelac* Appeals Judgment, note 6, para 51.

the principal but must be 'aware of the discriminatory context in which the crime is to be committed and know that his support or encouragement has a substantial effect on its perpetration'.[9] The same is obviously true for genocide, yet another specific intent crime.[10] In the *Krstic* case the ICTY distinguished between aiding and abetting and broader forms of complicity in genocide, the latter requiring the accomplice to possess the specific intent to destroy a protected group. The Appeals Chamber found no evidence that the accused ordered or directly participated in the crimes amounting to genocide, but held him liable for aiding and abetting genocide on the basis that 'he knew that those murders were occurring and that he permitted the Main Staff to use personnel and resources under his command to facilitate them'.[11]

A particular manifestation of aiding and abetting, the so-called 'approving spectator', was identified by the ICTR. This is identical in all other respects with the generic form of aiding and abetting with the exception that it requires actual presence during the commission of the crime or at least presence in its immediate vicinity, such that is perceived by the actual perpetrator as approval of his conduct. Liability arises where the 'approving spectator' knows that his presence would be perceived by the perpetrator as encouragement or support, particularly where he occupies a position of authority.[12]

The ICTY has on a few occasions, following the 1999 *Tadic* Appeals Judgment in which the concept of 'joint criminal enterprise' (JCE) was formulated, discussed the differences between aiding and abetting and JCE. Where a person substantially contributes to the commission of a crime by a single principal, or a plurality thereof, and this is all that he is aware of, he becomes an accomplice (by aiding and abetting) as regards those particular offences. This is so even if the principal is part of a JCE involving the commission of further crimes. Where, however, the aider is aware that his assistance is supporting the crimes of a group of persons involved in a JCE and shares that intent, he may be held liable for the crimes committed in furtherance of that common purpose as a whole (as a co-perpetrator) and not simply for the crimes in which he assisted.[13] His overall awareness of the criminal design and willing participation therein suffices to establish oblique intent as to the perpetration of the objectives of the design.

---

9   Op cit, *Krnojelac* Appeals Judgment, note 6, para 52.
10   *Prosecutor v Krstic*, Appeals Chamber Judgment (19 April 2004), para 140.
11   Ibid, paras 142, 144; *ICTY Prosecutor v Krajisnik*, Trial Chamber Judgment (27 Sept 2006), para 865.
12   *ICTR Prosecutor v Semanza*, Trial Chamber Judgment (15 May 2003), paras 385–89.
13   Op cit, *Vasiljevic* Appeals Judgment, note 1, para 102; op cit, *Krnojelac* Appeals Judgment, note 6, para 33; *Prosecutor v Kvocka*, Appeals Chamber Judgment (28 Feb 2005), para 90.

2.2 ORDERING

An order is a command for action or omission that is issued by a superior to a subordinate, irrespective of whether the context of the relationship is military or civilian. The relationship itself need not be formally established, but could exist *de facto*, as long as the addressee perceives the order as a binding command. It may be written or oral and addressed to either a specific individual or to unknown recipients, and it may also be channelled to its addresses through a number of intermediaries. The *actus reus* of ordering consists of the transmission of an unlawful command to one or more subordinates.[14] An order is unlawful where it violates international humanitarian or general international criminal law, even if it is in conformity with the domestic law of the State of the person who issued it. Although this conclusion is consistent with the customary principle that domestic law may not be invoked to justify violation of an international rule, it does little to aid a subordinate who dutifully acted within the boundaries of his domestic law. As a result, domestic law should itself be characterised as an order, so that its implementing recipients may benefit from the international law relating to superior orders and duress.

Equally, not all orders whose content is unlawful entail the liability of the person who issued, or transmitted them. The general *mens rea* standard for ordering requires knowledge of the order's illegal character, coupled with direct intent to fulfil its content. Where the order was not known to the issuer to be unlawful, or where it was not manifestly unlawful that person will not be liable for the harm caused by the order.[15] This would, therefore, exclude negligence, which may be defined as lacking awareness as to an unlawful risk or a criminal consequence. Thus, where superiors are aware of the illegality of the order, or are reckless (ie they are conscious as to the taking of an unjustifiable risk) as to its consequences and nonetheless transmit it through the chain of command they are just as liable as the person who initially issued the order.[16] In the absence of a standard lower than direct intent in Art 7(1) of the ICTY Statute, the ICTY was forced to decide whether recklessness or *dolus eventualis* pertain to ordering. The methodology employed by the *Blaskic* Appeals Chamber involved an examination of the common law recklessness and civil law *dolus eventualis* as a matter of general principle of domestic laws. It found that in common law jurisdictions, the *mens rea* of recklessness – which

---

14 This much has been established without controversy by all ICTY Chambers. See, eg, op cit, *Brdjanin* Trial Judgment, note 2, para 270; I Bantekas, *Principles of Direct and Superior Responsibility in International Humanitarian Law*, 2002, Manchester: Manchester University Press, 50–53.

15 See Art 33 ICTY Statute, on the defence of superior orders.

16 *USA v von Leeb* (*High Command* case) 11 Trials of War Criminals before the Nuremberg Military Tribunals under Control Council Law No 10 [TWC] 510.

attaches to serious crimes equivalent to ordering – incorporates 'the awareness of a risk that the result or consequence will occur or will probably occur [but it must not be virtually certain that they will occur, otherwise it is oblique intent], and the risk must be unjustifiable or unreasonable. The mere possibility of a risk that a crime or crimes will occur as a result of the actor's conduct generally does not suffice to ground criminal responsibility'.[17] The Appeals Chamber's findings with regard to the civil law conception of *dolus eventualis* make no significant departure. In general terms it requires that the accused perceived or foresaw the harm as possible, but not remote, and although he may not have intended to bring it about, he accepted the possibility that it may well occur.[18] Thus, besides direct intent, the Appeals Chamber expressly grounded in addition the existence of a lower *mens rea* standard that is more akin to common law recklessness, despite the civil law composition of the Court, in the following terms:

> A person who orders an act or omission with the awareness of the substantial likelihood that a crime will be committed in the execution of that order, has the requisite *mens rea* for establishing liability under Art 7(1) [of the ICTY Statute]. Ordering with such awareness has to be regarded as accepting that crime'.[19]

The matter is not clarified in the International Criminal Court (ICC) Statute, Art 30(1)(b) of which states that a person has intent in relation to a consequence where 'that person means to cause that consequence or is aware that it will occur in the ordinary course of events'. The language and terminology in the latter part of this provision is more akin to recklessness than oblique intent, but whereas oblique intent in English common law requires that the perpetrator perceive the risk as 'virtually certain', the ICC provision only speaks of awareness 'in the ordinary course of events'. With some caution, we have to accept that Art 30(1)(b) refers to oblique intent because the purpose of this provision is to designate the various contours of intent as to a consequence.

In the absence of written orders as evidence before a court, ordering may be inferred from a variety of circumstantial evidence, particularly the number of illegal acts, the number, identity and type of troops involved, the effective command and control exerted over these troops, the logistics involved, the widespread occurrence of the illegal acts, the tactical tempo of operations, the location of the superior and his knowledge of crimes committed under

17 Op cit, *Blaskic* Appeals Judgment, note 1, para 38.
18 Ibid, para 39.
19 Ibid, para 42; now firmly accepted as part of the ICTY's jurisprudence. See *Prosecutor v Kordic*, Appeals Chamber Judgment (17 Dec 2004), para 30.

his command, and others.[20] Equally, there may exist confusion as to the unlawful nature of a written order, as was the case in the *Blaskic* Appeals Judgment where a preventive attacking order against a village inhabited by civilians was found by the Trial Chamber to lack a military objective. In reversing the Trial Chamber's determination of the nature of the order, the Appeals Chamber held that in fact the village had a strategic significance because it was very close to a road linking two major cities and on which enemy combatants frequently travelled.[21]

The issuer of an illegal order who satisfies the requisite *actus reus* and *mens rea* is as liable as if he himself had perpetrated the eventual crime. The same applies *mutatis mutandis* with regard to attempts, in accordance with Art 25(3)(b) of the ICC Statute.[22]

2.3 PLANNING/PREPARATION

Several legal terms have been employed since the end of the Second World War to describe a concerted effort between multiple participants to commit one or more crimes. Article 6(a) of the Nuremberg Charter imposed liability for the planning, among others, of crimes against peace as well as for participation in 'a common plan or conspiracy' to commit war crimes and crimes against peace. Equally, Art 3(b) refers to liability arising from a conspiracy to commit genocide, without making any reference to planning. Finally, while the concept of conspiracy is absent from the ICTY and ICC Statutes, planning exists in Art 7(1) of the Statute, but not in its ICC counterpart. As will be examined later in this chapter, the ICTY has developed the 'joint criminal enterprise' (JCE) liability, which shares many of the characteristics of common law conspiracy. The latter, although omitted from the ICC Statute, was nonetheless compensated by the compromise provision of Art 25(3)(d) in that Statute.

Although we shall be dealing with the concept of conspiracy later in this chapter, it suffices to say that a significant difference between the two is that while the planning of a crime may be committed by a single person, conspiracy requires at least two.[23] Planning, therefore, involves 'one or several persons contemplating designing the commission of a crime at both the preparatory and execution phases'.[24] The existence of a plan, whether this is

---

20 *Prosecutor v Galic*, Trial Chamber Judgment (5 Dec 2003), para 171.
21 Op cit, *Blaskic* Appeals Judgment, note 1, para 330–32.
22 See R Cryer, 'General Principles of Liability in International Criminal Law', in D McGoldrick *et al, The Permanent International Criminal Court*, 2004, Oxford: Hart, 242–47, where he discusses the legal nature of liability incurred as a result of ordering.
23 *Prosecutor v Akayesu*, Trial Chamber Judgment (2 Sept 1998), para 480.
24 Ibid.

formal or informal, must be demonstrated by direct or circumstantial evidence.[25] The level of participation of the accused in the plan is an additional important factor. According to the *Brdjanin* Trial Judgment, planning liability arises only if it was 'demonstrated that the accused was substantially involved at the preparatory stage of that crime in the concrete form it took, which implies that he possessed sufficient knowledge thereof in advance'.[26] It is not a requirement, however, that the accused be intimate with every detail of the acts committed by the physical perpetrator.[27] Moreover, it is necessary that the accused devise the plan or be involved in the immediate preparation of the concrete crimes and not merely participate in its implementation by virtue of his authority.[28]

A person that plans a crime and moreover commits the planned crime will only be liable for its perpetration.[29] This factor demonstrates a further proximity with conspiracy/JCE in which participants in the conspiracy or common design are ultimately liable as perpetrators and not on account of their particular roles, which may not have involved perpetration of the crimes themselves. There is no guidance in the relevant international instruments or the jurisprudence of the ICTY/ICTR as to whether the planner is liable absent perpetration of the crime. It is probably imprudent to seek a solution to this query on the basis of general principles because planning liability has developed since its Nuremberg origins wholly within the realm of international law. In this light, since the complicity/JCE concepts do not require completion and given that planning belongs within this family of liability, it would be wise at least to provide for the liability of persons that are instrumental with regard to the formulation of a criminal plan even where it is dissolved against their will before being consummated.

The *mens rea* for planning requires that the accused intended the crime in question through the plan. Besides direct intent, the *Kordic* Appeals Judgment stated that in relation to planning, 'a person who plans an act or omission with the awareness of the substantial likelihood that a crime will be committed in the execution of that plan' has the requisite *mens rea* for planning, since this is regarded as accepting that crime.[30] This would refer to oblique intent rather than recklessness/*dolus eventualis*, which does not seem to be supported by any identifiable doctrinal basis.

25 *Prosecutor v Naletilic*, Trial Chamber Judgment (31 March 2003), para 59.
26 Op cit, *Brdjanin* Trial Judgment, note 2, para 357.
27 Ibid.
28 Ibid, para 358.
29 *ICTY Prosecutor v Blaskic*, Trial Chamber Judgment (3 March 2000), para 278.
30 Op cit, *Kordic* Appeals Judgment, note 19, para 31.

2.4 INSTIGATION

Liability through instigation arises by prompting another to commit an offence through action or omission.[31] The ICTY has held that omissions amount to instigation in circumstances where a commander has created 'an environment permissive of criminal behaviour by subordinates'.[32] If this amounts to negligence (in this instance defined as indifference or a 'couldn't care less attitude'), such negligence-based liability will be hard to justify in the case of instigation. Unlike ordering, which involves a superior–subordinate relationship no such relationship is required for an instigation to take place and will thus lack the elements of compulsion and command. A causal link must exist between the instigation and the perpetration of a crime, although it is not necessary to demonstrate that the crime would not have been perpetrated without the involvement of the accused.[33] The prosecution must show that the instigation 'was a factor substantially contributing to the conduct' of the principal.[34] Moreover, liability for instigation arises only where the offence has been committed, or attempted.[35] Where the crime has not been committed, the accused's conduct may be described as incitement, which does not generally entail liability, unless it concerns public and direct incitement to commit genocide.[36] In cases where instigation has not been followed by perpetration, the prosecution may well argue that the accused devised a plan or was a co-perpetrator in the context of a joint criminal enterprise. Because of the lack of compulsion involved in instigation, the physical perpetrator cannot invoke superior orders or duress to exculpate himself. On the contrary, the instigator may under particular circumstances invoke these defences, especially where the instigation was the result of a binding order given to the instigator by his superiors, provided that the other requisites for these defences are met.

The *mens rea* for instigation requires that the accused intended to provoke or induce the commission of the crime by the physical perpetrator (direct intent), or that he was aware of the substantial likelihood that the commission of the crime would be a probable consequence of his acts or omissions.[37] Again, this can only refer to oblique intent and not recklessness/*dolus eventualis*,

---

31 Op cit, *Akayesu* Trial Judgment, note 23, para 482.
32 Op cit, *Blaskic* Trial Judgment, note 29, para 337; op cit, *Galic* Trial Judgment, note 20, para 168.
33 Op cit, *Kordic* Appeals Judgment, note 19, para 27.
34 Ibid.
35 Op cit, *Akayesu* Trial Judgment, note 23, para 482; *Brdjanin* Trial Judgment, supra note 2, para 269.
36 Art 3(c) of the 1948 Genocide Convention; Art 25(3)(e) ICC Statute.
37 Op cit, *Blaskic* Appeals Judgment, note 1, para 42; op cit, *Kordic* Appeals Judgment, note 19, para 32.

but it is evident from the wording of these judgments that some Chambers are confused even when citing among themselves. The basic principle is that for serious violations of international law through ordering, instigating and planning no *mens rea* standard below direct/oblique intent should be accepted.

Just like incitement to genocide where the particular perception of the message by the intended audience is a critical aspect only for determining the perpetrator's awareness as to the understanding of the audience, the same is true with regard to instigation. If that were not so, a court would be justified in imposing liability on the basis of reckless behaviour by the accused where he was aware that a possibility did exist that the message may be perceived as instigating criminal activity. Recklessness, however, finds no place in the *mens rea* definition of instigation, nor indeed in the crime of genocide.

2.5 JOINT CRIMINAL ENTERPRISE

In both domestic and international criminal law a distinction is made between (general) joint perpetration and joint perpetration that involves a common purpose or a common design. The difference between the two is that where a common purpose has been established and roles have been allocated therein, each member of the common purpose is equally liable regardless of the nature and gravity of his or her participation and role. On the contrary, in the case of a joint perpetration absent a common purpose, the liability of each perpetrator is determined in accordance with the crime committed. Article 7(1) of the ICTY Statute does not explicitly establish liability involving common purpose perpetration, whereas Art 25(3)(d) does indeed do so in the following manner:

> [A person incurs liability where he] contributes to the commission or attempted commission of a crime by a group of persons acting with a common purpose. Such contribution shall be intentional and shall either:
>
> (i) be made with the aim of furthering the criminal activity or criminal purpose of the group, where such activity or purpose involves the commission of a crime within the jurisdiction of the Court; or
>
> (ii) be made in the knowledge of the intention of the group to commit the crime.

Since Art 25(3)(a) refers to a distinct form of liability consisting of committing a crime 'jointly with another', it is evident that the liability established under subparagraph (3)(d) is of a wholly different nature. In the absence of a similar provision in the ICTY Statute, the ICTY Appeals Chamber in the *Tadic* case in 1999 pronounced that so-called 'joint criminal enterprise' existed in customary international law,[38] rendering each and every member of a 'common design' equally liable regardless of the gravity of the crime or contribution of each participant.[39] According to the Appeals Chamber, a JCE consists of a common plan, design or purpose, and the participation of a plurality of persons therein, all of which are acting with the aim of committing one or more international crimes.[40] The ICTY chambers confirmed that participation in a joint criminal enterprise is a form of 'commission' within the meaning of Art 7(1) of the ICTY Statute, just like physical perpetration, aiding and abetting, planning, ordering, etc.[41] There is no need for the plan to be organised under a formal guise or structure, such as with organised crime; nor is there a requirement for the plan to be conceived before the crime is committed, thus rendering JCE formulation and participation therein a spontaneous event.[42] This would then render JCE liability in relation to genocide and crimes against humanity problematic if charged as 'spontaneous designs', since both require substantial planning and preparation. While a person sharing the objectives of a JCE, but without having any links to it, will not transfer his liability to the participants of that JCE, the situation is different where that person has forged links in pursuit of a common objective.[43] The *Krajisnik* Trial Chamber raised this point in order to negate the argument of the accused, who was the second in command in the Bosnian-Serb leadership, and according to which he had little or no link or actual authority over those military or paramilitary units that committed crimes against humanity. Thus, persons who do not participate in a common objective but are used, or indeed use, the JCE to achieve shared criminal purposes are liable for the crimes committed through the JCE and equally transfer their own liability to the JCE itself. Unlike common complicity where the accomplice shares the liability of the principal only when he or she significantly contributes to the execution of the *actus reus* of the offence, this is not a requirement for participants to a JCE. Instead, causation as to execution is irrelevant for the purposes of attributing liability.[44]

The Appeals Chamber distinguished between three JCE categories. The first, and more general, consists of cases where a group of persons possesses a shared intent to commit a crime and a common design is accordingly

---

38 *Prosecutor v Tadic*, Appeals Chamber Judgment (15 July 1999), paras 194 *et seq*. JCE liability was subsequently adopted unquestionably before other ICTY Chambers. See, eg, *Prosecutor v Vasiljevic*, Trial Chamber Judgment (29 Nov 2002), paras 63 *et seq*; *Prosecutor v Furundzija*, Appeals Chamber Judgment (21 July 2000), para 119.

39 Op cit, *Vasiljevic* Trial Judgment, note 38, para 67.

40 Op cit, *Tadic* Appeals Judgment, note 38, para 188.

41 Op cit, *Krnojelac* Appeals Judgment, note 6, para 73.

42 Op cit, *Tadic* Appeals Judgment, note 38, para 227.

43 Op cit, *Krajisnik* Trial Judgment, note 11, para 1083.

44 Op cit, *Tadic* Appeals Judgment, note 38, para 199.

formulated. Participants in the common design will inevitably assume differing roles and levels of responsibility, and, depending on the magnitude of the eventual crime, some participants will contribute to its planning and intermediate stages while others will play a significant role in its execution. JCE liability arises even for those that do not directly contribute to the execution of the crime, as long as they are found to enjoy a significant contribution in the perpetration of the common design. Contributions of this nature may vary, but can include all types of assistance at any stage of the design. A significant difficulty with JCE liability concerns the construction of an appropriate *mens rea* for those participants that did not take part in the execution of the crime. The *Tadic* Appeals Chamber was of the view that the participant must willingly contribute to at least one element of the common design and intend the result of the ultimate crime(s) undertaken by his co-perpetrators.[45]

The second category is more specific, derived by the *Tadic* Appeals Judgment from concentration camp JCE liability cases. After further refinement this category is now known as 'systemic', covering all cases 'relating to an organised system with a common criminal purpose perpetrated against the detainees'.[46] These consist of a common design in which multiple persons participate in a 'system of ill-treatment' of detainees in camps. The participants enjoy positions of authority in the camp and have either established or are aware of the system and contribute to its furtherance in whatever capacity each is called upon. Thus, tasks undertaken within such a system of ill-treatment will vary significantly. The participants must be aware of the system and intend to contribute to it.[47] Camps of this type will certainly be staffed with multiple persons and in the absence of an agreement to ill-treat detainees, the prosecution will have to infer the participation of each staff member in the common design.[48] The *Kvocka* Appeals Judgment agreed with the conclusions of the Trial Chamber in that the holding of an 'executive, administrative or protective role in a camp constitutes general participation in the crimes committed therein. An intent to further the efforts of the JCE so as to rise to the level of co-perpetration may also be inferred from knowledge of the crimes being perpetrated in the camp and continued participation which enables the camp's functioning'.[49] According to the *Kvocka* Appeals

---

45 Ibid, para 196.
46 Op cit, *Kvocka* Appeals Judgment, note 13, para 182.
47 Op cit, *Tadic* Appeals Judgment, note 38, paras 202–03.
48 The fact that abuses do take place in a camp does not necessarily mean that a systemic JCE has been established. In *ICTY Prosecutor v Limaj*, Trial Chamber Judgment (30 Nov 2005), para 669, the Chamber held that no evidence of a common design could be inferred in the absence of proof demonstrating that a group of individuals whose identities could be established at least by reference to their category as a group had furthered a common plan.
49 Op cit, *Kvocka* Appeals Judgment, note 13, paras 103, 184.

Judgment, inference of *mens rea* may be taken from the position of the accused in the camp, the amount of time spent there, his function, movement throughout the camp, and any contact he had with detainees, staff personnel, or outsiders visiting the camp, as well as through ordinary senses.[50] It is obvious that not every person staffing an abuse camp is necessarily a participant in the common design. This is especially true for those in the lower echelons who are not aware of the crimes, or who although aware of them take no part and have no capacity to prevent them. Persons who do commit crimes in camp-related common designs, but do so unwillingly as a result of duress or superior orders, cannot logically be deemed to share the intent of the other co-perpetrators. In this case, however, for the purposes of doctrinal consistency it may be best to say that they share the required direct intent but their culpability is negated by the defences they invoke.

The third category refers to common plans or designs in which the actions of one or more participants exceed the aim of the original design and as such the excessive action no longer coincides with the intention of all participants (so-called 'extended JCE'). Should all participants be equally liable for the unintended action, or only for that which they had originally intended? It is unlikely that an exception could plausibly be made for a standard lower than direct/oblique intent for such serious offences, but the *Tadic* Appeals Chamber is of a different opinion, although its choice of terms is unsatisfactory and confusing. It first noted that liability for the unintended deaths would arise where 'the risk of death was a predictable consequence . . . and the accused was either reckless or indifferent to that risk'.[51] Despite the 'predictability' element this standard may suggest recklessness. However, in para 228 the Chamber then goes on to say that liability arises if 'it was foreseeable that such a crime might be perpetrated by one or other members of the group and the accused willingly took that risk'. This smacks of oblique intent, leaving no room for reckless-based liability. Just when one thought the standard was clear, the Appeals Chamber notes in para 220 that:

> What is required is a state of mind in which a person, although he did not intend to bring about a certain result, was aware that the actions of the group were most likely to lead to that result but nevertheless willingly took that risk. In other words, the so-called *dolus eventualis* is required (also called 'advertent recklessness' in some national legal systems).

---

50 Op cit, *Kvocka* Appeals Judgment, note 13, paras 201–202.
51 Ibid, note 38, para 204.

What this means is that the Appeals Chamber introduces also recklessness/ *dolus eventualis* to the *mens rea* definition of the third JCE type.[52] It has now been accepted in the ICTY Appeals Chamber that the third type of JCE and the crime of genocide are compatible.[53] This is a dangerous precedent for a specific intent crime such as genocide, since if only the excessive and unintended crimes were to amount to genocide, the Court would not require the normal JCE participants to demonstrate the *dolus specialis* for genocide, but a *dolus eventualis* for genocide instead. This would work well for the vast majority of offences but would defeat the raison d'être of the *mens rea* for genocide.

Some criticism is rightly due to the formulation of JCE by the *Tadic* Appeals Chamber. For one thing, it is unacceptable for a criminal tribunal to come up *de novo* with a legal construction that is unfavourable to the accused, especially when it is not explicitly provided in its Statute. Secondly, it is equally unacceptable for the tribunal to claim the validity of this legal construction on conspicuously declared customary law[54] that itself is based on scattered post-Second World War case law that lay dormant during the Cold War, suddenly finding itself awake! Finally, it is by no means clear that the criminal liability grounded in Art 25(3)(d) of the ICC Statute is identical to the ICTY's JCE construction since it does not expressly equate the liability of each member of the group. Despite the JCE precedent within the context of the ICTY chambers and its elevation therein to a customary principle, it should not be lightly assumed that this statement is also true and final outside the ICTY framework.[55] It should be noted that the common purpose liability

---

52 In English criminal law, indifference as to the consequence (couldn't care less attitude) was until 2004 encompassed within the domain of recklessness, as an inadvertent species thereof, introduced by the House of Lords in *Caldwell* [1982] AC 341. Such inadvertent recklessness was rightly criticised because it lacked the element of awareness, even if that was down to the irresponsible character of the accused, and was applied by the courts in cases of criminal damage. It was finally repealed in *G* [2004] 1 AC 1034. As a result of these observations, its application in the third JCE type is highly problematic.

53 *ICTY Prosecutor v Brdjanin*, Appeals Chamber Decision on Interlocutory Appeal (19 March 2004), paras 9–10; *ICTY Prosecutor v Stakic*, Appeals Chamber Judgment (22 March 2006), para 38.

54 In *ICTY Prosecutor v M Milutinovic et al*, Appeals Chamber Decision on Ojdanic's Motion Challenging Jurisdiction: Indirect Co-Perpetration (22 March 2006), para 21, the Appeals Chamber declared the existence of JCE liability in customary international law since as early as 1992.

55 Some, but understandably, limited criticism of JCE liability has come even from within the ICTY. In *Prosecutor v Stakic*, Trial Chamber Judgment (31 July 2003), paras 438, 441, the Trial Chamber expressed its reservations about the doctrine, indicating that a 'more direct reference to commission in its traditional sense should be given priority before considering JCE liability'. Instead, it applied *de novo* (for the purposes of the ICTY) a form of liability it termed 'co-perpetratorship'. At the Appeals stage, the Appeals Judgment (22 March 2006), paras 58ff, dismissed co-perpetratorship, deeming it inconsistent with ICTY jurisprudence and outside the ambit of customary law. It thus reapplied the evidence on the basis of the JCE doctrine.

of Art 25(3)(d) of the ICC Statute has found a place in Art 2(4)(c) of the 2005 UN Convention for the Suppression of Acts of Nuclear Terrorism.

2.6 CONSPIRACY

References to conspiracies in international criminal law textbooks are most commonly included in the section concerning inchoate offences (ie crimes that incur liability without the perpetration of any principal offence). We should, however, distinguish the double life of the concept in domestic criminal laws and international law. The concept is only known in common law jurisdictions, and in general terms it consists of an agreement between two or more persons with the intention of carrying out a crime and playing a part in that course of conduct.[56] Significantly, this common law conspiracy need not be consummated and anyone found to have been a party to such agreement, absent perpetration of the principal crime, is liable. Liability is incurred with regard to the conspiracy itself, rendering it therefore a distinct offence. Its justificatory existence is apparently of a preventive nature. The concept of conspiracy in international law rests on different premises. Its inclusion in Art 6(a) of the Nuremberg Charter clearly aimed at formulating a particular form of perpetrating the crime of aggression. It is, therefore, not a crime at all.

Although the wording of Art 6(a) suggests that a crime against peace may be perpetrated through a conspiracy to commit (extensive) war crimes and crimes against humanity, the Nuremberg Tribunal declined to entertain that notion and instead confined conspiracy to crimes against peace. The Nuremberg and subsequent Second World War tribunals required three criteria for the existence of this hybrid international law conspiracy:

(a) the existence of a concrete plan involving the participation of at least two persons;
(b) clear outlining of the criminal purpose of the plan;
(c) the plan be not too far removed from the time of decision and action.[57]

Mens rea consisted of knowledge of the conspiracy and direct intention to play a part in its execution, but which was not eventually carried out.[58] Certainly, a good part of the elements of conspiracy were borrowed, as a matter of general principles, from common law legal systems, but it is equally undeniable that the armed conflict context of Nuremberg and subsequent

---

56 AP Simester, GR Sullivan, *Criminal Law: Theory and Doctrine*, 2004, Oxford: Hart, 271–95
57 See *Krupp* case, 10 Law Reports of Trials of War Criminals (LRTWC) 69, 110, 113.
58 *I.G. Farben* case, 10 LRTWC 1, 31, 40; Official Transcript of the Judgment of the IMTFE (*Tokyo* Trial), 1142–43. Although conspiracy was charged and found in the context of the Tokyo Trials, it did not sit well with some judges on the panel.

tribunals, as well as the fact that in international practice it was employed as a form of participation rather than as an inchoate crime, render international law conspiracy a distinct legal creature. The Nuremberg Tribunal required a very high threshold of participation and knowledge of the plan and limited the charge of conspiracy only against those that participated in preparatory acts materialising into actual acts of aggression.[59]

The conspiracy legacy of the Nuremberg Charter and Tribunal did not survive the Cold War, at least in most respects. Article 3(b) of the Genocide Convention, which criminalizes conspiracy as a particular inchoate crime pertinent to genocide – as is also the case with incitement and attempts – was hotly debated during the conference that preceded its adoption. It was agreed that genocide could not be charged for mere preparatory acts without some form of attempt or completion.[60] Similarly, Art 2(3)(e) of the ILC's 1996 Draft Code of Crimes required the implementation of the criminal plan in relation to conspiracy. Nonetheless, the inclusion of conspiracy in Art III of the Genocide Convention, together with the actual perpetration of genocide, is evidence enough that it was intended as an inchoate offence.

It is not, therefore, surprising that the ICTR Trial Chamber in the *Musema* case after defining genocidal conspiracy as 'an agreement between two or more persons to commit the crime of genocide' argued that since it is the agreement which is punishable, it is irrelevant whether or not it results in the actual commission of genocide.[61] It is obvious, moreover, that in this manner genocidal conspiracy is treated as an inchoate crime, rather than as a form of liability. As to the existence of a conspiratorial agreement, the *Nahimana* Trial Judgment considered that this may be inferred:

> . . . from coordinated actions by individuals who have a common pur-
> pose and are acting within a unified framework. A coalition, even an
> informal coalition, can constitute such a framework so long as those
> acting within the coalition are aware of its existence, their participation
> in it, and its role in furtherance of their common purpose. [A] conspiracy
> can be comprised of individuals acting in an institutional capacity as
> well as or even independently of their personal links with each other.
> Institutional coordination can form the basis of a conspiracy among those
> individuals who control the institutions that are engaged in coordinated
> action.[62]

---

59 Op cit, Bantekas, note 14, 47.
60 Ibid, 48.
61 *ICTR Prosecutor v Musema*, Trial Chamber Judgment (27 Jan 2000), paras 189, 193; *ICTR Prosecutor v Kajelijeli*, Trial Chamber Judgment (1 Dec 2003), paras 787–88. The latter argued that the agreement must be shown to have been reached and that the showing of a mere negotiation in progress will not suffice.
62 *ICTR Prosecutor v Nahimana*, Trial Chamber Judgment (3 Dec 2003), paras 1047–48.

The ICTR is, nonetheless, divided as to whether upon consummation of genocide, the accused should be convicted of both genocide and conspiracy on the basis of the same facts. The *Musema* Trial judgment took a negative approach to this question,[63] while in the *Niyitegeka* case the Trial Chamber was inclined to punish the accused for both.[64]

During the preparatory conferences on the ICC Statute it was suggested that the Nuremberg-type conspiracy be included because of its legacy. In this regard, two proposals were submitted; one where the conspirators simply plan but do not carry out the conspiracy themselves and another where it is the conspirators that perpetrate the overt act.[65] The compromise solution, as has already been stated, is now Art 25(3)(d) of the ICC Statute, which is akin to the Nuremberg concept of common plan (Art 6(a) thereof) since it requires attempt or completion, which was not the case with conspiracy as an inchoate crime, nor with the recent ICTR deliberations. Even if some sort of conspiracy is recognised, thus, in the ICC Statute, this is not an inchoate crime but a form of participation in crime and liability thereof.

2.7 COMMISSION THROUGH ANOTHER PERSON

This form of participation in crime is entertained in Art 25(3)(a) of the ICC Statute, but not in Art 7 of the ICTY Statute, despite its incorporation in the criminal justice systems of most States. It entails the employment or use of another person to commit a crime for which the 'behind the scenes' perpetrator commits no physical acts as to its execution. In the ICC context a commission of crime through another person must be distinguished from situations where an order is given to a subordinate for no other reason but for the existence of a distinct liability through ordering found in subparagraph 3(b) of Art 25. It is most likely that the perpetrator has a senior status in the political or military hierarchy, whereas the person used as a tool is the recipient of the perpetrator's authority. The liability of the perpetrator is not dependent on the liability of the person used as a tool, since the latter may not incur liability at all on account of his age, mental capacity, or his exoneration on the basis of particular defences, such as superior orders, duress and others. Indeed, the person used may be classified, as is the case in numerous legal systems, as an innocent agent.

---

63 Op cit, *Musema* Trial Judgment, note 61, para 197.
64 *ICTR Prosecutor v Niyitegeka*, Trial Chamber Judgment (16 May 2003), paras 429, 480, 502.
65 Op cit, Bantekas, note 14, 49, citing from the official records of ICC Preparatory Commissions.

2.8 COMMAND/SUPERIOR RESPONSIBILITY

2.8.1 The nature of command responsibility

The doctrine of command responsibility is a particular creature of international law, although academic writings trace similarities with analogous concepts in domestic criminal laws. Its fundamental purpose is to concretize through criminal law the duty of superiors to supervise the activities of their subordinates, to such a degree that the acts of subordinates are to be attributed in the same manner to the superior. In this sense, the actions of the subordinate become those of the superior, but not vice versa. If there did not exist any recognizable limits to the application of the command responsibility doctrine, then the liability of superiors for acts of subordinates would be tantamount to vicarious liability – where irrespective of the personal circumstances and efforts of the superior to avert the consequences of the crime, once the crime is committed by the subordinate it is also attributed to the superior.[66] It is obvious, however, that this is not the case, since the prosecuting authorities must prove that the superior intended or could have foreseen the consequences of subordinate criminality and that he failed to take any meaningful measures to prevent or punish. Equally, therefore, command responsibility is not a form of strict liability, since the mental element involving the knowledge of the accused must be well proven. Command responsibility is closer to what domestic criminal justice systems would term 'accomplice' liability, because the commander is liable in the same manner as the subordinate, just like an accomplice to crime would be equally liable as the direct perpetrator and his individual intent must also be demonstrated.[67]

The *Halilovic* Trial Judgment raised the question as to whether command responsibility encompasses liability for subordinate crimes only, or also for dereliction of duty.[68] The evidence surmounted by the Trial Chamber convinced it that for the purposes of the ICTY Statute, at least, dereliction of duty did not form part of the doctrine.[69] This position may prove to be problematic when we later examine the duties incumbent upon commanders, particularly the duty to prevent, which does entail a preventative duty, omission of which could be deemed tantamount to a dereliction of duty. Another particularity of command responsibility is that no proof of causality need be demonstrated between the commander's failure to prevent or punish and his

---

66 See *ICTY Prosecutor v Halilovic*, Trial Chamber Judgment (16 Nov 2005), paras 46–47, discussing the personal culpability element in command responsibility doctrine stemming from WWII jurisprudence.

67 I Bantekas, 'The Contemporary Law of Superior Responsibility', 93 *AJIL* (1999), 573, pp 575–77.

68 Op cit, *Halilovic* Trial Judgment, note 66, paras 49ff.

69 Ibid, para 53.

subordinates' criminal activity.[70] Nonetheless, it is suggested that causation should be required in a single case; where a superior fails in his duty to discipline subordinates who do not commit any crimes during that superior's tenure, but do so immediately following his departure and under the leadership of a new superior. Given that the command responsibility doctrine provides for the liability of multiple commanders for the same offence[71] – as effective control may rest with more than one person – the first superior should incur some liability for failing in his preventative duty under ordinary principles of justice. This can only be achieved by demonstrating a causal relationship between his omission and later criminality.

The definition of command responsibility in Art 28 of the ICC Statute best encapsulates the finer points of the doctrine and fills in the lacunae from the less detailed definition of Art 7(3) of the ICTY Statute. It reads as follows:

(a) A military commander or person effectively acting as a military commander shall be criminally responsible for crimes within the jurisdiction of the Court committed by forces under his or her effective command and control, or effective authority and control as the case may be, as a result of his or her failure to exercise control properly over such forces, where:

(i) that military commander or person either knew or, owing to the circumstances at the time, should have known that the forces were committing or about to commit such crimes; and

(ii) that military commander or person failed to take all necessary and reasonable measures within his or her power to prevent or repress their commission or to submit the matter to the competent authorities for investigation and prosecution.

(b) [In cases where a superior–subordinate relationship is not described in paragraph (a), but which is nonetheless subject to the same effective command and control, the superior is liable where:]

(i) the superior either knew, or consciously disregarded information which clearly indicated, that the subordinates were committing or about to commit such crimes;

(ii) the crimes concerned activities that were within the effective responsibility and control of the superior; and

(iii) the superior failed to take all necessary and reasonable measures within his or her power to prevent or repress their commission

---

70 Op cit, *Blaskic* Appeals Judgment, note 1, para 77.
71 *ICTY Prosecutor v Aleksovski*, Trial Chamber Judgment (25 June 1999), para 106; op cit, *Halilovic* Trial Judgment, note 66, para 62.

or to submit the matter to the competent authorities for investigation and prosecution.

Subparagraph (b) is a residual clause whose purpose is to encompass within its ambit non-military superior-subordinate relationships. Let us now examine in more detail the various aspects of the doctrine.

2.8.2 The superior–subordinate relationship

From the civilian President or Prime Minister of a country to the soldier on the battlefield there exist a large number of command layers. Persons that possess some authority in any of these layers are not responsible for the actions of everyone in all the command layers directly below them right down to the soldier on the battlefield. Instead, command responsibility requires that commanders are liable only for acts committed by persons who are their direct subordinates; that is, over persons they enjoy direct and effective command and control (effective control standard).[72] In order to numerically ascertain the persons subject to any given superior–subordinate relationship, one must proceed on the basis of both fact (*de facto*) and law (*de jure*).

A *de jure* superior–subordinate relationship is determined on the basis of the official (*de jure*) allocation of specific subordinates to a particular commander, whether in the context of a military or civilian administration. *De jure* command structures may be found in constitutional documents, administrative laws, military hierarchical charts, military orders, and others of this nature. It is of course possible that due to the exigencies of battle, or on account of other operational realities, the *de jure* relationship becomes inoperable or inactive. The determination of the superior–subordinate relationship then becomes a matter of fact and not law and is to be assessed on the basis of the 'effective control' standard. Four general layers may be delineated to demonstrate *de jure* command:[73]

(a) policy;
(b) strategic;
(c) operational;
(d) tactical.[74]

The person, or limited number of persons, exercising policy command, are most typically the Head of State and/or the Head of Government. This

---

72 *ICTY Prosecutor v Delalic et al [Celebici]*, Trial Chamber Judgment (16 Nov 1998), para 378; *Prosecutor v Strugar*, Trial Chamber Judgment (31 Jan 2005), para 360.
73 A plethora of other sub-layers exist within each layer, particularly at the lower end of tactical military command.
74 Op cit, Bantekas, note 67, 578–79.

person makes the final decision to enter into war. This decision is then channelled to a War Cabinet (strategic command) which is composed of both civilians and military officers of the highest possible rank whose task it is to formulate a viable war plan. This plan is further channelled to high-ranking officers on the battlefield (operational command) in order to implement it through their subordinate units, divisions, corps, etc. Tactical command is the final frontier on the battlefield, encompassing every officer and non-commissioned officer (NCO) that is physically present in the theatre of operations and who possesses one or more direct subordinates. The ICRC Commentary to the 1977 Protocols correctly notes that for the purposes of command responsibility, tactical command may be assumed even by a mere soldier/private where all the officers and NCOs in his unit have been killed or incapacitated by wounds and the soldier has assumed authority.[75] The latter would of course constitute a case of *de facto* command. Since the doctrine of command responsibility requires direct subordination, as well as particular knowledge on the part of the superior and a failure to act, it is evident that the construction of superior–subordinate relationships on the basis of the four general layers cannot involve situations where a superior is far removed from the acts committed by an alleged subordinate. Thus, a person exercising policy command does not exercise direct authority over a platoon on the battlefield because he cannot apprise himself of their activities and has for this reason delegated this task to senior military officers and they in turn to other officers, etc. The President's direct subordinates are certainly persons comprising strategic command, they themselves possessing direct authority over persons exercising operational command. It is not out of the question that strategic commanders are directly subordinate to policy commanders, particularly where the size of the army is small, or the magnitude of the military operations limited. Equally, staff commanders, ie high-ranking military officers that formulate battle plans, and who belong to the layer of strategic command, can never be subject to the doctrine of command responsibility because despite their rank they do not enjoy direct subordination over any subordinate units.

While *de jure* command structures may be found with regard to the political and military branches of State entities, the same is not true in relation to paramilitary units whose command structures are ad hoc, flexible and ever-changing. Moreover, even in the case of regular armies, it is not uncommon to experience quick command successions on the battlefield where casualties are high, or even where authority has been usurped *ultra vires*. In such cases the determination of direct subordination is no longer a matter of law – because no such law exists – thus necessitating a determination on the basis

---

75 C Pilloud *et al* (eds), *Commentary on the Additional Protocols of 8 June 1977 to the Geneva Conventions of 12 August 1949* (ICRC, 1987), para 3553.

of fact. Article 28(a) of the ICC Statute reflects customary international law, particularly that reflected in Art 87 of Protocol I of 1977 and the relevant jurisprudence of the ICTY, when it expressly states that subordination must be rooted in 'effective command and control'. The concept of command is much broader than that of control, in that whereas a policy or operational commander exercise command over all those in subordinate layers, they do not, however, necessarily exercise control over such persons, which is a more direct form of authority. Thus, it is the concept of 'control' that is determinative for the purposes of command responsibility, because it encompasses by its very nature direct subordination.[76] In every case, besides the directness of control, the control itself must be effective, otherwise a superior-subordinate relationship will not have been established, unless the superior intentionally renders the control ineffective. The concept of 'effective control' is also particularly important in cases where *de jure* command structures are well known, but additional troops were added informally to the superior's forces. This may take place, for example, where a military unit loses its commander on the battlefield and as a result joins the first available commander it comes across.[77] The *Celebici* Appeals Judgment defined effective control as 'the material ability to prevent and punish criminal conduct'.[78]

The experience of the ICTY is that the establishment of *de facto* effective control is extremely hard to prove. Where direct evidence is unavailable, for example in the form of a signed document demonstrating hierarchical structures, circumstantial evidence has successfully been utilised in the ad hoc tribunals to achieve the same purpose. The evidence that is more likely to be produced, and that which has carried the highest probative value in the proceedings of the ad hoc tribunals, has been both written and oral. Written evidence, particularly in the form of orders signed by the accused, helps provide circumstantial evidence as to one's power over other persons, not necessarily those to whom it is addressed. It should not be thought, however, that the signing of orders in all cases demonstrates a superior-subordinate relationship. This is true, for example, with regard to orders relating to logistics and administration.[79] For the purposes of command responsibility an order must demonstrate the existence of direct subordinates. Although the ICTY deemed otherwise in the *Celebici* case,[80] one should not rule out the possibility that the possession of significant powers of influence may under certain circumstances establish a superior-subordinate relationship. An influential individual who yields full respect and obeisance, whether out

76 *ICRC Commentary*, ibid, para 3544.
77 Ibid.
78 *Celebici* Appeals Chamber Judgment (20 Feb 2001), para 256.
79 Op cit, *Celebici* Trial Judgment, note 72, para 658.
80 *Celebici* Trial Judgment, ibid, paras 658, 669; op cit, *Celebici* Appeals Judgment, note 78, para 266.

of fear or otherwise, can as a result establish effective control over his subjects, having intentionally placed himself in a position of authority. There is sufficient precedent for this from the *Ministries* case,[81] but it is also a conclusion based on logic, which legal reasoning cannot ignore. Finally, oral evidence, particularly that provided by prisoners of war (POWs) and other camp detainees, has produced sufficient circumstantial evidence for the ICTY, such as to substantiate the distribution of tasks within a POW camp and thus distinguish those who hold superior positions within the camp.[82]

2.8.3 The mental element

The mental element in the definition of command responsibility requires that the superior either knew (ie that he had direct knowledge), or had reason to know on the basis of the circumstances at the time, that the subordinate(s) was about to commit, or had committed, a crime. Command responsibility does not require the commander to possess the same intent as the perpetrators. Article 28 of the ICC Statute seems to follow the *mens rea* standards contained in Art 7(3) of the ICTY Statute, albeit the wording is somewhat different. None of the judgments of past and present have given us a thorough exposition of the theoretical bases of *mens rea* for omissions entailing serious violations of international law. Domestic principles are of very little, if any, assistance, not only because of the divergence on omissions between common and civil law jurisdiction, but more so because of the context and magnitude in which command responsibility is applied in the international arena.

When we talk about the mental element (*mens rea*) of an offence we are in fact examining two distinct mental phases: (a) knowledge of the perpetrator as to a circumstance, or of a risk; and (b) going beyond the mental barrier (just before any physical action) with the intention, or some degree of foreseeability, to bring about the consequence or the risk, or accepting that it will occur. In the vast majority of offences, the two elements are contemporaneous and simultaneous and are treated as such by the criminal courts. In command responsibility, however, they are seldom contemporaneous, since, for example, the duty to prevent requires the commander to ascertain information as to impending criminal activity before he can take any action. This, depending on the circumstances, can take days, weeks or months, during which time the commander's knowledge of the criminal circumstance or risk may be obscure or inadequate to justify prosecution for failing to prevent. Let

---

81 *USA v von Weizsaecker* [*Ministries* case], 14 *Trials*, 684.
82 *Prosecutor v Nikolic*, Review of the Indictment pursuant to Rule 61 of the Rules of Procedure and Evidence (20 Oct 1995), para 24.

us, therefore, first examine what degree of knowledge is sufficient and how this is ascertained.

Direct knowledge is pretty straightforward, whereas the 'had reason to know' standard is less so. The latter derives its contemporary origin from Art 86(2) of Protocol I of 1977, where it is understood as 'being in possession of sufficient information, such as to be put on notice of subordinate criminality'.[83] According to settled ICTY jurisprudence, a person incurs superior responsibility 'only if information was available to him which would have put him on notice of offences committed by subordinates'.[84] The superior may in fact demonstrate that he was not at all aware of subordinate crimes, but if the prosecutor shows that the accused did not take the necessary and reasonable measures to apprise himself of available and specific information,[85] his truthful ignorance does not constitute a valid defence. The information need not be such that 'by itself, suffices to compel the conclusion of the existence of [subordinate] crimes . . . it is sufficient that the superior was put on further inquiry by the information'.[86] The Yugoslav Tribunal jurisprudence also clearly stipulates that neglect to acquire such information that would put a commander on notice of offences is not part of the 'had reason to know' component of Art 7(3) of the ICTY Statute.[87] As a result, the ICTY succeeds in averting the establishment of a negligence test with regard to the formation of knowledge element of command responsibility,[88] but is silent as to whether liability would arise where the lack of knowledge may be attributed to recklessness. To rule otherwise would be inconsistent with the preventative duty[89] of commanders and the diligence required in apprising oneself of available information (as already discussed), the failure of which can only be deemed as culpably reckless behaviour. What we are suggesting is not an imputation of knowledge for failing to discover clues and information, but recklessness

83 Op cit, *Celebici* Trial Judgment, note 72, para 393; op cit, *Strugar* Trial Judgment, note 72, para 369.

84 Op cit, *Celebici* Appeals Judgment, note 78, para 241; op cit, *Krnojelac* Appeals Judgment, note 6, para 151; op cit, *Blaskic* Appeals Judgment, note 1, para 62.

85 The superior is not, however, liable for failing to acquire such information in the first place, if it is not available to him through the normal course of events. See, op cit, *Blaskic* Appeals Judgment, note 1, para 62; op cit, *Celebici* Appeals Judgment, note 78, para 226; op cit, *Strugar* Trial Judgment, note 72, para 369.

86 Op cit, *Strugar* Trial Judgment, note 72, paras 369, 370.

87 Op cit, *Celebici* Appeals Judgment, note 78, para 226; op cit, *Blaskic* Appeals Judgment, note 1, para 62.

88 *Blaskic* Appeals Judgment, ibid, para 63.

89 In the *Halilovic* Trial Judgment, op cit, note 66, para 86, the Trial Chamber stated that it 'transpires from the jurisprudence of the Tribunal that some preventative measures may be required of a superior'. If this is indeed so, failure to take such measures can only amount to a dereliction of duty.

(both advertent and inadvertent)[90] for failing to institute mechanisms required under international law and of equally failing to apprise oneself of otherwise available information. A commander, for example, who does not institute reporting mechanisms and makes no use of information available to him is either aware of the risk to some degree and yet does nothing (advertent recklessness), or consciously renders himself completely oblivious to the risk (couldn't care less attitude, or indifference), in which case he is not aware (inadvertent recklessness). For the purposes of this chapter, we shall treat this aspect of the 'had reason to know' standard as either advertent or inadvertent recklessness, as the case may be.

The test of recklessness under the ICC Statute, Protocol I, as well as under customary international law, is clearly a subjective one ('circumstances at the time'). Paragraph (b)(i) of Art 28 of the ICC Statute, which refers to a 'conscious disregard of information' that clearly indicates subordinate criminality is somewhat problematic. It is not clear whether this is a particular manifestation of the 'had reason to know' standard, or whether it refers to the 'must have known' standard. Given the customary-oriented nature of the ICC Statute, the genre of Art 28 and the recklessness-based outlook concerning disregard of information, we are of the opinion that paragraph (b)(i) refers to the 'had reason to know' standard. The onus for proving the commander's recklessness, advertent or otherwise, rests with the prosecutor, who will attempt to demonstrate that the commander did not have a mechanism in place through which to monitor the behaviour of his troops. The same is true even if a mechanism was in place but the incumbent superior did not reinforce it, or took lukewarm measures to apprise himself of the results of said monitoring. Following from our discussion on the ICTY's rejection of duty dereliction as part of the 'had reason to know' standard, it would be inconsistent to hold a superior liable for 'disregarding available information' when there exists no duty to collect it in the first place. Where, therefore, superiors have a mechanism in place to monitor subordinate behaviour and apprise themselves accordingly, then even if crimes do occur, the said superiors will not have behaved recklessly.

Besides actual knowledge and recklessness ('had reason to know' standard), a third test has surfaced, whose normative value, however, is under fierce debate and which has gained no support in the ICTY. This is the so-called presumption of knowledge standard, or otherwise known as 'must have known' test. This test stipulates that whenever subordinate criminality is widespread and notorious it must be presumed that the incumbent superior knew about it.[91] As a result, the burden of proof is shifted from the prosecutor

90 See, however, op cit, note 52, for a brief exploration of the theoretical and practical problems in the classification of inadvertent recklessness in English criminal law.
91 Op cit, Bantekas, note 67, 588–89.

to the accused superior, but this is a presumption that is subject to rebuttal. The 'must have known' standard has not received recognition in the ICTY, but this has nothing to do with its normative value as such, but is instead predicated on the rightly conservative mandate of the ad hoc tribunal, whose authority extends to the application of law that is beyond any doubt part of customary international law. In this light, the ICTY exercised caution in the *Celebici* case when it rejected the customary nature of the 'must have known' test.[92] Evidence clearly suggests that the test has a normative history equal to that of its 'had reason to know' counterpart. One must keep in mind, however, that when these *mens rea* formulations were used in the aftermath of the Second World War, it was a time when command responsibility was a sketchy concept that was under development and thus it is not wise to expect neat categorisations and exact legal constructions. What is of interest in the present analysis is not the legal expressions employed in the past, but what the tribunals actually meant when using them. Thus, in the *Yamashita* case before a US Military Commission, the widespread nature and notoriety of crimes perpetrated by Japanese forces prompted the Commission to conclude that the accused 'either knew or had the means of knowing'.[93] This presumption of knowledge was reaffirmed by another US military tribunal in the *Hostages* case, although the test employed was not premised on widespread occurrence and notoriety, but on the superior's failure to acquire and obtain complete information.[94] Equally, in the *High Command* case, the superior's knowledge was found by the military tribunal to be presumed through numerous reports received at his headquarters. Moreover, the ICRC Commentary on Arts 86 and 87 of Protocol I of 1977 affirms that widespread, publicly notorious, numerous, geographically and temporarily spanned breaches 'should be taken into consideration in reaching a presumption that the persons responsible could not be ignorant of them'.[95]

Even if Art 28 of the ICC Statute is construed as excluding the presumption of knowledge standard – something that is not totally clear – on the basis of the overwhelming aforementioned evidence, the standard can still validly be applied before other courts and tribunals, be they domestic or international. The major difficulty in applying this test lies in the subjective determination of what constitutes widespread and notorious, such as to trigger the presumption against the superior. Although it is impossible to remove all subjectivity from the domain of criminal law, in the present case there are simply insufficient binding criteria available. In the *Yamashita* case, the

92 Op cit, *Celebici* Trial Judgment, note 72, paras 384–85.
93 *Trial of General Yamashita* (US Military Commission, Manila, 8 Oct–7 Dec 1945), 4 Law Reports of Trials of War Criminals (1945), 1, 34, 94.
94 *USA v List, et al* [*Hostages* case], 11 *Trials* 759, 1281.
95 Op cit, *ICRC Commentary*, note 75, para 3548.

accused was far removed from the field of operations where the crimes took place and his lines of communication had been severed by enemy forces. The crimes may indeed have been widespread and notorious, but under the specific circumstances of Yamashita he certainly had very little scope for obtaining information. This, after all, was the whole purpose of the severing of his communication lines. More than a century later it is evident that not only communications are better, but that the mass media has access to a significant amount of information that is available in the public domain, but also contemporary military operations are far less restricted in respect of location, with the exception of occupations.

2.8.4 The duty to prevent or punish

The doctrine of command responsibility requires the existence of three cumulative criteria: superior–subordinate relationship, knowledge of subordinate criminal activity by the superior (whether actual or through recklessness) and a subsequent failure to prevent or punish such crimes. It is evident that the duties are disjunctive, requiring action in different temporal phases; ie the duty to prevent arises prior to the perpetration of crimes, whereas the duty to punish arises after a crime has been committed. International law consistently obliges commanders to take only such measures as are within their powers; this refers to actual, physical powers,[96] as opposed to legal powers, since a commander may not have legal authority over the actions of subordinate units, but could at the same time possess sufficient physical power and influence upon them so as to punish or prevent their behaviour. Thus, the actual power of a superior will be determined by a court on the basis of the subjective circumstances of the accused.

The ICC Statute requires that the accused take all 'necessary and reasonable' measures to prevent or punish. Again, the test in this case concerns the specific person of the superior in question. One can imagine two different scenaria; one in which a superior has been overshadowed by other subordinates and has lost his influence and authority, and another where the accused is a dominant personality who yields fear and respect from units other than his own. The law is, after all, applicable to natural persons, whose private circumstances are subject to continuous change, and not automatic robots. What constitutes necessary and reasonable measures on the basis of actual power in the two situations is certainly very different. The duty to prevent arises upon the preparation or planning of a crime, which suggests that the superior's duty at this stage is supervisory and disciplinary. A superior cannot be expected to foil every plan of his subordinates to commit a crime, but only

---

96 *ICTY Prosecutor v Kordic*, Trial Chamber Judgment (26 Feb 2001), para 443; op cit, *Strugar* Trial Judgment, note 72, para 372.

those for which he has acquired information or for which he has *i* grounds to suspect that a crime is about to be committed.[97] The *d* component of the duty to prevent includes an obligation to maintain *..* impose general discipline, train one's troops on the laws of war and secure an effective reporting system. In cases where information exists that a crime is planned or is in progress, the superior must issue and enforce orders to the contrary, protest against it and its protagonists, or criticise criminal action and/or insist before a superior authority that immediate action be taken.[98] If all these measures are diligently performed and one's subordinates nonetheless engage in violations of humanitarian law their superior will bear no liability for their actions. Therefore, the duty to prevent should not be conceived as a general police duty, particularly taking in mind the additional combat functions of the superior, but rather as a supervisory and disciplinary duty. The other aspect of the duty to prevent concerns preventing the crime from materialising when it is in its final stages, or when it is in the process of being attempted.

On the contrary, the duty to repress or punish requires specific action. It arises not at the time a subordinate offence takes place, because even a diligent commander may not be aware of the offence, but from the time the offence becomes known to the superior, or at a time when the superior would have known about it, in accordance with the *mens rea* standards applicable to the command responsibility doctrine. Thereafter, depending on the exigencies of battle the superior is obliged to investigate the case with a view to submitting it further to his competent authorities. There may be situations in which superiors are physically unable to seize, detain or investigate a subordinate. Even so, they can at least notify their immediate superiors of the situation.[99]

2.9 INTERNATIONAL CORPORATE CRIMINAL LIABILITY

There is no doubt that *general* corporate criminal liability does not exist in international law. Its existence is fragmentary, context-specific and subject to qualification. One could argue that because the concept is found in some legal systems, it may in fact amount to a general principle of criminal laws and thus a source of international law. This is not true, because it does not exist in every, or most, legal systems, but even where it does exist, the objective and subjective elements are significantly divergent. Another argument as to the possible general applicability of corporate criminal liability could be

---

97 Op cit, *Blaskic* Appeals Judgment, note 1, para 83; op cit, *Strugar* Trial Judgment, note 72, para 373.
98 *Strugar* Trial Judgment, ibid, para 374.
99 Op cit, *Kordic* Trial Judgment, note 96, para 446.

predicated on Arts 9 and 10 of the Charter of the Nuremberg Tribunal, which gave authority to the Tribunal to assess and declare groups or organisations as being criminal in nature. These provisions, however, were intended to target membership therein and not the legal entity itself. Article 10 is instructive of the purposes of its drafters.

> In cases where a group or organization is declared criminal by the Tribunal, the competent national authority of any signatory shall have the right to bring individuals to trial for membership therein before national, military or occupation courts. In any such case the criminal nature of the group or organisation is considered proved and shall not be questioned.

The fact that corporate criminality was not envisaged in the post-Second World War international instruments may also be discerned from the fact that in the so-called industrialist trials it was personal participation at the highest levels that was targeted and not the corporation itself.[100]

In the post-Cold War era, while it is true that legal persons have been the subject of suits before some national courts even for extraterritorial acts, the impact of these suits has remained exclusively at the civil and not the criminal level.[101] The two are quite distinct and no arbitrary similarities may be inferred as to criminal implications from civil suits and the reach of the criminal law thereof. This conclusion is further reinforced by the plethora of non-binding international legal instruments pertaining to the role and function of corporations.[102]

What we do have, however, is the seed of exceptional corporate criminal liability regionally or with regard to particular international offences. As regards the latter, recent Framework Decisions falling within the Third Pillar of the European Union (EU), while obliging Member States to promulgate legislation entailing corporate liability, all that such instruments do is to harmonize the sanctions and leave the nature of the liability to the law of each Member State.[103] This is understandable, given the lack of uniformity in

---

100 Op cit, *Krupp* case, note 57; op cit, *I.G. Farben* case, note 58; *USA v Flick*, 6 *Trials* (1948) 1217.

101 See I Bantekas, 'Corporate Social Responsibility in International Law', 22 *Boston U Intl LJ* (2004), 309.

102 2000 OECD Guidelines for Multinational Enterprises, OECD Doc OECD/GD(97)40 (2000); and the UN Norms on the Responsibilities of Transnational Corporations and other Business Enterprises with regard to Human Rights, UN ESCOR CHR, 55th Sess, 22nd mtg, UN Doc E/CN.4/Sub.2/2003/12/Rev.2 (2003).

103 For example, Arts 7 and 8 of Council Framework Decision of 28 May 2001 on Combating Fraud and Counterfeiting of Non-Cash Means of Payment, OJ L 149, 02/06/01; Arts 8 and 9 of Council Framework Decision of 29 May 2000 on Increasing Protection by Criminal Penalties and Other Sanctions against Counterfeiting in connection with the Introduction of the Euro, OJ L 140, 14/06/00; Art 4, Council Framework Decision of 19 July 2002 on Combating Trafficking in Human Beings (2002/629/JHA), OJ L 203, 01/08/2002.

the Member States' legal systems on this matter and as a result the principle of 'functional equivalence' is applied (ie that Member States may use any principle of law consistent with their domestic legal order, as long as the sanctions against the legal person satisfy the criteria under the particular convention). Hence, criminal corporate liability in this context becomes a national imperative and not an international obligation. With regard to crime-specific corporate criminality, some degree of liability is prescribed in anti-corruption treaties, such as Arts 2 and 3(2) of the 1997 OECD Convention on Bribery in International Business Transactions and Art 26 of the 2003 UN Convention against Corruption.[104] It is true that these provisions do not oblige Member States to promulgate the criminal liability of legal persons, but only to adopt 'effective, proportionate and dissuasive' sanctions, whether of a civil, administrative or criminal nature in conformity with their legal systems. Nonetheless, the conventions do provide for the criminal liability of the natural persons that committed the offences, where they were acting as agents of the legal person.[105] Therefore, as a result of treaty law – under which only signatories are bound – corporate criminal liability with respect to corruption entails: (a) criminal liability of the legal person only where this is possible in the law of the signatory and under the terms of that law; and (b) the criminal liability of corporate agents for the crime they committed (as principals or accomplices) as a matter only of international law. Such agents would be subject to the usual rules of principal or accomplice liability, and as such they could also be tried before the ICC in their personal capacity. Their link to the legal person, although not wholly relevant for ICC criminal proceedings except only for evidentiary purposes, could provide the backbone for a subsequent civil suit brought by victims and their families against the legal person.[106]

---

104 See Chapter 12, section 12.2 on the criminal liability of legal persons under the domestic law of the 1997 OECD Convention's Member States.
105 Art 26(3), 2003 UN Convention; Art 3(1), 1997 OECD Convention.
106 See I Bantekas, 'Corruption as an International Crime and Crime against Humanity: An Outline of Supplementary Criminal Justice Policies' 4 JICJ (2006), 466.

Chapter 3

Defences in international criminal law

3.1 THEORETICAL UNDERPINNINGS OF CRIMINAL DEFENCES

The concept of 'defence' in international criminal law is neither self-evident, nor does it clearly possess an autonomous meaning. Instead, it derives its legal significance as a result of its transplantation from domestic criminal justice systems through the appropriate processes of international law. Nonetheless, its definition, elaboration, evolution or application do not depend on the relevant processes of any single criminal justice system – nor combinations thereof – although these may have persuasive value. This is even more so in the context of a self-contained, highly elaborate and sophisticated legal system, such as the International Criminal Court (ICC), where reliance on domestic rules is the exception – or at least, a judicial act of last resort – rather than the norm.[1] Despite these observations, however, the fact remains that the underlying theoretical underpinnings of the concept of 'defences' is premised on well established notions of criminal law, originating from both the common law and the civil law traditions. Despite the elaborate character of the ICC Statute, its drafters have been wise in detecting the inadequacy of the fledgling international criminal justice system, thus necessitating recourse to national legal concepts and constructs. This is well evident as far as defences are concerned.[2]

In its most simple sense, a defence represents a claim submitted by the accused by which he or she seeks to be acquitted of a criminal charge. The concept of defences is broad, and this may encompass a submission that the prosecution has not proved its case. Since a criminal offence is constituted through the existence of two cumulative elements, a physical act (*actus reus*) and a requisite mental element (*mens rea*), the accused would succeed with a claim of defence by disproving or negating either the material or the

---

1 ICC Statute, Art 21(1)(c).
2 Ibid, Art 31(3).

mental element of the offence charged. Domestic criminal law systems generally distinguish between defences that may be raised against any criminal offence (so called general defences), and those that can only be invoked against particular crimes (so called special defences).[3] Another poignant distinction is that between substantive and procedural defences. The former refer to the merits, as presented by the prosecutor, while the latter are used to demonstrate that certain criminal procedure rules have been violated to the detriment of the accused, with the consequence that the trial cannot proceed to its merits. This distinction is not always clear cut, but one may point to the following often claimed procedural defences: abuse of process,[4] *ne bis in idem*,[5] *nullum crimen nulla poena sine lege scripta*,[6] passing of statute of limitations,[7] retroactivity of criminal law, although these are not typically classified as defences in domestic criminal laws.[8] This chapter will focus only on substantive defences. Although our analysis covers substantive defences as these have evolved through domestic and international developments, the detailed ICC legal framework will serve as the basis of discussion.

Another seminal aspect of any discussion on defences relates to the allocation of the burden of proof. Article 66 of the ICC Statute postulates the 'presumption of innocence' until proven guilty beyond reasonable doubt. This means that, and in accordance with universal standards of justice, the prosecution carries the onus of proving the material and mental elements constituting an offence. On the other hand, facts relating to a defence raised by the accused, and being peculiar to his or her knowledge, must be established by the accused.[9] Article 67(1)(i) at first glance seems to possibly attack the burden of proof set out in Art 66, by declaring that 'the accused shall be entitled . . . not to have imposed on him or her any reversal of the burden of proof or any onus or rebuttal'. This would not be a correct interpretation, as it would run contrary to the object and purpose of the ICC Statute and

3 An example of a special defence is that of the 'battered wife syndrome', although this itself is based on an expanded defence of provocation. See C Wells, 'Battered Woman Syndrome and Defences to Homicide: Where Now?', 14 *LS* (1994), 266.
4 See *Barayagwiza v Prosecutor*, Appeals Decision (3 November 1999), Case No ICTR–98–34–S, as well as the reversal of parts of the latter decision by the Appeals Chamber in its decision of 31 March 2000.
5 ICC Statute, Art 20.
6 Ibid, Arts 22 and 23.
7 Ibid, Art 29. The crimes contained in the ICC Statute are not subject to a statute of limitations under general international law. See 1968 United Nations (UN) Convention on the Non-Applicability of Statutory Limitations to War Crimes and Crimes Against Humanity, 754 UNTS 73.
8 Ibid, Art 24.
9 *Prosecutor v Delalic and Others* (*Celebici* case), Judgment (16 Nov 1998), 38 ILM (1998), 57, para 1172. In English law, the burden of proof is always on the prosecution even with regard to defences raised by the defendant, with the exception of insanity and certain statutory exceptions (including diminished responsibility). See R May, *Criminal Evidence*, 1999, London: Sweet & Maxwell, 53–60.

general international law. The correct view is that Art 67(1)(i) should be read in conjunction with Arts 31(3) and 21, which, as explained in the following section, give authority to the Court to introduce defences existing outside the Statute, only if they are consistent with accepted treaty and custom or general principles of domestic law. Thus, no defence introduced by the Court in the proceedings under Art 31(3) can ever override the burden of proof established in accordance with Art 66. Essentially therefore, while the accused has the burden of proving the particular claim invoked in his or her defence (for example, that he faced death if he did not execute the order of his superior), the burden is on the prosecutor to prove the overall guilt of the accused.

All substantive defences represent claims that the material element of the offence was indeed committed by the accused, but for a reason which is acceptable under the relevant criminal justice system. In this respect, domestic legal systems distinguish between two types of defence in which the accused claims to lack the requisite *mens rea* to commit the underlying crime: justification and excuses. Defences operating as justifications usually regard the act as harmful but not as wrong in its particular context, whereas excuses are grounded on the premise that although the particular act was indeed wrongful, its surrounding special circumstances would render its attribution to the actor unjust.[10]

Despite the existence of the aforementioned distinctions in both common and civil law traditions, they were not included in the ICC Statute, whose drafters agreed instead to use the general term 'exclusion of criminal responsibility', thus avoiding the need to insert terminology distinguishing between the two. Whether this intentional omission has any legal significance remains to be seen, judged on the appropriate sources of the Court's jurisdiction. The Rules of Procedure and Evidence provide that the accused must lodge his or her defence claim no later than three days before the date of the hearing.[11] The next section, therefore, explores the general conception of defences in the ICC Statute, with particular emphasis on primary and secondary sources.

3.1.1 Is there a place for domestic defences in the ICC Statute?

During the preparation of the Preparatory Committee (Prep Com) draft Statute there was strong divergence over the inclusion of an exhaustive or

---

10 Several theories have been elaborated in this respect, such as the 'character theory' and the 'fair opportunity theory'. See W Wilson, *Criminal Law*, 1998, London: Longman, 206–19; see Draft Code of Crimes against the Peace and Security of Mankind, Art 14 (Comment 2), in *ILC Report on the Work of its Forty-Eighth Session*, UN GAOR 51st Sess, Supp No 10, UN Doc A/51/10 (1996), 14.
11 Rules of Evidence and Procedure, r 121(9).

open list of defences. Naturally, the proponents of an exhaustive list were apprehensive of the Court's freedom and latitude were it to be authorised to determine defences beyond those enumerated in the Statute. The opposite side, however, stressed the impossibility of reaching precise definitions of all desired defences, thus necessitating an open list. There was considerable support for a middle ground, whereby although there would be an enumerated list, the Court could under special circumstances introduce viable defences existing outside the Statute, in such a way that it would not make, but rather apply, the law.[12] Preference for this latter solution was finally reflected in Art 31(3), which reads:

> At trial, the Court may consider a ground for excluding criminal responsibility other than those referred to in paragraph 1 [ie, mental incapacity, intoxication, self-defence, duress] where such a ground is derived from applicable law as set forth in Article 21.

Article 21 sets out the sources available to the Court in its judicial function; in the same fashion this is prescribed for the International Court of Justice in Art 38 of its Statute. Article 21 is premised on a hierarchy of rules, on top of which lie the Statute, supplemented by the Elements of Crimes and the Rules of Procedure and Evidence. Where the aforementioned sources fail to produce an appropriate result, the Court may turn to treaties and the principles and rules of international law, and, failing that, to general principles of law derived from the national laws of the world's legal systems. The examination of these sources does not fall within the purview of this chapter, but a brief discussion of the third source (that is, general principles) is warranted, because of the potential use by the Court of defences existing outside the Statute. General principles of municipal law are practices or legal provisions common to a substantial number of nations encompassing the major legal systems (common, civil and Islamic law). Under customary international law, reliance upon principles deriving from national legal systems is justified either when rules make explicit reference to national laws, or when such reference is necessarily implied by the very content and nature of the concept under examination. However, even within these confines, the freedom of extrapolation of general principles by a court is open to abuse, as was the case in the *Furundzija* judgment, decided by an International Criminal Tribunal for the Former Yugoslavia (ICTY) Chamber.[13] It is evident that if the court possesses authority to freely employ general principles,

---

12 UN Doc A/CONF 183/C 1/WGGP/L 4/Add 1/Rev 1 (1998), commentary to Art 31(3).

13 *Prosecutor v Furundzija*, Judgment (10 Dec 1998), 38 ILM (1999), 317, paras 182–86. See I Bantekas, *Principles of Direct and Superior Responsibility in International Humanitarian Law*, 2002, Manchester: Manchester UP, 28.

the theoretical underpinnings of the distinction between 'justifications' and 'excuses' (constituting part and parcel of any domestic discussion on defences) is pertinent when general principles are used.

As a result of a compromise reached during the 1998 conference, whereby some delegations insisted that domestic law, especially that of the accused's nationality or that of the territorial State, should be directly applicable apart from general principles,[14] the Statute extended the sources available to the Court. The compromise was basically a middle ground, whereby such domestic law could, if the Court deemed it appropriate, be included in the pool of sources. Article 21(1)(c) articulates the following sources, failing paragraphs 2 and 3:

> [G]eneral principles of law derived by the Court from national laws of legal systems of the world, *including, as appropriate, the national laws of states that would normally exercise jurisdiction over the crime*, provided that those principles are not inconsistent with this Statute and with international law and internationally recognised norms and principles [emphasis added].

A logical and realistic interpretation of this clause suggests that in the event the Court is unable to fill a legal lacuna on an issue pertaining to international law – in both a broad and narrow sense – it may turn to individual legal systems. Therein, the Court may not choose a particular law or provision for application or transplantation before the ICC; rather, it is bound to extract relevant principles from the rules of the legal system under consideration. This is an exercise that may turn out to be so cumbersome that it negates the initial utility of recourse to a particular legal system. A more realistic interpretation would reflect ICTY practice such as where the ad hoc tribunals take heed of the sentencing practices and legislation of the former Yugoslavia and Rwanda, unless these conflict with general international law.[15] The ICC could extend the direct application of domestic law to determination of procedural matters that have taken place on the territory of a State, where this is relevant to ICC proceedings (for example, in relation to testimony and other evidence taken by the surrendering State), as well as to elements of defences that are ill-defined in the Statute, as will become apparent in this chapter. Let us now proceed to examine in detail the substantive defences set out in the Statute, that is, superior orders, duress/

---

14 See P Saland, 'International Criminal Law Principles', in RS Lee (ed), *The International Criminal Court: The Making of the Rome Statute: Issues, Negotiations, Results*, 1999, Boston: Kluwer Law International, 214–15.

15 Art 24(1) of the ICTY Statute states that '[i]n determining the terms of imprisonment, the Trial Chambers shall have recourse to the general practice regarding prison sentences in the courts of the former Yugoslavia'.

necessity, self-defence, intoxication, mistake of fact and law, and mental incapacity.

As a matter of safeguard against abuse by the defendant of the rule enunciated in Art 31(3), the Rules of Procedure and Evidence require that the defence give notice to both the Trial Chamber and the prosecutor if it intends to raise a ground for excluding responsibility under Art 31(3). This must be done 'sufficiently in advance of the commencement of the trial'.[16] Following such notice, the Trial Chamber shall hear the prosecutor and the defence before deciding whether the defence can raise a ground for excluding criminal liability. If the defence is eventually permitted to raise the ground, the Trial Chamber may grant the Prosecutor an adjournment to address that ground.[17]

3.2 SUPERIOR ORDERS

Since discipline is the cornerstone of military doctrine, it follows that obedience to superior orders is paramount. But a subordinate receiving an order may find that the order conflicts with his or her duty to obey criminal or military law. From the point of view of a strict hierarchy of rules, a neutral observer will have little problem in articulating an objection to the order, but for the ordinary military subordinate used to the discipline described, the choice is not obvious. The dilemma is simple: submit to the illegal order and you commit a crime, defy the order and face the wrath and penalties imposed by your superiors.[18] One should not forget that in time of war disobedience often carries a penalty of summary execution, with little time or credence given to the subordinate to make his or her claim during the exigencies of conflict. These thoughts represent personal moral imperatives. What sense does the law make of all this?

From the time that national authorities prosecuted violations of the *jus in bello*, and were subsequently faced with claims of 'superior orders', they themselves first encountered the aforementioned dilemma of the military subordinate. As a result, two schools of thought emerged on the subject. The first, premising its argument primarily on notions of justice, opined the invocation of superior orders to constitute a complete defence,[19] while the second

---

16 ICC Rules of Procedure and Evidence, r 80(1).

17 Ibid, r 80(2) and (3).

18 Y Dinstein, *The Defence of Obedience to Superior Orders in International Law*, 1965, Leiden: Stjthoff, 5–7. See generally MJ Osiel, 'Obeying Orders: Atrocity, Military Discipline, and the Law of War', 86 *California Law Review* (1998), 939; MJ Osiel, *Obeying Orders*, 1999, Brunswick: Transaction.

19 1845 Prussian Military Code; see also the adoption of the doctrine of '*respondeat superior*' by Oppenheim in his early treatises: L Oppenheim, *International Law: Disputes, War and*

articulated a doctrine of 'absolute liability' which gave no merit to claims of obedience.[20] Amidst these two extremes a more conciliatory position was adopted at both a national and international level. From the 1845 Prussian Military Code to the *Leipzig* trials at the close of the First World War a consistent principle has emerged recognising the relevance of 'moral choice' in such circumstances. In accordance with the 'moral choice' principle, a subordinate would be punished, if in the execution of an order, he or she went beyond its scope, or executed it in the knowledge that it related to an act which aimed at the commission of a crime and which the subordinate could avoid.[21] The German Supreme Court affirmed this principle at the *Leipzig* trials on the basis of Art 47 of the 1872 German Military Penal Code, which provided that superior orders were of no avail where subordinates went beyond the given order or were aware of its illegality.[22] In the *Dover Castle* case, the defendant Karl Neuman, the commander of a German submarine, claimed he was acting pursuant to superior orders when he torpedoed the *Dover Castle*, a British hospital ship, according to which orders the Germans believed that Allied hospital ships were being used for military purposes in violation of the laws of war. The accused was acquitted because he was not found to have known that the *Dover Castle* was not used for purposes other than as a hospital ship.[23] In the *Llandovery Castle* case, however, involving the torpedoing of a British hospital ship and subsequent murder of its survivors, the Supreme Court did not readily accept a defence of superior orders. It emphatically pointed out that although subordinates are under no obligation to question the orders of their superior officer, this is not the case where the 'order is universally known to everybody, including also the accused, to be without any doubt whatever against the law'.[24]

Thus, the 'moral choice' principle encompassed an objective test, whereby an order whose illegality was not obvious to the reasonable man and was executed in good faith could be invoked as a viable defence. This was later also termed 'manifest illegality' principle. Where the subordinate is aware of the unlawfulness of the order, although the order itself is not manifestly

---

Neutrality, 1912, 264–70; H Kelsen, 'Collective and Individual Responsibility in International Law with Particular Regard to the Punishment of War Criminals', 31 *California Law Review* (1943), 556–58.

20 *R v Howe and Others* [1987] 1 AC 417, *per* Lord Hailsham, 427. See also op cit, Dinstein, note 18, 68–70. Contemporary expressions of this doctrine, but for the varying reasons described below, are also embodied in the Charter of the International Military Tribunal at Nuremberg, Art 8, Control Council Law No 10, Art II(4)(b), as well as the ICTY and ICTR Statutes, Arts 7(4) and 6(4), respectively. In all these instruments, a successful plea of superior orders could serve to mitigate punishment.

21 *USA v Ohlendorf and Others* (*Einsatzgruppen* case) (1949) 15 ILR 656; 15 ILR 376.

22 Cited in *USA v Von Leeb and Others* (*High Command* case) (1949) 15 ILR 376.

23 *Dover Castle* case, 16 *AJIL* (1921), 704.

24 *Llandovery Castle* case, 16 *AJIL* (1922), 708.

illegal, the subjective knowledge of the accused is relevant in the attribution of liability, as any other conclusion would lead to absurdity. It would, moreover, disregard the significance of *mens rea* in the definition of crimes. Similarly, no irrebuttable presumption exists in this field of law suggesting that universal knowledge of the order's illegality will automatically prove the accused's awareness of it.[25] Following the end of the Second World War, both the 'moral choice' and the 'manifest illegality' test were abandoned by the Allies in their quest for swift military justice. As already mentioned, the doctrine of absolute liability prevailed in the Nuremberg Charter, Control Council Law No 10, and did not feature either in the Genocide Convention[26] or the 1949 Geneva Conventions.[27] On this basis alone, it has wrongly been asserted that since 1945 the defence of superior orders has been abrogated.[28] The fallacy of this argument will be proven shortly. For one thing, international tribunals constitute self-contained systems, whose sources of law do not necessarily follow the evolution of law outside of that system; rather, their legal route is drawn by their drafters. The Nuremberg Tribunal was not an exception to this rule, since the Allies did not want to be faced with mass claims of superior orders, all leading back to Hitler. However, the Tribunal took it for granted that all of the accused were fully aware of the orders received, and stated:

> The true test, which is found in varying degrees in the criminal law of most nations, is not the existence of the order, but whether *moral choice* was in fact possible [emphasis added].[29]

Similarly, subsequent Second World War military tribunals, especially those applying Control Council Law No 10 while upholding the validity of Art II(4)(b), did not also fail to mention that to plead superior orders one

25 Op cit, Dinstein, note 18, 28.
26 1948 Convention on the Prevention and Punishment of the Crime of Genocide, 78 UNTS 277.
27 Convention for the Amelioration of the Condition of the Wounded and Sick in Armed Forces in the Field (No I), 75 UNTS 31; Convention for the Amelioration of the Condition of the Wounded, Sick, and Ship-Wrecked Members of Armed Forces at Sea (No II), 75 UNTS 85; Convention Relative to the Treatment of Prisoners of War (No III), 75 UNTS 135; Convention Relative to the Protection of Civilian Persons in Time of War (No IV), 75 UNTS 287.
28 P Gaeta, 'The Defence of Superior Orders: The Statute of the International Criminal Court Versus Customary International Law', 10 *EJIL* (1999), 172. For the better view that the ICC Statute provision on superior orders is in conformity with customary law, see C Garraway, 'Superior Orders and the International Criminal Court: Justice Delivered or Justice Denied?', 836 *IRRC* (1999), 785.
29 IMT judgment, 22 (1946), p 466.

must show an excusable ignorance of their illegality.[30] The tribunals in these cases made it clear that if a defence was available to an accused under such circumstances, that would be the defence of duress, which would be brought about as a direct consequence of the severity and force of the order. The concept of duress will be examined below in another section. Further evidence of the existence of the duress-related 'moral choice' doctrine re-emerged in 1950, when the International Law Commission (ILC) codified, after a request by the General Assembly, the Principles of the Nuremberg Charter and Tribunal.[31] Principle IV provided, or more importantly, reaffirmed, that obedience to superior orders did not relieve the subordinate from responsibility, provided a 'moral choice' was in fact available. The concept of 'moral choice' in Principle IV is somewhat removed from the defence of superior orders, constituting as it does a particular defence in its own context.[32] Unlike the 'manifest illegality' principle associated with the defence of superior orders, where personal knowledge of the illegal nature of the order is crucial, the application of the 'moral choice' principle assumes from the outset such knowledge, predicating the defence instead on the possibility of action. After an intense Cold War period fuelled by endless disagreements, the final version of the Draft Code of Crimes against the Peace and Security of Mankind,[33] finally shelved in 1996, reverted to the absolute liability doctrine.[34] Interestingly, the Draft Code, especially in its final stages from 1981 to 1996, was a significant influence on the ICC Statute, which, as shall be seen, did not eventually adopt the stringent absolute liability doctrine.[35]

The evolution of national case law since the end of the Second World War has seen the domination of the principle of 'manifest illegality'. This was clearly articulated in the judgment of the District Court of Jerusalem in the *Eichmann* trial, confirmed also by that country's Supreme Court.[36] Moreover, the US, who is not a party to the ICC Statute, has consistently upheld the defence of superior orders under strict application of the manifest illegality test in both the Korean[37] and the Vietnam Wars.[38] The 1956 US Military

---

30 *Einsatzgruppen* case (1949) 15 ILR 656; 15 ILR 376; *Re Eck and Others (The Peleus)* (1945) 13 AD 248.

31 Reprinted in *Yearbook of the International Law Commission* (2nd session, 1950), Vol II, 374.

32 This is confirmed by the fact that while the first ILC rapporteur on the Draft Code of Crimes submitted his report in 1950 suggesting the viability of the defence of superior orders under certain circumstances, a subsequent report submitted in 1951 adopted the 'moral choice' principle found in Principle IV. See op cit, Dinstein, note 18, 241–51.

33 UN Doc A/CN 4/L 522 (31 May 1996).

34 Draft Art 5.

35 ICC Statute, Art 33.

36 36 ILR (1962), 277.

37 *USA v Kinder*, 14 CMR 742, 776 (1954).

38 *USA v Calley*, 46 CMR 1131 (1973), *aff'd*, 22 USCMA 534, 48 CMR 19 (1973). See also JJ Paust, 'My Lai and Vietnam: Norms, Myths and Leader Responsibility', 57 *Military Law Review* (1972), 99.

Manual, in fact, not only recognises the plea of superior orders as a valid defence;[39] it also obliges courts to take into consideration the fact that subordinates 'cannot be expected, in conditions of war discipline, to weigh scrupulously the legal merits of the orders received'.[40] Similarly, the Canadian Supreme Court in the *Finta* case recognised the defence of superior orders to war crimes and crimes against humanity as having been incorporated in the Canadian criminal justice system, and firmly accepted the manifest illegality rule.[41]

We have already made reference to the fact that Art 33 of the ICC Statute permits, subject to certain stringent conditions, a defence of superior orders. Because of the divergence of doctrine – from absolute liability to manifest illegality before international and domestic tribunals – it is worthwhile examining the process leading to Art 33 from the purview of the participating States. During the 1996 Prep Com it was generally felt that the absence of the defence in three seminal contemporary instruments, that is, the ICTY and International Criminal Tribunal for Rwanda (ICTR) Statutes, as well as the Draft Code, rendered any discussion on the matter redundant. With the insistence of Canada and France as regards the requirement of knowledge, supplemented with the 'manifest illegality' criterion, the matter gradually resurfaced.[42] By December 1997 the inclusion of the defence had gained strong support, but disagreement remained over the quantum of 'knowledge' required, whether or not the defence should cover orders received from the Security Council.[43] There was strong support, however, in excluding the defence vis-à-vis crimes against humanity and genocide.[44] During the Rome conference the two opposing schools of thought clashed for the final time. The US and Canada vehemently argued that the defence of superior orders, in those cases where the subordinate was not aware that the order was unlawful or where the order was not manifestly unlawful, was widely recognised in international law.[45] This proposal was particularly criticised by the UK, New Zealand and Germany who argued that in cases where superior orders could otherwise be invoked, an accused could raise a plea of duress and mistake of

39 US Dept of Army FM 27–10, *The Law of Land Warfare*, 1956, US Dept of Army. In accordance with para 509(a) the defence exists as long as the accused 'did not know and could not reasonably have been expected to know that the act ordered was unlawful'.
40 Ibid, para 509(b).
41 *R v Finta* (1994) 104 ILR 284.
42 *Report of the Preparatory Committee*, UN Doc A/51/22 (12–30 Aug 1996), Art Q, p 518, cited in M Scaliotti, 'Defences Before the International Criminal Court: Substantive Grounds for Excluding Criminal Responsibility (Part I)', 1 *ICLR* (2002), 111, 135–36.
43 During the March–April 1998 Prep Com, the proposal absolving subordinates from liability for orders received by the Security Council was dropped. Ibid.
44 Decisions Taken by the Preparatory Committee at its Session held from 1–12 October 1997, UN Doc A/AC 249/1997/L 9/Rev 1 (1997), Art M, pp 18–19, cited in Scaliotti, ibid.
45 UN Doc A/CONF 183/C 1/WGGP/L 2 (16 June 1998), ibid, p 137.

fact or law. Although the parties came up with a compromise formula agreed by an informal working group, which became the basis of Art 33, the German as well as other delegations were still unsatisfied as a matter of principle. Having thereafter the support of the US and its NATO allies, the US proposal was adopted by the Committee of the Whole by consensus, and finally also by the plenary of the Diplomatic Conference.[46]

What has now emerged as Art 33 of the ICC Statute recognises the defence on the basis of the three qualifications that exist in customary international law. The first presupposes an existing loyalty or legal obligation, while the other two refer to the requisite standards of knowledge, consisting of both the subjective knowledge of the accused, and an objective test based on the 'manifest illegality' rule. The article thus reads as follows:

1 The fact that a crime within the jurisdiction of the Court has been committed by a person pursuant to an order of a Government or of a superior, whether military or civilian, shall not relieve that person of criminal responsibility unless:

(a) The person was under a legal obligation to obey orders of the Government or the superior in question;

(b) The person did not know that the order was unlawful; and

(c) The order was not manifestly unlawful.

2 For the purposes of this article, orders to commit genocide or crimes against humanity are manifestly unlawful.

The presumption of knowledge inserted in para 2 seems to be irrebuttable. However, since the commission of genocide and crimes against humanity involve large scale action, often requiring minor operations in which the offender cannot always be expected to be aware of the eventual aim, justice necessitates this presumption to be a rebuttable one. Let us now proceed to examine the defence of 'duress', which has a strong affiliation and is closely related to the defence of superior orders.

3.3 DURESS AND NECESSITY

The poor drafting of Art 31(1)(d) has its roots not in the ignorance of its drafters, but rather on the divergent and inflexible views of the negotiating parties. It therefore reflects, like many provisions in the Statute, a clause founded among other things on compromise. What is not clear in the text of sub-para (d) is primarily the definition of 'duress' and 'necessity' as two

46 Ibid.

related but distinct concepts, as well as the question whether this defence is also available to a charge of murder. The legislative history of the Statute suggests that although initially the two concepts were included in different articles, by 1998 they had been moved to a single provision where moreover 'necessity' had been subsumed within the concept of 'duress'.[47] Furthermore, during discussions before the Committee of the Whole, it was decided that the combined defence encompassed in Art 31(1)(d) was available also to a charge of murder, since the prior requirement necessitating an intention not to cause death had been deleted.[48] Some isolated proposals to the effect that duress/necessity apply also in cases of threats to property were unanimously rejected.[49]

Sub-paragraph (d) offers a definition of an offence caused as a result of duress, where this 'result[s] from a threat of imminent death or of continuing or imminent serious bodily harm against that person or another person'. According to this provision, a person is exculpated from the underlying offence where:

(a) the threat is not brought about by actions attributed to the accused, but by other persons, or as a result of circumstances beyond the control of the accused (necessity);

(b) the accused has taken all necessary and reasonable action to avoid this threat; and

(c) the accused does not intend to cause a greater harm than the one sought to be avoided.

The ICTY Trial Chamber in the *Erdemovic* case confirmed the conclusion of the post-Second World War War Crimes Commission that duress constitutes a complete defence subject to the aforementioned conditions.[50] In fact, the ICTY recognised that one of the essential elements of the post-war jurisprudence was the 'absence or not of moral choice'. In the face of imminent physical danger, a soldier may be considered as being deprived of his moral choice, as long as this physical threat (of death or serious bodily harm) is clear and present, or else imminent, real and inevitable.[51] The ad hoc tribunal, moreover, spelled out certain criteria which are to be used by the court in order to conclude whether or not moral choice was in fact available. These are the voluntary participation of the accused in the overall criminal operation, and

---

47 Op cit, Saland, note 14, 207–08.
48 Although under traditional English law, duress may never excuse the killing of an innocent person. See *R v Howe* [1987] 1 AC 417 and *Abbott v R* [1977] AC 755.
49 Op cit, Saland, note 14, 208.
50 *Prosecutor v Erdemovic*, Sentencing Judgment (29 Nov 1996), para 17. These were identified in the *Trial of Krupp and Eleven Others*, 10 LRTWC (1949), 147.
51 Ibid, para 18, citing post-Second World War case law.

the rank held by the person giving the order as well as that of the accused, which includes the existence or not of a duty to obey in a particular situation.[52]

Cassese J has convincingly argued that since law is based on what society can reasonably expect of its members, it 'should not set intractable standards of behaviour which require mankind to perform acts of martyrdom, and brand as criminal behaviour falling below these standards'.[53] This philosophical approach to duress merits consideration because of its practical implications. In the *Erdemovic* Appeals Decision, the Chamber, while agreeing that no special rule of international law existed regulating duress where the underlying crime was the taking of human life, its members strongly disagreed on whether the general rule on duress should apply or whether some other domestic principle should be introduced. Judges McDonald and Vohrah unsuccessfully argued that in the absence of a special rule on duress, common law (as it turned out) was applicable, concluding thus that duress does not afford a complete defence to homicides. Cassese and Stephen JJ made the case that the general rule applies, which based on a case-to-case examination does afford a defence. The dissenting opinion of Cassese J that the general international law rule on duress be applied[54] was not only internationally respected but moreover influenced ICC developments. One of the essential elements in a successful plea of duress is that of proportionality (doing that which is the lesser of two evils). In practical terms this will be the hardest to satisfy, the burden of proof being on the accused, and may never be satisfied where the accused is saving his own life at the expense of his victim. Conversely, where the choice is not a direct one between the life of the accused and that of his victim, but where there is high probability that the person under duress will not be able to save the life of the victim, the proportionality test may be said to be satisfied.[55] Although duress has been admitted as a defence against homicides,[56] post-Second World War case law suggests that courts have rarely allowed duress to succeed in cases involving unlawful killing, even where they have in principle admitted the applicability of this defence. This restrictive approach has its roots in the fundamental importance of human life to law and society, from which it follows that any legal endorsement of attacks on, or interference with, this right will be very strictly construed and only exceptionally admitted.[57] The result would be

---

52 Ibid, paras 18–19.
53 *Erdemovic* case, Appeals Chamber Decision (7 Oct 1997), Dissenting Opinion of Judge Cassese, para 47.
54 Ibid, paras 12, 40.
55 Ibid, para 42.
56 It was only in the *Holzer* case, cited ibid, para 26, that both the prosecutor and the Judge Advocate contended that duress can never excuse the killing of innocent persons, relying however, on English law.
57 *Erdemovic*, Appeals Decision (7 Oct 1997), para 43.

different where the homicide would have been committed in any case by a person other than the one acting under duress.[58] This was the case with Erdemovic who argued that had he not adhered to his superiors to execute Bosnian civilians, not only would he have been shot but others would have taken his place as executioners. In such cases the requirement of proportionality is satisfied because the harm caused by not obeying the illegal order is not much greater than the harm that would have resulted from obeying it.[59] This requirement of proportionality is clearly a subjective one, irrespective of whether the greater harm is in fact avoided.

The concept of necessity is broader than duress, encompassing threats to life and limb generally, and not only when they emanate from another person.[60] There is a subjective element in the definition of necessity in that the person should reasonably believe that there is a threat of imminent or otherwise unavoidable death or serious bodily harm to him or to another person. This should be combined with an objective criterion, that the person acted necessarily and reasonably to avoid the threat and moreover did not voluntarily expose him or herself to the threat or danger. Since the defence of 'necessity' is encompassed within the general concept of duress in sub-para (d), it necessarily follows that it is used to merely qualify the 'threat or danger' giving rise to a defence of duress. Therefore, duress in sub-para (d) is broader than the equivalent concept found in general international law. This is not, however, the end of the story, since, as already noted, Art 21(1)(c) of the Statute empowers the Court to delve into domestic law in cases where all other sources have failed to extract satisfactory solutions. In such cases the Court would find itself unable to extrapolate general principles because of the divergence of national legislation on necessity between the common law[61] and civil law systems.[62] Depending on relevant circumstances, and after deeming it appropriate, the Court in a scenario of this type might very well be

---

58 *Erdemovic*, Appeals Decision (7 Oct 1997), para 43.
59 Ibid.
60 Ibid, para 14. See also 1958 British Manual of Military Law, *The Law of War on Land*, para 630, which puts forward the case of one who in extremity of hunger kills another person to eat him or her.
61 The failure of this defence in English law is premised on unclear and ill-defined case law that requires reinterpretation. In the classic case of *Dudley and Stephens* (1884) 14 QBD 273, necessity was not upheld to a charge of murder where a cabin boy was eaten by other shipwrecked crew members. The justification for the decision, however, is not clear. That case did not say that a deliberate killing could not be justified, only that a person could not justifiably kill an innocent to save his life. 'Neither did it say that a deliberate killing could not be excused, only that an excuse would not be available where there was no immediate necessity.' Op cit, Wilson, note 10, 289.
62 Civil law systems generally allow this defence. See, for example, Arts 122–27 of the French Penal Code, and Art 54(1) of the 1930 Italian Penal Code, cited in op cit, Scaliotti, note 42, 143–45.

inclined to decide that the application of the principles of a particular legal system be applicable before the case at hand.

3.4 SELF-DEFENCE

A contemporary international definition of self-defence, provided by an international tribunal, is that propounded by the ICTY in the *Kordic* case. The Tribunal pointed out that the notion of self-defence:

> May be broadly defined as providing a defence to a person who acts to defend or protect himself or his property (or another person or person's property) against attack, provided that the acts constitute a reasonable, necessary and proportionate reaction to the attack.[63]

The Trial Chamber in that case noted that although the ICTY Statute did not provide for self-defence as a ground for excluding criminal responsibility, defences form part of the general principles of criminal law that are binding on the Tribunal. It went on to note that the definition of self-defence enshrined in Art 31(1)(c) of the ICC Statute reflects provisions found in most national criminal codes 'and may be regarded as constituting a rule of customary international law'.[64]

Despite this general definition which is almost identical to that found in the ICC Statute, there are issues related to this defence that are not straight-forward. These problem areas include the relationship between the UN Charter and self-defence,[65] the invocation of self-defence with regard to property, proportionality, and whether force can be used in cases of pre-emptive self-defence or only when the danger is present or imminent. We shall examine each of these issues individually.

Where a State entity commits an act of aggression in violation of Art 2(4) of the UN Charter, that country will incur responsibility pertaining to States. Moreover, under the ICC Statute,[66] pending a definition on aggression, the initiators of the aggression will be held criminally liable. Since a definition of aggression is bound to be premised on the relevant provisions of the UN Charter, persons in the highest civilian and military echelons of a State apparatus resorting to the use of military force will be able to invoke

---

63 *Prosecutor v Kordic and Others* (*Kordic* case), Judgment (26 Feb 2001), Case No IT–95–14/2-T, para 449.

64 Ibid, para 451.

65 Of particular relevance is the concept of unlawful use of force under Art 2(4) of the UN Charter, as well as legitimate responses to such force in accordance with Arts 42 (collective enforcement action) and 51 (unilateral or collective self-defence).

66 ICC Statute, Art 5(2).

self-defence (as a claim aiming to exclude criminal liability) only where the force used is lawful, that is, it is permitted under Arts 42 and 51 of the UN Charter. What is more, such force, even if lawful, will exclude criminal liability only where it satisfies the requirements for self-defence, that is, it is proportionate, the danger is present, and the response does not constitute a crime against humanity or genocide. Article 31(1)(c) is clear that:

> The fact that the person was involved in a defensive operation conducted by forces shall not in itself constitute a ground for excluding criminal responsibility [under the rubric of self-defence].[67]

Although most delegations raised reservations as regards the availability of self-defence to defend property, at the insistence of the US and Israel, reference to this effect was eventually included. Sub-paragraph (c) reflects the unanimous feeling of all delegates that the commission of crimes against humanity and genocide can never justify the protection of property. Self-defence with regard to property can only be raised where the defensive action involved the perpetration of war crimes, where the property concerned 'is essential for the survival of the person or another person or property which is essential for accomplishing a military mission'. Thus, stringent and narrow criteria apply. The result is not a happy one, at least as far as the second part of the sentence is concerned, since under customary international law the concept of 'military necessity', which is akin to 'property which is essential for accomplishing a military mission',[68] does not permit the commission of war crimes.[69] Since the concept of 'belligerent reprisals' is not encompassed within the notion of self-defence,[70] it stretches the imagination to conceive of a war crime committed in defence of property essential for military operations, which is moreover proportionate! The only possible scenario would be where an unlawful attack against military property was repelled with unlawful weapons used against the attackers – the defending party possessing no other or appropriate weaponry – or where protected property was counterattacked as a result. The use of unlawful weapons or the perpetration of attacks in defence of such property

---

67 Enunciated also in the *Kordic* judgment (26 Feb 2001), para 452.
68 Ibid, para 451.
69 1977 Protocol I to the Geneva Conventions of 1949 (International Armed Conflicts), Art 51(4) and (5), 1125 UNTS 3. Kalshoven has correctly argued that deviations from the rules contained in Protocol I cannot be justified with an appeal to military necessity, unless a given rule expressly admits such an appeal. See F Kalsnoven, *Constraints on the Waging of War*, 1987, Geneva: ICRC, 73.
70 It is unlawful to subject civilians to belligerent reprisals, in accordance with the customary rule encapsulated in the 1977 Protocol I, Art 51(6).

against innocent civilians is not only contrary to *jus cogens*, it is certainly not warranted by any construction of the principle of 'proportionality'.[71]

As far as the decision to engage in defensive action is concerned (which includes the determination that force has been used), the test applied in sub-para (c) is an objective one. The person must act 'reasonably'. This will depend on relevant external circumstances, but the Court is not excluded from assessing the personal state and characteristics of the accused on the basis of domestic law permitting the evaluation of such subjective criteria, in accordance with Arts 31(3) and 21(1)(c). Similarly, the degree of force applied is predicated on the objective test of proportionality.

3.5 INTOXICATION

Legal systems usually distinguish between voluntary and involuntary intoxication. Moreover, English law differentiates, for the purposes of the present discussion, between *mens rea* offences and non-*mens rea* offences. The former, known also as specific intent offences, are characterised by the requirement of intention in the definition of their mental element, where adducing evidence of voluntary intoxication will negate *mens rea*, although voluntary intoxication does not generally excuse criminal liability. For crimes of negligence, strict liability and crimes of recklessness, adducing such evidence will be ineffective. Likewise, involuntary intoxication does not generally excuse criminal liability, unless the effect of the involuntary intoxication is to negate the *mens rea* of the underlying crime, but this would find application only with regard to crimes of specific or basic intent.[72] A claim of involuntary intoxication would be unsuccessful with regard to crimes of negligence and strict liability.[73] The ICC Statute does not purport to make this distinction, but it is clear that all the offences in the Statute require some form of intent, although depending on the form of participation in these offences strict liability may suffice.[74] The terms of the defence of intoxication contained in Art 31(1)(b) are simple, and the provision does not make such a distinction of *mens rea* and strict liability offences. Intoxication will be considered involuntary under English law if it is coerced,[75] or

---

71 Y Sandoz *et al* (eds), *Commentary on the Additional Protocols of 8 June 1977*, 1987, Geneva: ICRC, 625–26.

72 Crimes of basic intent in English law are those that can be committed recklessly, including those forms where foresight or awareness must be proved. This encompasses assault, malicious wounding, manslaughter and rape, among others. See op cit, Wilson, note 10, 258.

73 Ibid, 253–56.

74 See I Bantekas, 'The Contemporary Law of Superior Responsibility', 93 *AJIL* (1999), 573, 586, regarding liability of superiors who are commanders of occupied territories.

75 GR Sullivan, 'Involuntary Intoxication and Beyond', *Crim LR* [1994], 272.

where the accused entirely mistakes what he is consuming. Doubt exists whether a self-induced mistake renders intoxication involuntary, or whether the mistake must be induced by the unlawful acts of another person. Both causes should excuse as long as the accused is deprived of a fair opportunity to conform.[76]

The aforementioned state of the law in England reflects in general terms the practice of most States, and hence its inclusion in Art 31(1)(b) of the ICC Statute does not depart from these principles. Thus, involuntary intoxication will excuse liability where *mens rea* is negated as a result, whereas voluntary intoxication will only produce the same effect if 'the person knew, or disregarded the risk, that, as a result of the intoxication, he or she was likely to engage in conduct constituting a crime'.[77]

3.6 MISTAKE OF FACT OR MISTAKE OF LAW

There were widely divergent views on this provision. Two options were initially inserted, whereby delegates were divided over whether mistake of law or fact should be a ground for excluding liability or not. Some delegations were of the view that mistake of fact was not necessary because it was covered by *mens rea*.[78] The view eventually accepted was that both mistake of fact and law constitute valid grounds for excluding criminal responsibility only if the mistake under consideration negates the mental element required by the crime.[79] However, a mistake of law 'as to whether a particular type of conduct is a crime' shall not be a ground for excluding criminal responsibility.[80] Paragraph 2 of Art 32, moreover, makes the necessary connection between mistake of law and superior orders. Where a subordinate receives an unlawful order which is not manifestly unlawful and which he or she is under an obligation to obey, the subordinate will be exculpated where he or she believed the order to lie within the confines of legitimacy.

A situation not covered in Art 32 is that of the doctrine of 'transferred intent'. Where A plans to kill B, but mistakenly assumes C for B, and

---

76 Op cit, Wilson, note 10, 254–55.
77 During the preparatory discussions two approaches to voluntary intoxication surfaced: if it was decided that voluntary intoxication should in no case be an acceptable defence, provision should nonetheless be made for mitigation of punishment with regard to persons who were not able to form a specific intent, where required, towards the crime committed due to their intoxication; if voluntary intoxication were to be retained as a valid defence, as was finally accepted, an exception would be made for those cases where the person became intoxicated in order to commit the crime in an intoxicated condition. UN Doc A/CONF 183/2/Add 1 (14 April 1998), p 57.
78 Ibid, pp 56–57.
79 ICC Statute, Art 32.
80 Ibid, Art 32(2).

proceeds to kill C, A's mistake as to a charge of murder is irrelevant. His mistake did not prevent him from forming *mens rea* for the crime of murder. The 'transferred intent' doctrine should also find application before the ICC in situations analogous to the conduct just described. As for the applicable test for either a mistake of fact or of law, the wording of the Statute suggests that this is a subjective one. This is in line with English law, for example, where mistakes as to justificatory/definitional defences[81] need only be honest.[82]

3.7 MENTAL INCAPACITY

A defence of mental incapacity necessarily develops and evolves alongside medical/psychiatric advances. Although this is recognised in domestic legal systems, in essence because serious mental incapacity negates the mental element of crime, law-making institutions and courts are not bound in incorporating such scientific evidence into the criminal law. Article 31(1)(a) of the ICC Statute exculpates from criminal responsibility where the defence of mental incapacity is proven. However, besides a general qualification of the scope of mental incapacity, none of the variants recognised in the different legal systems are employed, and for good reason. In the limited spatial confines of the Prep Com, agreement would have been impossible, and by that time, para 3 of Art 31 had been inserted, or was imminent, whereby the Court could *proprio motu* derive any additional appropriate defence by reference to general principles of law. In fact, it is very likely that the elaboration of this defence before the ICC will depend almost exclusively on such principles.[83]

The defence was raised in the *Celebici* case, where an ICTY Trial Chamber established a two-tier test of 'diminished responsibility'. This consists of an 'abnormality of mind' which the accused must be suffering at the time of the crime, which must moreover 'substantially impair' the ability of the accused to control his or her actions.[84] This test was essentially constructed on the basis of English law.[85] On the facts of the case, the Court, although

---

81 That is, defences operating within the parameters of the offence definition, such as consent.
82 *R v Williams* (1984) 78 Cr App R 276; *Beckford v R* [1988] AC 130. See op cit, Wilson, note 10, 203.
83 The lack of international jurisprudence was also evident during the drafting of the ICTY Statute, where the UN Secretary General's report, although silent on the specific issue, left it to the Tribunal to decide the fate of 'mental incapacity, drawing upon general principles of law recognised by all nations'. UN Doc S/25704 (1993), reprinted in 32 ILM (1993), 1159, para 58.
84 *ICTY Prosecutor v Delalic and Others* (*Celebici* case), Judgment (16 Nov 1998), Case No IT–96–21–T, paras 1165–70.
85 *R v Byrne* [1960] 3 All ER 1, 4.

recognising that the accused Landzo suffered from an abnormality of mind, rejected his claim because in its opinion he failed to prove that the impairment was substantial. The basis of this judgment does represent at a minimum the incorporation of the defence in the various legal systems, and as such was deemed appropriate for the purposes of the ICC Statute. It may successfully be raised where:

> The person suffers from a mental disease or defect that destroys that person's capacity to appreciate the unlawfulness or nature of his or her conduct, or capacity to control his or her conduct to conform to the requirements of law.

It is uncertain whether this may serve as a complete or partial defence, but there is no reason why both cannot be applicable. As for the burden of proof, based on discussions in previous sections of this chapter, this is an affirmative defence whose elements must be raised and satisfied by the accused on a balance of probabilities.[86]

In its determination of the factual criteria relating to this defence, the Court will have recourse to expert witnesses, provided by both parties,[87] and also from a list of experts approved by the Registrar, or an expert approved by the Court at the request of a party.[88] This intricate interplay between law and psychiatry/forensics, coupled with (a) the relatively wide definition of Art 31(1)(a), and (b) the liberal rules on the production of evidence (as long as probative value can be demonstrated), ensures that technical consultants will be a substantial guide for the Court.[89]

---

86 *Celebici*, Judgment (16 Nov 1998), paras 78, 1160, 1172.
87 ICC Rules of Procedure and Evidence, r 135(1).
88 Ibid, r 135(3).
89 See generally, P Krug, 'The Emerging Mental Incapacity Defence in International Criminal Law: Some Initial Questions of Implementation', 94 *AJIL* (2000), 317, 322–35.

Chapter 4

State jurisdiction and immunities

4.1 CRIMINAL JURISDICTION: AN INTRODUCTION

Jurisdiction refers to the power of each State under international law to prescribe and enforce its municipal laws with regard to persons and property. This power is exercised in three forms, which correspond to the three branches of government. Hence, legislative or prescriptive jurisdiction relates to the competence to prescribe the ambit of municipal laws, judicial jurisdiction relates to the competence of courts to apply national laws and enforcement jurisdiction refers to the ability of States to enforce the fruits of their legislative or judicial labour (for example, gathering of evidence, arrest and infliction of sanctions). While prescriptive and judicial jurisdiction may assume an extra-territorial character, enforcement jurisdiction generally cannot.[1] In the sense described, jurisdiction may be both civil and criminal. With the growth of interstate commerce and movement of persons across international borders since the 18th century, Lord Halsbury's assertion that, 'All crimes are local . . . jurisdiction is only territorial',[2] must be viewed as obsolete today. Until recently, there did not exist even a general set of rules delineating conflicts of criminal jurisdiction. While conduct occurring solely on the territory of one country could logically fall within that country's competence, a conflict of criminal laws existed where harmful conduct, or its effects, were perpetrated or felt in more than one State. At the same time, the application of the general rule whereby a State may unilaterally lay claim to jurisdiction in a particular case, with the sole proviso that no other rule of international

---

1 Exceptionally, some common law countries do not object to foreign consuls serving writs to persons on their territory. Furthermore, visiting Heads of State have been permitted to perform their official functions while abroad, such as signing decrees. See M Akehurst, 'Jurisdiction in International Law', 45 *BYIL* (1972–73), 145, pp 146, 150.
2 *Macleod v AG for New South Wales* [1891] AC 455, p 458, *per* Lord Halsbury.

law is opposed to it,[3] creates further conflicts.[4] Not surprisingly, there does not exist a general agreement resolving issues of concurrent criminal jurisdiction. Problems of concurrent legislative jurisdiction, and in particular with regard to criminal matters, are satisfactorily dealt with only where they have been regulated by treaty,[5] but even these subject-specific treaties provide for a variety of jurisdictional bases with no clear hierarchical order. The jurisdictional principles contained in criminal treaties are the product of national criminal practice and, to the extent they are uniformly applied, they may be regarded, albeit with caution, as reflecting general principles of national law. These are the principles of territoriality, active personality (or nationality), passive personality, universality and the protective principle.

Issues of criminal jurisdiction remain a highly contentious area of international relations. Even where specific conduct has been regulated by treaty, jurisdiction cannot be said to constitute a settled matter, since not only non-States parties might oppose the said rule, but also States parties may disagree over its ambit, execution, or hierarchical status.[6] This chapter examines the scope and nature of prescriptive and judicial jurisdiction, as well as possible immunities available as exceptions to it being exercised in individual cases.

3 *France v Turkey (Lotus* case) (1927) PCIJ Reports, Ser A, No 10; see W Estey, 'The Five Bases of Extra-Territorial Jurisdiction and the Failures of the Presumption against Extra-Territoriality', 21 *Hastings Int'l & Comp L Rev* (1997), 153; R Higgins, *Problems and Process: International Law and How We Use It*, 1994, Oxford: OUP, 77, who takes the opposite view by contending that the *Lotus* presumption should not be relied on because it is based on a much dissented judgment.

4 It is not clear whether *Nottebohm (Guatemala v Liechtenstein)* (1955) ICJ Reports 4 and *AngloNorwegian Fisheries (UK v Norway)* (1951) ICJ Reports 116, which limited the unilateral competence of States to confer nationality and delimit the territorial sea through the use of straight baselines respectively, have invalidated the *Lotus* presumption in the field of criminal jurisdiction, which now seems firmly established in a plethora of treaties providing for the exercise of national jurisdiction akin to 'universal'.

5 1998 Amsterdam Treaty Amending the Treaty on the European Union, Art K3(d), reprinted in 37 ILM (1998), 56, provides that European Union (EU) States are to prevent conflicts of criminal jurisdiction arising among themselves; in similar fashion, and for the first time articulated in an anti-terrorist treaty, Art 7(5) of the 2000 United Nations (UN) Convention for the Suppression of the Financing of Terrorism obliges States parties, in cases of jurisdictional conflicts, to strive to co-ordinate their actions appropriately, 'in particular concerning the conditions for prosecution and modalities for mutual legal assistance'. Reprinted in 39 ILM (2000), 270.

6 See FA Mann, 'The Doctrine of Jurisdiction in International Law', 111 *RCADI* (1964), 44, p 82, who formulated the theory of 'reasonable link', according to which jurisdiction should be dependent upon the strongest possible connection between the conduct and the claimant forum; see I Brownlie, *Principles of Public International Law*, 1998, Oxford: OUP, 313, who also adds the general principles of non-intervention and proportionality; MS McDougal and WM Reisman, *International Law in Contemporary Perspective*, 1981, Mineola, New York: Foundation Press, 1274, claim that a State may exercise its prescriptive jurisdiction only when it is substantially affected by an act.

4.2 TERRITORIAL JURISDICTION

States have traditionally, on account of their sovereignty, exercised a primary right of criminal jurisdiction over offences perpetrated upon their territory.[7] Assumption of such jurisdiction has the advantage of immediate accessibility to sources of evidence and relevant witnesses and subsequent minimisation of expenses and judicial time. In many cases, it may also prove to be politically expedient, where competing claims for jurisdiction involve delicate questions of interstate relations; especially where the exercise of extra-territorial jurisdiction would be viewed as encroachment of another State's sovereignty. The territoriality principle operates well and without interstate friction only when all the elements of an offence have taken place on the territory of the prosecuting State. In the classic example of one person firing a shot across a frontier and subsequently causing the death of another on the other side, the principle of territoriality proper gives rise to questions of primacy between two competing jurisdictions. State practice has illustrated that in such situations municipal authorities will resort either to extra-territorial principles of jurisdiction, or consider an element of the *actus reus* (firing of the shot) or the ensuing result (death) as having occurred on their territory, thus finding application for the territoriality principle. This latter expansion of the territoriality principle is termed 'qualified'.

With regard to the qualified territorial principle, various tests are operated by different States as to whether this requires the actual commission of the offence or its effects to have occurred in the claimant State. Two principles have generally been applied to address this situation, namely, the subjective and objective principles of territoriality.

4.2.1 Subjective territoriality

States applying this principle assert, in general, that when an element of an offence either commences or in any other way takes place on their territory, they may validly assert jurisdiction over that offence.[8] This principle was early

7 *Compania Naviera Vascongando v SS Cristina* [1938] AC 485, p 496, *per* Lord Macmillan. See M Hirst, 'Jurisdiction over Cross-Frontier Offences', 97 *LQR* (1981), 80; in *Bankovic and Others v Belgium and Sixteen Others*, Admissibility Decision (13 Dec 2001), Application No 52207/99, European Court of Human Rights (ECHR), the Court was seized with a complaint brought by six Yugoslav nationals against North Atlantic Treaty Organisation (NATO) Member States with regard to the bombing campaign against Yugoslavia and the killing of the applicants' family members. The Court found the application inadmissible, holding that the crucial events occurred outside the Convention's juridical space, stating also that under international law State jurisdiction is primarily territorial, all others being exceptional.

8 See G Gilbert, 'Crimes *Sans Frontieres*: Jurisdictional Problems in English Law', 63 *BYIL* (1992), 415, p 430, who makes reference to the 'doctrine of ubiquity', which allows States to assume jurisdiction over an offence, as well as any connected inchoate offences, if a part of the offence or its effects are felt in the prosecuting State.

recognised in two international treaties, although not widely regarded as a general principle of national law.[9] These were the 1929 Convention for the Suppression of Counterfeiting Currency and the 1936 Convention for the Prevention of Illicit Drug Traffic, which bound the contracting parties to assume jurisdiction over the prescribed offences, irrespective of the locus where the offence materialised, as long as an attempt, commission or conspiracy was perpetrated on their territory.

While, at the interstate level such a rule may be formulated in accordance with the needs of its drafters in order to effectively combat certain illegal activities, such as counterfeiting and drug-trafficking, its application at the national level with respect to municipal offences seems to warrant that not only a significant portion of the offence take place in the claimant State, but also that there exists a 'real and substantial link' between the offence and that State.[10] In *Libman*, the accused committed fraud in Canada by selling worthless shares over the telephone to buyers in the US who, as directed, sent the money to Central America, which was finally received by Libman back in Canada. The Canadian Supreme Court exercised jurisdiction on the basis of the 'real and substantial link' theory and the perpetration of the largest part of the offence in Canada.[11]

It is evident that where the application of this principle pays no attention to the consequences of the offence for the prosecuting State it resembles more a rule of extra-territorial rather than territorial jurisdiction. A strong argument for territorial jurisdiction would best be served if the claimant State were to demonstrate it had suffered harmful consequences as a result of the crime concerned. This is the basis of objective territoriality.[12] However, the exercise of subjective jurisdiction in some cases may serve as a good deterrent with regard to criminal conduct that is not penalised or adequately policed in the country where its consequences are felt, especially transnational fraud and sex-related offences in developing countries.

---

9   I Shearer, *Starke's International Law*, 11th edn, 1994, London: Butterworths, 186; as an example of municipal law, ibid, Gilbert, note 8, p 431, cites s 7 of the New Zealand Crimes Act 1961.

10 *Libman v R* (1986) 21 DLR 174, p 200, *per* La Forest J.

11 On the same basis, and without proof of damage to the interests of the prosecuting State, an Australian Criminal Appeals Court assumed jurisdiction over an offence of grievous bodily harm with intention, committed by the mailing of poisoned food from Australia to Germany: *R v Nekuda* (1989) 39A Crim R 5, NSW, CCA; similarly, an act of murder committed in Mexico by a US citizen was held to fall within the jurisdiction of Arizona courts because the crime had been premeditated in Arizona, this being a substantial element of first degree murder: *State of Arizona v Willoughby* (1995) 114 ILR 586.

12 See generally JJ Paust *et al, International Criminal Law: Cases and Materials*, 1996, Durham, NC: Carolina Academic Press, 123–28.

4.2.2 Objective territoriality

This principle allows for jurisdiction where conduct committed abroad produces effects in a third State. The classic example associated with this principle involved the *Lotus* case before the Permanent Court of International Justice.[13] In that case, eight Turkish crewmen perished as a result of a collision on the high seas between a French and Turkish vessel. Upon arrival in Turkish territorial waters, the captain of the *Lotus* was apprehended and charged with the death of the crewmen. The majority of the Court ruled that since the Turkish vessel was flying the flag of that country it was to be assimilated to Turkish territory. Hence, under this theory, it was as if the ensuing manslaughter was committed on Turkish soil, in which case it was thereafter justified in exercising jurisdiction over the French captain. That part of the judgment was heavily criticised and, in any event, does not represent the law today.[14]

The magnitude of the consequences which different States require is felt in their territory as a prerequisite to exercising objective territorial jurisdiction are issues that have evolved through municipal case law and legislation. In international law, jurisdiction with regard to these inchoate offences could be based, depending on the particular facts, on the protective principle with which it overlaps. US courts consider that the existence of any two of the following are sufficient to trigger the application of objective territoriality jurisdiction: perpetration of particular elements of the *actus reus*; demonstration of intent or the production of effects within the US.[15] US case law has correctly recognised that because criminal acts may be consummated through agents, whether knowing or unknowing, such as through accomplices or postal and telephone services, a defendant will be subject to US jurisdiction if he or she knowingly uses such agents to carry out an act within that country.[16]

Another alternative employed by US federal courts, again similar to the protective principle, is the so-called 'effects doctrine', which has empowered the courts of that country to assume jurisdiction, especially in anti-trust cases, on the basis that the economic or other consequences of the offence were

---

13 *France v Turkey* (1927) PCIJ Reports, Ser A, No 10.
14 In his dissenting opinion, ibid, p 53, Lord Finlay argued that criminal jurisdiction for negligence causing a collision belongs to the Flag State, unless the accused is of a different nationality, in which case it is his or her own country that may also assume jurisdiction. This is the rule adopted in Art 27 of the 1982 United Nations Law of the Sea Convention (UNCLOS), 21 ILM (1982), 1261.
15 Op cit, Paust *et al*, note 12, p 124.
16 Op cit, Paust *et al*, note 12; *Ford v USA*, 273 US 593 (1927), p 621; *McBoyle v USA*, 43 F 2d 273 (1930).

directly felt in the US.[17] Notwithstanding the municipal merits for such jurisdiction, its far-reaching application may be injurious to the trading or other interests of third States[18] and public economic organisations.[19] International protestation against the broad use of the 'effects doctrine' in the US culminated in *Timberlane Lumber Co v Bank of America*,[20] where it was held that jurisdiction under the doctrine had to consider the economic interests of other States and the scope of the relationship between the US and the defendants.[21] The EU has reacted vociferously to the promulgation of extraterritorial legislation of this kind, calling on its Member States to take appropriate measures to protect themselves.[22] If the doctrine is to be applied in accordance with international law, the relevant courts must be satisfied that the 'effect' is not only substantial and direct, but also that the executive has exhausted all consultative or other means with the conflicting State in order to settle the dispute.

A third alternative form of the objective territoriality principle is the 'continuing act' doctrine. This stipulates that a State enjoys jurisdiction over an offence which, although committed abroad, is continuing to produce results within that State. In *DPP v Doot*,[23] the accused were charged with conspiring to import cannabis into the UK. Although the conspiracy was fully carried out abroad, and UK courts would not normally entertain jurisdiction in such

17 See Sherman (Anti-Trust) Act 1890, 15 USC § 1; *USA v Aluminium Co of America*, 148 F 2d 416 (1945); *Mannington Mills Inc v Congoleum Corp*, 595 F 2d 1287 (1979); *Hartford Fire Insurance Co v California*, 113 S Ct 2891 (1993); see also DHJ Hermann, 'Extra-Territorial Criminal Jurisdiction in Securities Laws Regulation', 16 *Cumberland L Rev* (1985–86), 207; in 1996 Congress passed the US Cuban Liberty and Democratic Solidarity Act (Helms Burton Act), 22 USC § 6021. Title III of the Act concerns nationals of third States 'trafficking' in nationalised US property by the Cuban authorities in 1959, imposing on such persons penalties such as treble damages and denial of entry to the US. See A Qureshi, *International Economic Law*, 1999, London: Sweet & Maxwell, 67–69; BM Clagett, 'Title III of the Helms Burton Act is Consistent with International Law', 90 *AJIL* (1996), 434; AV Lowe, 'US Extra-Territorial Jurisdiction: The Helms-Burton and D'Amato Acts', 46 *ICLQ* (1997), 378.

18 It is not surprising that such jurisdiction has been ardently opposed by a number of countries. See UK Protection of Trading Interests Act 1980; AV Lowe, 'Blocking Extra-Territorial Jurisdiction: The British Protection of Trading Interests Act 1980', 75 *AJIL* (1981), 257.

19 The EU generally assumes jurisdiction over anti-competitive activities performed outside its boundaries, either on the basis of relevant subsidiaries situated in the EU or by finding that such activity was implemented in the EU, although originating outside it. See *ICI v Commission* (*Dyestuff* case) [1972] ECR 619; *Ahlstrom v Commission* (*Wood Pulp* case) [1988] 4 CMLR 901; DGF Lange and JB Sandage, 'The *Wood Pulp* Decision and its Implications for the Scope of EC Competition Law', 26 *CML Rev* (1989), 137.

20 (1976) 66 ILR 270.

21 Restatement (Third) of the Foreign Relations Law of the USA 1986, § 403 further requires that the exercise of jurisdiction be 'reasonable'.

22 Joint Action 96/668/CFSP (1996 OJ L309, 29 Nov, p 7).

23 [1973] 1 All ER 940.

case,[24] the House of Lords rejected the defendants' plea by stating that the offence continued to occur in England since the result of the conspiracy was ongoing.

Finally, reference should also be made to jurisdiction over legal persons, particularly multinational corporations, although this is not connected to any form of criminal liability. These are normally constituted by a parent company and a multitude of subsidiaries, the latter acting as independent entities in the country within which they have been incorporated. Despite this structure of multinational corporations, US courts have consistently upheld their jurisdiction over foreign-based subsidiaries in cases where the actions of the parent company produce effects in the US.[25] However, as this is an area not yet sufficiently regulated by rules of international law, it is individual countries that have unilaterally formulated jurisdictional competence.

4.2.3 The ambit of national territory

For the purposes of normal territorial jurisdiction, national criminal law applies beyond a State's land territory, until the outermost part of its contiguous zone at sea. Under customary international law, the Flag State has been responsible for exercising criminal jurisdiction upon both its merchant and public vessels for acts committed in the territorial waters of a foreign State. While this rule was absolute with regard to public vessels and warships, merchant vessels could fall within the jurisdiction of the coastal State, depending on the reach of local laws, if the act on board the vessel was considered injurious to the safety or other welfare interests of the coastal State.[26]

Merchant vessels are now subject to the regime established under Art 27 of the 1982 UNCLOS. This makes a distinction, with regard to the jurisdiction of the coastal State, between internal and territorial waters. Internal waters are the landward part of the sea from a State's baseline, which includes ports and river mouths,[27] while territorial waters stretch from the baseline seaward until a distance not exceeding 12 nautical miles.[28] All merchant vessels enjoy a

---

24 This requirement no longer applies, on account of the Criminal Justice Act (CJA) 1993, ss 1–2.
25 *USA v Aluminium Co of America*, 148 F 2d 416 (1945). The European Court of Justice has adopted an approach that views the parent company and its subsidiary as a single entity, allowing for jurisdiction over the parent company by the State where the subsidiary is incorporated: *United Brands Co v Commission* [1978] ECR 207; 1 CMLR 429.
26 In the *Wildenhus'* case, the murder of a Belgian crewman by his compatriot on board a Belgian merchant vessel in a US port was held by the US Supreme Court to be subject to local prosecution. Reported in 120 US 1 (1887); in *R v Anderson* (1868) 11 Cox Crim Cases 198, the UK Court of Criminal Appeals upheld the jurisdiction of the courts of the Flag State for offences on board its merchant vessels in foreign territorial waters, but recognised that this jurisdiction was concurrent to that of the coastal State.
27 UNCLOS, Art 8.
28 Ibid, Art 3.

right of innocent passage through internal waters and territorial sea, but, whereas coastal States enjoy an almost unrestricted criminal competence in internal waters,[29] such competence is more limited in their territorial sea. In order to properly justify its exercise of jurisdiction in the latter zone of sea, the coastal State must demonstrate that a crime has either disturbed or affected its land territory, or that the measures taken were intended for the suppression of illicit traffic of drugs, or that it received the consent of the Flag State.[30]

Public ships are generally immune from coastal State jurisdiction under the traditional notion of an 'implied licence' to enter internal waters, which secures them immunity.[31] Exception to this rule may be effectuated only through an express waiver of immunity by the Flag State.[32] In cases where the coastal State deems the action of foreign public vessels and warships injurious to itself it has the power to declare them *non grata* and expel them from its territorial sea.[33] A coastal State has also some limited jurisdiction in a belt of sea contiguous to its territorial sea, and which does not exceed 24 nautical miles from its baselines. This is known as the 'contiguous' zone.[34] Coastal jurisdiction in the contiguous zone is limited to powers of preventive enforcement of the coastal State's fiscal, sanitary, immigration or customs laws, as well as offences already perpetrated within its territorial waters.[35] Contrary to the ruling in the *Lotus* case, in cases of collision or any other penal or disciplinary incidents on the high seas,[36] jurisdiction lies with the Flag State or the State of which the accused is a national.

As regards offences committed in airspace, without prejudice to specific multilateral conventions and concurrent jurisdiction specified therein, the general rule is that primary jurisdiction lies with the subjacent State.[37] This rule was enforced in the case of the Pan Am flight bombing over Lockerbie, Scotland, through the establishment of a criminal tribunal in The Netherlands with the application of Scots criminal law.[38]

The question of criminal jurisdiction with regard to succession of States is a problematic one. In the *Former Syrian Ambassador to the German*

---

29 UNCLOS, Art 27(2).
30 Ibid, Art 27(1).
31 *Schooner Exchange v MacFaddon* (1812) 7 Cranch 116.
32 See *Chung Chi Cheung v R* [1939] AC 160.
33 UNCLOS, Art 30.
34 Ibid, Art 33.
35 Ibid, Art 33(1)(a) and (b).
36 Ibid, Art 97(1).
37 See *Smith v Socialist People's Libyan Arab Jamahiriya* (1997) 113 ILR 534, p 541.
38 See 1998 Agreement Between the Government of the Kingdom of The Netherlands and the Government of the United Kingdom of Great Britain and Northern Ireland Concerning a Scottish Trial in The Netherlands, 38 ILM (1999), 926.

Democratic Republic (GDR) case,[39] the Syrian Ambassador to the GDR was charged with fostering and co-ordinating a terrorist bombing in the Federal Republic of Germany (FRG). The Federal Constitutional Court upheld the jurisdiction of German courts (after unification), first because the acts had been committed in West Berlin, and secondly because it deemed federal criminal law applicable even prior to German reunification. Whatever the merits of this decision, its application should not offend the general principles of prohibition of retroactive criminal laws and double jeopardy.

4.3 THE ACTIVE PERSONALITY PRINCIPLE

The active personality principle (or nationality) of jurisdiction is based on the nationality of accused persons.[40] It allows States to prescribe legislation regulating the conduct of their nationals abroad and in some cases it has also been applied to persons with residency rights.[41] For such purposes, although the granting of nationality is considered a matter of domestic law,[42] its application and recognition in international fora is premised on principles of international law.[43] This competence of States to prosecute their nationals on the sole basis of their nationality is based on the allegiance that is owed to one's country under municipal law.[44] Although the active personality principle is mostly prevalent in civil law jurisdictions, it is generally recognised also in common law States.[45] In the UK, the nationality principle applies to a limited number of offences, such as treason,[46] murder and manslaughter,[47] bigamy,[48]

---

39 (1996) 115 ILR 597, pp 604–05.
40 GR Watson, 'Offenders Abroad: The Case for Nationality-Based Criminal Jurisdiction', 17 *Yale J Int'l L* (1992), 41.
41 UK War Crimes Act 1991, s 1(2) brings to the jurisdiction of English courts persons who are accused of committing war crimes during the Second World War, if at the time of prosecution they are either residents or citizens of the UK. See *R v Sawoniuk* (1999) unreported.
42 930 Hague Convention on Certain Questions Relating to the Conflict of Nationality Laws, Art 1, 179 LNTS 89.
43 In the *Nottebohm* case (1955) ICJ Reports 4, Second Phase, the International Court of Justice (ICJ) pointed out that a State claiming protection on behalf of one of its naturalised nationals against a respondent State needed to establish an effective and genuine link.
44 Harvard Research, *Draft Convention on Jurisdiction with Respect to Crime*, reprinted in 29 *AJIL* (1935 Supp), 480, p 519.
45 *Blackmer v USA*, 284 US 421 (1932), p 436; *USA v Columba-Colella*, 604 F 2d 356 (1979), p 358.
46 Treason Act 1351 and Official Secrets Act 1989, s 15(1); see also *R v Casement* [1917] 1 KB 98; *Joyce v DPP* [1946] AC 347, where the offence of treason was upheld even though Joyce's allegiance to the UK was made possible through a fraudulently obtained passport.
47 Offences Against the Person Act 1861, s 9.
48 Ibid, s 57; *Trial of Earl Russell* [1901] AC 446.

offences on board foreign merchant vessels[49] and, more recently, conspiring or inciting sexual offences against children.[50]

Until recently, the active personality principle was utilised in order to protect State interests from being harmed abroad, the primary example being the offence of treason. With increased efforts in recent years to combat transnational crime, in conjunction with expanding human rights awareness since 1945, the use of the nationality principle has been extended to encompass activities that do not directly endanger individual State interests. Hence, by prosecuting its nationals who organise illegal sexual tourism, the UK adheres not only to pressure from public opinion, but also to its obligations under international human rights law. In this manner, States refuse to portray themselves as facilitating safe havens for those nationals committing crimes abroad.[51]

The application of this principle in civil law jurisdictions is not only a common statutory feature; it has itself also been expansively construed.[52] In *Public Prosecutor v Antoni*, the Swedish Supreme Court found the criminal provisions of the Traffic Code of that country to be applicable against Swedish nationals abroad.[53] The reason for such generous construction may be justified by the refusal of civil law States, in accordance with their Constitutions, to extradite their nationals. European experience has demonstrated variations in the application of this principle. Some States impose an obligation of double criminality, others that the act constitute a crime in both itself and the *locus delicti commissi*,[54] while some States extend their criminal laws against nationals whose acts were committed in places lacking an effective criminal justice system.[55] The adoption of the European Arrest Warrant (EAW) by Member States of the European Union has effectively put an end to the invocation of nationality as a bar to extradition. Conflicts between national constitutions and the EAW did arise before some constitutional courts, particularly where national Constitutions had not been amended, but this had to do with the choice of instrument employed by the Commission, ie Framework Decision, rather than any perceived inviolability of the nationality

---

49 Merchant Shipping Act (MSA) 1995, s 281. In *R v Kelly* [1981] 2 All ER 1098, the House of Lords admitted charges under the purely internal Criminal Damage Act 1971 (then under MSA (1894), s 686(1)), against UK passengers for damage caused by them on board a Danish vessel.

50 Sexual Offences Act 1956 and Sexual Offences (Conspiracy and Incitement) Act 1996. See P Alldridge, 'The Sexual Offences (Conspiracy and Incitement) Act 1996', *Crim LR* [1997], 365.

51 See *Re Gutierez* (1957) 24 ILR 265.

52 See LS Green, 'The German Federal Republic and the Exercise of Criminal Jurisdiction', 43 *U Toronto LJ* (1993), 207.

53 (1960) 32 ILR 140.

54 See op cit, Gilbert, note 8, p 417.

55 1985 Hellenic Criminal Code, Art 5.

rule itself. The adoption of the UK Sexual Offences (Conspiracy and Incitement) Act (SOA) 1996 is evidence that States are now willing to bring within their jurisdiction offences which, on account of socio-economic reasons in developing countries, would not be prosecuted there. The active personality principle features also, in conjunction with other jurisdictional bases, in a large number of multilateral treaties.[56] This confirms not only its international acceptance, but, foremost, its effectiveness in combating impunity.

4.4 THE PASSIVE PERSONALITY PRINCIPLE

Criminal jurisdiction under the passive personality principle is exercised by the State of the nationality of the victim where the offence took place outside its territory.[57] Assumption of jurisdiction under this principle was criticised in the early part of the 20th century and was not included in the 1935 Harvard Research Draft on Jurisdiction. Common law States had initially opposed it ardently, but with the rise in transnational terrorist activity such inhibitions have given place to the enactment of statutes entertaining the principle.

The justification for exercising it in national fora has to do with each country's interest in protecting the welfare of its nationals abroad, where the *locus delicti* State either neglects, refuses, or is unable to initiate prosecution. In this context alone the passive personality principle may be deemed as a lawful, but auxiliary, form of jurisdiction.[58] In the *Cutting* case, a US citizen was arrested in Mexico for a libel charge against a Mexican national.[59] The action for which the alleged libel was charged had been committed whilst its author was in the US, but his arrest was effectuated much later during the author's subsequent trip to Mexico. The US Government vigorously opposed Mexico's claim of jurisdiction and the case was finally discontinued. The principle later received the same rejection by the Permanent Court of International Justice in the *Lotus* case.

In the early part of the 20th century, at a time when nation States ardently asserted their sovereignty, the application of any extra-territorial principle would have met strong opposition. This is true even more in the above-mentioned cases where passive personality was statute-based and not treaty-based. As noted, the advent of transnational crimes, especially terrorist-related, necessitated the enactment of both statute and treaty-based

---

56 1988 Convention for the Suppression of Unlawful Acts Against the Safety of Maritime Navigation, Art 6(1)(c), 27 ILM (1988), 668; 1984 Convention Against Torture and Other Cruel Inhuman or Degrading Treatment or Punishment (Torture Convention), Art 5(1)(b), 1465 UNTS 85.

57 See GR Watson, 'The Passive Personality Principle', 28 *Texas ILJ* (1993), 1.

58 See op cit, Shearer, note 9, p 211.

59 IA Moore, *Moore's Digest of International Law*, 1906, Vol 2, 228.

instruments promulgating jurisdiction on the basis of the victim's nationality. Following the *Achille Lauro* incident and the subsequent murder of a US citizen, the US Congress enacted the Omnibus Diplomatic Security and Anti-Terrorism Act 1986, which grants US courts, *inter alia*, jurisdiction over persons charged with the extra-territorial murder of US nationals, where the intention of the perpetrator has been to intimidate, coerce or retaliate against any government or people.[60] Similar provisions include s 3(4) of the UK Taking of Hostages Act 1982[61] and Art 689(1) of the French Code of Penal Procedure. Even though the US did not generally recognise this form of jurisdiction,[62] in fact, in *USA v Yunis*,[63] it was unequivocally upheld by a Court of Appeals.[64] Passive personality jurisdiction over the accused, for hijacking a Jordanian airliner in Beirut with two US citizens on board, was assumed on the basis of the Anti-Hijacking Act 1974[65] and the HTA 1984. Despite its recent acceptance in domestic fora, statute-based passive personality has not received general consensus regarding its delimitation[66] and national judiciaries should apply it only as an auxiliary form of jurisdiction where other competing *fora* lay claim to the accused under territorial grounds.

The case is different with treaty-based jurisdiction, since this supersedes any domestic provision to the contrary. This is allotted in two ways: either by directly granting a concurrent right of jurisdiction based on the nationality of the victims,[67] or indirectly by not excluding any criminal jurisdiction exercised in accordance with national law.[68] This latter form is necessarily secondary, as can be ascertained from its inclusion and purpose in the relevant treaties.

---

60 18 USC § 2331. This particular *mens rea* component of the Act may, in fact, render such jurisdiction more akin to the protective, rather than the passive personality, principle.

61 In *Rees v Secretary of State for the Home Department* [1986] 2 All ER 321, the House of Lords accepted extradition to FRG of a British national accused of participating in the kidnapping of a German citizen in Bolivia.

62 Op cit, Paust *et al*, note 12, p 121.

63 (1991) 88 ILR 176.

64 Hostage Taking Act (HTA) 1984, 18 USC § 1203. Jurisdiction was based on the passive personality principle under § 1203(b)(1)(A); similarly, *In the Matter of Extradition of Atta* 104 ILR 52, the accused, a US national, was implicated by Israel in an attack against an Israeli bus in the West Bank resulting in the death of two civilians. The accused challenged an Israeli request for extradition, but a US District Court recognised a claim under s 7(a) of the 1977 Israeli Penal Code, providing for passive personality jurisdiction.

65 49 USC App § 1472(n).

66 See op cit, Gilbert, note 8, p 419, who points to the relevant provisions in various European penal codes.

67 Eg, 1973 Convention on the Prevention and Punishment of Crimes Against Internationally Protected Persons, Including Diplomatic Agents, Art 3(1)(c), 13 ILM (1974), 42; 1984 UN Torture Convention, Art 5(1)(c); 1988 UN Convention for the Suppression of Unlawful Acts Against the Safety of Maritime Navigation, Art 6(2)(b).

68 Eg, 1971 Montreal Convention for the Suppression of Unlawful Acts Against the Safety of Civil Aviation, Art 5(3), 10 ILM (1971), 1151.

4.5 THE PROTECTIVE PRINCIPLE

It is unequivocally accepted that every country is competent to take any measures that are compatible with the law of nations in order to safeguard its national security interests. This implication of State sovereignty is the basis for the protective or security principle.[69] The necessity for the protective principle may be demonstrated by the lack of adequate measures in most municipal legal systems through which to criminalise harmful behaviour or prosecute persons for acts which, although committed abroad, are directed against the security of a foreign State.[70] The problem with this theory is that national parliaments enacting the protective principle may take a very expansive, or at least subjective, view of what is actually injurious to their national interests. For example, State A might consider that avoiding military service by residing abroad harms national security because it decreases its defensive capacity. In contemporary international law the extent to which the *forum deprehensionis* can extradite a person on the basis of the protective principle is limited by the list of extraditable crimes in extradition treaties and fundamental human rights norms, especially the rule of non-extradition for political offences. If the accused is not in the custody of the prosecuting State, a request for extradition may hinge on a denial to extradite in case no offence has been committed in the *forum deprehensionis*, in order to safeguard its own national interests. As alliances come and go, a similar situation may be accommodated through the rules of comity, by recognising the requesting State's protective jurisdictional competence.

Case law suggests that the executive and judiciary perceive 'national interests' quite broadly. Espionage and treason are classic examples of the application of the protective principle, since they have traditionally been viewed as acts endangering internal security. In *Re Urios*,[71] a Spanish national was convicted of espionage on account of his contacts against the security of France but whilst in Spain during the First World War. In *Joyce v DPP*,[72] the House of Lords, in a rather confusing judgment, took the view that an alien with a fraudulently obtained British passport owed allegiance to the Crown and was liable for treason with regard to the broadcast of propaganda during the Second World War, notwithstanding that nationality is irrelevant in

---

69 See generally I Cameron, *The Protective Principle of International Criminal Jurisdiction*, 1994, Aldershot: Brookfield, VT.
70 Op cit, Harvard Research, note 44, p 552.
71 (1920) 1 AD 107.
72 [1946] AC 347, p 372, *per* Lord Jowitt. Jurisdiction was also upheld based on the basis of the active personality principle. See also H Lauterpacht, 'Allegiance, Diplomatic Protection and Criminal Jurisdiction over Aliens', 9 *CLJ* (1947), 330.

enforcement of the protective principle.[73] Relying on *Joyce*, the District Court of Jerusalem upheld, *inter alia*, protective jurisdiction in the *Eichmann* case.[74] The accused was responsible for implementing Hitler's 'Final Solution' programme. After the war he fled to Argentina and was abducted by Israeli agents to stand trial in Israel under the 1951 Nazi and Nazi Collaborators Law for war crimes, crimes against the Jewish people and crimes against humanity. The judgment of the District Court, which was subsequently affirmed by the Israeli Supreme Court,[75] held that a country whose 'vital interests' and ultimately its existence are threatened, such as in the case of the extermination of the Jewish people, has a right to assume jurisdiction to try the offenders.[76]

The protective principle was used by western European States during the Cold War in cases involving enlistment or espionage which resulted in a threat to the interests of allied countries. In *Re Van den Plas*,[77] for example, a Belgian national was held liable for acts of espionage against Belgium by a French tribunal on the basis that his acts were injurious to the interests of both France and Belgium. US jurisprudence has perceived the ambit of 'national interests' under the protective principle as encompassing acts which do not necessarily require a direct or actual effect within the territory of the US.[78] This has had considerable impact on cases involving the breach of US immigration law, where the breach was perpetrated outside US territory.[79] US courts have approached the issue of immigration as vital to the security of the State, especially as regards the executive function determining who should be permitted to enter.[80] Applying the protective principle in cases involving the extra-territorial apprehension of drug-traffickers[81] or suspected terrorists[82] has proved less arduous, since a threat to security or other national interests can be easily discerned and proven. It is generally agreed that in order to

---

73 Nonetheless, in *R v Neumann* (1949) 3 SA 1238, cited in op cit, Paust *et al*, note 12, p 149, a South African Special Court convicted a South African national of treason on account of his participation on the German side during the Second World War. The judgment of the court stated that jurisdiction was obtained due to the impairment of national security caused by the act of treason.

74 *AG of the Government of Israel v Eichmann* (1961) 36 ILR 5.

75 (1962) 36 ILR 277.

76 See H Silving, 'In re *Eichmann*: A Dilemma of Law and Morality', 55 *AJIL* (1961), 307; JES Fawcett, 'The *Eichmann* Case', 38 *BYIL* (1962), 181.

77 22 ILR 205; op cit, Akehurst, note 1, p 158, argues that such decisions are defensible only where the accused are nationals of allied powers.

78 *USA v Pizzarusso*, 388 F 2d 8 (1968), p 11; *USA v Keller*, 451 F Supp 631 (1978), p 635. See the opposite view espoused op cit, by Paust *et al*, note 12, p 129.

79 *Rocha v USA*, 288 F 2d 545 (1961); *USA v Pizzarusso*, 388 F 2d 8 (1968), p 11; *Giles v Tumminello*, 38 ILR 120.

80 See Restatement (Third) of the Foreign Relations Law of the USA 1986, § 402(3).

81 *Rivard v USA*, 375 F 2d 882 (1967); *USA v Bright-Barker*, 784 F 2d 161 (1986).

82 *USA v Yunis* (1991) 88 ILR 176; Omnibus Diplomatic Security and Anti-Terrorism Act 1986, 18 USC § 2331.

restrict possible abuse, the use of statute-based protective principle jurisdiction should be limited to cases where both significant national interests are at stake and, moreover, where its application in each particular case is permissible under international law.[83]

4.6 UNIVERSAL JURISDICTION

The four forms of jurisdiction discussed above require some kind of link or connection with the prosecuting State, whether that link is based on the territory where the offence took place, the nationality of the perpetrator or the victim, or involving a threat to the interests of the State concerned. The application of universal jurisdiction to a particular offence does not require any such link, and any State may assert its authority over offences that are subject to universal jurisdiction.[84] Due to the broad extra-territorial competence encompassed by the exercise of the principle of universal jurisdiction, it is reasonable that only a very limited number of offences can be subject to the application of this principle.

Before we proceed with this analysis, it is imperative that some clarifications be made. A criminal offence, for example torture, is established as such within a State by its competent authority, namely its parliamentary body. In this sense, torture becomes an offence under national law. The same offence of torture, however, can also be promulgated by the competent sources of international law; that is treaty and custom.[85] In this latter context, torture is defined as an offence under international law, and even though both its subjective and objective elements may be identical to the national provision, a crime under international law is subject to the interpretation and limitations of the international legal regime that formulates it.

Crimes under international law (international crimes) have customarily attracted universal jurisdiction in two independent ways: (a) based on the heinous, repugnant nature and scale of the offence, as is the case with grave breaches of humanitarian law[86] and crimes against humanity;[87] or (b) on the

---

83 Op cit, Paust *et al*, note 12, p 128.

84 See K Randal, 'Universal Jurisdiction Under International Law', 66 *Texas LR* (1988), 785; ES Kobrick, 'The *Ex Post Facto* Prohibition and the Exercise of Universal Jurisdiction Over International Crimes', 87 *Columbia LR* (1987), 1515.

85 General principles of the law of nations have never in the past been used to establish an international offence, but only to clarify the scope of existing international offences.

86 1949 Geneva Conventions and both Additional Geneva Protocols 1977 to the 1949 Conventions. See also C Joyner, 'Arresting Impunity: The Case for Universal Jurisdiction in Bringing War Criminals to Accountability', 59 *LCP* (1996), 153.

87 *Federation Nationale de Deportes et Internes Resistants et Patriotes and Others v Barbie*, 78 ILR 125, p 130; see also *Re Pinochet*, 93 AJIL (1999), 700, Brussels Tribunal of First Instance, pp 702–03.

basis of the inadequacy of national enforcement legislation with regard to offences committed in locations not subject to the authority of any State, such as the high seas. Extension of universal jurisdiction over piracy under international law (piracy *jure gentium*) has substantially contributed to combating this scourge.[88] It cannot be overemphasised that these two bases for attracting universal jurisdiction are independent and conjunctive. The practical significance of this observation is that to discern whether or not an international crime is subject to universal jurisdiction, one must first ascertain which of the two bases, nature and scale, or that of an act perpetrated on the high seas, is appropriate. Thus, in *Re Rohrig*,[89] although war crimes of a serious and repugnant nature did and do attract universal jurisdiction, a Dutch Special Cassation Court wrongly assimilated the basis for asserting universal jurisdiction over war crimes to that of piracy. In *Re Pinochet (No 3)*,[90] Lord Millet succinctly argued that international crimes attract universal jurisdiction where they violate a rule of *jus cogens* and, at the same time, are so serious and perpetrated on such a large scale that they can be regarded as an attack against international legal order.[91] This statement, correct though it may be, lacks a most essential ingredient: the consent of States to subject an offence to universal jurisdiction through treaty or custom. The vast majority of international crimes violate *jus cogens* norms. Can it seriously be contended that all States parties to these international criminal law conventions intended to confer universal jurisdiction over the relevant crimes? Furthermore, what is the legal position of non-States parties to these conventions?

The first question can only be answered by contrasting the various international provisions. Article 105 of UNCLOS, and relating to piracy, states:

> On the high seas, or in any other place outside the jurisdiction of any State, *every State* may seize a pirate ship or aircraft, or a ship or aircraft taken by piracy and under the control of pirates, and arrest the persons and seize the property on board [emphasis added].

Notice now the difference in wording in Art 99 of the same Convention, which prohibits the transport of slaves on the high seas:

---

88 In *Re Piracy Jure Gentium* [1934] AC 586, Lord Macmillan confirmed the application of universal jurisdiction over piracy *jure gentium* and noted that a pirate 'is no longer a national, but *hostis humani generis* and as such he is justiciable by any State anywhere', p 589.

89 (1950) 17 ILR 393, p 395.

90 *R v Bow Street Metropolitan Stipendiary Magistrate and Others ex p Pinochet Ugarte (No 3)* [1999] 2 All ER 97; see H Fox, 'The *Pinochet* Case No 3', 48 *ICLQ* (1999), 687.

91 Ibid, p 177.

Every State shall take effective measures to prevent and punish the transport of slaves in ships authorised to fly *its flag* and to prevent the unlawful use of *its flag* for that purpose [emphasis added].

Although it is obvious that Art 99 renders slave-trafficking an international crime, whether by criminalising it, or acknowledging its prior existence, it does not confer on States parties universal jurisdiction as a matter of international law, regardless of the undoubtedly repugnant character of slavery. On the contrary, it is clear that Art 105 does confer universal jurisdiction on States parties with regard to piracy *jure gentium*. The conclusion is, thus, that the repugnant nature or the *locus commissi* of an offence may determine its subjection to universal jurisdiction, but this process also requires the unequivocal consent of the international community; that is, it is not an automatic process.

On the grounds of the preceding analysis, only grave breaches of international humanitarian law (including crimes against humanity) and piracy *jure gentium* are, beyond any doubt, international crimes subject to universal criminal jurisdiction.[92] This conclusion is confirmed by reference to both treaty and customary law. As for non-parties to UNCLOS and the 1949 Geneva Conventions, the *jus cogens* character of the offences involved precludes even persistent objection.[93] It is submitted that the *jus cogens* nature of these crimes necessarily entails the peremptory character of the jurisdiction they carry under international law; that is, an international crime is always accompanied by its jurisdiction under international law. This narrow view of universal jurisdiction was confirmed, albeit *obiter dicta*, by the ICJ in the *Belgian Arrest Warrant* case. In that case, a Belgian Investigating Judge issued in April 2000 an international arrest warrant against the then incumbent Congolese Foreign Minister, on the basis of the Belgian 1993 Law Relative to the Repression of Grave Breaches, charging him for grave breaches in violation of the 1949 Geneva Conventions, Protocols I and II of 1977, as well as crimes against humanity. The ICJ did not view universal jurisdiction as central to the issue, but in his Separate Opinion, Judge Guillaume took a narrow

92 We are, thus, in disagreement with the US Court of Appeals Judgment in *USA v Yunis (No 3)*, 924 F 2d 1086 (1991); 88 ILR 176, p 182, that hijacking is a clear case of an international crime endowed with universal jurisdiction; similarly, Principle 2(1) of the Princeton Principles of Universal Jurisdiction lists the following as serious international crimes subject to universal jurisdiction: piracy, slavery, war crimes, crimes against peace, crimes against humanity, genocide and torture, without necessarily excluding it with regard to other offences. The Princeton Principles, the final version of which was adopted in 2001, were formulated through a series of meetings by a group of experts claiming to represent current international law.

93 1969 Vienna Convention on the Law of Treaties, Art 53, 1155 UNTS 331; see also J Charney, 'The Persistent Objector Rule and the Development of Customary International Law', 56 *BYIL* (1985), 1.

view of universal jurisdiction, finding it applicable in limited cases and certainly not *in absentia*.[94] Equally, in *Jones and Others v Kingdom of Saudi Arabia*, the House of Lords held that no evidence exists whereby States recognise an international obligation to exercise universal jurisdiction over claims arising from breaches of *jus cogens*, nor is there any judicial opinion that they should.[95]

The fact that an international crime does not attract universal jurisdiction under international law does not necessarily mean that it may not attract broad extra-territorial jurisdiction (similar to universal) under domestic law. In fact, relevant international treaties encourage parties to assert expansive jurisdiction with respect to the offences contemplated, very much akin to universal jurisdiction. Such jurisdiction, even if termed universal, is established after incorporation into municipal law of the international offence. In this case, it is delineated in scope according to domestic legislation. This is evident in, for example, Art 5 of the 1984 UN Torture Convention, which primarily establishes territorial (and State of registration),[96] nationality[97] and passive personality jurisdiction.[98] Art 5 further confers jurisdiction on:

> (2) Each State party [to] take such measures as may be necessary to establish its jurisdiction over such offences in cases where the alleged offender is present in any territory under its jurisdiction and it does not extradite him to any of the States mentioned in para 1 of this article.
>
> (3) This Convention does not exclude any criminal jurisdiction exercised in accordance with internal law.

Art 5(2) and (3) thus permits the exercise of universal jurisdiction with respect to the incorporated domestic offence of torture. Section 134 of the UK CJA 1988 incorporates this type of universal jurisdiction with regard to torture. It is not clear whether such universal jurisdiction is primary or secondary to those mentioned in Art 5(1). In terms of international comity, at least, the *locus delicti* State must enjoy primary jurisdiction, unless the apprehending State asserts its own right over the accused. There is a further natural limitation to the 'universality' espoused in Art 5(2) and (3), which is encountered neither in piracy *jure gentium* nor grave breaches. This is the requirement that the alleged offender actually be on the territory of the State embarking on an exercise of universal jurisdiction, as enshrined in Art 5(2).

---

94 *Democratic Republic of Congo v Belgium* (Arrest Warrant of 11 April 2000), Judgment (14 Feb 2002), Separate Opinion of Judge Guillaume.
95 [2006] UKHL 26, *per* Lord Bingham, para 27.
96 1984 Torture Convention, Art 5(1)(a).
97 Ibid, Art 5(1)(b).
98 Ibid, Art 5(1)(c).

Where the alleged offender is apprehended in a State that does not wish to initiate criminal proceedings and is, therefore, obliged to extradite to a third State (if a bilateral extradition treaty exists), extradition will generally take place only to a country with sufficiently close connection to the offence.[99] In the case of international crimes subject to universal jurisdiction, on the other hand, any extradition requests must be treated as legitimate by the requested country[100] and are to be dismissed only on account of human rights concerns. Another difference between 'internal' and 'international' universal jurisdiction is that, in order for the former to be lawfully prescribed by the national legislature, it must not conflict with any other generally agreed rule of international law.

The traditional common law view seems to have been that no presumption of universal jurisdiction be read in criminal statutes,[101] but both English and US courts assert that they have always enjoyed jurisdiction for personal violations of international norms.[102] The best approach is that adopted by § 443 of the Restatement (Third) of the Foreign Relations Law of the USA, which provides that:

> A State's courts may exercise jurisdiction to enforce the State's criminal laws which punish universal crimes (§ 404) or other non-territorial offences within the State's jurisdiction to prescribe (§§ 402–03).

Indeed, unless a prohibitory international rule to the contrary exists, a State may assert any form of jurisdiction over an alleged offence. In fact, some States have gone so far as to prosecute aliens for common offences that are perpetrated in, and subject to, the ordinary criminal law of third countries. In the *Austrian Universal Jurisdiction* case,[103] the accused had fled his native Yugoslavia and was convicted in Austria for offences committed there. While serving his sentence, Yugoslavia requested his extradition for common crimes perpetrated while he was still a resident of that country, but Austria refused because the accused was in danger of being subjected to political persecution in Yugoslavia. Instead, the Supreme Court of Austria argued that the judicial authorities of that country could exercise universal jurisdiction over the accused's alleged offences in Yugoslavia, because it deemed them punishable

---

99 Ibid, Art 8(4).
100 Obviously, in the event of conflicting extradition requests, the executive may reach its conclusion on the basis of relevant connecting factors.
101 *R v Jameson* [1896] 2 QB 425, p 430, *per* Lord Russell, who noted that 'an act will not be construed as applying to foreigners in respect of acts done by them outside the dominions of the sovereign power enacted'. See also *USA v Baker* (1955) 22 ILR 203.
102 *Ex p Quirin*, 317 US 27 (1942); *Re Pinochet (No 3)* [1999] 2 All ER 97, p 177, *per* Lord Millet.
103 28 ILR 341.

under Austrian law if committed in Austria. The exercise of such jurisdiction was based on Art 40 of the Austrian Criminal Code, which provided that where competent foreign authorities refuse to prosecute, or prosecution by them is impossible, this task is to be undertaken by Austrian courts in accordance with Austrian criminal law.[104] In similar fashion, in the *Universal Jurisdiction Over Drug Offences* case,[105] the FRG Federal Supreme Court upheld universal jurisdiction over drug-trafficking offences committed abroad on the basis of Art 6(5) of the 1998 Federal Criminal Code, which made the criminal law of that country applicable to drug-trafficking abroad and regardless of the law of the *locus delicti commissi*. The Supreme Court found Art 6(5) compatible with international law in the absence of a contrary special treaty provision, and as implementing Art 36 of the 1961 Single Convention on Narcotic Drugs, which calls on States parties to ensure that every relevant offence receives appropriate punishment.[106]

In similar manner, national courts have upheld the universality principle with regard to crimes defined under municipal criminal statutes, for a number of offences, such as war crimes,[107] crimes against humanity[108] and genocide.[109] These statutes incorporate into national law the obligations undertaken by a particular treaty.[110] As the *Austrian Universal Jurisdiction* case has indicated, some States are willing to prosecute offences under the universality principle not on the basis of their international obligations, but on a desire to combat impunity or protect prospective future interests, even where the offences concerned do not violate *jus cogens* norms.[111] Nonetheless, not all countries are willing to apply the universality principle in every case. In *Re Munyeshyaka*, a French court asserted that no universal jurisdiction was directly established by the 1949 Geneva Conventions and that Art 689 of the French Penal Code

---

104 28 ILR 341–42.

105 28 ILR 166.

106 In similar reasoning, it was held in *USA v Marino-Garcia*, 679 F 2d 1373 (1982), that USC § 955(a), s 21 gives the federal Government criminal jurisdiction over all stateless vessels on the high seas engaged in the distribution of controlled substances, noting that this exercise of jurisdiction is not contrary to international law.

107 *Public Prosecutor v Djajic* (German), 92 *AJIL* (1998), 528; *Public Prosecutor v Grabec* (Swiss), 92 *AJIL* (1998), 78.

108 *AG of Israel v Eichmann*, 36 ILR 5; *In re Demjanjuk*, 457 US 1016 (1986).

109 *Re Pinochet*, 93 *AJIL* (1999), 690, Spanish National Court, Criminal Division. Judicial Branch Act of 1985, Art 23(4) establishes universal jurisdiction of Spanish courts over genocide, terrorism, piracy, unlawful seizure of aircraft, as well as any other international crime which must be prosecuted in Spain.

110 UK Geneva Conventions Act 1957 and Geneva Conventions (Amendment) Act 1995. See P Rowe and M Meyer, 'The Geneva Conventions (Amendment) Act 1995: A Generally Minimalist Approach', 45 *ICLQ* (1996), 476; US War Crimes Act 1996, 18 USC § 2401.

111 In *Giles v Tumminello*, 38 ILR 120, the Supreme Court of South Australia upheld jurisdiction over aliens for common offences committed on the fringe of its territorial sea, 'for the control and protection' of its residents.

was not a basis for the application of universal jurisdiction in the French legal order.[112] Principle 3 of the so-called Princeton Principles of Universal Jurisdiction rather wishfully asserts the right of national courts to rely on universal jurisdiction in the absence of national legislation. Certainly, the application of universal jurisdiction by a domestic court in defiance of the laws of that country would nullify its judgment as a matter of domestic law. To reverse this result, it must be proven either that: (a) the judge is applying unimplemented treaty obligations; or (b) that customary law is automatically incorporated in the internal law of that country, that the offence in question is subject to universal jurisdiction, and that the court was applying that rule.

4.7 *AUT DEDERE AUT JUDICARE* PRINCIPLE

The vast majority of multilateral conventions dealing with international crimes contain a special clause, through which the *forum deprehensionis* is under an obligation to either prosecute or extradite those persons who are suspected of having committed the prescribed offence. The *aut dedere aut judicare* principle is, itself, subject to the conventional and customary limitations attached to extradition.[113] This principle, which is established only by treaty,[114] creates an affirmative obligation on parties to multilateral criminal law conventions to prosecute or extradite, but the treaties which contain it do not *per se* constitute an independent and sufficient legal basis for extradition. Extradition is dependent on the existence of specific bi- or multilateral treaties. Under the various international criminal law conventions, Member States enjoy a discretion as to which extradition request will be satisfied upon refusal to prosecute. As the *Lockerbie* case has demonstrated, the *aut dedere* component of the principle requires that prosecution be carried out independently of the executive and in accordance with international standards. In that case, Libya refused to extradite two of its nationals accused by the US and UK of detonating an explosive device on a Pan Am flight over Lockerbie, Scotland, arguing, instead, that it had discharged its obligation

---

112 *Re Javar and Re Munyeshyaka*, 93 *AJIL* (1999), 525.
113 CM Bassiouni and EM Wise, *Aut Dedere Aut Judicare: The Duty to Extradite or Prosecute in International Law*, 1995, Dordrecht: Martinus Nijhoff. The earliest multilateral treaty to encourage the prosecution of non-extradited nationals was the 1929 Convention for the Suppression of Counterfeiting Currency, 112 LNTS 371.
114 The House of Lords in *T v Secretary of State for the Home Department*, 107 ILR 552, p 564, noted that the *aut dedere* principle was to a limited extent a feature of the 1937 League of Nations Convention for the Prevention and Suppression of Terrorism (Arts 9 and 10); surprisingly, the Australian Federal Court in *Nulyarimma v Thompson* [1999] FCA 1192; 39 ILM (2000), 20, p 23, stated that the *aut dedere aut judicare* principle was imposed by customary law on Australia in connection with the crime of genocide.

under Art 7 of the 1971 Montreal Convention for the Suppression of Unlawful Acts Against the Safety of Civil Aviation (Montreal Convention), having already investigated the possible involvement of the accused. Although the subsequent Libyan investigation acquitted the two accused, there was ample evidence to suggest that both were agents of the Libyan Government, which as it turned out was the orchestrator of that terrorist attack.[115]

It is very likely that this principle constitutes an obligation *erga omnes* arising from the status of the offences to which it is applied, as being universal crimes.[116] It follows from this discussion that failure to enforce the *aut dedere aut judicare* obligation entails the international responsibility of the apprehending State. This would not be the result where either no extradition request existed, or if it did, it was not compatible with extradition law or the general rights of the accused. In such situations, prosecution does not seem to be obligatory even if in abuse of a State's ability to do so. It should also be noted that because the *aut dedere aut judicare* principle is established solely through treaty, it is only applicable as between States parties to a multilateral convention in which it is contained, regardless of the customary nature of the offence concerned. Two recent anti-terrorist treaties have facilitated extradition of nationals with respect to those countries whose Constitution forbids such extradition. Articles 8(2) and 10(2) of the 1998 UN Convention for the Suppression of Terrorist Bombings[117] and the 2000 UN Convention for the Suppression of the Financing of Terrorism,[118] respectively, release a State from its obligation to extradite where it does not prosecute, agreeing, instead, to extradite a national on the condition that such person will be returned to the requested State to serve the sentence.

4.8 JURISDICTION WITH RESPECT TO CRIMES AGAINST CIVIL AVIATION

The widespread seizure or hijacking of civil aircraft in the 1960s, mainly for political purposes, culminated in the adoption of several treaties regulating specific aspects of air terrorism. These agreements do not abandon the customary rule granting criminal jurisdiction to the subjacent State; they merely supplement it by conferring competence also to third countries. The first major attempt to combat a specific aspect of terrorism was made by the 1963

---

115 *Libya v USA*, 'Questions of interpretation and application of the 1971 Montreal Convention arising from the aerial incident at Lockerbie (interim measures)' (1992) *ICJ Reports* 3.
116 CM Bassiouni, 'International Crimes: *Jus Cogens* and *Obligatio Erga Omnes*', 59 LCP (1996), 63.
117 37 ILM (1998), 249.
118 39 ILM (2000), 270.

Tokyo Convention on Offences and Certain Other Acts Committed on Board Aircraft.[119] Article 4 of this instrument endowed the State of registration with competence over the prescribed offences and, further, permitted jurisdiction under the nationality (including the State of the lessee where the aircraft was leased without a crew) and passive personality principles, as well as to the State where the accused took refuge. Similarly, Art 4(1) of the 1970 Hague Convention for the Suppression of Unlawful Seizure of Aircraft (1970 Hague Convention)[120] confers criminal jurisdiction over hijacking and associated acts of violence to the State of registration, the State of landing (when the accused is on board)[121] and the State of the lessee's nationality. Paragraph 2 of Art 4 permits the exercise of criminal jurisdiction by any State on whose territory the alleged offender is present, but only in respect of acts of hijacking, and para 3 allows the exercise of criminal jurisdiction on any national legal basis.

The 1971 Montreal Convention adds two new jurisdictional elements in comparison with the 1970 Hague Convention. First, it covers relevant acts perpetrated not only 'in flight', but also 'in service'.[122] Secondly, because the objective of the 1971 Montreal Convention was to supplement the provisions of the 1970 Hague Convention in order to encompass, beyond acts of hijacking, also armed attacks, sabotage and other forms of violence and intimidation against civil aviation, Art 5(1)(a) provides a further ground of jurisdiction when the offence is committed in the territory of a contracting State.

4.9 INTERNATIONAL CRIMINAL JURISDICTION

The five principles discussed above address the ambit of the prescriptive competence of States, as this emanates from treaties, custom and national legislation. As a corollary, judicial and enforcement jurisdiction is limited in accordance with the scope of municipal prescriptive competence. International criminal tribunals are not susceptible to all these limitations. Their competence is derived from their constitutive instrument and is not at all confined by the jurisdictional principles and constraints applicable to municipal courts. This form of jurisdiction is termed 'international'. As a result of

---

119 704 UNTS 219.
120 S Shubber, 'Aircraft Hijacking under the Hague Convention 1970 – A New Regime?', 22 *ICLQ* (1973), 687, p 714.
121 This was the basis of jurisdiction asserted by a Dutch District Court regarding the hijacking of a British aircraft, whose crew was forced to land in Amsterdam: *Public Prosecutor v SHT*, 74 ILR 162.
122 Under the 1971 Montreal Convention, Art 2(b), an aircraft is considered to be in service from the beginning of pre-flight preparation until 24 hours after landing.

receiving their mandate from the international community, international tribunals are expressly authorised to disregard the principle of immunity for Heads of State, which otherwise applies in the relations between sovereign States.[123]

Both the International Criminal Tribunal for the Former Yugoslavia (ICTY) and that of Rwanda (ICTR) are the product of Chapter VII Security Council resolutions. In theory, the Security Council could have prescribed a very wide jurisdictional competence, whether *ratione materia* or *ratione temporis*, which would otherwise have been *ultra vires* for national courts, but not for a tribunal established under a Security Council resolution. The same would apply to a tribunal established through treaty, such as the International Criminal Court (ICC), but only where its Statute received global ratification. Since every international tribunal is a self-contained system, its jurisdictional powers can only be limited by its constitutive instrument, but only to the extent that such limitation does not endanger its judicial character.[124] Although the ICTY is a subsidiary organ of the Security Council, the Appeals Chamber in the *Tadic Jurisdiction* case correctly pointed out that it is a special kind of subsidiary organ, a tribunal endowed with judicial functions.[125] By implication of its judicial nature, a tribunal enjoys a certain degree of 'inherent' or 'incidental' jurisdiction. One element of this inherent jurisdiction, which is exercisable even if not mentioned in its Statute, is an international tribunal's competence to determine its own jurisdiction.[126] The ICTY has further held that it may, in the exercise of its incidental jurisdiction, examine the legality of its establishment by the Security Council, but only so far as this is needed to ascertain the scope of its 'primary' jurisdiction.[127]

We have already seen that even where a treaty delimits the prescriptive competence of States, there is no clear jurisdictional hierarchy. International tribunals do not face such conflicts. Article 9(1) of the ICTY Statute provides

---

123 Special Court for Sierra Leone (SCSL), *Prosecutor v Taylor*, Appeals Chamber Judgment (31 May 2004), para 51. We do not take the view, however, that the SCSL is an international tribunal, but a domestic tribunal with international elements. See also, *ICTY Prosecutor v Milosevic*, Decision on the Preliminary Motions, Kosovo (8 Nov 2001), paras 26–34, rejecting the validity of Head of State immunity.

124 *ICTY Prosecutor v Tadic*, Decision on the Defence Motion for Interlocutory Appeal on Jurisdiction 105 ILR 453, para 11; see also *ICTR Prosecutor v Kanyabashi*, Decision on Jurisdiction, 92 *AJIL* (1998), 66; I Bantekas, 'Head of State Immunity in the Light of Multiple Legal Regimes and Non-Self Contained System Theories: Theoretical Analysis of ICC Third Party Jurisdiction against the Background of the 2003 Iraq War' 10 *JSCL* (2005), 21.

125 Ibid, *Tadic* Appeals decision on jurisdiction, para 15.

126 Advisory Opinion on the Effect of Awards of Compensation Made by the United Nations Administrative Tribunal (1954) ICJ Reports 47, p 51. This power is termed 'Kompetenz Kompetenz'.

127 Op cit, *Tadic* Appeals decision on jurisdiction, note 124, para 21.

for concurrent jurisdiction with national criminal courts. However, para 2 emphatically establishes primacy for the ICTY by stating:

> The International Tribunal shall have primacy over national courts. At any stage of the procedure, the International Tribunal may formally request national courts to defer to the competence of the International Tribunal in accordance with the present Statute and the Rules of Procedure and Evidence of the International Tribunal.

It is evident that the ICTY enjoys primacy in an emphatic manner.[128] This is not, however, the case with the ICC. The ICC's jurisdiction is premised on the concept of complementarity with national courts, whose primary competence it may exceptionally override only where a State is shielding an accused,[129] or where the State party is genuinely unable to carry out an investigation or prosecution.[130] The ICC is burdened with further limitations. Upon becoming a party to its Statute, a State automatically accepts the jurisdiction of the Court with respect to the four core crimes,[131] subject to the qualification of Art 124 regarding the transitional period.[132] Under Art 12, the Court may exercise jurisdiction if it has the consent of the State on whose territory the offence was perpetrated, *or* of which the accused is a national. However, if a situation is referred to the Court by the Security Council, the Court will have jurisdiction even if the acts concerned were committed on the territory of non-parties or nationals of non-parties and in the absence of consent by the territorial State or the State of nationality of the accused.[133] In any other case, non-States parties must make a declaration accepting the Court's jurisdiction, as a precondition to the exercise of jurisdiction.[134]

The difference in the powers vested in the ICTY and ICC can be explained by the fact that the former was the product of a Security Council resolution under Chapter VII of the UN Charter, whereas the ICC was established as a result of a multilateral treaty, which necessarily entailed a great deal of compromise. The enforcement jurisdiction of the ICTY under Art 29 of its Statute is, thus, significantly enhanced, since it has the power, *inter alia*, to order the arrest and surrender of persons and the production of documents

---

128 See G Aldrich, 'Jurisdiction of the International Criminal Tribunal for the Former Yugoslavia', 90 *AJIL* (1996), 64.
129 ICC Statute, Arts 17(1)(a), (b) and 2(a).
130 Ibid, Art 17(1)(a), (b).
131 Ibid, Art 12(1).
132 According to Art 124, a State party may declare its non-acceptance of the Court's jurisdiction for a period of seven years after the entry into force of the Statute, with respect to war crimes alleged to have been committed by its nationals or on its territory.
133 M Arsanjani, 'The Rome Statute of the International Criminal Court', 93 *AJIL* (1999), 22, pp 26–27.
134 ICC Statute, Art 12(2) and (3).

irrespective of the nationality of persons or the location of documents or other evidentiary material.[135] Because international tribunals are limited by their Statute, the application of the *Lotus* rule by national courts, whereby national criminal jurisdiction under any basis is permissible subject only to a contrary binding rule of international law, does not apply to the subject matter jurisdiction of the ICTY nor the ICC. The subject matter jurisdiction of these international tribunals cannot be extended through construction of their Statutes under the jurisdictional principles applicable to municipal courts, nor as part of these Courts' incidental jurisdiction.

'International jurisdiction' is enjoyed by tribunals established through interstate agreements and Security Council resolutions. Unlike the International Military Tribunal at Nuremberg (IMT) the various 'subsequent' tribunals established by the allies in Germany after 1945 were not the product of treaty making. Despite the application of international law by some of them, their legal basis was domestic legislation, such as the Allied Control Council Law for Germany No 10, the British Royal Warrant and various US Theatre Regulations and Directives. These tribunals were, therefore, obliged to observe the internationally acceptable rules pertaining to the exercise of national judicial jurisdiction.

4.10 IMMUNITIES FROM CRIMINAL JURISDICTION

4.10.1 General conception of immunity in international law

As a general rule, a State enjoys absolute and complete authority over persons and property situated on its territory. Indeed, without directly intervening in the internal affairs of another country it is difficult to see how a sovereign may assert authority over persons or property situated in a foreign land. Even before the establishment of the modern sovereign States, it was recognised that if State-like entities were effectively to interact in commercial, diplomatic and other fields, there was a need for a formula granting their official representatives freedom from arrest or suit in the receiving State. The granting of such privileges and immunities are, in fact, limitations on State sovereignty, whose reciprocal nature is, nonetheless, beneficial for the receiving State in the exercise of its foreign relations.

If it is agreed that a State enjoys absolute territorial competence, immunity from civil or criminal suit is possible only by the forum's waiver of competence over certain persons or property located on its territory. This also means that immunity is an exception to a 'normative rule that would otherwise apply

---

135 *ICTY Prosecutor v Blaskic*, Appeals Judgment on the Request of the Republic of Croatia for Review of the Decision of Trial Chamber II (1997) 110 ILR 607.

[that is, to the ordinary jurisdiction of States]'.[136] This State-centred concept can be discerned as early as *Schooner Exchange v McFaddon*,[137] where Marshall J explained that a foreign public vessel would not enter the ports of another State if it was not satisfied that it benefited from not being sued in the courts of the coastal State. This voluntary waiver of jurisdiction amounts to an 'implied licence' from the judicial, executive and enforcement claws of the receiving State. This is the primary legal basis for the concept of immunity. The fact that sovereign States are juridically equal under international law does not alone suffice as a basis for granting an 'implied licence', despite the maxim *par in parent non habet imperium*.[138] In an era where a significant number of humanitarian norms have attained *jus cogens* and *erga omnes* character, equality has not prevented suits against States and their officials before municipal courts for both tort and criminal prosecutions,[139] although as will become evident in this chapter, tort suits have generally not succeeded. Similarly, although designed to enhance interstate relations and limit the reach of the receiving State's judicial and executive machinery the concept of State immunity is not based on comity. State practice at the international level suggests that what was once an implied licence has now evolved to a legal obligation on the part of the receiving sovereign. A realistic approach to immunity may elucidate some of the reasons associated with it, but not its basis in law.

The fact that adjudication of a case by a domestic court would raise issues of policy involving a foreign State[140] may explain why national judiciary has on many occasions been reluctant to exercise jurisdiction. It does not of itself evince waiver of jurisdiction. Notwithstanding this observation, the nature of some sovereign acts, under the rule of equality of States, cannot become the subject of municipal judicial proceedings. Thus, in *Buck v AG*,[141] the Court of Appeal refused to make a declaration on the validity, or not, of the Constitution of Sierra Leone. Other similar sovereign acts which would be excluded from the consideration of national courts have included governmental acts dealing with purely internal issues or issues pertinent to a State's external affairs.[142] These issues have fallen under the umbrella of non-justiciable acts

---

136 Op cit, *Arrest Warrant* case, note 94, Separate Opinions of Judges Higgins, Kooijmans and Buergenthal, para 71.

137 (1812) 7 Cranch 116.

138 One sovereign cannot exercise authority over another by means of its legal system.

139 *Re Pinochet (No 3)* (1999) 17 ILR 393; *Prefecture of Voiotia and Others v Federal Republic of Germany*, 92 *AJIL* (1998), 765, where acts of atrocity committed by German troops during their occupation of Hellas in the Second World War were held to be violations of *jus cogens* norms, hence susceptible to the civil jurisdiction of Hellenic courts (subsequently upheld in cassation by the Hellenic Supreme Court in 2000). Reported in 95 *AJIL* (2001), 375.

140 *Rahimtoola v Nizam of Hyderabad* [1958] 3 All ER 961.

141 [1965] Ch 745; 42 ILR 11. The same has been held as regards the validity of treaties where the issue does not raise questions of national law. *Ex p Molyneaux* [1986] 1 WLR 331.

142 See *Kuwait Airways Corp v Iraqi Airways Co* [1995] 1 WLR 1147.

and have precluded national courts from asserting their jurisdiction. Immunity, on the other hand, refers to those situations where, although the court would normally enjoy competence over a particular case, it is averted from doing so because one of the litigants is a sovereign State or a legitimate extension thereof.

It seems doubtful, however, that all traditional non-justiciable acts are beyond the ambit of national courts, since if the prevention or punishment of specific conduct is classified as an *erga omnes* obligation, it necessarily follows that if a violation of such a norm were embodied in a parliamentary act, the courts of a third State would be under an obligation to declare that act unobservable in the forum and therefore allow it to continue. For example, if a case comes before the courts of State A, whereby an alien has acted in accordance with a law in State B allowing the practice of torture, the courts of State A may declare that law to be contrary to international law and invalidate any legal effects arising within the territory of State A. In *Oppenheim v Cattermole*, for example, one issue that arose was whether a decree adopted in Nazi Germany in 1941 depriving Jews who had emigrated from Germany of their citizenship should be recognised by the English court. Lord Chelsea pointed out that the courts should be very reluctant to pass judgment on foreign sovereign acts, but because the Nazi law was not only discriminatory but deprived German Jews of their property and citizenship, 'a law of this sort constitutes so grave an infringement of human rights that the courts of this country ought to refuse to recognise it as a law at all'.[143]

Until very recently, States could not be sued at all before the courts of other States. This rule of absolute immunity rested on the customary assimilation of the sovereign and its officials with the represented State, regardless of the function served in each particular case. The personal dignity of the monarch, thus, precluded impleading him or her before a foreign jurisdiction. Before the 1920s, this rule of absolute immunity suggested that every State act was immune from domestic litigation. With the rapid growth of interstate commerce, there was a need to procure guarantees to private enterprises that trading with State entities would be on an equal basis. Indeed, the erosion of absolute immunity rested on financial considerations. The granting of sovereign immunity has since been premised only on the public nature of the act (acts *jure imperii*), thus excluding those acts serving private functions, such as commercial activities (acts *jure gestionis*). With the dissolution of the USSR and the communist system generally in Europe, only China and a few South

---

143 *Oppenheim v Cattermole* [1976] AC 249, p 277; in *The Queen on the Application of Abbasi and Another v FCO Secretary of State and Others*, Judgment [2002] EWCA Civ 1598, the Court of Appeal agreed with this position, but on the facts of the case, it had no power to compel the US to grant *habeas corpus* relief to the applicant, who was a British national held at Guantanamo Bay as a suspected Al-Qaeda member.

American States continue to apply a doctrine of absolute immunity. Each State is free to develop its own criteria determining whether an act serves a public or private function, as is the case with the UK State Immunity Act (SIA) 1978. However, since the distinction is not always clear-cut, several theories have subsequently been adopted by national courts. Examining the 'purpose of the act', that is, whether or not it was intended for a commercial or a public transaction, has not attracted favour from UK and US courts.[144] It was, nonetheless, incorporated in a subsidiary role in Art 2 of the International Law Commission (ILC) Draft Articles on Jurisdictional Immunities, since its role as a complementary test in a number of jurisdictions could not be overlooked.[145] Although the 'nature of the act' test has found some support,[146] it is unambiguous that certain commercial contracts can only be made by States and not by private parties, such as the supply of military material. The more common approach seemed to suggest that a list of detailed exceptions was preferred by municipal courts in order to avoid making personal determinations on the basis of either test.[147] This, to a large extent, is reflected in the UK SIA 1978. Section 3 of the Act provides for a catalogue of exceptions to State immunity as follows:

3(1) A State is not immune as respects proceedings relating to –

    (a) commercial transactions entered into by the State; or

    (b) an obligation of the State which by virtue of a contract (whether a commercial transaction or not), falls to be performed wholly or partly in the United Kingdom.

(2) This section does not apply if the parties to the dispute are States or have otherwise agreed in writing; and sub-s (1)(b) above does not apply if the contract (not being a commercial transaction) was made in the territory of the State concerned and the obligation in question is governed by its administrative law.

(3) In this section 'commercial transaction' means –

    (a) any contract for the supply of goods or services;

    (b) any loan or other transaction for the provision of finance and any guarantee or indemnity in respect of any such transaction or of any other financial obligation; and

---

144 *Trendtex Trading Corp v Central Bank of Nigeria* [1977] 1 All ER 881; *I Congreso del Partido* [1981] 2 All ER 1064; *Victory Transport Inc v Comisaria General De Abastecimientos y Transpertos*, 35 ILR 110.
145 *USA v The Public Service Alliance of Canada*, 32 ILM (1993), 1.
146 *Trendtex* [1977] 1 All ER 881.
147 In the *Victory Transport* case, 35 ILR 110, the District Court of Appeals listed as acts *jure imperii* internal administrative acts, such as the expulsion of aliens and the passing of national laws, acts concerning military and diplomatic affairs, and public loans.

(c) any other transaction or activity (whether of a commercial, industrial, financial, professional or other similar character) into which a State enters or in which it engages otherwise than in the exercise of sovereign authority, but neither paragraph of sub-s (1) above applies to a contract of employment between a State and an individual.

The 1978 Act represents a good example of a restrictive immunity statute since it is not only similar to the US Foreign Sovereign Immunities Act (FSIA) 1976, but it also implements the 1972 European Convention on State Immunity.[148] A foreign sovereign may waive its immunity privileges either expressly or by conduct. Such waiver need not necessarily extend to measures of execution.[149] US and UK courts require genuine submission to the competence of their judiciary and have rejected the invocation of 'implied waivers', even with respect to conduct constituting a violation of *jus cogens*.[150]

Thus far, we have briefly examined the general conception of immunity in international law. These rules are useful in discerning whether or not a foreign State may be impleaded in civil suits before the courts of other nations. We will now proceed to examine the international law of immunity from criminal jurisdiction afforded specifically to natural persons.

4.10.2 Immunity from criminal jurisdiction

In general terms, immunity from jurisdiction means that a court cannot entertain a suit, not that the defendant is immune from criminal liability altogether.[151] In practical terms, this means that once the procedural bar is removed (ie, immunity from suit because the person is an incumbent office holder), the person is liable for criminal prosecution. In customary law, there are two reasons as to why foreign nationals have been granted immunity from municipal courts for alleged perpetration of criminal offences. The first reason relates to the status of certain persons. Thus, it is recognised that individuals who hold certain public office enjoy absolute criminal immunity. Its basis is not the nature of the action, but the official status of the person

---

148 ETS 74.
149 Op cit, Brownlie, note 6, p 343; J Crawford, 'Execution of Judgments and Foreign Sovereign Immunity', 75 *AJIL* (1981), 75, p 86.
150 *Hirsch v State of Israel and State of Germany*, 113 ILR 543; in *Smith v Socialist People's Libyan Arab Jamahiriya* (1997) 113 ILR 534, the Court of Appeals stated further that FSIA, § 1605, did not contemplate a dynamic expansion whereby immunity could be removed by action of the UN Security Council; *Kahan v Pakistan Federation* [1951] 2 KB 1003, rejecting a claim that a waiver had been established from a prior contract to submit to the jurisdiction of UK courts.
151 *Dickinson v Del Solar* [1930] 1 KB 376, p 380, *per* Lord Hewart CJ; similarly, *Belgian Arrest Warrant* judgment (14 Feb 2002), paras 47–55.

concerned. This type of immunity is known as *ratione personae*, and is available to a limited number of individuals: serving Heads of State, heads of diplomatic missions, their families and servants.[152] It is not available to serving Heads of Government who are not also Heads of State, Foreign Minsters, or military commanders and their subordinates.[153]

Immunity *ratione materiae*, on the other hand, is subject-matter immunity. It serves to protect governmental acts of one State from being adjudicated before the courts of another and, therefore, only incidentally confers immunity on the individual. It is immunity from the civil and criminal jurisdiction of foreign national courts, but only in respect of governmental or official acts. Subsequently, it is open to any person exercising official functions, from a former Head of State to the lowest public official. The reason for granting this type of immunity is to protect the person of the foreign dignitary in order to carry out his or her State functions and to represent that country abroad without any hindrance. This means that once the person is removed from office and no longer represents State interests abroad, he or she may thereafter become subject to criminal prosecution for offences committed at any time in the past. The fact that such immunity may be abused while the holder is in office is regrettable, but does not alter that person's protected status, as this remains a well established rule of international law. In the *Belgian Arrest Warrant* judgment, the ICJ confirmed that no distinction could be drawn between acts undertaken by the Congolese Foreign Minister as falling within an official or private capacity, because his immunity was *ratione materiae*. It clearly noted that customary international law did not provide an exception to the granting of immunity *ratione materiae*, even in cases of war crimes and crimes against humanity.[154] The case is obviously different where such immunity is removed by the State of the protected person's nationality, or by treaty – including Security Council resolutions – as was the case with the prosecution of former President Milosevic before the ICTY, within the context of international criminal jurisdiction exercised by an international judicial body.

These immunity rules have emerged as a result of State practice in the form of domestic immunity statutes and case law. They are not relevant to a discussion on immunity with respect to the jurisdiction of international criminal tribunals, to which separate mention will be made further below. We will now

---

152 SIA 1978, s 14(1) extends immunity *ratione personae* to: (a) the sovereign or other Head of that State in his public capacity; (b) the government of that State; and (c) any department of that government (but not every executive entity). In *Propend Finance Pty Ltd and Others v Sing and Others* (1998) 111 ILR 611, the UK Court of Appeals held that the correct interpretation of the word 'government' in s 14(1) be in light of the concept of sovereign authority, thus, encompassing police functions.

153 See SIA 1978, s 20(1).

154 Op cit, *Belgian Arrest Warrant* judgment (14 Feb 2002), note 94, paras 47–55.

proceed to analyse the contemporary scope of subject matter and personal immunity.

4.10.3 Act of State doctrine

This has been developed mainly by common law courts, which have generally refused to pass judgment on the validity of acts of foreign governments performed within their national territory.[155] This doctrine is akin to the concept of 'non-justiciability', having been viewed as a function of the separation of powers with the aim of not hindering the executive's conduct of foreign relations.[156] The difference between the doctrines of State immunity and 'act of State' is that the former being a procedural bar to the jurisdiction of a court can be waived, while the latter being a substantial bar cannot.

The classic expression of the doctrine was stated in *Underhill v Hernandez*[157] and reaffirmed by US courts on several occasions. In *Banco Nacional de Cuba v Sabbatino*,[158] the Court refused to examine the legality of the Cuban Government's expropriation of US property in that country. The doctrine requires the defendant to establish that the performed activities were undertaken on behalf of the State and not in a private capacity. While any personal commercial transactions would clearly not be attributable to the State,[159] the extent to which individuals may purport to be acting for their sovereign has been limited in recent years. What is relevant for the purposes of the present analysis is the refusal of courts to accept the sovereign character of criminal acts in furtherance of personal aims. In *Jimenez v Aristeguieta*,[160] the accused had used his position as former President and dictator of Venezuela to commit financial crimes for his own benefit. He claimed that, criminal though these actions may have been, they were, nonetheless, acts that should be attributable to Venezuela. The Fifth Circuit court rejected this claim stating that offences perpetrated for private financial benefit constitute 'common crimes committed by the Chief of State in violation of his position

---

155 For a discussion of a civil law approach, see *Border Guards Prosecution* case, 100 ILR 364, where the German Federal Supreme Court found the act of State doctrine to be a rule of domestic law concerning the extent to which the acts of foreign States were assumed to be effective. See also JC Barker, 'State Immunity, Diplomatic Immunity and Act of State: A Triple Protection Against Legal Action?', 47 ICLQ (1998), 950.

156 See *Kirkpatrick v Environmental Tectonics*, 493 US 403 (1990).

157 168 US 250 (1897), p 252; see also the earlier decision *of Hatch v Baez* 7 Hun 596 (1876), where the New York Supreme Court was prevented from reviewing acts of the former President of the Dominican Republic done in his official capacity.

158 376 US 398 (1964).

159 *Alfred Dunhill of London Inc v Republic of Cuba*, 425 US 682 (1976).

160 311 F 2d 547 (1962).

and not in pursuance of it. They are as far from being an act of State as rape'.[161]

Similarly, in *USA v Noriega*,[162] the District Court held that acts of drug trafficking committed even by a *de facto* leader of a country do not constitute sovereign acts, on the same basis as *Jimenez*. The District Court further correctly noted that because the doctrine was designed to preclude the hindrance of foreign relations, if the executive, as in the case of *Noriega*, had indicted the defendant, no danger of conflict would exist, and could, therefore, decide the case. However, whether the extension of immunity under the FSIA covers a Head of State was considered by the US Court of Appeals for the Seventh Circuit as a matter for the Executive Branch to determine.[163] More recently, in *Doe v Unocal*, it was held that the act of State doctrine did not preclude US courts from considering claims based on legal principles on which the international community had reached unambiguous agreement, such as slavery.[164] It should be noted that, besides the prosecution of Noriega, all the aforementioned cases concerned actions in tort.

4.11 IMMUNITY UNDER DOMESTIC LAW AND *JUS COGENS* NORMS

As explained above, foreign Heads of State have customarily enjoyed immunity from criminal prosecution as a matter of the respect afforded to their person and the State they represent.[165] This was true, irrespective of the criminal offence they were alleged to have committed. For crimes ordered or tolerated in a leader's own State, the rule on non-intervention in the domestic affairs of other States, as enshrined in Art 2(7) of the UN Charter, precluded considerations of criminal liability even where fundamental human rights were seriously abused.

It seems that with the erosion of an unfettered absolute discretion previously associated with Art 2(7) in the sphere of human rights, immunity *ratione materiae* has also suffered considerable limitation. The majority of the House of Lords in the *Pinochet (No 3)* case[166] admitted that while the immunity of a former Head of State persists with respect to official acts, the

---

161 Ibid, pp 557–58; similarly, in *Sharon v Time Inc*, 599 F Supp 538 (1984), it was held that the Israeli Defence Minister's alleged support of a massacre could not constitute the policy of the Israeli Government and, therefore, an act of State.

162 99 ILR 143.

163 *Wei Ye v Jiang Zemin and Falun Gong Control Office*, 383 F. 3d 620 (7th Cir. 2004), at 20–21.

164 963 F Supp 880 (1997).

165 In *Lafontant v Aristide* (1994) 103 ILR 581, the Eastern District Court of New York held that a recognised Head of State enjoys absolute immunity even in exile, unless such immunity has been explicitly waived.

166 [1999] 2 WLR 827, pp 880, 906.

determination of what constitutes an official act is to be made in accordance with customary law. It held that international crimes, such as torture, cannot constitute official acts of a Head of State.[167] Indeed, since Art 1(1) of the 1984 Torture Convention defines torture as an act that can only be inflicted by a public official, the mere invocation of immunity *ratione materiae* would render the Torture Convention redundant. Article 1(1) has to be read, hence, as excluding such immunity. The situation is different in relation to an acting Head of State, who enjoys absolute immunity from criminal prosecution before national (but not international tribunals sanctioned by the UN Security Council) irrespective of the crimes committed.

The few prosecutions that have taken place before national courts do not support a consistent general trend or rule, but instead seem to have been motivated by individual instances of political enmity and available opportunity. We shall cite them, nonetheless, because they are evidence of some State practice. In February 2000, a court in Senegal indicted Hissene Habre, the Head of State in Chad from 1982–90, for acts of torture during his reign in that country, but on 20 March 2001 the Cour de Cassation of that country held that Habre could not be tried under torture charges in Senegal.[168] Whatever the precise scope of Head of State immunity, in *USA v Noriega* it was held that illegitimate assumption of power does not carry immunity benefits.[169] This statement, welcomed as it may be, should be approached with caution, because the US Government has not hesitated in the past to afford full immunities and support to illegitimate dictatorial regimes. Interestingly, the ECHR, in the *Al-Adsani* case, took the view that even *jus cogens* norms, such as the prohibition against torture, must be construed as existing in harmony with other recognised principles of international law, namely state immunity. The applicant was tortured by government agents in Kuwait and pursued civil claims before British courts for a period of 10 years, which rejected his claims on the basis of immunity afforded under the SIA 1978. Thereafter, he sought refuge before the ECHR, arguing that the SIA violated his right of access to judicial remedies. The Court rejected his claim, arguing that immunity is inherent in the operation of international law, and cannot be regarded as imposing a disproportionate restriction on the right of access to court.[170]

---

167 See G Garnett, 'The Defence of State Immunity for Acts of Torture', 18 *Australian YIL* (1997), 97.
168 F Kirgis, 'The Indictment in Senegal of the Former Chad Head of State' (February 2000) *ASIL Insight*; in the *Honecker Prosecution* case, 100 ILR 393, the issue of the criminal liability of a former Head of State for human rights violations authorised while in office was not considered because of the ill health of the accused.
169 99 ILR 143, pp 162–63.
170 *Al-Adsani v UK*, Judgment (21 Nov 2001) (2002) 34 EHRR 11, paras 55–66; for an overview, see E Voyakis, 'Access to Court v State Immunity', 52 *ICLQ* (2003), 279.

As already noted, until very recently, human rights abuses were perceived as issues exclusive to the domestic jurisdiction of the concerned State. US courts have attempted to detach human rights violations from the range of official acts which may lawfully be attributed to the State, but only where public officials acted independently, either in pursuance of personal interests as in the case of Noriega and Marcos, or beyond the level of abuse authorised by the State they represent. In *Forti v Suarez-Mason*, acts of torture and disappearances committed by an Argentine General who was an official of the military regime, did not, *ipso facto*, assimilate his actions to the Argentine State.[171] The general trend seems to be that national courts and the executive are very reluctant to waive the immunity of States and their officials with respect to tort suits, even for serious human rights violations perpetrated in a third country.[172] On the other hand, the wide acceptance of *Pinochet (3)* by the House of Lords and the similar conclusions reached by the ICJ in the *Arrest Warrant* case, confirm that while acting Heads of State enjoy absolute immunity from criminal prosecution, other persons may be prosecuted for international offences.

It has been widely advocated that States are obligated under international law to punish serious human rights breaches by a former regime.[173] As in the case of Chile, the promulgation of amnesty laws exonerating culpable individuals of prior regimes is incompatible with the duty of States to investigate human rights infractions and provide appropriate remedies. This is true, at least, of amnesties granted after crimes have been perpetrated,[174] and those favouring State security forces (self-amnesties).[175]

In order for the judicial authorities of a State to waive immunity with respect to human rights abuses, they must first determine whether there is a

---

171 672 F Supp 1531 (1987). These cases have been brought under the Aliens Tort Claims Act 1789, 18 USC § 1350, and so the criminal elements involved are incidental to the principal character of such claims, which is a claim in tort.

172 In *Jones and Others v Saudi Arabia*, supra note 95, paras 30–31, the House of Lords dismissed the argument upheld by the Court of Appeals, whereby the State enjoys immunity but not the agent. Equally, in *Bouzari v Islamic Republic of Iran* (2004), 124 ILR 427, the Ontario Court of Appeals could find no exception to the general rule of immunity for acts of torture committed outside the forum State.

173 D Orentlicher, 'Settling Accounts: The Duty to Prosecute Human Rights Violations of a Prior Regime', 100 *Yale LJ* (1991), 2537; M Scharf, 'Swapping Amnesty for Peace: Was There a Duty to Prosecute International Crimes in Haiti?', 31 *Texas ILJ* (1996), 1; nonetheless, in *Azanian Peoples Organisation v President of the Republic of South Africa*, 91 *AJIL* (1997), 360, the RSA Constitutional Court held that international human rights law did not compel domestic criminal prosecution of human rights abuses.

174 UN Human Rights Committee, General Comment No 20, UN Doc CCPR/C/21/Rev 1/Add 3 (7 April 1992), para 15, regarding the interpretation of Art 7 of the ICCPR; see also N Roht-Arriaza and L Gibson, 'The Developing Jurisprudence on Amnesty', 20 *HRQ* (1998), 843.

175 K Ambos, 'Impunity and International Law', 18 *HRLJ* (1997), 1, pp 7–8.

national law in place regulating the relevant conduct and whether or not they may lawfully exercise judicial jurisdiction. The House of Lords in the *Pinochet (No 3)* case upheld its subject matter jurisdiction over acts of torture committed after 1988 when the Torture Convention was enacted into British law. Another route would have been to recognise the prohibition of torture under customary law and avoid limiting the temporal scope of the charges. As regards jurisdiction, where the offence in question is subject to universal jurisdiction under international law, as in the case of piracy *jure gentium* and grave breaches, the prosecution of public officials by any State should not be a very difficult exercise. It would seem that where immunity is excluded from multilateral treaties, such as in Art IV of the 1948 Convention on the Prevention and Punishment of the Crime of Genocide (Genocide Convention) and in respect of offences that do not attract universal jurisdiction under treaty or customary law, any State is free to assert criminal jurisdiction as long as this does not conflict with the competence afforded to other States under the relevant treaty or custom.

4.12 FOREIGN AND MULTINATIONAL ARMED FORCES ABROAD

Since time immemorial, foreign armed forces have been allowed to pass through or station on the territory of allied or other States. Where a State allows a foreign force passage or sojourn on its territory, it does so, in the words of Justice Marshall in the *Schooner Exchange* case, under an implied waiver of jurisdiction.[176] The rationale for such a waiver by the receiving State is justified for the maintenance of the efficiency and integrity of the foreign force.[177] In the absence of a specific agreement, the law seems to be that immunity from the receiving State's criminal jurisdiction is not absolute. The sending State exercises exclusive jurisdiction over internal disciplinary or other offences committed by its forces when on duty, while the receiving State enjoys jurisdiction in respect of all other offences.[178] In cases where the distinction is not clear cut, in connection to an offence committed by a member of the force out of duty, Brownlie suggests that immunity should be complemented by principles of interest or substantial connection.[179] It is usual, however, for States to regulate such matters through the conclusion of special agreements and make detailed arrangements. The 1951 NATO Status

---

176 (1812) 7 Cranch 116. This case concerned the passage of foreign troops.
177 *Wright v Cantrell* (1943–45) 12 AD 37; *Chow Hung Ching v R* (1948) 77 CLR 449; 15 AD 47.
178 Op cit, Brownlie, note 6, p 374; op cit, Shearer, note 9, p 208.
179 Op cit, Brownlie, note 6, p 374.

of Forces Agreement (NATO SOFA)[180] provides in general for the exercise of concurrent jurisdiction over the civilian and military personnel of a NATO visiting force. The sending State enjoys primary criminal jurisdiction over offences and persons falling within the ambit of its military law, as well as over any act or omission done in the performance of official duty, whereas the receiving State has jurisdiction with respect to persons and offences under its own municipal law. In *Public Prosecutor v Ashby*, a US Army aeroplane, part of a NATO contingent in Italy, crashed in a residential area causing substantial material damage and killing several civilians.[181] The Italian court held that, in cases where jurisdiction is concurrent, priority goes to the sending State where the offence is solely against the interests of that State (Art VII, § 3(a)(i) of the 1951 NATO Agreement) or committed in the performance of official duty (Art VII, § 3(a)(ii)). In the case at hand, the offence in question, brought about by a flight in the course of a training mission, was determined to have arisen in the performance of official duty under Art VII, § 3(b)(ii) of the 1951 NATO SOFA.

As for UN peace-keeping forces, other than those constituted as a means of enforcement action, deployment is based only on the consent of the receiving State, unless there is an absence of government authority to grant such consent, as was the case with Somalia in 1993. In the post–1945 era, peace-keeping agreements have secured broad terms of immunity for UN forces.[182] As a matter of internal organisation, with respect to UN and other multi-national forces, jurisdiction over offences committed in the context of such operations remains with the State of the nationality of the accused. This represents well established customary law,[183] and is recognised in s 4 of the UN Secretary General's 'Observance by United Nations Forces of International Humanitarian Law', which subjects all infractions to national prosecution.[184] As already explained in Chapter 21, following the adoption of the 1998 ICC Statute, the US sought to immunise its armed forces from the jurisdiction of the ICC by concluding so called 'Impunity Agreements' with other countries, by which these countries agreed to refrain from prosecuting or transferring to the jurisdiction of the ICC any US nationals accused of relevant offences. These agreements clearly violate Art 86 of the ICC Statute,

---

180 48 *AJIL* (1954 Supp), 83; H Rouse and GB Baldwin, The Exercise of Criminal Jurisdiction under the NATO Status of Forces Agreement', 51 *AJIL* (1957), 29; J Woodliffe, The Stationing of Foreign Armed Forces Abroad in Peacetime', 43 *ICLQ* (1994), 443. See also the UK Visiting Forces Act 1952.

181 93 *AJIL* (1999), 219.

182 See DS Wijewardane, 'Criminal Jurisdiction over Visiting Forces with Special Reference to International Forces', 41 *BYIL* (1965–66), 122.

183 I Bantekas, 'The Contemporary Law of Superior Responsibility', 93 *AJIL* (1999), 573, p 579.

184 Secretary General's Bulletin ST/SG-B/1999/13 (6 Aug 1999), reprinted in 836 IRRC (1999), 812.

which obliges Member States to co-operate with the Court in investigating and prosecuting alleged perpetrators. In any event, these bilateral immunity agreements would not bind third States.

4.13 DIPLOMATIC AND CONSULAR IMMUNITIES [185]

According to the more correct view, the immunity enjoyed by diplomatic envoys is functional, its rationale being to allow them to perform their duties without interference or other hindrance.[186] In fact, under Art 29 of the 1961 Vienna Convention on Diplomatic Relations (Vienna Convention)[187] the receiving State has an obligation to safeguard the freedom and dignity of diplomatic agents.[188] Their immunity from local criminal jurisdiction under Art 32 of the 1961 Vienna Convention does not render them also immune from liability under the law of the receiving State.[189] The practical significance of this observation is that if the sending State waives the diplomatic immunity of its agent, as it may under Art 32 of the 1961 Vienna Convention, criminal liability may thereafter arise.[190]

Diplomatic immunity, in accordance with Art 39(1) and (2), exists from the moment the person enters the territory of the receiving State until such time as the privileges and immunities are revoked by the sending State. Under Art 39(2) the diplomatic agent enjoys continuing immunity for acts performed 'in the exercise of his or her functions as a member of the mission'. However, since the conferment of diplomatic immunity is dependent on the consent of the receiving State, the correct view is that any immunity granted by the latter will not bind third States. In the *Former Syrian Ambassador to the GDR* case, the German Federal Constitutional Court found no general rule of customary international law whereby this principle of continuing immunity would be binding on third States, other than the receiving one, and, therefore, have *erga omnes* effect.[191] This immunity *ratione materiae*, the court further held, was effective in the receiving State even after the termination of diplomatic status, but only in respect of acts performed in the exercise of

---

185 See J Brown, 'Diplomatic Immunity: State Practice Under the Vienna Convention on Diplomatic Relations', 37 *ICLQ* (1988), 53.

186 See SE Nahlik, 'Development of Diplomatic Law: Selected Problems', 222 *RCADI* (1990 III), 187.

187 500 UNTS 95.

188 Affirmed by the ICJ in *USA Diplomatic and Consular Staff in Tehran (USA v Iran)* (1980) ICJ Reports 3.

189 *Dickinson v Del Solar* [1930] 1 KB 376, p 380, *per* Lord Hewart CJ; similarly, *Empson v Smith* [1966] 1 QB 426.

190 1961 Vienna Convention, Art 32(2) requires that the waiver be express. See Diplomatic Privileges Act 1964, s 2(3); *Engelke v Musmann* [1928] AC 433; *R v Madan* [1961] 2 QB 1.

191 115 ILR 597, pp 605–12.

official duties, with the provision of assistance in a bomb attack being excluded from such official function.

It is not rare for persons entitled to diplomatic immunity under Art 37 of the 1961 Vienna Convention to abuse their status.[192] In these cases, the receiving State is free to declare such persons *non grata*. Things become problematic when diplomatic agents are known to be in the course of committing an offence injurious to the interests of the receiving State, since Art 29 of the 1961 Vienna Convention prohibits any arrest or detention. The privileges in Art 29 are distinct from the absolute immunity from criminal jurisdiction contained in Art 31(1). Furthermore, there does not seem to exist any rule restraining the receiving State from maintaining internal order through the arrest or detention of diplomatic agents that violate local criminal law. No criminal proceedings may thereafter be instituted against protected diplomatic personnel and the only subsequent avenue is to expel them by declaring them undesirable in the host State.[193]

The law applicable to consular agents, who as a rule perform purely administrative functions, is quite different from that applied to their diplomatic counterparts.[194] Under Art 41 of the 1963 Vienna Convention on Consular Relations,[195] consular agents do not enjoy absolute immunity from the criminal jurisdiction of the receiving State, since in cases of 'grave crimes' they may be liable to arrest and judicial proceedings. Nonetheless, under Art 43 they are entitled to immunity in respect of acts performed in the exercise of consular functions.[196]

Persons attached to special international missions are also subject to a regime of privileges and immunities. This is dependent on the consent of the receiving State either on an *ad hoc* basis, or as a result of a relevant treaty obligation. In its *Advisory Opinion on Interference Relating to Immunity from Legal Process of a Special Rapporteur of the Commission on Human Rights*,[197] the ICJ held that a UN rapporteur was immune from the criminal jurisdiction of the receiving State for the contents of an interview premised on the subject matter of his investigation. This obligation incumbent on Malaysia to recognise the immunity of the rapporteur was based on Art VI,

---

192 See R Higgins, 'The Abuse of Diplomatic Privileges and Immunities: Recent United Kingdom Experience', 79 *AJIL* (1985), 641; JS Parkhill, 'Diplomacy in the Modern World: A Reconsideration of the Bases for Diplomatic Immunity in the Era of High-Tech Communications', 21 *Hastings Int'l & Comp L Rev* (1998), 565.

193 E Denza, *Diplomatic Law*, 1976, New York: Oceana, p 135; JS Beaumont, 'Self-Defence as a Justification for Disregarding Diplomatic Immunity', 29 *Can YIL* (1991), 391.

194 CJ Milhaupt, 'The Scope of Consular Immunity Under the Vienna Convention on Consular Relations: Towards a Principled Interpretation', 88 *Col L Rev* (1988), 841.

195 596 UNTS 261.

196 *Waltier v Thomson*, 189 F Supp 319 (1960); see *Honorary Consul of X v Austria*, 86 ILR 553.

197 93 *AJIL* (1999), 913.

s 22(b) of the 1946 Convention on the Privileges and Immunities of the United Nations.[198]

4.14 IMMUNITY FROM INTERNATIONAL CRIMINAL JURISDICTION

As already noted, the jurisdiction of an international judicial body is dependent on its constitutive instrument. Although this instrument will adhere to international human rights and fundamental principles of international law, it need not follow those principles which, although firmly established, generally bind only national institutions, such as immunities and other privileges. This has had primary application as regards subject matter jurisdiction and immunity *ratione materia* and *ratione personae*. The invocation of official status of any kind was rejected in the Charter of the International Military Tribunal at Nuremberg. Article 7 read:

> The official position of defendants, whether as Heads of State or responsible officials in Government Departments, shall not be considered as freeing them from responsibility or mitigating punishment.[199]

This position was also adopted in Art II(4)(a) of the 1945 Control Council Law for Germany No 10, which was the legislation utilised by allied military tribunals acting in Germany at the end of the Second World War. The ILC's formulation of the Nuremberg Principles and the 1996 Draft Code of Crimes Against the Peace and Security of Mankind also followed this approach, although it is true that the Nuremberg Principles did not explicitly preclude this defence in mitigation of punishment.[200] Similarly, Arts 7(2) and 6(2) of the Statutes of the ICTY and ICTR respectively, rejected this plea as a defence.[201] In the instruments enumerated in this section, a claim of Head of State or of other official status was categorised as a defence assertion, which, if sustained, would have the effect of precluding the liability of the accused. It is clear, therefore, that any claim to official status in international criminal litigation would not be directed against the jurisdiction of the relevant tribunal, as this can only be served by invoking one's immunity. Immunity constitutes a procedural bar to the jurisdiction of a court; it does not waive or

---

198 1 UNTS 15.
199 Charter of the International Military Tribunal for the Far East, Art 6 provided that, although an individual's official position did not constitute a defence, it could be used in mitigation of punishment.
200 See M Ratner and J Abrams, *Accountability for Human Rights Atrocities in International Law*, 1997, Oxford: OUP, pp 124–25.
201 Similarly rejected in the 1948 Genocide Convention, Art IV.

excuse an accused's potential liability. Although the rejection of the defence of official status is found in Art 27(1) of the ICC Statute, para 2 of that Article further provides that:

> Immunities or special procedural rules which may attach to the official capacity of a person, whether under national or international law, shall not bar the Court from exercising jurisdiction over such a person.

This is the first instance of an international criminal tribunal addressing the issue of immunity and also distinguishing its legal nature from a defence claim on similar grounds. There is no doubt, however, that Art 27(2) is a superfluous provision, even for an elaborate Statute such as that of the ICC, since if official status cannot constitute a defence to criminal liability, it necessarily follows that immunity regarding jurisdictional competence will have already been denied.

It should not be thought that because international tribunals are capable of exercising broad jurisdictional powers and rejecting immunity pleas, the same can by implication apply before national courts. It is the consent of States that has shaped the relevant mechanisms in national and international judicial institutions. Until there is a clear and unambiguous statement that a rule has developed rejecting Head of State immunity before national courts, the presumption is that the preservation of such immunity, albeit in light of the developments noted, represents the law.

Chapter 5

War crimes and grave breaches

5.1 GRAVE BREACHES OF THE 1949 GENEVA CONVENTIONS

The *jus in bello* has conventionally been categorised as 'Geneva' law, that is, international humanitarian, and 'Hague' law, which is concerned with the regulation of the means and methods of warfare. International humanitarian law is itself concerned with the protection of victims of armed conflict, which includes those rendered *hors de combat* by injury, sickness or capture, as well as civilians. This division is purely artificial and there is a wide measure of overlap between the two.[1] The Geneva Conventions recognise two types of violations, in accordance with the gravity of the condemned act, namely, 'grave breaches'[2] and other prohibited acts not falling within the definition of grave breaches. Although both grave breaches and all other infractions of the Conventions are outlawed under international humanitarian law, the distinguishing feature of grave breaches is that they can only be committed in international armed conflicts against protected persons or property as designated by the Conventions and are moreover subject to universal jurisdiction.[3] As a result, they entail the criminal responsibility of the perpetrator under international law. The same is not *ipso facto* true with regard to infractions that are not grave breaches and the same applies to violations of 'the laws and customs (usages) of war'. There is no clear criminal basis for these in the Geneva Conventions and criminalisation will only accrue where such violations are penalised in any domestic legal order or in the Statute of an international tribunal. These processes in time may give rise to a customary

---

1 H McCoubrey, *International Humanitarian Law: The Regulation of Armed Conflicts*, 1990, Aldershot: Dartmouth, 1–2.
2 Convention I, Art 50; Convention II, Art 51; Convention III, Art 130; Convention IV, Art 147.
3 1977 Protocol I added new 'grave breaches' to the list of the 1949 Geneva Conventions and further introduced a new set of such breaches. C Van den Wyngaert, 'The Suppression of War Crimes under Additional Protocol I', in AJM Delissen and GJ Tanja (eds), *Humanitarian Law of Armed Conflict*, 1991, Dordrecht: Martinus Nijhoff, 197.

rule that provides for international criminal liability of those perpetrating a non-grave breach.

The 'grave breaches' provisions are applicable where the victims are clearly defined as 'protected persons' under the relevant Geneva Conventions.[4] In the (International Criminal Tribunal for Rwanda) ICTY context, civilian populations during the Yugoslav conflicts were made the target of attacks with a view to either being exterminated or expelled. Article 4 of Geneva Convention IV provides that protected persons are those belonging to another party to the conflict. When this provision was drafted in 1949, it did not envisage the transformation and unprecedented eruption of internal or mixed armed conflicts in their contemporary form, and its purpose was to protect civilian persons held by the adversary, these being in their majority enemy nationals. The concept of nationality, belying a formal legal bond between an individual and a State, would not serve the protective function of Geneva Convention IV as both victims and attackers possessed the same nationality, even though the ensuing conflict was in most part international in character. The *Tadic* Appeals judgment correctly observed that since 1949 the legal bond of nationality has not been regarded as crucial in determining protected person status, further adding that in the particular case of the former Yugoslavia it was 'allegiance' to a party or 'control' over persons by a party that was perceived as crucial.[5] In a nation that had crumbled, ethnicity became more important than nationality in determining loyalties.[6] Therefore, civilian persons in Bosnia who fell into the hands of belligerents possessing the same nationality as they did, but who associated themselves with a different ethnic group, were entitled to protected status under Art 4 of Geneva Convention IV. The *Tadic* Appeals judgment further identified as recipients of the same protection persons in occupied territory who, while possessing the nationality of their captor, are refugees and thus no longer benefit from the protection of Geneva Convention IV.[7] A possible scenario would be that of German Jews fleeing to France before 1940 to avoid persecution and who subsequently fall into German hands when Germany occupies France. It should be noted that whatever the defining element of loyalty may be in each particular case, under Art 4(2) of Geneva Convention IV 'nationals' of co-belligerent States are not entitled to benefit from protected status. In the case of the fragile and, on many occasions, interrupted alliance between the Bosnian Croats and the Bosnian Moslems, the *Blaskic* judgment found the two parties not to be co-belligerents.[8] Although the Trial Chamber in the latter case rebuffed the existence of an alliance *in toto*, at least as this was relevant to determining

---

4 Art 13, Convention I; Art 13, Convention II; Art 4, Convention III; Art 4, Convention IV.
5 *ICTY Prosecutor v Tadic*, Appeals Chamber Judgment (15 July 1999), paras 165–66.
6 *ICTY Prosecutor v Blaskic*, Trial Chamber Judgment (3 March 2000), paras 125–33.
7 Op cit, *Tadic* Appeals Judgment, note 5, para 164.
8 Op cit, *Blaskic* Trial Judgment, note 6, paras 137–43.

protected status, this alliance undoubtedly existed on various occasions despite its instability and on this basis co-belligerency must be formally recognised as a fact.

We have already seen that a war crime is a crime that takes place in the particular context of a conflict and against a protected person. This does not, however, tell us who may commit a war crime. Obviously, those taking a direct part in hostilities incur liability for a war crime by either intentionally attacking protected persons, employing prohibited weapons or particular means of combat, or by altering the status of civilians (such as by altering the demographics of occupied territories). Civilians in occupied territory who intentionally attack the enemy and who do not satisfy the four criteria for lawful combatant status[9] do commit a war crime because they act in a perfidious manner.[10]

According to the *Tadic* Appeals jurisdiction decision an armed conflict exists where there is 'resort to armed force between States or protracted armed violence between governmental authorities and organised groups or between such groups within a State'.[11] The Appeals Chamber further affirmed that the temporal and geographical scope of an armed conflict extends beyond the exact time and place of hostilities and covers the entire territory or territories in which an armed conflict is taking place.[12] This means that, although actual fighting may not be taking place in certain parts of a territory plagued by war, any breaches committed in these locations against protected persons or property may warrant the application of humanitarian law if the breaches are connected in some way to the armed conflict.

5.2 CLASSIFICATION OF ARMED CONFLICTS

An armed conflict may be classified as being international and to have commenced in accordance with the requirements of common Art 2 of the 1949 Geneva Conventions where, in addition to armed violence between two or more States, there has been a declaration of war – even without any hostilities – or partial or total occupation even if it meets with no resistance. Moreover, an international armed conflict exists in situations of *levee en masse*, that is where the inhabitants of a non-occupied territory spontaneously take up

---

9 In accordance with Art 4(2), Geneva Convention III, these consist of: being commanded by a responsible superior; having a fixed distinctive sign recognisable at a distance; carrying arms openly; conducting overall operations in compliance with humanitarian law.

10 Art 37, Protocol I.

11 *ICTY Prosecutor v Tadic*, Appeals Chamber Interlocutory Decision on Jurisdiction (2 Oct 1995), para 70; *ICTY Prosecutor v Kovac, et al*, Appeals Chamber Judgment (12 June 2002), para 57.

12 *Tadic*, ibid, para 67.

arms against an approaching enemy.[13] Equally, for those States that have ratified the 1977 Protocol I, an international armed conflict arises in cases of protracted armed violence in which peoples are fighting against colonial domination, alien occupation and racist regimes, in accordance with Art 1(4) of the Protocol. Besides these situations described in treaty law, an international armed conflict exists where a State directly intervenes militarily in a non-international armed conflict on the side of either party, or when a State exercises 'overall control' over a rebel entity as to justify attributing its actions to the controlling State. The Appeals Chamber in its judgment in the *Tadic* case rebuffed the 'effective control' test propounded by the International Court of Justice (ICJ) in the *Nicaragua* case, which held that organised private individuals whose action is co-ordinated or supervised by a foreign State and to whom specific instructions are issued are considered *de facto* organs of the controlling State. Although this test had found application by the ICJ vis-à-vis 'Unilaterally Controlled Latino Assets' who were non-US nationals, but acting while in the pay of the US, on direct instructions and under US military or intelligence supervision to carry out specific tasks, it was not applied to the Nicaraguan contra rebels because they had not received any instructions.[14] The ICTY Appeals Chamber held that the ICJ's 'effective control' test was at variance with both judicial and State practice and could only apply with regard to individuals or unorganised groups of individuals acting on behalf of third States, but was generally inapplicable to military or paramilitary groups.[15] The ICTY's departure from the stringent 'effective control' test was duly replaced with an 'overall control test' which simply requires co-ordinating or helping in a group's general military planning, besides equipping or possibly financing the group, in order to establish a relationship of agency between the group and the aiding State.[16] Thus, in overturning the much criticised Trial Chamber's judgment which had found the Bosnian Serb Army (VRS) not to be an agent of the Federal Republic of Yugoslavia (FRY),[17] the Appeals Chamber held the VRS to constitute a military organisation under the overall control of the FRY, finding the latter not only to have equipped and financed the VRS, but to have also participated in the planning and supervision of its military operations.[18] Until the *Tadic* Appeals judgment in 1999, the various ICTY Chambers had, as a direct result of interpreting differently in each case the test propounded in the *Nicaragua* judgment, reached inconsistent

---

13 Art 1(2), Regulations attached to the 1907 Hague Convention No IV [Hague Regulations].
14 Op cit, *Tadic* Appeals Judgment, note 5, paras 109, 114.
15 Ibid, para 124.
16 Ibid, para 131.
17 T Meron, 'Classification of Armed Conflicts in the Former Yugoslavia: Nicaragua's Fallout', 92 *AJIL* (1998), 236.
18 Op cit, *Tadic* Appeals Judgment, note 5, para 131.

determinations as to the nature of the Bosnian armed conflicts. The 'overall control' test, correct on its merits, certainly set a precedent and is now accepted as good law by ICTY Chambers in their evaluation of both FRY and Croat intervention on behalf of rebel entities.[19]

5.3 TYPES OF INTERNATIONAL ARMED CONFLICT WAR CRIMES

The ICTY Statute clearly provides for criminal jurisdiction over grave breaches of the Geneva Conventions in its Art 2, but is not at all clear as to the context of the offences encompassed in its Art 3. As the *Tadic* Appeals Jurisdiction Decision later explained, Art 3 of the ICTY Statute, entitled 'Violations of the laws or customs of war', is a residual clause that covers international armed conflict war crimes other than grave breaches, as well as certain violations committed in non-international armed conflicts.[20] The specific grave breaches which entail individual responsibility under Art 2 of the ICTY Statute and which must further be sufficiently linked to the armed conflict are:

(a) wilful killing;
(b) torture or inhuman treatment, including biological experiments;
(c) wilfully causing great suffering or serious injury to body or health;
(d) extensive destruction and appropriation of property, not justified by military necessity and carried out unlawfully and wantonly;
(e) compelling a prisoner of war or a civilian to serve in the forces of a hostile power;
(f) wilfully depriving a prisoner of war or a civilian of the rights of fair and regular trial;
(g) unlawful deportation or transfer or unlawful confinement of a civilian;
(h) taking civilians as hostages.[21]

Although the International Committee of the Red Cross (ICRC) commentary to the 1949 Geneva Conventions states that the list of grave breaches therein is not exhaustive and that criminality itself may extend beyond grave breaches,[22] such construction cannot have any application to Art 2 of the ICTY Statute whose list of grave breaches is exhaustive. The same is not true, however, with regard to Art 3 of the ICTY Statute.

19 *ICTY Prosecutor v Aleksovski*, Appeals Chamber Judgment (24 March 2000), para 145; op cit, *Blaskic* Trial Judgment, note 6, para 100.
20 Op cit, *Tadic* Appeals Jurisdiction Decision, note 11, paras 87–92
21 These also appear verbatim in Art 8(2)(a) of the ICC Statute.
22 JS Pictet, *Commentary: IV Geneva Convention Relative to the Protection of Civilian Persons in Time of Armed Conflict*, 1958, 305.

In general terms, four broad categories of war crimes – other than grave breaches – may be said to exist: targeting crimes; prohibited weapons; prohibition of particular means of combat; and altering the status of particular civilians. Article 8(2)(b) of the ICC Statute aptly reflects these categorisations. Targeting crimes (paras (i), (ii), (iii), (iv), (v), (ix), (xii) and (xxiv)) are premised on the customary principle that the warring parties should distinguish between civilians/civilian objects[23] and combatants/military objects and must only target the latter.[24] Given that only subsection (iv) mentions military necessity, while subparagraph (2)(b) states that all war crimes in that subsection are to be viewed within 'the established framework of international law', it is assumed that customary international law and the relevant provisions of Protocol I on military necessity apply *mutatis mutantis* in the absence of other normative guidance in the Statute. Within the same framework, the Court will have to judge some grey areas of combatant status, particularly civilians working at ammunition factories, children throwing petrol bombs at occupying forces and others. Although we are in favour of a narrow interpretation of combatant status, neat categorisations are not always feasible when boundaries are blurred.

As regards prohibited weapons, there is some agreement under customary law as to which are prohibited, while for others there is substantial dissention. This is aptly reflected in the ICC Statute, which criminalizes the employment of poison or poisoned weapons,[25] asphyxiating or poisonous gases and other analogous materials,[26] expanding bullets[27] and finally 'some' weapons that are inherently indiscriminate, or which are of a nature to cause superfluous injury or unnecessary suffering.[28] The latter category, while valid without any reservations under international law for the majority of conventional weapons, is explicitly conditioned in the context of the ICC Statute by the existence of a comprehensive prohibition and a yet to be formulated annex. This leaves out of the Rome Statute, therefore, bacteriological weapons,[29] anti-personnel

---

23 This includes also widespread, long-term and severe damage to the natural environment, in accordance with Art 8(2)(b)(iv) ICC Statute; Art 55, Protocol I.
24 Arts 51, 52, Protocol I.
25 Art 8(2)(b)(xvii), ICC Statute; Art 2(3), 1907 Hague Regulations.
26 Art 8(2)(b)(xviii), ICC Statute; 1925 Protocol for the Prohibition of the Use in War of Asphyxiating, Poisonous or Other Gases and of Bacteriological Methods of Warfare (1925 Gas Protocol).
27 Art 8(2)(b)(xix), ICC Statute; 1899 Hague Declaration No III Concerning Expanding Bullets.
28 Art 8(2)(b)(xx), ICC Statute.
29 But see the relevant parts of the 1925 Gas Protocol and the 1972 Convention on the Prohibition of the Development, Production and Stockpiling of Bacteriological and Toxic Weapons and on their Destruction.

mines,[30] blinding laser weapons[31] and nuclear weapons. This policy of particular, as opposed to general, weapons prohibition is consistent with treaty and other State practice, as well as the ICJ's *Advisory Opinion on the Legality of the Threat or Use of Nuclear Weapons*. This Opinion, however, stressed the irreconcilable conflict, from a practical perspective, between the principles of discrimination and prohibition of unnecessary suffering on the one hand and the non-prohibition of inherently indiscriminate weapons.[32]

The rule expressed in Art 35(1) of the 1977 Protocol I that the choice of means and methods of war is not unlimited dates back many centuries. The acts concerned constitute war crimes only when committed against enemy combatants or civilians in occupied territory and not against the perpetrator's own forces. We shall confine ourselves to the ICC Statute list of prohibited means of combat war crimes, as follows: killing or wounding a combatant who has laid down his arms;[33] improper use of truce flags, insignia or the distinctive emblems of the Geneva Conventions;[34] undertaking physical mutilation or medical or scientific experiments not justified by the person's medical interests and which cause death or serious injury;[35] killing or wounding treacherously enemy personnel;[36] denial of quarter;[37] pillaging;[38] outrages upon personal dignity;[39] rape, sexual slavery, enforced prostitution, forced pregnancy, enforced sterilisation, or other forms of sexual violence;[40] using civilian populations as human shields or to immunise locations from attacks;[41] starvation of civilians or wilful impediment of supplies;[42] conscripting or enlisting children under the age of 15 into the armed forces or using them to participate actively in hostilities.[43]

---

30 Nonetheless, many States are parties to either the 1997 Ottawa Convention on the Prohibition of the Use, Stockpiling, Production and Transfer of Anti-Personnel Mines and on their Destruction, or the 1980 Protocol II on Prohibitions or Restrictions on the Use of Mines, Additional to the UN Convention on Prohibitions on the Use of Certain Conventional Weapons (CCW).

31 1995 CCW Protocol IV on Blinding Laser Weapons.

32 See Art 35, Protocol I (1977).

33 Art 8(2)(b)(vi), ICC Statute; Art 41(2)(b), Protocol I (1977).

34 Art 8(2)(b)(vii), ICC Statute; Art 39, Protocol I (1977), which does not, however, require that 'death or serious personal injury' ensue, as does the ICC Statute provision.

35 Art 8(2)(b)(x), ICC Statute; Art 32, Geneva Convention IV (1949); Art 11, Protocol I (1977).

36 Art 8(2)(b)(xi), ICC Statute; Art 37, Protocol I (1977).

37 Art 8(2)(b)(xii), ICC Statute; Art 40, Protocol I (1977).

38 Art 8(2)(b)(xvi), ICC Statute; Arts 28, 47, Hague Regulations (1907).

39 Art 8(2)(b)(xxi), ICC Statute.

40 Art 8(2)(b)(xxii), ICC Statute; Art 76(1), Protocol I (1977).

41 Art 8(2)(b)(xxiii), ICC Statute; Art 28, Geneva Convention IV (1907).

42 Art 8(2)(b)(xxv), ICC Statute; Art 55, Geneva Convention IV (1949); Art 54, Protocol I (1977).

43 Art 8(2)(b)(xxvi), ICC Statute; Art 77(2), Protocol I (1977); Art 38(2)–(3), 1989 Convention on the Rights of the Child.

The last category of war crimes involves no direct harm or personal injury to enemy combatants or civilian populations, but by abolishing fundamental rights such acts are capable of destroying the fabric of particular nations or communities. These include: the transfer by the occupying power, directly or indirectly, of its own civilian population into the territory it occupies, or the deportation or transfer of all or parts of the population of the occupied territory within or outside this territory;[44] declaring abolished, suspended or inadmissible in a court of law the rights and actions of the nationals of the hostile party;[45] compelling enemy nationals to take part in operations against their own country.[46]

5.4 VIOLATIONS OF THE LAWS OR CUSTOMS OF WAR IN INTERNAL CONFLICTS

Until the promulgation of Art 4 of the International Criminal Tribunal for Rwanda (ICTR) Statute in 1994 that criminalized violations committed in internal armed conflicts, this possibility was deemed contrary to the principle of non-interference and the case of Rwanda was considered somewhat exceptional. This view was even more reinforced by the fact that Art 3 of the ICTY Statute, a possible basis for internal armed conflict criminalization, was initially unclear as to this possibility. Although the title of Art 3 of the ICTY Statute, 'Violations of the laws or customs of war' suggests that the intention of its drafters was to limit this provision to the 1907 Hague Convention IV and the Regulations annexed to it, the Appeals Chamber in the *Tadic* jurisdiction decision held that Art 3 in fact covers all violations of international humanitarian law other than grave breaches. This therefore includes the 1907 Hague Convention, non-grave breaches provisions of the 1949 Geneva Conventions, violations of common Art 3 of the four Geneva Conventions, as well as other customary law applicable to internal conflicts and violations contained in agreements entered into by the parties to the conflict.[47] The implication of this construction of Art 3 of the ICTY Statute, which is nonetheless consistent with relevant Security Council deliberations, has been the recognition for the first time by an international judicial institution of individual criminal responsibility for offences committed in the context of non-international armed conflicts.

The *Tadic* Appeals Chamber did not hesitate to assert that violations of common Art 3 of the 1949 Geneva Conventions entail individual criminal responsibility under customary international law.[48] It is true, as categorically

44 Art 8(2)(b)(viii), ICC Statute; Art 49, Geneva Convention IV (1949).
45 Art 8(2)(b)(xiv), ICC Statute; Art 23(h), Hague Regulations (1907).
46 Art 8(2)(b)(xv), ICC Statute; Art 23(h), Hague Regulations (1907).
47 Op cit, *Tadic* Appeals Jurisdiction Decision, note 11, paras 87, 89.
48 Ibid, para 134.

noted by the ICJ, that the norms prescribed in common Art 3 constitute minimum considerations of humanity.[49] Similarly, the ICTY Appeals Chamber found at the time that customary international law prohibited all attacks against civilian objects and persons no longer taking part in hostilities, as well as certain means and methods of warfare applicable to internal armed conflicts.[50] Although the international community's concern over such issues seemingly violates the rule against interference in the domestic affairs of States, it is evident that a State sovereignty-oriented approach has been gradually superseded by a human being-oriented approach.[51] Notwithstanding this universal character of international humanitarian norms governing internal conflicts, it seems unlikely that there ever existed a customary rule entailing the penalisation of these norms under international law, especially since both common Art 3 and the 1977 Protocol II were drafted purposively, that is, as minimum humanitarian considerations whose criminal aspects and prosecution would be determined exclusively at the domestic level.[52] In fact, the drafting history of the 1949 Geneva Conventions demonstrates that ICRC proposals to apply the Conventions to non-international armed conflicts were almost unanimously rejected by participating delegates. The ICRC then proposed that Convention No IV (the Civilians Convention) be applied to internal conflicts in order to better protect civilians, but delegates noted the political and technical difficulties this would entail. The conference rejected a considerable number of alternative drafts and after much effort adopted common Art 3.[53] The aforementioned discussion seeks merely to highlight the fact that, contrary to the Appeals Chamber conclusion, customary international law had not until 1995 penalised violations of the laws or customs of war occurring in internal conflicts. This notwithstanding, it is undeniable that the pronouncement of such liability is laudable and is in fact now supported by a much larger number of States than prior to the establishment of the ICTY. Whatever the merits of the Appeals Chamber ruling on the criminal

---

49 *Nicaragua v USA*, Military and Paramilitary Activities in and Against Nicaragua (Merits) (1986) ICJ Reports 14, para 218.

50 Op cit, *Tadic* Appeals Jurisdiction Decision, note 11, para 127.

51 Ibid, para 97.

52 The view common among jurists is that by 1994 there was no such consensus at the interstate level. See D Plattner, 'The Penal Repression of Violations of International Humanitarian Law Applicable in Non-International Armed Conflicts', 20 *IRRC* (1990), 414; T Meron, 'The Case for War Crimes Trials in Yugoslavia' (1993 Summer) *Foreign Affairs*, 124, p 128; 'Letter dated 24 May 1994 from the Secretary General to the President of the Security Council', UN Doc S/1994/674 (1994), para 52, which reads: 'It must be observed that the violations of the law or customs of war . . . are offences when committed in international, but not in internal armed conflicts', in JV Mayfield, 'The Prosecution of War Crimes and Respect for Human Rights: Ethiopia's Balancing Act', 9 *Emory Int'l L Rev* (1995), 573.

53 See DE Elder, 'The Historical Background of Common Article 3 of the Geneva Conventions of 1949', 11 *Case W Res J Int'l L* (1979), 37.

nature of common Art 3 in October 1995, that decision has subsequently been relied upon as authoritative by both ICTY and ICTR Chambers;[54] it has influenced the national prosecution of common Art 3 offences committed abroad, and has culminated in the incorporation of an analogous and much more extensive provision in the Statute of the International Criminal Court (ICC).[55]

Under international law there exist two types of non-international armed conflicts: internal armed disputes of any kind attaining the threshold of armed conflicts (common Art 3 conflicts); and armed disputes under Art 1(1) of the 1977 Protocol II which require that rebels occupy a substantial part of territory, attain a sufficient degree of organisation, and hostilities reach a certain degree of intensity.[56] Although the 1977 Protocol II was purposely excluded from the ambit of the ICTY, it was expressly included in Art 4 of the ICTR Statute. The application of common Art 3 and Protocol II as criminal provisions is triggered by the cumulative existence of a non-international armed conflict, a link between the accused and the armed forces, the civilian nature of the victims, and a nexus between the crime and the armed conflict. The accused need not necessarily be a member of the armed forces, since 'individuals legitimately mandated and expected as public officials or agents or persons otherwise holding public authority or *de facto* representing the government in support of the war effort' are deemed to be sufficiently linked to the armed forces.[57] As for the victims, although the definition of 'civilian population' is usually given negatively as consisting of persons who are not members of the armed forces,[58] the concept of 'civilians' includes those accompanying armed forces, those who are either attached to them, or those who are among combatants engaged in hostilities.[59] In accordance with Art 13(3) of Protocol II, 'civilians' enjoy protection unless and for such time as they take a direct part in hostilities. 'Civilian populations' by their very nature are presumed not to take part in hostilities and are, therefore, entitled to general protection. In the *Kayishema* case, the ICTR ascertained the existence of a Protocol II type conflict between governmental Rwandan forces (FAR) and dissident armed forces (RPF). It found the RPF to be under the responsible command of General Kagame, to have exercised control over part of Rwanda and to have been able to carry out sustained and concerted

54 *ICTR Prosecutor v Akayesu*, Trial Chamber Judgment (2 Sept 1998), para 617.
55 Art 8(2)(c) and (e), ICC Statute.
56 See D Turns, 'War Crimes Without War? The Applicability of International Humanitarian Law to Atrocities in Non-International Armed Conflicts', 7 *RADIC* (1995), 804; HP Gasser, 'International Non-International Armed Conflicts: Case Studies of Afghanistan, Kampuchea and Lebanon', 31 *AmULRev* (1982), 911.
57 Op cit, *Akayesu* Trial Judgment, note 54, para 631; *ICTR Prosecutor v Kayishema and Ruzindana*, Trial Chamber Judgment (21 May 1999), para 175.
58 1977 Protocol I, Art 50.
59 Op cit, *Kayishema* Trial Judgment, note 57, para 180.

military action, as well as implement international humanitarian law.[60] It found, however, the Tutsi victims of the specific assault not to have been attacked by either the FAR or the RPF at the localities they sought refuge in Kibuye prefecture. It held the massacres to have been undertaken by civilian authorities as a result of an extermination campaign against the Tutsis, with no proof that either the victims or the offences against them were directly related to the conflict and thus concluded that Protocol II was inapplicable in that case.[61]

5.5 SPECIFIC INTERNAL ARMED CONFLICT WAR CRIMES

Having overcome the obstacle of international criminal liability in the context of international armed conflicts, one is concerned with the applicable crimes. A wholesale importation of grave breaches and other war crimes into the realm of non-international armed conflicts is precluded by the following considerations:

(a) treaty limitations, particularly the specific applicability of grave breaches to international conflicts. The same is true for the majority of pre-1995 treaties[62] or lack thereof, none of which categorically provides for criminal liability. Thus, reliance can only be placed on the existence of customary war crimes, or a revision of these treaties, or their re-interpretation by States – which would probably amount to a new custom anyway;

(b) the status of participants and the general legal context of international armed conflicts are determined solely by international law. In domestic conflicts these elements are determined to a very large degree by domestic law. Thus, in a domestic conflict, while government forces are obliged to treat members of the dissident group humanely, they may validly declare the dissident cause/struggle, and participation therein as a criminal offence, irrespective of whether dissident forces satisfy the four criteria of combatant status enunciated in Art 4 of Geneva Convention III. As a result, whereas such persons would be lawful combatants and benefit from prisoner of war (POW) status in international armed conflicts, they would not benefit from POW status while engaged in non-international conflicts. Thus, the largest part of Geneva Convention III (POW Convention) is automatically inapplicable to domestic conflicts.[63] Equally, the

---

60 Ibid, para 172.
61 Ibid, paras 602–03.
62 One notable exception is Art 1 of the 1993 Chemical Weapons Convention.
63 However, Rowe correctly suggests that due to the lack of combatant status in domestic armed conflicts, a member of a dissident group detained by his own side will benefit from the relevant provisions and any harm caused to him will be deemed a war crime. P Rowe, 'War Crimes', in D McGoldrick *et al*, *The Permanent International Criminal Court*, 2004, Oxford: Hart), 229.

international law of occupation cannot apply to government forces anywhere in the territory of the State;

(c) finally, dissident forces are unlikely to be able to establish lawfully constituted and impartial tribunals, because for reasons noted above they have
no authority to establish tribunals under domestic law. Equally, they
cannot occupy territory for the purposes of the law of occupation and as
such, for example, cannot commit the offence described in Art 49 of the
Geneva Convention IV (1949) of transferring their own populations to
change the demographics of a particular area.

The aforementioned considerations, therefore, severely restrict the importation of the whole range of international conflict war crimes into domestic
armed disputes. The drafters of the ICC Statute wisely balanced these realities with the need to protect all human beings from the calamities of war and
the corruption of authority where impunity is present. Much like other war
crimes, therefore, the ICC Statute recognises two types of internal armed
conflict war crimes, depending on their source in law:

(a) common Art 3 violations;[64] and
(b) 'other serious violations of the laws and customs' applicable to non-
international armed conflicts.[65]

As these two categories are meant to be exhaustive in their enumeration of
war crimes, it is sensible from a purely legal point of view that there are no
prohibited weapons provisions analogous to those applicable in international
conflicts. The other three categories are, nonetheless, present. Targeting
crimes comprise those in Art 8(2)(e), subparagraphs (i), (ii), (iii), (iv), while
means and methods of combat crimes include Art 8(2)(c), subparagraphs (i),
(ii), (iii), (e)(v), (e)(vi), (e)(vii), (e)(ix), (e)(x), (e)(xi), (e)(xii). Status of civilians
war crimes encompass the following: passing of sentences and executions
without previous judgment of a lawfully constituted court affording all
judicial guarantees;[66] ordering the displacement of the civilian population for
reasons related to the conflict, unless this is demanded by imperative military
necessity; and the security of the civilians.[67]

---

64 Art 8(2)(c), ICC Statute.
65 Art 8(2)(e), ICC Statute.
66 Art 8(2)(c)(iv), ICC Statute.
67 Art 8(2)(e)(vii), ICC Statute.

Chapter 6

Crimes against humanity

6.1 ORIGINS OF THE CONCEPT

The concept of crimes against humanity was first articulated as an international offence in Art 6(c) of the Charter of the Nuremberg Tribunal in 1945.[1] This read as follows:

> Crimes against Humanity: namely, murder, extermination, enslavement, deportation, and other inhuman acts committed against any civilian population, before or during the war, or persecutions on political, racial or religious grounds in execution of, or in connection with, any other crime within the jurisdiction of the Tribunal, whether or not in violation of the domestic law of the country where perpetrated.

Prior to the Nuremberg Charter, reference to the laws of humanity and the dictates of public conscience was expressly made in the preamble to the 1907 Hague Convention IV – otherwise known as the Martens clause – the aim of which was to extend additional protection to both combatants and civilian populations where the law was silent or in development, until such time as more comprehensive rules were adopted. Following the massacre of at least 1.5 million Armenian civilians under the orders of what was then the Ottoman Empire, the governments of Great Britain, France and Russia issued a declaration denouncing the atrocities as 'crimes against humanity and civilisation', further noting the criminal culpability of all members of the Turkish Government and its agents.[2] This formulation, however, was not the result of normative considerations and the initial proposal was to

---

1 1945 Agreement for the Prosecution and Punishment of the Major War Criminals of the European Axis, 82 UNTS 279. See E Schwelb, 'Crimes Against Humanity', 23 BYIL (1946), 178; B Van Schaack, 'The Definition of Crimes Against Humanity: Resolving the Incoherence', 37 *Columbia J Trans L* (1999), 787.
2 R Clark, 'Crimes Against Humanity at Nuremberg', in G Ginsburg, VN Kudriavtsev (eds), *The Nuremberg Trial in International Law*, 1990, Dordrecht: Martinus Nijhoff, 177.

treat the offences as 'crimes against Christianity', to which France objected on the grounds that it would offend the Muslim subjects of France and Britain. The 1920 Peace Treaty of Sevres which made provision for the trial of those Turkish officials responsible for violating the laws and customs of war and of engaging in the Armenian massacres during the war, but excluding reference to the 'laws of humanity',[3] was superseded by the 1923 Treaty of Lausanne which contained a declaration of amnesty for all offences committed between 1914 and 1922.[4] However, as Cherif Bassiouni points out, the political motivations behind this compromise could not disguise the fact that amnesties are only granted for crimes, which even if not prosecuted does not negate their legal existence.[5] It is true, nonetheless, that up to that point the term 'humanity' and its link to 'crime' had no fixed legal meaning.

Immediately upon conclusion of the First World War, the Allied and Associated Powers established in 1919 a Commission on the Responsibility of the Authors of the War and Enforcement of Penalties.[6] The majority of the Commission supported the establishment of a tribunal with criminal jurisdiction over all persons belonging to enemy countries that were found to have violated the laws of war or the laws of humanity.[7] US dissent over the precision and uncertain scope of the term 'laws of humanity' prevailed against endorsing the Commission's position, and so the 1919 Peace Treaty of Versailles excluded reference to crimes against humanity.[8] The rationale for constructing this particular international offence stems from the aftermath of the Second World War whereupon the victorious nations came to the realisation that international law did not protect the nationals of a State from the excesses of its government and its agents. Thus, although international humanitarian law protected enemy civilians and combatants and treated offences against them as war crimes, such protection was missing with regard to persecuted German citizens, such as Jews, gypsies, members of the church and others. The introduction of the new offence was meant to remedy this lack of protection. The offence, however, was restricted by the fact that a

---

3 Treaty of Peace between the Allied Powers and Turkey (Treaty of Sevres), Arts 226, 230, reprinted in 15 *AJIL* (1921 Supp), 179.
4 Treaty of Peace between the Allied Powers and Turkey (Treaty of Lausanne), 28 LNTS 12.
5 CM Bassiouni, *Crimes Against Humanity in International Criminal Law*, 1992, Dordrecht: Martinus Nijhoff, 175–76.
6 Commission on the Responsibility of the Authors of the War and on Enforcement of Penalties, *Report Presented to the Preliminary Peace Conference, Versailles, 29 March 1919*, reprinted in 14 *AJIL* (1920), 95.
7 'All persons belonging to enemy countries, however high their position may have been, without distinction or rank, including Chiefs of Staff, who have been guilty of offences against the laws and customs of war or the laws of humanity, are liable to criminal prosecution.' Ibid, p 123.
8 2 Bevans 43

link was required with armed conflict and any of the other two offences (ie, war crimes and crimes against peace) in the Tribunal's Statute. These limitations have since been lifted in both treaty and customary law.

Until the establishment of the International Criminal Tribunal for the former Yugoslavia (ICTY) in 1993 and the incorporation therein of Art 5 no other international definition of crimes against humanity reappeared since the Nuremberg Statute.[9] Nonetheless, a number of national prosecutions did take place through the use of domestic statutes, which, although influenced by the Nuremberg articulation, proved to be significant factors in the gradual development of the concept of crimes against humanity.[10]

6.2 THE FUNDAMENTAL ELEMENTS OF THE OFFENCE

The crime against humanity provision in the ICTY Statute, Art 5, was the first post-Cold War international normative formulation of the offence. The relevant ICTY and International Criminal Tribunal for Rwanda (ICTR) jurisprudence has been largely responsible for its rapid evolution and detailed elaboration. In the present section of this chapter we shall confine our analysis to the ad hoc tribunals' articulation of the offence, and in the latter part of the chapter we shall analyse the particularities of the International Criminal Court (ICC) definition.

Article 5 of the ICTY Statute encompasses offences committed in armed

---

9 Unlike the Nuremberg Charter, Control Council Law No 10, enacted by the Allied Control Council for Germany (hence, it did not have the attributes of a treaty), excluded the requirement that crimes against humanity be committed in execution of or in connection with war crimes or crimes against peace. While some military tribunals entertaining cases pursuant to Control Council Law No 10 accepted that crimes against humanity could also be committed in time of peace, others did not. See WJ Fenrick, 'Should Crimes Against Humanity Replace War Crimes?', 37 *Columbia J Trans L* (1999), 767, p 775; both the 1968 UN Convention on the Non-Applicability of Statutory Limitations to War Crimes and Crimes Against Humanity, 754 UNTS 73, as well as the 1974 European Convention on the Non-Applicability of Statutory Limitations to Crimes Against Humanity and War Crimes, ETS 82, 13 ILM (1974), 540, referred to the definitions of the Nuremberg Charter and the 1948 Genocide Convention respectively.

10 In the *Barbie* case, French Court of Cassation Judgment (1988) 100 ILR 330, pp 332, 336, the accused, who was the Head of the Gestapo in Lyon from 1942 to 1944, was convicted of crimes against humanity for his role in the deportation and extermination of Jewish civilians. The court held that the definition of crimes against humanity within the meaning of the Nuremberg definition consisted of enumerated inhumane acts against civilians 'performed in a systematic manner in the name of the State practising by those means a policy of ideological supremacy'; see also *Touvier* case, French Court of Cassation Judgment (1992) 100 ILR 337, and *R v Finta*, Canadian Supreme Court Judgment (1994) 104 ILR 284.

conflict, whether international or internal in character, being part of an overall attack against any civilian population. Hence, the five elements that comprise this offence under the ICTY Statute are:

(a) existence of an attack;
(b) the perpetrator's acts must be part of the attack;
(c) the attack must be directed against any civilian population;
(d) the attack must be widespread or systematic; and
(e) the perpetrator must know of the wider context in which his acts occur and know that his acts are part of the attack.

It is obvious that the ICTY definition has retained the armed conflict nexus of the Nuremberg Charter, but has accepted jurisdiction irrespective of the nature of the conflict. Furthermore, there exists no requirement, unlike Art 6(c) of the Nuremberg Charter, that crimes against humanity be connected to any other offences. The ICTY Appeals Chamber in the *Tadic* case held that Art 5 was narrower than customary international law, which no longer requires any nexus to armed conflict.[11] This aspect of customary law (that is, the absence of a nexus to armed conflict) is reflected in Art 3 of the ICTR Statute, which, however, requires the existence of a discriminatory intent on national, political, ethnic, racial or religious grounds. Discriminatory intent in Art 5 of the ICTY Statute is required only with regard to the specific offence of persecution.

Article 3 of the ICTR Statute further qualifies an attack as a crime against humanity when it is perpetrated in either widespread or systematic fashion. This last element requiring a 'widespread or systematic' attack, although not expressly articulated in Art 5 of the ICTY Statute, follows the customary definition of crimes against humanity and was early elaborated by ICTY Chambers.[12] The concept of 'attack' in the definition of crimes against humanity is significantly broader than that used in the context of the laws of war, and particularly Art 49(1) of the 1977 Additional Protocol I, since it 'may also encompass situations of mistreatment of persons taking no active part in hostilities, such as someone in detention'.[13] The underlying offence does not need to constitute an attack (ie, it need not be widespread or systematic), but must form part of, or be linked with the attack, which itself is the crime against humanity.[14] An 'attack' is therefore an accumulation

---

11 *ICTY Prosecutor v Tadic*, Appeals Jurisdiction Decision (2 Oct 1995), paras 140–41.
12 *ICTY Prosecutor v Nikolic*, R 61 Decision (20 Oct 1995), para 26.
13 *ICTY Prosecutor v Kunarac and Others*, Trial Chamber Judgment (22 Feb 2001), para 416.
14 *ICTY Prosecutor v Mrksic (Vukovar Hospital)*, R 61 Decision (3 April 1996), para 30; *ICTY Prosecutor v Tadic*, Appeals Judgment (15 July 1999), para 248; *ICTY Prosecutor v Kunarac*, Appeals Judgment (12 June 2002), para. 96; *ICTY Prosecutor v Blaskic*, Appeals Judgment (29 July 2004), para 102.

of various crimes which may be perpetrated in different times and places, the sum total of all reflecting a clear widespread or systematic nature. In terms of ICTY temporal jurisdiction, although the attack must be part of the armed conflict, it can outlast it.[15] The list of offences which may constitute an 'attack' under the concept of crimes against humanity in the ICTY and ICTR Statutes is both exhaustive and identical. They comprise of the following:

(a) murder;[16]
(b) extermination;[17]
(c) enslavement;[18]
(d) deportation;[19]
(e) imprisonment;[20]
(f) torture;[21]
(g) rape;[22]

15 Op cit, *Kunarac* Trial Judgment, note 13, para 420.
16 The ICTY jurisprudence requires: (a) the victim to have died; (b) his death to be caused by an act or omission of the accused, or of a person or persons for whose acts or omissions the accused bears criminal responsibility, and; (c) the act was done, or the omission was made, by the accused, or by a person or persons for whose acts or omissions the accused bears criminal responsibility, with an intention: (i) to kill, or (ii) to inflict serious injury, in reckless disregard of human life. See *ICTY Prosecutor v Delalic et al* (*Celebici* case) Trial Judgment (16 Nov 1998), para 439.
17 Extermination may be defined as 'killing on a large scale', which includes 'subjecting a widespread number of people, or systematically subjecting a number of people to conditions of living that would inevitably lead to death. Equally, the *mens rea* for extermination requires the intent to kill on a large scale or to systematically subject a large number of people to conditions of life that would lead to their deaths. See *ICTR Prosecutor v Ntakirutimana*, Appeals Chamber Judgment (13 Dec 2004), paras 516, 522; *ICTY Prosecutor v Stakic*, Appeals Chamber Judgment (22 March 2006), paras 259–60.
18 Enslavement consists of the intentional exercise of any, or all, powers of ownership over a person. See *ICTY Prosecutor v Krnojelac*, Trial Chamber Judgment (15 March 2002), para 350.
19 Deportation means 'the forced displacement of persons by expulsion or other forms of coercion from the area in which they are lawfully present, across a *de jure* State border or, in certain circumstances, a *de facto* border, without grounds permitted under international law'. There is no requirement that the perpetrator intend a permanent displacement. See op cit, *Stakic* Appeals Judgment, note 17, para 278. On the other hand, 'forcible transfer' refers to displacement but within national boundaries and can be classified under 'other inhumane acts'.
20 The ICTY jurisprudence has found the following elements as essential for a finding of the crime of imprisonment: (a) deprivation of liberty; (b) such deprivation is imposed arbitrarily, that is without any legal justification; (c) the act or omission leading to such deprivation of physical liberty is performed with the intent to deprive one arbitrarily of his or her physical liberty, or in the reasonable knowledge that his act or omission is likely to cause arbitrary deprivation of physical liberty. See op cit, *Krnojelac* Trial Judgment, note 18, para 15.
21 See Chapter 8.
22 See Chapter 19, section 20.3.2.

(h) persecutions on political, racial and religious grounds;[23]
(i) other inhumane acts.[24]

6.2.1 The widespread or systematic element

As already observed, the offences enumerated above constitute crimes against humanity when they are perpetrated against any civilian population in a widespread or systematic manner. Evidence of either a 'widespread' or 'systematic' element suffices, although in practice it will not be unusual for both to co-exist. International law requires – with the exception of Art 7 ICC Statute – that only the overall attack, and not the underlying offences, be widespread or systematic. This means that a single offence could be regarded as a crime against humanity if it takes place under the umbrella of a widespread or systematic attack against a civilian population.[25]

The *Blaskic* judgment held that the term 'systematic' requires the following ingredients:

(a) the existence of a political objective, a plan pursuant to which the attack is perpetrated or an ideology that aims to destroy, persecute or weaken a community;
(b) the perpetration of a crime on a large scale against a civilian group, or the repeated and continuous commission of inhumane acts linked to one another;
(c) the preparation and use of significant public or private resources, whether military or other; and
(d) the implication of high-level political and/or military authorities in the definition and establishment of the plan.[26]

The *Akayesu* judgment defined a systematic attack as one that is 'thoroughly

---

23 The *actus reus* of persecution in the ICTY jurisprudence consists of an act or omission that discriminates in fact and which denies or infringes upon a fundamental right laid down in international customary or treaty law. The *mens rea* requires that the act was carried out deliberately with the intention to discriminate on the basis of religion, race or politics. See op cit, *Blaskic* Appeals Judgment, note 14, para 131.
24 These were designed deliberately as a residual category whose exhaustive enumeration would create opportunities for evasion. Inhumane acts as a crime against humanity must satisfy the following conditions: (a) the victim must have suffered serious bodily or mental harm; (b) the suffering must be the result of an act or omission of the accused or his subordinate, and; (c) when the offence was committed, the accused or his subordinate must have been motivated by the intent to inflict serious bodily harm or mental harm upon the victim. See *ICTY Prosecutor v Kordic and Cerkez*, Appeals Chamber Judgment (17 Dec 2004), para 117.
25 *ICTY Prosecutor v Kupreskic*, Trial Chamber Judgment (14 Jan 2000), para 550; op cit, *Kunarac* Trial Judgment, note 13, para 431.
26 *ICTY Prosecutor v Blaskic*, Trial Chamber Judgment (3 March 2000), para 203; *ICTY Prosecutor v Kordic and Cerkez*, Trial Chamber Judgment (26 February 2001), para 179.

organised and following a regular pattern on the basis of a common policy involving substantial public or private resources'.[27] Unlike the French *Cassation* judgments, the ICTR affirmed that there is no requirement that such policy be formally adopted as the policy of the State.[28] Moreover, the existence of a plan does not have to be expressly declared, nor clearly and precisely stated, in order to prove the 'systematic' element of crimes against humanity, although if such is found it will be useful from an evidentiary point of view.[29] This does not mean that crimes against humanity may be the work of private individuals acting alone, but they can be orchestrated and executed also by organised non-State entities.[30] This was the conclusion reached by an ICTY Trial Chamber in its r 61 Review of the evidence against the leader of the Bosnian Serbs, Radovan Karadzic. The ICTY ascertained the existence of a policy of 'ethnic cleansing' as consisting of a systematic separation of non-Serbian men and women with subsequent internment in detention facilities, extensive damage to sacred symbols with intent to eradicate them, shelling of Sarajevo in order to expel non-Serbian residents, and establishment of camps devoted to rape, enforced pregnancy and enforced prostitution of non-Serbian women. The purpose of these camps and the policy of sexual assaults in general was found to be the displacement of civilians and the incurring of shame and humiliation to the victims and their communities, thus forcing them to leave.[31] As evidence of plans of this nature will seldom be retrieved in writing, it suffices if such planning can be inferred from relevant circumstances, even if not expressly declared or stated clearly and precisely. Such circumstances include the overall prevailing political background, the general content of a political programme, the role of the media and incendiary propaganda, intentional alterations to ethnic compositions, the imposition of discriminatory measures and the scale of acts of violence.[32] Since the concept of crimes against humanity refers not to a particular act but to a 'course of conduct', a single act may constitute a crime against humanity when the

---

27 *ICTR Prosecutor v Akayesu*, Trial Chamber Judgment (2 Sept 1998), para 580.

28 Ibid; op cit, *Nikolic*, R 61 Decision, note 12, para 26; op cit, *Kupreskic* Trial Judgment, note 25, para 551.

29 Op cit, *Blaskic* Trial Judgment, note 26, para 204; op cit, *Kordic and Cerkez* Trial Judgment, note 26, para 181; op cit, *Kunarac* Appeals Judgment, note 14, para 98; op cit, *Blaskic* Appeals Judgment, note 14, para 120.

30 ILC Report, *Draft Code of Crimes Against the Peace and Security of Mankind*, UN Doc A/51/10 (1996) Supp No 10, p 94; in *ICTR Prosecutor v Kayishema*, Trial Chamber Judgment (21 May 1999), para 125, the ICTR convicted the accused Ruzindana, a local businessman, of crimes against humanity because he partook in the overall Hutu extremist policy to exterminate the minority Tutsis.

31 *ICTY Prosecutor v Karadzic and Mladic*, R 61 Decision (11 July 1996), paras 60–64.

32 Op cit, *Blaskic* Trial Judgment, note 26, para 204; *ICTY Prosecutor v Jelisic*, Trial Chamber Judgment (14 Dec 1999), para 53.

perpetrator has the requisite *mens rea* and the offence is part of either a widespread or systematic attack against a civilian population.[33]

6.2.2 The nature of the targeted 'civilian population'

The 'widespread' element of crimes against humanity is probably easier to substantiate, as it necessarily refers to the scale of the acts perpetrated and the number of victims.[34] The *Akayesu* judgment defined the element of 'widespread' as 'massive, frequent, large scale action, carried out collectively with considerable seriousness and directed against a multiplicity of victims'.[35] The status and nature of the civilian population that is the target of an attack is also very important, since it is this which differentiates crimes against humanity from random attacks against civilian populations without any defining characteristics in the mind of the attacker. Civilian populations, defined generally as people not taking an active part in hostilities, can never become legitimate objects of attack. The *Kunarac* Appeals Judgment further elaborated on the fact that an attack could still be classified as systematic even where some members of the civilian population were not targeted, by stating that:

> . . . the use of the word 'population' does not mean that the entire population of the geographical entity in which the attack is taking place must have been subjected to that attack. It is sufficient to show that enough individuals were targeted in the course of the attack, or that they were targeted in such a way as to satisfy the Chamber that the attack was in fact directed against a civilian 'population', rather than against a limited and randomly selected number of individuals.[36]

Possible presence of non-civilians in such populations does not deprive them of their civilian character,[37] provided that these are not regular units with fairly large numbers.[38] The general approach in the ICTY has been to construe the term 'civilian population' broadly, encompassing persons who have been involved in resistance movements and also former combatants who no longer take part in hostilities at the time the attack against the civilian population took place, either because they had left their units, no longer bore

---

33 Op cit, *Kupreskic* Trial Judgment, note 25, para 550.
34 Op cit, *Blaskic* Trial Judgment, note 26, para 206.
35 Op cit, *Akayesu* Trial Judgment, note 27, para 580.
36 Op cit, *Kunarac* Appeals Judgment, note 14, para 90.
37 1977 Protocol I, Art 50. See C Pilloud *et al* (eds), *Commentary on the Additional Protocols of 8 June 1977 to the Geneva Conventions of 12 August 1949* (ICRC, 1987), para 1922; affirmed in op cit, *Akayesu* Trial Judgment, note 27, para 582.
38 *ICRC Commentary*, ibid; op cit, *Blaskic* Appeals Judgment, note 14, para 116.

arms, or because they had been rendered *hors de combat*.[39] This is certainly the contemporary position in customary international law, which itself is reflected in Art 7 of the ICC Statute. Nonetheless, the *Blaskic* Appeals Judgment placed a very logical limitation to the broad construction of civilian populations for the purposes of crimes against humanity. The Trial Chamber had wrongly suggested that the assessment of civilian status depends on the 'specific situation of the victim at the moment the crimes were committed, rather than his status'.[40] The implication of this suggestion is that a combatant under Art 4(A) of Geneva Convention III and Art 50 of Protocol I (1977) switches to a civilian every time he is not engaged in actual active combat (eg, at sleep, dinner, breaks, etc). The Appeals Chamber expressly refuted this suggestion, adding that if a person is 'indeed a member of an armed organisation, the fact that he is not armed or in combat at the time of the commission of crimes does not accord him civilian status'.[41] Unlike the Nuremberg definition which required that the civilian population be composed of nationals or allies of the offending State, the contemporary stance is that – and given that the ICC Statute no longer requires any link to an armed conflict – crimes against humanity may be committed against all civilian populations (whether nationals or non-nationals).

6.2.3 The subjective element

Crimes against humanity differ from other war crimes from the fact that their perpetrators are engaging in particular unlawful acts with the knowledge and approval that such acts are committed on a widespread scale or based on a policy against a specific civilian population. Hence, it is the knowledge of the 'overall context' within which an underlying crime is committed that makes a perpetrator criminally liable for a crime against humanity, combined with his intent to contribute thereof through the commission of an underlying crime. It is the widespread or the policy elements that establish this overall context and not the perpetrator personally through multiple acts of violence, and hence the perpetrator need not share or be identified with the ideology or plan that supports the attack against the targeted population. The *Kunarac* Appeals Judgment succinctly stated that:

> It is irrelevant whether the accused intended his acts to be directed against the targeted population or merely against his victim. It is the attack, not the acts of the accused, which must be directed against the

---

39 Op cit, *Vukovar Hospital* R 61 Decision, note 14, paras 29–32; op cit, *Blaskic* Trial Judgment, note 26, paras 210, 216; op cit, *Kayishema* Trial Judgment, note 30, para 127.
40 Op cit, *Blaskic* Trial Judgment, note 26, para 214.
41 Op cit, *Blaskic* Appeals Judgment, note 14, para 114.

target population and the accused need only know that his acts are part thereof.[42]

Therefore, as explained above, a single unlawful act perpetrated with the knowledge that it is part of an overall attack against a civilian population constitutes a crime against humanity. In the *Jelisic* case, the accused was the commandant of a Bosnian Serb POW camp in Brcko. He was eventually convicted of serious offences against prisoners and other detainees amounting to crimes against humanity. The ICTY Trial Chamber inferred Jelisic's knowledge of a Bosnian Serb policy of annihilation of non-Serb populations in the Brcko area on the basis of his appointment to the Brcko camp and his active participation in the operations against Moslems in the region.[43]

As already observed, a discriminatory intent is required in the definition of crimes against humanity contained in the ICTR Statute, but not in the ICTY Statute. Both provisions, however, include 'persecution' as an offence capable of producing crimes against humanity. This is triggered by the existence of a widespread or systematic attack against a civilian population, gross or blatant denial of a fundamental right reaching the same level of gravity as other acts contained in Arts 5 and 3 of the ICTY and ICTR Statutes, respectively, and the imposition of discriminatory grounds. The *Kurpeskic* judgment held that the *actus reus* for persecution in the ICTY Statute does not require a link to crimes enumerated elsewhere in the Statute, but being a broad offence its definition may encompass crimes not listed in the Statute. However, there must be 'clearly defined limits on the expansion of the types of acts which qualify as persecution'.[44] *Mens rea* for the particular act of persecution is higher than ordinary offences falling within the ambit of crimes against humanity, but lower than genocide. In the crime of persecution the discriminatory intent may take many inhumane forms, while in genocide it must strictly be accompanied by the specific intent (*dolus specialis*) for genocide, that is, to destroy in whole or in part a specific group.[45]

6.3 CRIMES AGAINST HUMANITY IN THE ICC STATUTE

The definition of this offence under Art 7 is different in a number of respects from that found in the statutes of the ICTY and ICTR, as a result of a compromise in accommodating varying demands regarding the threshold

---

42 Op cit, *Kunarac* Appeals Judgment, note 14, para 103.
43 Op cit, *Jelisic* Trial Judgment, note 32, para 57.
44 Op cit, *Kupreskic* Trial Judgment, note 25, paras 581, 618; op cit, *Kordic and Cerkez* Trial Judgment, note 26, paras 193–94.
45 See *Kupreskic* Trial Judgment, ibid, paras 627, 636.

standard for this offence. The general threshold for crimes against humanity is set out in Art 7(1), comprising any act contained in an exhaustive list of offences when committed 'as part of a widespread or systematic attack' against any civilian population. Up to this point the definition is identical to the jurisprudence of the ad hoc Tribunals. However, since it was agreed by all participants at the Rome Conference that not every inhumane act should amount to a crime against humanity, the concept of an 'attack' in the ICC Statute is elaborated in Art 7(2)(a), meaning a 'course of conduct involving the multiple commission of acts pursuant to or in furtherance of a State or organisational policy to commit such attack'. To substantiate a charge of crime against humanity, the prosecutor would have to demonstrate that an attack against a civilian population involves multiple crimes, all of which are themselves widespread or systematic, in addition to the requirement that the overall attack be widespread or systematic.[46] The *mens rea* for crimes against humanity in Art 7(1) requires that the perpetrator act with knowledge that his or her particular underlying offence was part of an overall widespread or systematic attack against a civilian population. While the perpetrator must be aware of the overall attack, it is also necessary that the elements of the particular offence be proven. For example, a person killing two civilians from group A is guilty of a crime against humanity only if it can be proven that the *mens rea* elements for the offences of extermination or murder have been satisfied and also that either of these offences was committed with the knowledge that group A was specifically targeted by the perpetrator's affiliate organisation. It must also be demonstrated that the murders and exterminations were themselves either widespread or systematic. Likewise, and following the jurisprudence of the ad hoc tribunals, crimes against humanity can be committed by State entities and their agents, as well as by non-State entities. However, unlike the ICTY and ICTR Statute, Art 7 of the ICC Statute does not require a nexus to an armed conflict, or a discriminatory intent.

The list of offences included in Art 7 comprises certain acts which had in the past received recognition as crimes against humanity and whose status was reaffirmed in the ICC Statute as depicting customary law. Of particular significance are the offences of 'apartheid' and 'enforced disappearance', both of which have been identified as crimes against humanity in earlier instruments. 'Apartheid' is defined in Art 7(2)(h) as:

> . . . inhumane acts [intentionally causing great suffering, or serious injury to body or to mental health] committed in the context of an institutionalised regime of systematic oppression and domination by one racial group

---

46 D Robinson, 'Defining Crimes Against Humanity at the Rome Conference', 93 *AJIL* (1999), 43, p 51.

over any other racial group or groups and committed with the intention of maintaining that regime.

This definition and characterisation as a crime against humanity is consistent with Art I of the 1973 Convention on the Prevention and Suppression of Apartheid,[47] as well as Art 1(b) of the 1968 Convention on the Non-Applicability of Statutory Limitations to War Crimes and Crimes Against Humanity. Although apartheid could, and does in the context of the ICC, fall within the ambit of 'inhumane acts' of Art 7(1)(k), it was purposely included as an individual offence in order to reaffirm universal condemnation of this practice.[48] Similarly, the enumeration of 'enforced disappearances', reflecting policies exercised mainly by South American dictatorial regimes, echoes vociferous condemnation already found in international instruments and the case law of international human rights judicial organs.[49] It is defined in Art 7(2)(i) as:

> . . . the arrest, detention or abduction of persons by or with the author-isation, support or acquiescence of, a State or a political organisation, followed by a refusal to acknowledge that deprivation of freedom or to give information on the fate or whereabouts of those persons, with the intention of removing them from the protection of the law for a pro-longed period of time.

The inclusion of 'persecution' in the list of enumerated acts contained in Art 7 of the ICC Statute follows well-established precedent stemming from both Nuremberg and the ad hoc tribunals. It is defined, however, for the first time in para 2(g) as the 'intentional and severe deprivation of fundamental rights contrary to international law by reason of the identity of the group or collectivity'. Many delegates at the Rome conference expressed concern that this provision could be used to criminalise all forms of discrimination. To alleviate such fears it was finally agreed that persecution as a crime against humanity in the ICC context refers only to extreme forms of discrimination with a clearly criminal character. Furthermore, persecution can only be

---

47 1015 UNTS 243.
48 See RC Slye, 'Apartheid as a Crime Against Humanity: A Submission to the South African Truth and Reconciliation Commission', 20 *Mich J Int'l L* (1999), 267.
49 *Velasquez Rodriguez* case (Merits) (29 July 1988) (1994) 95 ILR 232; UN Human Rights Committee, General Comment No 20, regarding ICCPR, Art 7, para 15, UN Doc CCPR/C/21/Rev 1/Add 3 (7 April 1992); see GA Res 47/133 (18 Dec 1992), entitled Declaration on the Protection of all Persons from Enforced Disappearances; the preamble to the 1994 Inter-American Convention on the Forced Disappearance of Persons affirms that the systematic practice of forced disappearances constitutes a crime against humanity. Reprinted in 33 ILM (1994), 1259.

characterised as a crime against humanity if it is connected to any of the other 10 enumerated acts articulated in Art 7 or any other offence within the Court's jurisdiction (that is, war crimes, genocide, or aggression), notwithstanding that such nexus is required neither by the ICTY and ICTR, nor customary law.[50] There is no need to prove that the connected acts themselves were committed on a widespread or systematic scale; however, if found to be connected to severe criminal persecution, this, in effect, furnishes evidence of either widespread crimes or a particular policy. The ICC Statute includes 'political, racial, national, ethnic, cultural, religious and gender' in its list of discriminatory grounds, as well as 'other grounds that are universally recognised as impermissible under international law'.[51] The latter, although an open-ended sub-provision, introduces a high threshold category of acts, whose existence the Court can ascertain only if they are clearly established under the competent sources of international law.

The ambit of offences of a sexual nature comprising crimes against humanity has been considerably expanded in comparison to the ICTY and ICTR, including besides rape, 'sexual slavery, enforced prostitution, forced pregnancy, enforced sterilisation, or any other form of sexual violence of comparable gravity'.[52] Fears from western countries that reference to 'forced pregnancy' might be interpreted as affecting national laws relating to the right to life of the unborn or that of a mother regarding the termination of her pregnancy were removed with the addition of para 2(f). Similarly, to allay concern of Moslem countries that the definition of torture might affect their practice of corporal punishment, para 2(e) excludes pain or suffering arising from lawful sanctions.

---

50 Op cit, Robinson, note 46, pp 53–55.
51 ICC Statute, Art 7(1)(h). The term 'gender' in Art 7(3) refers to 'the two sexes, male and female, within the context of society'. The inclusion of gender-related crimes acknowledges the distinction between sex and gender, the latter referring to socially constructed rather than biological differences. See *Report of the Secretary General on Integrating the Human Rights of Women throughout the UN System*, UN Doc E/CN4/1997/40 (1996), para 10.
52 Art 7(1)(g), ICC Statute.

Chapter 7

Genocide

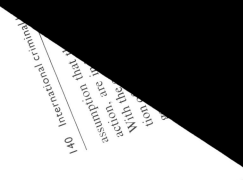

7.1 HISTORICAL ORIGINS AND LEGAL S̄

Genocide has been described as the 'ultimate crime'.[1] Although the Armenian massacre of 1915 did not result in any serious criminal proceedings,[2] revulsion caused by the Jewish Holocaust eventually led to the adoption in 1948 of the Genocide Convention.[3] Although the acts covered by the Genocide Convention could be encompassed under the definition of crimes against humanity, there was a compelling reason, not necessarily related to any imperative legal justification, for the two offences to be differentiated. The drafters of the crime of genocide wanted to emphasise the particular gravity of targeting members of a specific group with a view to their intentional physical or biological extermination. Emphasis is therefore on the destruction of the group, whereas the victimisation of group members in their individual capacities takes second place.

The prohibition of genocide as a matter of *jus cogens* has been confirmed by the International Court of Justice (ICJ),[4] as has the non-contractual character of the 1948 Genocide Convention, that is, its capacity in creating obligations even vis-à-vis non-affected States (*erga omnes* obligations) – that is, States whose nationals are not victims of genocide – on the basis of its compelling humanitarian nature.[5] The only two effective means of enforcing the *erga omnes* obligation arising from the prohibition of genocide, on the

1 P Akhavan, 'Enforcement of the Genocide Convention: A Challenge to Civilization', 8 *Harvard Human Rights Journal* (1995), 229.
2 VN Dadrian, 'Genocide as a Problem of National and International Law: The World War I Armenian Case and its Contemporary Legal Ramifications', 14 *Yale J Int'l L* (1989), 221.
3 78 UNTS 277.
4 *Advisory Opinion Concerning Reservations to the Genocide Convention* (1951) ICJ Reports 15, p 23; *Belgium v Spain, Barcelona Traction Light and Power House Co Ltd* (*Barcelona Traction* case) (1970) ICJ Reports 3, Second Phase.
5 *Barcelona Traction* case, ibid, p 32, paras 33–34. See R Provost, 'Reciprocity in Human Rights and Humanitarian Law', 65 *BYIL* (1994), 383.

the State engaged in it will take neither legal nor material ...dividual or collective use of force, and interstate litigation.[6] ...exception of the Vietnamese invasion of Cambodia and the convic-... ...f former Prime Minister Pol Pot by a people's revolutionary tribunal of ...enocide *in absentia*, there have been no other cases of humanitarian intervention in order to suppress the occurrence of genocide,[7] even though a rapporteur of the UN Sub-Commission on Prevention of Discrimination and Protection of Minorities pointed out in his 1985 report on genocide that a significant number of genocidal incidents had taken place after 1945; namely, the Hutu massacres by Tutsis in Burundi in 1965 and 1972, the 1974 Paraguayan eradication campaign of the Ache Indians, the Khmer Rouge massacres in Cambodia in 1975 and 1978 as well as the extermination of Baha'is in Iran – although in the case of the Baha'is their persecution commenced in the mid-19th century when they were first established as a religious minority.[8]

The contentious jurisdiction of the ICJ, even if one assumes that such consent would exist in each case, offers little help to the victims of an ongoing genocide, irrespective of the severity of provisional measures ordered, and can at best serve to determine the existence of a genocidal plan or action for the purposes of State responsibility or its use in subsequent criminal proceedings. This has been illustrated in the case brought by the Republic of Bosnia and Herzegovina against the Federal Republic of Yugoslavia (FRY) in 1993 on charges of genocide, which continued to persist – at least in the form of acute persecution against Bosnian Muslims – despite the ICJ's imposition of interim measures.[9] Notwithstanding these incidents of genocide, to date no non-affected State has held another accountable before the ICJ, thus failing to give substance to the Genocide Convention's *erga omnes* nature.

7.2 DESTRUCTION OF THE GROUP 'IN WHOLE OR IN PART'

The definitions of genocide and enumeration of punishable acts under Arts 2 and 4 of the International Criminal Tribunal for Rwanda (ICTR) and International Criminal Tribunal for the former Yugoslavia (ICTY) Statutes,

---

6 See L Kuper, *The Prevention of Genocide*, 1985, New Haven, London: Yale UP.
7 See H Hannum, 'International Law and Cambodian Genocide: The Sounds of Silence' 11 *HRQ* (1989), 82.
8 Question of the Prevention and Punishment of the Crime of Genocide, UN Doc E/CN4/Sub2/1985/6 (1985), p 9.
9 *Bosnia and Herzegovina v FRY*, 'Case Concerning Application of the Convention on the Prevention and Punishment of the Crime of Genocide (Order on the Request for Provisional Measures)' (1993) ICJ Reports 3.

respectively, constitute a *verbatim* reproduction of Arts II and III of the 1948 Genocide Convention. Article II of this Convention defines genocide as:

> ... any of the following acts committed with intent to destroy, in whole or in part, a national, ethnical, racial or religious group, as such:
>
> (a) killing members of the group;
> (b) causing serious bodily harm or mental harm to members of the group;
> (c) deliberately inflicting on the group conditions of life calculated to bring about its physical destruction in whole or in part;
> (d) imposing measures intended to prevent births within the group;
> (e) forcibly transferring children of the group to another group.

Article III penalises, besides principal participation in genocide, conspiracy, direct and public incitement, attempt and complicity in acts of genocide. What is evident from this definition is that it is exhaustive and much more specific than that articulated for other grave offences, namely, crimes against humanity. Its specificity is not exhausted solely on the four groups that may become the target of genocide, but more importantly it is based on the particular *mens rea* of the perpetrator, whose intention must be to destroy in whole or in part a particular group designated under the terms of the Convention. This element renders genocide a specific intent crime (*dolus specialis*) and differentiates it from other offences of mass destruction and extermination.

The *actus reus* of genocide requires the perpetration of acts that aim to destroy a group in whole or in part. The 'in part' element does not characterise the destruction of the group, but refers instead to the intent of the perpetrator in destroying the group within the confines of a limited geographical area.[10] Thus, if an individual possesses the intent to destroy a distinct part of a group within a limited geographical area, as opposed to an accumulation of isolated individuals within it, that person would be liable for genocide. On this basis, the ICTY Trial Chamber convicted General Krstic of genocide for his participation in the extermination of thousands of Bosnian Muslim males in the area of Srebrenica in 1995.[11] Since genocide is a mass-victim offence, the part targeted must be a substantial part of the group. In terms of victim numbers, ICTY and ICTR jurisprudence suggest that the intent to destroy a part of the group must affect a considerable number of individuals that make

---

10 *ICTY Prosecutor v Krstic*, Trial Chamber Judgment (2 Aug 2001), paras 582–84.
11 This view was adopted by two recent German judgments: *Jorgic* case, Dusseldorf Supreme Court, 3 StR 215/98 (30 April 1999), upheld by the FRG Federal Constitutional Court, and the *Djajic* case, Bavarian Appeals Court (23 May 1997), 92 *AJIL* (1998), 528, cited with approval in the *Krstic* Trial Judgment, ibid, para 589.

up a 'substantial' part of that group.[12] In such cases the prosecutor must prove both the intent to destroy the targeted group in the particular geographical area, as well as the intent to destroy a substantial part of that group as such.[13] In the *Krstic* case, the accused argued that the Bosnian Muslim population of Srebrenica did not constitute a significant part of the overall Muslim population in Bosnia. The ICTY Appeals Chamber pointed out, however, that in the present instance this was not an overriding consideration because: (a) Srebrenica was of huge strategic importance to the Bosnian Serbs, as it was an obstacle to an ethnically pure Bosnian Serb State; (b) Srebrenica was the only area in that region which the Serbs were able to control and thus extermination of other Muslims elsewhere was not physically possible under the circumstances.[14]

It is possible in some cases for the accused to validly argue that although many members of the targeted group were killed while under his authority, many others under similar authority were allowed to leave. In the context of the Srebrenica massacre, while the Bosnian Serbs rounded up and executed all Bosnian Muslim male civilians (around 8,000 souls), they transferred all other women, children and the elderly to Muslim armed forces. The *Krstic* Appeals Chamber gave no significance to this act, putting it down to the fact that such an action could not have been kept an eternal secret or disguised as a military operation and thus carried an increased risk of international exposure.[15] It was sufficient that the intent to exterminate a part of the group without being detected existed, further making sure that without its males, the Srebrenica female community would not be able to reconstitute itself.

A significant number of killings and a pattern of ethnic cleansing, as in the case of the Muslim population targeted by Bosnian Serbs, may not always be sufficient to infer a particular accused's genocidal intent. In the *Krajisnik* case, the ICTY Trial Chamber took note of the senior position of the defendant in the Bosnian-Serb political hierarchy – second only to President Karadzic – as well as the 3,000 brutal killings of Muslim civilians and other crimes committed against the Muslim civilian population. It moreover rejected his arguments that he was not aware of this situation from the arming of the first militias right until the ethnic cleansing itself. Despite this bulk of evidence, the Trial Chamber refused to infer a genocidal intent and instead convicted the accused for participating in a joint criminal enterprise

---

12 *ICTR Prosecutor v Kayishema and Ruzindana*, Trial Chamber Judgment (21 May 1999), para 97; *ICTR Prosecutor v Bagilishema*, Trial Chamber Judgment (7 June 2001), para 64; op cit, *Krstic* Trial Judgment, note 10, paras 586–88; *ICTY Prosecutor v Krstic*, Appeals Chamber Judgment (19 April 2004), paras 8–12.

13 *ICTY Prosecutor v Sikirica*, Trial Chamber Judgment (3 Sept 2001), para 61.

14 Op cit, *Krstic* Appeals Judgment, note 12, paras 15–17.

15 Ibid, para 31.

in connection with crimes against humanity.[16] It would not be surprising if a differently composed court, whether national or international, decided the existence of a genocide under the circumstances differently.

7.3 THE SPECIFIC INTENT (*DOLUS SPECIALIS*) REQUIRED FOR GENOCIDE

The ICTY had not, until January 2001, made a finding on the occurrence of genocide with regard to the former Yugoslavia nor, of course, did it convict any accused of this offence.[17] It did, however, urge the prosecutor in the *Nikolic* case to consider also charging the accused with genocide[18] and inferred Karadzic's genocidal intent from a variety of factors.[19] In the *Jelisic* case, the accused was the commandant of a Bosnian Serb camp that was charged, *inter alia*, with participating in a campaign of genocide against Muslims. The Trial Chamber initially acquitted him of genocide on the grounds that the prosecutor had failed to prove Jelisic's genocidal intent beyond reasonable doubt.[20] It had reached this conclusion because the evidence (random acts of violence, albeit solely against Bosnian Muslims) and the disturbed personality of the accused (eg, narcissistic tendencies) did not demonstrate a *dolus specialis* against Brcko Muslims beyond a reasonable doubt. The Appeals Chamber disagreed with this evaluation of the evidence, finding instead that genocidal intent clearly existed, but did not see it in the interest of justice to order a retrial and thus declined to reverse the acquittal.[21] The ICTY has been reluctant to convict lower-ranking personnel of genocide, despite the large number of victims in particular cases.[22]

The ICTR was established primarily to address the issue of genocide and in the *Akayesu* case authoritatively determined that genocide against the Tutsi did, in fact, take place in Rwanda in 1994.[23] The judicial assessment of the *dolus specialis* by the ad hoc tribunals begins by first examining the existence of a genocidal plan and the commission of genocide, then inquiring into the genocidal intent of the accused, which is distinct but yet interrelated to that of

---

16 *ICTY Prosecutor v Krajisnik*, Trial Chamber Judgment (27 Sept 2006), para 857 *et seq*; for a more extensive discussion of joint criminal enterprise liability, see Chapter 2, section 2.5.

17 On 2 August 2001, Bosnian-Serb General Krstic was convicted at first instance of genocide for his role in the planning and execution of the Srebrenica massacre in 1995. On appeal, his conviction was upheld in relation to aiding and abetting genocide.

18 *ICTY Prosecutor v Nikolic*, R 61 Decision (20 Oct 1995), para 34.

19 *ICTY Prosecutor v Karadzic*, R 61 Decision (11 July 1996), para 95.

20 *ICTY Prosecutor v Jelisic*, Trial Chamber Judgment (14 Dec 1999), paras 97–98.

21 *ICTY Prosecutor v Jelisic*, Appeals Chamber Judgment (5 July 2001), paras 70–77.

22 *ICTY Prosecutor v Sikirica and Others*, Trial Chamber Judgment on Defence Motions to Acquit (3 Sept 2001).

23 *ICTR Prosecutor v Akayesu*, Trial Chamber Judgment (2 Sept 1998), para 126.

the underlying plan.[24] A genocidal plan is not a normative ingredient of the crime of genocide, but ICTY Chambers have consistently argued that it could nonetheless provide evidential assistance in proving the intent of the authors.[25]

The *dolus specialis* of genocide necessitates that the intention to commit this crime be formed prior to the execution of genocidal acts, although the individual offences themselves do not require any such premeditation.[26] The execution of genocide involves two levels of intent: that of the criminal enterprise as a collectivity and that of the participating individuals. In such cases of joint participation the intent to commit genocide must be discernible in the criminal act itself, apart from the intent of particular perpetrators. The next step is to establish whether the accused shared the intention that genocide be carried out.[27] The *Jelisic* judgment opined that genocidal intent may manifest itself through a desire to exterminate a very large number of group members, or by killing a more limited number of persons selected for the impact their disappearance or extermination will have upon the survival of the group as such.[28] In most cases, there will be no direct proof of genocidal intent and, so, this must be inferred through circumstantial evidence. Jean Paul Akayesu, the first person to be convicted of genocide by the ICTR, was the Bourgmestre of Taba commune, a position that afforded him a very significant amount of influence and authority over all the public institutions of the commune. The accused had delivered passionate speeches against the Tutsi and moderate Hutus, whereby he advocated their extermination and was found to have ordered other acts of violence against his victims. These actions could only be classified as genocide if discriminatory intent could be demonstrated with the aim of destroying the perceived group in whole or in part. The ICTR reached this inference on the basis of the general context of other culpable acts systematically directed against the Tutsi, the multiplicity of offenders across Rwanda, the general nature of the crimes and the deliberate targeting of victims on account of their particular membership, while excluding others.[29] The *Kayishema* judgment added further elements, such as the use of derogatory language towards group members, methodical planning and systematic killing, and the number of victims exterminated.[30] None of

24 G Verdirame, 'The Genocide Definition in the Jurisprudence of the Ad Hoc Tribunals', 49 *ICLQ* (2000), 578, p 588.

25 Op cit, *Krstic* Trial Judgment, note 10, para 572; op cit, *Jelisic* Appeals Judgment, note 21, para 48.

26 Op cit, *Kayishema* Trial Judgment, note 12, para 91.

27 Op cit, *Krstic* Trial Judgment, note 10, para 549.

28 Op cit, *Jelisic* Trial Judgment, note 20, para 82.

29 Op cit, *Akayesu* Trial Judgment, note 23, para 523; reaffirmed in *ICTR Prosecutor v Rutaganda*, Trial Chamber Judgment (6 Dec 1999), para 399.

30 Op cit, *Kayishema* Trial Judgment, note 12, para 93; the *Karadzic* R 61 Decision, op cit, note 19, para 95, inferred the accused's genocidal intent from the combined effect of his speeches, the massive scale of crimes, all of which were aimed at undermining the foundation of the

these factors alone can provide credible proof of genocidal intent; what is needed is a combination demonstrating the overall context of atrocities against a specific group of which the accused can only have been a substantial actor on account of his or her unlawful acts against the targeted group.

7.4 MEMBERSHIP OF THE TARGETED GROUP

Genocide requires that the accused intended to destroy a particular group, but is silent as to membership and acceptance in such group. Moreover, there is no guidance as to whether membership of a group is an objective factor, or if it is the accused's particular perception of membership that is crucial. Although the case law of the Permanent Court of International Justice (as did also the early jurisprudence of the ICJ) suggested that membership of a specific group was a question of fact,[31] the *Akayesu* tribunal assessed such membership solely on subjective criteria, in accordance with recent developments in human rights law.[32] This approach is desirable in the construction of membership with regard to genocide, since each specific culture and society maintains its own distinct perception of membership to particular groups, which is not easily visible to outside observers, and in the case of Rwanda there was an even more compelling reason to do so, since the Tutsi did not fit into any of the four enumerated groups, sharing as they did the same language, culture and race as the Hutus.[33] However, this approach does not necessarily conform to the *travaux* of the 1948 Genocide Convention, nor with subsequent ICTY/ICTR judgments. The Trial Chamber in the *Akayesu* case, on the basis of its aforementioned approach, resorted to an interpretation of particular membership in light of the preparatory work of the 1948 Genocide Convention, which intended to ensure the protection of only 'stable' groups.[34]

---

group; the *Krstic* Appeals Judgment, op cit, note 12, para 35, inferred genocidal intent from the scale of killings, awareness by senior Military Staff and from the actions of senior Staff to ensure the targeted group's physical demise.

31 *Germany v Poland*, 'Rights of minority schools in Upper Silesia' (1928) PCIJ Reports, Ser A, No 15; *Liechtenstein v Guatemala* (*Nottebohm* case) (Merits) (1955) ICJ Reports 4.

32 See *Lovelace v Canada*, UN Human Rights Committee (1981) 68 ILR 17.

33 The term 'ethnic' is derived from the Greek word 'ethnos', meaning 'nation'. Thus, although the terms 'ethnic' and 'national' appear to be identical, the contemporary semantic application of the word 'ethnic', especially in minority law, refers to a category of people possessing some degree of coherence, being aware of their common origin and cultural interests. 'National', on the other hand, refers to the bond of nationality. See G Welhengama, *Minorities' Claims: From Autonomy to Secession, International Law and State Practice*, 2000, Aldershot: Ashgate, 64–65.

34 *Akayesu* Trial Judgment, supra note 23, paras 510–11, 516. In fact, the 1948 Genocide Convention has come under increased criticism for excluding from its ambit political and other socially vulnerable groups.

This interpretation was supported in *Rutaganda*, decided *obiter dicta*, but was not directly referred to in either of the judgments rendered in *Kayishema, Ruzindana* or *Jelisic*.[35] The *Krstic* Trial judgment actually disagreed altogether, arguing that the Genocide Convention does not protect all types of human groups, its application being confined solely to national, ethnical, racial or religious groups.[36] This seems to be the position that most conforms to the Genocide Convention and the ICTY/ICTR Appeals Chamber.

What, however, of the proposition that the personal perception of membership by the perpetrator is equally important, particularly where he perceives membership through a 'negative' assessment or 'positive criteria'? A negative assessment refers to the lack of certain group characteristics in the mind of the accused, while a positive assessment entails the accumulation of certain characteristics. Some ICTY and ICTR chambers have given normative credence to the accused's personal assessment of membership on the basis of negative criteria.[37] In the *Stakic* case, the ICTY Appeals Chamber was faced with a situation that possessed all the elements of genocide, but where the accused did not target any particular group as such; only anyone who was not a Serb. This negative approach by the accused, although admitted in the *Jelisic* case to demonstrate that the accused possessed genocidal intent against a prescribed group, was expressly rejected by the *Stakic* Appeals Chamber, which stated:

> Given that negatively defined groups lack specific characteristics, defining groups by reference to a negative would run counter to the intent of the Genocide Convention's drafters. . . . Unlike positively defined groups, negatively defined groups have no unique distinguishing characteristics that could be destroyed.[38]

As regards positive subjective stigmatisation of group membership by the perpetrator, although this can be used as a criterion when defining target groups, it cannot be used as the sole criterion. Although national, ethnic, racial and religious identity is largely subjective, ICTY and ICTR chambers have consistently held that although an act may constitute genocide on the basis of the perpetrator's perception of the victim as belonging to the target group, a subjective definition alone is insufficient to determine victim groups.[39]

---

35 Op cit, *Rutaganda*, Trial Judgment, note 29, para 58; the *ICTR Prosecutor v Musema*, Trial Chamber Judgment (27 Jan 2000) also seems to agree with the *Akayesu* Trial Judgment, op cit, note 23, paras 161–63.
36 Op cit, *Krstic* Trial Judgment, note 10, para 554.
37 Op cit, *Jelisic* Trial Judgment, note 20, paras 70–71; op cit, *Rutaganda* Trial Judgment, note 29, para 56.
38 *ICTY Prosecutor v Stakic*, Appeals Chamber Judgment (22 March 2006), paras 22–23.
39 Op cit, *Rutaganda* Trial Judgment, note 29, paras 56–57; *Stakic* Appeals Judgment, ibid, para 25.

7.4.1 Acts constituting genocide

Genocide is limited to any act seeking the physical or biological destruction of all or part of the group, and thus 'an enterprise attacking only the cultural or sociological characteristics of a human group in order to annihilate these elements which give to that group its own identity distinct from the rest of that community' would not fall under the definition of genocide.[40] The enumerated criminal acts against members of a group on the basis of their membership in the group as such are exhaustive, but their ambit had not been tested in practice prior to the ICTR's jurisprudence. 'Killing members of the group'[41] includes only homicides committed with intent to cause death.[42] 'Causing serious bodily or mental harm'[43] to members of the group does not require, contrary to what the USA has been arguing since the adoption of the 1948 Genocide Convention,[44] that the harm be permanent or irremediable.[45] This provision is not limited to specific well known practices causing bodily or mental harm, such as torture, but is open, as the Israeli Supreme Court pointed out in the *Eichmann* case, to any acts designed to cause degradation, deprivation of humanity and cause physical or mental suffering.[46] However:

> Failure to provide adequate accommodation, shelter, food, water, medical care or hygiene sanitation facilities will not amount to the *actus reus* of genocide if the deprivation is not so severe as to contribute to the destruction of the group, or tend to do so.[47]

'Deliberately inflicting on a group conditions of life calculated to bring about its physical destruction'[48] has been described as a method of slow death, of which rape can constitute a means of its accomplishment.[49] The *Akayesu* judgment stated that this category comprises the methods of destruction that are not immediately aimed at killing the members of the group, but which do

---

40 Op cit, *Krstic* Trial Judgment, note 10, para 580; cited with approval by the *Krstic* Appeals Judgment, op cit, note 12, para 25.
41 ICTR Statute, Art 2(2)(a).
42 Op cit, *Akayesu* Trial Judgment, note 23, paras 500–01; op cit, *Musema*, Trial Judgment, note 35, para 155.
43 ICTR Statute, Art 2(2)(b).
44 Op cit, Verdirame, note 24, pp 580–81.
45 Op cit, *Akayesu* Trial Judgment, note 23, paras 502–04.
46 *Public Prosecutor v Eichmann*, Judgment (1962) 36 ILR 277, p 340. This passage from the court's judgment refers to the charge of 'crimes against the Jewish people', which is equivalent to that of genocide. The judgment rendered by the District Court of Jerusalem was subsequently upheld by the Israeli Supreme Court.
47 Op cit, *Krajisnik* Trial Judgment, note 16, para 863.
48 ICTR Statute, Art 2(2)(c).
49 Op cit, *Kayishema* Trial Judgment, note 12, para 116.

so ultimately. This includes, *inter alia*, subjecting a people to 'a subsistent diet, systematic expulsion, and the reduction of essential medical services below minimum requirement'.[50] 'Imposing measures intended to prevent births within a group'[51] includes, but is not limited to, obvious practices such as sexual mutilation, sterilisation, forced birth control, separation of sexes, or prohibition of marriages. As was noted by the ICTR, in patriarchal societies children follow the lineage of the father. Thus, impregnation of a woman by a rapist belonging to another group with the intention that the victim bear a child from his group would constitute genocide – provided obviously that all other criteria are present. Likewise, the mental effect of rape by which a woman is so traumatised that she refuses to procreate would also amount to genocide.[52] 'Forcibly transferring children of the group to another group'[53] encompasses not only forceful physical transfer but also the causing of serious trauma to the parents or guardians that would necessarily lead to such transfer.[54]

In the *Krstic* Trial judgment, the ICTY noted that besides the physical destruction of a group, the same result may also be achieved by a 'purposeful eradication of [the group's] culture and identity, resulting in the eventual extinction of the group as an entity distinct from the remainder of the community'.[55] Although the Trial Chamber found that cultural genocide was excluded from the ambit of the 1948 Genocide Convention, it nonetheless pointed to some recent developments outside the ICTY/ICTR context that support criminalisation of this form of genocide. It finally determined that cultural genocide was not part of customary international law and thus did not fall within the ICTY Statute, but since acts of genocide usually involve attacks against cultural and religious property, such attacks may be seen as evidence of genocide.[56]

Art III of the Genocide Convention enumerates the various modalities through which a person may be convicted of genocide. These include: genocide, conspiracy, direct and public incitement, attempt and complicity to commit genocide. Whereas these would constitute different forms by which a person participates in a criminal offence, in the Genocide Convention they play the role of inchoate crimes – apart from the perpetration of genocide itself which is a principal offence, and complicity which requires the existence of either a principal or an inchoate offence. The equivalent of Art III of the Genocide Convention has been omitted from the ICC

---

50 Op cit, *Akayesu* Trial Judgment, note 23, paras 505–06.
51 ICTR Statute, Art 2(2)(d).
52 Op cit, *Akayesu* Trial Judgment, note 23, paras 507–08.
53 ICTR Statute, Art 2(2)(e).
54 Op cit, *Akayesu* Trial Judgment, note 23, paras 509–10.
55 Op cit, *Krstic* Trial Judgment, note 10, para 574.
56 Ibid, paras 576–80.

Statute, which transformed all the aforementioned inchoate offences into modes of participation and forms of liability, as is evident, for example, with Art 25(3)(e) relating to incitement to commit genocide. In Chapter 2 the reader can find a more extensive discussion on conspiracies, complicities and joint criminal enterprise relating to genocide. The next subsection will deal with incitement to commit genocide, which is not covered elsewhere in this book.

7.4.2 Incitement to commit genocide

The Rwandan genocide was conceived at the highest level by Hutu officials and was executed by lower level individuals, including Hutu youth teams and private individuals who had been incited through the mass media and public speeches. The seminal role of the media as a means of instigating hatred and calling for extermination of the Tutsi by falsifying or exaggerating events was made clear in the case of former Prime Minister Kambanda, but more so in the case of *Georges Ruggiu*, a Belgian national who was responsible for broadcasting these messages on Rwandan radio.[57] Public speeches given by influential individuals were found to have had the same effect, as was evident in the case of Akayesu's rallies with which he intended to directly create a particular state of mind in his audience that would lead to the destruction of the Tutsi. The ICTR defined incitement as 'encouraging, persuading or directly provoking another through speeches, shouts, threats or any other means of audiovisual communication to commit an offence'.[58] Incitement to commit genocide must further be committed in public and be direct as to what its author wants to achieve. However, the 'directness' element, as correctly propounded by the *Akayesu* Trial Chamber, should be assessed in light of its cultural and linguistic content and the particular perception of each individual audience.[59] The *Akayesu* Trial Judgment defined the *mens rea* of incitement to genocide as existing:

> . . . in the intent to directly prompt or provoke another to commit genocide. It implies a desire on the part of the perpetrator to create by his actions a particular state of mind necessary to commit such a crime in the minds of the person(s) he is so engaging. That is to say that the person who is inciting to commit genocide must have himself the specific intent to commit genocide.[60]

---

57 *ICTR Prosecutor v Ruggiu*, Trial Chamber Judgment (1 June 2000), paras 17, 44, 50.
58 Op cit, *Akayesu* Trial Judgment, note 23, para 555.
59 Ibid, paras 557, 559.
60 Ibid, para 560.

Since, as previously observed, the various forms of participation in genocide contained in Art 2(3) of the ICTR Statute, of which 'incitement' is one, do not require consummation of actual genocide in order to entail the criminal liability of the participants, it follows that unsuccessful incitement to commit genocide is a punishable act.

Chapter 8

Offences against the person

8.1 INTRODUCTION

This chapter examines offences against the person with an international or transnational element. Many of these, however, constitute *erga omnes* obligations, and as such their violation even within a single State creates a legal interest for every State in the world. Here we examine the following offences: slavery and related practices; torture; apartheid; and enforced disappearances. Other offences against the person, such as grave breaches, war crimes, crimes against humanity and genocide are covered in other chapters, in accordance with the judicial institution in which they are framed. Other international offences that offend the person, albeit where the effect on the person is incidental to the primary aim of the perpetrator, which is either financial or socio-political, such as piracy, terrorism and organised crime are covered in other distinct chapters. All of these offences, by their very nature, constitute serious human rights violations. Although reference is made to the various international human rights instruments, these were not designed to deal with the individual responsibility of the perpetrators. This does not mean that they are irrelevant in the international criminalisation process; rather, caution should be exercised when human rights notions are transplanted in the international criminal process, as will be evident throughout this chapter.

8.2 SLAVERY AND RELATED PRACTICES

A study conducted by the non-governmental organisation Anti-Slavery International revealed the conclusion of some 300 international agreements concerning the suppression of slavery between 1815 and 1957. These were, however, largely ineffective mainly due to the lack of national mechanisms in evaluating incidences of slavery between States parties.[1] Although by the late

---

1 Report of the Working Group on Contemporary Forms of Slavery, UN Doc E/CN4/Sub2/ 1999/17 (20 July 1999), para 41.

18th century many States had formally abolished slavery[2] and considered such practice as being contrary to the law of nations, they nonetheless tolerated the slave trade in countries where it was permitted by law and by nationals of such countries on the high seas.[3] In the dispute arising between the US and Great Britain in the *Creole* cases, the arbiter assigned to settle the ensuing claims held that in cases of *force majeure* which force a slave vessel to put in in the territorial waters of an abolitionist State, the latter is obliged to respect the law of the Flag State.[4] The arbitral award was, nonetheless, criticised on humanitarian grounds. National courts refused to recognise that slave trade on the high seas was tantamount to the offence of piracy.[5] At the time, search and seizure of private vessels on the high seas was dependent on bilateral treaties granting reciprocal rights and, so, it is of no surprise that the first multilateral treaties of this kind, the 1885 General Act of the Conference of Berlin Concerning the Congo,[6] as well as the 1890 Brussels General Act Relative to the African Slave Trade,[7] contained limited enforcement prerogatives. Despite the limitations in search and seizure arising from these instruments and the continuation of unrestricted engagement in the slave trade in certain countries, the above mentioned agreements and relevant State practice suggested in unequivocal terms that, by the late nineteenth century, the slave trade was an international offence that was treated as such by national criminal legislation.[8]

As a matter of customary law, it is now settled that all persons are entitled to be free from slavery or servitude,[9] as well as from forced or compulsory labour.[10] It is equally true that all persons have a right to be free from institutions and practices similar to slavery, and that the enjoyment of such rights

---

2 See Abolition of Slavery Act 1833, which by abolishing slavery in the British colonies rendered the slaves apprentices and ordered their compensation by public funds paid by their owners.

3 *The Fortuna* (1811) 165 ER 1240; *The Diana* (1813) 165 ER 1245; *San Juan Nepomuceno* (1824) 166 ER 94; *The Antelope*, 23 US 66 (1825).

4 *The Creole* (1853); IA Moore, *Moore's Digest of International Law*, 1906, Vol 2, p 352; see DP O'Connell, *The International Law of the Sea*, 1984, Oxford: Clarendon, pp 854–55.

5 *Le Louis* (1817) 2 Dods 213, p 218, *per* Scott J.

6 Declaration Concerning the Slave Trade, Art 9, allowed interdiction on land and sea in the territories forming the conventional basin of the Congo. Reprinted in 82 BFSP 55.

7 1890 Brussels General Act Relative to the African Slave Trade, Art XXII granted reciprocal rights of search and seizure to States parties, but only in the Persian Gulf and the Red Sea (Art XXI), over vessels of less than 500 tonnes (Art XXIII). Reprinted in 1 Bevans 134.

8 Berlin Act, Art 9 and Brussels Act, Arts V and XIX.

9 1927 Slavery Convention, Art 2(b), 60 UNTS 253, amended by 1953 Protocol Amending the 1927 Slavery Convention, 182 UNTS 51; Universal Declaration on Human Rights, Art 4, GA Res 217A (10 Dec 1948); 1966 International Covenant on Civil and Political Rights (ICCPR), Art 8(1), (2), 999 UNTS 171.

10 1927 Slavery Convention, Art 5; 1966 ICCPR, Art 8(3); 1930 International Labour Organization (ILO) Forced Labour Convention (No 29), Art 2(1).

constitutes an obligation *erga omnes*, that is, all States have a legal interest in the fulfilment of these rights worldwide.[11] Article 1(1) of the 1927 Slavery Convention defines slavery as 'the status or condition of a person over whom any or all of the powers attaching to the right of ownership are attached'. The plethora of anti-slavery conventions and the detailed framework of rights contained in each obfuscates the distinction that should be drawn in every case between the granting of a right and the intentional promulgation of an offence to be implemented at either national or international level. In this treatise, an act is deemed to acquire criminal character either when explicit reference to this effect is made in a relevant treaty, or when through sustained State practice or by reasonable implication a right can only be enforced through the penalisation of the behaviour that impedes it. Such reasoning implies, further, that although a form of behaviour may not have been treated in the context of an international treaty, it could, nonetheless, as a rule of customary law, be defined as an international offence on account of its penalisation in a large number of States. Alternatively, marginal ratification of a treaty containing express criminal provisions may render the said provisions ineffective in terms of producing a general rule of international law, but slightly ratified treaties which prohibit reservations do not necessarily evince absence of general norms, as it is possible that States may refuse to ratify on the basis of an objection to procedural or other provisions unrelated to penalisation.[12]

8.2.1 The slave trade and similar institutions

Article 1(2) of the 1927 Slavery Convention defines the slave trade as including:

> . . . all acts involved in the capture, acquisition or disposal of a person with intent to reduce him to slavery; all acts involved in the acquisition of a slave with a view to selling or exchanging him; all acts of disposal by sale or exchange of a slave acquired with a view to being sold or exchanged, and, in general, every act of trade or transport in slaves.

It is also well settled that conveying, attempting, or being an accessory to the conveyance of slaves from one country to another constitutes a serious

---

11 *Belgium v Spain (Barcelona Traction Light and Power House Co Ltd)* (1970) ICJ Reports 3, Second Phase, p 32.

12 Eg, the UK has refused to ratify the 1949 Convention for the Suppression of the Traffic in Persons and of the Exploitation of the Prostitution of Others, 96 UNTS 271, although it has passed legislation conforming to most provisions contained in the Convention. The reason for the UK's refusal is that the Convention penalises more acts than are penalised under UK law. See op cit, note 1, para 37.

offence under international law.[13] Although the definition of slave trade contained in Art 1(2) of the 1927 Slavery Convention seems to encompass a wide range of acts, it, in fact, excluded a number of similar practices that affected and still affect a substantial part of the population of developing countries. Extreme poverty compounded by the lack of social and administrative structures soon revealed a different facet of slavery; one where the individual was forced to submit to exploitation or risk extinction.

The 1956 Supplementary Convention on the Abolition of Slavery, the Slave Trade, and Institutions Similar to Slavery (Supplementary Slavery Convention) was designed purposely to fill that lacuna. Article 1 prohibits the institutions of debt bondage, serfdom, 'bride-price' and the illegal transfer of children. Debt bondage arises from a pledge by a debtor of his personal services or of persons under his or her control as security for a debt. This transaction becomes unlawful under Art 1(a) of the 1956 Supplementary Slavery Convention where either the value of those services as reasonably assessed are not applied towards the liquidation of the debt, or the length and nature of those services are not respectively limited and defined. The Ad Hoc Committee established by the Economic and Social Council (ECOSOC) of the United Nations (UN) in 1949 to formulate this Convention was of the view that debt bondage was also constituted where the bondsman and the debtor submit to conditions not allowing the exercise of rights enjoyed by ordinary individuals within the framework of local social custom,[14] as would necessarily be the case of an undefined in nature and unlimited in time contract of servitude. Debt bondage is endemic in the majority of developing nations and a 1995 study estimates the existence, in India alone, of in excess of 15 million child labourers, incurred by a debt of a parent.[15] These debts cannot be easily paid off as a result of astronomical interest rates and low wages, and so children may work throughout their youth without having managed to repay the loan, which could subsequently be inherited by another family member, typically a younger child. Despite the passing of the 1976 Bonded Labour System (Abolition) Act (No 19), which obliges the governments of the various Indian States to release the bonded labourers and rehabilitate them, further occasioned by similar judgments of the Indian Supreme Court,[16] debt bondage continues with impunity. The penalisation of debt bondage against children below the age of 18 is also prescribed by the 1999 International Labour Organization (ILO) Convention for the

---

13 1956 Supplementary Slavery Convention, Art 3(1), 266 UNTS 3.
14 JAC Gutteridge, 'The Supplementary Slavery Convention 1956', 6 *ICLQ* (1957), 449, p 452.
15 L Tucker, 'Child Slaves in Modern India: The Bonded Labour Problem', 19 *HRQ* (1997), 572, p 573.
16 *Chaudhary v State of Madhya Pradesh* (1948) 3 SCC 243, p 255; see ibid, Tucker, p 622.

Prohibition and Immediate Action for the Elimination of the Worst Forms of Child Labour (No 182).[17]

The prohibition of bride-price in Art 1(c) of the 1956 Supplementary Slavery Convention penalises the acquisition of girls by purchase disguised as payment of dowry for marriage. This institution becomes a criminal offence where the female is either denied the right to consent and is given to marriage on the basis of a financial transaction of any kind by familial or any other persons, or where upon death of her husband, family or clan members transfer her to another person, thus, basically reducing her to an object of inheritance. Bride-price and, indeed, all the institutions and practices penalised in the 1956 Convention were so deeply rooted in traditional rural societies in the developing world that the western delegates agreed, despite the vehement opposition of many non-governmental organisations (NGOs), to allow for progressive abolition of these practices, rather than impose an immediate prohibition. States are generally free to prescribe a minimum age of marriage and although the 1962 Convention on Consent to Marriage, Minimum Age for Marriage and Registration of Marriages[18] is not widely ratified, the principle of full and free consent of both parties declared in Art 1 therein is undoubtedly a rule of customary international law on account of its presence in the widely ratified 1956 Supplementary Slavery Convention.

The practice of bride-price should be distinguished from that of 'bride-wealth'. The latter constitutes a substantial and obligatory payment from the groom's kin to the bride's family, not to the bride. Bride-wealth represented both marital cement and an assurance for both partners against the bad behaviour of the other and was to be returned if the marriage ended on account of the wife's 'fault'. Although the material elements of bride-wealth did not traditionally fit within supply/demand market notions, during the 20th century this institution has been distorted as its ingredients have acquired national currency values. As the material 'gifts' associated with bride-wealth acquired modern money value, the prospect always loomed that bride-wealth would, indeed, become transformed into bride-price. For this reason, many African countries have now regulated the cash value of bride-wealth. As the 1956 Supplementary Slavery Convention only intended to penalise and prevent the downgrading of marriage to a financial transaction lacking the consent of the bride, traditional bride-wealth does not violate the Convention.

The transfer of children under the age of 18 by their natural parents or guardian to another person, whether for financial benefit or not, with a view to exploiting the child or its labour is an international offence under Art 1(d) of the 1956 Convention. A number of international instruments under the

17 1999 ILO Convention, Arts 3(a) and 7, 38 ILM (1999), 1207.
18 521 UNTS 231; see also GA Res 2018(XX) (1 Nov 1965) endorsing this principle.

same terms expressly prohibit the trafficking, more specifically the sale or exploitation of children in any form, such as the 1989 Convention on the Rights of the Child,[19] the 2000 Optional Protocol II thereto on the Sale of Children, Child Prostitution and Child Pornography,[20] and the 1999 ILO Worst Forms of Child Labour Convention.[21] These instruments do not intend to punish those adoptions which the parents earnestly believe are in the best interest of their children and which are moreover completed lawfully and without any personal benefit to the parents, in accordance with Arts 1 and 21 of the 1993 Hague Convention on Protection of Children and Co-operation in Respect of Inter-Country Adoptions[22] and the 1989 Convention on the Rights of the Child, respectively. Interpol research suggests that illicit foreign adoptions are carried out through the falsification of birth certificates, followed by abductions or deceit of uneducated mothers by organised criminal rings.[23]

It is equally undisputed that the acts of procuring or offering of children in sexual activities for remuneration or any other form of consideration (child prostitution), or for representation of children engaged in real or simulated explicit sexual activities or any representation of the sexual parts of a child for sexual purposes (child pornography) constitute international offences.[24] This would include procurers and clients engaged in sex tourism, as well as distributors and possessors of pornography through postal services or the Internet.[25] It should be stressed that the Special Rapporteur on the Sale of Children, Child Prostitution and Child Pornography identified four causes related to the sexual exploitation of children; namely, ineffective justice systems, the role of the media, lack of education, but foremost she emphasised that besides cases of kidnapping it was the family of the children that was responsible for their eventual exploitation in the hands of others.[26]

Serfdom is also prohibited and is an international offence under Art 1(b)

---

19 1989 Convention on the Rights of the Child, Arts 35 and 36, 28 ILM (1989), 1448.
20 Contained in GA Res 54/263 (25 May 2000), Art 2(a).
21 ILO Worst Forms of Child Labour Convention, Art 3(a).
22 32 ILM (1993), 1134.
23 Y Bird, *The Trafficking of Children for Sexual Exploitation and Foreign Adoption: Background and Current Measures*, 1999, Paris: Interpol; see also 'Adoptions of Smuggled Mexican Babies (1999) *Associated Press* , 25 July.
24 2000 Optional Protocol II to the Convention on the Rights of the Child, Arts 2(b), (c) and 3; 1999 ILO Worst Forms of Child Labour Convention, Art 3(a), (b); 1989 Convention on the Rights Of the Child, Art 34; ECOSOC Res 1996/26 (24 July 1996), entitled 'Measures to Prevent Illicit International Trafficking in Children and to Establish Penalties Appropriate to Such Offences'.
25 See LM Jones, 'Regulating Child Pornography on the Internet: The Implications of Article 34 of the United Nations Convention on the rights of the Child', 6 *Int'l J Children's Rights* (1998), 55.
26 UN Doc E/CN4/2000/73 (14 Jan 2000).

of the 1956 Supplementary Slavery Convention. This refers to the condition of a tenant who is bound to live and labour on land belonging to another person and provide determinate service to the landowner, whether for reward or not, and who is not free to change that condition. In *Van Droogenbroeck v Belgium*, the European Commission of Human Rights observed, *obiter dictum*, that the notion of servitude embraces, in addition to the obligation to perform certain acts for others, 'the obligation for the serf to live on another person's property and the impossibility of altering his condition'.[27] Contemporary serfdom resembles the existence of the feudal system in medieval Europe, where, in the absence of an industrial middle class and the accumulation of land by the few, two social classes were established: the dominant class (*domini, nobiles*) and the vassals. The vassals gradually became animate objects tied to the land (*servi terrae*). The same medieval elements are present in cases of contemporary serfdom taking place in developing countries, whose eradication can only be premised on courageous land reform and industrial development. Since, in most cases, the vassal will have consented to his or her status, the institution of serfdom is illegal no matter how it has come about.

Traffic in persons, especially for purposes of sexual exploitation, is a specific form of slavery related institution. One treaty has, in the past, penalised 'trafficking' in persons without defining the term. Article 1 of the 1949 Convention for the Suppression of the Traffic in Persons and of the Exploitation of the Prostitution of Others (1949 Convention), which supersedes several previous instruments relating to the traffic of women and children ('white slavery'), penalises any person who in order to gratify the passions of another:

1   procures, entices or leads away, for purposes of prostitution, another person, even with the consent of that person;
2   exploits the prostitution of another person, even with the consent of that person.

This provision aims at eradicating both the initial enticement into prostitution, which usually commences as a result of socio-financial hardships, as well as the eventual procuring of prostitution in urban or other centres. The relevant discussions in the various human rights bodies of the UN have revealed two schools of thought on this issue; one maintains that controlled and lawfully registered prostitution should be allowed and that only the initial trafficking should be punished, while the other argues for a total ban and penalisation of prostitution. This division among States, further reinforced with the penalisation of the financing or maintenance of brothels or places facilitating prostitution in Art 2 of the 1949 Convention, is manifested by the

---

27 Application No 7906/77, Decision (5 July 1979) (1982) 4 EHRR 443.

limited ratifications this instrument has received.[28] This number should not lead one to believe that prostitution in all its manifestations is lawful except where it is prohibited by States parties to the 1949 Convention. Rather, although exploitation of the prostitution of others not culminating to a condition of ownership over a person and performed with the prostitute's consent does not draw consensus to warrant its characterisation as an international offence, the procurement or enticement of a person for the purposes of prostitution does constitute an international or transnational offence.[29] This conclusion is derived, first, from the fact that the latter facet of prostitution is a criminal offence, if not in all States, then at least in the vast majority, and, secondly, by the declarations of non-parties to the 1949 Convention to the effect that ratification of this instrument is problematic only because their national laws permit organised, State-controlled prostitution.[30]

The ineffectiveness of the 1949 Convention necessitated the adoption of a specific instrument in November 2000, the UN Protocol to Prevent, Suppress and Punish Trafficking in Persons, Especially Women and Children.[31] The Protocol applies with regard to cases of trafficking involving duress and a transnational aspect (movement of people across borders or exploitation within a country by a transnational organised crime group) and is intended to prevent and combat trafficking, facilitate international co-operation, as well as provide certain measures of protection and assistance to victims. Article 3(a) defines 'trafficking in persons' as:

> The recruitment, transportation, transfer, harbouring or receipt of persons, by means of the threat or use of force or other forms of coercion, of abduction, of fraud, of deception, of the abuse of power or of a position of vulnerability or of the giving or receiving of payments or

---

28 74 parties, as of Feb 2003.
29 See also 1979 Convention on the Elimination of All Forms of Discrimination Against Women, Art 6, 19 ILM (1980), 33 which requires States to suppress all forms of traffic in women and exploitation of the prostitution of others; ECOSOC Res 1999/40 (26 April 1999) urged States to criminalise traffic in women and girls, whether the offence was committed in their own or third countries; para 24 of the Organisation for Security and Co-operation in Europe Charter for European Security prescribes an undertaking by this organisation to eliminate all forms of trafficking and sexual exploitation of human beings, 39 ILM (2000), 255: strategic objective D3 of the Beijing Platform for Action of the Fourth World Conference on Women (Report of 15 Sept 1995), UN Sales No E96.IV.13, aiming to eliminate trafficking in women.
30 Possible ratification of the 1949 Convention by retentionist States with the inclusion of relevant reservations would run counter to the purpose and object of the treaty and would be null, in accordance with the 1969 Vienna Convention on the Law of Treaties, Art 19(c), 1155 UNTS 331.
31 UN Doc A/55/383 (2 Nov 2000).

benefits to achieve the consent of a person having control over another person, for the purpose of exploitation.

The term 'exploitation' is further elaborated as exploitation of prostitution and other forms of sexual exploitation, forced labour, slavery and related practices, as well as the removal of organs. There is great expectation that the Protocol, as well as the 2000 UN Convention Against Transnational Organized Crime, will be effective in its preventive and punitive aspects and succeed where its predecessors failed.

There does exist one final form of slavery related practice, which is an offence only when committed by State entities: forced or compulsory labour. Article 2(1) of the 1930 ILO Forced Labour Convention (No 29) (1930 ILO Convention) defines forced labour as:

> All work or service which is exacted from any person under the menace of any penalty and for which the said person has not offered himself voluntarily.

This definition of forced labour excludes military service, civic duties, work arising from lawful conviction properly supervised, labour as a result of natural calamities or other emergencies and other cases of minor communal services.[32] All forms of forced labour constitute penal offences under the 1930 ILO Convention,[33] and wide ratification of this instrument has rendered the offence a rule of customary international law. In June 1999, the ILO decided to boycott commercial or other activities in Myanmar (Burma) for its 'grave and persistent' violation of the 1930 ILO Convention,[34] while in 1998 this country was barred from the Organisation.[35] It is estimated that more than 800,000 civilians, particularly from ethnic minorities, have been forcibly recruited by the Myanmar Government to work on public projects, resulting, moreover, in the displacement of between 5 and 10 per cent of the Burmese population.[36]

The UN Working Group on Contemporary Forms of Slavery stated in its reports that slavery, in all its forms and manifestations, is a crime against

---

32 1930 ILO Convention, Art 2(2).
33 Ibid, Art 25.
34 ILO Resolution, 'The Widespread Use of Forced Labour in Myanmar of 14 June 1999', 38 ILM (1999), 1215.
35 Report of the Commission of Inquiry Regarding the Observance by Myanmar of the 1930 Forced Labour Convention (2 July 1998).
36 In *Doe v Unocal*, 963 F Supp 880 (1997), a US District Court held that two American private corporations engaged in commercial activities involving the use of forced labour in Burma could be found liable under the 1789 Aliens Tort Claims Act, 18 USC § 1350.

humanity.[37] It is difficult to uphold this statement in every case of slavery, unless there is proof of widespread or systematic action in this regard, whether it originates from agents or organs of a State or from non-State entities. It is evident, however, that most cases of slavery and related institutions are the result of well organised criminal elements with international connections, who exploit vulnerable elements of society and rely heavily in their evil schemes on the corruption of State officials.

8.2.2 Remedies and international enforcement measures

All relevant treaties coincide and prescribe an obligation not only to treat the objects of all forms of slavery as victims, but also and – as far as possible – to rehabilitate them in a way that is beneficial to such persons. This is facilitated by the inclusion of either normative obligations in the relevant treaties, or through the establishment of technical co-operation organisations, such as the ILO's International Program on the Elimination of Child Labour.[38] ECOSOC, too, is monitoring the issue closely and has set up a Working Group on Contemporary Forms of Slavery, appointing a Special Rapporteur on the Sale of Children, Child Prostitution and Child Pornography. Slavery occupies the agenda of a multitude of other specialised agencies of the UN, while a large number of NGOs, especially Anti-Slavery International, provide comfort to victims and endeavour to inform international as well as national authorities of the magnitude of this scourge.[39]

States may lawfully extend their domestic criminal legislation to cover extra-territorial offences of those slavery related practices described as offences under international law, as long as prosecution of this kind does not conflict with a more substantial jurisdiction asserted by other States, to which they must give priority. The fact that slavery may be permitted *de facto* or *de jure* in the country of the accused is of no relevance to the rights of the accused, as slavery is an international offence and an *erga omnes* obligation, the suppression of which is in the interest of every State.

As for direct international enforcement, Art 99 of UNCLOS obliges States to prevent and punish transportation of slaves on vessels flying their flag, while Art 110(1)(b) of this Convention confers on warships of all nations a

---

37 UN Doc E/CN4/Sub2/1997/13 (11 July 1997), para 80 and UN Doc E/CN4/Sub2/1999/17 (20 July 1999), para 103.
38 MJ Dennis, 'The ILO Convention on the Worst Forms of Child Labour', 93 *AJIL* (1999), 943, p 947.
39 With the passing of GA Res 46/122 (17 Oct 1991), a UN Voluntary Trust on Contemporary Forms of Slavery was established with the aim of funding NGO participation in the meetings of the Working Group and also to provide assistance to victims of slavery.

right of visit aboard any vessel on the high seas where there is reasonable ground for suspecting that it is engaged in the slave trade. There does not exist, however, a general right to seize foreign slave trading vessels on the high seas, nor arrest its crew, as this prerogative belongs only to the Flag State, in contrast to piracy.[40] The only available option is to report such findings to the Flag State, which is thereafter under an obligation to promptly initiate criminal proceedings.

A more appropriate means of deterring recalcitrant States from utilising or tolerating the use of slave labour would be by barring the purchase of goods or services from companies engaged in any such practice. Any scrutiny of this nature, however, would be inconsistent with most countries' obligations under the World Trade Organization (WTO) Agreement on Government Procurement, thus clearly positing trading interests above fundamental human rights considerations. This obligation under the WTO Agreement is indirectly incompatible and contrary to the *jus cogens* character of slavery and related institutions.

8.3 TORTURE AS A CRIME UNDER INTERNATIONAL LAW

The prohibition of torture in international law is regulated by instruments whose primary purpose is the establishment of appropriate preventive and deterrent mechanisms. This forms part of a wider obligation undertaken by States in the context of human rights law.[41] Although these treaties envisage the application of criminal laws against the perpetrator, the purpose of these instruments is to form the basis of implementing domestic legislation and engage the responsibility of States parties. It should not, therefore, be assumed that these treaties apply *mutatis mutandis* to assess the criminal liability of the perpetrator under international law. The prohibition of torture as laid down in human rights treaties entails a right from which no derogation is permitted. This is confirmed by the fact that: it has been construed as such by domestic and international judicial bodies;[42] it has not been denied by any country; and, in Europe, at least, States are not permitted to return or extradite to another country persons who are in danger of being subjected to

---

40 RR Churchill and AV Lowe, *The Law of the Sea* , 1999, Manchester: Manchester UP, 171.
41 ICCPR, Art 7.
42 Human Rights Committee, General Comment No 24 (4 Nov 1994), para 10; *Siderman de Blake v Argentina*, 965 F 2d 699 (1992) *cert denied; Argentina v De Blake*, 507 US 1017; *Xuncax and Others v Gramajo*, 886 F Supp 162 (1995); *ICTY Prosecutor v Furundzija*, Judgment (10 Dec 1998), 38 ILM (1999), 317, paras 153–57.

torture or to practices that have the same effect as torture.[43] The *Furundzija* judgment logically, therefore, concluded that international law not only prohibits torture, but also strictly regulates '(i) the failure to adopt the national measures necessary for implementing the prohibition and (ii) the maintenance in force or passage of laws which are contrary to the prohibition'.[44]

8.3.1 Defining torture

The definition of torture under customary international law remains ambiguous. It is of course contained in one universal and a number of regional treaties, but the precise extra-conventional nature of these treaties and the crystallisation of a customary definition is itself doubtful. While the various instruments enjoy common elements, there is divergence generally on two issues: (a) the range of acts and the effect of acts that constitute torture; and (b) whether torture may be committed by persons other than State agents. We shall examine these issues in the following sections. It is useful, first of all, to consider the definition of torture under the most widely ratified of the aforementioned instruments, the 1984 UN Convention Against Torture and Other Cruel, Inhuman or Degrading Treatment or Punishment (UN Torture Convention). Article 1(1) defines the offence to mean:

> Any act by which severe pain or suffering, whether physical or mental, is intentionally inflicted on a person for such purposes as obtaining from him or a third person information or a confession, punishing him for an act he or a third person has committed or is suspected of having committed, or intimidating or coercing him or a third person, or for any reason based on discrimination of any kind, when such pain or suffering is inflicted by or at the instigation of or with the consent or acquiescence of a public official or other person acting in an official capacity. It does not include pain or suffering arising only from, inherent in or incidental to lawful sanctions.

This definition coincides to a very large extent with the 1975 General Assembly Declaration on Torture, which was adopted by consensus.[45] However, the definition contained in Art 3 of the 1985 Inter-American Torture

---

43 1984 UN Convention against Torture and Other Cruel, Inhuman or Degrading Treatment or Punishment, Art 3, 1465 UNTS 85; 1969 Inter-American Convention on Human Rights, Art 13(4); *Soering v UK*, Judgment (7 July 1989), EurCtHR, Ser A, No 161, para 91; *Chahal v UK*, Judgment (5 Nov 1996), EurCtHR, SerA, No 22; *C v Australia*, Human Rights Committee, Com No 900/1999.

44 Op cit, *Furundzija* Judgment note 42, para 148.

45 GA Res 3452 (XXX) (9 Dec 1975), Declaration on the Protection of All Persons Being Subjected to Torture and Other Cruel, Inhuman or Degrading Treatment or Punishment.

Convention[46] is broader than that of the 1984 UN Torture Convention, in that it does not require any threshold of pain or other suffering for an act of ill-treatment to constitute torture. In actual fact, neither physical nor mental suffering is required if the intent of the perpetrator is 'to obliterate the personality of the victim or to diminish his physical or mental capacities'. This definition, moreover, does not contain an exhaustive list of purposes that can be pursued by the perpetrator but instead provides examples of such purposes and adds 'or any other purpose'. The European Court and Commission of Human Rights have construed torture as constituting an aggravated and deliberate form of inhuman treatment which is directed at obtaining information or confessions, or at inflicting a punishment.[47] This definition echoes Art 1 of the 1975 Declaration on Torture. International Criminal Tribunal for the Former Yugoslavia (ICTY) jurisprudence has put forward the proposition that under customary international law there is no requirement that the conduct be solely perpetrated for one of the prohibited purposes.[48] Thus, in the *Furundzija* judgment, the Court held that the intentional humiliation of the victim is among the possible purposes of torture, since this would be justified by the general spirit of international humanitarian law, whose primary purpose is to safeguard human dignity.[49] The Trial Chamber further justified this proposition by noting that 'the notion of humiliation is, in any event, close to the notion of intimidation, which is explicitly referred to in the [1984] Torture Convention's definition of torture'.[50] This statement should be approached with extreme caution, since if true it would render the offences of 'outrages upon personal dignity' and 'inhuman and degrading treatment' redundant. This is more so because Trial Chamber II in the *Krnojelac* case rejected the proposition espoused in the above mentioned judgments that intentional humiliation may constitute torture under customary law.[51] The common denominator of all the instruments to which reference has been made points to the conclusion that the underlying act must be instrumental to achieve a particular purpose set out by the perpetrator. It is contentious whether customary law permits other forms of ill-treatment to constitute torture, but increasingly the use of rape,

---

46 25 ILM (1986), 519.
47 *Ireland v UK*, Judgment (18 Jan 1978) (1978) 2 EHRR 25, para 167; *Greek* case (1969) ECHR Yearbook 134, p 186.
48 *ICTY Prosecutor v Delalic and Others* (*Celebici* case), Judgment (16 Nov 1998), 38 ILM (1998), 57, para 470; *ICTY Prosecutor v Kunarac and Others* , Judgment (22 Feb 2001), para 486.
49 Op cit, *Furundzija* Judgment note 42, para 162. The judgment in the same case recognised that being forced to watch serious sexual attacks inflicted on a female acquaintance was torture for the forced observer, as is the presence of onlookers, particularly family members, on the person being raped, para 267.
50 Ibid, para 162.
51 *ICTY Prosecutor v Krnojelac*, Judgment (15 March 2002), Case No IT–97–25-T, para 186.

in particular, in the course of detention and interrogation as a means of intimidating, punishing, coercing or even humiliating the victim, or for obtaining information, or a confession, from the victim or a third person, has been recognised.[52] In the *Krnojelac* judgment, the ICTY held that where confinement of the victim can be shown to pursue one of the prohibited purposes of torture and to have caused the victim severe pain or suffering, the act of putting or keeping someone in solitary confinement may amount to torture, and the same would be true in analogy of the deliberate deprivation of sufficient food.[53]

The distinguishing characteristic between torture and other lesser forms of ill-treatment is the severity of the pain or suffering of the victim. A precise threshold would be impractical to delineate and thus the task of assessment is left to the discretion of the judge. ICTY and European Court of Human Rights (ECHR) jurisprudence does not clearly set out a single test, whether objective or subjective. Rather, they are in agreement that: (a) the severity of the harm rests on an objective test; whereas (b) the mental or physical suffering requires subjective assessment, involving consideration of factors such as the victim's age, health, sex and others.[54] The objective test regarding the severity of the harm may be triggered by beating, sexual violence, prolonged denial of sleep, food, hygiene, and medical assistance, as well as threats to torture, rape, or kill relatives, as well as mutilation of body parts.[55]

Torture in times of armed conflict is specifically prohibited by the 1949 Geneva Conventions[56] and the two Additional Protocols of 1977.[57] As we shall see below, the *Kunarac* judgment concluded that whether or not international human rights law generally recognises that only public officials or State agents can commit the crime of torture, international humanitarian law makes no such distinction, thus rendering any individual culpable of the offence, as long as the appropriate *mens rea* and *actus reus* have been satisfied.[58]

---

52 *Aydin v Turkey* (1998) 25 EHRR 251, paras 82–84; *Fernando and Raquel Mejia v Peru*, Decision (1 March 1996), Report No 5/96, Case No 10,970, Annual Report of the IACHR (1995), Doc OEA/Ser L/V/II 91, pp 182–88; op cit, *Furundzija* Judgment note 42, para 163.

53 Op cit, *Krnojelac* Judgment note 51, para 183.

54 *Ireland v UK*, Judgment (18 Jan 1978) (1978) 2 EHRR 25, para 162; *ICTY Prosecutor v Kvocka and Others*, Judgment (2 Nov 2001), para 143.

55 *Kvocka* Judgment, ibid, para 144; confirmed also in the views of the UN Human Rights Committee in *Grille Motta*, Com No 11/1977; *Miango Muiyo v Zaire*, Com No 194/85; *Kanana v Zaire*, Com No 366/89; *Herrera Rubio v Colombia*, Com No 161/1983.

56 Common Art 3; Arts 12 and 50, Geneva I; Arts 12 and 51, Geneva II; Arts 13, 14 and 130, Geneva III; Arts 27, 32 and 147, Geneva IV.

57 Protocol I, Art 75; Protocol II, Art 4.

58 Op cit, *Kunarac* Judgment note 48, paras 490–96.

8.3.2 The 'public official' requirement of torture

As already examined, the definition of torture in Art 1 of the 1984 UN Torture Convention requires that the offence was perpetrated at the instigation, consent, or acquiescence of a public official. If this constitutes a generally mandatory requirement under treaty and customary law, the ambit of the offence becomes very narrow, with the result of excluding all cases of torture committed by non-State actors, such as guerrillas, paramilitaries and terrorists. We must distinguish between torture in the context of international humanitarian law and torture generally.

Under international humanitarian law, in particular the 1949 Geneva Conventions and the two 1977 Protocols, the presence, involvement or acquiescence of a State official or any other authority-wielding person is not required for the offence to be characterised as torture. The same is true of Arts 3 and 5 of the ICTY Statute. This conclusion was correctly drawn by the *Kunarac* judgment, which examined in detail all the relevant provisions of humanitarian law.[59] Moreover, Art 7(2)(e) of the International Criminal Court (ICC) Statute, concerning torture as a crime against humanity, does not impose the State actor requirement.

The inclusion, on the other hand, of non-State actors outside the ambit of humanitarian law is less clear. In a recent decision, the UN Committee Against Torture (CAT) held that a civilian pogrom against Roma settlers in Yugoslavia, which was tolerated by the police, constituted a violation of Art 16 of the 1984 UN Torture Convention (inhuman and cruel treatment). In a common dissenting opinion, two Committee members expressed the view that the acts could also be described as torture under Art 1.[60] The jurisprudence of the ECHR[61] and the UN Human Rights Committee[62] clearly articulates that Arts 3 and 7 of the European Convention on Human Rights and of the International Covenant on Civil and Political Rights (ICCPR) respectively may also apply in situations where organs or agents of the State are not involved in the violation of the rights protected under these provisions. Although both the European Convention on Human Rights and the ICCPR are primarily human rights instruments and the jurisprudence of their respective enforcement mechanisms does not directly involve reference to criminal liability, it would be absurd to uphold one definition for human rights purposes and another with regard to international criminal law. The

---

59 Ibid; the following concurred with this statement: op cit, *Krnojelac* Judgment note 51, para 187; op cit, *Kvocka* Judgment note 54, paras 138–39.

60 *Hajrizi and Others v Yugoslavia*, Com No 161 /2000, CAT Doc CAT/C/29/D/161/2000.

61 *HLR v France*, Judgment (29 April 1997) (1997) 26 EHRR 29, para 40; *Costello-Roberts v UK*, Judgment (25 March 1993) (1993) 19 EHRR 112, paras 27–28; *A v UK*, Judgment (23 September 1998) (1998) 27 EHRR 611, para 22.

62 General Comment No 7/16 (27 July 1982), para 2.

only doubtful issue in this scenario is whether the perpetration of torture by non-State agents would entail the responsibility of the State in which the offence took place. This question has been answered in the affirmative by the UN Human Rights Committee in all cases where the State does not protect individuals from interference by private parties.[63]

Finally, mention should be made to the distinction identified by the *Furundzija* judgment between complicity in torture and complicity in other offences. It held that co-perpetrators of torture are persons participating in an integral part of the torture process and who partake in the purpose behind its infliction (that is, confession, punishment, etc), whereas aiders and abettors in acts of torture assist the principal in a way that has a substantial effect on the perpetration of the crime, with knowledge that torture is taking place. In that case, the accused was held liable as co-perpetrator of a rape by virtue of his interrogation of the victim, which was found to constitute an integral part of the rape.[64]

8.4 APARTHEID

The official policy of racial segregation and discrimination practised by the white minority regime of South Africa up until the early 1990s had sparked worldwide repugnance and condemnation by both the UN General Assembly and the Security Council. Article 3 of the 1965 Convention on the Elimination of All Forms of Racial Discrimination (CERD)[65] first obliged parties to prevent, prohibit and eradicate racial segregation and apartheid, as well as all practices of that nature from territories under their jurisdiction. This general obligation was specifically articulated as entailing a duty to enact legislation criminalising all forms of advocacy of racial superiority or hatred, criminalise groups advocating the aforementioned, as well as personal participation therein, and moreover prevent all public bodies from practising or promoting such forms of discrimination.[66] Reference in the CERD to apartheid and racial segregation was meant to underline them as particular manifestations of the wider offence of racial discrimination. Moreover, apartheid was practised officially in South Africa and the CERD emphasised its repugnant nature and the will of the international community to declare it illegal.

Notwithstanding the fact that all forms of racial discrimination constitute

63 General Comment No 20/44 (3 April 1992), para 2.
64 Op cit, *Furundzija* Judgment note 42, paras 257, 267; see I Bantekas, *Principles of Direct and Superior Responsibility in International Humanitarian Law* , 2002, Manchester: Manchester UP, 62–66.
65 660 UNTS 195.
66 CERD, Art 4.

offences under international law, the crime of apartheid has established a particular dynamic. The 1974 International Convention on the Suppression and Punishment of the Crime of Apartheid (Apartheid Convention)[67] recognised it as a crime against humanity.[68] Although the Convention possesses a universal character, it was drafted solely with South Africa in mind. The offence is completed, in accordance with Art II, by the commission of inhuman acts 'with the purpose of establishing and maintaining domination by one racial group of persons over any other racial group of persons and systematically oppressing them'. Although Art II contains a very broad and detailed list of underlying inhuman acts giving rise to the practice of apartheid, this list is merely indicative and may encompass other offences. Both the CERD and the Apartheid Convention recognise that apartheid is an institutional policy, borne by the State. This means that private individuals participating in the implementation of a policy of racial segregation – for example, a South African business conforming with domestic law in not recruiting black people or agreeing to use them under conditions of forced labour – do so because this policy has been formally established and institutionalised by State machinery. Article III suggests, however, that even under such circumstances, that is, of apartheid as binding domestic law, not only State agents but also private individuals incur international criminal responsibility. Since apartheid is a crime against humanity, the contours of which are not described in the Apartheid Convention, it must be assumed that the elements of crimes against humanity pertaining to apartheid will depend on the judicial context in which it is examined. Thus, the definition of crimes against humanity is different in the ICTY, International Criminal Tribunal for Rwanda (ICTR) (although neither of these makes reference to apartheid) and ICC Statutes, as well as in customary international law and domestic laws. Depending on the forum, determination of apartheid as a crime against humanity will vary. To illustrate its application to the South African experience under existing customary law, the policy of segregation would constitute the 'attack' against the indigenous black population. Because of its proclaimed official status, the 'systematic' element of crimes against humanity would be clearly established. Perpetrators include not only those persons in government that instituted and formulated the policy, but also all private individuals that implemented the policy to the detriment of the rights of the victims, with knowledge of the overall 'attack'. The Apartheid Convention establishes broad jurisdictional competence on the basis of the *erga omnes* obligation, the prevention and punishment of which the offence of apartheid necessarily entails. In any event, crimes

---

67 1015 UNTS 243.
68 Similarly, para 15 of the 2001 Durban Declaration Against Racism, Racial Discrimination, Xenophobia and Related Intolerance.

against humanity are subject to universal jurisdiction under customary international law.

Apartheid is also recognised as a crime against humanity by Art 7(1)(j) of the ICC Statute. In accordance with para 2(h), it encompasses:

> Inhumane acts [intentionally causing great suffering, or serious injury to body or to mental health] committed in the context of an institutionalised regime of systematic oppression and domination by one racial group over any other racial group or groups and committed with the intention of maintaining that regime.

The definition is very similar to that contained in the Apartheid Convention, but the concept of crimes against humanity in the ICC context is narrower than that established under customary international law. In conclusion, apartheid constitutes a very specific crime against humanity, based solely on racial discrimination. It is relevant even after the collapse of the South African apartheid State, and much will depend on the anthropological definition of 'race', in particular judicial fora.

8.5 ENFORCED OR INVOLUNTARY DISAPPEARANCES

The problem of enforced or involuntary disappearances first received international attention through the UN General Assembly Resolution 33/173 in 1978.[69] The situation was endemic and an integral part of the South American dictatorships. Despite their demise, however, by at least the mid-1980s, the problem has not only persisted, but has spread all over the world. As a result, the UN Human Rights Commission established in 1980 a Working Group on Enforced or Involuntary Disappearances. The mandate of the work has been renewed ever since, and its latest reports clearly manifest an increase in individual communications with only few cases resolved.[70] Because of its prevalence in South America, the Assembly and Commission of the Organisation of American States (OAS) have repeatedly referred to the practice of disappearances since 1978, urging all cases be investigated and the practice stopped.[71] In the US, in two civil suits tried under the 1789 Aliens Tort Act,

---

69 GA Res 33/173 (20 Dec 1978); see also ECOSOC Res 1979/38 (10 May 1979).

70 UN Human Rights Commission Res 2002/41 (23 April 2002).

71 AG Res 443 (IX–0/79) (31 Oct 1979); Inter-American Commission on Human Rights, *Annual Report*, 1978, pp 24–27.

the courts ruled that the prohibition against enforced disappearances had assumed the status of *jus cogens*.[72]

In 1983 the OAS Assembly stated that the practice of enforced disappearances constitutes a crime against humanity.[73] Without a legal instrument criminalising this practice, or mentioned as prohibited under a human rights instrument within its jurisdiction, the Inter-American Court of Human Rights in the *Velasquez Rodriguez* case, although noting that its classification as a crime against humanity may be possible, held that the disappearance of 150 persons in Honduras between 1981 and 1984, and carried out as part of a systematic practice by that country's armed forces, amounted to a violation of three distinct human rights contained in the 1969 Inter-American Convention on Human Rights.[74] These were: Art 7 (right to personal liberty); Art 5 (right to humane treatment); Art 4 (right to life).[75] The most comprehensive international definition of the offence of enforced disappearance is that contained in the preamble to the UN General Assembly's 1972 Declaration on the Protection of All Persons from Enforced Disappearance.[76] Under this instrument, such illegal disappearances occur when:

> Persons are arrested, detained or abducted against their will or otherwise deprived of their liberty by officials of different branches or levels of government, or by organised groups, or private individuals acting on behalf of, or with the support, direct or indirect, consent or acquiescence of the government, followed by a refusal to disclose the fate or whereabouts of the persons concerned, or a refusal to acknowledge the deprivation of the liberty, which places such persons outside the protection of the law.

This definition elaborates with more precision the elements of the offence found in Arts II and 7(2)(i) of the 1994 Inter-American Convention on the Forced Disappearance of Persons[77] and the ICC Statute respectively. However, although the 1994 Convention and the ICC Statute treat this practice as a crime against humanity, the 1992 Declaration makes no such statement, but instead provides that it shall be considered as an offence under domestic criminal law (Art 4), to which the defence of superior orders is not applicable (Art 6).

By its very nature, the 'practice' of enforced disappearances is a serious and

---

72 *Re Estate of Marcos*, 25 F 3d, at 1745; *Forti v Suarez-Mason*, 672 F Supp 1531, at 1542 (1987), *amended*, 694 F Supp 707, at 710–11 (1989).
73 AG/Res 666 (18 Nov 1983).
74 9 ILM (1970), 673.
75 *Velasquez Rodriguez* case (Merits) (29 July 1988) (1988) 95 ILR 232.
76 GA Res 47/133 (18 Dec 1992).
77 33 ILM (1994), 1259.

systematic attack against a dissenting civilian population, within a State, and as such qualifies as a crime against humanity. However, although the jurisprudence of the ad hoc tribunals and the ICC Statute clearly suggest that crimes against humanity can be committed by non-State agents, enforced disappearances can only be committed by public officials or persons authorised by the State. Abduction of persons by non-State actors would constitute the offence of kidnapping or hostage taking, depending on the facts of each case, but not the offence of involuntary disappearances. The *actus reus* of the offence may commence lawfully, that is through initial arrest of the victim by duly authorised government forces. The crime is not completed with the unlawful arrest or abduction of the victim by government agents, but by the intentional and unlawful deprivation of the victim's liberty, coupled with a refusal to disclose his or her whereabouts. The latter component of the crime (that is, non-disclosure) may take place while the victim is otherwise lawfully detained. In its General Comment No 20, the Human Rights Committee held that in order to guarantee the effective protection of detained persons, provision should be made by States for detainees to be held in places officially recognised as places of detention, as well as for the names of persons responsible for their detention to be kept in registers made available to those concerned, including relatives and friends. Furthermore, the time, place and names of all present in the interrogation must be recorded.[78]

Besides qualifying as a crime against humanity, the practice of enforced disappearances may well qualify as torture if the relevant criteria pertaining to the crime of torture are satisfied. As already noted, the crime of torture need not be committed only by State agents, but also by private individuals. Although involuntary disappearances do not constitute a particular violation of the European Convention of Human Rights, the ECHR pointed out in the case of *Kurt v Turkey* that forced disappearance is a violation of Art 3 of the Convention, prohibiting torture, cruel and inhuman treatment, which as a result caused extreme suffering to the victim's mother.[79] Although all offences against the person have an emotional impact on the family or circle of friends of the victim, this is usually incidental to the underlying crime. In the case of forced disappearances, one of the aims of the perpetrators is to terrorise or otherwise intimidate those close to the victim but also, in a significant number of cases, a larger segment of the population. Thus, the practice of disappearance as torture could be substantiated not only vis-à-vis the victim, but also against his or her relatives or friends.

Finally, mention should be made of the jurisdictional aspects of the offence. Both the Draft Convention on Enforced Disappearances, currently

---

78 General Comment No 20, UN Doc CCPR/C/21/Rev1/Add3 (7 April 1992), para 11; similar provision is stipulated in Arts 8–12 of the 1992 Declaration.
79 *Kurt v Turkey*, Judgment (25 May 1998), Case No 15/1997/799/1002, para 134.

contemplated by the United Nations, and the 1994 Inter-American Convention proclaim a broad jurisdictional basis, which however fall short of universal jurisdiction. Much like Art 14 of the 1992 Declaration, these instruments at best provide for the exercise of permissive rather than compulsory jurisdiction. Only one of these instruments is legally binding, the 1994 Inter-American Convention on the Forced Disappearance of Persons, and that is limited to eight States. On the other hand, if a particular case of enforced disappearance is classified as a crime against humanity, universal jurisdiction would be available under customary international law. Whereas the same is not true with regard to the same practice characterised as torture, the broad exercise of jurisdiction, akin to universal, would be permissible as long as other States claiming closer links with the case do not raise objections.

Chapter 9

International criminal law of the sea

9.1 INTRODUCTION: THE LAW OF THE SEA

Before we set out to explore maritime crime it is useful to remember the sources of the law of the sea, namely customary law and treaty law. Most of the former has been codified in the 1982 United Nations Convention on the Law of the Sea (UNCLOS), as well as its precursor, the 1958 Geneva Conventions. Other treaties, however, both bilateral and multilateral, address issues relating to the seas. States have certain rights and duties with regard to the seas, depending on the maritime belt under consideration. UNCLOS clearly sets out the various maritime belts. The measurement of maritime belts seawards commences from what are known as baselines. UNCLOS provides for two types of baselines, normal and straight. Where a coastline is not heavily indented, the officially recognised low water mark point represents the normal baseline and thus the starting point for measuring the breadth of the various maritime belts. In the case of indented coastlines, the method of drawing straight lines between points on the coast or at sea may be used. The territorial sea may extend up to 12 nautical miles seaward from the baselines, whereas all waters landward from the baselines are considered internal waters. States retain sovereignty in both internal waters and territorial sea but there is an obligation to grant a right of 'innocent passage' in the latter, provided that such passage is not detrimental to the security of the coastal State. UNCLOS also introduced a regime for archipelagic States, that is States made up of a group of closely spaced islands, such as Indonesia. For those States, the territorial sea is a 12 mile zone extending from a line drawn joining the outermost points of the outermost islands of the group that are in close proximity to each other. The waters between the islands are declared archipelagic waters, where ships of all States enjoy the right of innocent passage. As regards international straits, the regime of 'transit passage' retains the international status of the straits and gives naval powers the right to unimpeded navigation and overflight. In all matters other than transient navigation, straits are considered territorial waters. Coastal States are also empowered to implement certain rights in an area beyond the territorial sea, extending 24 nautical miles from their baselines for the purpose of preventing certain violations and enforcing police powers. This area, known as the 'contiguous zone', may be used to curtail offenders violating the laws of the coastal State within its territory or its territorial sea. The exclusive economic zone (EEZ) extends up to 200 nautical miles from the baselines. The coastal State retains sovereign rights but not sovereignty in the EEZ. The continental shelf comprises the seabed and its subsoil that extend beyond the limits of the territorial sea throughout the natural prolongation of the coastal State's land territory to the outer edge of the continental margin, or to a distance of 200 miles from the baselines, where the outer edge of the continental margin does not extend up to that distance. In cases where the continental margin extends further than 200 miles, States may claim a continental shelf up to 350 miles from the baseline or 100 miles from the 2,500 metre depth isobath. The coastal State possesses exclusive rights of exploration and exploitation of the continental shelf's natural resources. The rights of the coastal State over the continental shelf do not affect the legal status of the superjacent waters or of the air space above those waters. Finally, the high seas are open to all States and for a number of purposes, such as navigation, over-flight, laying of submarine cables and fishing, subject to certain restrictions. The international seabed, too, is not subject to the sovereignty of any State, and is part of the 'common heritage of mankind'.

In this chapter we examine the crimes of piracy *jure gentium*, mutiny, maritime terrorism, damage to submarine cables, unauthorised broadcasting and the right of hot pursuit – although the last relates to enforcement, it was included in this chapter for reasons of coherency. Maritime crime is also explored in other chapters, especially those dealing with jurisdictional issues (Chapter 4), the transport of slaves and the smuggling of migrants on the high seas by organised criminal groups (Chapters 8 and 11).

9.2 PIRACY *JURE GENTIUM*

To those who believe that sea piracy is a romantic remnant of past centuries, it may come as a surprise to discover that the International Maritime Organisation's (IMO) statistics on piracy and armed robbery at sea from 1984 to 31 December 1999 reported 1,751 known incidents.[1] The areas that are currently most affected by piratical attacks are: the Far East, in particular

---

1 *Reports on Acts of Piracy and Armed Robbery Against Ships*, First Quarterly Report (January–March 2000), IMO Doc MSC/Circ 944 (1 April 2000), p 1; see International Chamber of Commerce (ICC), *Piracy and Armed Robbery Against Ships: 2002 Annual Report*, 2002, London: ICC, which recorded an increase in incidents from 253 in the first nine months of 2001 to 271 for the corresponding period in 2002.

the South China Sea and the Malacca Strait;[2] South America and the Caribbean; the Indian Ocean; and West and East Africa. The increase in piracy can be explained on several grounds, such as the need for small crews on large technologically advanced vessels, which renders them vulnerable, lack of adequate diplomatic representation where vessels fly flags of convenience and the existence of poor countries with large coastlines that are unable to afford adequate patrol of their territorial waters, let alone the adjacent high seas.

Contemporary pirates can be classified into two categories. First are those who operate on a small scale, interested either in the possessions of the crew (the captain usually keeps a substantial amount of money for payroll, maintenance and port fees), or various equipment on board the vessel. The majority of such pirates operate when ships are anchored in, or pass through, territorial waters. The second category involves well-organised groups whose operations go far beyond random attacks at sea. Organised piracy aims either at the cargo of merchant vessels or the vessel itself. When ships are stolen in this way they are repainted, renamed and re-registered. Temporary registration certificates may be obtained through consulate offices, whether by bribery or presentation of false documents, or both. The pirates will then look for a shipping agent with a letter of credit that has almost expired and will offer the services of their ship, upon which the ship is loaded and the shipper receives the bill of lading. The pirates then sail to a different destination than the one specified on the bill of lading. There they may unload the cargo to an accomplice, or an unsuspecting buyer and change the temporary registration certificate again. Low freight rates and financial recession has created an upsurge in organised piracy in South East Asia, not only in the form of attacks against merchant vessels, but also in defrauding insurance companies through acts of piracy against ships owned by criminal groups such as the Chinese Triads.[3] Contemporary organised piracy is also believed to be heavily involved in the illicit traffic of narcotic drugs and arms, while reports indicate that corruption in a number of countries is responsible for both the lack of prosecutions and enforcement, as well as for facilitating the disposal of stolen vessels and cargo.[4]

2 T Arbuckle, 'Scourge of Piracy Returns to Southeast Asia', 29 *Jane's International Defence Review* (1996), 26.
3 'Upsurge in South East Asia Cases of Piracy' (1998) *Lloyd's List*, 3 Dec, p 3; 'Rogue Owners Colluding in Piracy Attacks' (1999) *Lloyd's List*, 13 May, p 5.
4 J Hitt, 'Bandits in the Global Shipping Lines' (2000) *New York Times Magazine*, 20 August, where the author furnishes information implicating Chinese authorities in the release of captured pirates.

9.2.1 Definition of piracy under international law

Piracy under international law, otherwise known as piracy *jure gentium*, is the oldest international offence. Until the 1536 Statute of Henry VIII,[5] piracy was punished in England only when committed within the realm of the Admiralty of the Crown and, then, merely as a civil offence. The 1536 Statute changed the jurisdictional element of piracy but not the nature of the offence as robbery at sea. It was well recognised by the 17th century that the common law definition was in no essential respect different from that of the law of nations.[6]

Although jurisdiction for piracy *jure gentium* under customary law was acknowledged as belonging to all States,[7] no authoritative definition existed as to its substantial elements.[8] Hence, until the adoption of an international definition in the 1958 Geneva Convention on the High Seas,[9] national statutes, the majority of which purported to incorporate the concept of piracy under customary international law,[10] were interpreted in accordance with each domestic judiciary's understanding of the prevailing elements of piracy.[11]

The earliest element in the definition of piracy was *animus furandi*, the intention to rob a vessel on the high seas – or, as in the case at hand, in any waters within the jurisdiction of UK admiralty.[12] It was later held, in other plagued jurisdictions, that robbery or an intention thereof was not an essential element and that acts of revenge, hatred, or abuse of power against another ship were tantamount to piracy. In the *Malek Adhel* case, the rather mentally disturbed captain of a commercial ship made it a habit of aggressively forcing other merchant vessels on the high seas to halt their course, without however robbing or looting them, except only to claim the gunpowder used to force them to stop.[13] The US Supreme Court stressed that a piratical act is an act of aggression unauthorised by the law of nations, being hostile and criminal in character and commission and without sanction from

---

5 Offences at Sea Act 1536, Chapter 15.
6 *USA v Smith*, 18 US 153 (1820), p 159, *per* Story J.
7 *Talbot v Jansen*, 3 US 153 (1795); *Turkey v France* (*Lotus* case) (1927) PCIJ Reports, Ser A, No 10, p 10, *per* Moore J.
8 M Halberstam, 'Terrorism on the High Seas: The *Achille Lauro*, Piracy and the IMO Convention on Maritime Safety', 82 *AJIL* (1988), 269, p 272.
9 450 UNTS 82, Arts 13–22.
10 This is true for the vast majority of contemporary statutes, if not all. See the US Piracy and Privateering Act 1948, 18 USC, § 1651.
11 In some countries slave-trading was considered an act of piracy (Imperial Act, 5 Geo IV, Chapter 113, §§ 9 and 10), but there was no such consensus between the international community. See Paust *et al, International Criminal Law: Cases and Materials*, 1996, Durham, NC: Carolina Academic Press, 1229.
12 *Rex v Dawson* (1696) 13 St Tr 451.
13 *USA v Cargo of the Brig Malek Adhel*, 43 US 210 (1844).

public or sovereign authority. This was so irrespective of whether the aim of the perpetrator was plunder, hatred, revenge, or wanton abuse of power.[14]

Since the time of Grotius a pirate has been considered to be *hostis humanis generis*, an enemy of mankind. This is not a rhetorical statement, it carries legal substance; for, if a person commits otherwise unlawful acts against persons and property of one country on the high seas, that person cannot readily be characterised as an enemy of mankind, only of that specific country. This issue was encountered when courts determined cases involving interference with maritime commerce not for private ends but as part of political or ideological struggles. The law in the nineteenth century, as it also stands today, was that insurgents fighting for a political cause should not be treated as pirates as long as, in their struggle against the target government, they attack only vessels and persons of that State.[15] This did not mean, of course, that the existence of political motives justified any act of insurgency. It was clear that common crimes, regardless of their motive, would result in the liability of the perpetrator.[16] Although now obsolete with the advancement of international humanitarian law, especially common Art 3 of the 1949 Geneva Conventions, the recognition of insurgency or belligerent status was of seminal importance both for the relations between belligerents, but also for the law of neutrality. Insurgency referred to a state of conflict where the dissident group, even though of considerable strength, did not receive international recognition as a legal entity under international law. Belligerency, on the other hand, existed when an armed conflict was recognised as taking place between two legal entities.[17] Having established a set of criteria for its recognition,[18] it was accepted by the end of the 19th century that belligerency was viewed as a question of fact rather than as one of law.[19] The relevant jurisprudence seems to suggest that the absence of belligerency did not render politically motivated acts by rebel groups piratical. In the *Ambrose Light*, the New York District Court held that unrecognised insurgents (that is,

14 Ibid, p 230; in *Re Piracy Jure Gentium* [1934] AC 856, the Privy Council held that actual robbery was not an essential element, as a frustrated attempt to commit piratical robbery is equally piracy *jure gentium*.

15 See C Hyde, *International Law Chiefly as Interpreted by the United States*, 1945, Boston: Little, Brown, Vol 2; *Dole v New England Mutual Marine Insurance Co* (1864) 7 F Cas 838, p 847; *Republic of Bolivia v Indemnity Mutual Marine Assurance Co Ltd* [1909] 1 KB 785, p 795.

16 *Magellan Pirates* (1853) 1 A&E 81.

17 A Arend and R Beck, *International Law and the Use of Force*, 1993, London: Routledge, 81–2.

18 These consisted of the existence of a generalised armed conflict, occupation and administration of a substantial portion of territory, organised armed forces under a responsible leadership and circumstances justifying recognition. H Lauterpacht, *Recognition in International Law*, 1948, Cambridge: CUP, 176.

19 L Moir, 'The Historical Development of the Application of Humanitarian Law in Non International Armed Conflicts to 1949', 47 *ICLQ* (1998), 347.

belligerents) were deemed to be pirates, even though in that case there was no proof of violence or depredation beyond that required for the group's political aims against the Venezuelan Government.[20] This judgment was vociferously rejected by the US executive and overturned by its judiciary shortly after it was issued, having no standing in international law.[21] The Harvard Draft Convention on Piracy, which was relied upon heavily by the International Law Commission's (ILC) rapporteur for the 1958 Convention on the High Seas, found that under customary law an attack by an unrecognised group is not piratical if, had the group received recognition, the contested act would not have been one of piracy.[22]

The elements described constitute the offence of piracy *jure gentium* under customary law and, as such, they were incorporated in the relevant definition in Arts 14 and 101 of the 1958 Geneva Convention on the High Seas and the 1982 UNCLOS respectively. The latter provides that:

Piracy consists of any of the following acts:

(a) any illegal acts of violence or detention, or any act of depredation, committed for private ends by the crew or the passengers of a private ship or a private aircraft, and directed:

   (i)   on the high seas, against another ship or aircraft, or against persons or property on board such ship or aircraft;
   (ii) against a ship, aircraft, persons or property in a place outside the jurisdiction of any State;

(b) any act of voluntary participation in the operation of a ship or of an aircraft with knowledge of facts making it a pirate ship or aircraft;[23]

(c) any act of inciting or of intentionally facilitating an act described in paras (a) or (b).

This definition is in line with customary law as explained above. The *actus reus* of the offence is not dependent on factors such as gravity or an intention to act openly. Hence, in *Athens Maritime Enterprises Corp v Hellenic Mutual War Risks Association Ltd*, the court erred when it held that a clandestine attempt to rob a ship anchored three miles from the coast of Bangladesh did not constitute piracy simply because the culprits intended to steal without recourse to violence.[24] It is also clear that the offence requires two vessels or

---

20 (1885) 25 Fed 408.
21 See LC Green, 'The Santa Maria: Rebels or Pirates', 37 *BYIL* (1961), 496, p 502; op cit, Hyde, note 15, p 774.
22 Harvard research in international law, comment to the Draft Convention on Piracy, 26 *AJIL* (1932 Supp) 749, p 857; see 1 *Yearbook ILC* (1955), p 41.
23 *Talbot v Jansen*, 3 US 153 (1795), p 156, *per* Paterson J.
24 [1983] 1 All ER 590. The court would have been right, however, had it stated that the incident did not constitute piracy *jure gentium* because it occurred in territorial waters.

aircraft: the piratical and the victim vessel or aircraft. It is, thus, evident that piracy under international law cannot be born through an act of mutiny, unless the mutineers subsequently engage in acts of violence or depredation against other vessels or aircraft on the high seas. Likewise, the perpetration of piratical acts, as defined in Art 101 of UNCLOS, by a warship, government ship or government aircraft whose crew has mutinied and taken control of the ship or aircraft are assimilated to acts committed by a private ship or aircraft.[25]

Unlike in the 19th century, the contemporary interpretation of the 'private ends' proviso logically suggests that illegal violence, detention or depredation against another vessel or its passengers on the high seas, even for political ends of any kind, entails the criminal liability of the perpetrators if they violate any of the universal anti-terrorist conventions. However, an act of violence on the high seas for political ends cannot be characterised as piratical, because it lacks the required private aim; it may, nonetheless, fall within the ambit of a specialised terrorist offence, as these treaties contain clauses specifically renouncing the political character of the crimes contained therein.

Finally, it should be stressed that UNCLOS only addresses the repression of acts of piracy taking place on the high seas and, owing to the reference in Art 58(2) of UNCLOS, also those acts which are perpetrated in the EEZ. Individual countries may freely limit or expand the international definition as regards acts of piracy committed in their territorial sea. The United Nations (UN) General Assembly and IMO usually refer to such incidents as 'armed robbery'.

9.2.2 Mutiny and other violence against ships not amounting to piracy

As is evident from the definition of Art 101 of UNCLOS and, indeed, customary law, illegal acts of violence, detention or depredation originating from within a vessel, or other acts of interference with maritime commerce not involving an attacking ship, do not constitute piracy *jure gentium*.[26] The same is true with regard to acts of mutiny.[27] Such incidents, although of some concern, did not attract the attention of international institutions because they were perceived as existing on a small local scale which did not pose too serious a threat to maritime safety. This perception radically altered in October 1985 when the Italian cruise ship *Achille Lauro* was seized by members of a Palestinian militant organisation while the ship was en route from Alexandria to Port Said. The hijackers boarded the cruiser in Genoa and

---

25 UNCLOS, Art 102.
26 See *USA v Palmer*, 16 US 610 (1818), p 635.
27 *The Creole* (1841); IA Moore, *Moore's Digest of International Law*, 1906, Vol 2, pp 352, 358.

threatened to blow it up and kill the passengers unless the Government of Israel released 50 Palestinian prisoners. When their demands were not met they killed a Jewish-American passenger who was in a wheelchair and threw his body overboard.[28] Despite the branding of the whole incident as piratical by the US President,[29] this was a case of vessel hijacking or 'boatjacking', which was not regulated by international law. The offences committed could well have been punished on the basis of domestic statutes prohibiting interference with maritime safety or that of committing a homicide or other offences against the person, but terrorist acts on board private vessels did not constitute an international offence at the time.

In March 1988 the IMO adopted a Convention on the Suppression of Unlawful Acts Against the Safety of Maritime Navigation,[30] which covered offences against maritime safety not falling under UNCLOS. Individuals are liable under the Convention if they unlawfully seize or exercise control over a ship or endanger its safe navigation by either violence against persons on board, destruction or damage to a ship or its cargo, destruction of its navigational facilities or interference with their operation, placing of a device likely to destroy a ship, or by communicating false information to a ship.[31] This wide-ranging international crime in fact resembles a combination of the 1970 Hague Convention for the Suppression of Unlawful Seizure of Aircraft[32] and the 1971 Montreal Convention for the Suppression of Unlawful Acts Against the Safety of Civil Aviation,[33] applicable to merchant vessels on the high seas. Article 11 of the IMO Convention obliges Member States to render the contemplated offences extraditable ones, thus removing any doubt that politically motivated acts of seizure and violence could be justified. Unfortunately, the Convention has not received wide ratification, despite calls to that effect from the IMO and the General Assembly.[34]

9.2.3 International maritime terrorism

Since the terrorist events of 11 September 2001, the US had made it a priority to combat those terrorist operations on the high seas that were aimed at land-based targets, whether on US territory or elsewhere. At the time no international agreement existed on maritime terrorism and the provisions of

---

28 See op cit, Halberstam, note 8, pp 269–70.
29 24 ILM (1985), 1515.
30 27 ILM (1988), 668; see also 'Protocol for the Suppression of Unlawful Acts Against the Safety of Fixed Platforms Located on the Continental Shelf', 27 ILM (1988), 685.
31 1988 Convention on the Suppression of Unlawful Acts Against the Safety of Maritime Navigation, Art 3(1).
32 860 UNTS 105.
33 974 UNTS 177.
34 See GA Res 53/32 (24 Nov 1998) and 54/31 (18 Jan 2000).

the 1988 IMO Convention were far too restricted to serve this purpose. As a result, the US government embarked on a twofold objective: (a) to conclude bilateral ship-boarding agreements; and (b) to revise the terms of the 1988 IMO Convention to encompass terrorist operations. These bilateral agreements were modelled on existing bilateral treaties, particularly in the fields of drug-trafficking and smuggling, and generally provide for the consent of the flag State to a request of another State to board and search a ship of concern on the high seas. A presumption is often inserted in such bilateral agreements to the effect that if the requested State does not respond within a given time, then consent is deemed to have been given. Since 2001 the US has concluded such bilateral agreements with the major convenience flag States, such as Panama, Cyprus, Liberia, Marshall Islands and Belize.

The other major development has been the expansion of the 1988 IMO Convention through two distinct Protocols adopted in 2005; the Protocol for the Suppression of Unlawful Acts against the Safety of Maritime Navigation (Protocol I) and the Protocol for the Suppression of Unlawful Acts against the Safety of Fixed Platforms located on the Continental Shelf (Fixed Platforms Protocol). Although the title of Protocol I makes no claim to a terrorist connection, the body of the Protocol and Art 7 – which refers to all existing relevant anti-terrorist treaties – makes it abundantly clear that the Protocol focuses on both terrorist and nuclear threats. Article 4(5) of Protocol I establishes a new Art 3*bis* offence to the 1988 IMO Convention as follows:

1. Any person commits an offence within the meaning of this Convention if that person unlawfully and intentionally:

(a) when the purpose of the act, by its nature or context, is to intimidate a population, or to compel a government or an international organisation to do or abstain from doing any act:

   (i) uses against or on a ship or discharges from a ship any explosive, radioactive material or BCN [biological, chemical, nuclear weapons or devices] weapon in a manner than causes or is likely to cause death or serious injury or damage; or

   (ii) discharges, from a ship, oil, liquefied natural gas, or other hazardous or noxious substance, which is not covered by subparagraph (a)(i), in such quantity or concentration that causes or is likely to cause death or serious injury or damage; or

   (iii) uses a ship in a manner that causes death or serious injury or damage; or

   (iv) threatens, with or without a condition, as is provided for under national law, to commit an offence set forth in subparagraph (a)(i), (ii) or (iii); or

(b) transports on board a ship:

(i) an explosive or radioactive material, knowing that it is intended to be used to cause, or in a threat to cause, with or without a condition, as is provided under national law, death or serious injury for the purpose of intimidating a population, or compelling a government or an international organisation to do or to abstain from doing any act; or

(ii) any BCN weapon, knowing it to be a BCN weapon as defined in Art 1; or

(iii) any source material, special fissionable material, or equipment or material especially designed or prepared for the processing, use or production of special fissionable material, knowing that it is intended to be used in a nuclear explosive activity or in any other nuclear activity not under safeguards pursuant to an IAEA comprehensive safeguards agreement; or

(iv) any equipment, materials or software or related technology that significantly contributes to the design, manufacture or delivery of a BCN weapon, with the intention that it will be used for such purpose.

The Protocol does not apply to the maritime operations of States parties to the Treaty on the Non-Proliferation of Nuclear Weapons, or to the activities of armed forces. Article 3*quater* introduced by the Protocol sets out in detail the various forms of criminal liability – instead of entrusting this task to national law – a trend which is apparent in recent anti-terrorist treaties. Of particular importance is the incorporation of 'common purpose' or 'joint criminal enterprise' liability, first introduced by the ICTY in the 1999 *Tadic* Appeals Judgment[35] and later codified in Art 25(3)(d) of the ICC Statute and Art 2(4)(c) of the 2005 UN Convention for the Suppression of Acts of Nuclear Terrorism.[36] This is further evidence that a corpus of general criminal international law – especially that related to forms of liability and defences – is perceived as applicable to all international crimes. The terrorist element of the offence in Art 3*bis* of the Protocol is apparent in the *mens rea* requirement that the accused intended to intimidate or compel a specified body or entity to do or abstain from particular action.

Of particular importance in the Protocol are its enforcement provisions. Article 8*bis* retains the customary rule that the permission of the flag State is imperative for the purposes of boarding and search. However, pursuant to the co-operation envisaged in the bilateral ship-boarding agreements mentioned in the start of this section, the US was successful in incorporating a similar, albeit narrower, provision in the Protocol. Article 8*bis* 5(d) permits

---

35 *ICTY Prosecutor v Tadic*, Appeals Chamber Judgment (15 July 1999), paras 194 *et seq.*
36 See Chapter 2, section 2.5.

State parties, following ratification, to notify the IMO Secretary-General that a requesting State party may presume that flag State consent to board, search and question persons on board has been given where there is no response from the flag State within four hours of acknowledgment of receipt of a request to confirm nationality. Equally, under subparagraph 5(e) a notification may also be made whereby a requesting State party is permitted to board and search a foreign vessel under any circumstance within the scope of the Protocol. Such notifications may be withdrawn at any time. The Protocol obliges Member States to cater for the liability of legal persons (although not necessarily criminal) and to provide for effective and dissuasive penalties.[37] The provisions on other forms of cooperation, including extradition and mutual legal assistance, although detailed, do not depart from relevant practice in international criminal law treaties.

9.2.4 Mechanisms for the prevention and eradication of piracy

It cannot be overemphasised that piracy can only be combated by interstate co-operation. Parties to UNCLOS, in particular, are under an express obligation to this effect.[38] On the high seas, any State may seize a pirate ship and prosecute its crew,[39] as well as assert a right of visit upon vessels suspected to be engaged in piracy.[40] Both seizure and visit can be enforced solely by warships, or other governmental vessels that are authorised to do so.[41] Article 27 of UNCLOS further entitles coastal States to exercise criminal enforcement jurisdiction over foreign ships passing through their territorial sea in order to conduct an investigation or to make arrests, if a crime committed on board that ship is of a kind to disturb the peace of the country or the good order of the territorial sea.

Close co-operation in matters of piracy was never a priority in State agendas. The rapid increase in attacks has resulted in the mobilisation of maritime employees, ship-owners and insurance agencies, calling for the implementation of mechanisms safeguarding the shipping industry and its people. At a meeting on piracy convened by the International Chamber of Commerce's International Maritime Bureau (IMB) in 1992, it was proposed that a Piracy Reporting Centre (PRC) be set up, whose aim would be to assist in the reporting of incidents and the collation of information for the benefit of both the maritime industry and law enforcement agencies worldwide. As a result, the

37 Art 5*bis*.
38 UNCLOS, Art 100.
39 Ibid, Art 105.
40 Ibid, Art 110.
41 Ibid, Art 107.

IMB with the support of IMO and the International Mobile Satellite Organisation (INMARSAT) – the latter is now a private corporation – established the PRC on 1 October 1992. The Centre is financed by voluntary contributions from shipping and insurance agencies and its services are free of charge to all vessels irrespective of ownership or flag. The Centre receives information on suspicious or unexplained craft movement as well as piracy reports from around the world and broadcasts daily accounts of piracy on secured satellite channels. It further liaises with enforcement agencies, collates and analyses relevant information and issues quarterly reports to interested bodies.

The Maritime Safety Committee, an organ of the IMO, has studied the problem of piracy and has passed two significant recommendations; one is addressed to governments[42] and the other to ship-owners, shipmasters and crews.[43] The former stresses the need for governments to establish incident command systems for both tactical and operational responses, integrated with other security matters, such as smuggling, drug-trafficking and terrorism. This should be followed by the development of sound action plans, the establishment of necessary infrastructure and operational arrangements, as well as detailed and accurate databases of relevant incidents and statistics with a view to disseminating this information to interested parties in a format that is understandable and usable. It is strongly advised, moreover, that the victim ship not be detained unnecessarily for investigation purposes. The latter recommendation calls moreover for reducing pirate temptations by avoiding the use of cash for the ship's businesses and by not transmitting through the radio information regarding the ship's cargo and other valuable items on board, because attackers are able to intercept communications. It further advises ships operating in waters where attacks have occurred to adopt a security plan, which should cover matters such as: the need for enhanced surveillance and the use of lighting and detection equipment; crew responses; radio alarm procedures;[44] reports to be made after an attack. This circular recommends against the use of firearms, but favours the employment of evasive manoeuvres and water hoses, only in situations where the captain is convinced he or she can use them to his or her advantage and without risk to those on board.

---

42 IMO Doc MSC/Circ 622/Rev 1 (16 June 1999).
43 Ibid.
44 The International Telecommunications Union and INMARSAT have included 'piracy/ armed robbery attack' as a category of distress message which ships can now transmit through either their digital selective calling or INMARSAT equipment by pressing a button. The message can be received automatically by shore stations and ships in the immediate vicinity. See IMO Doc MSC/Circ 805 (6 June 1997); op cit, the 2002 ICC Piracy Report, note 1, mentions a newly introduced device, called 'Secure-Ship', which consists of a 9,000 volt, non-lethal electrifying fence surrounding the ship, specifically adapted for maritime use.

In recent years proposals have suggested the establishment of an international naval force under the auspices of the UN to patrol danger areas. Others have proposed more realistic action, such as the employment of private security forces, highly equipped and acting as rapid response forces in cases of piracy.[45]

9.3 OFFENCES AGAINST SUBMARINE CABLES AND PIPELINES

The era of submarine transmission cables was launched in 1850 when the first telegraph cable was laid across the English Channel, connecting England with France. Within days, however, a French fisherman who had stumbled upon it proceeded to carve it, assuming he had discovered a peculiar seaweed. Although a boom in the laying of submarine cables followed, it was not until August 1858 that a third attempt to lay the first trans-Atlantic cable was crowned with success. The cable was operational for only a month and it was in 1866 that the first enduring trans-Atlantic cable was finally laid. For a period of 30 years since the 1920s, radio carried the bulk of the globe's communications, but was unreliable in adverse weather conditions and had a limited capacity. The development in the 1950s of a lightweight co-axial cable, which was reinforced with a high-tensile steel core and a polythene outer skin meant that it did not require armouring in deep water. Since the first fibre optic submarine cable was laid in the 1980s, underwater cables have overtaken satellites as the leading means of overseas communication. Cables now carry more than two-thirds of all telephone, fax and data transmissions crossing oceans, with over 150,000 miles of fibre optic cable already laid on the seabed, and rapidly increasing.[46]

The general freedom to lay submarine cables beneath the high seas and on the seabed thereof is expressly recognised under UNCLOS,[47] as well as its predecessor, the 1958 Geneva Convention on the High Seas,[48] and was acknowledged as such under customary international law prior to the 20th century. No such freedom exists with regard to another State's territorial sea and internal waters, or, indeed, in archipelagic waters in accordance with

---

45 PT Bangsberg, 'Gurkhas Offered for On-board Protection' (2000) *Journal of Commerce Online*, 28 January.

46 See HM Field, *The Story of the Atlantic Telegraph*, 1972, New York: C Scribner; LB Tribolet, *The International Aspects of Electrical Communications in the Atlantic Area*, 1929, Baltimore: John Hopkins University; see International Cable Protection Committee website: <http://www.iscpc.org>.

47 UNCLOS, Arts 87(1)(c) and 112. Art 58 further extends this freedom to the EEZ, although strictly speaking this does not form part of the high seas.

48 Geneva Convention on the High Seas, Arts 2(3) and 26(1).

Art 51 of UNCLOS, except with the coastal State's consent. For the purposes of legal protection, two types of submarine cable exist: 'trans-territorial' systems, which transcend the oceans and are therefore deployed on the high seas, and 'festoon' systems, which are laid along several coastlines and, thus, are in large part contained in territorial or internal waters. The 1884 Convention for the Protection of Submarine Cables (1884 Convention),[49] which has not been superseded by other instruments and is still the basis for most national statutes, was adopted to suppress, punish and compensate breaking or injury to cables outside of territorial waters. Article 2(1) of the 1884 Convention made it a punishable offence to:

> ... wilfully or through culpable negligence, [commit any act] resulting in the total or partial interruption or embarrassment of telegraphic communication.

In accordance with Art 2(2) of the 1884 Convention, any injuries to cables inflicted with the sole purpose of saving one's life or vessel, after all necessary precautions have been taken to avoid such occurrences, negate the criminal character of the act.[50] The application of Art 2(1) extends also to cable owners, presumably through the actions of their agents who wilfully or negligently break or injure another cable while laying or repairing their own.[51] Both the 1958 Geneva Convention on the High Seas[52] and UNCLOS[53] encapsulated the *actus reus* and *mens rea* contained in Art 2(1) of the 1884 Convention and extended it to cover also submarine pipelines and high-voltage power cables. Significantly, Art 113 of UNCLOS features an additional sentence, whereby it penalises not only wilful commission and negligence, but also 'conduct calculated or likely to result in such breaking or injury'.[54]

Unlike piracy *jure gentium*, which, too, is an offence committed on the high seas, judicial jurisdiction for injuries to submarine cables under Art 8 of the 1884 Convention and, indeed, customary law, is not universal but belongs to the Flag State, or that of the nationality of the offender, in cases where the

---

49 1 Bevans 89.
50 Similarly, 1958 Geneva Convention on the High Seas, Art 27 and UNCLOS, Art 113.
51 1884 Convention, Art 4, 1958 Geneva Convention on the High Seas and UNCLOS, Arts 28 and 114 respectively, removed reference to criminal liability in such cases, but this should not be viewed as absolving them of such if they act wilfully or negligently.
52 Ibid, 1958 Convention, Art 27.
53 UNCLOS, Art 113.
54 In a Supplementary Declaration to the 1884 Convention, signed in 1886, the parties to the former construed the term 'wilfully' contained in Art 2(1) of the 1884 Convention as not imposing penal responsibility 'to cases of breaking or of injuries occasioned accidentally or necessarily in repairing a cable, when all precautions have been taken to avoid such breakings or damages'. Reprinted in 1 Bevans 112.

Flag State is unable to act.[55] The same is true with respect to Art 113 of UNCLOS. Article 10(2) of the 1884 Convention makes a minor departure from the rule of exclusive enforcement jurisdiction of the Flag State on the high seas by granting the limited right to other States parties to approach but not board suspected vessels in order to determine their nationality.[56] Both the British Submarine Telegraph Act 1885[57] and the US Submarine Cable Act 1888,[58] enacted to implement the 1884 Convention, reproduce almost verbatim the elements of the offence, as well as its jurisdictional clause. The light penalties provided in the British and US statutes, which have remained the same since their enactment, may well account for the lack of criminal prosecutions and reluctance to engage in costly financial litigation with little benefit on the horizon.

In time of armed conflict, although it is permissible to sever the adversary's submarine cables,[59] it is prohibited to seize or destroy submarine cables connecting an occupied territory with a neutral State, except in situations of absolute necessity.[60] In a case tried by a British–American Claims Arbitral Tribunal in 1923, a British corporation claimed compensation for repairs incurred in repairing the Manila–Hong Kong and the Manila–Cadiz submarine telegraph cables cut by the US naval authorities during the Spanish–American War in 1898. The tribunal dismissed the claim by stating that not only was the cutting of cables not prohibited by the rules of international law applicable to warfare at sea, but 'such action may be said to be implicitly justified by that right of legitimate defence which forms the basis of the rights of any belligerent nation'.[61]

Protection and prosecution of cases involving injury to submarine cables and pipelines is dependent on each individual State, both by application and adaptation of domestic statutes to contemporary exigencies, as well as by international co-operation and rigid police enforcement action. State action has unfortunately proven inadequate. For this purpose an International Cable Protection Committee (ICPC) was established in 1958 by cable owners with the purpose of promoting the protection of submarine cables against natural and man-made hazards. Since the largest threat to cables is encountered from fisheries activities, especially trawl fishing and shellfish dredging, the ICPC

---

55 MS McDougal and WT Burke, *The Public Order of the Oceans: A Contemporary International Law of the Sea*, 1962, New Haven: Yale UP, 1079.
56 See RR Churchill and AV Lowe, *The Law of the Sea*, 1999, Manchester: Manchester UP, 175.
57 Chapter 49, ss 3, 6(5).
58 47 USC §§ 21, 22, 33.
59 1884 Convention, Art 15.
60 1907 Hague Regulations, Art 54.
61 *Eastern Extension, Australasia and China Telegraph Co Ltd Claim* (1923–24) 2 AD 415, p 417; see also *Cuba Submarine Co Ltd Claim* (1923–24) 2 AD 419, p 419, whose facts and judgment were similar to the previous case.

has issued and distributed cable warning and cable awareness charts, as well as notices to mariners, and has developed standard procedures for activities such as cable routing and cable/pipeline crossing, in an effort to foster cable awareness in the fishing and offshore industries.

9.4 UNAUTHORISED BROADCASTING FROM THE HIGH SEAS

The rigid regulation of broadcasting in Western Europe in the early 1960s and the inability of private individuals to be granted broadcasting licences, resulted in the establishment of 'pirate' radio stations outside the jurisdiction of coastal States, on the high seas. Because of the customary rule permitting only Flag State jurisdiction on the high seas for offences other than piracy *jure gentium*, Member States of the Council of Europe adopted in record time in 1965 the European Agreement for the Prevention of Broadcasts Transmitted from Stations Outside National Territories (1965 Agreement).[62] Article 2 of the 1965 Agreement, which was widely ratified, criminalises the establishment or operation of broadcasting stations, as well as any acts of collaboration knowingly performed, such as the provision of services concerning advertising for the benefit of the stations.[63] The 1965 Agreement provided for jurisdiction based on the nationality and territoriality principles.[64] The entry into force of the 1965 Agreement and its enforcement by Member States caused most stations to cease their operations.[65]

Art 109 of UNCLOS has a broader spectrum than the 1965 Agreement. It defines unauthorised broadcasting as:

> . . . the transmission of sound, radio or television broadcasts from a ship or installation on the high seas intended for reception by the general public contrary to international regulations, but excluding the transmission of distress calls.

It provides for the following bases of judicial jurisdiction: (a) Flag State, depending on whether the broadcasting emanates from a vessel or a structure not amounting to a vessel; (b) nationality; (c) the State receiving the unauthorised transmissions, or that whose authorised radio communications suffer as a result. States that enjoy judicial jurisdiction further enjoy

---

62 ETS 53.
63 1965 Agreement, Art 2(2)(e).
64 Ibid, Art 3.
65 See JC Woodliffe, 'The Demise of Unauthorised Broadcasting from Ships in International Waters', 1 *IJECL* (1986), 402; NM Hunnings, 'Pirate Broadcasting in European Waters', 14 *ICLQ* (1965), 410.

enforcement jurisdiction, including a right of visit as well as a right to seize the offending vessel and crew. In accordance with Arts 109(4) and 110 of UNCLOS only warships of the States having jurisdiction are permitted to visit and seize the offending vessels and crew members, but if it is proven that the vessel under suspicion was not in fact at fault, it is entitled to compensation.

Although it is only the States listed in Art 109 that have jurisdiction over offending vessels, para 1 of this provision obliges all States parties to UNCLOS to co-operate in the suppression of this particular offence. This would not, obviously, involve any enforcement action, but it would necessitate police co-operation, extradition procedures, etc. With the privatisation and private licensing of all types of telecommunications transmissions, 'pirate' stations seem to have disappeared. However, as Churchill and Lowe correctly point out, UNCLOS retains its importance as it may be applicable to other forms of illegal broadcasting, such as unofficial propaganda broadcasts from the high seas.[66] Under these circumstances and depending on the severity of the underlying offence under repression, the obligation for all States to co-operate may involve the use of radio-jamming techniques that would interfere with the illegal broadcasts and render the message inaudible.[67] In the extreme case where the broadcast is deemed to attempt to incite a group of people to commit genocide, it is possible for every State to seize the vessel and prosecute the offenders. This would not be premised on the 1948 Genocide Convention, which does not expressly provide for universal enforcement jurisdiction, but on the basis of customary law, to the extent that no significant objections to such jurisdiction are posited by interested States.[68]

9.5 THE RIGHT OF HOT PURSUIT

9.5.1 Introduction

The right of hot pursuit is well established under customary law, as well as in the 1958 Geneva Convention on the High Seas and UNCLOS.[69] It gives coastal States the right to pursue and arrest foreign vessels that have

---

66 Op cit, Churchill and Lowe, note 56, p 212.
67 JF Meltz, 'Rwandan Genocide and the International Law of Radio Jamming', 91 *AJIL* (1997), 628.
68 See I Bantekas, *Principles of Direct and Superior Responsibility in International Humanitarian Law*, 2002, Manchester: Manchester UP, pp 57–62.
69 1958 Geneva Convention on the High Seas, Art 23; Art 111 UNCLOS; see op cit, Churchill and Lowe, note 56, pp 214–16. States are increasingly concluding bilateral or regional multilateral treaties providing for co-operation in the exercise of the right of hot pursuit, such as the 1993 Conakry Convention on Sub-regional Co-operation in the Exercise of Hot Pursuit and Protocol.

committed an offence within their maritime zones onto the high seas as an exceptional measure departing from the rule of exclusive Flag State jurisdiction on the high seas. Before considering the details of this right, it is useful to scrutinise its justificatory basis. Under the relevant treaties, it is not only an exceptional measure; its exercise is also subject to certain limitations, such as that the pursuit must be continuous and uninterrupted. Moreover, other sea-trafficking treaties stress the primacy of Flag State jurisdiction, the security of the foreign vessel, safety of life at sea, as well as the commercial interests of the Flag State.[70] On the other hand, hot pursuit operates as a right of necessity for the enforcement of the laws and regulations of the coastal State, which would otherwise be unpunished in accordance with the aforementioned general rule.[71] It would seem that, unless otherwise explicitly permitted by new rules of customary law or unilateral acquiescence, hot pursuit must be exercised only in accordance with the strict requirements of UNCLOS.

It is clear from the text of Art 111 of UNCLOS, and the *travaux* of the 1958 Geneva Convention on the High Seas,[72] that States are not restricted in the list of offences that may be subject to hot pursuit. This is a matter for the coastal State's domestic law. This general freedom is subject to two limitations. First, hot pursuit may be exercised in any one of the coastal State's areas of maritime jurisdiction – including the continental shelf – provided that the pursuit is in response to a violation for the protection of which the particular maritime belt was established. For example, since Art 33 of UNCLOS permits the establishment of a contiguous zone in order to prevent the infringement of the coastal State's customs, fiscal, immigration or sanitary laws, hot pursuit is available only if the foreign vessel has, while in the contiguous zone, violated any such laws. Similarly, the non-prescribed but limited sovereign rights granted to coastal States under Art 56 of UNCLOS restrict hot pursuit to a small range of environmental, illegal fishing, and similar offences. Secondly, while international comity suggests that hot pursuit should be avoided with regard to trivial infringements,[73] violation of less serious offences such as illegal fishing has in the past given rise to legitimate pursuit.[74] Irrespective of whether a crime has in fact been committed by a foreign vessel in a maritime belt, hot pursuit is lawful only where the pursuing

---

70 1988 UN Convention Against the Illicit Traffic in Narcotic Drugs and Psychotropic Substances, Art 17, 28 ILM (1989), 493; Council of Europe Agreement on Illicit Traffic by Sea, Implementing Art 17 of the UN Convention Against Illicit Traffic in Narcotic Drugs and Psychotropic Substances, ETS 156.

71 RC Reuland, 'The Customary Right of Hot Pursuit Onto the High Seas: Annotations to Article 111 of the Law of the Sea Convention', 33 *Va J Int'l L* (1993), 557, p 558.

72 *YBILC* (1956), Vol II, p 285.

73 Op cit, Reuland, note 71, p 558.

74 *The North* case, 11 Ex Rep (1905) 141, Canada.

vessel 'has good reason to believe'[75] that the particular violation has taken place. What is thus required is either actual knowledge or reasonable suspicion, but mere suspicion would not suffice.[76] This proposition that mere suspicion is an insufficient basis for asserting a right of hot pursuit was reinforced by the judgment in the *M/V Saiga (No 2)* case, where the International Tribunal for the Law of the Sea (ITLOS) stated that when the Guinean pursuing ship made its 'initial decision to pursue, it had insufficient grounds for hot pursuit. Guinea could have had no more than a suspicion that the *Saiga* had violated its laws in the EEZ'.[77] The argument that the flight of a foreign vessel to the high seas upon its visual or radar contact with a ship belonging to the authorities of the coastal State constitutes reasonable suspicion of committing a crime[78] is incompatible with the justificatory principle of hot pursuit enunciated above. In any event, the test of reasonable suspicion should be interpreted to encompass particular criminal activity, as opposed to suspicion about general criminal activity.

Hot pursuit represents enforcement action by the coastal State, and as such the use of force is permissible in two cases: (a) for the purposes of self-defence; and (b) in order to stop the offending vessel and arrest those on board. Force, however, must conform with the principles of proportionality and reasonableness. In the *I'm Alone* case,[79] a Canadian ship was pursued by a US Customs vessel onto the high seas, and upon refusing to surrender, she was fired upon with more than 100 shots resulting in her sinking and the death of one crew member. The Mixed Committee of Arbitration ruled that the sinking of the pursued vessel must be incidental to the exercise of necessary and reasonable force. Similarly, in the *M/V Saiga* case, the ITLOS observed that considerations of humanity must apply in the law of the sea, pointing out that since the *Saiga* was fully laden and its maximum speed was 10 knots it could have easily been overrun and boarded by the Guinean warship, without excessive force.[80]

75 UNCLOS, Art 111(1).
76 Op cit, McDougal and Burke, note 55, p 896; NM Poulantzas, *The Right of Hot Pursuit in International Law* (1969), 155; op cit, Reuland, note 71, p 569.
77 *Saint Vincent and the Grenadines v Guinea* (The *M/V Saiga*) *(No 2)*, Judgment (1 July 1999) (Merits), 38 ILM (1999), 1323, para 147.
78 Op cit, Reuland, note 71, p 570.
79 *I'm Alone* case (*Canada v USA*) (1935) III UNRIAA 1609.
80 *M/V Saiga* Judgment (Merits), paras 153–57; see also *The Red Crusader* case (1962) 35 ILR 485, and 1995 Agreement for the Implementation of the Provisions of UNCLOS, Art 22(1)(f), Relating to the Conservation and Management of Straddling Fish Stocks and Highly Migratory Fish Stocks, 34 ILM (1995), 1542.

9.5.2 Commencement and continuous nature of hot pursuit

Under Arts 111 of UNCLOS and 23 of the 1958 Geneva Convention on the High Seas respectively, the right of hot pursuit commences where a foreign vessel has committed an offence in a maritime belt, is moreover present therein and the pursuing public ship has ordered the foreign vessel to stop at a distance which enables it to be seen or heard by the foreign vessel. Refusal to stop would give rise to pursuit onto the high seas. As Art 111 of UNCLOS speaks only in terms of 'ship' and not persons, hot pursuit would be available for offences committed by passengers on board a foreign ship only where they are acting under the authority of those in charge of the ship. The coastal State may thereafter lay claim for the offenders to be tried before its courts on the basis of the law of extradition.[81] Moreover, although the wording of both UNCLOS and the 1958 Geneva Convention on the High Seas suggest that only a completed offence justifies pursuit, the *travaux* to the 1958 Geneva Convention on the High Seas clearly illustrate that the special rapporteur perceived any reference to 'attempts' as superfluous, as they were implied in the text.[82]

Once the pursuit commences, it must remain continuous and uninterrupted. A pursuit is deemed to have been interrupted in the following cases:

(a) where the pursued vessel has entered the territorial sea of a third State,[83] although other maritime belts are assimilated to high seas for the purposes of hot pursuit;[84]

(b) where the warship has abandoned pursuit, pursuit cannot be thereafter resumed. Although UNCLOS is silent, case law suggests that only significant interruptions can invalidate a right of hot pursuit. Thus, if the warship momentarily stops to pick the mother ship's dories, this should not terminate pursuit;[85]

(c) finally, since UNCLOS requires that the foreign vessel be given an audible or visual signal to stop, it is necessary that the pursuing ship maintain some sort of visual observation of the foreign vessel. This requirement of visual observation would have to be fulfilled despite the

---

81 Op cit, Reuland, note 71, p 570.

82 Op cit, Poulantzas, note 76, p 154.

83 In *R v Mills* (unreported), Croydon Crown Court adopted a more liberal view. See WC Gilmore, 'Hot Pursuit: The Case of *R v Mills and Others*', 44 *ICLQ* (1995), 949.

84 *YBILC* (1956), vol I, p 52. Op cit, Poulantzas, note 76, p 580 argues that a short stay of passage through a third State's territorial waters, with the aim of evading the law, does not preclude the resumption of hot pursuit. He notes, however, that in all other instances, where the fleeing vessel has entered the territorial waters of a third State, at that moment the jurisdictional link between the pursuing and pursued vessel has been broken.

85 *The North* case, 11 Ex Rep (1905), 141, Canada.

existence of radars which make observation possible without the need for visual proximity.[86]

Pursuit is possible by either a warship or aircraft duly authorised. UNCLOS permits a warship to take over the pursuit from an aircraft, but is silent on whether an aircraft can continue the pursuit commenced by a warship. Juristic opinion generally takes the view that this is possible.[87] Furthermore, in accordance with UNCLOS, it is not necessary that, at the time when the foreign ship within the territorial sea or the contiguous zone receives the order to stop, the warship or aircraft giving the order be within the territorial sea or the contiguous zone.

A pursuit is lawful only where, as already stated, the foreign vessel does not respond to a clearly audible or visual signal to stop. In *USA v Postal*,[88] the fifth circuit court ruled that the arrest of a foreign vessel on the high seas was unlawful because, *inter alia*, the giving of visual or auditory signals to stop did not occur until after a second boarding of the fleeing vessel, by which time the foreign vessel was outside US territorial waters. It is argued that since the signal requirement is intended to give the foreign vessel time to heave and await inspection, it may be dispensed with where the foreign vessel attempts to flee upon sighting the warship or aircraft.[89] Although Art 111(4) of UNCLOS allows only visual or auditory signals, recent case law has accepted the use of signals given by radio.[90]

9.5.3 The doctrine of constructive presence

The practice of States has, at least since the latter part of the 19th century, accepted that the presence of a mother ship beyond the crucial maritime belt – or on the high seas – would still give rise to a right of hot pursuit against it where boats belonging to, or associated with, the mother ship commit offences in the coastal State's maritime zones of jurisdiction.[91] This is known as the doctrine of constructive presence, whereby for the purposes of hot pursuit the mother ship, otherwise not lawful prey, is deemed to be within the enforcement jurisdiction of the coastal State.[92] The doctrine has been codified in both

---

86 Op cit, Poulantzas, note 76, p 212.

87 Op cit, Churchill and Lowe, note 56, p 215.

88 589 F 2d 862 (1979).

89 *The Newton Bay* case, 36 F 2d 729 (1929). The recent Judgment (Merits) in the *M/V Saiga* case, however, supports a stricter view, para 148.

90 *R v Mills* (unreported); *R v Sunila and Soleyman*, (1986) 28 DLR 450.

91 *Araunah* (1888) Moore, *Int Arb* 824; *Grace and Ruby*, 283 F 475 (1922).

92 See WC Gilmore, 'Hot Pursuit and Constructive Presence in Canadian Law Enforcement', 12 *Marine Policy* (1988), 105.

UNCLOS and the 1958 Geneva Convention on the High Seas, and Art 111(4) of UNCLOS provides that hot pursuit is not deemed to have commenced:

> . . . unless the pursuing ship has satisfied itself . . . that the ship pursued or one of its boats or other craft working as a team and using the ship pursued as a mother ship is within the limits of the territorial sea, or, as the case may be, within the contiguous zone or the exclusive economic zone or above the continental shelf.

Although the doctrine of constructive presence was born to challenge situations involving a mother ship and smaller boats operating from the mother ship (eg, *Araunah* involved canoes engaged in sealing within Russian territorial waters and operating from a British Columbian schooner on the high seas), in recent years it has become common practice for a number of large vessels to be co-operating in illegal activities (especially drug-trafficking and smuggling) without the existence of a mother ship in the traditional sense. Thus, in the case of *R v Mills*, a ship registered in St Vincent was smuggling cannabis into the UK by transferring the drugs through the high seas to Ireland and from there to a British trawler which subsequently sailed into British waters. Croydon Crown Court was not troubled by the fact that the British trawler was not one of the boats of the pursued St Vincent vessel. Although this case does not conform to the spirit of Art 111 of UNCLOS, its evolution will undoubtedly depend on relevant State protests and consensus emanating from recent international criminal co-operation initiatives in the spheres of organised crime, drug-trafficking and terrorism.

Chapter 10

Terrorism

10.1 INTRODUCTION

The term 'terrorism' is commonly and widely used in everyday parlance with varying political and criminal connotations,[1] but at the same time it remains a designation which is elusive and one that has never been singly defined under international law,[2] at least at the global level. The first ever international attempt at codification was made in 1937 through the League of Nations by the adoption of a Convention for the Prevention and Punishment of Terrorism.[3] Article 1(2) of that Convention, which required merely three ratifications to come into force, but received only one and was subsequently abandoned, defined:

> . . . acts of terrorism [as] criminal acts directed against a State and intended or calculated to create a state of terror in the minds of particular persons, or groups of persons or the general public.[4]

Such a definition does not accurately describe a criminal act of terrorism as distinct from a common crime and leaves a wide margin of discretion as to the specific *mens rea* of a terrorist offence, that is, the creation of a state of terror. What is further problematic, and more so in 1937, was determining when an otherwise criminal offence is deemed to have been committed for a political purpose and not in the context of a purely criminal enterprise. Since in the majority of countries the characterisation of a criminal offence as a

---

1 'Tibetan Leader Accused of Terrorism' (1999) *The Times*, 23 October, where China accused the Dalai Lama of masterminding several explosions and assassinations in Tibet.
2 See generally A Evans and J Murphy, *Legal Aspects of International Terrorism*, 1978, Lexington, Mass Heath: Teakfield; MT Franck and BB Lockwood, 'Preliminary Thoughts Towards an International Convention on Terrorism', 68 *AJIL* (1974), 69.
3 (1938) 19 LNOJ 23.
4 See A Cassese, 'The International Community's Legal Response to Terrorism', 38 *ICLQ* (1989), 589, p 591.

political one removes personal culpability, the so-called 'political offence exception' is therefore of seminal importance.[5] The distinction between political and non-political offences was more difficult in the past than at present, exemplifying the tension and variety of opinion in international relations, resulting in a seeming impossibility of agreement on politically sensitive issues.

The regulation of terrorism in international law has been shaped by terrorist events, whose force and impact in certain periods of world history outraged the international community, prompting its members to conclude subject specific anti-terrorist agreements. Events of this nature were initially the alarming number of incidents regarding seizure or interference with civil aviation in the 1960s and 1970s by private individuals, proffering either financial or political demands. This led to the adoption of three distinct international treaties: the 1963 Tokyo Convention on Offences and Certain Other Acts Committed on Board Aircraft;[6] the 1970 Hague Convention for the Suppression of Unlawful Seizure of Aircraft;[7] and the 1971 Montreal Convention for the Suppression of Unlawful Acts Against the Safety of Civil Aviation.[8]

The lack of a single definition has resulted in a thematic consideration and codification of criminal acts deemed to be terrorist by the international community.[9] This is clearly exemplified by the various subject specific conventions relating to hijacking, hostage taking, bombings, financing of terrorist operations and others. This thematic approach is still the preferred route in concluding counter-terrorism treaties among States,[10] with organs of international organisations increasingly taking an active part in reinforcing and crystallising those rules that are common to all these treaties.[11]

Besides the issue of a single definition of terrorism and the determination of political crimes, other related problem areas have arisen, such as the relationship between terrorism and human rights and that between national liberation movements and terrorist violence. A thorough examination of these issues is necessarily dependent on the recognition and application of certain *jus cogens* norms, especially those emanating from the realm of international

---

5 CM Bassiouni (ed), *International Terrorism and Political Crimes*, 1975, Springfield: Thomas.
6 2 ILM (1963), 1042.
7 860 UNTS 105; 10 ILM (1971), 133.
8 974 UNTS 177; 10 ILM (1971), 1151.
9 In *Tel-Oren v Libyan Arab Republic* 726 F 2d 795 (1984), where an action for tort against an alleged terrorist attack on a bus in Israel was dismissed, Edward J noted the lack of international consensus on terrorism and stated that, besides those acts which are already prohibited by international conventions, no other terrorist action can be regarded as a crime under international law.
10 1998 UN Convention for the Suppression of Terrorist Bombings 37 ILM (1998), 249, and 2000 UN Convention for the Suppression of the Financing of Terrorism 39 ILM (2000), 270.
11 See, eg, GA Res 49/60 (1994).

human rights law. Furthermore, one should not overlook contemporary forms of terrorist activity beyond the private domain, namely, the involvement and support of States, or agencies thereof, to persons or organisations involved in terrorism. Such 'State-sponsored terrorism' has resulted in the promulgation in some jurisdictions of laws sanctioning the culprit State both internally and extraterritorially.[12] Finally, it has been observed, especially by the United Nations (UN), that terrorist activity exhibits in many cases a link with organised crime,[13] even though it should be acknowledged that, whatever its manifestation, terrorism always involves some kind of political element, whilst organised crime does not.

Following the terrorist attacks of 11 September 2001 against the US, and subsequent related terrorist activity through the attempted use of chemical and biological agents, the use of the mail, as well as terrorist bombings against tourist resorts, some States have taken measures to adopt legislation that either departs from human rights standards or disregards fundamental principles of international law, such as that relating to the use of force. In this chapter we argue that the vast majority of States agree that there is no special need to depart from human rights standards or fundamental principles of international law. On the contrary, legality at all levels should be fortified.

10.2 THE THEMATIC APPROACH IN INTERNATIONAL LAW

Following an attack against Israeli athletes during the 1972 Munich Olympic Games, the General Assembly of the UN commenced discussions on a US draft treaty proposal for the prevention and suppression of certain acts of international terrorism. This proposal was outvoted by developing and communist countries which, with the urging of Syria, desired to see the adoption of a convention containing a single definition of terrorism. Western States argued that a general definition would not only be impossible to obtain, but would further serve the purposes of certain organisations, such as the Palestine Liberation Organisation (PLO), which would try to distinguish between terrorism and national liberation movements in order to further their causes. Moreover, it was feared by the West that a wide embracing

---

12 US Anti-Terrorism and Effective Death Penalty Act 1996, 28 USC § 1605(a)(7); reprinted also in 36 ILM (1997), 759.
13 Resolution of the UN Commission for the Prevention of Crime and Criminal Justice, Ninth Cairo Congress on the Prevention of Crime and Treatment of Offenders, UN Doc A/CONF 169/16 (12 May 1995), p 17; see also 10th Vienna Congress, UN Doc A/CONF 187/4/Rev 3 (15 April 2000), p 4, adopting the Vienna Declaration on Crime and Justice.

definition would result in subsuming Israel under the rubric of State terrorism. Nonetheless, a compromise was reached and an Ad Hoc Committee was established by the General Assembly under Resolution 3034, adopted on 18 December 1972, to examine the matter. The Committee met three times between 1972 and 1979. During this time developing nations argued that terrorism should be viewed from its root causes, such as racism, colonialism, occupation and apartheid and be differentiated from action undertaken by national liberation movements. Nothing concrete emerged from these discussions as Western States vociferously opposed the above proposals. From 1979 onwards it was the Sixth (Legal) Committee of the General Assembly that became the forum for discussions on terrorism and since 1985 the Syrian proposal has either been raised in brief or abandoned from the Committee's agenda. Between 1972 and 1989 the General Assembly, upon request of the then Secretary General Kurt Waldheim, had been discussing the issue of terrorism on an annual basis under the title 'Measures to Prevent International Terrorism which Endangers or Takes Innocent Human Lives or Jeopardises Fundamental Freedoms, and Study of the Underlying Causes of Those Forms of Terrorism and Acts of Violence Which Lie in Misery, Frustration, Grievance and Despair and Which Cause Some People to Sacrifice Human Lives, Including their Own, in an Attempt to Effect Radical Changes'. The title of the series is significant because it underpins its Arab and developing world sponsorship and because it places emphasis on the underlying causes of terrorism, a taboo subject in current legal and political discourse. In recent years, however, there have been renewed discussions on the drafting of a comprehensive convention on terrorism under the aegis of the General Assembly; this topic is currently under discussion.

The only anti-terrorist convention that does not follow a purely thematic approach is the 1976 European Convention on the Suppression of Terrorism.[14] However, far from adopting a single definition, Art 1 of this European Convention enumerates all existing counter-terrorism treaties and reiterates the obligation of States parties not to characterise the acts therein as political offences for the purposes of extradition. As is evident, the adoption of a single definition on terrorism, just like Pandora's box, raises a variety of issues with substantial implications which most States are not prepared to discuss. The thematic route, despite current discussions on a single comprehensive convention, so far appears the only vehicle guaranteeing both international co-operation and relative consensus.

14 ETS 90; 15 ILM (1976), 1272.

10.3 THE SPECIALISED ANTI-TERRORIST CONVENTIONS

10.3.1 Offences against civil aviation

The first international agreement to emerge on the subject was the 1963 Tokyo Convention on Offences and Certain Other Acts Committed On Board Aircraft (Tokyo Convention).[15] Its application extends to any act, whether a recognised offence or not, which jeopardises the safety of an aircraft or 'of persons or property therein or which jeopardise[s] good order and discipline on board'.[16] Such acts become offences under the Tokyo Convention only if they are committed by a person on board an aircraft in flight or on the surface of the high seas.[17] An aircraft is considered to be 'in flight', for the purposes of the Tokyo Convention, 'from the moment when the power is applied for the purpose of take-off until the moment when the landing run ends'.[18] Although not clear from the wording of the Convention, an act taking place solely on the territory of one State does not substantiate an international offence under the scheme of the Convention. Similarly, the Convention does not apply to three types of public aircraft: military, custom and police.[19] Unlike other anti-terrorist treaties, the 1963 Tokyo Convention was not designed to address urgent problems and was generally viewed as reflecting customary law; yet it was frugally ratified by signatory States.[20]

The plethora of attacks against aircraft in the 1960s and the inadequate hortatory anti-hijacking provision contained in Art 11 of the 1963 Tokyo Convention rendered imperative the adoption of a new instrument which would not only elaborate the elements of the offence, but would moreover affirm and reinforce interstate mechanisms towards effective suppression and eradication.[21] Since, at the time, airport security was not equipped with sophisticated detection machinery, nor was surveillance or other security safeguards high on the agenda of most national airport authorities, the majority of attacks against civil aviation took place by persons embarking an aircraft with weapons and seizing control of it when its external doors had

---

15 See generally M Mendelsohn, 'In-Flight Crime: The International and Domestic Picture Under the Tokyo Convention', 53 *Virginia Law Review* (1967), 509.
16 1963 Tokyo Convention, Art 1(1).
17 Ibid, Art 1(2). It is also required that the aircraft in question be registered in a contracting State.
18 Ibid, Art 1(3).
19 Ibid, Art 1(4).
20 E McWhinney, *Aerial Piracy and International Terrorism*, 1987, Dordrecht, Lancaster: Martinus Nijhoff, pp 39–40.
21 1963 Tokyo Convention, Art 16(2) noted that nothing in the Convention 'shall be deemed to create an obligation to grant extradition'.

closed.[22] This specific problem of aircraft hijacking was the focal point of the 1970 Hague Convention for the Suppression of Unlawful Seizure of Aircraft (Hague Convention). The 1970 Hague Convention deals exclusively with acts of international hijacking committed by persons on board an aircraft in flight.[23] The notion of an aircraft 'in flight' is wider in the 1970 Hague Convention than in the 1963 Tokyo Convention since its temporal application encompasses the period of time when all external doors are closed following embarkation until the moment any such door is opened for disembarkation.[24] The offence of aircraft hijacking under the 1970 Hague Convention is consummated by a person who:

(a) unlawfully, by force or threat thereof, or by any other form of intimidation, seizes, or exercises control of [an] aircraft, or attempts to perform any such act; or

(b) is an accomplice of a person who performs or attempts to perform any such act.

The phrase 'any other form of intimidation' seems to be superfluous, since there can be no other form of unlawfully taking over an aircraft without the use or threat of force,[25] so it seems as though the drafters intended to cover every possible future situation, even if it was unknown to them at the time. It is possible, nonetheless, that seizure be perpetrated without use of force, through bribery or collaboration with the aircraft's pilots or cabin crew. An Australian proposal to include such non-forceful seizure in the 1970 Hague Convention was rejected by the Legal Committee of the International Civil Aviation Organisation (ICAO) by 25:7. Shubber argued in 1973 that a reasonable interpretation, compatible with the aim and purpose of the Convention, requires a wide construction, one which would define non-forceful seizure as hijacking.[26] This inference seems to be arbitrary, especially in light of its previous rejection and the highly specialised nature of this and

22 See ICAO Resolutions A17–3 (1970), A17–4 (1970), A17–5 (1970) and A17–6 (1970), reprinted in YO Elagab, *International Law Documents Relating to Terrorism*, 1997, London: Cavendish Publishing, 443–45.

23 1970 Hague Convention, Art 1; in *Public Prosecutor v SHT* 74 ILR 162, the accused was charged with hijacking a British aircraft in flight from Beirut to London, forcing it to land in Amsterdam. The Dutch court applied the 1971 Dutch Penal Code, Art 385(a), which implemented the 1971 Montreal Convention and which provides for the punishment of persons 'who by force, threat thereof or intimidation seize or exercise control over an aircraft, and cause it to change course'.

24 1970 Hague Convention, Art 3(1).

25 S Shubber, 'Aircraft Hijacking under the Hague Convention 1970 – A New Regime?', 22 *ICLQ* (1973), 687, p 691.

26 Ibid, pp 692–93.

all other terrorist conventions, which cannot, accordingly, allow any room for interpretations of this kind.

For the purposes of the Hague Convention, the seizure must originate and be perpetrated by the principal from within the aircraft. Likewise, an accomplice falls within the ambit of the Convention only if such person provides assistance while on board the aircraft in flight. Accomplices whose participation in the offence takes place outside the aircraft are subject only to local criminal jurisdiction.[27] To meet the growing refusal of certain recalcitrant States to counter the aforementioned terrorist offences, the delegates to the 1978 Bonn Economic Summit issued a Joint Statement whereby they agreed to cease all incoming and outgoing flights to those countries that refused to extradite or prosecute hijackers and/or did not return illegally seized aircraft. It is worth noting that a joint US–Canadian draft sanctions treaty to the same effect was rejected by the Legal Committee of the ICAO in 1972.[28] The Bonn Declaration was subsequently enforced against Iran, Afghanistan and later Libya.[29]

A very specific form of unlawful aircraft seizure is that of 'air piracy', as defined under Art 15 of the 1958 Geneva Convention on the High Seas[30] and Art 101 of the 1982 UN Convention on the Law of the Sea (UNCLOS)[31] – although the term is also used generally to describe offences under the three anti-terrorist civil aviation conventions. Unlike aerial hijacking under the Hague Convention, air piracy under UNCLOS involves an illegal act of violence, namely an unlawful diversion to a destination other than that envisaged in the target aircraft's original flight plan, and originating from outside the attacked aircraft – thus requiring an aircraft of assault – and occurring in a place outside the jurisdiction of any State. Although the Hague Convention obliges States parties to consider the offences described therein as extraditable offences,[32] in effect denying the culprits a political motive excuse, the application of this rule to 'air piracy' under UNCLOS would be problematic, since piracy exists only where the illegal act of violence was committed for private ends, thus excluding action undertaken on political grounds. One is therefore presented with the regulation of this issue by two distinct legal regimes: on the one hand, UNCLOS and, on the other, the anti-terrorist treaties. The former allows the invocation of a political motive, whereas the latter does not. Clearly, the two regimes are contradictory and

---

27 Ibid, pp 704–05.
28 Op cit, McWhinney, note 20, pp 48–62.
29 See 1981 Ottawa Economic Summit (Point 3); 1986 Tokyo Economic Summit (Point 4).
30 450 UNTS 82.
31 Both UNCLOS, 21 ILM (1982), 1261, and the 1958 Convention reflect well established customary law; S Shubber, 'Is Hijacking of Aircraft Piracy in International Law?', 43 *BYIL* (1968–69), 193.
32 1970 Hague Convention, Art 8(1).

there do not exist any discernible guidelines as to which should prevail. However, in light of the by now customary prohibition of unlawful interference with civil aviation it is uncertain whether the illegal diversion of a civil aircraft, even for political purposes, would not amount to an international offence under UNCLOS.[33]

With the signing of the 1971 Montreal Convention for the Suppression of Unlawful Acts Against the Safety of Civil Aviation (Montreal Convention), the international community supplemented the legislative structure initialled by its two precursor conventions.[34] The aim of the 1971 Montreal Convention was to combat the scourge of attacks and other forms of aerial sabotage endangering the safety of civil aviation. Under Art 1, an offence is committed where a person unlawfully and intentionally:

(a) performs an act of violence against a person on board an aircraft in flight if that act is likely to endanger the safety of that aircraft; or

(b) destroys an aircraft in service or causes damage to such an aircraft which renders it incapable of flight or which is likely to endanger its safety in flight; or

(c) places or causes to be placed on an aircraft in service, by any means whatsoever, a device or substance which is likely to destroy that aircraft, or to cause damage to it which is likely to endanger its safety in flight; or

(d) destroys or damages air navigation facilities or interferes with their operation, if any such act is likely to endanger the safety of an aircraft in flight; or

(e) communicates information which he knows to be false, thereby endangering the safety of an aircraft in flight.

The concept of an aircraft 'in flight' is identical to that contained in the 1970 Hague Convention,[35] while an aircraft is considered to be 'in service' from the beginning of its pre-flight preparation until 24 hours after landing; the duration of an aircraft 'in service' cannot be shorter than that 'in flight'.[36] Besides this latter innovation and the various offences it covers, the 1971 Montreal Convention is similar to its Hague counterpart in all its other procedural provisions, that is, jurisdiction,[37] rendering proscribed offences extraditable, incorporation of the *aut dedere aut judicare* principle, mutual legal

33 See, to this effect, Council of Europe Resolution 450 (1970) on Air Piracy, reprinted in op cit, Elagab, note 22, p 440.

34 CS Thomas and MI Kirby, 'Convention for the Suppression of Unlawful Acts Against the Safety of Civil Aviation', 22 ICLQ (1973), 163.

35 971 Montreal Convention, Art 2(a).

36 Ibid, Art 2(b).

37 See Chapter 4.

assistance, and other forms of interstate co-operation and the obligation to adopt implementing legislation. It is fair to say that, solely from the point of view of the offences stipulated by the Hague and Montreal Conventions combined, the 1963 Tokyo Convention has, in fact, but not in law, been superseded.

The enhancement of security services in airports worldwide since the early 1980s has made hijacking far less frequent than in previous years.[38] This has resulted, however, in an increase in remote controlled detonations using plastic explosives and has rendered the application of the 1971 Montreal Convention all the more relevant. Observation of the Montreal Convention without other combined efforts to prevent the production and distribution of plastic explosives would be futile. Hence, under the aegis of ICAO, a Convention on the Marking of Plastic Explosives for the Purpose of Detection was adopted in 1991,[39] which obliges States parties to introduce detection agents into explosive products, whether manufactured in that State or simply imported therein, in order to render such explosives detectable – this process is termed 'marking' of explosives.[40]

At the same time, the provisions of the 1971 Montreal Convention have been triggered by clandestine or confessed attacks against civil aircraft by State entities. The most notorious attack of the latter kind, which was subsequently admitted to by the culprit State, concerned the downing of Iranian Airbus Flight 655, on 3 July 1988, by two surface to air missiles launched from USS Vincennes, causing the death of the 290 passengers and crew. Iran brought the case to the International Court of Justice (ICJ), claiming the US had violated the 1971 Montreal Convention by refusing to prosecute or extradite those responsible.[41] The US argued that the Convention was not applicable to acts committed by the armed forces of a State. The two parties finally resolved their dispute through a Settlement Agreement on 9 February 1996.[42] In another incident, North Korea was implicated in the destruction of a South Korean airliner on 29 November 1987. Although there was sufficient

---

38 A supplementary Protocol to the Montreal Convention on the Suppression of Unlawful Acts of Violence at Airports Serving International Civil Aviation was also agreed in 1988, reprinted in 27 ILM (1988), 627. Article II(1) criminalises unlawful and intentional acts of violence against persons at international airports which cause serious injury or death, as well as acts of destruction or serious damage to facilities of such airports, where such acts endanger or are likely to endanger safety at said airports.

39 30 ILM (1991), 721.

40 Ibid, Arts II, III and IV. The terms of the Convention do not apply to authorities performing military or police functions, unless they are used for purposes inconsistent with the objectives of the Convention (Arts III(2) and IV(1)).

41 *Islamic Republic of Iran v USA*, Aerial Incident of 3 July 1988. Iran instituted proceedings on 17 May 1989. Text reprinted in 28 ILM (1989), 843.

42 Reprinted in 35 ILM (1996), 572. By an order of 22 Feb 1996, the ICJ struck the case off its docket: (1996) ICJ Reports 9.

evidence demonstrating that a North Korean woman was responsible for the bombing,[43] that country did not assume responsibility for the incident, nor, of course, did it launch an investigation against the alleged offender.

One case that has attracted widespread public opinion has been the Lockerbie incident. On 21 December 1988, Pan Am flight 103A with direction from London to New York exploded above Lockerbie in Scotland, killing all its passengers and crew, as well as 11 unsuspecting Lockerbie residents from the falling debris. Three years later two Libyans were indicted in the US. Libya refused to extradite the accused, claiming it had investigated the case against them and had found no indication of criminal liability.[44] The case was, moreover, complicated by the fact that both the US and UK argued that the two men were Libyan agents ordered by the government of that country to sabotage the aircraft. From the point of view of its accusers this meant that any Libyan prosecution or, indeed, criminal investigation was, thereafter, an exercise in futility. Continued intransigence through Libya's refusal to extradite prompted the Security Council to pass Resolution 731 on 21 January 1992, urging Libya to co-operate with the US and UK in establishing responsibility for the terrorist acts. Rather than complying with the Security Council's request, on 3 March 1992 Libya lodged two separate complaints against the two countries, claiming violation of Arts 5(2)–(3), 7 and 11(1) of the 1971 Montreal Convention and asked the Court to order provisional measures. Meanwhile, on 31 March 1992, and pre-empting the World Court's decision, the Security Council acting under Chapter VII of the UN Charter adopted Resolution 748 with which it demanded Libya extradite the two accused, denounce terrorism and, further, imposed a number of sanctions. On 14 April 1992 the ICJ ruled that under Arts 25 and 103 of the UN Charter, Security Council resolutions take precedence over all other treaty commitments, including Libya's claim for refusal to extradite under the Montreal Convention, which, as most of the judges determined, would have probably been in the right had it not been for Resolution 748.[45] Despite an ICJ ruling on 27 February 1998 finding jurisdiction over the merits of the dispute,[46] for the purposes of international criminal law the above cases

---

43 See European Parliament Resolution of 10 March 1988 on Terrorist Attacks on Civil Aviation, reprinted in op cit, Elagab, note 22, p 440.

44 See C Joyner and W Rothbaum, 'Libya and the Aerial Incident at Lockerbie: What Lessons for International Extradition Law', 14 *Michigan JIL* (1992–93), 643.

45 *Libya v UK, Libya v USA*, Questions of Interpretation and Application of the 1971 Montreal Convention Arising from the Aerial Incident at Lockerbie (Provisional Measures), Order of 14 April 1992 (1992) ICJ Reports 3, p 114.

46 *Libya v UK, Libya v USA*, Questions of Interpretation and Application of the 1971 Montreal Convention Arising from the Aerial Incident at Lockerbie (Preliminary Objections), Judgment of 27 February 1998 (1998) ICJ Reports 115; see F Beveridge, 'The Lockerbie Cases', 48 *ICLQ* (1999), 658; V Debbas-Gowland, 'The Relationship between the International Court

exemplify the difficulties in the application of the 1971 Montreal Convention to situations of terrorist attacks involving States, which the Convention in question was not envisaged to cover. By 1998 the deadlock regarding the criminal prosecution of the two accused had been broken and an agreement was reached whereby a court established in The Netherlands and composed of Scottish judges applying Scottish law would sit in trial of the two Libyans.[47] Whether due to the stringent and effective security measures at airports worldwide, enhanced interstate co-operation, or simply because air offences do not attract the attention of public opinion as in the past, air travel is now far safer. At the second meeting of its 156th Session, on 22 February 1999, the ICAO Council reported a sharp decline in the number of incidents of unlawful interference with international civil aviation.[48] The events of 11 September 2001 revealed the extent to which fundamentalist terror groups are prepared to employ civilian aircraft for terrorist action. Although this incident has no bearing on the legal effect of the various civil aviation treaties, the industry itself reviewed internal procedures and has restricted access to the pilots' cabin, among other measures.

10.3.2 Hostage taking and attacks against internationally protected persons

The practice of hostage taking for political ends, especially prevalent in the 1970s and 1980s among terrorist organisations active in the Middle East, Western Europe and South America,[49] has once again resurfaced in the territories of the former Soviet Union and in the various civil wars in South America. Under Art 1(1) of the 1979 International Convention Against the Taking of Hostages, the offence of taking hostages is committed by:

> . . . any person who seizes or detains and threatens to kill, to injure or to continue to detain another person (hereinafter referred to as the 'hostage') in order to compel a third party, namely, a State, an international intergovernmental organisation, a natural or juridical person, or a group

---

of Justice and the Security Council in the Light of the Lockerbie Case', 88 *AJIL* (1994), 643; K Kaikobad, The Court, the Council and Interim Protection: A Commentary on the Lockerbie Order of 19 April 1992', 17 *Australian YIL* (1996), 87.

47 Agreement between the Government of the Kingdom of The Netherlands and the Government of the United Kingdom of Great Britain and Northern Ireland, Concerning a Scottish Trial in The Netherlands, 18 September 1998, reprinted in 38 ILM (1999), 926.

48 Report of the Secretary General, *Measures to Eliminate International Terrorism,* UN Doc A/54/301 (3 Sep 1999), p 7.

49 SC Res 579 (18 Dec 1985), 618 (29 July 1988) and 638 (31 July 1989); Organisation of American States (OAS) GA Res 4(I-E 170) (30 June 1970); see also TH Sponsler, 'International Kidnappings', 5 *International Lawyer* (1970), 25.

of persons, to do or abstain from doing any act as an explicit or implicit condition for the release of the hostage.

As is evident, acts of hostage taking overlap with offences encountered in other counter-terrorist treaties. The provisions of the Convention are not applicable to purely internal situations of hostage taking, thus requiring at least one international element.[50] The Convention, like all its other anti-terrorist predecessors, recognises the grave nature of the offence[51] and obliges States parties to define it as an extraditable crime under their domestic laws.[52] The Convention is inapplicable to situations involving armed conflicts, but in any event hostage taking is prohibited in armed conflicts by both customary law and relevant conventions.[53]

Although the 1979 Convention makes no provision regarding the handling of hostage situations once these have occurred, it requires parties to take all appropriate measures, such as to 'ease the situation of the hostage, in particular, to secure their release'[54] and subsequently return to them any object which the offender has obtained as a result of the offence.[55] Most States have adopted a policy of refusing to yield to terrorist demands,[56] a practice which is compatible with Art 3(1) of the Convention by discouraging an endless chain of abductions. Even non-yielding States are under an obligation not to abandon a hostage situation. To this end, both peaceful as well as forceful means are permitted and, in many cases, whether openly or secretly, mounting domestic political pressure forces States to concede to kidnappers' demands, as was the case with the US hostages in Iran during the 1979 crisis.[57]

A more specialised international offence against the person is that formulated by the 1973 UN Convention on the Prevention and Punishment of

---

50 1979 International Convention Against the Taking of Hostages, Art 13.
51 Ibid, Art 2.
52 Ibid, Art 10(1); likewise, all forms of unlawful detention constitute offences under the 1976 European Convention on the Suppression of Terrorism, Art 1(d), which the Member States are obliged to regard as extraditable.
53 1949 Geneva Convention Relative to the Protection of Civilian Persons in Time of War, Arts 3(1)(b) and 34, 75 UNTS (1950) 287; *USA v List* (*Hostages* case) 8 LRTWC (1949), 34; see also SC Res 674 (29 Oct 1990), demanding, under the 1945 UN Charter, Chapter VII, that Iraq release all hostages in occupied Kuwait.
54 1979 International Convention Against the Taking of Hostages, Art 3(1).
55 Ibid, Art 3(2).
56 The participating nations in the G8/Russia 1995 Ottawa Anti-terrorist Summit, agreed, *inter alia*, to deny demands from kidnappers.
57 The two countries negotiated an agreement whereby Iran was to release, *inter alia*, the hostages under the condition that the US unfreeze Iranian assets and an arbitral tribunal be established to settle individual claims for compensation arising from the 1979 coup. See op cit, Elagab, note 22, pp 615–49.

Crimes Against Internationally Protected Persons, Including Diplomatic Agents.[58] This Convention penalises what has been an ancient customary obligation to protect the person and property of diplomatic agents and other foreign public officials,[59] as was reaffirmed in the year-long hostage incident involving 59 US diplomatic personnel in Iran.[60] Article 1 of the Convention distinguishes two categories of internationally protected persons. The first is Heads of State, Heads of Government or Foreign Affairs Ministers, whenever such persons are in a foreign State, as well as accompanying family members.[61] This protection exists regardless of official capacity and extends under customary law only to immediate family members.[62] The second category includes representatives of States or intergovernmental organisations who are entitled to special protection under general international law; that is, diplomats, consuls, accredited officials of States and international organisations on official visits.[63] The offence is completed through the intentional commission, threat, attempt of, or complicity in the murder, kidnapping, attack upon the person or liberty thereof, or a violent attack against the official premises, private accommodation, or transportation of internationally protected persons likely to endanger their person or liberty.[64] Additionally, the accused must be aware of the protected status of the person when perpetrating the *actus reus* of the offence, hence a fatal road traffic accident does not necessarily fall within the scope of Art 2.[65]

The rise in attacks against internationally protected persons accelerated concerted international efforts towards acknowledging the seriousness of the

---

58 13 ILM (1974), 41.

59 1961 Vienna Convention on Diplomatic Relations, Arts 29, 30, 500 UNTS 95; 1971 OAS Convention to Prevent and Punish the Acts of Terrorism Taking the Form of Crimes Against Persons and Related Extortion that are of International Significance, Art 2, reprinted in 10 ILM (1971), 255, makes kidnapping, murder and other assaults against the life or integrity of internationally protected persons 'common crimes of international significance'. Therefore, unlike the 1973 Convention, the relevant offences contained in the 1971 OAS Convention are not considered international offences.

60 *USA v Iran* (*US Diplomatic and Consular Staff in Iran* case), Judgment (24 May 1980), ICJ Reports 3.

61 1973 UN Convention on the Prevention and Punishment of Crimes Against Internationally Protected Persons Including Diplomatic Agents, Art 1(a).

62 CL Rozakis, 'Terrorism and the Internationally Protected Persons in the Light of the ILC's Draft Code', 23 *ICLQ* (1974), 32, p 43.

63 In *R v Donyadideh and Others*, 101 ILR 259, 11 persons were charged with offences against representatives of Iran in Australia. The Australian Supreme Court convicted the culprits under that country's Internationally Protected Persons Act 1976, s 8(2) and (3), incorporating the relevant 1973 UN Convention for offences against the liberty and damage to property of said officials; see also UK Internationally Protected Persons Act 1978, s 1.

64 1973 Convention, Art 2; see also 1976 European Convention on the Suppression of Terrorism, Art 1(c).

65 Op cit, Rozakis, note 62, pp 49–50.

problem and taking measures to give effect to the 1973 Convention. The Venice Economic Summit Conference of 1980 contained a Statement on the Taking of Diplomatic Hostages (the Venice Statement), noting the duty of States to adopt appropriate policies and criminal legislation and refrain from taking a direct or indirect part in such acts. The Venice Statement was reaffirmed in the Ottawa Summit of 1981, which further addressed the resolve of participating States to take prompt action in cases of State support of related terrorist activities. Moreover, a reporting procedure was established by the General Assembly in 1980, urging Member States to submit reports on offences against protected persons, as well as the application of domestic laws and measures taken to effectively implement them.[66] This procedure was supplemented in 1987 by a request for more detailed information to be supplied to the Secretary General with regard to his *Annual Report* on the subject.[67]

10.3.3 Terrorist bombings and nuclear terrorism

The Ad Hoc Committee on Terrorism established by the General Assembly in 1996[68] examined the drafting of three distinct treaties on specific issues of international terrorism: terrorist bombings, terrorist financing and nuclear terrorism. Agreement on the first two was swift, but nuclear terrorism was of a far thornier nature and a treaty was only agreed in 2005. The issue of urban terrorist bombings was never placed on the international agenda before the end of the Cold War because the vast majority of such attacks were committed within a single State by persons or groups that were nationals of that State. Countries also felt that such incidents were of purely domestic concern for an additional reason. They were reluctant to trigger debate over the possible application of the laws of armed conflict in their battle against terrorist organisations, subsequently giving rise to questions of self-determination. This was particularly the case with the provisional Irish Republican Army (IRA) in the UK and the Kurdistan Workers' Party (PKK) in Turkey. Such cases assumed an international element either when governmental forces acted clandestinely abroad,[69] or the said States requested the extradition of alleged perpetrators apprehended elsewhere.[70] This practice of branding groups as terrorist organisations and refusing to recognise the existence of a non-international armed conflict and combatant status vis-à-vis enemy belligerents, where the criteria were satisfied under common Art 3 of the 1949

---

66 GA Res 35/168 (15 Dec 1980).
67 GA Res 42/154 (7 Dec 1987), operative para 9.
68 GA Res 51/210 (17 Dec 1996) and affirmed by GA Res 53/108 (8 Dec 1998).
69 *McCann v UK* (1996) 21 EHRR 97.
70 *Re Croissant* (1978) 74 ILR 505, Conseil d'Etat.

Geneva Conventions,[71] resulted in appalling human rights abuses both for belligerents and civilian populations.[72]

With the demise of communism and the concentration of politics and commerce in supra-national institutions, terrorist organisations began conducting urban warfare across borders, as restrictions in cross-border crossings were also declining in many parts of the world. Common interests, therefore, should preclude isolationist politics on issues of terrorism, unless these involve strictly domestic incidents without any international elements or repercussions. In 1998, the UN Convention for the Suppression of Terrorist Bombings (Terrorist Bombings Convention) was adopted by the General Assembly of the UN. This instrument made it an offence to unlawfully and intentionally deliver, place, discharge or detonate an explosive or other lethal device in, into or against a place of public use, a State facility, a public transportation system or infrastructure facility, with intent to cause death or bodily injury, or extensive destruction, resulting or likely to result in major economic loss.[73] In order to avoid the political shortcomings identified above, Art 3 of the Convention requires that the operation leading to a terrorist bombing involve at least one extraterritorial element; that is, it must not be performed solely within one country, or where the offender and victim are nationals of the same country.

Both the terrorist bombings and financing conventions view terrorism as a series of pre-planned operations carried out by persons participating in multifaceted organisational webs, and oblige Member States to take specific measures in such a way as to curb terrorism from its roots. Building on a growing de-politicisation of terrorist-related activities, the Terrorist Bombings Convention makes it clear that no justification is to be provided under domestic law for the offences contemplated, regardless of political, philosophical, ideological, religious, or other motive involved.[74]

Finally, with the growth of criminal organisations, the issue of nuclear terrorism has once again resurfaced. The 1979 Convention on the Physical Protection of Nuclear Material,[75] an instrument indirectly related to terrorism, was adopted with a twofold objective: to establish levels of physical

---

71 Common Art 3 is a norm of customary international law. See *Nicaragua v USA* (Military and Paramilitary Activities in and against Nicaragua) (Merits) (1986) ICJ Reports, para 218; affirmed in *ICTY Prosecutor v Tadic*, Decision on Interlocutory Appeal on Jurisdiction 105 ILR 453, para 98.

72 See E Yuksel, 'Cannibal Democracies, Theocratic Secularism: The Turkish Version', 7 *Cardozo J Int'l & Comp L* (1999), 423.

73 1998 Terrorist Bombings Convention, Art 2(1). It is also an offence to attempt (Art 2(2)), participate (Art 2(3)(a)), organise or direct (Art 2(3)(b)), or act in a common purpose (Art 2(3)(c)) to commit any of the offences contained in Art 2(1).

74 1998 Terrorist Bombings Convention, Art 5.

75 18 ILM (1979), 1422.

protection of nuclear material used for peaceful purposes while in international nuclear transport,[76] and to provide for measures against unlawful acts (for example, the requirements that relate to making specified acts criminal offences under national law, establishing jurisdiction over those offences, and prosecuting or extraditing alleged offenders) with respect to such material while in international transport, as well as in domestic use, storage and transport.[77] The adoption in 2005 of the UN Convention on the Suppression of Acts of Nuclear Terrorism was a response to the possibility that nuclear or radioactive material may fall into the hands of terrorists. Indeed, the gravity of illicit trafficking in nuclear material has alarmed the International Atomic Energy Agency (IAEA) since the early 1990s. To this end, the IAEA's Illicit Trafficking Database (ITDB) programme for incidents involving nuclear materials and other radioactive sources dates from August 1995 when the IAEA Secretariat invited governments to participate in its database programme and to identify points of contact for that purpose. In its 2005 Report, the IAEA confirmed 103 incidents of illicit trafficking and unauthorised activities concerning nuclear and radioactive material for that year alone. However, the Report stressed the fact that these incidents did not involve a terrorist element or threat thereof, not even criminal liability in the vast majority of cases, but highlighted security vulnerabilities in nuclear-handling facilities.[78]

A person commits an offence within the meaning of the Nuclear Terrorism Convention if that person unlawfully and intentionally:

(a) Possesses radioactive material or makes or possesses a device:

   (i) With the intent to cause death or serious bodily injury; or
   (ii) With the intent to cause substantial damage to property or to the environment;

(b) Uses in any way radioactive material or a device, or uses and damages a nuclear facility in a manner which releases or risks the release of radioactive material: [with intent to cause death, serious bodily injury, substantial damage to property or the environment]

   (i) With the intent to compel a natural or legal person, an international organisation or a State to do or refrain from doing an act.[79]

---

76 1979 Convention on the Physical Protection of Nuclear Material, Arts 2 and 3.
77 Ibid, Arts 7–11.
78 IAEA, Illicit Trafficking and Other Unauthorised Activities Involving Nuclear and Radioactive Material (2005), available at: <http://www.iaea.org/NewsCenter/Features/RadSources/PDF/fact_figures2005.pdf>.
79 Art 2(1), Nuclear Terrorism Convention.

A person commits an offence within the meaning of Art 2 if he threatens to employ nuclear or radioactive material, or unlawfully demand such material, device or nuclear facility under circumstances indicating the credibility of a threat. The offence may be consummated through an attempt, accomplice and common purpose liability,[80] as well as by ordering or organising others to do so.[81] In accordance with Arts 3 and 4 the Convention is inapplicable where the offence takes place on the territory of a single country, or where the offender and victims are nationals of the same country, etc, nor is it applicable where it concerns the activities of armed forces during an armed conflict, or in their exercise of official duties. This provision was included to alleviate the concerns of nuclear powers over the activities of their military personnel, but it should not be read as condoning nuclear theft or threats to use nuclear or radioactive material by the intelligence services of States during peace time.[82] In all other respects the Convention resembles the post–1998 generation of anti-terrorist treaties, granting thus wide territorial and extraterritorial jurisdiction[83] and rejecting all possible defences or justifications offered by the perpetrators. On the other hand, the provisions on co-operation are weak and subject to numerous exceptions.

10.3.4 Terrorist financing and Security Council Resolution 1373 (2001)

Prior to the collapse of communism it was not uncommon for terrorist groups to be funded by particular States. This was achieved through direct funding or logistical support and by allowing or tolerating the use of their territory by such groups as a base for launching and planning illegal acts. The New World Order, following the end of the Cold War, created a vacuum with regard to State-financing and thus terrorist groups turned increasingly to other means of self-preservation. Since the early 1990s the UN General Assembly had identified possible links between terrorism and organised crime.[84] The 2000 UN Convention Against Transnational Organized Crime (CATOC)[85] exemplifies this connection between terrorism and organised

---

80 For an analysis of these types of liability, see Chapter 2.
81 Art 2(2)–(4), Nuclear Terrorism Convention.
82 See Art 4(3) of the Convention.
83 Art 9(2)(b) provides jurisdiction even to the State whose government facilities abroad, including embassies or consular premises, were the target of an offence.
84 GA Res 49/60 (9 Dec 1994); the Vienna Declaration and Program of Action, adopted at the World Conference on Human Rights, emphasised that the linkage between terrorism and drug-trafficking aims at the 'destruction' of human rights and democracy, UN Doc A/CONF 157/23 (14–25 June 1993).
85 40 ILM (2001), 335.

crime, but despite the acknowledged and manifest links between the two[86] the insertion of terrorist acts in the definition of organised crime was finally avoided. Nonetheless, some groups such as the Colombian FARC and the Taliban, who at the time sheltered Al-Qaeda in Afghanistan, were known to cultivate and traffic illicit narcotic substances.[87] In other instances, terrorists had formed alliances with organised criminal rings in order to conduct trafficking of arms, drugs and women, launder illicit proceeds, and infiltrate legitimate banking and commercial markets. Security Council Resolution 1333 determined that proceeds from narcotics strengthened the Taliban's capacity in harbouring terrorists and imposed a sanctions regime.[88]

In January 2000, the General Assembly of the UN opened for signature an International Convention for the Suppression of the Financing of Terrorism.[89] This Convention makes it an offence to directly or indirectly, unlawfully and wilfully: provide or collect funds with the intention or knowledge they are used, in full or in part, to carry out acts described in the various anti-terrorist conventions; commit other criminal acts with the aim of intimidating a population; or compel a government to do or abstain from a certain act.[90] The Convention establishes a distinct offence of terrorist financing, which is constituted by 'directly or indirectly, unlawfully and wilfully providing or collecting funds with the intention that they should be used or in the knowledge that they are to be used, in full or in part', in order to carry out an offence described in any one of the nine counter-terrorist treaties, or to commit any other violent act with the intent of intimidating a population or of compelling a government to act in a certain way.[91] While the criminalisation of funding of acts falling within the ambit of previous counter-terrorist treaties requires ratification of those treaties by the State concerned, that is not the case with regard to 'other violent intimidating acts', as described in sub-para 1(b). This wide definition may well encompass offences encountered

86 Second session of the Ad Hoc Committee (8–12 March 1999), UN Doc A/AC 254/4 Rev 1 (10 Feb 1999).
87 SC Res 1214 (8 Dec 1998).
88 SC Res 1333 (19 Dec 2000).
89 GA Res 54/109 (25 Feb 2000); see V Morris and A Pronto, 'The Work of the Sixth Committee at the Fifty-Fourth Session of the UN General Assembly', 94 *AJIL* (2000), 582, p 585; see also EC Council Recommendation of 9 December 1999 on Co-operation in Combating the Financing of Terrorist Groups (OJ C373, 23 Dec 1999).
90 2000 Terrorist Financing Convention, Art 2(1). It is also an offence to participate in, organise or direct, act in a common purpose (Art 2(5)), or attempt (Art 2(4)) any of the offences described in Art 2(1).
91 Art 2(1)(a) and (b); Art 2(d) of the 1999 Convention of the Organisation of the Islamic Conference (OIC) on Combating International Terrorism, states, *inter alia*, that 'all forms of international crimes, including illegal trafficking in narcotics and human beings, money laundering, aimed at financing terrorist objectives shall be considered terrorist crimes'.

in the nine counter-terrorist treaties. For example, the provision of financial assistance by an individual who is a national of country A, with the aim of kidnapping a Head of State, becomes an international offence only if country A has ratified both the 2000 Terrorist Financing Convention and the 1973 Convention on the Prevention and Punishment of Crimes Against Internationally Protected Persons, Including Diplomatic Agents.[92] The effect of sub-para (1)(b), however, is to establish such an act as an offence under the 2000 Terrorist Financing Convention, where it is understood that the kidnapping in question was either intended to intimidate the civilian population or compel a government to do or abstain from doing a certain act.[93] As regards the definition of 'financing', it was pointed out during the deliberations in the Sixth Committee that while the Convention focused on the financing of the most serious terrorist acts, all means of financing were covered, including both 'unlawful' means (such as racketeering) and 'lawful' means (such as private and public financing, financing provided by associations).[94] The Convention obliges parties to take appropriate measures in order to identify, detect, freeze, or seize terrorist-related funds as well as the proceeds derived from such offences.[95] A number of intergovernmental bodies, as well as domestic enforcement agencies, have called or imposed stricter client identification on financial institutions, as well as an obligation to file Suspicious Transactions Reports (STRs). The so called 'Know Your Client' (KYC) principle, which has been derived from counter-money laundering procedures, requires that financial institutions verify in as much detail as possible all their clients, whether these are natural or legal persons.[96]

Following the 11 September 2001 terrorist attack in the US, the Security Council adopted Resolution 1373 on 28 September 2001. This establishes a general – that is, not specifically directed against Al-Qaeda and their associates – financial regime which: criminalises all activities falling within the remit of terrorist financing; obliges States to freeze all funds or financial assets of persons and entities that are directly or indirectly used to commit terrorist acts or that are owned and controlled by persons engaged in, or associated with, terrorism; obliges States to prevent their nationals (including private financial institutions) from making such funds available, thus imposing strict

92 3 ILM (1979), 41.
93 Report of the Ad Hoc Committee established by GA Res 51/210 (1996), GAOR 54th Session, UN Doc A/54/37/Supp No 37 (5 May 1999), p 3.
94 Ibid.
95 2000 Terrorist Financing Convention, Art 8(1).
96 Ibid, Art 18(1)(b)(ii) requires, with regard to legal persons, the following: proof of incorporation, including information concerning the customer's name, legal form, address, directors, and provisions regulating the power to bind the entity. Sub-paragraph 1(b)(iv) further requires that 'financial institutions maintain, for at least five years, all necessary records on transactions, both domestic or international'.

client detection measures, requirements relating to the filing of STRs, and subordination to other intergovernmental institutions in order to receive the names of designated terrorist organisations or individuals;[97] and imposes substantive and procedural criminal law measures at the domestic level, including an obligation to co-operate in the acquisition of evidence for criminal proceedings.[98] In order to implement and monitor the terms of the Resolution, the Council decided to establish a subsidiary organ, the Counter-Terrorism Committee.[99] Member States were obliged to report to the Committee, within 90 days, on the steps they had taken to implement the Resolution. By late May 2002 the Committee had received more than 150 reports from States,[100] as well as reports from the Organisation for Security and Co-operation in Europe (OSCE)[101] and the European Union.[102] While the vast majority of States had criminalised terrorist financing, this did not necessarily entail the functioning of an adequate regulatory and enforcement regime and the CTC asked States to remedy these weaknesses.

The Security Council proceeded to impose so-called targeted sanctions against persons associated with terrorist-related funds, much in the same way it had done with other international crimes prior to 9/11. UN targeted sanctions operate through the delegation of the task by the Council to a subsidiary organ, a sanctions committee, which proceeds to draw a list of targeted persons or organisations, which list is thereafter binding on States and private entities. In the case of terrorist financing, the sanctions committee established under Council Resolution 1267[103] – whose mandate originally encompassed the Taliban regime and which was later extended to cover Al-Qaeda terrorist financing blacklisting – imposed a number of obligations, such as asset freezing, travel bans and others. This expansion of the 1267 Committee's work was achieved through the adoption of Resolution 1390,[104] which does not impose a time limit, nor require a link between the targeted individual/group and a State. The Security Council later provided a definition of 'association with' Al-Qaeda, through Resolution 1526,[105] because a number of States thought it wise to report political dissidents to the sanctions committee.[106] The Sanctions Committee receives its information through

97 Operative para 1; although in practice this also includes national law enforcement author-
    ities, such as the FBI, CIA and OFAC (Office of Foreign Assets Control).
98 Operative para 2.
99 Operative para 6.
100 Available at <http://www.un.org/docs/sc/committees/1373/reptse.htm>.
101 UN Doc S/2002/34 (8 Jan 2002).
102 UN Doc S/2001/1297 (28 Dec 2001).
103 SC 1267 (15 Oct 1999).
104 SC 1390 (16 Jan 2002)
105 SC 1526 (30 Jan 2004).
106 I Cameron, 'Terrorist Financing in International Law' in I Bantekas (ed), *International and
    European Financial Criminal Law*, 2006, Butterworths.

secret intelligence and although a recommendation to list a particular person/ group must be accompanied by an account of some evidence, the Committee does not possess the technical capacity to assess the veracity of the submitted information.[107] Besides the UN list issued by the 1267 Committee, various US government agencies, in particular OFAC, as well as the UK, EU[108] and others have issued their own lists, which in some cases are more extensive than the UN list. Although these have no binding effect on other States, let alone private financial institutions, in practice the latter are obliged to conform because of their business relations with the issuing States and possible consequences in cases where they are not seen to comply.

In practical terms, both the 2000 Convention and Resolution 1373 must be construed in accordance with the findings and Recommendations of the OECD's Financial Action Task Force (FATF). The FATF had warned about the channelling of funds to terrorists from money laundering, underground remittance systems (*hawala*), disguised charities and trusts. Most of these activities are difficult to detect, and so it is the duty of financial or other institutions to implement appropriate monitoring mechanisms (such as KYC and the filing of STRs). At an extraordinary plenary, held on 29 and 30 October 2001, the FATF expanded its mandate to encompass terrorist financing – apart from money laundering. During the plenary it was agreed that the FATF would issue Special Recommendations on Terrorist Financing. These commit members to:

- ratify counter-terrorism treaties;
- criminalise terrorist financing;
- freeze and confiscate terrorist assets;
- report suspicious transactions;
- provide related assistance to other countries;
- impose anti-money laundering requirements on alternative remittance systems;

---

107 The Committee has set up Guidelines for assessing listing and de-listing. Available at: <http://www.un.org/Docs/sc/committees/1267/1267_guidelines.pdf>.

108 EU freezing measures are predicated on the electronic-Consolidated Targeted Financial Sanctions List (e-CTFSL) database, which represents a joint initiative between the EC Commission and European banks, containing all persons and entities subject to EU financial sanctions. See also Council Regulation 2580/2001 of 27 Dec 2001 on Specific Restrictive Measures directed against certain Persons and Entities with a view to Combating Terrorism (OJ L 344, 28/11/2001); Council Regulation 881/2002 of 27 May 2002, imposing certain specific Restrictive Measures directed against certain Persons and entities associated with Osama bin Laden, the Al-Qaeda network and the Taliban . . . and extending the Freeze of Funds and other Financial Resources (OJ l 139, 29/05/2002). This Regulation authorises the EC Commission to supplement and amend the list on the basis of Security Council resolutions or the Sanction Committee's determinations through the adoption of subsequent EC Regulations.

- strengthen customer identification measures in international and domestic wire transfers;
- ensure that non-profit organisations cannot be misused to finance terrorism.[109]

The Special Recommendations, which although not binding are of extremely persuasive value, were followed by an Action Plan that included the completion of a self-assessment exercise by all FATF members. This included: the issuance of additional FATF Guidance for Financial Institutions in Detecting Terrorist Financing;[110] the identification of and measures to be taken vis-à-vis jurisdictions that lack appropriate measures; regular publication of frozen terrorist assets; provision of technical assistance to non-FATF members.

10.3.5 Establishment of regional mechanisms

The thematic approach to terrorism facilitates the international community's efforts in finding means to curtail its impact on regional and global stability. If this thematic approach adequately describes a definitional consensus among nations, the key feature of anti-terrorist treaties is the establishment of a framework of international co-operation in a way that principles such as *aut dedere aut judicare*, promulgation of criminal laws and prevention, exchange of information and mutual legal assistance, are reiterated in every instrument.[111] At the same time, regional anti-terrorist treaties are born out of regional needs and their aim is to consolidate and strengthen co-operation among the States concerned. Thus, following its 1996 Declaration and Plan of Action of Lima to Prevent, Combat and Eliminate Terrorism, the General Assembly of the Organisation of American States adopted Resolution 1650 (1999), whereby it decided to establish the Inter-American Committee Against Terrorism (CICTE), whose purpose is to develop sufficient co-operation in order to prevent and combat terrorism.[112] Similarly, the Member States to the South Asian Association for Regional Co-operation (SAARC) adopted in 1987 a Regional Convention on Suppression of Terrorism with the aim of promoting the mechanisms existing in the various multilateral treaties and facilitate more effective co-operation through the establishment of a supervisory organ. This organ is the SAARC Terrorist Offences

---

109 FATF Special Recommendations on Terrorist Financing (31 Oct 2001); see I Bantekas, 'The International Law of Terrorist Financing', 97 *AJIL* (2003) 315.
110 FATF Guidance for Financial Institutions in Detecting Terrorist Financing (24 April 2002), pp 2–3.
111 See JF Murphy, 'The Future of Multilateralism and Efforts to Combat International Terrorism', 25 *Columbia J Trans L* (1986), 35.
112 OAS GA Res 1650 (XXIX–0/99), operative para 3.

Monitoring Desk, created in 1992, which is mandated to collate, analyse and disseminate information on terrorist incidents, tactics, etc. Likewise, The League of Arab States adopted in 1998 the Arab Anti-Terrorism Agreement, which contains 43 clauses, organising trial and extradition procedures for those accused and convicted in terrorist incidents. It also deals with co-ordination between the security services in Arab countries and exchange of information, as well as the adoption of measures to prevent infiltration across borders. There is no indication that regionalism of this type has reinforced global standards under the United Nations international treaties or the efforts of the Security Council.

Of particular interest is the legal framework created in the context of the European Union. Under Arts K1–K9 of the 1992 Treaty on European Union (TEU),[113] terrorism was defined as an issue of 'common interest'. An inter-governmental body, the Executive Committee, was further established, which controls and co-ordinates these points of common interest (unofficially named 'K4 Committee'). The 1998 Amsterdam Treaty amending the TEU[114] retained terrorism in the Third Pillar of the EU (Title IV), promoting it from a point of common interest to an 'objective' of the EU through the adoption of common action between national law enforcement agencies, Europol and judicial authorities, as well as through approximation of criminal laws.[115] Following the 11 September 2001 terrorist attacks, on 27 December 2001, the Council adopted Common Position 931, which obliged both the EU and Member States to freeze the funds and financial assets of named terrorists and organisations, as well as enhance police and judicial co-operation, affording each other the 'widest possible assistance in preventing and combating terrorist acts'.[116] The definition of 'persons' and 'groups' involved in terrorism supplied in Art 1(2) of the Common Position has now been supplemented by the primary terrorist instrument in the EU, Council Framework Decision 2002/475/JHA on Combating Terrorism (2002). Article 1 defines terrorist offences as intentional acts committed with the aim of:

- seriously intimidating a population, or
- unduly compelling a government or international organisation to perform or abstain from performing any act, or
- seriously destabilising or destroying the fundamental political, con-stitutional, economic or social structures of a country or an inter-national organisation, [involving]

  (a) attacks upon a person's life which may cause death;

113 31 ILM (1992), 247.
114 37 ILM (1998), 56.
115 1998 Amsterdam Treaty, Art K1.
116 2001/931/CFSP of 27 Dec 2001 (OJ L 344, 28/12/2001), Art 4.

    (b) attacks upon the physical integrity of a person;

    (c) kidnapping or hostage taking;

    (d) causing extensive destruction to a government or public facility, a transport system, an infrastructure facility, including an information system, a fixed platform located on the continental shelf, a public place or private property likely to endanger human life or result in major economic loss;

    (e) seizure of aircraft, ships or other means of public or goods transport;

    (f) manufacture, possession, acquisition, transport, supply or use of weapons, explosives or of nuclear, biological or chemical weapons, as well as research into, and development of, biological and chemical weapons;

    (g) release of dangerous substances, or causing fires, floods or explosions the effect of which is to endanger human life;

    (h) interfering with or disrupting the supply of water, power or any other fundamental natural resource the effect of which is to endanger human life;

    (i) threatening to commit any of the acts listed.

Article 2 defines a 'terrorist group' as a structured group of more than two persons with some degree of permanency, defined roles, continuity of membership and acting in concert to commit terrorist offences. The main trait of EU counter-terrorism legislation lies not so much in the production of definitions as in the capacity of its members to agree and enforce a sophisticated and effective system of co-operation. Among others, the principle of mutual recognition of judicial decisions between Member States in the fields of extradition,[117] freezing orders[118] and imposition of financial penalties[119] precludes the requested State from examining the decision of the requesting State's court, or addressing the issue of double criminality. This principle is applicable to a listed number of offences, including terrorism.

10.4 STATE-SPONSORED TERRORISM

Too many political intricacies have so far obstructed the attainment of a single definition of terrorism; it is no wonder therefore that there does not

---

117 Council Framework Decision of 13 June 2002 (2002/584/JHA), on a European Arrest Warrant, (OJ L 190/1, 18/07/02).

118 Council Framework Decision of 22 July 2003 (2003/577/JHA) on Execution of Orders Freezing Property or Evidence, (OJ L 196, 02/08/03).

119 Council Framework Decision of 24 February 2005 (2005/214/JHA) on the Application of the Principle of Mutual Recognition to Financial Penalties, (OJ L 76/16, 22/03/05).

exist a single provision in any of the aforementioned anti-terrorist treaties setting out the criteria for branding a State as such. Starting in the late 1960s the West was disinclined to accept claims made by developing and Arab countries to the effect that Israel was a 'terrorist State', believing that only individuals or groups could be classified as terrorists. However, since the 1980s, and with evidence that some countries were behind terrorist activities, this stance was altered and 'State-sponsored terrorism' became a reality. The main concern in these cases should be the degree of support actually enjoyed; however, both direct and indirect assistance are prohibited and render a State liable.[120] This can include: the deployment of State agents or other persons controlled by that State; groups or persons independent from the State, but in receipt of financial aid or weapons, or only of logistic support; and persons or groups receiving no active support, but in respect of which a State acquiesces in their use of its territory.[121] When a State lends any form of support from the aforementioned list to terrorist armed activities, it not only violates the *jus cogens* principle of non-intervention;[122] it further risks retaliatory action from the target State. Indeed, in an extreme case of a State being equated with a terrorist organisation,[123] and whose actions amount to an armed attack, the target State is entitled to reply with force against the aggressor State in order to repel the attack.[124] However, since the criteria for determining both an armed attack and an agency require military operations and support of a very high threshold, it is doubtful that the acts of a terrorist organisation, even if an agency relationship could be established, could ever amount to an armed attack.

This latter view has vehemently been objected to by the US and Israel, the former, since the 1980s, and the latter from the 1970s, arguing that terrorist attacks justify the use of force in order to defend, but also for pre-emptive reasons.[125] On 7 August 1998, US embassies in Nairobi and Dar-es-Salam were devastated by bomb blasts that killed approximately 300 people, including 12 American nationals. Investigations led US authorities to suspect the involvement of Al-Qaeda which at that time was based in Afghanistan. In retaliation, on 20 August 1998, the US launched 79 Tomahawk Cruise missiles

---

120 See GA Res 49/60 (9 Dec 1994).
121 Op cit, Cassese, note 4, p 598.
122 *Nicaragua v USA* (Military and Paramilitary Activities in and against Nicaragua) (Merits) (1986) ICI Reports, para 205; ILC Draft Code of Crimes Against the Peace and Security of Mankind, draft Art 14, reprinted in 18 *HRLJ* (1997), 96.
123 For the requirements of an 'agency' relationship, see ibid, *Nicaragua* judgment, para 108.
124 1945 UN Charter, Art 51.
125 Op cit, Cassese, note 4, pp 600, 603; see Israeli claim of pre-emptive self-defence regarding the interception of a Libyan civil aircraft in 1986, UN Doc S/PV 2655/Corr 1 (18 Feb 1986); see US Presidential Directives 62 (on combating terrorism), 22 May 1998, and 63 (on critical infrastructure protection), 22 May 1998.

against paramilitary camps in Afghanistan and a Sudanese pharmaceutical plant in Sudan, claiming the latter produced chemical weapons. In his report, President Clinton stated that the US acted in the exercise of its right of self-defence under Art 51 of the 1945 UN Charter, pointing out that the strikes were necessary and proportionate to an imminent terrorist threat, further arguing that they were intended to prevent and deter future attacks.[126] The day following the 11 September 2001 attack against the US by Al-Qaeda, the Security Council adopted Resolution 1368, which made reference to the inherent right of self-defence. The connotation was adamantly clear, since the Resolution was adopted on the basis of a terrorist attack; thus, its drafters adhered to the view that the particular terrorist attack was tantamount to an armed attack, therefore justifying recourse to armed force. Alternatively, one can take a counter-restrictionist stance and consider the Resolution to imply that it is irrelevant whether or not the terrorist act amounted to an armed attack, as pre-Charter law allows the use of retaliatory force under such circumstances. This is highly unlikely, and in any event is a dangerous path to follow.

The Security Council itself has condemned the involvement of States in certain incidents related to terrorism,[127] but even where, as in the Lockerbie incident, it acted under Chapter VII of the 1945 UN Charter, it has never used the term 'State sponsor' of terrorism, preferring instead to demand that culprit States desist from all forms of terrorist action and all assistance to terrorist groups.[128] The inclusion of terrorism within the ambit of Chapter VII necessarily equates some forms of terrorist activity with either a threat to the peace, breach of the peace or an act of aggression, making them theoretically susceptible to collective enforcement action.[129] Some commentators have argued that terrorist action of this kind is tantamount to 'low intensity aggression',[130] but on a level of scale and effect only a sizeable terrorist army that is deployed and equipped through a State is capable of launching an armed attack.

In light of controversies and ambiguities highlighted, it is highly unlikely whether cases involving direct or indirect State support of terrorism can be solved through the mechanisms envisaged in anti-terrorist treaties. In contesting the existence of the dispute in the *Lockerbie* case, the US and UK argued that the element of State-sponsored terrorism in that case placed the situation

126 SD Murphy, 'Contemporary Practice of the US Relating to International Law', 93 *AJIL* (1999), 161.

127 Eg, SC Res 461 (31 Dec 1979); SC Res 731 (21 Jan 1992); SC Res 1044 (31 Jan 1996).

128 SC Res 748 (31 March 1992); SC Res 883 (11 Nov 1993); SC Res 1054 (26 April 1996).

129 1945 UN Charter, Art 39.

130 See SS Evans, 'The Lockerbie Incident Cases: Libyan Sponsored Terrorism, Judicial Review and the Political Question Doctrine', 18 *Maryland JIL & Trade* (1994), 20, p 70.

outside the framework of the 1971 Montreal Convention.[131] Indeed, these conventions were premised on interstate co-operation under the assumption that terrorists acted against the interests of all States. The involvement of States in terrorist attacks on the territory of other States triggers, instead, the application of Art 2(4) of the 1945 UN Charter and international humanitarian law.

In its fight against State-sponsored terrorism, the US Congress amended the 1976 Foreign Sovereign Immunities Act (FSIA) in 1996 through the adoption of the AEDPA, permitting civil suits for compensatory and punitive damages against a foreign State, or its State agency or instrumentality that either committed the terrorist act or provided aid to the culprit group.[132] A terrorist act includes torture, extra-judicial killings, aircraft sabotage and hostage taking, provided that the victim is a US national and the offence occurs outside the US. The terrorism exception to the FSIA 1976 applies only vis-à-vis States that are designated by the State Department as State sponsors of terrorism.[133] Significantly, the AEDPA 1996 permits the claimant to execute a judgment against State-owned property that is used for a commercial activity in the USA, even if the property cannot be connected to the terrorist act.[134] Successful suits were brought under the Act against Cuba,[135] Iran,[136] and Libya.[137] No money was paid in the case of Iran and Cuba because the US government decided it was best to use frozen assets as a leverage when negotiating with these States. With regard to Libya, in reaching agreement to prosecute the two Libyan agents and lift US sanctions, the Libyan government also agreed to pay each victim's family an amount of $10 million. It should be stressed that the State Department has objected to the passing of AEDPA by Congress, believing that the terrorism exception to immunity is incompatible with US treaty obligations and that it will negatively impact on the country's ability to use frozen assets to negotiate with recalcitrant States.[138]

---

131 Op cit, Beveridge, note 46, p 660.
132 AEPDA 1996, 28 USC §§ 1603(b) and 1605(a)(7).
133 The Secretary of State is authorised to determine whether a foreign country has provided repeated support to international terrorism, and if it should therefore be designated as a State sponsor of terrorism. See the 1979 Export Administration Act, 50 USC § 2405(j); 1961 Foreign Assistance Act, 22 USC § 2371.
134 28 USC §§ 1610(a)(7) and (b)(2).
135 *Alejandre v Republic of Cuba,* 996 F Supp 1239 (1997).
136 *Flatow v Islamic Republic of Iran,* 999 F Supp 1 (1998); *Cicippio v Islamic Republic of Iran,* 18 F Supp 2d 62 (1998); see also SD Murphy, 'Contemporary Practice of the US Relating to International Law', 94 *AJIL* (2000), 117.
137 *Rein v Socialist People's Libyan Arab Jamahiriya,* 162 F 3d 748 (1998) *cert denied,* 119 S Ct 2337 (1999).
138 M Vadnais, The Terrorism Exception to the Foreign Sovereign Immunities Act: Forward Leaning Legislation or Just Bad Law?', 5 *UCLA J Int'l L & For* Aff (2000), 199, p 201.

10.5 TERRORISM AND NATIONAL LIBERATION MOVEMENTS

Contemporary terrorism has primarily manifested itself through ideological and revolutionary movements.[139] The earliest revolutionary movements appeared in the 1920s in South America following the establishment of autocratic regimes that were assisted through external intervention. Contemporary movements are less inclined to remove anti-democratic governments as they are to bringing revolutionary terrorism to the masses,[140] which is also the cause for numerous illicit operations such as drug-trafficking. The erosion of the South American revolutionary movements began with the death of Ernesto 'Che' Guevara, which saw terrorist operations conducted for the first time in urban centres and the adoption of Marxist/Leninist teachings advocating that the execution of terrorist acts was within the purpose of uprooting political power.[141] These movements, detached from Che Guevara's idealist socialist society, ultimately failed, while their successors in this region of the world seem to be fighting regular armed conflicts against governmental forces, their operations widely linked to organised criminal activity.

Ideological movements in Europe had until very recently been inspired by Marxist and, to a lesser degree, by fascist theories. Other groups such as Baader Meinhof and the Red Brigades drew their motivation from the theories of anarcho-communism as formulated by Kropotkin and Bakunin, the latter especially advocating the abolition of capitalism and collectivisation of production and consumption.[142] Were ideological and revolutionary movements to disseminate their agenda without the use of violence, the invocation of international human rights law would certainly aid their plight against any oppressive regimes. Nonetheless, the mere fact that violence has been used by a group does not automatically render that group a terrorist organisation. Since the principle of self-determination of peoples is well established in international law,[143] a certain degree of violence must necessarily be legitimised to pursue it when all other peaceful means have failed. Article 1(4) of the 1977 Additional Protocol I to the Geneva Conventions of 1949 and Relating to the Protection of Victims of International Armed Conflicts (Protocol I) equates to international armed conflicts those struggles in which peoples are fighting against colonial domination, alien occupation and racist regimes in

---

139 See generally G Schwarzenberger, 'Terrorists, Hijackers, Guerillas and Mercenaries', 24 CLP (1971), 257.
140 See E Halperin, *Terrorism in Latin America*, 1976, London: Sage.
141 Ibid, Halperin, pp 32–33.
142 Ibid, pp 35–39.
143 1945 UN Charter, Arts 1(2) and 55; 1966 International Covenant on Civil and Political Rights, Art 1, 999 UNTS 171.

the exercise of their right to self-determination.[144] The three conditions contained in Art 1(4) are exhaustive, thus being applicable only to a limited number of groups. Article 1(4) was earlier preceded by the General Assembly Declaration on Principles of International Law Concerning Friendly Relations and Co-operation among States in Accordance with the Charter of the UN, which affirmed not only a duty to refrain from forcible action depriving peoples of their right to self-determination, but made it clear that in their actions against, and resistance to, such forcible action, peoples are entitled to seek and receive support in accordance with the 1945 UN Charter.[145] These legal developments offer the conclusion that organised groups and members thereof enjoy legitimate combatant status under international law as long as their struggle falls within Art 1(4) of the 1977 Protocol I.[146] The level of violence permitted in an ensuing armed conflict with government forces is thereafter regulated by international humanitarian law – and not the various anti-terrorist treaties – and applies equally to both parties. Not only acts of terrorism,[147] but all acts of violence to life or property are prohibited against non-combatants.[148]

With the demise of the major racist, colonial and occupation regimes by the late 1980s the General Assembly's Sixth Committee resolutions on terrorism continued to affirm the legality of all national liberation struggles in their exercise of self-determination,[149] but in practice these rights were not afforded to such movements. In fact, the reasons for dropping draft Art 24 (on terrorism) from the International Law Commission's Code of Offences in 1996 concerned definitional problems and the precise relationship between terrorism and self-determination.[150] Despite some clear-cut acts of terrorism perpetrated by their members, it is obvious that groups such as the IRA, PKK and the PLO fall squarely within the parameters of Art 1(4) of the 1977 Protocol I. However, none of these groups were recognised as having this status, although the PLO was admitted with observer status in international organisations. It should be noted that, on the insistence of Turkey, an Annex

---

144 1125 UNTS 3 (1979).
145 GA Res 2625 (24 Oct 1970); similarly GA Res 3103 (12 Dec 1973), affirmed the legitimate character of self-determination struggles and the fact that ensuing armed conflicts are of an international nature and covered by the 1949 Geneva Conventions.
146 See C Pilloud *et al, Commentary on the Additional Protocols of 8 June 1977 to the Geneva Conventions of 12 August 1949*, 1987, Geneva: Martinus Nijhoff, 41–56.
147 1977 Protocol I, Art 4(d).
148 Ibid, Arts 4, 48.
149 GA Res 36/109 (10 Dec 1981); GA Res 38/130 (19 Dec 1983); GA Res 40/61 (9 Dec 1985); GA Res 42/159 (7 Dec 1987); GA Res 44/29 (4 Dec 1989); GA Res 46/51 (9 Dec 1991); GA Res 49/60 (9 Dec 1994); GA Res 50/53 (11 Dec 1995); GA Res 51/210 (17 Dec 1996); GA Res 52/165 (15 Dec 1997).
150 ILC, *Report on the Work of Its 48th Session*, UN Doc A/51/10, Supp No 10 (6 May–26 June 1996).

was attached to General Assembly Resolution 49/60 (1994) identifying terrorism as a factor endangering friendly relations and territorial integrity. Turkish insistence on the maintenance of 'territorial integrity' relates to its interest in labelling Kurdish rebel fighters as terrorists, refusing to allow them recognition of their legitimate struggle under international law.[151]

A similar troublesome situation has arisen with regard to the treatment by the US military of captured Taliban and Al-Qaeda members. Despite a series of confusing statements in early 2002, the US Government's position differentiated between Taliban and Al-Qaeda members, characterising the latter as unlawful combatants, while recognising that the former belonged to the forces of a State that was a party to the Geneva Conventions.[152] Both the Military Order of 13 November 2001 and the US position in general make it clear that the protection and guarantees afforded under the Geneva Conventions will not apply to Al-Qaeda members. Certainly, the characterisation of Al-Qaeda fighters as unlawful combatants may to a certain degree be justified, and on account of the gravity of the situation and the strength of this organisation particular security measures may have to be employed. However, this does not mean that they are not entitled to fair trial guarantees under the Geneva Conventions and Protocol I of 1977, Art 75 of which obliges parties to grant fundamental guarantees to those combatants that do not benefit from more favourable provisions. Similarly, the use of military commissions against individuals deemed to fall outside the ambit of armed conflict and humanitarian law presents a serious contradiction in criminal procedure terms.[153] That is, if one is classified as falling outside the scope of the laws of war, then the offences accused of having been committed are common criminal offences, even if extremely serious, but which in any event are subject to the jurisdiction of ordinary courts.

The US government attempted to sever the detainees from the reach of the US justice system by detaining them outside US territory and by classifying them as unlawful combatants. In a series of judgments the US Supreme Court held that US courts possess authority to decide the *habeas corpus* claims of unlawful combatants that are US nationals,[154] as well as of non-US

---

151 Even if the PKK is considered to be outside the context of 1977 Protocol I, Art 1(4), the scale of military operations between government and rebel forces is unquestionably within the ambit of the 1949 Geneva Conventions, common Art 3, a provision that is part of customary law.

152 Both are to be tried by military commissions, in accordance with the Military Order of 13 November 2001, Detention, Treatment and Trial of Certain Non-Citizens in the War Against Terrorism, F Reg 57833, vol 66, No 222

153 See generally DA Mundis, 'The Use of Military Commissions to Prosecute Individuals Accused of Terrorist Attacks', 96 *AJIL* (2002), 320; HH Koh, 'The Case Against Military Commissions', 96 *AJIL* (2002), 337.

154 *Hamdi v Rumsfeld*, 542 US 507 (2004).

nationals held in territory under the authority and control of the USA.[155] As a response to the *Hamdi* judgment, the US Department of Defence instituted Combatant Status Review Tribunals (CSRT), which grossly lack the credentials of impartial tribunals mandated by Art 5 of Geneva Convention III (1949) and customary international law relating to due process rights. Indeed, the US Supreme Court in *Hamdan v Rumsfeld* held that military commissions were neither authorised by federal law (including particularly the Uniform Code of Military Justice), nor military necessity, being moreover contrary to the Geneva Conventions.[156] In order for military commissions to conform with the rule of law, the Court continued, they must either operate by the rules of regular courts-martial or the government should ask Congress for specific permission to proceed differently.[157] The Supreme Court held that a military commission can be regularly constituted 'only if some practical need explains deviation from courts-martial practice'.[158]

As a conclusion to this section, the fact that legitimate national liberation movements may conduct some urban operations by violating domestic criminal law or international norms – this is not the case with Al-Qaeda obviously – does not entail the passing of such groups into the sphere of terrorist organisations. Rather, any infractions should be attributed to persons taking a direct or indirect part in these infractions of the law, in the same way that armies are not outlawed in cases where their members violate international humanitarian law.

10.6 ORGANISED CRIME AND ITS RELATION TO TERRORISM

In recent years concerns have been raised regarding possible links between terrorism and organised crime. Narco-terrorism (illicit trafficking in drugs), unlawful arms trade, money laundering and smuggling of nuclear and other lethal material feature prominently among activities linked to terrorism in the

---

155 *Rasul v Bush*, 542 US 466 (2004). In *Gherebi v Rumsfeld*, the US Court of Appeals for the Ninth Circuit, in its judgment of 18 Dec 2003, assessed the Treaty with Cuba over Guantanamo Bay, holding that the US exercised complete jurisdiction and control over Guantanamo for over a century and as a result the US courts have *habeas corpus* jurisdiction and the detainees recourse to legal remedies, pp 8, 17, 23.

156 Judgment of 29 June 2006, 548 US (2006), pp 62–68. Rather confusingly the Court relied on common Art 3 of the Geneva Conventions on the premise that Al-Qaeda was not a party to the Geneva Conventions, ignoring the fact that Afghanistan was.

157 Ibid. As a response to the *Hamdan* judgment, on 29 Sept 2006 Congress adopted the Military Commissions Act, whereby the President may designate certain people as enemy combatants, subjecting them to military commissions.

158 Ibid, *Hamdan* judgment, pp 69–70.

Annex attached to General Assembly Resolution 49/60 (1994).[159] In that year, the World Ministerial Conference on Organised Transnational Crime adopted the Naples Political Declaration and Global Action Plan Against Organised Transnational Crime, which, *inter alia*, recognised the existence of links between transnational organised crime and terrorist acts.[160] A later General Assembly Resolution pointed out that organisations financing terrorists are usually also engaged in unlawful activities, such as the ones described in Resolution 49/60, for the purpose of funding terrorist operations.[161] These observations are not useful for ascertaining legal principles, *per se*, since despite the similarity in organisation and violence between terrorist organisations and organised crime, terrorism involves a political element which is absent from organised crime. Article 2(a) of the CATOC[162] is instructive:

> 'Organised criminal group' shall mean a structured group of three or more persons, existing for a period of time and acting in concert with the aim of committing one or more serious crimes or offences established in accordance with this convention, in order to obtain, directly or indirectly, a financial or other material benefit.

Some delegations participating in the preparatory working groups of the Transnational Organized Crime Convention, including those of Algeria, Egypt and Turkey, were of the view that the scope of the Convention should specifically include crimes committed in order to obtain, directly or indirectly, moral benefit. Other delegations, however, were of the view that this concept was ambiguous. During the Eighth Session the delegation of Algeria proposed the addition of the words 'or any other purpose', which was supported by Egypt, Morocco and Turkey. In the same Eighth Session, the Turkish representative stated that his country could not accept the present formulation of the paragraph, which excluded not only crimes committed for purposes other than financial or material benefit, but also omitted any mention to the links between transnational organised crime and terrorist acts, as established in the 1994 Naples Political Declaration, which Turkey strongly favoured annexing to the Draft Convention.[163] Although this position was supported by some delegations at the Ninth Session of the Ad Hoc Committee, including Algeria, Egypt and Mexico, the eventual definition of organised crime

---

159 Similarly GA Res 50/186 (22 Dec 1995).

160 UN Doc A/49/748 (23 Nov 1994).

161 GA Res 51/210 (17 Dec 1996).

162 UN Doc A/55/383 (2 Nov 2000).

163 Ad Hoc Committee on the Elaboration of a Convention Against Transnational Organised Crime, Revised Draft United Nations Convention Against Transnational Organised Crime, 10th Session (Vienna, 17–28 July 2000), UN Doc A/AC 254/4/Rev 9 (29 June 2000), p 3.

contains neither express nor tacit reference to terrorism.[164] This is not only reasonable; it also prevents unnecessary future confusion, since it is unquestionable that a group which is involved in drug-trafficking, or bribing of foreign officials for financial or related benefit does not constitute a terrorist organisation under any of the anti-terrorist conventions. The Convention does not address the situation of groups engaging in certain offences described therein (especially trafficking in arms and bribery of officials) for financial benefit, which they ultimately intend to allocate for charitable purposes. In such remote cases, one should not dismiss the possibility of an organisation with political or ideological motives.

Our previous analysis of national liberation movements helps us better comprehend the political benefits associated with the insistence of countries such as Turkey, Algeria and Egypt regarding possible connections between terrorism and organised crime. Indeed, the branding of a national liberation movement either as a terrorist group, or as a collectivity involved in organised crime, on the basis of its participation in offences aimed at financing its otherwise legitimate struggle, justifies political manoeuvres targeted at removing all legitimacy from that movement before international fora. On the one hand, it is unarguable that terrorist groups engaged in prohibited acts for financial benefit do enter the sphere of organised crime. On the other hand, prohibited acts committed by national liberation movements, where the financial benefit is intended only to finance a movement's struggle, do not necessarily render that group illegal, as long as the prohibited acts in question do not violate *jus cogens* norms and depending on the extent of politicisation (that is, to what degree they are viewed as political offences) afforded to such offences.

10.7 TERRORIST ACTS AS POLITICAL OFFENCES

As previously stated, terrorism involves an ideological or political element. For the purposes mainly of extradition, but also immigration, many countries regard political offences as non-extraditable, while the international impetus is to depoliticise most acts and, thus, render them extraditable. The relevant jurisprudence shows that a political offence must primarily satisfy the so-called 'incidence test', as formulated in *Re Castioni*.[165] Stephen J noted, in that case, that offenders are not to be extradited if the crimes concerned

---

164 The Ad Hoc Committee's interpretative notes on Art 3 (scope of application) emphasised 'with deep concern the growing links between transnational organised crime and terrorist crimes', taking into account the 1945 UN Charter and relevant General Assembly resolutions; UN Doc A/55/383/ Add 1 (3 Nov 2000), p 2.
165 [1891] 1 QB 149.

were 'incidental to and formed a part of political disturbances'.[166] In fact, there must exist a close nexus between the violence and the political objective of forcing a regime to resign or change its policies, taking place in the course of a violent disturbance.[167] In determining whether the political aspect of the offence is of a predominant character, domestic courts have enquired whether the offender could reasonably expect that the offence would yield a result directly related to the political goal.[168] This query has since become more explicit by making it clear that the political motive of an offence is irrelevant where it is likely to involve killing or injuring members of the public.[169] It is evident, however, from the Good Friday Agreement, reached between the political branch of the IRA and the UK Government, that, although indiscriminate violent attacks may constitute criminal offences, a subsequent amnesty agreement may lift criminal liability where a political element was involved.[170]

This jurisprudence is in conformity with the various anti-terrorist conventions, despite its outward liberal appearance. These conventions demand that Member States criminalise the relevant acts and further render them extraditable.[171] However, all the offences described in anti-terrorist conventions refer to acts which either directly or indirectly are intended to cause or likely to inflict indiscriminate death or injury to members of the public, and which are not committed in the context of violent disturbances. Despite broad ratification of anti-terrorist treaties since 1963, covering a wide spectrum of areas, national judges still enjoy some discretion in deciding on a case-by-case basis the political character of an offence in relation to the motive involved and the means pursued to achieve it. Such judicial determination may well depend on certain occasions on a common sense of justice prevalent at any given time in a particular community, due to its affiliation and sympathy to the offenders

---

166 [1891] 1 QB 166.
167 *R v Governor of Brixton Prison ex p Schtraks* [1964] AC 556, pp 583–84, *per* Lord Reid; *Gil v Canada* (1994) 107 ILR 168, Canadian Federal Court of Appeal, p 170; *In the Matter of Extradition of Atta,* 104 ILR 52, p 87; *McMullen v INS* 788 F 2d 591 (1986), 9th Cir, a refugee determination case.
168 *Folkerts v Prosecutor* (1978) 74 ILR 498, Dutch Supreme Court.
169 *T v Secretary of State*, 107 ILR 552, a refugee determination case; *Re Croissant* (1978) 74 ILR 505, Conseil d'Etat; *Yugoslav Terrorism* case (1978) 74 ILR 509, FRG Federal Supreme Court; *Galdeano* case (1984) 111 ILR 505, Conseil d'Etat; *In the Matter of Extradition of Atta*, 104 ILR 52; *Gil v Canada* (1994) 107 ILR 168, Canadian Federal Court of Appeal; in the *Baader-Meinhof Group Terrorist* case (1977) 74 ILR 493, FRG Constitutional Court, p 498, the court stated that membership of a politically motivated organisation constituted an offence where it executed its objective through the perpetration of serious offences.
170 Good Friday Agreement (10 April 1998), reprinted in 37 ILM (1998), 751, Strand 10(1), provides for the release of prisoners convicted of scheduled offences in Northern Ireland, or in the case of those sentenced outside Northern Ireland, similar offences.
171 Eg, 1998 Terrorist Bombings Convention, Arts 5, 9 and 11, and 2000 Terrorist Financing Convention, Arts 6, 7, 11, 13–14.

and their aims. Some States, however, have limited this judicial discretion through amendment to their extradition treaties. The US–UK Extradition Treaty of 1977[172] provided in Art 5 a political offence exception to extradition. This served as the basis by US courts to deny the extradition of members of the IRA. These decisions were criticised by both the US and the UK, the former fearing adverse effect on law enforcement and foreign relations, the latter as condoning terrorism. Subsequently, a Supplementary Treaty was agreed in 1985 as a means of limiting the political offence exception by making reference to a list of offences that no longer may be regarded as political.[173] The 1985 Supplementary Treaty endows, under Art 3(a), US judges with a limited judicial inquiry into the fairness and guarantees of trial in the UK.[174] Despite the signing of such agreements and the promulgation of laws limiting judicial discretion, the majority of constitutions contain a clause obliging their independent judiciary not to apply laws that are in conflict with the constitution.[175] Thus, since the concepts of fairness, justice and civil rights form an integral part of every constitutional tradition and, as we have seen, some countries wilfully manipulate the issue of terrorism for 'social control' purposes,[176] national judges are under an obligation to disregard laws that violate these principles.

10.8 TERRORISM AND HUMAN RIGHTS

We have already examined a number of human rights issues related to terrorism; now we shall briefly look at the problem of human rights and the role of non-State actors (reference to which has already been made), as well as procedural guarantees prescribed for those persons accused of terrorist offences. Article 14 of the 1966 International Covenant on Civil and Political Rights (ICCPR) guarantees the right to a fair trial as well as other pre-trial protections to those accused or arrested in relation to criminal offences.[177] Many countries suffering from sustained terrorist attacks promulgate legislation that falls below the standard set by the ICCPR. Beginning in 1973, the UK enacted sweeping emergency legislation in its effort to counter violence arising from the Northern Ireland conflict.[178] This legislation eliminated a

172 28 UST 227.
173 Art 1, reprinted in TIAS 12050.
174 See *USA v Artt* 38 ILM (1999), 100.
175 1975/86 Hellenic Constitution, Art 93(4).
176 N Chomsky, 'Human Rights Priorities and Responsibilities for Citizens', in D Barnheizer (ed), *Effective Strategies for Protecting Human Rights*, 2002, Aldershot: Ashgate.
177 See also 1950 European Convention for the Protection of Human Rights and Fundamental Freedoms, Art 6, 213 UNTS 221.
178 See Northern Ireland (Emergency Provisions) Act 1978, Chapter 5.

number of pre-trial procedural safeguards typically available to criminal defendants in the UK. It also established an alternative system of tribunals to try those accused of 'scheduled offences', that is, certain politically motivated criminal offences. These 'Diplock courts' employed abbreviated trial procedures, eliminating trial by jury and significantly relaxing evidentiary standards. Such practice, irrespective of the gravity of the alleged offence, violates fundamental pre-trial procedural safeguards as these are formulated in international instruments. Likewise, on the basis of derogation provisions contained in human rights treaties, States are afforded a certain degree of discretion as to the suspension of certain rights in times of public emergency.[179] The European Court of Human Rights' jurisprudence evinces the enjoyment of a margin of discretion which Member States may utilise in order to determine a state of emergency. Such discretion is not unlimited but subject to control by the Court.[180] A new trend is now emerging in the form of so-called 'control orders'. These are provided for in domestic legislation, such as the 2005 UK Prevention of Terrorism Act, which allows for control orders against suspected terrorists whether acting in the UK or abroad, with the aim of restricting use of particular objects (eg, internet or telephone communications) or of movement.[181]

Anti-terrorist conventions contain minimum procedural safeguards entitling the accused to fair treatment and ensuring communication with an appropriate person, either a representative of his State or another.[182] The 1976 European Convention on the Suppression of Terrorism included a provision whereby a requested State is not bound to extradite if it has substantial grounds for believing that the request is a guise for prosecution or punishment on account of a person's race, religion, nationality, ethnic origin or political opinion.[183] This is known as '*clause française*', and one of its purposes is to protect the concept of asylum. This clause has been inserted

179 1950 European Convention for the Protection of Human Rights, Art 15, and ICCPR, Art 4.
180 In *Ireland v UK* (1978) 2 EHRR 25, although UK interrogation techniques violated the European Convention for the Protection of Human Rights, Art 3, the court ruled that, due to the wave of terrorist attacks prevalent in 1972, the UK could validly decide that its legislation was insufficient under the European Convention for the Protection of Human Rights, Art 15.
181 *SSHD v AF* [2007] EWHC 651 and *SSHD v E* [2007] EWHC 233; see S Nash and A Boon 'Special Advocacy: Political Expediency and Legal Roles in Modern Judicial Systems' (2006) *Legal Ethics* 101–124.
182 1970 Hague Convention, Art 6(3);1971 Montreal Convention, Art 6(3);1973 Internationally Protected Persons Convention (the latter guaranteeing fair treatment), Arts 6(2) and 9; 1979 Hostages Convention, Art 6(3), (4); 1998 Terrorist Bombings Convention (the latter guaranteeing fair treatment), Arts 7(3) and 14; 2000 Terrorist Financing Convention, Art 9(3).
183 1976 European Convention on the Suppression of Terrorism, Art 5.

in all subsequent international anti-terrorist treaties.[184] In general, there is unanimous agreement from international bodies that procedural guarantees should not be set aside when investigating terrorist-related offences.[185]

States with particular terrorist problems, such as Turkey, Algeria and Russia, have consistently argued that terrorism violates human rights. This, itself, is a contradictory statement since the whole rationale of human rights is based on the State being the transgressor and not private entities. To address these concerns, the Vienna Declaration and Programme of Action adopted by the World Conference on Human Rights in 1993 condemned terrorism as an act aiming at the 'destruction' of human rights, democracy and territorial integrity.[186] This new terminology is hardly reconcilable with human rights philosophy, and was sadly included on the insistence of States with poor human rights records. The 1993 Vienna Declaration was followed up by annual decisions of the Third Committee of the General Assembly, which were subsequently endorsed by the Assembly under the title 'Human Rights and Terrorism'. These resolutions recognise the 'destruction' of human rights through terrorist acts, ascertain its connection to organised crime and further demand for measures consonant with 'international human rights standards'.[187] The term 'standards' was preferred because most developing countries are not parties to the major international human rights instruments. Sadly, States non-parties to customary human rights treaties are allowed to regress back to an unacceptable state of affairs where they not only defy international institutions accusing them of gross rights violations; they also establish new 'human rights' regimes which entitle them to abuse those whom they are under a customary obligation to protect.[188] The Third Committee's initiative to engage in an examination of terrorism has unofficially been contested vehemently by the Sixth Committee, which has demanded without success an end to the Third Committee's involvement in the issue. Finally, the role of non-State actors has been addressed by the special rapporteur on human rights and terrorism, Kalliopi Koufa. In her 1999 report she noted that terrorism puts under threat those social and political values that relate, either directly or indirectly, to the full enjoyment of human rights and fundamental freedoms, namely the areas of: (a) life, liberty

---

184 1979 Hostages Convention, Art 9(1); 1998 Terrorist Bombings Convention, Art 12; 2000 Terrorist Financing Convention, Art 15.
185 *Report of the Inter-American Commission on Human Rights on Terrorism and Human Rights*, OAS Doc OEA/Ser L/V/II 116, Doc 5/Rev 1/Corr (22 Oct 2002).
186 UN Doc A/CONF 157/23 (12 July 1993), para 17.
187 GA Res 48/122 (20 Dec 1993); GA Res 49/185 (23 Dec 1994); GA Res 50/186 (22 Dec 1995); GA Res 51/210 (17 Dec 1996); GA Res 52/133 (27 Feb 1997); some CSCE/OSCE Concluding Documents make a connection between terrorism and human rights, however, on the basis of State-sponsored terrorism. The latest 1999 Istanbul Summit, Chapter I(4), made reference only to a 'challenge to security' emanating from terrorism.
188 This new terminology is also contained in GA Res 49/60 (9 Dec 1994).

and dignity of the individual; (b) democratic society; and (c) social peace and public order. While emphasising that terrorism prevents individuals from fully enjoying human rights, and whereas recent developments in international law render individual perpetrators liable under international law, the special rapporteur pointed out that the 'relevance and adequacy of international and human rights law with regard to terrorist activities of non-State actors is questionable. For non-State actors are not, strictly speaking, legally bound by the supervisory mechanisms of international and human rights law'.

Chapter 11

Transnational offences

11.1 TRANSNATIONAL ORGANISED CRIME

Until the collapse of the USSR, and the subsequent cataclysmic effects, organised crime was essentially a domestic affair, even though transnational patterns were evident. Some States chose to see the phenomenon holistically,[1] while others preferred to view each underlying offence in isolation from the organised nature of the group. Similarly, requests for international co-operation such as extradition and mutual legal assistance were made on the basis of the underlying offence. The post–1990 era, with the advent of globalised trade and physical movement of persons, witnessed an increase in organised crime, originating especially from the former Eastern bloc, necessitating a different approach to the problem.[2] Two factors have generally contributed to the eruption of organised crime at the dawn of the 21st century: the emergence of 'weak' States and corruption.[3] The former refers to the institutional capacity of States to govern legitimately, effectively administer justice and demand obeisance from the entire population. To the effect that the vast majority of South American States and Russia have been unsuccessful in achieving these ends, they are seen as 'weak'. Moreover, in this environment of a weak State, a thriving poor population provides the cauldron in which criminality multiplies. Corruption further exacerbates the situation,[4] as does the ability of such groups to launder their criminal proceeds in tax havens where banking regulations are relaxed.[5]

---

1 Eg, the 1951 US Racketeering Act, 18 USC § 1951 *et seq.*

2 N Passas, 'Globalisation and Transnational Crime: Effects of Criminogenic Asymmetries', 4 *Transnational Organized Crime* (1998), 2.

3 W Rensselaer and I Lee, 'Transnational Organised Crime: An Overview', in T Farer (ed), *Transnational Crime in the Americas*, 1999, New York: Routledge, 4.

4 JM Waller and VJ Yasmann, 'Russia's Great Criminal Revolution: The Role of the Security Services', 11 *Journal of Contemporary Criminal Justice* (1995), 282.

5 RE Grosse, *Drugs and Money: Laundering Latin America's Cocaine Dollars*, 2001, Westport: Praeger; J Blum, 'Offshore Money', in op cit, Farer, note 3, p 57.

Since the early 1990s the United Nations (UN) General Assembly had detected the increase and expansion of organised criminal activity worldwide, and made reference to the emergent links between organised crime and terrorism.[6] In 1994, the World Ministerial Conference on Organised Transnational Crime adopted the Naples Political Declaration and Global Action Plan Against Organised Transnational Crime,[7] which, *inter alia*, addressed the issue of convening a conference for the negotiation of a convention on the matter. By Resolution 53/111 the General Assembly established an Ad Hoc Committee for the purpose of elaborating a convention and three additional protocols.[8] After a series of 11 sessions between 1999 and 2000, the UN Convention Against Transnational Organized Crime (CATOC)[9] and two Additional Protocols were adopted in late 2000, while another one on firearms was adopted on 31 May 2001.[10] CATOC establishes four distinct offences: (a) participation in organised criminal groups;[11] (b) money laundering;[12] (c) corruption;[13] and (d) obstruction of justice.[14] Under Art 3, the Convention applies to the four aforementioned offences, as well as to any 'serious crime', as defined by Art 2(b),[15] if cumulatively the offence is 'transnational in nature' and 'involves an organised criminal group'. In accordance with Art 3(2), offences are transnational in nature if they are: committed in more than one State; committed in only one State, but are prepared, planned, directed, controlled or have substantial effects in other States; and committed in one State by an organised criminal group that engages in criminal activities

---

6 GA Res 49/60 (9 Dec 1994), and 50/186 (20 Dec 1995). See E Mylonaki, 'The Manipulation of Organised Crime by Terrorists: Legal and Factual Perspectives', 2 *ICLR* (2002), 213.

7 UN Doc A/49/748 (1994), approved by GA Res 49/159 (23 Dec 1994). This was followed by the 1995 Buenos Aires Declaration on Prevention and Control of Organised Transnational Crime, UN Doc E/CN 15/1996/2/Add 1 (1996) and the 1997 Dakar Declaration on the Prevention and Control of Organised Transnational Crime and Corruption, UN Doc E/CN 15/1998/6/Add 1 (1998), and the 1998 Manila Declaration, UN Doc E/CN 15/1998/6/Add 2 (1998).

8 GA Res 53/111 (9 Dec 1998).

9 40 ILM (2001), 335.

10 Protocol to Prevent, Suppress and Punish Trafficking in Persons, especially Women and Children, 40 ILM (2001), 377; Protocol Against the Smuggling of Migrants by Land, Sea and Air, 40 ILM (2001), 384; Protocol Against the Illicit Manufacturing of and Trafficking in Firearms, their Parts and Components, and Ammunition.

11 CATOC, Art 5.

12 Ibid, Art 6.

13 Ibid, Art 8.

14 Ibid, Art 23.

15 This means any conduct constituting an offence punishable by at least a four-year incarceration or a more serious penalty. The main criminal activities of criminal organisations are: racketeering, fraud, robberies, car theft, armed assault, drug trafficking, trafficking in arms and radioactive materials, trafficking in human beings, alien smuggling, smuggling of goods, extortion for protection money, gambling, embezzling from industries and control of black markets.

in more than one State.[16] It is evident that the relationship between the 2000 Convention and other sectoral agreements, especially those relating to narcotics and corruption,[17] is complementary but at the same time the convention is independent of those agreements. Because of its unique scope it finds application only where the underlying offence possesses a transnational element and involves an organised criminal group. The only other reference to organised crime in previous sectoral treaties is found in the 1988 UN Convention Against Illicit Traffic in Narcotic Drugs and Psychotropic Substances (Narcotics Convention). Article 3(1)(a)(v) of the latter instrument obliges States to 'criminalise the organisation, management or financing of the offences listed' therein, and relating to the various processes, from cultivation to final distribution. Moreover, sub-s (c)(iv) criminalises 'participation in, association or conspiracy to commit' any of the listed offences, while sub-s (5) of Art 3 requires that Member States adopt legislation requiring courts to take into account the involvement of organised criminal groups and individual membership therein as rendering the offence 'serious' in nature. Not all of the offences established under CATOC, however, have in the past been subject to universal regulation, particularly, money laundering,[18] participation in organised criminal groups and obstruction of justice, and States parties are under an obligation to criminalise these activities. For the purposes of CATOC, an 'organised criminal group' is defined as:

A structured group of three or more persons, existing for a period of time and acting in concert with the aim of committing one or more serious crimes or offences established in accordance with this Convention, in order to obtain, directly or indirectly, a financial or other material benefit.[19]

The *travaux preparatoires* construe the term 'direct or indirect benefit' to be a broad one, encompassing, for example, crimes in which the predominant motivation may be sexual gratification, such as the receipt or trade of materials by members of child pornography rings, the trading of children by members of paedophile rings or cost sharing among ring members.[20]

16 See GOW Mueller, 'Transnational Crime: Definitions and Concepts', 4 *Transnational Organised Crime* (1998), 14.
17 1988 UN Convention Against Illicit Traffic in Narcotic Drugs and Narcotic Substances 28 ILM (1989), 497; 1997 OECD Convention on Combating Bribery of Foreign Officials in International Business Transactions, 37 ILM (1998), 1.
18 See 1990 Council of Europe Convention on Laundering, Search, Seizure and Confiscation of the Proceeds from Crime, ETS 141; 1991 EC Council Directive on Prevention of Use of the Financial System for the Purpose of Money Laundering, 91/308/EEC, OJ L166/77, as amended by the new EC Directive 2001/97/EC.
19 CATOC, Art 2(a).
20 Interpretative Notes, UN Doc A/55/383/Add 1 (2000), p 2.

Although a group falls within the scope of CATOC if it is 'structured', this would exclude randomly formed groups, but would include groups with a hierarchical or other structure, as well as non-hierarchical groups, where the roles of the members of the group need not be formally defined.[21]

The offence of participating in an organised criminal group under Art 5 of CATOC is constituted by taking part in the activities of such a group, either with the knowledge of the group's aims, or in the knowledge that one's activities will somehow contribute to the achievement of those aims. Moreover, a person is also culpable by organising, directing, aiding, abetting, facilitating or counselling the commission of serious crime involving an organised criminal group. Under Art 23 of CATOC, parties are obliged to criminalise any form of obstruction of justice, including the use of corrupt or coercive methods in order to influence testimony, other evidence or the actions of any law enforcement or other justice official at both pre-trial and trial stage. This would not, however, cover those countries whose legislation grants natural persons the privilege not to give evidence.[22]

The main purpose behind CATOC was the enhancement of co-operation between States, and calls for assistance and co-operation were echoed by most developing countries, since organised crime was seen by many as a serious destabilising threat.[23] Co-operation has a twofold dimension in the Convention. First, law enforcement agencies are required to assist one another in general and specific terms, while the usual forms of co-operation are also provided, such as extradition and mutual legal assistance,[24] as well as more specialised measures, such as collection and exchange of information.[25] Secondly, since States are required to maintain adequate expertise in dealing with transnational organised crime, it is only developed countries that can afford to efficiently comply. For that purpose, both CATOC and the Protocols envisage the creation of technical assistance projects, whereby developed nations would provide material and financial assistance to developing nations, while calling also for the establishment of a fund to which regular and voluntary contributions would be paid.[26] Moreover, States parties are obliged to adopt domestic laws and practices that would prevent

---

21 See also P Williams, 'Organising Transnational Crime: Networks, Markets and Hierarchies', 4 *Transnational Organised Crime* (1998), 57.

22 Op cit, Interpretative Notes, note 20, p 9.

23 *Report of the Ad Hoc Committee on the Work of its First to Eleventh Sessions*, UN Doc A/55/ 383 (2000), p 18.

24 CATOC, Arts 16 and 18; police co-operation in the context of the 1990 Schengen Agreement on the Gradual Abolition of Checks at Common Borders, 30 ILM (1991), 68; Member States have agreed to allow pursuit over national frontiers for, *inter alia*, breach of laws relating to explosives and arms, illicit traffic in narcotic drugs, traffic in human beings, etc, in accordance with Arts 40 and 41.

25 Ibid, Arts 27 and 28.

26 Ibid, Art 30(2)(b) and (c).

organised crime-related activities. Some of these are already contained in other international instruments and deal mainly with money laundering,[27] such as maintaining accurate bank records, lifting of bank secrecy with regard to organised crime investigations,[28] while under the 2001 Protocol Against the Smuggling of Migrants by Land, Sea and Air (Smuggling Protocol), minimum standards for the issuance and verification of passports and other travel documents are required.[29]

11.1.1 The additional CATOC Protocols

The three additional Protocols are supplementary and subordinate to CATOC. Under Art 37(2) of CATOC, before a State can become a party to any of the Protocols it must first ratify CATOC. It is obvious and explicit that the offences stipulated in the Protocols are both transnational in nature and must be committed in the context of an organised criminal group or operation. The structure of CATOC is such that its provisions relating to co-operation and technical assistance are applicable to the Protocols; however, each Protocol establishes in addition specific provisions supplementing and adapting the general rules found in CATOC. Reference to the Trafficking Protocol is made elsewhere in this book.[30] The Smuggling Protocol obliges States to criminalise the smuggling of migrants, which includes the procurement of either illegal entry or illegal residence with the aim of financial benefit, as well as the procurement, provision, possession or production of a fraudulent travel document, where this was done for the purpose of smuggling migrants.[31] In addition to the co-operation procedures established under the Smuggling and Trafficking Protocols, both instruments require parties to take measures to protect trafficked and smuggled persons, whether by giving them access to medical, welfare, social and other facilities and programmes, or by entitling them to confidentiality and protection against offenders where they provide evidence to prosecutorial authorities.[32] Of particular importance is Pt II of the Smuggling Protocol which refers to the taking of measures against vessels at sea. This was drafted in conformity with the 1982 UN

---

27 FATF 40 Recommendations; SC Res 1373 (29 Sept 2001); 1999 International Convention for the Suppression of the Financing of Terrorism, Art 18, 39 ILM (2000), 270.

28 CATOC, Arts 7 and 12(6).

29 2001 Smuggling Protocol, Arts 12 and 13.

30 See Chapter 5, section 5.2.1.

31 2001 Smuggling Protocol, Art 2. The IMO Maritime Safety Committee's 2002 *Report on Unsafe Practices Associated with the Trafficking or Transport of Migrants by Sea*, IMO Doc MSC 3/Circ 3 (30 April 2002), noted that by that date 276 incidents had been reported to the Organisation, involving 12,426 migrants.

32 Trafficking Protocol, Arts 4–6; 2001 Smuggling Protocol, Arts 16 and 18. Art 5 of the Smuggling Convention further provides that migrants will not become subject to criminal prosecution.

Convention on the Law of the Sea (UNCLOS) and the 1988 Narcotics Convention. The general rule is that no action can be taken in the territorial sea of a State without the coastal State's consent. Similarly, no action can be taken against a vessel at sea without the approval of the Flag State. However, the Protocol requires parties to 'co-operate to the fullest extent possible'. In cases where a State has credible evidence that a vessel registered in another State is involved in the smuggling of migrants, it must acquire the permission of that Flag State in order to board, search and, if evidence of smuggling is found, to take other action with the consent always of the Flag State.[33] The Flag State must respond to such requests expeditiously and may impose conditions upon the requesting State. Although the conditions set by the Flag State must be respected, the requesting State may take other remedial action only where this is necessary in order to relieve imminent danger to the lives of persons, or in the existence of a bilateral or multilateral agreement that rules otherwise.[34] It would not be inconsistent with the Protocol and UNCLOS to assimilate a smuggling vessel to a slave vessel, thereby granting the right to any other ship to liberate the migrants, even without the consent of the Flag State.[35]

In May 2001 the Protocol Against the Illicit Manufacturing of a Trafficking in Firearms, their Parts and Components, and Ammunition (Firearms Protocol) was adopted. The origins of this instrument can be traced back to the 1997 Organisation of American States (OAS) Convention Against the Illicit Manufacturing of and Trafficking in Firearms, Ammunition, Explosives and Other Related Materials. Article 5 of the Protocol criminalises illicit manufacturing and trafficking of firearms, components and ammunition, as well as falsification or illicit obliteration, removal or alteration of the marking on firearms. The Protocol sets out comprehensive procedures for the import, export and transit of firearms, their components and ammunition. It is a reciprocal agreement requiring States to provide authorisation to each other before permitting shipments of firearms to leave, arrive or transit across their territory and enables law enforcement authorities to track the movement of shipments through record-keeping and unique marking in order to prevent theft and diversion.[36] The Protocol does not apply to interstate transactions relating to the transfer of arms, nor does it prejudice or have any impact upon national security.[37]

33 Smuggling Protocol, Art 8(2).
34 Ibid, Art 8(5).
35 UNCLOS, Art 99. However, only the Flag State may seize the slave vessel and arrest those engaged in slave trade.
36 2001 Firearms Protocol, Arts 7–12.
37 Ibid, Art 2.

11.2 DRUG TRAFFICKING

Drug trafficking generates large financial profits for criminal organisations. The creation of wealth has provided an opportunity for these organisations to infiltrate legitimate commercial businesses, undermine weakened economies and corrupt the structures of government. The recognition that drug trafficking is linked to other serious criminal activity, including terrorism, has raised concern in the international community that trafficking has the potential to destabilise society. Thus problems related to drug taking and drug trafficking have become a major preoccupation for governments and law enforcement agencies. The social problems caused by the use of illicit drugs are difficult to quantify, but include health problems and the loss of people participation in ordinary society. Individuals who are heavy users or addicts of drugs may resort to crime to fund their drug use, thus burglary, prostitution and shop theft are all common problems associated with drug use. Trafficking drugs is an illegal activity and, therefore, not subject to the normal regulation of commercial and contract law that legitimate business abides by. Violence and intimidation are the tactics of 'enforcement' in the drug-trafficking industry. Trafficking of illicit drugs is a lucrative market and large scale operations are the business of organised crime groups. It has also been the case that States themselves have been implicated in illicit drug trafficking in various ways. History shows that Britain encouraged the opium trade in Asia for national profit and that the US and French Governments aided and abetted drug trafficking in Laos for political reasons during the course of the Vietnam War. Furthermore, there is evidence to show that the governments in some South American States, such as Bolivia and Colombia, have been influenced or even run by drug-trafficking cartels and that the US was involved with cocaine traffickers in order to provide covert assistance to insurgent activities in Nicaragua. The US has also apprehended the Head of State of Panama, General Noriega, who was subsequently convicted of drug-trafficking offences.[38]

Other significant problems associated with drug trafficking are the bribery and corruption of public officials so as to ease trafficking or avoid the scrutiny of police and customs. Furthermore, the object of illicit drug trafficking is to make profit. The proceeds of drug trafficking cannot be accounted for in an ordinary legitimate way and, therefore, need to be disguised so that they can be used. This chapter will also consider the problem of money laundering. Debate is ongoing and discussion exists over the decriminalisation or legalisation of some of the drugs currently outlawed. Commentators argue that by allowing the sale and consumption of some drugs currently considered

---

38 L Sunga, *The Emerging System of International Criminal Law*, 1997, Dordrecht: Kluwer, 206–12.

illegal, thereby removing their illicit nature, State authorities would be able to regulate those drugs to a more effective degree and consequently mitigate the network of crime that is currently associated with drug trafficking. International legal efforts to counter drug trafficking should be viewed in concert with other aspects of international legal co-operation including police co-operation during investigations and extradition and mutual legal assistance in preparing prosecutions.

11.2.1 Development of international measures to control drug trafficking

International efforts to control drug trafficking were ongoing throughout the 20th century. In 1909, the US president Theodore Roosevelt called together 13 countries to establish the International Opium Commission, which subsequently produced a range of resolutions which recommended the gradual suppression of opium smoking 'with due regard to the circumstances of each country concerned'. Formal treaty measures followed a few years later.[39] Subsequent multilateral conventions were developed to regulate the production of narcotic drugs for medical and scientific purposes under the League of Nations.[40]

Following the Second World War and the creation of a new international order under the auspices of the UN, it was apparent that the framework of international instruments relating to drug trafficking was insufficient to meet the modern scale and nature of the problem. Furthermore, international diplomatic relations had changed greatly after the war and much of the work of the League of Nations had little remaining practical legal value. The control of illicit drugs was an issue of concern to the UN from the outset following the Second World War. In 1946, the UN Economic and Social Council, at its First Session, established the Commission on Narcotic Drugs to work towards effective implementation of measures controlling illicit drugs.[41] The UN continued to develop legal mechanisms for the control of illicit drugs.[42]

---

39 Convention Relating to the Suppression of the Abuse of Opium and Other Drugs, 23 January 1912, 38 Stat 1912; 8 LNTS 187.
40 See, eg, Convention for Limiting the Manufacture and Regulating the Distribution of Narcotic Drugs, Geneva, 13 July 1931.
41 Resolution of the First Session of the Economic and Social Council, Official Records, ECOSOC, First Session, 1946, Vol I, p 168.
42 See, eg, Protocol Bringing Under International Control Drugs Outside the Scope of the Convention of 13 July 1931 for Limiting the Manufacture and Regulating the Distribution of Narcotic Drugs, as amended by the Protocol signed at Lake Success, New York on 11 December 1946, signed at Paris, 19 November 1948, 44 UNTS 277; The Protocol for Limiting and Regulating the Cultivation of the Poppy Plant, the Production of, International and Wholesale Trade in, and Use of Opium, signed at New York, 23 June 1953, 456 UNTS 56.

The UN has subsequently created a new framework of provisions relating to illegal drug trafficking.[43] Controls were extended to drugs used for illicit purposes by the 1961 Single Convention on Narcotic Drugs (1961 Convention). Aspects of the 1961 Convention were developed by a protocol in 1972.[44] During the 1960s, stimulants such as amphetamines, hallucinogens such as LSD and depressant drugs such as barbiturates and tranquillisers became more widely available. These drugs, known as psychotropic drugs, were not controlled by the 1961 Convention and, in 1971, the UN concluded a Convention on Psychotropic Substances (1971 Convention).[45] These initiatives were strengthened by the 1988 UN Convention Against Illicit Traffic in Narcotic Drugs and Psychotropic Substances.[46] It was anticipated that by confiscating the proceeds of crime the incentive for drug trafficking would be eliminated. Contracting parties are required to criminalise not only the organisation, management and financing of drug trafficking but also the conversion, transfer and concealment of the proceeds of drug trafficking.

In addition to drafting international treaties for the control of illegal drug trafficking, the UN has also created a number of agencies with specific responsibilities in relation to the control of illicit drugs. The Commission on Narcotic Drugs was established in 1946 as an organ of the Economic and Social Council (ECOSOC). Its task is to consider and report on all aspects of international drug control and it can initiate work and make recommendations to ECOSOC and to national governments. A particular role of the Commission is to achieve effective implementation of the provisions set out under the 1961 Convention and 1972 Protocol. The International Narcotics Control Board was established by the 1961 Convention and is comprised of members elected by the ECOSOC on the basis of their impartiality. The Board is in charge of controlling the international trade in narcotic drugs and for taking measures to ensure the execution of the provisions of the 1961 Convention. The Board manages the estimates and statistics systems set up under the 1961 and 1971 Conventions. The UN Fund for Drug Abuse Control was established in 1971 and is funded by State contributions. Its primary function is to provide professional and technical assistance to governments on law enforcement and social measures for drug control.[47]

43 See generally C Bassiouni, 'The International Narcotic Control Scheme', in C Bassiouni (ed), *International Criminal Law: Crimes*, 1986, New York: Transnational, 507–24.
44 Protocol Amending the Single Convention on Narcotic Drugs, 25 March 1972, TIAS No 8118, 976 UNTS 3.
45 Convention on Psychotropic Substances, 10 ILM (1971), 261.
46 Reprinted at 28 ILM (1989), 497.
47 See generally M Lopez-Ray, *A Guide to United Nations Criminal Policy*, 1985, Aldershot: Gower.

11.2.1.1 1961 Single Convention on Narcotic Drugs

The overall effect of the 1961 Convention was to codify and amalgamate previous multilateral drugs conventions.[48] International measures were extended over the cultivation of plants grown as raw materials for the production of natural narcotic drugs, and existing restrictions on the production of opium and its derivatives were continued. The 1961 Convention includes the requirement that State parties should control and license individuals and commercial entities involved in the trade or distribution of licit drugs. Parties are obliged to 'prevent the accumulation in the possession of traders, distributors, State enterprises or duly authorised persons . . . of quantities of drugs and poppy straw in excess of those required for the normal conduct of business, having regard to the prevailing market conditions'.[49] There are provisions in the Convention ensuring that licit drugs are issued under prescription, are properly labelled, and that trade in drugs is regulated and conforms with the estimates system, as well as encouraging full legal and administrative co-operation between countries.

11.2.1.2 1972 Protocol Amending the 1961 Single Convention on Narcotic Drugs

Further development of the initiatives set out in the 1961 Convention were brought about through the measures of the 1972 Protocol. The International Narcotics Control Board will seek to limit the cultivation, production, manufacture and use of drugs to amounts necessary for medical and scientific purposes.[50] Article 12 of the Protocol strengthens measures concerning the illicit cultivation of opium and cannabis under the 1961 Convention, in that parties are not only obliged to take measures prohibiting illicit cultivation, but also to seize and destroy plants used for illicit production. Article 18 of the Protocol widens the duties of the parties to inform and provide information relating to domestic enforcement to the Secretary General of the UN. Article 14 of the Protocol complements Art 36 of the Single Convention in that it provides that parties should, as an alternative, or as an addition to punishment of narcotic drug offences, provide measures of treatment, education, aftercare, rehabilitation and social reintegration. Finally, the Protocol also provides that the offences set out in the 1961 Convention shall be extraditable offences and that the 1972 Protocol may act as a basis for extradition where no other provision exists.

48 Op cit, Lopez-Ray, p 52.
49 1961 Convention, Art 30(2)(a).
50 1972 Protocol, Art 2. The Board is not permitted to interfere with national law, merely to give advice to a government. Commentary on the Protocol Amending the Single Convention on Narcotic Drugs 1961 (UN, New York), p 13, para 11.

11.2.1.3 1971 UN Convention on Psychotropic Substances

In setting out measures to control the illicit use of what were a 'new' range of drugs, the 1971 Convention adopts a range of preventative and prohibitive provisions. Thus, the Convention includes measures under which the parties will adopt strict measures for the control of the trade, manufacture and production of the listed psychotropic substances.[51] These restrictions also apply to materials used in preparation or manufacture of these drugs. The Convention requires parties to ensure that offences are punishable under domestic law.[52]

11.2.1.4 1988 UN Convention Against Illicit Traffic in Narcotic Drugs and Psychotropic Substances

Despite these international agreements being widely ratified, a view emerged during the 1980s that the existing conventions focused primarily on controlling the production of licit drugs and the prevention of their diversion into the illicit market place.[53] To this end, the UN General Assembly began a process of consultation in 1984 which resulted in the 1988 UN Convention Against Illicit Traffic in Narcotic Drugs and Psychotropic Substances (the Vienna Convention)[54] which had as its stated aim to 'promote co-operation among the parties so that they may address more effectively the various aspects of illicit traffic . . . having an international dimension'.[55] The Vienna Convention is the most comprehensive international agreement on the control of drug trafficking. The Convention recognises that, whilst drug trafficking is an international criminal activity, State parties should develop procedures in domestic law to identify, arrest, prosecute and convict those who traffic drugs across national boundaries. These measures include establishing drug-related offences and sanctions under domestic criminal law, providing for extradition in respect of those offences, providing for mutual legal assistance and co-operation on investigating and prosecuting those offences and establishing measures to seize and confiscate the proceeds from illicit drug trafficking.[56] The Convention provides for stringent controls on the international trade of constituent chemicals and equipment (precursors) used in manufacturing illicit drugs and that State parties take measures to prevent and eradicate the illicit cultivation of plants used to manufacture drugs. The

---

51 1971 Convention, Art 2.
52 Ibid, Art 22.
53 UN Draft Convention Against Illicit Traffic in Narcotic Drugs and Psychotropic Substances, 10th Congress, First Session, Committee Print, S Prt 100–64, p iii.
54 Reprinted at 28 ILM (1989), 497.
55 Vienna Convention, Art 2(1).
56 For further discussion on the measures to prevent money laundering.

Convention is not only concerned with tightening legal controls on drug trafficking, but also recognises that measures need to be taken to reduce demand for illicit drugs and thereby introduces provisions to promote treatment, education, aftercare, rehabilitation and social reintegration of drug offenders.[57] The Vienna Convention was adopted by consensus and entered into force on 11 November 1990. A particularly innovative feature of the Vienna Convention is the introduction of controls set down on precursor chemicals and equipment used to manufacture synthetic drugs.

Chemicals are imperative to the manufacture of illicit drugs. The production of heroin and cocaine relies on essential chemicals, which are used in the processing and refining of the drug. The production of synthetic drugs relies on precursor chemicals that become part of the resulting product.[58]

Commentators have pointed out that the misuse of precursor chemicals has challenged the traditional perception of the nature and origin of the drug problem. The common perception is that drugs emanate from producer countries in Asia and South America; however, evidence suggests that, in relation to precursor drugs, the situation is different and that it is 'the industrialised countries of Europe and the USA and Japan that manufacture the essential and precursor chemicals'.[59] In discussions prior to the Vienna Convention, an Iranian delegate reported that his country's experience was that precursors which were essential for drug manufacture were being easily and illegally imported from industrial European countries into countries of the Middle East and the Far East, where raw materials were available for their conversion into heroin and other narcotic drugs by simple chemical processes.[60] In the light of these developments, the Vienna Convention adopts two main strategies in respect of precursor drugs. The first is to require parties to criminalise the intentional 'manufacture, transport or distribution of equipment, materials or of substances listed in [two tables annexed to the Convention], knowing that they are to be used in or for the illicit cultivation, production or manufacture of narcotic drugs or psychotropic substances'.[61] The second prong of the Convention's strategy against precursors is to prevent diversion of these chemicals from legitimate medical, scientific and commercial origins into the illicit production of narcotic drugs, both by way of domestic law and regulation and international co-operation.[62]

57 Vienna Convention, Art 14(4).
58 Chemical Action Task Force, *Final Report*, June 1991, Washington DC.
59 European Parliament, *Report on the Spread of Organised Crime Linked to Drugs Trafficking in the Member States of the EC*, 1992 A3–0358/91, p 26.
60 *Official Records: UN Conference for the Adoption of a Convention Against Illicit Traffic in Narcotic Drugs and Psychotropic Substances*, 1991, New York: UN, Vol II, p 248.
61 Vienna Convention, Art 3(1)(a)(iv).
62 Ibid, Art 12.

11.2.1.5 Measures preventing the trafficking of illicit drugs at sea and other initiatives

Due to the problems of establishing an effective framework of jurisdiction over drug trafficking at sea in international waters, Art 17 of the 1988 Vienna Convention introduced a scheme whereby a party to the Convention may request from the Flag State of a vessel permission to board, search and take appropriate measures against vessels suspected of trafficking drugs. Such actions should be carried out by military vessels or aircraft or other vessels authorised for the purpose, and caution must be taken not to endanger life, the security of the vessel or interests of the Flag State. The measures under Art 17 have been implemented by the Council of Europe in its Agreement on Illicit Traffic by Sea Implementing Art 17 of the UN Convention Against Illicit Drugs and Psychotropic Substances.[63]

Whilst the UN has established a legal and administrative framework to counter the problems of illicit drug trafficking and associated problems of drug use, there is a plethora of other anti-drug measures. The European Union (EU) has taken a range of measures aimed at a range of criminal problems, including drug trafficking, not least the improvement of police co-operation culminating in the establishment of Europol Initiatives against drugs which is a specific priority to the Council of Ministers for Justice and Home Affairs.[64] Under the 1990 Schengen Implementing Convention, provisions are included to improve judicial and police co-operation and the Convention provides a means of implementing the measures set out in the UN conventions of 1961, 1971 and 1988 in the Member States to the Schengen *Acquis*.[65]

11.2.2 Drug trafficking as a crime against international law

Following the conclusion of the Vienna Convention in 1988, the UN General Assembly adopted a resolution requesting the International Law Commission to address the question of establishing an international criminal court, which would have jurisdiction over international offences including illicit trafficking in narcotic drugs across national frontiers.[66] Further discussions

---

63 For discussion on these measures and their operation, see W Gilmore, 'Drug-Trafficking at Sea: The Case of *R v Charrington and Others*', 49 *ICLQ* (2000), 477.

64 See, eg, *Action Against Designer Drugs*, Council Meeting – Justice and Home Affairs, Brussels, 26–27 May 1997 (Pres/97/166); *Report on Drugs and Drug Related Issues*, Council Meeting – Justice and Home Affairs, 3–4 Dec 1998 (Pres/98/427); Strategy on Drugs 2000–2004 (Pres/99/288).

65 H Meijers, *Schengen, Internationalisation of Central Chapters of the Law on Aliens, Refugees, Privacy, Security and the Police*, 1991, Dordrecht: Stichting Noem-Beokerij, 107.

66 Adopted by the General Assembly, UN Doc A/44/39 (4 Dec 1989).

on the criminalisation of drug trafficking in international law took place in the course of the drafting of the Draft Code of Crimes against the Peace and Security of Mankind. Whilst the crime of drug trafficking was included in the 1991 Draft Code, doubts expressed by States on the provision saw its exclusion from the revised 1996 Draft.[67] Reviewing these developments, Sunga has claimed that, '[t]he proliferation of international agreements designed to suppress trafficking in illicit drugs indicates that the international community has recognised the need for international rather than purely domestic solutions to the drug problem'.[68] This view was borne out by discussion on the inclusion of the crime of drug trafficking in the Rome Statute for the International Criminal Court.[69] In the frenzied discussion of the Rome Conference and the search for common agreement as to the crimes that should fall under the International Criminal Court (ICC)'s jurisdiction and their definitions, interest in including drug trafficking in the Statute waned during final negotiations. Drug trafficking was not included in the final Statute; however, the parties adopted a resolution recommending that State parties consider reaching agreement on a definition and on including both drug trafficking and terrorism at a future review conference.[70]

During the course of the 20th century, measures against drug trafficking developed from regulatory measures controlling the transit and quantities supplied, to measures which criminalise and prevent production and distribution. The UN initiatives are an acknowledgment that the growth in drug trafficking adversely affects the economic, cultural and political foundations of society. Recently, there has been increasing awareness that drug trafficking generates large financial profits enabling criminal organisations to penetrate and corrupt structures of government. By focusing on the proceeds from the sale of drugs, law enforcement agencies can develop an effective mechanism for disrupting major drug-trafficking networks. Thus, an important development has been the emergence of an international strategy to combat drug trafficking through measures to address money laundering. The realisation that laundering dirty money is necessary in order to provide drug traffickers and other organised criminal organisations with capital for developing illegal activities has resulted in the rapid increase in the international effort to tackle the problem.

67 Op cit, Sunga, note 38, pp 216–19.
68 Op cit, Sunga, note 38, p 216.
69 ICC Statute, 37 ILM (1998), 999.
70 *Rome Statute of the ICC, Background Information*, UN Diplomatic Conference of Plenipotentiaries on the Establishment of an International Criminal Court, UN Doc A/CONF 183/9 (17 July 1998).

11.3 MONEY LAUNDERING[71]

11.3.1 Introduction

While the increased interest in money laundering as an international crime has been engendered by the rapid growth in criminal activities linked to international drug trafficking, money laundering is the natural consequence of many other large scale international organised criminal activities including corruption, fraud and terrorism. The term money laundering is used to describe the process whereby the proceeds of crime are converted for the purpose of concealing or disguising their illicit origin.[72] This process is necessary in order to sever the link between the original criminal conduct and the proceeds of the crime. Several common factors can be identified: the conversion or transfer of property; the concealment or disguise of the source of the property; and the need to regain access to the money. Thus, money laundering is generally a three stage process: first, the placement phase where the profits generated by the criminal activity must become separated from the criminal activity itself; secondly, the layering phase when steps must be taken to disguise the route which the money takes during the laundering process; and, finally, the integration phase where the money must become available for use by the criminal organisation. During the placement phase, 'dirty' money is usually placed with other legitimate money in the financial system. However, before a criminal organisation gains access to the money it needs to be satisfied that the money cannot be traced back to the original offence. It is at the layering phase that the real separation from the origin of the money is generally achieved.

Globalisation of the economy and the development of high tech communication systems that facilitate the international transfer of money have created a near perfect environment for the growth in money laundering. The electronic movement of money across national boundaries makes financial transactions difficult to trace and has produced problems for law enforcement

---

71 For further discussion of money laundering generally, see P Birks, *Laundering and Tracing*, 2003, Oxford: OUP; W Gilmore (ed), *International Efforts to Combat Money Laundering*, 1992, Cambridge: Grotius; and G Stessens, *Money Laundering: A New International Law Enforcement Model*, 2000, Cambridge: CUP; W Gilmore, *Dirty Money, the Evolution of International Measures to Counter Money Laundering and the Financing of Terrorism*, 2004, Council of Europe; D Masciandaro, *Global Financial Crime: Terrorism, Money Laundering, and Off Shore Centres*, 2004, Aldershot: Ashgate Publishing; G Stessons, *Money Laundering*, 2005, Cambridge: CUP.

72 Money laundering is defined in Art 3(1)(b) of the 1988 UN Convention Against Illicit Traffic in Narcotic Drugs and Psychotropic Substances as the conversion or transfer of property, knowing that such property is derived from offences specified in the Convention, or the concealment or disguise of the nature, source, location, disposition, movement, rights or ownership of property, knowing that such property is derived from a specified offence.

agencies. In order to combat the problem, money laundering has been criminalised, national law enforcement agencies have been empowered to trace, freeze, seize and confiscate the proceeds of criminal conduct, and international mutual legal assistance schemes have been introduced.[73] Furthermore, the realisation that banks and other financial institutions are used, albeit unwittingly, as intermediaries for the transfer or deposit of money derived from criminal activity, has generated a range of national and international initiatives aimed at preventing the banking system from being employed in this manner.[74] These include the 1988 UN Convention Against Illicit Traffic in Narcotic Drugs and Psychotropic Substances,[75] the 1990 Council of Europe Convention on Laundering, Search, Seizure and Confiscation of the Proceeds from Crime,[76] and EC Directives on prevention of the use of the financial system for the purpose of money laundering.[77] There are also several significant self-regulatory regimes including those published by the Basle Committee on Banking Supervision and the Financial Action Task Force (FATF) on Money Laundering. Many of these initiatives have been co-ordinated through the UN Office for Drug Control and Crime Prevention (ODCCP) within the framework of its global programme against money laundering. Arising from the growth in international terrorism, many international and national anti-money laundering initiatives now include measures to combat the financing of terrorism.[78]

11.3.2 Self-regulation

In order to prevent the laundering of money through the financial system, banks and financial institutions have introduced a range of self-regulatory regimes. In its report in June 1980, the Committee of Ministers of the Council of Europe observed that the banking system could play a significant preventative role and suggested that increased co-operation with the police and judicial authorities could assist in the repression of criminal acts. Initially, the international effort to combat the growth in money laundering was

---

73 For further discussion of mutual legal assistance, see Chapter 15.
74 For an overview of the UN Conventions and other International Standards see http://www.imolin.org/pdf/imolin/overview%20update_0107.pdf (accessed on 11 April 2007).
75 Reprinted at 28 ILM (1989) 497.
76 ETS 141.
77 Directive 2001/97/EC of the European Parliament of the Council of 4 Dec 2001 amending Council Directive 91/308/EEC on prevention of the use of the financial system for the purpose of money laundering OJ 2001 L 344/76.
78 See for example Directive 2005/60/EC on the prevention of the use of the financial system for the purpose of money laundering and terrorist financing and the 2005 Council of Europe Convention on Laundering, Search, Seizure and Confiscation of the Proceeds from Crime and the Financing of Terrorism, OJ 2005 L 309/15. For further discussion of terrorist financing see Chapter 10.

addressed by banking regulations and codes of conduct rather than through legislative reform. In the late 1980s, representatives of the central banking authorities from 10 States met to consider how the institutions could assist in the suppression of money laundering. At the outset, the members of the Basle Committee on Banking Regulations and Supervisory Practices[79] observed that the primary function of banking supervisory authorities is to maintain the overall financial stability of banks, rather than to ensure that individual transactions conducted by bank customers are legitimate. Further, national banking supervisory authorities do not necessarily have the same role and responsibilities in relation to the suppression of money laundering. In some States, supervisors have a specific responsibility; in others they may have no responsibility. Nevertheless, the Committee acknowledged that, as a consequence of the inadvertent association between banks and criminal activity, public confidence in the banking system could be undermined and the stability of the system threatened.

The Basle Committee agreed to draft a general statement of ethical principles in order to encourage banks worldwide to develop procedures to encourage customer due diligence and to discourage money laundering.[80] The Committee recommended that banks take reasonable steps to determine the true identification of persons conducting business with their institutions, including those using safe custody facilities, and should refuse to conduct business transactions with customers who fail to provide evidence of identity. However, while banks should be encouraged to co-operate with national law enforcement authorities and should close or freeze the accounts of persons suspected of depositing money which derived from criminal activity, the Committee observed that the Statement of Principles was not binding in international law and its implementation would depend upon national law and practice. However, the drafting of the Statement demonstrated a commitment to encourage ethical standards of professional conduct among banks and other financial institutions. This initiative has been acknowledged by the EU Council as a major step towards preventing the use of the financial system for money laundering.

Further Committee publications, issued in 1997 and 1999, recommend that banks develop policies which 'promote high ethical and professional standards in the financial sector and prevent the bank from being used, intentionally or unintentionally, by criminal elements'.[81] The Committee also

---

79 The original committee comprised of banking representatives from Belgium, Canada, France, Germany, Italy, Japan, Luxembourg, The Netherlands, Sweden, Switzerland, the UK and USA.

80 Basle Committee on Banking Supervision, *Prevention of Criminal Use of the Banking System for the Purpose of Money-Laundering*, 1988, Basle: Basle Committee.

81 Basle Committee on Banking Supervision, *Core Principles for Effective Banking Supervision and Core Principles Methodology*, 1997, Basle: Basle Committee.

strongly supports the recommendations of the Financial Action Task Force on Money Laundering (FATF) relating to customer identification, record keeping and reporting and the need to take measures to deal with States that do not have effective anti-money laundering procedures in place. A further publication, issued in October 2001, reinforced the principles established in earlier publications and provided precise guidance on the essential elements of 'Know Your Customer' (KYC) standards and their implementation.[82] It warns that without adequate controls and procedures in place to check customer credibility, banks risked damage to their reputation and might fail to meet requirements imposed by national anti-money laundering legislation. It considered that effective KYC safeguards required banks to formulate a customer acceptance policy and a tiered customer identification programme which involved increased due diligence for higher risk accounts, and included proactive account monitoring for suspicious activities. The Basle Committee considers that similar guidance should be developed for both non-bank financial institutions and the professions frequently engaged in financial services, such as lawyers and accountants.

The increasing international dimension of organised criminal activity has also prompted a range of intergovernmental self-regulatory initiatives. In 1989, the FATF, a multi-disciplinary body established by the Heads of State of the seven major industrialised nations, known as the G7 countries, set out to develop and promote anti-money laundering policies. These policies aim to prevent the proceeds of crime from being used for future criminal activities and from affecting legitimate economic activities. In 1990, a report was circulated setting out 40 recommendations for increasing co-operation in this area which aimed to establish a framework for anti-money laundering activities. They cover the areas of law enforcement, financial regulation and international co-operation and are accompanied by a set of interpretative notes which clarify the application of specific recommendations. Member States are required to monitor the implementation of the recommendations through a self-assessment exercise and a mutual evaluation process. This development is regarded as a benchmark in the field of international standards for combating money laundering. Currently membership of FATF includes the European Commission, the Gulf Co-operation Council and 31 States from the major financial centre countries in Europe, North and South America and Asia. It works in co-operation with other like-minded bodies including the Caribbean Financial Action Task Force and the ODCCP. In 2005 the Eurasia Group (EAG), which includes the People's Republic of China, Kazakhstan, Kyrgyzstan and Tajikistan, was granted observer status.

---

82 Basle Committee on Banking Supervision, *Customer Due Diligence for Banks,* 2001, Basle: Basle Committee.

In the general framework to the recommendations, Member States are encouraged to implement the 1988 UN Convention Against Illicit Traffic in Narcotic Drugs and Psychotropic Substances (the 1988 UN Convention) to adopt an effective anti-money laundering programme, which should include mutual legal assistance initiatives, and to ensure that rules protecting financial confidentiality do not inhibit the operation of the FATF initiative. The remainder of the recommendations address both the role of national systems and the financial system in tackling money laundering. Thus States are encouraged to adopt measures similar to those set out in the 1988 UN Convention including criminalising money laundering activities and establishing procedures for tracing, seizing and confiscating assets. Acknowledging the important role that is played by financial institutions, States are also urged to introduce a range of anti-money laundering regulations including customer identification, record keeping and reporting requirements. These regulations should be applied to all branches and foreign subsidiaries of financial institutions, especially in States identified as having a poor anti-money laundering regime. It is recommended that international co-operation between law enforcement agencies be strengthened to facilitate the gathering and exchange of information. Further, mutual legal assistance measures should be introduced which include arrangements for co-ordinating seizure and confiscation, which may include the sharing of assets, and procedures to address conflicts of jurisdiction and extradition. These recommendations were revised in 2003 to take account of changes in money laundering trends. Among the areas identified as requiring further consideration were customer identification and suspicious transaction reporting and regulation, identification of beneficial ownership of companies, trusts and foundations and the increased use of professional advice or other assistance with laundering criminal assets. The FATF has now extended its activities to include anti-terrorism initiatives and has issued special recommendations that address terrorist financing which Member States are urged to implement. There are currently Forty Recommendations and Nine Special Recommendations. In August 2004, its mandate was reviewed and extended for a further eight years. In October 2006, the FATF published a study which assessed the risks caused by new payment methods. It analysed internet and mobile payment systems to determine whether the current FATF Recommendations adequately addressed the potential increase in money laundering opportunities. Although satisfied that these do provide appropriate guidance, the study suggested that further work should be done to assess the effect of the new technologies on cross-border and domestic regulatory frameworks to ensure compatibility with the FAFT Recommendations.

11.3.3 UN initiatives

The 1988 UN Convention Against Illicit Traffic in Narcotic Drugs and Psychotropic Substances[83] was the first international instrument to address confiscation of the proceeds of crime and to require States to criminalise money laundering. This Convention has been used as a framework for several important international anti-money laundering initiatives including work undertaken by the Council of Europe, the EU and the FATF. Further, its provisions are frequently mirrored in national anti-money laundering legislation. The primary purpose of the Convention is to weaken the economic power of criminal organisations by promoting international co-operation to combat drug trafficking. The preamble to the Convention notes that drug trafficking generates large financial profits which enable criminal organisations to penetrate legitimate financial businesses, corrupt the structures of government and destabilise society. It was anticipated that by confiscating the proceeds of crime the incentive for drug trafficking would be eliminated. Contracting parties are required to criminalise not only the organisation, management and financing of drug trafficking but also the conversion, transfer and concealment of the proceeds of drug trafficking. States must ensure that measures are adopted which enable the authorities to confiscate these proceeds. Thus States should introduce measures allowing the authorities to identify, trace and freeze or seize the proceeds of drug trafficking, which may require the examination of relevant records held by banks and financial institutions.[84]

Although the 1988 Convention limited its anti-money laundering provisions to the proceeds from drug trafficking, these measures were eventually extended to include the proceeds from serious crime. Thus in a UN General Assembly Resolution, States and other relevant global and regional organisations were urged to develop effective international co-operation against the 'threats posed by organised transnational crime in relation to measures and strategies to prevent and combat money laundering and to control the use of the proceeds of crime'.[85] This Resolution was followed by the Political Declaration adopted at a Special Session of the UN General Assembly which expressed concern at the link between drug production, trafficking and terrorism and resolved to strengthen international and regional anti-money laundering initiatives. It recommended that by 2003 all States should have in place national anti-money laundering regimes in accordance with the measures set out in the UN action plan entitled 'Countering Money Laundering'.[86] In this plan, States are urged to establish 'a legislative framework to

---

83 28 ILM (1989), 497.
84 Ibid, Art 5(3).
85 GA Res 49/159.
86 GA Res s–20/4D.

criminalise the laundering of money derived from serious crimes in order to provide for the detection, investigation and prosecution of the crime of money laundering'.[87] Thus States should introduce measures to identify, seize and confiscate the proceeds of crime, facilitate international co-operation and implement mutual legal assistance measures, and establish an effective financial and regulatory regime to prevent criminals laundering 'dirty' money through the financial system. The plan also recommended introducing 'KYC' procedures which included customer identification and record keeping.

The scope of money laundering was eventually extended to include the proceeds from serious crime in the 2000 UN Convention against Transnational Organised Crime (CATOC).[88] In addition to requiring States to adopt legislative and regulatory measures to criminalise the laundering of the proceeds of crime, this Convention emphasises the importance of customer identification, record keeping and the reporting of suspicious transactions.[89] This applies not only to banks but also to other bodies particularly susceptible to money laundering. States are required 'within the parameters of national law' to ensure that administrative, regulatory and law enforcement authorities have the ability to co-operate and exchange information at the national and international level, and should contemplate establishing a financial intelligence unit to serve as a national centre for the collection, analysis and dissemination of information.[90] In order to monitor the movement of cash across borders, States may implement measures which include a requirement that individuals and businesses report the cross-border transfer of substantial amounts of cash and negotiable instruments.[91] In establishing a domestic regulatory and supervisory regime, contracting parties are advised to refer to the relevant initiatives of regional and multilateral organisations involved in combating money laundering.[92] The 2003 UN Convention against Corruption also contains provisions which require State Parties to adopt legislative measures to criminalise money laundering.

Work undertaken by the FATF indicated that terrorists could manipulate the financial system in much the same way as other criminal groups. It was also noted that terrorist financing might not be encompassed within the definition of money laundering used in the framework of many national and international anti-money laundering initiatives. FATF experts were of the opinion that terrorism should be considered to be a serious crime and recommended that States should take immediate steps to ratify the 1999 UN

---

87 Ibid, para 2(a).
88 CATOC, Art 1.
89 Ibid, Art 7(1)(a).
90 Ibid, Art 7(1)(b).
91 Ibid, Art 7(2).
92 Ibid, Art 7(3).

International Convention for the Suppression of the Financing of Terrorism. This Convention acknowledges that financing is at the heart of terrorist activity and applies to the provision or collection of funds which are intended to be used for the purpose of committing a terrorist act. Other steps taken by the UN to address the problem of terrorist financing include Security Council Resolutions 1368 and 1373 on combating financing which require States to take measures to stop the financing and training of terrorists. These initiatives require States to identify, detect, freeze and seize the funds. Thus many of the measures used to combat other forms of serious crime are now employed in the fight against terrorism.

As part of its anti-money laundering programme, the UN Office on Drugs and Crime introduced model legislation which facilitates the drafting of national legislative provisions designed to combat money laundering and to promote international co-operation between judicial and law enforcement agencies. While the model legislation incorporates many of the existing measures found in national and international instruments, it proposes several innovative provisions in order to improve the effectiveness of international co-operation. Adaptation of model legislation can present national legislative bodies with many difficulties. In order to address this problem, the model legislation presents optional or variant provisions. In 1999, UNODC introduced Model Legislation on Laundering, Confiscation and International Co-operation in Relation to the Proceeds of Crime, which was designed primarily for use in civil law systems. This was revised in 2005. The new initiative is the 2005 Model Legislation on Money Laundering and Terrorist Financing, which is based on the relevant international instruments concerning money laundering and terrorist financing and incorporates the FATF 40+9 recommendations. In addition to providing definitions for 'proceeds of crime', 'terrorist', 'terrorist act' and 'terrorist organisation', the 2005 model legislation covers the prevention of money laundering and financing of terrorism; detection of money laundering and financing of terrorism; investigation; penal matters and international co-operation. The definition of money laundering and terrorist financing are contained in Art 5 of the 2005 model law which creates the criminal offences of money laundering and terrorist financing. Article 5.2.1 provides that:

(1) For the purposes of this law, money laundering is defined as follows:
(a) The conversion or transfer of property,
Variant 1: by any person who knows or should have known
Variant 2: by any person who knows or suspects
Variant 3: by any person who knows, should have known or suspects that such property is the proceeds of crime, for the purpose of concealing or disguising the illicit origin of such property or of assisting any person who is involved in the commission of the predicate offence to evade the consequences of his or her actions;

(b) The concealment or disguise of the true nature, source, location, disposition movement or ownership of or rights with respect to property,
Variant 1: by any person who knows or should have known
Variant 2: by any person who knows or suspects
Variant 3: by any person who knows, should have known or suspects
that such property is the proceeds of crime.

(c) The acquisition, possession or use of property,
Variant 1: by any person who knows or should have known
Variant 2: by any person who knows or suspects
Variant 3: by any person who knows, should have known or suspects
[Option: at the time of receipt] that such property is the proceeds of crime.

Article 5.2.2 defines terrorist financing as 'an act by any person who . . . provides or collects funds . . . with the intention that they should be used a) to carry out a terrorist act, or b) by a terrorist, or c) by a terrorist organisation.

Two further anti-money laundering Model Bills also address the problem of terrorist financing. The first of these is the UN Model Money Laundering, Proceeds of Crime and Terrorist Financing Bill 2003[93] which is designed for use in common law systems. This bill covers financial regulatory requirements and provides for the seizing and freezing of assets and the confiscation of terrorist-related property. It provides for the creation of a Financial Intelligence Unit (FIU) which should receive reports of suspicious transactions issued by financial institutions and send them to law enforcement authorities. The second bill deals specifically with terrorist financing and implements the provisions of the 1999 UN International Convention for the Suppression of the Financing of Terrorism[94] and associated Security Council Resolutions.[95] The UN Model Terrorist Financing Bill 2003[96] contains provisions on the definition of terrorist financing, the collection, use or possession of property obtained by crime, information sharing, extradition and mutual assistance. It sets out the circumstances when it would be appropriate for national law enforcement agencies to exchange information about terrorist groups and terrorist acts with law enforcement agencies in other states.

93 <http://www.unodc.org/pdf/report_money_laundering_2003–09.pdf> (accessed on 15 Dec 2006).
94 Adopted by General Assembly Resolution 54/109 of 25 Feb 2000. <http://www.unodc.org/unodc/resolution_2000–02–25_1.html> (accessed on 15 Dec 2006).
95 Security Council Resolutions 1368 and 1373.
96 <http://www.imolin.org/imolin/tfbill03.html> (accessed on 15 Dec 2006).

11.3.4 Council of Europe initiatives

In June 1987, the Committee of Ministers of the Council of Europe author-ised a Select Committee of Experts to examine the applicability of existing international instruments to the tracing, seizure and forfeiture of the pro-ceeds from crime. The Committee considered the problem from the stand-point of international co-operation and examined a range of international criminal law initiatives, including work undertaken by the UN into drug trafficking. It noted that criminal investigations were sometimes hampered by lack of harmonisation in national criminal law and practice, and expressed concern that there were significant differences in national approaches to the confiscation of criminal proceeds. Further, existing initiatives introduced within the framework of the Council of Europe did not adequately address the problem. Thus the 1959 European Convention on Mutual Assistance in Criminal Matters did not apply to the search and seizure of property with a view to its subsequent confiscation, and the 1972 European Convention on the Transfer of Proceedings in Criminal Matters raised problems of jurisdic-tion. The Committee's recommendations included the need to have in place effective mechanisms of international co-operation during all stages of the criminal investigation and the need for Member States to harmonise criminal law and adopt measures to confiscate criminal proceeds. The European Committee on Crime Problems of the Council of Europe (CDPC) eventually approved the draft proposal for an anti-money laundering convention which establishes a common criminal policy and lays down principles for inter-national co-operation. Reflecting the global nature of the problem, this instrument, unlike most others drafted by the Council of Europe, omits the word 'European' from the title. The 1990 Convention on Laundering, Search, Seizure and Confiscation of the Proceeds from Crime was eventually opened for signature in November 1990 by Member States of the Council of Europe and other non-Council States which had participated in its drafting.[97]

The primary purpose of this initiative was to extend international co-operation initiatives between law enforcement agencies to prevent criminals from gaining an economic advantage from their involvement in crime. Contracting parties agreed to adopt measures which criminalise money laundering,[98] and to facilitate the identification,[99] confiscation[100] and seiz-ure[101] of the proceeds of crime. National legislation was enacted which makes it an offence to be knowingly involved in the conversion, transfer, conceal-ment, acquisition or use of criminal proceeds. States were also encouraged to

97 ETS 141.
98 1990 Convention, Art 6.
99 Ibid, Art 3.
100 Ibid, Art 2.
101 Ibid, Art 4.

implement legislation, regulations and administrative decisions which empowered the courts and other competent authorities to order that bank, financial or commercial records be made available in order to identify and trace property which may be confiscated. Contracting parties are urged to introduce measures which enable the authorities to use special investigative techniques to gather evidence related to the tracing of assets derived from criminal activity. Further, to increase the effectiveness of national anti-money laundering initiatives, the 1990 Convention includes provision for international co-operation procedures to assist law enforcement agencies, including operational assistance in the identification and tracing of the proceeds of crime. In addition, to prevent the disposal of property, parties should implement the necessary provisional measures which permit the authorities to freeze assets to enable confiscation to be enforced. The 1990 Convention, which is designed to complement other international initiatives, does not affect rights and undertakings given in respect of other mutual assistance treaties.[102]

Further Council of Europe schemes include an initiative by the Committee of Ministers of the Council of Europe which in 1997 set up a committee to conduct an assessment of the anti-money laundering measures adopted in non-FATF States within the Council of Europe. The Select Committee of Experts on the Evaluation of Anti-Money Laundering Measures (PC-R-EV) is a sub-committee of the CDPC, which meets regularly to determine whether States are achieving the agreed anti-money laundering standards. It has developed a procedure for the conduct of mutual evaluations and a set of procedures and guidelines to deal with States which fail to comply with the FATF standards. The Committee publishes summaries of the mutual evaluations. In June 2003 the Council of Europe instructed the Committee of Experts to update and expand the 1990 Convention to include measures to prevent the financing of terrorism. The Committee recommended so many amendments that it was decided to draft a new Convention rather than just add an additional Protocol. At a meeting in May 2005 the Committee of Ministers formerly adopted a new Convention, which was opened for signing on 16 May 2005. The 2005 Council of Europe Convention on Laundering, Search, Seizure and Confiscation of the Proceeds from Crime and on the Financing of Terrorism takes into account other international anti-money laundering instruments including the FATF Recommendations and the third EC Money Laundering Directive.[103] It includes provisions that allow for the disclosure of bank account details including information about transactions. These provisions may be extended to include other financial institutions. Interestingly, in order to avoid incompatibility with future EU developments in this area, the 2005 Convention has

---

102 Ibid, Art 39.
103 Directive 2005/60/EC of the European Parliament and of the Council of 26 Oct 2005 on the prevention of the use of the financial system for the purpose of money laundering and terrorist financing, OJ 2005 L 309/15.

a disconnection clause that allows EU Member States to apply the corresponding EU rules rather than the rules set out in this Convention.[104] The European Community is permitted to be a party to this Convention and will be a member of the committee responsible for monitoring its implementation.

11.3.5 EU initiatives

Since the Tampere European Council summit in 1999, the EU has introduced a range of anti-money laundering legislation which set out a framework for credit and financial institutions. Money laundering and organised crime have been identified as a political priority of the EU based on the need to protect the financial system and, since 11 September 2001, the international consensus to target terrorist financing. Accordingly, in addition to three Money Laundering Directives and a Framework Decision, several measures have been introduced which strengthen the role of Europol and enhance co-operation and information exchange between law enforcement agencies.[105] The 1991 Directive,[106] which is based on the original FATF Recommendations, defines money laundering as the conversion or transfer of property, knowing that such property is derived from criminal activity or from an act of participation in such activity, for the purpose of concealing or disguising the illicit origin of the property or of assisting any person who is involved in the commission of such activity to evade the legal consequences. The definition embraces the acquisition, possession or use of such property and includes forms of secondary participation. The Directive requires financial institutions to identify their customers, to keep appropriate records, to report suspicious transactions, and to establish anti-money laundering training programmes. Bank secrecy rules could also be suspended. The Directive required Member States to introduce legislative and other methods necessary to ensure compliance with these provisions before 1 January 1993.

In order to increase the effectiveness of EU anti-money laundering measures, a second Money Laundering Directive was introduced in 2001, amending

---

104 Art 52(4).

105 A Directive is binding on Member States. However the manner in which the results are achieved is left to the discretion of national authorities. Failure to comply can result in a referral to the European Court of Justice (ECJ). Framework Decisions do not have direct effect and the Commission cannot take legal action before the ECJ for non-compliance. However, a ruling can be sought if there is a dispute between Member States regarding interpretation or application. In C–105/03 *Criminal Proceedings against Maria Pupino*, ECR [2005] I–5285 the ECJ held that the principle of indirect effect applies to framework decisions, ie, domestic judges must interpret national law, as far as is possible, in the light of framework decisions. See further B Kurcz, A Lazowski, 'Two Sides of the Same Coin? Framework Decisions and Directives Compared' 26 YEL (2007) forthcoming.

106 Council Directive 91/308/EEC of June 1991 on the prevention of the use of the financial system for the purpose of money laundering, OJ 1991, L 166/77.

the 1991 Directive, which broadens the definition of criminal activity to include a wider range of serious offences including terrorism. The amended Directive applies to non-financial professional service providers and allows for the establishment of financial intelligence units (FIU's) which collect and analyse information. These units facilitate the sharing of money laundering data between the public and private sectors. Criminal activity now covers any kind of involvement in the commission of a serious crime which includes organised crime, corruption, and fraud against the European Community.[107] Further, the obligations incurred by financial institutions under the 1991 Directive are now imposed on members of the legal profession, accountants working in financial or allied industries, estate agents, art and antique dealers and casinos.[108] States must ensure that persons subject to the Directive undertake customer identification procedures,[109] report suspicious transactions to a designated authority[110] and establish appropriate training and internal reporting procedures.[111] The amended Directive, which should have been incorporated into domestic law by June 2003, is still causing problems. Not only have Member States been reluctant to implement it, but also the Council of the Bars and Law Societies of Europe are concerned that reporting obligations will prejudice a lawyers' ability to represent clients. Lobbying by the professional bodies resulted in an acknowledgment of the need for lawyers in the UK to abide by legal professional privilege rules.[112] Following concerns raised by the Belgian Bar Association, the Belgian court referred a question to the ECJ asking whether the 2001 Directive is compatible with the right to a fair trial which is guaranteed by Article 6 of the European Convention for Human Rights.[113] Belgian lawyers have argued that the reporting obligations adversely affect their ability to act independently.

Despite these problems a Third Money Laundering Directive was adopted in October 2005 which incorporates revisions made to the FATF recommendations in June 2003 and covers financial transactions which may be linked to terrorist activities.[114] The Third Directive, which replaces the amended Directive in its entirety, strengthens the area of 'customer due diligence' by

---

107 Ibid, Art 1(E).
108 Ibid, Art 2a.
109 Ibid, Art 3.
110 Ibid, Art 6.
111 Ibid, Art 11.
112 Under these rules communications between a legal adviser and a client for the purposes of obtaining legal advice are privileged. Thus legal professional privilege will apply when a lawyer is giving advice relating to contemplated legal proceedings, or if proceedings are not contemplated, the advice relates merely to the client determining their legal position.
113 Case C–305/05, 2005/C 243/15.
114 Directive 2005/60/EC of the European Parliament and of the Council of 26 Oct 2005 on the prevention of the use of the financial system for the purpose of money laundering and terrorist financing, OJ 2005 L 309/15.

requiring identity checks to be carried out on customers opening accounts and increases penalties for failing to report suspicious transactions. Obligations are imposed on insurance intermediaries, company service providers and dealers in high value goods where payments are made in cash. The Third Directive must be implemented in all Member States by December 2007. In addition to these Directives, the EU introduced a Framework Decision on money laundering in 2001.[115] This initiative aims to strengthen and support other anti-money laundering initiatives by dealing with the seizing and confiscation of the proceeds of crime. Member States are required not to make reservations in respect of the 1990 Council of Europe Convention which requires them to provide for confiscation measures and to criminalise the laundering of the proceeds of serious crime.[116] In its report in May 2006, the Commission noted that several Member States had not yet complied with all the provisions of the Framework Decision, and some had not provided sufficient information for the Commission to assess compliance.[117]

All Member States are expected to comply with this initiative by June 2007. In order to supplement the arrangements provided for by the 2001 Framework Decision, the Council adopted a further Framework Decision in 2005 requiring Member States to take measures to confiscate the proceeds of crime.[118] This initiative entered into force in March 2005. Other EU developments include extending the competence of Europol to money laundering,[119] the addition of a Protocol to the Convention on Mutual Assistance in Criminal Matters which requires authorities to provide details of bank accounts,[120] and introducing customs controls on the movement of large sums of money across external borders of the EU. Anyone entering or leaving the EU with cash to the value of EUR 10,000 or more will be required to declare it to customs authorities.[121] Many of the EU initiatives introduced to address the problem of money laundering and organised crime raise questions regarding

---

115 Council Framework Decision of 26 June 2001 on money laundering, the identification, tracing, freezing, seizing and confiscation of the instrumentalities and the proceeds of crime. COM(2006) 72 final.

116 1990 Convention on Laundering, Search, Seizure and Confiscation of the Proceeds from Crime ETS 141.

117 COM(2006)72, 21.02.2006.

118 The Council Framework Decision 2005/212/JHA of 24 Feb 2005 on Confiscation of Crime-Related Proceeds, Instrumentalities and Property, OJ L 68.

119 Council Act of 30 Nov 2000 drawing up on the basis of Article 43(1) of the Convention on the establishment of a European Police Office (Europol Convention) of a Protocol amending Art 2 and the Annex to the Europol Convention, OJ 2000/C358/01.

120 Council Act of 16 Oct 2001 establishing, in accordance with Article 34 of the Treaty on European Union, the Protocol to the Convention on Mutual Assistance in Criminal Matters between Member States of the EU, OJ 2001/C 326/1.

121 Regulation (EC) No 1889/2005 of the European Parliament and of the Council of 26 Oct 2005 on controls of cash entering or leaving the Community, OJ 2005 L 309/9.

whether a fair balance has been achieved between the need to protect national and international security and the need to guarantee individual privacy rights. Banking and other financial institutions, and lawyers, maintain that on occasion disclosure and reporting requirements impose an unreasonable burden.

11.3.6 National initiatives to combat money laundering[122]

11.3.6.1 The United Kingdom

Money laundering was initially criminalised in the UK with respect to the proceeds of drug trafficking. The confiscation regime introduced by the Drug Trafficking Act 1986 provided the trial judge with the power to confiscate from convicted defendants proceeds from drug trafficking activities. When assessing the amount to be paid, the court can assume that assets accrued by the defendant in the six years prior to the commencement of proceedings were derived from criminal conduct. Arguments that this statutory assumption infringes the European Convention on Human Rights have so far been unsuccessful.[123] Although the confiscation regime was initially limited to drug-trafficking cases, it has subsequently been extended to cover other offences. The 1986 Act has now been replaced by the Drug Trafficking Act 1994. Further anti-money laundering provisions appeared in a range of legislation, including the Criminal Justice Act 1993, which took account of the Council Directive 91/308/EEC.[124] Subsequently, with a view to increasing the efficiency of the confiscation procedure, the Prime Minister requested an assessment of the recovery of illegally obtained assets regime. The report prepared by the Performance and Innovation Unit (PIU) in the Cabinet Office was published in 2000 and recommended the consolidation of existing

---

122 For a comprehensive account of the law and practice in the UK, see B Rider and C Nakajima, *Anti-Money Laundering Guide*, 2003, Bicester: CCH.

123 In *Phillips v UK* (2002) 11 BHRC 280, the Strasbourg Court considered that although an issue relating to fairness may arise in circumstances where a confiscation order was based on hidden assets, in this case the relevant provisions were confined within reasonable limits, given the importance of what was at stake, and the Court was unanimous in holding that the operation of the statutory assumption did not violate the notion of a fair hearing. Similarly, in *R v Benjafield and Rezvi* [2001] 3 WLR 75, the appellant argued that a confiscation order imposed under Pt VI of the Criminal Justice Act 1988 did not accord with his rights under the Convention. In dismissing the appeal, the House of Lords considered that the legislation amounted to a proportionate response to the problem it was designed to address and represented a fair balance between the interests of the individual and the public. However, when considering an application for an order the trial judge must avoid any serious or real risk of injustice. If there was such a risk, the court should not make an order.

124 OJ 1991, L 166/77.

legislation dealing with confiscation and money laundering. In 2001, the Proceeds of Crime Bill was introduced which incorporated many of the recommendations from the PIU report.

The Proceeds of Crime Act 2002, which came into force in February 2003, consolidates the existing confiscation provisions relating to drug trafficking and other criminal offences and creates new powers of civil forfeiture without conviction. In addition to creating three specific money laundering offences, this legislation removes the distinction between laundering money from drug trafficking and laundering the proceeds of other forms of criminal activity. This legislation also provides prosecuting authorities with a range of measures, including new powers of investigation, restraint orders and confiscation orders, which will make the recovery of unlawfully held assets more effective; it also includes provisions on international co-operation and mutual legal assistance. The three principal money laundering offences, which apply to the laundering of the offender's own proceeds of crime as well as the proceeds of other people's criminal activity,[125] criminalise concealing,[126] arranging,[127] acquiring, using or possessing[128] criminal property. These offences all carry a maximum penalty of 14 years' imprisonment. The offence of concealing is committed when a person conceals, disguises, converts, transfers or removes from the jurisdiction criminal property. Similarly, it is an offence for someone to be concerned in arrangements which they know or suspect would make it easier for another person to acquire, retain, use or control criminal property. Criminal property is defined as being property which the alleged offender knows or suspects constitutes or represents benefit from any criminal conduct.[129]

This legislation creates a new offence of failing to disclose suspicions that someone is engaged in money laundering activities. However, the duty to report is restricted to persons who receive information in the course of a business in the regulated sector, which is defined in Schedule 9 to the Act.[130] Regulated sector businesses are required to nominate a Money Laundering Reporting Officer[131] who will incur criminal liability for failing to disclose an employee's suspicion to the National Criminal Intelligence Service (NCIS) as soon as is practicable.[132] It is also an offence to disclose information likely to prejudice a money laundering investigation.[133] The maximum penalty for

125 Proceeds of Crime Act 2002, s 340.
126 Ibid, s 327.
127 Ibid, s 328.
128 Ibid, s 329.
129 Ibid, s 340.
130 Ibid, s 330.
131 Money Laundering Regulations 1993, reg 14.
132 Proceeds of Crime Act 2002, s 331. NCIS has been replaced by the Serious and Organised Crime Agency (SOCA).
133 Ibid, s 333.

these offences is five years' imprisonment. The Act provides for confiscation of proceeds derived from the defendant's criminal conduct. If the court is satisfied that the defendant has a criminal lifestyle, the confiscation order can relate to the proceeds of any criminal conduct whenever it occurred.[134] In line with earlier confiscation legislation, the court is permitted to make assumptions in respect of the amount the defendant has benefited from criminal conduct.

The Proceeds of Crime Act 2002 also introduces specific coercive powers to assist with investigations into money laundering. These powers are more intrusive than were previously available in an investigation into the proceeds of crime and have been justified on the ground that the government is committed not only to prosecuting crime but also to confiscating the proceeds of crime. A code of practice provides guidance to the agencies exercising these powers.[135] The 2002 Act provides that in confiscation and money laundering investigations, applications can be made to a circuit judge for production orders, warrants for entry, search and seizure, and customer information and account monitoring orders. Amendments which relate to both the substantive money laundering offences in Part 7 of the 2002 Act and the reporting and disclosure obligations have now been introduced by the Serious and Organised Crime Act 2005. In order to deal with problems relating to double criminality, unless the Secretary of State orders to the contrary, overseas conduct will not be classed as 'criminal conduct' if it is lawful in another jurisdiction. There is no longer a reporting obligation unless information discloses the identity of an alleged offender or the whereabouts of criminal property, and a defence of reasonable excuse is introduced for failing to disclose. The 2005 Act provides for the creation of the Serious and Organised Crime Agency, which replaces the National Criminal Intelligence Service and the National Crime Squad. This agency will now receive Suspicious Activity Reports (SARs) and conduct criminal investigations into money laundering activities and other serious criminal activity.

11.3.6.2 Money Laundering Regulations

Exercising powers conferred under s 2(2) of the European Communities Act 1972, the Government introduced the Money Laundering Regulations 1993[136] to give effect to the Council Directive 91/308/EEC[137] which relates to measures on prevention of the use of the financial system for the purpose of money laundering. This Directive was one of the early international initiatives

---

134 Ibid, s 6.
135 Ibid, s 377.
136 SI 1993/1933.
137 Council Directive 91/308/EEC on prevention of the use of the financial system for the purpose of money laundering OJ 2001 L 344/76.

in the fight against money laundering. Under the 1993 Regulations, financial institutions are required to establish and maintain procedures which would deter money laundering activities. The Regulations were designed to ensure persons engaged in relevant financial business activities in the UK took appropriate measures to help staff identify and prevent money laundering. Financial institutions were required to establish reporting systems and to set up training programmes for employees on the law and practice relating to anti-money laundering measures. The Regulations also required institutions to obtain adequate evidence of the identity of new applicants for business and, where persons were acting on behalf of another person, to take reasonable measures to obtain satisfactory evidence of the identity of the other person. Failure to comply with these regulations was punishable by a fine or imprisonment. The 1993 Regulations which were updated in 2001 have now been replaced by the 2003 Regulations.[138]

Money laundering for the purpose of the 2003 Regulations 'means an act which falls within s 340(11) of the Proceeds of Crime Act 2002 or an offence under s 18 of the Terrorism Act 2000'.[139] Under these Regulations, persons seeking to form a business relationship, or conduct a one-off transaction in the course of a relevant business, must ensure compliance with a variety of procedures. These include: record keeping and internal reporting procedures; identification checks on applicants for business; and training to enable staff to recognise money laundering transactions. Casino operators are required to obtain satisfactory evidence of identity of all high spending customers. Failure to maintain these procedures will result in criminal liability. The Regulations require the Commissioners of Customs & Excise to keep a register of money service operators and a register of high value dealers and provide the Commissioners with powers to enter, search and seize documents and, in some circumstances, to impose a civil penalty. The Regulations also impose a duty on a 'supervisory authority' to inform the police if it knows or suspects that someone has been involved in money laundering. For the purposes of the Money Laundering Regulations, the Bank of England, the Office of Fair Trading and the Gaming Board of Great Britain are supervisory authorities.

---

138 SI 2001/3641.
139 A draft of 5 Nov 2002; SI 2003; Money Laundering Regulations 2003, reg 2.

Chapter 12

Other transnational offences

12.1 CYBERCRIME

Recent developments in the field of information technology have given rise not only to rapid expansion in e-commerce but also to innovative forms of criminal behaviour and have provided new methods by which traditional criminal offences can be committed.[1] Using the Internet and other computer networks to commit crime has created serious problems for national legislative bodies and national law enforcement agencies. The rapid growth in cyber-crime may restrict the development of e-commerce, which depends on safe systems for money transactions, as businesses struggle to make their computer networks and data more secure. Undoubtedly, self-regulation by the high tech industry can play an important role in preventing the proliferation of com-puter and Internet-related crime.[2] In addition to implementing technical measures to protect computer systems, legal and non-legal measures must be introduced to prevent and deter criminal activities. While self-regulatory mechanisms to combat misuse of the new technologies have many advantages over external regulation, to be effective self-regulation needs to be supported by appropriate national legislation and international agreements. However, many of the measures proposed by both national and international agencies to tackle the problem of cybercrime arguably inhibit the legitimate use and

---

1 See generally Y Akdeniz, C Walker and D Wall (eds), *Internet, Law, and Society*, 2000, Har-low: Longman; P Norman, 'Policing "High-Tech Crime" in the Global Context: The Role of Transnational Policy Networks', in D Wall (ed) *Crime and the Internet: Cybercrimes and Cyberfears*, 2001, London: Routledge, pp 184–94; V Ruggiero, 'Criminals and Service Pro-viders: Cross-National Dirty Economies', 28 *Crime, Law and Social Change* (1997), 27–38; C Walker and Y Akdeniz, 'The Governance of the Internet in Europe with Special Reference to Illegal and Harmful Content', *Crim LR* [1998], December Special Edition: *Crime, Criminal Justice and the Internet*, pp 5–19; D Wall (ed) *Crime and the Internet*, 2001, London: Routledge.

2 See, eg, the Internet Service Providers Association (ISPA) which requires members to abide by a Code of Practice, the Internet Watch Foundation (IWF) and work undertaken by Microsoft's anti-counterfeiting team.

development of information technology and violate the right to freedom of expression and the right to privacy.

Cybercrime offences can include: using the Internet for illegal money transactions; violation of copyright by means of a computer system; gaining unauthorised access to data held on a computer with the intention of committing a serious criminal offence; computer-related fraud, forgery or money laundering; intentionally hindering the functioning of a computer system by transmitting viruses or deleting computer data; and the distribution of child pornography. Attacks against information systems which form part of the critical infrastructure of States is referred to as cyber terrorism. The transnational nature of computer-related crime, which is generally committed in 'cyberspace', adds a jurisdictional complexity to the investigation and prosecution of cybercrime. Substantive criminal law and procedure varies from State to State and police investigative powers usually do not extend beyond national borders.[3] Lack of harmonisation in criminal legislation has led to difficulty in establishing a common definition of cybercrime, and criminal investigations are hampered because cross-border evidence gathering is dependent upon both formal and informal international police co-operation.[4] However, while the law and practice in relation to mutual legal assistance in criminal matters has been notoriously slow and laborious, cybercrime is a rapidly developing phenomenon.

Concerned at the acceleration of high tech crime, and keen to signal the need to intensify international co-operation in the fight against cybercrime, ministers from the G7/G8 States[5] recommended at the French summit in 1996 that:

> States should review their laws in order to ensure that abuses of modern technology that are deserving of criminal sanctions are criminalised and the problems with respect to jurisdiction, enforcement powers, investigation, training, crime prevention and international co-operation are adequately addressed – States are urged to negotiate bilateral or multilateral agreements to address the problems of technological crime investigation.

---

3 For further discussion see DL Speer, 'Redefining Borders: The Challenges of Cybercrime', 34 *Crime, Law and Social Change* (2000), 259.

4 See, for example, 'League Against Racism and Antisemitism (LICRA), French Union of Jewish Students v Yahoo! Inc. USA, Yahoo! France', 1(3) *Electronic Business Law Reports* [2001], 110–20. Case analysis by Y Akdeniz at <http://www.cyber-rights.org/documents/yahoo_ya.pdf>.

5 The Group of Eight (G8) is comprised of the Heads of State of the major industrial democracies. This group holds an annual summit to discuss significant economic and political issues. Summit decisions can generate new initiatives to deal with global issues. At the time of the Lyon summit, the group was comprised of seven states and Russia. Since 1998 Russia has been admitted as a full partner. The G8 states are Canada, France, Germany, Italy, Japan, Russia, USA and the UK.

Subsequently, at the Denver Summit in 1997 the G8 leaders issued a *communiqué* stating its intent to focus on the 'investigation, prosecution and punishment of high-tech criminals, such as those tampering with computer and telecommunications technology, across national borders'. Further meetings have resulted in establishing an action plan to combat high tech crime, which has been endorsed by the EU Justice and Home Affairs Council, and a network of law enforcement experts.

While the G8 States continue to develop recommendations to combat the problem of crime in cyberspace, many other initiatives have been launched at both the international and national level. These include the Council of Europe Convention on Cybercrime[6] and the Additional Protocol, the European Commission Communication on Cybercrime,[7] the EU Forum on Cybercrime, the Organisation for Economic Co-operation and Development Guidelines for the Security of Information Systems and Networks,[8] the Australian Cybercrime Act 2001, and the National High Tech Crime Unit in the UK. Whether these schemes represent an adequate response to the problem of cybercrime and also achieve a balance between the interests of the information technology industry and the consumer, the needs of the law enforcement agencies and the protection of fundamental rights is open to question.

12.1.1 Council of Europe initiatives

12.1.1.1 Council of Europe Convention on Cybercrime

This Convention (Cybercrime Convention) is the first international treaty to address the commission of crime committed via the Internet and other computer networks. It aims to facilitate the detection, investigation and prosecution of cybercrime and to provide arrangements for efficient and reliable international co-operation. This initiative introduces a range of substantive, procedural and mutual legal assistance measures designed to deter the misuse of computer systems, networks and computer data. Following four years of discussions and many drafts, the Cybercrime Convention was opened for signature in November 2001. States eligible to sign and ratify the Convention include Member States of the Council of Europe and non-Member States which have participated in the drafting process. It entered into force on 1 July 2004 when it was ratified by at least five States, which included three States from the Council of Europe. Currently, the Convention has been signed but not ratified by 25 States, including the UK, and signed and ratified by 18 states including the US.[9] By adopting appropriate legislation and encouraging

6 ETS 185.
7 COM (2000) 890.
8 DSTI/ICCP/REG (2002) 6.
9 The US Senate voted to ratify the Cybercrime Convention on 1 Aug 2006.

international co-operation, the Convention aims to establish a common criminal policy which will protect society from cybercrime. Opposition to ratification has focused on concerns about the lack of legal safeguards for privacy rights and the absence of a double criminality provision. In the preamble reference is made to the need to maintain a balance between the interests of law enforcement and respect for fundamental rights. Its provisions supplement existing multilateral and bilateral mutual legal assistance and extradition treaties. In addition to providing law enforcement agencies with powers to search and intercept computer networks, the Convention addresses infringements of copyright, computer-related fraud, child pornography and violations of network security. On 7 November 2002, the Council of Ministers adopted an Additional Protocol to the main Cybercrime Convention which makes it an offence to use the Internet to publicise racist and xenophobic propaganda.

The Convention has four chapters. Chapter I provides common definitions of some basic concepts including 'computer system', 'network', 'computer data' and 'service provider'. Chapter II, which is subdivided into three sections, deals with substantive criminal law and procedure and matters of jurisdiction. The list of offences set out in s 1 include offences against the confidentiality, integrity and availability of computer data systems, computer-related fraud and forgery, offences related to child pornography and offences related to infringements of copyright. Contracting parties are also required to implement legislation which makes it an offence to attempt, aid and abet the commission of the substantive offences. Measures must be taken to provide national authorities with appropriate powers and procedures to undertake effective criminal investigations and prosecutions. Thus measures must be taken to allow the prompt preservation of stored computer data and disclosure of traffic data, production orders, search and seizure of data stored in a computer, real-time collection of traffic data and the interception of content data. However, these powers must be balanced by procedural protections, which may include judicial or other independent supervision. This chapter concludes with provisions relating to jurisdiction.

Chapter III calls for parties to make liberal use of existing mutual legal assistance agreements and extradition arrangements for the purpose of investigating and prosecuting criminal offences. However, in the absence of a mutual assistance treaty, parties can use the provisions set out in Art 27 of this Convention. Requests for assistance may not be refused solely on the ground that the request relates to a fiscal offence and the rules relating to double criminality are relaxed. Specific mutual assistance provision is made in relation to expedited stored computer and traffic data and the accessing of stored computer data. Mutual assistance is not required for parties to gain access to publicly available stored computer data located in the territory of another party. Provided consent is obtained from the person with lawful authority to disclose data through a computer system, transborder access is also available without recourse to mutual assistance measures. Acknowledging that assistance can be required at any time, provision is made for a '24/7 Network'. Chapter IV contains the standard provisions relating to signature, entry into force, territorial application and reservations which are generally found in Council of Europe treaties.

12.1.2 EU initiatives

12.1.2.1 European Commission Cybercrime Communication[10]

The EU Action Plan to combat organised crime, which was adopted in May 1997 by the Justice and Home Affairs Council and endorsed by the European Council, contained a request for a study to be undertaken into computer-related crime. The European Commission, the executive body of the EU, presented the findings of this study, known as the COMCRIME study, to the Council in April 1998. It provided the European Commission with reliable, current information on legal aspects of computer-related crime and established a database of relevant national criminal statutes on computer crime.[11] The Cybercrime Communication, which was issued in 2001 considers the recommendations made by this study, is entitled *Creating a Safer Information Society by Improving the Security of Information Infrastructures and Combating Computer-Related Crime*.[12] One of the main issues addressed by this initiative was the need for effective action to deal with threats to the integrity, confidentiality and availability of information systems. It was considered necessary to take account of the views of all interested parties including service providers, network operators, consumer groups, data protection authorities and law enforcement agencies. Privacy issues should also be addressed. This Communication was the European Commission's first comprehensive policy statement on cybercrime which included proposals for EU Framework Decisions relating to child pornography and the spread of computer viruses. Taking account of this Communication, the European Parliament published a Recommendation entitled a Strategy for Creating a Safer Information Society.[13] The main aim of the COMCRIME study was to analyse the legal issues and to recommend a range of strategies to tackle the problem of computer crime. The researchers noted that, at the time, most legislation dealing with computer-related crime was linked to economic offences such as computer fraud and theft of intellectual property. However, public concern

10 COM (2000) 890.
11 The report of the study *Legal Aspects of Computer-Related Crime in the Information Society – COMCRIME* is available at <http://europa.eu.int/ISPO/legal/en/crime/crime.html>.
12 COM (2000) 890.
13 A5-0284/2001.

regarding the availability of illegal material on computer networks was on the increase. National authorities seldom considered using non-legal remedies to solve the problem, preferring to use the criminal law. Research revealed a lack of harmonisation with respect to the substantive criminal law, the range of coercive powers given to prosecuting authorities to investigate and prosecute computer crime and criminal jurisdiction. Nationally, there was also a lack of consistency regarding responsibilities imposed on the computer industry. While international responses to the problem were improving, the co-ordination of these activities remained a cause for concern. Suggestions made by international organisations were criticised as being too vague and for tending to focus too much on legal issues.

The research indicated that the international dimension of computer-related crime required international measures to combat it. It was submitted that the amount of data transferred via the Internet meant that national strategies would most likely fail and could create havens for cybercriminals. Consideration should be given to non-legal solutions, which would include measures to foster self-regulation by the computer industry and education of both business and private users. These measures were considered likely to be more effective than criminal law solutions and presented less risk to civil liberties. In addition, it was recognised that the problem created by the new information technologies would not be solved by recourse to tradition legal remedies. An effective solution required a new doctrine of information law which dealt with a new range of rights and responsibilities. Thus tackling the problem of computer crime would involve introducing measures which made use of a range of both legal and non-legal remedies which included technology, education, industry and the law.

Using these four remedies, the report listed specific recommendations. Non-legal recommendations included: improving intelligence with respect to the analysis of the links between high tech crime and organised crime; raising awareness and educating the consumer; increasing research with respect to computer security and international codes of conduct for the industry. Legal measures under the First and Third pillars of the Treaty of European Union (TEU)[14] should focus on directives which would identify the responsibility of Internet service providers and require Member States to create effective sanctions against clearly defined offences. Further, joint action and framework decisions should be adopted with respect to fostering transborder investigations, jurisdictional conflicts should be addressed and a set of common rules for record keeping in police and judicial statistics should be created. It was suggested that the European Commission should start its work by organising an international conference involving all parties interested in the fight against computer crime.

14 1993 OJ L293/61.

Taking account of these recommendations and the work undertaken by the Council of Europe and other international bodies including the G8, the European Commission issued a Communication which highlighted the need for a comprehensive EU policy initiative which aimed to improve the security of information infrastructures and to combat cybercrime. Prior to drafting the Cybercrime Communication, the Commission consulted with representatives from law enforcement agencies throughout the Member States, the EU advisory body on data protection[15] and members of the telecommunications industry. The Commission identified the need for an EU instrument to ensure Member States had in place effective sanctions to combat child pornography on the Internet. It would also seek to bring forward legislative proposals under Title VI of the 1992 TEU to harmonise substantive criminal law in the area of high tech crime. This would include offences related to hacking and denial of service attacks. In addition to promoting the creation of specialised police computer crime units at local level, it aimed to introduce measures to facilitate computer-related investigations involving more than one Member State. Non-legislative measures would include establishing an EU Forum on Cybercrime which would raise public awareness of the risks posed by cybercrime and would facilitate co-operation between all parties interested in tackling computer crime.

The forum is now operational and provides a website, a series of plenary sessions and expert group meetings. This initiative assists law enforcement agencies, civil liberty organisations, consumer representatives, ISP providers, telecommunications operators and data protection authorities to consider methods of promoting best practice to increase computer security and combat cybercrime. In addition, the Commission intended to continue to promote security awareness in the context of the *e*Europe initiative.[16] In June 2001, the European Commission issued a further communication entitled 'Network and Information Security: Proposal for A European Policy Approach',[17] which developed some of the matters addressed in the Cybercrime Communication. In addition to emphasising the importance of international co-operation and the need to increase public awareness, this Communication provided an overview of threats posed to security. The focus of the latter Communication was on preventative measures and technical support. While examining the range of options open to the EU, the Commission has warned that the solutions chosen should not hinder the development of the Internal Market nor undermine the protection of fundamental rights. Thus any measures taken to prevent and combat misuse of the new technologies must comply with the EU Charter on Fundamental Rights, Art 6 of the TEU and the jurisprudence of the ECJ.

---

15 See Directive 95/46/EC, Arts 29 and 30.
16 See *Europe 2002: An Information Society for All*, 14 June 2000.
17 COM (2001) 298.

Responding to these initiatives, the European Parliament recommended that the Council and Commission establish a coherent strategy aimed at maintaining international communication networks as a global, free market place in order to allow everyone to pursue lawful activities and to prevent criminal activities which interfere with civil liberties and the public interest. It also recommended that the Commission draw up common definitions and proposals to resolve conflicts of jurisdiction between Member States in order to make it easier to prosecute and punish those responsible for cyber-crime offences.[18] It was further recommended that the Commission propose legislative and non-legislative initiatives to enable a general framework to be established for a policy on computer-related crime. In order to encourage self-regulation, the Council and the Commission were encouraged to obtain the co-operation of those working in the field of information technology and urged to ensure that legislation did not place excessive burdens on the industry. Research into preventative techniques, such as encryption, should be encouraged and security should be developed and implemented by the industry. The scope for user self-protection should be increased and preventative technology measures implemented by the consumer.

The recommendation proposed that the Council clearly define the role of Europol and Eurojust in respect of cybercrime to avoid duplication of internal databases and to increase co-ordination of activities, and to ensure that these bodies remained subject to democratic control and comply with the *acquis communutaire* on the protection of personal data.[19] Further, leading jurists from Member States should be invited to attend a conference to discuss all aspects of cybercrime including problems associated with jurisdiction, human rights issues, evidential questions and the setting up of specialised 'cyber-courts'. Insofar as the EU is responsible, the Council and Commission were recommended to define clearly the measures available to law enforcement agencies for the collection of evidence in order to comply with the rules set out in existing instruments addressing mutual legal assistance provision. The recommendation emphasised that any coercive measures must strike a balance between effective prevention and punishment of offences, the legitimate interests of users and respect for fundamental rights, which includes the right to privacy and the protection of personal data. Thus, while international initiatives should be encouraged, care must be taken to maintain a balance between the interests of law enforcement and the need to safeguard

---

18 Recommendation by the European Parliament on the Strategy for Creating a Safer Information Society by Improving the Security of Information Infrastructures and Combating Computer-related Crime (2001/2070/COS).

19 The Council of the EU has expressed concern that the definition of computer crime in the Annex to the 1995 Europol Convention is insufficiently precise and proposed adding a specific definition which would include all forms of attack on automated data processing systems.

fundamental rights and freedoms of citizens. Accordingly, no one may be forced to incriminate themselves by revealing encryption codes and data must not be transferred to a State which will not guarantee an equivalent degree of protection as guaranteed by Art 8 of the European Convention on Human Rights.

12.1.2.2 European Union Safer Internet Action Plan

Several EU initiatives have focused on the issue of self-regulation within the computer industry. In January 1999, the European Parliament adopted a four-year Community action plan designed to promote 'safer use of the Internet by combating illegal and harmful content on global networks'.[20] This Safer Internet Action Plan initiative, which was allocated a budget of EUR 25 million, recognised the need not only to support and promote self-regulation mechanisms within the industry but also to co-ordinate the work of the self-regulating bodies and to raise public awareness. The action plan covered four areas of activity which included creating a safer environment, developing filtering and rating systems, encouraging awareness and a range of supporting activities such as addressing legal questions arising from Internet use. In order to achieve the objective of promoting safer use of the Internet, a range of activities would be undertaken in Member States under the guidance of the Commission. Thus funding allocated to the action plan is available to establish a network of hotlines to receive calls from users finding offensive material on-line and to develop European guidelines on codes of conduct for the industry. Financial support is also available for projects that encourage the industry to introduce content monitoring schemes, filtering tools and rating systems which allow parents and teachers to select appropriate content for children. In addition support was given to projects fostering international co-operation and exchange of best practice at both the European and inter-national level and which aim to co-ordinate self-regulating activities across Europe. At the end of the first two years of the Action Plan, the Commission was required to submit an evaluation report to the European Parliament.

In March 2002, the Commission submitted a proposal to the European Parliament to amend and extend the action plan for a further two years. The Commission sought to include EU candidate States in the action plan's activities and to extend its coverage to include new online technologies including mobile and broadband content, online games and all forms of real-time communication. It also wanted to give more attention to other forms of illegal and offensive material communicated via the Internet including child pornography, racism and violence. Before approving this request, Parliament is required to assess the progress of the original Action Plan and examine the

---

20 Council Decision 276/1999/EC.

new proposal. Accordingly, the Commission's proposal was referred to the Committee on Citizens' Freedoms and Rights, Justice and Home Affairs for its opinion. The Committee appointed a rapporteur to assist with the task of evaluating the achievements and shortcomings of the current Action Plan and to examine the new tasks mentioned in the proposal. In the Committee's draft report on the new proposal it was noted that, although many projects had received funding, many of the goals set out in the original Action Plan remained unfulfilled.[21] It was noted that the Commission's evaluation report revealed that although a network of hotlines had been established in some Member States, contact details were not readily available. While the University of Oxford had been contracted to conduct research into self-regulatory attempts in the media and to develop models of self-regulation which, hopefully, would lead to proposals for a European Code of Conduct, no project was looking specifically at the quality labelling system for suppliers of Internet services. Further, although several filtering projects had been financed, no project focused on validating existing filtering software and conducting security tests against counterattacks, and the awareness-raising projects failed to make best use of the new media to distribute information. Finally, the Commission's report did not indicate whether there had been a response to the European Parliament's call for tenders for an assessment of the legal questions raised by either the content or the use of the Internet, and no conference had been organised in the past four years. In the light of these shortcomings, the rapporteur considered it would be inappropriate to extend the original Action Plan beyond introducing amendments which emphasised the importance of the measures still to be taken and to include co-operation with the candidate States.

In March 2003, the European Parliament and the Council of the European Union acknowledged that more time was needed for actions to be implemented to achieve the objectives of the original Action Plan and to take account of the new online technologies, and agreed to amend the original Community Safer Internet Action Plan.[22] The activities to be undertaken in the second phase of the Action Plan include: completing the hotline network in all Member States and adapting best practice guidelines to new technology; promoting self-regulation through the systematic reporting of legal and regulatory issues and providing assistance to candidate States keen to set up regulatory bodies; focusing on benchmarking of filtering software services and providing assistance for developing filtering technology; encouraging user-friendly content rating by bringing together the industry, content providers, regulatory and self-regulatory bodies and consumer associations; providing support for awareness-raising initiatives and to exchange best

21 COM (2002) 152-C5-0141/2002–2002/0071 (COD).
22 COM 2002/0071 (COD).

practice on new-media education; providing support for sociological research into children's use of the new technologies in order to develop educational and technological means for protecting them from harm; supporting networking and information sharing and developing methods which promote international co-operation including establishing a Safer Internet EU Forum. A further EUR 13.3 million was set aside for the second phase of the Action Plan. In 2006 an independent evaluation by a team of experts found that the Safer Internet programme had been effective in improving safer internet use, particularly for children, and that it also took account of the need to respect freedom of expression.[23] Its main achievements included the European network of national hotlines for end users to report illegal content anonymously and the creation of national awareness nodes. In order to consolidate these outcomes, the Commission is due to implement the Safer Internet plus programme in 2007–2008 which will promote combined hotlines and awareness nodes. Acknowledging the need to encourage parental awareness of filtering tools, the Commission is funding an assessment of the filtering software and filtering services currently available. It will also fund pilot projects to encourage co-operation between hotlines and law enforcement agencies. The Commission has also established the eEurope 2005 Action Plan to develop an effective environment for e-business. This programme includes maintaining a secure information infrastructure and increasing Internet security. Following the adoption of Regulation (EC) No 460/2004, the European Network and Information Security Agency (ENISA) was established to respond to information security problems.[24] This agency became operational in September 2005. In addition to assisting the European Commission in the technical aspects of updating and developing Community legislation in the field of network and information security, its main aim is to provide assistance and advice to Member States and businesses on network security issues.

12.1.2.3 Council Framework Decisions

In April 2002 the European Commission adopted a proposal for a Council Framework Decision on attacks against information systems.[25] Member States were required to implement it no later than 31 December 2003. The main objective of this initiative was to harmonise the substantive criminal law in the area of high tech crime, which would facilitate police and judicial co-operation within the EU. The definition of 'information systems' for the purpose of this proposal covers not only networks and Internet servers but

---

23 The final evaluation of the project can be accessed at <http://europa.eu.int/information_society/activities/sip/programme/evaluations/index_en.htm> (accessed on 1 Dec 2006).
24 Further information is available at <http://www.enisa.europa.eu>.
25 OJ C 203E (27 Aug 2002).

also personal computers and mobile phones. It addresses illegal access to and interference with electronic networks and computer data, and covers both hardware and software. It deals with international hacking, distribution of viruses and website defacement. The Framework Decision which was eventually adopted on 24 February 2005[26] creates a common set of legal definitions and criminal offences and supplements other European initiatives, including EC Directives on telecommunications and data protection.[27] The criminal offences covered by the Framework Decision require an intention to unlawfully access or interfere with information systems. It aims to criminalise serious attacks against information systems and does not cover minor offences. Member States must ensure that the offences attract sentences of at least 12 months' imprisonment, which should be increased to at least two years if committed within the framework of a criminal organisation. States must also establish a point of contact for the exchange of information which must be available around the clock. Consequently, this has become known as the 24/7 Network.

In order to address the problem of online child exploitation, the Council adopted the text of a Framework Decision on combating the sexual exploitation of children and child pornography.[28] This initiative, which was adopted in December 2003 aims to achieve a common level of approximation of criminal law in this area by penalising most forms of possession and distribution of child pornography. Member States are required to introduce legislation to makes it a criminal offence for individuals or legal persons to use a computer system to produce, distribute, disseminate or transmit child pornography. Similarly, the Framework Decision requires states to penalise the acquisition and possession of child pornography. It is also an offence to instigate, aid, abet or attempt to commit these offences, which will be aggravated if the victim is below the age of consent under national law, or if serious harm is caused to the child or a criminal organisation is involved. The penalty for these offences, which the Decision states should be 'effective, proportionate and dissuasive,' is usually a sentence of imprisonment for 12 months to three years, or five to ten years for the aggravated offence. States are required to take the necessary measures to comply with this initiative by 20 January 2006. The Commission will assess compliance by 20 January 2008.

26 Framework Decision 2005/222/JHA, OJ L 69 (16 March 2005).
27 Directive 95/46/EC OJ L 281 and Directive 97/66/EC OJ L 024.
28 Council Framework Decision 2004/68/JHA OJ L 13/44.

12.1.3 International initiatives

12.1.3.1 The Organisation for Economic Co-operation and Development Security Guidelines[29]

Users of global information systems and networks have been aware for some time of the risks created by lack of security. However, until recently security was not always at the forefront for those responsible for designing, managing and providing information systems. Similarly, business and private users did not always appreciate the extent of the risk. Following the events of 11 September 2001, cyber security became an international matter. In 2002, the Organisation for Economic Co-operation and Development (OECD) issued a revised set of guidelines entitled *Guidelines for the Security of Information Systems and Networks: Towards a Culture of Security*.[30] These non-binding guidelines, which were the result of lengthy discussions between government experts, representatives of the information technology industry, business users and consumer groups, aim to develop a 'culture of security' among all participants who develop, service, manage and use global information networks by raising awareness of security risks and promoting sound security practices. The Guidelines, which were adopted as a Recommendation of the OECD Council in July 2002, have been taken into account by both national and international bodies concerned with improving the security and reliability of information network systems.

The Guidelines encourage governments, businesses and individual users of information networks to take account of nine basic principles. These principles refer to the need to promote awareness, responsibility and co-operation in the matter of information network security and to respect ethical and democratic values. Account should also be taken of the need to reduce vulnerability by regular risk assessment and to incorporate security design in information networks. All participants are urged to review and reassess the security of existing systems and to make the necessary modifications to security policies, measures and practices. Additionally, the promotion of a culture of security requires the implementation of initiatives to encourage international co-operation. These Guidelines formed the basis of a UN Resolution on cybercrime which has been adopted by the 57th session of the UN General Assembly.[31]

29 The OECD is an intergovernmental organisation established in 1961 to facilitate the harmonisation of national economic policies. In order to achieve its main objective of promoting economic growth, trade and development, it makes available to its members information which facilitates the process of rational policy making.

30 DSTI/ICCP/REG (2002) 6.

31 A/RES/57/239.

12.1.4 National initiatives

Drafting specialist legislation that not only provides prosecuting authorities with sufficient coercive powers to investigate and prosecute cybercrime but also adequately preserves fundamental rights has presented national legislative bodies with a significant challenge. Unless legislation designed to combat cybercrime is clear, comprehensive and well focused, competent cybercriminals will be able to exploit loopholes and avoid prosecution. Although several States have created a specific legislative framework to deal with computer and Internet-related crime, including offences designed to protect the integrity of computer data, developments in computer and Internet technology frequently outstrip the legislative process. In 2001, the Australian Federal Government introduced legislation which focuses on activities directed at computer technology rather than the more traditional criminal offences which are committed via the computer. The Cybercrime Act 2001, which entered into force in December 2001, contains provisions relating to the dissemination of computer viruses, computer hacking and unauthorised access to or modification of data held in a computer or unauthorised impairment of communications to or from a computer with the intention of committing a serious offence. The offence of unauthorised impairment of electronic communications, which carries a maximum penalty of 10 years' imprisonment, makes it an offence to circulate a diskette containing a computer virus that aims to infect a target computer through an innocent agent. This legislation also makes it an offence to obstruct communication links. Thus sending a high volume of emails to an address with the intention of crashing a computer system is an offence. Further, it is an offence to gain unauthorised access to restricted data held in a computer and to assist others to commit a computer offence. In order to assist police officers gather evidence held on electronic equipment, prosecuting authorities are given the power to access data held on computers at locations other than the address on the search warrant.

Encryption and computer passwords can cause problems for police officers seeking access to computer data. The Cybercrime Act 2001 provides the prosecuting authorities with compulsory powers to obtain information or assistance sufficient to enable an officer to gain access to computer data. Thus a person with the requisite knowledge can be compelled, in appropriate circumstances, to provide the authorities with the necessary information. This provision may give rise to problems relating to the privilege against self-incrimination. Following a Parliamentary Joint Commission into recent trends in the practice and methods of cybercrime in 2004, the Australian Crime Commission recommended a legislative package which penalises the grooming of children for sexual exploitation and detects and prosecutes those who use information technology for the trade of child pornography.[32]

Over the last six years, the UK government has also introduced legislation aimed at dealing with cybercrime. Under the Computer Misuse Act 1990 it is an offence to gain unauthorised access to computer material, known as hacking, or to use a computer system with intent to commit or facilitate the commission of a serious crime. The 1990 Act also created the offence of unauthorised modification of computer material. The Police and Justice Act 1996, ss 35–37 has introduced several amendments to the 1990 Act including increasing the sentence for hacking from five to ten years, re-working the offence of unauthorised modification to cover the denial of service attacks and creating a new offence of making, supplying or obtaining articles for use in computer misuse offences. Several measures have been introduced in the UK to tackle the problem of the sexual exploitation of children via the Internet, including the creation in April 2006 of the Child Exploitation and Online Protection Centre. Further, using the Internet to groom children for sex is an offence under the Sexual Offences Act 2003, and the Police and Justice Act 2006 provides for the forfeiture of indecent photos of children.[33]

Practical challenges to the successful investigation and prosecution of cybercrime can range from lack of technical training for police officers to issues relating to jurisdiction arising from the transnational nature of Internet-related crime. Local police forces may lack the resources to equip personnel with the necessary high level of technical expertise and specialist investigative skills necessary to tackle computer and Internet-related crime. In common with many other States, the UK's approach to this problem has been to establish specialist units which are staffed by personnel equipped with the necessary investigative, forensic and computer skills. These units not only deal with the investigation and prosecution of cybercrime but also provide advice and support at the local level. Police forces throughout the UK now have computer crime units which deal with computer-based fraud and other computer-related crime. These units work in conjunction with other specialist police units and the National Infrastructure Security Co-ordination Centre (NISCC) which provides an emergency response team. NISCC, which was set up in 1999 is an inter-departmental centre using expertise from a range of government departments, including Defence and Trade, and law enforcement agencies. Its website provides information and advice on threats to IT systems. In 2001 a National High-Tech Crime Unit was established to provide police forces and businesses throughout the UK with information, advice and

---

32 The Australian Criminal code, s 218A prohibits the use of electronic communication with the intent to procure a person under the age of 16, or expose such a person to any indecent matter.
33 The Sexual Offences Act 2003, s 15 makes it an offence for a person aged 18 or over to meet a child under 16 in any part of the world if he has met or communicated with the child on at least two earlier occasions and intends to commit a 'relevant offence'.

assistance on computer crime and crime prevention. This unit, which was staffed by personnel from the National Crime Squad, HM Customs & Excise and the National Criminal Intelligence Service, was divided into four sections dealing with investigations, intelligence, support, and forensic retrieval. Its jurisdiction was restricted to investigations into the distribution of illegal and offensive material, computer hacking and computer-related fraud, offensive electronic communications and the dissemination of computer viruses. Since 1 April 2006 this unit became part of the Serious Organised Crime Agency (SOCA) and now operates under the title of SOCA e-Crime.[34]

12.2 BRIBERY OF FOREIGN PUBLIC OFFICIALS

Corruption and, in particular, bribery of foreign public officials was until recently considered merely an issue pertinent to each country's domestic laws and commercial practices. Another reason for industrialised States not extending extra-territorial jurisdiction against nationals or domestically registered corporations known to have bribed public officials of third nations was because the prospects of investments abroad were obviously perceived as boosting national economies, regardless of their unethical acquisition. On a short-term scale, this may be true for a local economy, but IMF studies have revealed that corruption is negatively linked to the level of investment and economic growth.[35] Moreover, bribery may also constitute an act of unfair competition[36] and also have a serious impact on the enjoyment of fundamental human rights.[37]

The US was the first country to enact extra-territorial legislation prohibiting bribery of foreign public officials by US nationals or corporations of any type, which are either controlled by US nationals, or which have their principal place of business in the US, or are organised under US laws.[38] 'Bribery', under the Foreign Corrupt Practices Act (FCPA) 1977, is the offer of

---

34 This agency was established under the Serious and Organised Crime Act 2005 to manage criminal intelligence and undertake national and international investigations into serious crime. This unit merges NCIS (National Criminal Intelligence Service), NCS (National Crime Service, which included the National High Tech Crime Unit) and parts of Customs and Excise and the Immigration Service.

35 V Tanzi and H Davaodi, 'Corruption, Public Investment and Growth', IMF Working Paper 97/139, 1997.

36 International Chamber of Commerce, *Revisions to the International Chamber of Commerce Rules of Conduct on Extortion and Bribery in International Business Transactions*, 35 ILM (1996), 1306, p 1307.

37 *Report of the Working Group on Contemporary Forms of Slavery*, UN Doc E/CN4/Sub2/1999/17 (20 July 1999), para 53, which describes corruption as an inescapable element in the struggle against contemporary forms of slavery.

38 1977 FCPA, 15 USC, §§ 78a, 78dd-1, 78dd-2 (Supp 1997).

payment of money or anything in value to an official of a foreign government or a political party with corrupt intent for business purposes. This definition excludes so called 'facilitating payments' intended to expedite otherwise lawful government action, as well as any payments permitted in accordance with the laws of the foreign State.[39] This legislation, although a bright light in the darkness of international business corruption, was rightly seen by US corporations and their foreign subsidiaries as placing them at an onerous disadvantage against their international competitors who were not susceptible to such laws.

US-led efforts to achieve global normative consensus on the international criminalisation of foreign bribery prompted various organisations to confront this issue for the first time. In 1975, the General Assembly of the UN passed Resolution 3514 condemning bribery by transnational and multinational corporations and the United Nations Economic and Social Council (ECOSOC) was directed to formulate a code of conduct regarding payments in international trade. Although an ad hoc Working Group on Corrupt Practices was established and produced a draft Agreement on Corrupt Practices, lack of support from developed nations eventually shelved the project. At the same time, the OECD established a Committee on International Investment and Multinational Enterprises (CIME) with the purpose of drafting a relevant code of conduct. On 21 June 1975, the OECD Ministerial Conference adopted a Declaration on International Investment that prohibited the solicitation and payment of bribes to foreign officials, as well as other unlawful political contributions.[40] However, it was not until 1994, and the adoption by the OECD Council of a Recommendation on Bribery in International Business Transactions,[41] that mounting pressure had paved the way for establishing concrete normative guidelines on international corruption. This Recommendation called upon OECD Member States to deter bribery through their national legislation and practice, especially by amendment of any tax laws that permit or favour bribery and further urged them to facilitate international co-operation. CIME was designated as a monitoring body, ordered to review the status of the Recommendation after three years. On the instigation of the US, the OECD Council adopted, on 11 April 1996, a Recommendation calling upon States to re-examine their laws on tax deductibility concerning bribes paid to foreign public officials – preferably by treating such bribes as illegal – the majority of which were often listed as

---

39 See L H Brown, 'The Extra-Territorial Reach of the US Government's Campaign Against International Bribery', 22 *Hastings Intl & Comp L Rev* (1999), 407, pp 410–16; MK Hurst, 'Eliminating Bribery in International Business Transactions', 6 *JILP* (1997), 111.

40 Likewise, the International Chamber of Commerce issued a report in 1977 containing Rules of Conduct to Combat Extortion and Bribes in connection with retaining or obtaining business, requiring the adoption of codes of conduct and rigorous accounting controls by participating States. These Rules were revised in 1996, reprinted in 35 ILM (1996), 1306.

41 OECD Doc C(94)75/FINAL (27 May 1994), 33 ILM (1994), 1389.

commissions or fees.[42] In accordance with its mandate, on 23 May 1997 CIME submitted a Revised Recommendation on Combating Bribery in International Business Transactions, which the OECD Council subsequently adopted.[43] This instrument recommended the adoption of specific legislative proposals in every field of national laws – criminalisation of bribery, non-recognition of tax deductibility, enforcement of adequate accounting, independent external audit, internal company controls, transparency in public procurement and international co-operation – and eventually formed the basis for the OECD's 1997 Convention on Combating Bribery of Foreign Officials in International Business Transactions (OECD Convention).[44] Art 1(1) of this Convention makes it a criminal offence for any person:

> Intentionally to offer, promise or give any undue pecuniary or other advantage, whether directly or through intermediaries, to a foreign public official, for that public official or for a third party, in order that the official act or refrain from acting in relation to the performance of official duties, in order to obtain or retain business or other improper advantage in the conduct of international business.

It is also an offence under the Convention to be involved in instances of bribery through acts of complicity, incitement, aiding or abetting, attempts or conspiracy.[45] Article 1 also covers bribes paid for the benefit of third parties, otherwise one would avoid liability by forwarding the benefit to a third party, such as a political party. This definition of bribery of foreign public officials is entirely consistent with similar international instruments, such as the 1996 Organisation of American States (OAS) Inter-American Convention Against Corruption,[46] the 1997 EU Convention on the Fight Against Corruption Involving Officials of the EC or Officials of Member States of the

---

42 1996 Recommendation on the Tax Deductibility of Bribes to Foreign Public Officials, OECD Doc C(96)27/FINAL (17 April 1996), 35 ILM (1996), 1311; following publication in May 1997 of the OECD's Committee on Fiscal Affairs (CFA) *Report on the Recommendation on Tax Deductibility*, which noted that in 12 Member States bribes to foreign officials were 'in principle' deductible offences; the majority of these States re-examined their tax legislation. See op cit, Brown, note 39, p 494.

43 OECD Doc C(97) 123/FINAL (29 May 1997), 36 ILM (1997), 1016.

44 37 ILM (1998), 1; the most significant changes to the FCPA 1977 made by the International Anti-Bribery and Fair Competition Act 1998, which is intended to implement into US law the OECD Convention, are that it adds officials of public international organisations to the definition of 'foreign officials' and expands US jurisdiction both to acts committed by US nationals wholly abroad, without a nexus requirement to US interstate commerce, and also to acts committed by non-US nationals while in the USA: Pub L No 105–366, 112 Stat 3302 (1998). See SD Murphy, 'Contemporary Practice of the US Relating to International Law', 93 *AJIL* (1999), 161.

45 1997 OECD Convention, Art 1(2).

46 Art 4(1).

EU,[47] the 1999 Council of Europe Criminal Law Convention on Corruption[48] and the 2000 CATOC.[49] Although illicit enrichment is an offence in two of the above instruments,[50] advantages collected by foreign public officials are generally recognised as not constituting bribery if they are permitted by statute or case law of the official's country, or are in fact 'facilitation payments'.[51] The FCPA provides an exception to the foreign bribery offence for any facilitating or expediting payment whose purpose is 'to expedite or to secure the performance of a routine governmental action'. A few countries, namely Italy and Hungary provide a statutory defence to the bribery of a foreign official where such an official has coerced the individual to provide the benefit.[52]

The 1997 OECD Convention renders legal persons responsible for acts of bribery and subject to financial and administrative sanctions[53] and the 1997 EU Convention makes explicit reference to the criminal liability of heads of businesses – defined as the people having power to exercise control or take decisions – where an act of bribery was performed by a person under their authority acting on behalf of the business.[54] Significantly, as of 2006, 12 parties to the 1997 OECD Convention had established the criminal responsibility of legal persons (Australia, Belgium, Canada, Finland, France, Iceland, Japan, Korea, Norway, Switzerland, UK and the USA), while six a non-criminal form of responsibility (Germany, Greece, Hungary, Mexico, Italy and Sweden). Of the latter six, Hungary, Mexico and Sweden provide for criminal sanctions but do not consider the liability as criminal *per se*.[55] The liability of the legal person is generally linked to the acts of management or someone in a senior position (the 'directing mind' principle), but a newer trend has emerged whereby the legal person will still incur liability where senior management has delegated decision-making authority to lower level employees, or where such employees are under the direction or supervision of senior management.[56] The offence contemplated is an extraditable one,[57] subject to the usual qualification of bilateral extradition treaties between the parties concerned.

The relevant anti-bribery conventions confer territorial jurisdiction on

---

47 Arts 2 and 3, distinguishing between 'passive' and 'active' corruption. 1997 OJ C195/1, 37 ILM (1998), 12.
48 ETS 173.
49 Art 8, UN Doc A/55/383 (2 Nov 2000).
50 1996 OAS Convention, Art 11; GA Res 51/191 (16 Dec 1996), containing the UN Declaration against Corruption and Bribery in International Commercial Transactions.
51 'Commentaries on the 1997 OECD Convention', 37 ILM (1998), 8, p 9.
52 OECD Mid-Term Study on the 1999 Treaty, OECD Doc. DAF/INV/BR/WD(2005)19/REV5, paras 83–86.
53 1997 OECD Convention, Arts 2 and 3(2).
54 1997 EU Convention, Art 6.
55 OECD Mid-Term Study, op cit, note 52, para 116.
56 Ibid, paras 137–144. For an analysis of international corporate liability see Chapter 2, section 2.9.
57 1997 OECD Convention, Art 10; 1997 EU Convention, Art 8.

States parties where at least part of the offence takes place on their territory. The OECD has rightly criticised those States parties to the 1997 Convention whose legislation provides that prosecution can only commence where the victim or the government of the State where corruption took place file a complaint.[58] In the majority of cases, if not all, the government is complicit in the corrupt act and the legal standing of a victim – other than the government – is uncertain, but may include a competing corporation and the rightful owners of their country's resources, its people. The application of the nationality principle of jurisdiction to legal persons is determined:

(a) in accordance with the law of the place where the legal person is incorporated (common law countries);
(b) the effective seat of the legal person (civil law countries); or
(c) on the basis of the nationality of particular individuals.

The responsibility of the parent company for the acts of the subsidiary is a complex issue which finds inconsistent regulation in the various States. Some countries require a sufficient connection between the subsidiary and the parent, whereas in others it would be necessary to demonstrate direction or authorisation by a directing mind.[59] Interestingly, although possibly restricted in practice, four parties to the OECD Convention, namely Belgium, Hungary, Iceland and Norway, apply universal jurisdiction to foreign bribery.[60]

Besides the stress on interstate co-operation, treaties and non-binding instruments alike either urge or oblige parties to adopt sound economic regulatory and disclosure procedures, auditing, surveillance of public officials and initiate prosecutions in cases of corruption.[61] The 1997 OECD Convention established a monitoring mechanism under the supervision of the Working Group on Bribery in International Business Transactions, incorporating both a reporting system and an examination procedure for each Member State.[62] In 1996, the World Bank's Board of Executive Directors revised the organisation's Guidelines for Loans and Credits by requiring that all parties to a transaction that is financed by the Bank observe the highest standards of ethics and that in case of corrupt practice the Bank is to reject financing proposals.[63] The World Bank has taken concrete action regarding bribes allegedly paid to win contracts for the Lesotho Highlands Water Project, a dam construction

58 OECD Mid-Term Study, op cit, note 52, para 237.
59 Ibid, paras 247–48.
60 Ibid, para 252. For an analysis of universal jurisdiction see Chapter 4, section 4.6.
61 International Chamber of Commerce, *Revisions to the Rules of Conduct on Extortion and Bribery in International Business Transactions*, 35 ILM (1996), 1306; 1997 OECD Convention, Art 8; GA Res 51/191 (16 Dec 1996).
62 1997 OECD Convention, Art 12.
63 The World Bank, *Guidelines for Procurement under IBRD Loans and IDA Credits*, 1996, p 7.

venture partly funded by the Bank. It has provided financial assistance to the Lesotho Government's investigation into the corruption allegations, stating further that if a company were discovered to have paid bribes it could be excluded from participating in any World Bank projects elsewhere.[64] Another possible deterrent for States seeking to attract investment is the annual publication by Transparency International – a private organisation – of its *Corruption Perception and Bribe Payers Indexes*. A country's poor performance on the Index may result additionally in heavier loan guarantees for prospective investors, which in itself may turn out to be a primary disincentive.

It is obvious that bribery of foreign public officials has been finally recognised as a contemporary scourge, an international offence that is a threat to commerce, stability and the enjoyment of human rights. Whatever may be the domestic practice with regard to other international offences, the application of the 'act of State' and similar doctrines is incompatible with the purposes of the above anti-corruption treaties, as these instruments are, by their nature, intended to regulate acts of public officials. It would, thus, be absurd to hold that solicitation and receipt of bribes constitutes a public act of a foreign State committed on its territory, and, hence, not one susceptible to the criminal jurisdiction of other States, as this defeats the object and purpose of the relevant conventions.

Equally, a significant link must be recognised between the corrupt acts of a government that deprive its people from sustenance, or the means and resources of natural sustenance and crimes against humanity. Under Art 7(2)(b) of the ICC Statute, extermination as a crime against humanity may be perpetrated by the intentional deprivation of access to food that is calculated to bring about the destruction of part of a population. Article 30(2)(b) of the ICC Statute states that a person has intent 'in relation to a consequence, [where] that person means to cause that consequence or is aware that it will occur in the ordinary course of events'. Such *dolus eventualis* suffices to hold members of government responsible for crimes against humanity perpetrated against their own people in peacetime by placing them in conditions of life, which in the ordinary course of events would deprive them of access to sufficient food and medical care.[65]

12.3 INTERNATIONAL POSTAL OFFENCES

Although channels of postal communication had been established since at least 255 BC, it was not until the 17th century that the first postal treaty was

---

64 'Dam Builders Charged in Bribery Scandal', BBC News, 19 Nov 1999.

65 For an elaboration of this possibility, see I Bantekas, 'Corruption as an International Crime and Crime against Humanity: An Outline of Supplementary Criminal Justice Policies', 4 *Journal of International Criminal Justice* (2006), 466.

agreed, consisting of bilateral agreements governing the transit of mail within several European countries. The enormous growth in postal communications which subsequently ensued at a global level was later regulated on the basis of bilateral arrangements, using a multitude of postal rates, units of measurements and currencies, which by the mid-19th century warranted a radical reform in order to ensure some uniformity. At a conference convened in Berne between September and October 1874 and attended by representatives from 22 nations, an agreement establishing the General Postal Union was adopted. In 1878, and in reflection of growing membership, the organisation's name was changed to Universal Postal Union (UPU).

Although the aim of the UPU Conventions was to unify the regulation of postal activities, the 1878 Convention expressed the Union's concern over the unlawful use of the mails by private individuals.[66] Article 11 forbids the public to send by mail letters or packets containing gold or silver substances, pieces of money, jewellery, or precious articles, as well as any packets containing articles liable to customs duty. The successive UPU Conventions since 1878, each terminating its predecessor, clearly established two categories of offences: (a) the fraudulent use of counterfeit postage stamps or used stamps, as well as the fraudulent manufacture and distribution of forged or imitated stamps; and (b) the illegal use of the mails.[67] The list of objects falling in this latter category included, besides articles subject to customs duty and precious items, any other articles which by their nature would expose postal officials to danger, or damage the correspondence, as well as explosive, inflammable or other dangerous substances.[68] The list was later expanded to include narcotic drugs and obscene articles.[69] The wording of Arts 18(5) and 20 of the 1920 UPU Convention strongly suggests that only the acts of counterfeiting postage stamps and the insertion of narcotic drugs in the mails were recognised as constituting international offences, since, with respect to all other unlawful usages, there did not exist an express obligation to prevent and punish the offenders. This wording has been consistently applied in subsequent UPU Conventions[70] and the 1964 Final Protocol to the Universal Postal Union Constitution obliged Member States additionally to prevent and punish the insertion of explosives or other easily inflammable substances in postal

---

66 1 Bevans 51; 1885 Additional Act to the 1878 Convention, Art VIII, elaborated that the sending by mail of precious articles was prohibited only in case the legislation of the countries concerned forbade their being placed in the mails or being forwarded. Reprinted in 1 Bevans 97.

67 Eg, 1906 UPU Convention, Arts 16(3) and 18, 1 Bevans 492.

68 1906 UPU Convention, Art 16(3).

69 1920 UPU Convention, Art 18(1), 2 Bevans 282.

70 1924 UPU Convention, Arts 41 and 79, 2 Bevans 443; 1929 UPU Convention, Arts 45 and 80, 2 Bevans 873; 1939 UPU Convention, Arts 46 and 81, 3 Bevans 539; 1964 Final Protocol to UPU Constitution, Art 14, TIAS 5881.

articles.[71] With the adoption of the 1994 UPU Postal Parcels Agreement, it is clearly discernable that under customary international law it is an offence to:

(a) counterfeit stamps or international reply coupons, as well as to fraudulently manufacture or imitate such stamps and coupons;[72]
(b) insert narcotic drugs and psychotropic substances in postal items;[73] and
(c) insert explosive, flammable or other dangerous substances in postal items where their insertion has not been expressly authorised by UPU Conventions.[74]

As regards all other objects that are prohibited from being placed in postal items, the penalisation of the act itself is not addressed in the UPU Conventions and Protocols and is, therefore, dependent on the regulations employed by each individual country.[75] In any case, the sender of such objects incurs civil liability as a result of the UPU Conventions and Protocols, as long as the relevant instrument has been transposed into domestic law. Although no relevant mention is made in the UPU Conventions, jurisdiction over the aforementioned international postal offences is based primarily on the subjective territorial principle (that is, the place where the illegal postal item was mailed, or where the stamps were counterfeited), but also on objective territoriality (that is, the country of destination or the country of transit if the illegal item was discovered there, and the country where economic loss was suffered as a result of the counterfeiting). Other legitimate bases of jurisdiction cannot be excluded. In all cases of illegal use of the mails, it will hardly seem appropriate to national prosecutors to charge an accused with a postal offence usually carrying a lighter penalty, especially where other domestic provisions relating to drug offences or offences against the person can be applied instead.

Other postal offences such as mail fraud,[76] which in the US alone is responsible for defrauding private individuals of over USD100 million annually, constitute domestic crimes, albeit with a transnational character. The combating of this type of activity is at present pursued at an interstate level through the co-operation of the afflicted States. The UPU, recognising the need for postal security, established the Postal Security Action Group in 1989 with the aim of

---

71 1964 UPU Constitution Final Protocol, Art 14(e).
72 1994 UPU Postal Parcels Agreement, Art 58(1.1)–(1.3).
73 Ibid, Art 58(1.4); this is confirmed in the 1988 UN Convention against Illicit Traffic in Narcotic Drugs and Psychotropic Substances, Art 19, which obliges parties to adopt appropriate legislation in order to apply investigative and control techniques designed to detect illicit consignments of narcotic drugs in the mails. Reprinted in 1988 UST LEXIS 194.
74 Ibid, Art 58(1.4).
75 US federal law, eg, penalises the mailing of obscene or crime inciting matter. See Obscenity Act 1948, 18 USC § 1461; similarly, UK Postal Services Act 2000, s 85(3)–(5).
76 Mail Fraud Act 1948, 18 USC § 1341.

developing worldwide security standards, promoting the creation of internal security units in national postal administrations and establishing co-operation with other international organisations. For this purpose, it has been working closely with Interpol, drawing special emphasis on illicit drug-trafficking, child pornography and paedophile networks, as well as mail fraud and money laundering.

12.4 CIRCULATION AND TRAFFICKING IN OBSCENE PUBLICATIONS

Although most countries had, by the 19th century, enacted legislation out-lawing trafficking and possession of obscene publications,[77] it was not until 1910 that the first relevant treaty was adopted: the Agreement for the Suppression of the Circulation of Obscene Publications (the 1910 Agreement).[78] Prior to this Agreement, however, Member States to the 1906 UPU Convention could have relied on its Art 16(3)(2)(d) which prohibited the mailing of any articles whose importation or circulation was forbidden in the country of destination. This prohibition on the mailing of obscene material was later made explicit in Art 18(2)(d) of the 1920 UPU Convention and has been incorporated ever since in the international agreements of that organisation.[79] Despite the absolute prohibition in distributing obscene material established by the UPU Conventions and the 1910 Agreement, the elastic nature of the concept of obscenity from region to region has precluded international lawmakers from reaching a binding definition. The 1910 Agreement simply obliges parties to establish or designate a national authority charged with the duty of centralising and supplying information which would facilitate the repression of infringements under domestic law relative to obscene writings, drawings, pictures or articles, whose constitutive elements bear an international character.[80] The 1910 Agreement, therefore, did not intend to create an international offence, but merely to combat a transnational offence through domestic mechanisms. On the same basis, Art 1 of the 1923 Convention for the Suppression of the Circulation of and Traffic in Obscene Publications made it a punishable offence:

> (1) for purposes of or by way of trade or for distribution or public exhibition to make or produce or have in possession obscene writings, drawings, prints, paintings, printed matter, pictures, posters, emblems, photographs, cinematograph films or any other obscene objects;

77 Eg, UK Obscene Publications Act 1857.
78 1 Bevans 748.
79 1994 UPU Postal Parcels Agreement, Art 26(2), (5.3).
80 1910 Agreement, Art 1.

(2) for the purposes above mentioned, to import, convey or export or cause to be imported, conveyed or exported any of the said obscene matters or things, or in any manner whatsoever to put them into circulation;

(3) to carry on or take part in a business, whether public or private, concerned with any of the said obscene matters or things, or to deal in the said matters or things in any manner whatsoever, or to distribute them or to exhibit them publicly or to make a business of lending them;

(4) to advertise or make known by any means whatsoever, in view of assisting in the said punishable circulation or traffic, that a person is engaged in any of the above punishable acts, or to advertise or to make known how or from whom the said obscene matters or things can be procured either directly or indirectly.

It is evident that, although the participating States possessed a general understanding on what constituted obscenity, they were reluctant in reaching a definition, which, even if agreed upon, would involve such compromises that would only limit the scope of the Conventions.[81]

The complexity of this topic has subsequently raised threshold questions vis-à-vis the right to freedom of expression and legitimate commercial interests. In the *Handyside* case, a publisher was convicted under the UK's Obscene Publications Act (OPA) 1959 for distributing a children's book containing anti-authoritarian passages. Under Art 10(2) of the 1950 European Convention on Human Rights[82] the freedom of expression may be restricted, *inter alia*, as may be necessary in a democratic society for the protection of morals. The European Court of Human Rights held that, since it was impossible to find a uniform European conception of morals, Art 10(2) afforded national authorities a margin of appreciation, which, in the particular case, was legitimately aimed at protecting the morals of the young.[83] Likewise, the ECJ has held that, although Member States to the 1957 Treaty Establishing the European Economic Community[84] are free to make their own assessments of the indecent or obscene character of certain articles, they may not rely on the public morality provisions in the Treaty to prohibit the import of goods from other Member States when their own legislation contains no prohibition on the manufacture or marketing of the same goods on their territory.[85]

---

81 This did not change even with the latest instrument, the 1949 Protocol Amending the 1910 Agreement for the Suppression of the Circulation of Obscene Publications, TIAS 2164.

82 213 UNTS 221.

83 *Handyside* case (1976) 58 ILR 150.

84 298 UNTS 11.

85 *R v Hennand Darby* [1979] ECR 3795; *Conegate Ltd v HM Customs and Excise* [1986] ECR 1007.

As a transnational offence, individual countries are best suited to define obscenity and repress its distribution and circulation. In the UK the test of obscenity under s 1(1) of the OPA 1959 has been whether the contested article tends to deprave and corrupt persons who are likely to read, see or hear the matter contained or embodied in it. It is an offence under s 1(3) of the Act to publish an obscene article – including distribution, circulation, selling, letting on hire, giving, or lending – whether for gain or not.[86] Although not a strict liability offence, persons found to possess obscene material for the purpose of publication must prove that they had not examined them and had no reasonable cause to suspect their nature.[87] This statutory defence is limited to persons who were in possession of such material for a legitimate reason, or to individuals who were ignorant of and had no reason to believe that they were in possession of or distributing indecent material, as well as persons that had received it unsolicited and had got rid of it with reasonable promptness.[88]

Under US federal law, it is unlawful for anyone to bring into that country any 'obscene, lewd, lascivious, or filthy book, pamphlet, picture or other matter of indecent character . . . recording, [or] electrical transcription of the same nature'.[89] The test of obscenity procured by the Supreme Court is whether work taken as a whole appeals to prurient interest in sex, display of which is patently offensive, not serious literary, artistic, political or scientific value, based on community standards, not national.[90] Knowledge need only be of the general nature of the matter imported or transported, not whether it was known to be illegal.[91]

The growth of interstate communications and especially the potential which the Internet offers for the international transmission of pornography, has necessitated a re-examination of definitions and criminal jurisdiction. In the UK, s 84(3)(b) of the Criminal Justice and Public Order Act 1994 expanded the definition of photograph to include data stored on a computer disk or by other electronic means which is capable of conversion into a photograph. International repugnance against child pornography has developed a dynamic impetus as regards the suppression and criminalisation of all related

---

86 OPA 1959, s 2(1). An 'article' under s 1(2) of the Act can be anything embodying matter to be read or looked at, any sound recording and any other film or picture. Video cassettes were later found to fall within the ambit of this section. See *AG's Reference (No 5 of 1980)* [1985] 3 All ER 816.

87 Ibid, s 2(5); see also OPA 1964, s 1(3).

88 *Pepper v Hart* [1993] AC 593; this defence is not available to individuals who created the material or advertised its availability: *R v Land* (1998) 1 CAR 301.

89 Obscenity Act 1948, 18 USC § 1462 (importation or transportation of obscene matters).

90 *Miller v California,* 413 US 15 (1973).

91 *USA v Groner,* 494 F 2d 499 *cert denied*; similarly, persons who mailed prohibited material need not have produced it, being sufficient that they only knew of the general nature of the material when it was mailed. *USA v Thomas,* 726 F 2d 1191 (1982) *cert denied*.

activities.[92] Although child pornography constitutes a serious offence under the laws of all nations,[93] its circulation through the Internet poses jurisdictional problems where the offender is involved in transmitting material to a website which can be accessed by persons anywhere in the world. In a recent judgment, where the accused challenged the jurisdiction of UK courts on the basis that he had uploaded obscene material on a website in the US and, hence, there was no actual publication in England, the English Court of Appeal was of the opinion that publication could take place when uploaded onto a website abroad and downloaded elsewhere.[94] It is obvious that States wishing to suppress and prosecute child and other forms of pornography on the Internet can legitimately assert their jurisdiction based on the objective territorial principle, as all data uploaded on a website may be accessed from any national terminal, although other principles may alternatively be used.[95] Ratification of the 2000 Optional Protocol will undoubtedly make a significant impact in this regard, especially if participating States adhere to its provisions on effective co-operation.

---

92 See 2000 Optional Protocol to the Convention on the Rights of the Child on the Sale of Children, Child Prostitution and Child Pornography, Art 3(1)(c); on 6 Feb 1999 the EU adopted an Action Plan to combat illegal and harmful Internet contents such as child pornography and hate speech. Decision No 276/1999 (OJ L 33).

93 See, eg, *Osborne v Ohio*, 495 US 103 (1990).

94 *R v Graham* (2000) LTL, 6 April.

95 The 1923 Obscene Publications Convention, Art 2, permits both objective and subjective territorial jurisdiction, as well as nationality jurisdiction. The 2000 Optional Protocol, Art 4, establishes, in addition, broad jurisdictional competence following the language of the various anti-terrorist treaties.

Chapter 13

Extradition

13.1 INTRODUCTION

Extradition is the formal process whereby a fugitive offender is surrendered to the State in which an offence was allegedly committed in order to stand trial or serve a sentence of imprisonment. There is no general rule of international law that requires a State to surrender fugitive offenders and extradition arrangements proceed on the basis of a formal treaty or a reciprocal agreement between States. The increase in the mobility of suspects has resulted in the increased willingness of States to use this form of mutual legal assistance to enforce their domestic criminal law. While the US continues to prefer bilateral treaties as the legal basis for extradition, European States are increasingly reliant upon multilateral regional treaties. The process of extradition, which is founded on the concepts of reciprocity, comity and respect for differences in other jurisdictions,[1] aims to further international co-operation in criminal justice matters and strengthens domestic law enforcement. The absence of effective extradition arrangements can result in law enforcement agencies using extra-judicial and irregular forms of extradition. The law of extradition, which is a branch of international criminal law, is based on the assumption that the requesting State is acting in good faith and that the fugitive will receive a fair trial in the courts of the requesting State.[2] With regard to the principle *aut dedere aut judicare*, States embracing

---

1 *Kindler v Canada* (1991) 84 DLR (4th) 438, p 488.
2 However, in *Re Saifi* [2001] 4 All ER 168 the English Divisional Court was satisfied that it would be unfair and unjust to return the applicant to India on the ground that evidence supporting the request for extradition appeared to have been obtained in bad faith. See also *Gulay Asliturk v Government of Turkey* [2002] EWHC 2326, in which the English court held that it would be unjust or oppressive to return the applicant to Turkey in the absence of a denial by the Turkish Government that the accusation made against the applicant was political and not made in good faith. In *R v Secretary of State ex p Peter Elliot* [2001] EWHC 559, the court accepted that unless there was a real risk of denial of fair trial in the requesting State, issues affecting the fairness of the trial were best left to the trial itself.

the civil law tradition generally apply extra-territorial jurisdiction and prosecute persons for crimes committed in other jurisdictions in which their own nationals are either the offender or the victim. Thus, while the majority of Council of Europe States refuse to extradite their nationals, and some will also refuse to extradite their residents, States in the common law tradition such as the UK and Ireland cannot generally prosecute offences committed outside the jurisdiction.[3]

13.2 THE EXTRADITION PROCESS: GENERAL PRINCIPLES

While requests for extradition are traditionally made through diplomatic channels, extradition proceedings usually involve input from both the executive and the judiciary. Although a few States prefer to give exclusive control of the process to either the judiciary or the executive, most States prefer a hybrid system. In the UK, Canada and the US, for example, extradition is a two-step process involving a hearing at which a magistrate or judge considers whether the requesting State has complied with the formalities. Provided the court is satisfied that a legal basis for extradition exists, the fugitive will be committed to await surrender to the requesting State. The ultimate decision to surrender the fugitive is an act of executive discretion.[4] This decision lies with the Secretary of State in the UK and the US[5] and with the Minister of Justice in Canada. Arguably the law of extradition is procedural not substantive, and extradition proceedings are the means by which domestic criminal proceedings can be pursued abroad. The procedure governing the granting of extradition is subject to national law and is administered by national courts. States have adopted different rules with regard to the quality of evidence required before agreeing to a request for extradition. Some States adopt the rule of non-inquiry and refuse to inquire into the good faith or motive behind a request for extradition.

In order to facilitate international co-operation in the fight against serious crime, national courts have generally adopted a liberal interpretation of extradition treaties. In *R v Governor of Ashford ex p Postlethwaite*,[6] for example, the House of Lords considered that extradition legislation ought

---

3 The issue of jurisdiction was discussed in more detail in Chapter 4.
4 Acknowledging that the ultimate decision lay with the executive, in *St John v Governor of HM Prison Brixton* [2001] EWHC 543, the English Divisional Court observed that in extradition proceedings the potential issue of a violation of the European Convention of Human Rights arose when the Secretary of State decided to allow the request and not at the committal hearing.
5 The President delegates his authority to the Secretary of State.
6 [1988] AC 924, pp 946–47.

to be interpreted generously in order to facilitate extradition. Lord Bridge, referring to the *dictum* of Lord Russell in *Re Arton*,[7] considered this case to be good authority for the proposition that the court should not, unless constrained by the language used in the instrument, interpret any extradition treaty in a way that would hinder the working and narrow the operation of most salutary international agreements. This broad approach to the interpretation of treaties is consistent with current English practice. In *Re Ismail*,[8] for example, the German Government sought the return of a British national in connection with international fraud and issued a request for his extradition. Under the terms of the Extradition Act (EA) 1989 extradition could be granted in respect of an accused person.[9] It was submitted on behalf of the appellant that he was not a person accused within the meaning of the Act because he had not been formally charged. Lord Steyn considered that in transnational matters it was wrong to approach the construction of extradition treaties from the perspective of English criminal procedure. Without defining the term accused, their Lordships chose to adopt a purposive interpretation in order to accommodate differences between civil and common law systems.[10]

In some circumstances, States will refuse a request for extradition. Traditionally, extradition procedures have sought to offer a balance between judicial co-operation in the fight against crime and the need to protect the fundamental rights of the individual. Exemption from extradition generally provides the fugitive with some protection against unfairness. However, the rationale for exemption is often linked to the fact that extradition is still considered a sovereign act. Most modern extradition treaties seek to balance the rights of the individual with the need to ensure the extradition process operates effectively and are based on principles, regarded now as established international norms, which are designed not only to protect the integrity of the process itself, but also to guarantee the fugitive offender a degree of procedural fairness.[11] These principles include: the requirement that the fugitive has committed an extraditable offence, which is linked to the principle of double criminality; the rule of specialty; the political offence exception; the restriction on return for military and religious offences; the prohibition on return in death row cases; and the principle of double jeopardy.

---

7 [1896] 1 QB 108.
8 [1999] AC 320.
9 EA 1989, s 1(1)(a).
10 This approach to the meaning of 'accused' in an extradition treaty has also been applied by the Privy Council in *Rey v Government of Switzerland* [1998] 3 WLR 1.
11 See C Gane and S Nash, 'Illegal Extradition: The Irregular Return of Fugitive Offenders', 1 *Scottish Law & Practice Quarterly* (1996), 277.

13.2.1 Double criminality

The majority of extradition treaties require the double criminality rule to be satisfied. Traditionally, extradition proceedings have been reserved for persons who have allegedly committed a serious offence and thus, based on the maxim *nulla poena sine lege*, a request for extradition will only be granted if the alleged conduct of the fugitive amounts to a crime in both the requesting and the requested State. This is known as the double criminality rule. The principle of reciprocity has resulted in most States complying with the principle of double criminality, ensuring that a requested State is not forced to extradite a fugitive for conduct which it does not regard as criminal. Extradition can be challenged during the extradition proceedings on the basis that the offences mentioned in the request are not extradition crimes. While European extradition treaties generally define an extradition crime by reference to the minimum level of punishment in both States, it has been the usual practice in the UK and the US for extradition treaties to provide a list of specific extradition crimes. The list method has many drawbacks. Extradition can only be granted for offences included in the list, thus, treaties require constant updating to keep abreast of new offences. Furthermore, generally the requested State has no jurisdiction to inquire into the substantive criminal law of the requesting State to determine whether the conduct amounts to an extraditable offence.[12] In order to avoid problems, most modern treaties adopt the practice of defining extradition offences by reference to a minimum level of punishment. Accordingly, in order to determine whether the double criminality requirement has been satisfied, the requested State need only consider the seriousness of the penalty and is not required to examine whether the conduct amounts to a crime in both jurisdictions. In the UK, for example, s 2 of the EA 1989 limited extradition to conduct in the territory of a foreign State which, if it occurred in the UK, would constitute an offence punishable with imprisonment for a term of 12 months, or any greater punishment, and which, however described in the law of the foreign State, is so punishable under that law. The requesting State is required to provide information that enables the requested State to assess whether the principle of double criminality is satisfied. However, there is no obstacle to prevent a fugitive who returns voluntarily from being tried for non-extradition crimes. Having been advised, erroneously, that the offences in the extradition request were extradition crimes, the applicant in *Neil Walker v Governor of HM Prison Nottingham*[13] waived his right to an extradition hearing and agreed to return to the UK. The court found that he had returned voluntarily and thus had not been extradited. On arrival in the UK, he was in the same position as anyone

---

12 English courts are restricted to an examination of English law: see *Re Nielsen* [1984] AC 606.
13 [2002] EWHC 39.

arriving unescorted on a self-purchased ticket and there was no obstacle preventing him from being tried for the offences charged.

Where States exercise jurisdiction on the basis of territoriality, the double criminality rule can be problematic in respect of extra-territorial and transnational offences.[14] While civil law States generally prosecute regardless of whether the fugitive's conduct took place wholly or partially outside their territory, common law States have traditionally taken a different view. Difficulties arising in respect of extradition for extra-territorial offences have been addressed in some States by domestic legislation. In the UK, for example, Pt III of the EA 1989 provided that extradition can be granted provided the fugitive's conduct would constitute an extra-territorial offence against the law of the UK.[15] However, unless cases came under Pt III of the EA 1989, the concept of jurisdiction based on territoriality placed a limitation on extradition from the UK. In *Al-Fawwaz v Governor of Brixton Prison and Another*,[16] the US sought the applicant's extradition alleging that he conspired with others in an Islamic terrorist organisation to murder US citizens, diplomats and other internationally protected persons. The applicant objected to his extradition on the grounds that while it was accepted that the offence was within the jurisdiction of the US, the offence took place outside the territorial jurisdiction of the English court. The respondent submitted that, in order to be classed as an extraditable crime it was sufficient for the offence to be indictable in the UK, even if on an extra-territorial basis. The Divisional Court observed that Sched 1 to the EA 1989, which required that an extradition offence must be an offence under the domestic law of the requesting State and English law, governed extradition to the US. Accordingly, in this case it was not sufficient that the conduct alleged was indictable under the extra-territorial jurisdiction of the UK.[17] However, the court noted that, in special cases, English courts do have jurisdiction over crimes of an international nature. Section 1(3) of the Internationally Protected Persons Act 1978, for example, provides that it is an offence under domestic law for any person anywhere in the world to do prohibited acts in relation to an internationally protected person. Provided extradition was sought for this type of offence, domestic legislation provided for extradition in respect of offences

---

14 See G Mullan, 'The Concept of Double Criminality in the Context of Extra-Territorial Crimes', *Crim LR* [1997] 17.

15 See EA 1989, Pt III.

16 [2001] UKHL 69.

17 EA 1989, Sched 1, provided that where an Order in Council under the EA 1870, s 2, was in force in a foreign State, EA 1989, Sched 1, had effect in relation to that State subject to the limitations contained in the Order. The relevant Order was the USA (Extradition) Order 1976 SI 1976/2144 which provides that fugitives liable to be surrendered were persons accused or convicted of an extradition crime committed within the jurisdiction of the relevant foreign State.

committed within the jurisdiction of the requesting State. In dismissing this application, the Divisional Court was satisfied that the acts relied on by the US Government to found a case of conspiracy sufficed to establish the required jurisdiction.

The House of Lords was called upon to consider the double criminality principle in respect of extra-territorial offences in *R v Bow Street Metropolitan Stipendiary Magistrate ex p Pinochet Ugarte (Amnesty International and Others Intervening) (No 3)*.[18] The applicant was a former Head of State of Chile. Following his arrival in the UK in 1998, the Spanish Government issued a request for his extradition in respect of offences of torture and conspiracy to torture committed against Spanish citizens in Chile. The House of Lords was asked to consider, *inter alia,* whether the applicant had been accused of any extradition crime within the meaning of s 2 of the EA 1989. Their Lordships observed that none of the acts of torture were committed by or against citizens of the UK or occurred in the UK. Further, the court noted that whilst most of the charges had no connection with Spain, the Spanish courts were satisfied that they had jurisdiction over all the crimes alleged. Having considered the correct interpretation of the EA 1989, the House of Lords was satisfied that the principle of double criminality required the fugitive's conduct to be a crime under both the law of Spain and the UK at the date it was committed, not merely at the date of the request for extradition. Since torture committed outside the UK was not a crime under UK law until 29 September 1988, only conduct occurring after this date could be considered to amount to an extraditable crime. This decision has been criticised on the ground that the court's interpretation of the relevant legislation was questionable and hindered international co-operation in criminal matters.[19]

Prior to granting a request for extradition, many treaties require the requested State to hold a judicial hearing at which the requesting State can be required to produce sufficient evidence to establish a *prima facie* case. While the requesting State is the sole arbiter[20] of the quantity and quality of the evidence that it places before the court, the requested State generally has no power to seek further evidence as a condition precedent to committal for extradition. Unless the extradition treaty states otherwise, the procedure with regard to extradition is governed by the law and practice of the requested State. However, any conflict between the terms of an extradition treaty and national law is settled in favour of national law.[21] Failure to produce sufficient evidence to satisfy the relevant domestic extradition legislation will result in the request being refused. In extradition proceedings, the requested State

---

18　[1999] 2 All ER 97. This case is discussed in further detail at the end of this chapter.
19　See further C Warbrick, 'Extradition Law Aspects of Pinochet 3', 48 *ICLQ* (1999), 958.
20　*R v Governor of Pentonville Prison and Another ex p Lee* [1993] 3 All ER 504, p 508.
21　*In re Nielsen* (1984) AC 606.

applies national rules when considering the admissibility of evidence. In *Al-Fawwaz v Governor of Brixton Prison and Another*, the examining magistrate admitted evidence from an anonymous witness after finding that the witness's evidence was not so inherently incredible that no jury could properly convict on it and that it corroborated the remaining evidence.[22] The Divisional Court was satisfied that the magistrate had exercised his discretion correctly according to English law and practice. Notwithstanding a preference in common law jurisdictions for oral testimony, extradition proceedings usually involve consideration of documentary evidence and only in a minority of cases will witnesses be called. In the event of a witness giving oral testimony inconsistent with a sworn statement, it may still be appropriate for the court to recommend extradition on the basis of the statement.[23] Under the 1957 European Convention on Extradition,[24] Member States are not required to furnish evidence of a *prima facie* case unless the requested State has entered a reservation to this effect. Arguably, the *prima facie* evidence requirement added an unnecessary complexity to the extradition process.[25] Prior to granting a request for extradition from a Member State, the requested State is only required to determine whether the alleged conduct constitutes an extradition offence. Extradition between EU States has now been replaced by a surrender mechanism known as the European arrest warrant (EAW), which is based on the principle of mutual recognition of judicial decisions.[26] The EAW abolishes many of the traditional bars to extradition including the double criminality requirement for 32 serious types of offence provided these offences are punishable in the issuing State by a sentence of imprisonment exceeding three years.[27] Member States can also opt out of the double criminality requirement for other offences.[28]

13.2.2 Specialty

The majority of extradition treaties contain reciprocal specialty provisions requiring States to undertake to prosecute the fugitive only in respect of

---

22 (2001) *The Times*, 4 Feb.

23 *Alves v DPP* [1992] 4 All ER 787.

24 ETS 24 (1957).

25 See, eg, *Re Nielsen* [1984] AC 606.

26 Council Framework Decision of 13 June 2002 on the European arrest warrant and surrender procedures between Member States (2002/584/JHA) OJ 2002 L 190/1. For further discussion see N Keijzer, 'The Double Criminality Requirement' in R. Blekxtoon (ed), *Handbook on the European Arrest Warrant*, 2005, The Hague, The Netherlands: TMC Asser Press. For further discussion see S Alegre and M Leaf, 'European Arrest Warrant: A solution ahead of its time?', JUSTICE, 2003, at 11.

27 Council Framework Decision of 13 June 2002 on the European arrest warrant and surrender procedures between Member States (2002/584/JHA) OJ 2002 L 190/1, Art 2(2).

28 Ibid, Art 2(4).

extradition crimes set out in the extradition request. The specialty rule aims to provide the fugitive with protection against unfair treatment in the requesting State and is linked historically to the political offence exception. In order to comply with the rule, the requesting State must give the fugitive an opportunity to leave the country before instituting criminal proceedings for any other offence. Under Art 14 of the 1957 European Convention on Extradition, for example, a person had 45 days to leave before being charged with a new offence. However, in specific circumstances exceptions to the specialty rule were permitted under the 1995 and 1996 EU Conventions on extradition. While the EAW has not removed the speciality requirement entirely for surrender between Member States, it has been further eroded. Member States are now permitted to waive specialty on a reciprocal basis with states that have made the same declaration.[29] States can also waive speciality in respect of further extradition to other Member States.[30] The specialty principle is so broadly recognised in international law and practice that it has customary international law status, and applies to treaty-based extraditions as well as to extraditions predicated on other bases.[31] Traditionally, specialty provisions have been applied strictly. In *USA v Rancher*, for example, the fugitive had been surrendered for murder but was tried for offences of cruelty.[32] Notwithstanding that the allegation of cruelty was founded on identical facts, the Supreme Court refused to allow the prosecution to proceed on the ground that cruelty was not an extraditable crime under the treaty. However, generally, the addition or substitution of further offences is permitted without violating the specialty rule provided the new offence arises from the same set of facts as the original offence and is an extraditable crime.

In some circumstances, the specialty rule appears to offer fugitives minimal practical protection. Notwithstanding the existence of specialty assurances in extradition treaties, changes in the political complexion of the requesting State can have unforeseen consequences. In *R v Governor of Brixton Prison ex p Osman (No 3)*[33] it was suggested that the application of the specialty provision requires the requested State to focus not only on the date of the extradition request, but also to consider any political changes which could occur in the future. At the time of the hearing, the People's Republic of China was preparing to resume sovereignty over Hong Kong, and the UK did not have an extradition arrangement with China. The applicant argued that the Government of Hong Kong could not guarantee his continued enjoyment of the specialty protection provided by the current extradition treaty with the

---

29 Ibid, Art 27(1).
30 Ibid, Art 28(1).
31 CM Bassiouni, *International Criminal Law: Procedural and Enforcement Mechanisms*, 1999, New York: Transnational, 236.
32 119 US 407 (1886).
33 [1992] 1 All ER 122.

UK. Accepting that no State can give an undertaking beyond its sovereign powers, nor could the UK require a State to give an undertaking to bind a different State, Russell LJ considered it wholly inappropriate to look beyond the specialty provision given by the current government of the requesting State. Similarly, in *R v Governor of Pentonville Prison ex p Lee*,[34] the applicant was reluctant to return to Hong Kong fearing that protections in extradition arrangements would not survive the change of sovereignty. He argued that the changing political situation was relevant to the application of the specialty principle. Noting that this approach would drive a coach and horses through the principle of comity and reciprocity, which underlies the basis of extradition,[35] the court should not look outside the framework of the protection undertaken at the time of the request.[36] Generally the issue of undertakings given by the requesting State is not a matter for the courts but for the executive during the surrender stage of the extradition process. Thus, a request can be made to the Secretary of State to exercise his or her discretion to refuse the request for extradition on the ground that the specialty rule fails to offer the defendant sufficient protection.

13.2.3 Re-extradition

The problem of re-extradition to a third State can also arise in connection with the specialty principle. Article 15 of the 1957 European Convention on Extradition provides that a person should not be re-extradited to a third State in respect of offences committed before surrender without the consent of the requested State. In *Bozano v France*,[37] for example, an Italian court convicted the applicant in his absence of the murder of a 13-year-old Swiss girl. He was eventually arrested in France. Notwithstanding the refusal by a French court to surrender Bozano to the Italian authorities on the ground that French law did not allow extradition following a conviction *in absentia*, the French Government ordered his deportation. He was taken to the Swiss border and handed over to the Italian authorities. Although the European Court of Human Rights upheld the applicant's complaint that his abduction was neither lawful nor compatible with his right to security of the person,[38] provided there has been no collusion between the trial State and the State of refuge, this method of returning a fugitive offender did not seem to violate the 1957 Convention. In *R v Secretary of State ex p Johnson*,[39] the English Divisional Court was called upon to consider, *inter alia*, whether it could

---

34 [1993] 3 All ER 504.
35 Ibid, p 510.
36 Ibid, p 511.
37 (1986) 9 EHRR 297.
38 As guaranteed by the European Convention on Human Rights, Art 5.
39 [1999] 2 WLR 932.

conduct an inquiry into the requested State's consent to re-extradite the fugitive. In 1992, the applicant was extradited from Austria to the UK on charges of fraud. During the course of the criminal proceedings in the UK, the Australian authorities requested the applicant's extradition for offences allegedly committed in Australia between 1988 and 1990. In 1994, the UK authorities obtained the consent of the Austrian authorities to the applicant's re-extradition in the form of a diplomatic note. Notwithstanding his subsequent acquittal on the fraud charges, the applicant was arrested in anticipation of a formal request from the Australian authorities, which was made in 1995. An order was eventually made in 1997 for the applicant's return to Australia to face charges of conspiracy to defraud. In rejecting the applicant's appeal, the court was satisfied that the UK authorities were entitled to extradite the fugitive to Australia provided consent had been obtained from the Austrian authorities prior to surrender as required by Art 15 of the 1957 Convention. Article 14 dealt solely with the issue of specialty and did not explicitly or implicitly forbid re-extradition. Indeed, the wording was sufficiently wide to permit the requested State to remove the fugitive from its territory by way of re-extradition or deportation. While Art 15 required that requested States consent to re-extradition, the requesting State had no obligation to inquire into the validity of this consent. To do so would transgress the principle which prevents assessment of validity of the act of a sovereign State done abroad by a sovereign authority.[40] Despite providing the opportunity for Member States to waive the specialty requirement, the EAW contains provisions that limit re-extradition to a third state for offences committed before surrender.[41]

13.2.4 Political offence exception

Traditionally, a State is not obliged to surrender persons wanted in connection with an offence which it considers to be of a political nature.[42] The political offence exception is a universally recognised principle of extradition law and is related to the principle of sovereignty.[43] It is justified by the need for States to remain detached from political conflict and protects the right of States to grant asylum to political refugees.[44] While the inclusion of the

---

40 [1999] 2 WLR 942.
41 Ibid, Arts 27(4) and 28(3)(d).
42 For a general discussion of this topic see C Van Den Wyngaert, 'The Political Offence Exception to Extradition: How to Plug the Terrorists' Loophole Without Departing from Fundamental Human Rights', in J Dugard and C Van De Wyngaert (eds), *International Criminal Law and Procedure*, 1996, Aldershot: Dartmouth, 524.
43 See, eg, its inclusion as a mandatory ground for exclusion in the United Nations (UN) Model Treaty on Extradition 1990, Art 3(a).
44 For further discussion, see H Lauterpacht, 'The Law of Nations and the Punishment of War Crimes', 21 *BYIL* (1944).

political offence exception in extradition treaties has offered some protection to fugitives from States seeking to silence political opponents, arriving at a satisfactory definition of political offence is frequently fraught with difficulties.[45] Although extradition treaties do not necessarily define the term 'political offence', the phrase 'offence of a political character' has generally been accepted as suggesting some opposition on the part of the fugitive to the requesting State. Thus, in determining whether the offence amounts to an offence of a political nature, the requested State may be required to consider both the motive of the requesting State and of the fugitive before deciding whether the request for extradition is *bona fides*.[46] This process might conflict with the rule of non-inquiry.

Although courts in the UK have for some years demonstrated some consistency in their approach to the problem of interpretation,[47] the definition of political offence has now been further refined. Following the decision in *Ex p Dunlayici*,[48] to qualify as a political offence the fugitive's political purpose must be directed against the government of the requesting State and linked to an existing or contemplated political struggle.

Arguably, States should not be obliged to surrender persons for extradition if the offence mentioned in the extradition request is incidental to civil unrest. However, US extradition treaties have traditionally limited this exception to purely political offences, which have been described as offences of opinion, political expression or those which otherwise do not involve the use of violence.[49] Nevertheless, in several high profile cases involving members of the Irish Republican Army the political offence exception was applied successfully in respect of offences of violence, and extradition denied. In *USA v Mackin*,[50] for example, the UK requested the return of the applicant from the US for offences related to the attempted murder of a British soldier in Northern Ireland. Extradition was refused on the basis that the offences listed in the extradition request amounted to political offences. Similarly, in *Re McMullen*, the US court refused to extradite the applicant, who was wanted in connection with the bombing of an army installation in England,

---

45 For further discussion, see B Swart, 'Human Rights and the Abolition of Traditional Principles', in A Eser and O Lagodny (eds), *Principles and Procedures for a New Transnational Criminal Law*, 1991, Freiburg: Herstellung Barth, 505–34.

46 *R v Governor of Pentonville ex p Cheng* [1973] AC 931.

47 See, eg, *Re Castioni* [1891] 1 QB 149; *Re Meunier* [1894] 2 QB 415; *R v Governor of Brixton Prison ex p Kolczynski* [1955] 1 QB 540; *R v Governor of Brixton Prison ex p Schtraks* [1964] AC 556; *R v Governor of Pentonville ex p Cheng* [1973] AC 931; *T v Secretary of State for the Home Department* [1996] 2 All ER 865.

48 (1996) *The Times*, 22 August.

49 Op cit, Bassiouni, note 31, p 241.

50 Case No 3–78–1899 MG (ND Cal 11 May 1979). For further discussion of this and the case below, see op cit, Bassiouni, note 31, pp 195 and 241.

on the grounds that the offence came within the political offence exception.[51] The political offence exception has also been applied by the Irish Supreme Court in extradition proceedings involving terrorist activities in Northern Ireland. In *Finucane v Mahon*,[52] for example, the defendant was wanted in connection with offences relating to the escape of prisoners from the Maze prison in Northern Ireland. In refusing the UK's request for extradition, the court held that if the offences were committed in furtherance of the campaign to create a united Ireland, the political offence exception would apply.

However, the increase in international terrorism has led to the willingness of States to limit the extent of the political offence exception, which is generally no longer applicable to crimes against international law. Accordingly, while the political offence exception has been described as the most venerable of the mandatory exceptions to extradition,[53] there are so many offences excluded from consideration in most extradition treaties that in practice it is rarely used successfully. Within Member States of the Council of Europe, for example, the scope of the political offence exception has been reduced by the European Convention on the Suppression of Terrorism,[54] which lists a range of offences associated with terrorism that are precluded from being regarded as political offences, and the 1975 Additional Protocol to the 1957 European Convention on Extradition, which specifically excludes war crimes and crimes against humanity from the definition of political offence.[55] Although race, religion or political opinion was considered as a ground for refusal of a request for surrender, it was decided that the EAW would abolish the political offence exception in relation to surrender between Member States.[56] The reduction in the scope of the political offence exception is also reflected in the approach taken by the judiciary towards terrorism and other politically motivated offences. In *T v Immigration Officer*,[57] for example, Lord Mustill observed:

> . . . during the 19th century those who used violence to challenge despotic regimes often occupied high moral ground, and were welcomed in foreign countries as true patriots and democrats. Now, much has

---

51 668 F 2d 122 (1981), 2nd Cir.
52 [1990] IR 165.
53 C Gane, 'Human Rights and International Co-operation in Criminal Matters', in P Cullen and W Gilmore (eds), *Crime Sans Frontieres: International and European Legal Approaches*, 1998, Edinburgh: Edinburgh UP, 162.
54 ETS 90 (1977).
55 ETS 86 (1979).
56 For further discussion see M Planchta and W van Ballegooij, 'The Framework Decision on the European Arrest Warrant and Surrender Procedures between Member States of the European Union' in R. Blekxtoon (ed), *Handbook on the European Arrest Warrant*, 2005, The Hague, Netherlands: Asser Press, at pp 17–19.
57 [1996] AC 742, pp 752–53.

changed. The authors of violence are more ruthless, their methods more destructive and undiscriminating; their targets are no longer ministers and heads of state but the populace at large. What I regard as the exceptional difficulty of this appeal is that the courts here, as in other legal systems, must struggle to apply a concept which is out of date.

13.2.5 Capital punishment

Many extradition treaties do not oblige requested States to surrender persons to States which enforce the death penalty, unless the requesting State gives an undertaking not to implement it. The 1957 European Convention on Extradition, for example, provides that contracting parties may refuse to surrender a person if the offence for which extradition is requested is punishable by death under the law of the requesting party, and if in respect of such offence the death penalty is not provided for by the law of the requested party or is not normally carried out unless the requesting party gives such assurance as the requested party considers sufficient that the death penalty will not be carried out.[58] However, as a consequence of the decision of the European Court of Human Rights in *Soering v UK*[59] contracting parties to the European Convention on Human Rights are required not to surrender persons to States where the death penalty could be applied, unless the requested State is satisfied that it will not be carried out. In this case, the US requested the extradition of the applicant from the UK on charges of capital murder. If the UK agreed to surrender the applicant, he faced the possibility of spending a long time on death row. Exposure to the death row phenomenon, he argued, would amount to inhuman and degrading treatment and would violate a right guaranteed by Art 3 of the European Convention on Human Rights.[60] In finding for the applicant, the Court held that liability was incurred by the extraditing contracting State by reason of its having taken action which has as a direct consequence the exposure of an individual to proscribed ill-treatment. This case raises the vexatious question of conflicting treaty obligations.[61] In order to avoid problems with extradition to the US, contracting States have been willing to accept assurances from the US authorities. The UK Extradition Act 2003, for example, allows extradition to death penalty states provided a written assurance is given that a death sentence will not be imposed or, if

---

58 See 1957 European Convention on Extradition, Art 1, ETS 24 (1960).

59 (1989) 11 EHRR 439.

60 The Convention for the Protection of Human Rights and Fundamental Freedoms was signed at Rome on 4 Nov 1950 and is known as the European Convention on Human Rights, ETS 5 (1950); UKTS 71 (1953).

61 For further discussion of this matter, see C Van Den Wyngaert, 'Applying the European Convention on Human Rights to Extradition: Opening Pandora's Box', 39 ICLQ (1990), 212.

imposed, will not be carried out.[62] These undertakings have been sufficient to satisfy the European Court of Human Rights. Nevertheless, the position regarding parties to the European Convention on Human Rights and extradition to death penalty States is clear. There is an obligation on contracting parties to refuse a request for extradition where there are substantial grounds for believing that a person would face a real risk of being subjected to torture or ill-treatment in the receiving State.[63] A similar approach to death penalty States is taken by the Canadian Supreme Court in respect to Art 7 of the Canadian Charter. Thus in *USA v Burns and Rafay*,[64] a potential death penalty case, the Court disapproved a decision of the Minister of Justice to surrender a fugitive without first seeking assurances that the death penalty would not be carried out. The death penalty issue is less of a problem for States adhering strictly to the rule of non-inquiry, which prohibits courts in the requested States from inquiring into matters taking place outside the jurisdiction and, thus, prevents consideration of the treatment of offenders in the requested State.[65]

13.2.6 Fiscal offences and offences under military law

Arising from a reluctance to become involved in the enforcement of another State's fiscal law, extradition was traditionally refused in respect of tax and customs offences unless contracting parties had expressly agreed to the inclusion of fiscal offences in the treaty. However, the growth in financial crime generally, and drug-trafficking and money laundering specifically, has led to the increased willingness of States to include fiscal offences in extradition treaties.[66] States continue to be reluctant to extradite persons for offences under military law which are not also offences under ordinary domestic criminal law.[67]

13.2.7 Double jeopardy

Many extradition treaties acknowledge the principle of double jeopardy and include exemptions for persons who have already been tried and discharged

---

62 Extradition Act 2003, section 94.

63 *Hilal v UK* (2001) 33 EHRR 2.

64 QL (2001) SCJ 8.

65 For discussion of the position in the US, see op cit, Bassiouni, note 31, p 247.

66 See, eg, Second Additional Protocol to the 1957 European Convention on Extradition and the Council of Europe Convention on Laundering, Search, Seizure and Confiscation of the Proceeds of Crime, Art 2, 30 ILM (1991), 148. For further discussion of international measures to combat money laundering see Chapter 11.

67 See, eg, the UN Model Treaty on Extradition, Art 3 and the 1957 European Convention on Extradition, Art 4, ETS 24 (1960).

or convicted and punished for the same offence in another State.[68] Under the 1957 European Convention on Extradition, for example, Art 9 provides that extradition shall be refused if the competent authorities of the requested State have passed final judgment. While this principle has been held to apply to the actual trial, courts in the UK have considered that it does not apply to the extradition hearing.[69] In the US it has been held that a prosecution for the same offence in a foreign State does not necessarily infringe the principle of double jeopardy.[70] The Additional Protocols to the 1957 Convention created exemptions for persons who had been acquitted or pardoned[71] and in respect of offences of which an amnesty had been declared.[72] Extradition may also be refused if prosecuting authorities in the requested State have commenced a prosecution in respect of the offence for which extradition is sought. Similarly, extradition treaties generally contain provisions limiting the return of persons if it would be unjust or unfair to do so because of time considerations. Thus, if there is an unreasonable delay in seeking extradition, it is considered oppressive to agree to the request for extradition, and extradition will not be granted if the prosecution is barred by a statute of limitations. Under Art 10 of the 1957 Convention, for example, contracting parties are not obliged to extradite when the person has, according to the law of either the requesting or the requested party, become immune by reason of lapse of time from prosecution or punishment. The EAW includes a number of mandatory grounds for non-execution of a warrant refused. Surrender must be refused, for example, if it would infringe the rule against double jeopardy.[73] Art 3(3) provides that:

> if the executing judicial authority is informed that the requested person has been finally judged by a member state in respect of the same acts provided that, where there has been a sentence, the sentence has been served or is currently being served or may no longer be executed under the law of the member state.

The effect of this provision is to extend the rule against double jeopardy to cover all Member States in relation to surrender.

---

68 See *Atkinson v US Government* [1971] AC 197.
69 *Rees v Secretary of State for the Home Department* [1986] 2 All ER 321.
70 For further discussion of the position in the US, see op cit, Bassiouni, note 31, p 246, in which he cites *Blockburger v USA*, 52 S Ct 180 (1932).
71 1975 Additional Protocol to the European Convention on Extradition, Art 2, ETS 86.
72 Second Additional Protocol, Art 4, ETS 98 (1978).
73 For further discussion see H van der Wilt, 'The EAW and the principle *ne bis in idem* in Union' in R Blekxtoon (ed), *Handbook on the European Arrest Warrant*, 2005, The Hague, Netherlands: Asser Press.

13.2.8 Surrender of nationals

Many civil law States prefer to exercise criminal jurisdiction over their nationals whether an offence was committed on their own territory or abroad. The rationale for this exception is linked to sovereignty, and in some States it is considered to be a fundamental right. Indeed, in some States it is enshrined in national constitutions. In order to determine whether a person is a national, reference should be made to the relevant national law on nationality. Adopting a flexible approach, Nordic States, for example, consider all registered residents as nationals, raising concern that suspected terrorists seeking refuge in one of these States could avoid extradition on the grounds of residency. The preference for trying the offender in his or her own State is acknowledged in Art 6 of the 1957 European Convention on Extradition, which gives contracting parties the right to refuse extradition of its nationals. In the UK, nationality is not a bar to extradition and arguments in favour of exempting nationals from surrender have consistently been rejected. In *Re McAliskey*, for example, the German Government sought the extradition of a UK citizen from the UK. The Divisional Court refused to accept that extradition should be refused on the basis that Germany would not extradite its nationals to face trial in the UK. Adopting a purposive approach to the terms of the 1957 Convention, the Court held that if extradition proceeds on the basis of reciprocity, a State only has an obligation to do what it would do itself.[74] These opposing views are explained by the differing practice of the exercise of jurisdiction in Member States.[75] Refusal to extradite a national can limit the chances of bringing a successful prosecution against an offender who flees the country and may compromise the promotion of international co-operation of States in criminal matters. Cherif Bassiouni noted that States who refuse to extradite their own nationals have served as a consistent source of consternation to the US Congress, and suggests that such a denial of extradition should be conditional on the requested State prosecuting its national under the principle *aut dedere aut judicare*.[76] Although extradition can highlight the procedural diversity between civil law and common law jurisdictions, EU States have demonstrated a reluctance to let procedural differences restrict international co-operation. However, the optional clause in many extradition treaties which permits States to refuse a request for extradition of their own nationals is seen as a disincentive to cross-border law enforcement. The EAW which effectively removes the need for extradition between EU States was intended to solve any remaining problems relating to

---

74 (1997) *The Times*, 22 January.
75 For further discussion on jurisdiction, see Chapter 4.
76 Op cit, Bassiouni, note 31, pp 245–46. For further discussion of the principle, see C Bassiouni and EM Wise, *Aut Dedere Aut Judicare: The Duty to Prosecute or Extradite in International Law*, 1995, Dordrecht: Martinus Nijhoff.

the surrender of nationals within the EU. For further discussion see section 13.3.6 below.

13.2.9 The rule of non-inquiry[77]

The rule of non-inquiry is a rule of customary international law which has been defined as a rule that the courts will not inquire into the good faith of or motive for a request, or the treatment that a fugitive may receive upon surrender.[78] The decision not to enquire too closely into conduct taking place outside the jurisdiction reflects the traditional approach taken by courts in extradition cases. States engaging in strict observance of this rule do not allow the fugitive to produce any evidence to show that the requesting State will violate fair trial rights.[79] In jurisdictions adopting the rule of non-inquiry, the courts assume that the requesting State is acting in good faith and in the interests of justice. In *Jhirad v Ferrandina*, for example, the US Court of Appeals considered that it was not the business of their courts to assume responsibility for supervising the integrity of the judicial system of another sovereign nation.[80] The argument for adopting this rule stems from the assumption that States enter into extradition arrangements on the basis that the criminal justice system in the requesting State observes minimum standards of procedural fairness. While the US appears resistant to any relaxation of the rule,[81] there are developments in the UK which indicate a move away from a strict policy of non-inquiry. In recent years, courts in the UK have assumed a limited role of inquiry into human rights issues, including consideration of events taking place outside the jurisdiction.[82]

In *Re Saifi*, for example, a case considered before the enforcement of the Extradition Act 2003, the English Divisional Court was satisfied that it would be unfair and unjust to return the applicant to India on the ground that evidence supporting the request for extradition appeared to have been

---

77 In the UK, an inquiry is permitted for specific reasons: see EA 1989, ss 6(1)(c), (d) and 11(3).

78 C Nicholls, 'The Rule of Non-Inquiry in Extradition Cases', paper presented to the Oxford Conference on International Co-operation in Criminal Matters, 24–28 August 1998.

79 For discussion of the rule of non-inquiry, see CM Bassiouni, 'International Crimes: *Jus Cogens* and *Obligatio Erga Omnes*', 59 *LCP* (1996), 63; CM Bassiouni, *International Extradition: United States Law and Practice*, 3rd edn, 1996, New York: Oceana; see also op cit, Nicholls, note 78.

80 536 F 2d 478 (1976), pp 484–85.

81 *Ahmad v Wigen*, 910 F 2d 1063, 1967 (1990), 2nd Cir.

82 EA 1989, s 6(1), placed restrictions on return which arguably permits an inquiry into the requesting State's motive for the prosecution and requires the court to carry out a limited inquiry into the risk of prejudice at trial in the requesting State on the ground of race, religion, nationality or political opinion.

obtained in bad faith.[83] The case against the applicant depended upon the evidence of one witness who said his allegations had been obtained under circumstances of extreme duress. The court expressed concern that there was a significant risk that misbehaviour by the Indian police had so tainted the evidence as to render a fair trial impossible. Similarly, in *R v Secretary of State for the Home Department ex p Rachid Ramda*[84] the English court considered that the Secretary of State would effectively be bound to refuse extradition if satisfied that evidence supporting the request may have been obtained by oppression and that the requesting State would refuse to hear argument on the matter. This case involved an application for judicial review of a decision to order the extradition of an Algerian national to France for trial in relation to a series of terrorist bombings. The French Government's case was based almost entirely on the confession of a third party which had allegedly been obtained as a direct result of brutality.

13.3 INTERNATIONAL INITIATIVES

The escalation of both national and transnational crime and the acknowledgment that effective law enforcement is increasingly dependent upon international co-operation mechanisms has led to several important international initiatives which aim to standardise and simplify extradition procedures. The rise in terrorist-related offences has been an added incentive for States to negotiate efficient surrender mechanisms. Although some States have traditionally preferred bilateral treaties, there is a move amongst States in close geographical proximity to each other to make use of multilateral treaties.[85] Undoubtedly multilateral extradition treaties between States that share a common legal and cultural heritage generally present fewer procedural difficulties than extradition arrangements between States that are culturally, politically and geographically miles apart.

13.3.1 The UN Model Treaty on Extradition[86]

The UN Model Treaty on Extradition was adopted by the General Assembly of the UN in 1990 and is supplemented by the Complementary Provisions for the Model Treaty on Extradition. These instruments have been prepared as

---

83 For discussion of the UK's approach to extradition on grounds of bad faith see P Garlick 'The European Arrest Warrant and the ECHR' in R. Blekxtoon (ed), *Handbook on the European Arrest Warrant*, 2005, The Hague, the Netherlands: Asser Press at 180.
84 [2002] EWHC 1278; [2001] 4 All ER 168.
85 See, eg, the 1957 European Convention on Extradition, ETS 24 and the 1981 Inter-American Convention on Extradition, OASTS no 60.
86 Resolution 45/116, 30 ILM (1990), 1410.

part of a general UN initiative to promote the development of effective international co-operation in criminal matters and to encourage the implementation of national and international measures to tackle organised crime. The Model Treaty has been designed to provide a useful framework for States negotiating bilateral, regional and multilateral extradition arrangements. It also aims to encourage States to update existing extradition treaties in the light of recent developments in international law. In the preamble, the treaty emphasises that when drafting extradition treaties, States must take account of the protection of human rights. The provisions in the Model Treaty are similar to those found in the 1957 European Convention on Extradition.[87] Thus, subject to several mandatory and optional exceptions, States are obliged to extradite persons wanted for the extradition offences set out in Art 2 of the Model Treaty. In line with the modern approach, extradition offences are defined in terms of the minimum level of punishment.[88] The Model Treaty contains several mandatory and optional exceptions to extradition. The mandatory exceptions include the political offence exception, offences under military law and offences for which there has been a final judgment. States must also refuse to extradite if there are substantial grounds for believing that the request has been made for the purpose of prosecuting or punishing a person on account of that person's race, religion, nationality, ethnic origin, political opinions, sex, or status.[89] Extradition is also prohibited if the person extradited would be subjected in the requesting State to torture or cruel, inhuman or degrading treatment or punishment. The optional exceptions include a provision which allows States to refuse to extradite their own nationals, provided the offence is dealt with by appropriate action in the requested State. Further, in appropriate circumstances, States can refuse a request for extradition to a death penalty State and can reject a request for extradition on account of the fugitive's age, health or other personal circumstances.[90] Extradition may also be refused if the offence was committed outside the territory of the requested State, or if the requested State has made the decision not to prosecute.[91] The Model Treaty also includes provisions addressing specialty and simplified extradition procedures. In an attempt to introduce some flexibility for States negotiating extradition treaties, several provisions have optional clauses which allow for some modification to be incorporated into the text of a specific treaty.

87 ETS 24.
88 UN Model Treaty, Art 2.
89 Ibid, Art 3.
90 Ibid, Art 4.
91 Ibid.

13.3.2 1957 European Convention on Extradition[92]

In the early 1950s, the Committee of Ministers, the decision-making body of the Council of Europe, appointed a Committee of Experts to develop a scheme to facilitate extradition between Member States. Some concern had been raised in a memorandum from the Secretariat General in respect of the refusal of most European States to extradite nationals and the reluctance to extradite for fiscal offences. Following extended discussions, it was agreed to introduce a multilateral treaty, which, in addition to setting out procedures designed to simplify the process of extradition, contained several humanitarian provisions. The European Convention on Extradition was opened for signature in Paris on 13 December 1957. It is considered to be the most important multilateral treaty on extradition and has been used as a model for other conventions. Contracting parties undertake to extradite any person wanted in the requesting State for prosecution in respect of an extraditable offence, which is defined by reference to the minimum level of punishment in both States.[93] Parties are not obliged to extradite in respect of political offences, offences under military law or fiscal offences.[94]

Contracting parties have the right to refuse to extradite their own nationals[95] and, in certain circumstances, may refuse to extradite persons for offences which are punishable by death under the law of the requesting State.[96] The Convention prohibits extradition if a final judgment has been passed for the offence mentioned in the request. Contracting States agree to abide by the rule of specialty and will not, without the consent of the requested party, re-extradite a person to a third State.[97] If extradition is requested by more than one State, the requested State should communicate to the State to which the person is being surrendered indicating whether it consents or refuses to the re-extradition of the fugitive.[98] In order to supplement these provisions, an additional protocol was opened for signature in 1975, which added to the definition of political offence and addressed the effect of the *ne bis in idem* rule. Subsequently, a second additional protocol replaced Art 5 of the 1957 European Convention on Extradition, inserting provisions in relation to fiscal offences and addressing the matter of judgments *in absentia* and amnesty.[99] Extradition is also available under the 1977 European

---

92 For an overview of the background to the 1957 European Convention on Extradition, see C Gane and M Mackarel, *Human Rights and the Administration of Justice*, 1997, The Hague: Kluwer.
93 1957 European Convention on Extradition, Art 2.
94 Ibid, Arts 3, 4 and 5.
95 Ibid, Art 6.
96 Ibid, Art 11.
97 Ibid, Arts 14 and 15.
98 Ibid, Arts 17 and 15 and see Recommendation No R (96) 9.
99 ETS 98 (1978).

Convention on the Suppression of Terrorism. Although many European States were willing to sign and ratify the 1957 Convention, several entered reservations to some of its provisions which reduced its effectiveness. The UK did not ratify until February 1991. While this Council of Europe initiative undoubtedly assisted in simplifying extradition between European States, closer union within the EU resulted in moves to make the extradition process even easier. Following the implementation of the EAW, the 1957 Convention will only be applied in respect of extradition between signatories who are not Member States of the European Union.

13.3.3 EU initiatives[100]

Prior to the adoption of the Council Framework Decision on the EAW and surrender procedures between Member States,[101] extradition between Member States proceeded by international treaty. The Treaty of Amsterdam made provision for the framework decision as a new legal instrument to circumvent some of the difficulties arising from the existing EU conventions on extradition. Before this radical development, to assist effective legal co-operation in combating criminal activity, in 1996 the Justice and Home Affairs Council of the EU concluded two conventions to simplify and improve extradition procedures between Member States.[102] In doing so, the Council set in motion a process whereby existing arrangements for extradition were examined with a view to making them more flexible.[103] In 1995, the Council recommended that a convention on simplified extradition be adopted in order to fulfil the aim of efficiency in the field of criminal justice. Its aim was to speed up extradition in cases where persons consented to be extradited. However, after further discussion concerning other aspects of extradition the Council eventually recommended that Member States adopt far more radical procedures. The 1996 Convention appears to bypass several procedures designed to offer a degree of protection for the fugitive offender. Traditionally, extradition procedures have sought to offer a balance between judicial co-operation in

---

100 For further discussion, see M Mackarel and S Nash, 'Extradition and the European Union', 46 *ICLQ* (1997), 948.

101 Council Framework Decision of 13 June 2002 on the European arrest warrant and surrender procedures between Member States (2002/584/JHA) OJ 2002 L 190/1.

102 Convention on Simplified Extradition Procedure Between Member States of the European Union, adopted on 10 March 1995, 1995 OJ C78/1 (the 1995 Convention); Convention Relating to Extradition Between the Member States of the European Union, adopted 27 Sept 1996, 1996 OJ C313/11 (the 1996 Convention).

103 While extradition in Europe was largely based on the 1957 Convention and its two protocols, other arrangements had been formed under the 1990 Convention Implementing the Schengen Agreement (Schengen Implementing Convention) and regional agreements such as the 1962 Benelux Convention on Extradition and Mutual Assistance in Criminal Matters.

the fight against crime and protecting the fundamental rights of the individual, and these concerns are acknowledged within the preambles to both the new EU Conventions. However, the new Conventions made several alterations to what can be regarded as established extradition procedures. It was suggested that these developments shifted the balance too far in favour of law enforcement at the expense of fundamental legal protections.[104]

In order to extend arrangements already established under the Council of Europe, in 1977 France suggested proposals to extend European judicial co-operation. However, these proposals were largely unsuccessful and in 1990, in answer to a written question about the harmonisation of extradition arrangements, the European Community (EC) Commission accepted that there were still no plans for community legislation in this area. Measures to co-ordinate extradition procedures, which were necessary to compensate for the removal of border controls, would be greatly assisted if the Member States were to ratify the 1957 Council of Europe European Convention on Extradition and its two Protocols.[105] The European Ministers of Justice declared the improvement of extradition arrangements between EU States a priority[106] and a working group was established shortly after the Maastricht Treaty.[107] While the drafting of the EU Conventions progressed quickly and the 1995 Convention was completed in March 1995, discussions relating to more comprehensive developments proved to be more protracted. However, in September the 1996 Convention was drawn up.

13.3.4 1995 Convention on Simplified Extradition Procedure

This Convention aimed to facilitate extradition between Member States by supplementing the 1957 Convention by increasing the efficiency of current procedures without affecting the application of more favourable arrangements already in force in some Member States. In cases where the arrested person consents to extradition and the requested State gives its agreement, formal extradition procedures are avoided. The Convention was designed to simplify extradition by providing a flexible legal framework among EU Member States that reduces delays produced by the present systems. Providing the conditions of the Convention are complied with, contracting parties agree to apply the simplified provisions for surrender of fugitives. The simplified process begins once the request for provisional arrest is received or, if the

---

104 Op cit, Mackarel and Nash, note 100, p 948.
105 Joint Answer to Written Questions Nos 1072 and 1236/90 OJ C303/38.
106 G Vermeulun and G Vander Beken, 'Extradition in the European Union: State of the Art and Perspectives', 4 *Eur J Crime Cr L Cr J* (1996), 200, pp 207–08.
107 31 ILM (1992), 247.

Schengen agreement applies, when a person was reported in the Schengen information system.[108] Adequate information should be communicated both to the fugitive and the requested State to enable them to consider the question of consent. This information should include the identity of the person sought and details of the offence. In cases of consent to extradition, the Convention also provides for renunciation of the specialty rule.

The person wanted for the purpose of extradition must be informed of the simplified procedure and its consequences. To ensure that the arrested person was adequately informed and consent obtained voluntarily, they should have access to legal representation. Consent and renunciation of the right to specialty cannot be revoked and, thus, will be recorded formally in accordance with national procedures. If the arrested person consents to be extradited, the requested State must notify the requesting State so that a request for extradition can be submitted. However, notwithstanding the consent of the arrested person, once an arrest is effected, the request for extradition must be received within 10 days. The requested State is required to consider the request in accordance with the usual national procedures. Notification of the decision to extradite should be communicated directly between the competent State authorities and surrender of the fugitive must be within 20 days of the notification of the decision. In the event of unavoidable delay, a new surrender date can be agreed; however, the person must be released after the expiry of this new date. In cases where the arrested person consents to extradition, the simplified procedure would be available. The 1995 Convention is generally intended to apply to two types of cases. The first type involves a request for provisional arrest, consent to extradition being obtained within 10 days of arrest. In these cases, the requested State has no other reason for detaining the fugitive. The other type of case would involve consent between 10 and 40 days after arrest, but before receipt of the formal request for extradition under the 1957 Convention.[109]

13.3.5 1996 Convention Relating to Extradition

The 1996 Convention also supplemented the 1957 Convention and made a number of significant adjustments to standard extradition procedures. Interestingly, States need not have signed the 1957 European Convention on Extradition as a prerequisite to being a party to the 1996 Convention. The preamble states that Member States seek to improve judicial co-operation 'with regard both to the prosecution and to the execution of sentences, and recognise the need for efficient extradition procedures in compliance with

---

108 1990 Schengen Implementing Convention, Art 96, 30 ILM (1991), 68.
109 See in general Select Committee on the European Communities (House of Lords), 17th Report, 1996–97, pp 27–32.

democratic standards and the European Convention on Human Rights'. However, some of the preamble statements are not reflected in the substance of the Convention. The 1957 Convention allows for extradition to be granted in respect of offences punishable with a term of imprisonment of at least one year under the law of the requesting and the requested State.[110] The 12-month threshold was designed to ensure that extradition was not used for minor offences. This threshold has been lowered by the 1996 Convention which allows for extradition provided the offence attracts a term of imprisonment of at least one year under the law of the requesting State, and at least six months in the requested State.[111] The practical benefit of this development is uncertain.[112]

The 1996 Convention addresses a problem relating to the application of the double criminality rule between common law and civil law systems. Under Art 3, extradition applies to offences which are considered by the requesting State to be offences of conspiracy or an association to commit offences. The requirement is that the offence is punishable by a term of detention of at least 12 months and that they are offences referred to in Arts 1 and 2 of the 1976 European Convention on the Suppression of Terrorism,[113] or that they are offences in the field of drug-trafficking and other forms of organised crime or other acts of violence against the life, physical integrity or liberty of a person, or creating a collective danger for persons.[114] Extradition may not be refused on the ground that the facts would not amount to an offence in the requested State. This provision was an attempt to address the lacuna which existed under the present arrangements.[115] The drafting of Art 3(1)(b) is noteworthy for its vagueness[116] and would have required some Member States to change their domestic law in order to ratify this Convention.

---

110 1957 European Convention on Extradition, Art 2(1), subject to reservations, see Art 2(3) and (4).
111 1996 Convention, Art 2(1).
112 Two reasons given for needing to define extraditable offences are that the inefficiencies of extradition for minor offences are avoided along with the political problems caused by States refusing extradition on public policy grounds. Bassiouni has observed that the requirement of classifying an offence within a category of extraditable offences is curious. He asks why, subject to the offence meeting the requirements of double criminality and not being a political offence, should the requested State have a concern as to the seriousness of the offence? C Bassiouni, *International Extradition and World Public Order*, 1974, New York: Oceana, 319.
113 1996 Convention, Art 3(1)(a).
114 Ibid, Art 3(1)(b).
115 Eg, the rules relating to conspiracy to commit an offence are significantly different in the Netherlands from those in England and Wales.
116 What is the extent of offences in the field of drug-trafficking and other forms of organised crime? Since there is no accepted legal definition of organised crime in the UK, one awaits the publication of the explanatory report to the 1996 Convention with interest.

With regard to the political offence exception, the 1996 Convention provided Member States with two options. Article 5(1) provides that 'no offence may be regarded by the requested Member State as a political offence, as an offence connected with a political offence or an offence with political motives'. Article 5(2) provides that Member States may enter a reservation to Art 5(1) declaring that only offences, including conspiracy or association to commit offences, referred to in Arts 1 and 2 of the 1976 European Convention on the Suppression of Terrorism will not be regarded as political offences, a substantial limitation. Article 5(4) states that reservations made by Member States under Art 13 of the European Convention on the Suppression of Terrorism do not apply to extradition between Member States. Article 6 provides that extradition may be granted for fiscal offences. However, Art 6(3) allows any Member State to declare that it will grant extradition in connection with a fiscal offence, only where it relates to acts or omissions which may constitute an offence in connection with excise, value added tax or customs. This is in accordance with the approach adopted by the 1990 Schengen Implementing Convention.[117]

Article 7 provides that extradition may not be refused on the ground that the accused is a national within the meaning of Art 6 of the 1957 European Convention on Extradition. However, Art 7(2) permits any Member State to declare that it will not grant extradition of its nationals. Similarly, under the 1957 European Convention on Extradition, Member States could enter a reservation in respect of the non-extradition of nationals. The principle of specialty has been modified in Art 10. Whereas, under Art 14(1)(a) of the 1957 Convention, the specialty provision could be waived by the requested State, provided offences are not punishable by deprivation of liberty, the new Convention permits the requesting State to prosecute for offences other than those mentioned in the extradition request. Further, if offences are punishable by deprivation of liberty, the accused can expressly waive the benefit of the rule of specialty. However, Member States are expected to adopt 'the measures necessary to ensure that this waiver is established in such a way as to show that the person has given it voluntarily and in full awareness of the consequences.[118] This development reflected a change in the status of individuals within the extradition process.[119] Article 16(2) of the 1995 Convention and Art 18(3) of the 1996 Convention provide for entry into force 90 days after the last Member State has notified the Council of their ratification. However, until the Conventions entered into force, any Member State could declare that the treaty shall apply to its relations with Member States

---

117 1990 Schengen Implementing Convention, Art 63, 30 ILM (1991), 68.
118 1996 Convention, Art 10(3).
119 See A Eser, 'Common Goals and Different Ways in International Criminal Law: Reflections from a European Perspective', 31 *Harvard Intl LJ* (1990), 125; op cit, Swart, note 45, p 505.

that have made the same declaration.[120] Such a system gave the Conventions a rolling ratification and meant that the treaties became operational, albeit on a limited basis, sooner rather than later.[121]

Thus the 1996 Convention represented a re-examination of the traditional restrictions on extradition. It effectively removed or reduced restrictions on the return of a fugitive offender. Some traditional limitations on extradition are concerned with protecting fundamental rights of the fugitive and prohibit extradition if a person is likely to be punished on account of race, religion, or ethnic origin, or where they might be subjected to torture, denied a fair trial or executed.[122] While the preamble acknowledges that all the systems of government of the Member States are based on democratic principles and comply with obligations laid down by the European Convention on Human Rights, there is no express obligation in the text to ensure that the new procedures conform to the human rights commitments contained within the European Convention on Human Rights or the International Covenant on Civil and Political Rights. The new procedures would undoubtedly have improved legal co-operation between Member States and increased the efficiency of existing extradition procedures. The question remained whether these developments would have reduced to an unacceptable level the procedural guarantees that provide fugitives with some protection from over-zealous States.

The UK Government did not immediately ratify the new extradition treaties. However, in September 2001 the EU Justice and Home Affairs (JHA) Council proposed that all EU States would ratify the treaties by 1 January 2002. By virtue of the UK's dualist[123] approach to international law, treaty obligations are generally binding only on the State and do not confer rights, or create obligations, which are justiciable within the State. Domestic legislation is required to allow international obligations to have 'direct effect'. Accession to both EU Conventions was given approval by both Houses of Parliament on 19 December 2001. The Conventions were implemented under powers in the Anti-Terrorism, Crime and Security Act 2001 which enables measures approved by the EU JHA Council to be introduced by secondary

---

120 1995 Convention, Art 16(3); 1996 Convention, Art 18(4).
121 The Council and some Member States annexed a number of declarations to the Convention text, including adopting the dispute settlement mechanism of the 1969 Vienna Convention on the Law of Treaties, Art 65.
122 All of these restrictions have received the tacit approval of the UN by way of their inclusion in the UN Model Treaty on Extradition. UN GA Res 45/116 (14 Dec 1990).
123 There are two approaches that States may take with respect to the position of international law. Dualist States recognise a schism between national and international law, whereas monist States recognise only one legal order, in which international law is usually of a higher order than national law. Rather than being an abstruse matter of public international law, the position taken by a State will have a fundamental impact on the methods by which international law is incorporated into the national system.

legislation. The EU Extradition Regulations,[124] which give effect to the 1995 and the 1996 Conventions, entered into force in March 2002. Parliament noted with approval the reduction in the extradition crime threshold, the abolition of the political offence exception, the removal of the exemption for fiscal offences and the modification to the specialty rule. Although the new Conventions would have facilitated extradition between EU States, they did not completely remove the right of States to refuse to extradite their own nationals, which is at times a significant limitation to international co-operation. However, formal extradition procedures between EU States are no longer necessary following implementation of the Council Framework Decision on the EAW and the surrender procedures between the Member States.[125] This framework decision is a follow up to the adoption at the Tampere Special European Council 1999 of the principle of mutual recognition of judicial decisions by Member States. In the light of the limited success of the EU conventions on extradition, the Commission chose the framework decision mechanism for reasons of effectiveness. It was hoped it would address some of the problems produced by traditional surrender procedures between Member States.

13.3.6 The Council Framework Decision on the European arrest warrant

The Tampere European Council conclusions stated that:

> ... the formal extradition procedure should be abolished among the Member States as far as persons are concerned who are fleeing from justice after having been finally sentenced, and replaced by a simple transfer of such persons, in compliance with Article 6 TEU. Consideration should also be given to fast-track extradition procedures, without prejudice to the principle of fair trial.[126]

This statement is in line with other EU initiatives to expedite the extradition process including Recommendation 28 of the strategy of the EU for the next millennium as regards the prevention and control of organised crime. However, the initiatives to reform the surrender mechanisms within Member States have themselves been expedited by the events that took place in the US in September 2001. At an Extraordinary European Council meeting held on 21 September 2001, the Heads of State of the EU, the President of the

---

124 SI 2002/419, as amended by EU Extradition (Amendment) Regulations 2002 SI 2002/1662.
125 Council Framework Decision of 13 June 2002 on the European arrest warrant and surrender procedures between Member States (2002/584/JHA) OJ 2002 L 190/1.
126 Tampere European Council, item 35.

European Parliament and the President of the European Commission called for the creation of a European warrant for arrest and extradition in accordance with the conclusions reached at the Tampere meeting. Consequently, the European Commission presented a Proposal for a Council Framework Decision on the European arrest warrant (EAW) and the surrender procedures between the Member States.[127] It was intended that the EAW should replace extradition within the EU with a system of surrender on the basis of mutual recognition of the warrant. The EAW is designed to facilitate law enforcement in Member States by speeding up the transfer of suspects and removing the political dimension to extradition.[128] This system of surrender only applies to Member States. The European Commission gave its assurance that persons detained under an EAW will not be surrendered to a third State.[129] This initiative is based on the principle of mutual recognition of judicial decisions and on mutual trust between the judicial authorities of Member States, which forms the cornerstone of future developments in judicial co-operation. Mutual recognition is based on the assumption that the criminal justice systems in all Member States conform to the standards of human rights set out in the European Convention on Human Rights. The success of this initiative will be a reference point for other mutual recognition initiatives including the European evidence warrant. Further, the approach taken by Member States to problems of implementation of the EAW will be seen as 'a test of the reality of respect for fundamental rights in the field of justice and home affairs'.[130]

The Council of the European Union adopted the Framework Decision establishing the EAW in June 2002. Article 1 of the Framework Decision provides:

> The European arrest warrant is a judicial decision issued by a Member State with a view to the arrest and surrender by another Member State of a requested person, for the purposes of conducting a criminal prosecution or executing a custodial sentence or detention order.

Implementation of the EAW makes significant changes to the practice of extradition between Member States. In addition to removing the double

127 Council Framework Decision of 13 June 2002 on the European arrest warrant and surrender procedures between Member States (2002/584/JHA) [2002] OJ L 190/1.
128 There was some disquiet regarding the involvement of the Home Secretary in the decision to refuse an extradition request by the Spanish authorities in the case of *R v Bow Street Metropolitan Stipendiary Magistrate and Others ex p Pinochet Ugarte* [1999] 2 All ER 97.
129 E–3359/01EN. Answer given by Mr Vitorino on behalf of the Commission.
130 S Alegre and M Leaf, *European Arrest Warrant: A solution ahead of its time?* JUSTICE 2003 at 11. This publication provides detailed discussion of the EAW and provides an overview of national approaches to implementation. See also R. Blekxtoon (ed), *Handbook on the European Arrest Warrant*, 2005, The Hague, Netherlands: Asser Press.

criminality requirement and the role of the executive, the EAW abolishes the political offence exception and the exception for surrender of own nationals. However, the Framework Decision does not alter existing obligations to respect fundamental rights and fundamental legal principles set out in Article 6 of the TEU. Similarly, the EAW will not alter Member States obligations with respect to extradition under other international human rights instruments. Nevertheless, national courts interpret these obligations differently and Member States are frequently found in violation of their obligations under the European Convention on Human Rights. Whether these obligations provide adequate protection for suspects throughout the EU remains to be seen.[131]

The arrest warrant is a standard form sent directly from one judicial authority to another. It can be issued in respect of all offences carrying a sentence of imprisonment of at least 12 months, or for persons already sentenced to a custodial or detention order exceeding four months.[132] Having received a request from a judicial authority for the surrender of a convicted person or a person wanted for prosecution, Member States must arrange transfer. The warrant imposes strict time limits to ensure rapid surrender.[133] Grounds for refusal to execute a warrant are very limited. For example, a request must be refused if its execution would infringe the principle of double jeopardy or the requested person is below the age of criminal responsibility under the law of the executing state.[134] The Framework Decision does provide some optional grounds for refusing a request.[135] A request may be refused, for example, in the case of a parallel prosecution, ie, where the requested person is being prosecuted in another State for the same act on which the warrant is based. Surrender can be made conditional if the requested State undertakes to execute the sentence.[136] The whole process takes place between the judicial authorities of the Member States with no executive or administrative discretion to refuse surrender and no exception for nationals. Persons arrested under a warrant cannot rely on either the double criminality rule for 32 serious offences[137] or the specialty rule. However, with the exception of the 32 offences, a warrant will only be issued if the acts on which it is based constitute an offence in the executing state. The European Court of Justice (ECJ) recently found that the removal of the double criminality requirement

---

131 For discussion on the proposal for a Framework Decision of the Procedural Safeguards for Suspects and Defendants in Criminal Proceedings see Chapter 15.
132 Council Framework Decision of 13 June 2002 on the European arrest warrant and surrender procedures between Member States (2002/584/JHA) OJ 2002 L 190/1, Art 2.
133 Ibid, Arts 17 and 23.
134 Ibid, Art 3.
135 Ibid, Art 4(2).
136 Ibid, Art 4(6).
137 Ibid, Art 2. The list of offences can also be found in Schedule 2 to the Extradition Act 2003.

in the EAW did not result in a breach of the fundamental right to equality before the law and to the legality of criminal proceedings.[138] The procedure for referring a case to the ECJ for a preliminary ruling made sure that there was a uniform interpretation of law within all Member States. The mechanism of the arrest warrant has replaced many of the instruments authorising extradition within the EU including provisions of the 1990 Schengen Implementing Convention. In its response to the Council Framework proposal, the English Criminal Bar Association concluded that:

> If the new European Warrant scheme rids us of a system the public perceive to be unnecessarily slow and cumbersome, we welcome it. We particularly endorse a system based on the principles of recognition. We caution, of course, against any new system, however, which deprives a defendant or requested person, of the proper opportunity to arrange his defence or fairly scrutinise the case against him. We accept and encourage these proposals which allow the Courts to continue to supervise and uphold individual rights, such as bail and access to a lawyer and court. Most importantly, as paragraph 11 of the preamble to the Framework proposal makes clear, a key condition is that the execution of the warrant does not lead to a violation of fundamental rights.[139]

Although the Framework Decision establishing the EAW entered into force on 1 January 2004, only eight Member States, including the UK, were ready to implement it. Most States missed the deadline and did not provide the Commission with details of national legislation until the end of 2004. The EAW is now operational in all Member States.

The Hague programme identified the importance of evaluation mechanisms to assess the application and implementation of mutual recognition initiatives such as the EAW. Two assessment mechanisms have been used to assess progress so far. The first is conducted under Art 34(3) of the Framework Decision which provides that the Commission should submit a report to the European Parliament and the Council evaluating the operation of the EAW, and if necessary to submit legislative proposals. The second is based on the Joint Action of 5 December 1997 which establishes a mechanism for evaluating the application and implementation of initiatives to tackle organised crime.[140] In February 2005, the Commission produced a report analysing national legislative developments. A revised report was submitted in January

---

138 Reference for a preliminary ruling of 13 July 2005 from the Arbitragehof (Belgium) in the proceedings between Advocaten voor de wereld, a non-profit-making association, and the Council of Ministers, Case C–303/05.

139 <http://www.criminalbar.co.uk/reports/dec01.cfm>.

140 OJ L 344.

2006, which took account of national legislation adopted after the presenta-tion of the first report.[141] Article 34(2) of the Framework Decision provides that Member States transmit the text of national legislation to the Council and the Commission. The Commission's report, which provides an overview of the manner in which Member States have adapted national law, was critical of many Member States' attempts at implementation, and in an annex to the report identifies errors in transposing the Framework Decision into national law. However, Member States have expressed doubts regarding the accuracy of the Commission's analysis. Although the report assists Member States to understand the mechanisms used in other States to implement the EAW, the Third Pillar does not provide the Commission with the power to take enforcement action before the ECJ.[142] As part of the evaluation pro-gramme, the Council collected quantative information on the practical appli-cation of the EAW from Member States. Since 1 January 2004 the UK received over 5,500 warrants and issued over 200.[143] The reasons for the dis-parity in inward and outward requests is due, in part, to the fact that many of the inward warrants were posted as alerts with Interpol or on the Schengen Information System and not necessarily targeted at the UK. In the period 1 January 2004 to 22 February 2006, the authorities in the UK issued 175 arrests and surrendered 88 people. Some of the requests for surrender were discharged because the judge considered that the offence mentioned in the warrant was not an extraditable offence, or considered the warrant to be insufficiently specific. In *Palar v Court of First Instance of Brussels*,[144] the Divisional Court drew a distinction between scrutinising the description of the conduct in an EAW and an inquiry into evidential sufficiency of the case. The Belgian authorities had issued a warrant alleging that the suspect was wanted for swindling offences. The warrant stated that another suspect had been found in Belgium in possession of store loyalty cards which had mag-netic strips containing information from the defendant's legitimately held cards. These cards were used to withdraw money. The warrant also referred to alleged telephone conversations between the appellant and other suspects in which they discussed money withdrawals and bankcard thefts. Discharg-ing the warrant, the Divisional Court noted that while the request should

---

141 Report from the Commission based on Art 34 of the Council Framework Decision of 13 June 2002 on the European arrest warrant and the surrender procedures between Member States COM(2006)8 final.

142 For a detailed discussion of the evaluation process see A Zarza, 'Evaluation of Member States in the Third Pillar of the European Union: The specific case of the European Arrest Warrant' in A Weyembergh and S de Biolley (eds), *Comment evaluer le droit penal europeen?*, 3rd edn, 2006, Brussels: Institut d'études européenes.

143 See the report from the UK House of Lords European Union Committee: European Arrest Warrant: Recent Developments, published April 2006, HL paper 156.

144 BLD 184051604.

proceed in the spirit of co-operation and comity, the court still needed to be satisfied that the description of the alleged conduct amounted to an offence. In this case no criminal activity was alleged against the suspect; the alleged criminal conduct of others was, by itself, insufficient to justify surrender.

As predicted, many Member States are experiencing problems transposing the Framework Decision into national law due to the abolition of the exception to surrender their own nationals. This issue presented problems during the negotiations to conclude the 1996 Convention relating to extradition between the Member States of the EU (see above). Traditionally many Member States from civil law systems have guarantees in national constitutions prohibiting the extradition of nationals. Domestic law authorising the surrender of nationals to the prosecuting authorities of another Member State will be unconstitutional. The Polish Constitutional Tribunal, for example, considered it necessary to annul national legislation implementing the EAW because it was incompatible with Art 55 of the Polish Constitution prohibiting extradition of Polish nationals.[145] The Supreme Court of Cyprus held that the EAW was incompatible with articles in the constitution prohibiting the surrender of its citizens for prosecution abroad. Similarly, the German Constitutional Court annulled national law implementing the EAW on the ground that there was no possibility of challenging the decision to extradite in a national court. In this case, the Spanish authorities issued a warrant requesting the surrender of a person suspected of terrorist changes. The suspect sought a ruling from the court as to whether the charges amounted to a criminal offence in other Member States. The German Constitutional Court considered that eliminating the right to review by a court effectively removed a fundamental right of German citizens.[146] Following this decision, the Spanish authorities refused to execute German EAWs on the ground that under the Spanish Constitution extradition was based on the principle of reciprocity. In a referral to the ECJ, the Belgian Court of Arbitration sought the Court's opinion on whether a Framework Decision was an appropriate legal instrument for surrender procedures between Member States. The Advocate General held that the Framework Decision establishing the EAW was a proper mechanism to achieve the objectives laid down by the TEU, which included the maintenance and development of an area of freedom, security and justice.[147] Member States have now agreed to introduce

---

145 For a discussion of this case see A Lazowski, 'Constitutional Tribunal on the Surrender of Polish Citizens under the European Arrest Warrant. Decision of 27 April 2005' (2005) 1 EuConst, 569.
146 Decision of 18 July 2005.
147 Reference for a preliminary ruling of 13 July 2005 from the Arbitragehof (Belgium) in the proceedings between Advocaten voor de wereld, a non-profit-making association, and the Council of Ministers, Case C–303/05.

amendments to national legislation and in some cases to amend their national constitutions in order to give effect to the EAW.

13.4 THE UK EXTRADITION ACT 2003[148]

In addition to making provision for new extradition procedures in the UK, the Extradition Act 2003 (the 2003 Act), which came into force on 1 January 2004, contains provisions implementing the Council Framework Decision on the European arrest warrant.[149] The 2003 Act gives effect to proposals set out in a UK Government consultation document entitled *The Law on Extradition; A Review* which was published in March 2001. This consultation exercise, which began in 1997, set out to consider the implications of the 1995 and 1996 EU Conventions on extradition and to review the operation of extradition law in the UK generally. The 2003 Act makes provision for a range of new extradition procedures, the adoption of the Framework Decision on the European arrest warrant, the retention with some modification to current arrangements for extradition to non-EU States, the abolition of the *prima facie* requirement in some cases and a simplified appeal process. States are placed in two categories. States in the first category are EU States, with all other States having existing extradition arrangements with the UK being placed in the second category. Part 1 of the 2003 Act deals with extradition arrangements from the UK to States in the first category, and its provisions implement the Framework Decision on the European arrest warrant. The legislative framework for incoming extradition requests from States with bi-lateral treaties with the UK is contained in Part 2. Part 3 deals with the procedure for applying for an EAW requesting surrender from a Category 1 State, and Part 4 sets out the powers available to the police in extradition cases. All EU States are designated Category 1 territories and the return of suspects to Member States takes place in accordance with Part 1 of the 2003 Act. Following the issue of a Part 1 warrant by the appropriate EU authority, a district judge decides whether the offence mentioned in the warrant is an extradition offence. Although under the new surrender procedures there is a right of appeal to the High Court and the House of Lords, the executive ceases to play a role. The bars to extradition under this part of the Act include the rule against double jeopardy, the person's age, the death penalty, specialty and the person's earlier extradition to the UK from either another first category State or a non-first category State. There is provision under s 87 of the Act for the judge to decide whether the person's extradition is

---

148 For discussion of the Extradition Act 2003 see *Blackstone's Guide to the Extradition Act 2003*, 2004, Oxford: OUP.
149 COM (2001) 0522.

compatible with the rights set out in the European Convention on Human Rights.[150] However, it is questionable whether this guarantee is insufficient to counteract the removal of many of the traditional safeguards.

The Act also creates a new extradition regime governing extradition from the UK to the US, a Category 2 State. This regime introduced modifications aimed at reducing duplication and complexity which included a simplified appeals process, strict time limits for hearings and the removal of the requirement to provide *prima facie* evidence in some cases. Home office statistics indicate a disparity in the number of incoming and outgoing extradition requests between the US and the UK. While the removal of the *prima facie* requirement has caused some alarm, without doubt the most contentious part of this legislation is the implementation of the EAW, which removes most of the traditional bars to extradition. On occasion, more than one State has jurisdiction to try a case, which can give rise to parallel prosecutions. At the moment, the 2003 Act does not contain a mechanism to determine satisfactorily where cross-border cases should be tried. Amendments to the 2003 Act will be introduced in the Police and Justice Bill, which aims to address this issue. The 2003 Act has been heavily criticised for failing to provide sufficient safeguards for defendants. Gareth Crossman, policy director of Liberty, the human rights organisation, considers that the Act 'undermines longstanding safeguards against unfair removal and unfortunately appears to be more about politics than law'.[151] In *United States of America v Berminghham and others*[152] it was argued that removal to the US for trial was in violation of Art 8 of the European Convention on Human Rights, which guarantees the right to private and family life. The court rejected the argument that where a trial in the UK was possible, removal to another State was unnecessary and therefore disproportionate. At the moment there is no obligation under the 2003 Act requiring a cross-border case to be heard in the UK. Arguably, the critics are correct and the creation of a two-tiered system for extradition has resulted in 'a lengthy, cumbersome, ill-considered and badly drafted piece of legislation which will sacrifice a number of human rights without providing any substantial benefits in return'.[153]

13.5 EXTRADITION AND INTERNATIONAL HUMAN RIGHTS INSTRUMENTS

While most modern extradition treaties appear to seek a balance between protecting the fundamental rights of the requested person and the need to

150 See *R (Kashamu) v Governor of Brixton Prison* [2002] QB 887.
151 See <http://www.liberty-human-rights.org.uk>.
152 [2006] EWHC 200 (Admin).
153 Liberty's Response to the Draft Extradition Bill, Oct 2002, para 4.

ensure that the extradition process operates efficiently and effectively, it is doubtful whether there is a rule of international law requiring extradition procedures to take account of general principles of human rights.[154] The 1957 European Convention on Extradition, for example, does not contain a general provision excluding extradition even if it would place the person at risk of human rights violations. Nevertheless, in practice, many extradition treaties do impose procedural protections restricting extradition if surrender would lead to gross violations of human rights. These include the 1950 European Convention for the Protection of Human Rights and Fundamental Freedoms; the 1961 European Social Charter; the 2000 Charter of Fundamental Rights; the 1966 International Convention on Civil and Political Rights; the 1984 UN Convention against Torture and other Cruel, Inhuman or Degrading Treatment or Punishment and the 1989 UN Convention on the Rights of the Child. The EAW system, which has replaced extradition between Member States of the EU, does not reduce existing obligations under these international human rights instruments.[155] Although, on occasion, human rights instruments do not contain specific provisions dealing with extradition, reluctance to include an express provision has not placed extradition beyond the scope of human rights treaties. Thus, fundamental human rights principles have been found to apply to extradition.

13.5.1 European Convention on Human Rights[156]

The European Convention on Human Rights was signed in Rome on 4 November 1950 and entered into force on 3 September 1953. It takes the form of a treaty, binding in international law, which sets out minimum international standards for the protection of human rights and provides effective enforcement procedures. The Convention established the first international complaints procedure and the first international court dealing exclusively with human rights. The substantive rights and freedoms guaranteed by the Convention and the procedures for enforcing these rights have subsequently been extended by the adoption of a series of protocols. It was not intended that the Convention should replace the protection of human rights at national level; indeed, before there is recourse to proceedings under the Convention all remedies at the domestic level must have been exhausted. In the event of an alleged breach of the Convention, the European Court of Human Rights (ECHR) can now receive applications from both States and

154 For further discussion, see op cit, Van den Wyngaert, note 61, pp 757–79.
155 For a discussion of the relationship of the EAW and the European Convention on Human Rights see P Garlick, 'The European Arrest Warrant and the European Convention on Human Rights' in R. Blekxtoon (ed), *Handbook on the European Arrest Warrant*, 2005, The Hague, Netherlands: Asser Press.
156 ETS 5, UKTS 71 (1953).

individuals claiming to be a victim of a violation. Although the UK was one of the first States to sign and ratify the Convention, it refused to recognise the right of individual petition and the jurisdiction of the ECHR until 1966. The right of individual complaint and recognition of the ECHR's jurisdiction are now mandatory.

The ECHR has acknowledged that contracting States have a right, subject to their various treaty obligations, to control entry, residence and expulsion of non-nationals. Moreover, the right to political asylum is not contained within the Convention or any of its protocols. Article 5(1)(f) of the European Convention on Human Rights specifically permits the lawful arrest or detention of a person to prevent his effecting an unauthorised entry into the country or a person against whom action is being taken with a view to deportation or extradition. Further, provided there is a legal basis for the fugitive's arrest, deportation in the disguise of extradition would not necessarily be contrary to the Convention.[157] Thus, the Convention does not guarantee the right not to be expelled from the territory of a contracting State. However, it is well established in the jurisprudence of the ECHR that extradition may give rise to consequences that adversely affect the enjoyment of a right guaranteed by the Convention.[158] It has also been accepted that in some circumstances an order for deportation would, if executed, give rise to a violation of the Convention.[159] The ECHR has demonstrated a willingness to resolve a conflict between obligations under an extradition treaty and obligations under the Convention in favour of protecting fundamental rights.[160] It would appear that the protection provided by Art 3 is wider than that provided by other international human rights instruments.[161] While there is a need to seek a balance between protecting the fundamental rights of the individual and the public interest, if the ECHR is satisfied that the applicant is at risk of being subjected to any of the forms of treatment proscribed by Art 3, the balance must be in favour of non-extradition. Accordingly, Art 3 of the European Convention on Human Rights can impose significant limitations on the use of the extradition process. All Member States of the EU have ratified the European Convention on Human Rights; indeed, ratification is a prerequisite for membership of the EU. However, the majority of EU States continue to have judgments against them in the ECHR.

---

157 *Illich Sanchez Ramirez v France*, Application No 28780/95.
158 *Soering v UK* (1989) 11 EHRR 439.
159 *Cruz Varas v Sweden* (1991) 14 EHRR 1.
160 For further discussion of this case and extradition and human rights generally, see op cit, Swart, note 45, pp 505–34.
161 In *Ahmed v Austria* (1996) 24 EHRR 278, para 41, it was noted that: 'The protection afforded by Art 3 is thus wider than that provided by Art 33 of the UN 1951 Convention on the Status of Refugees.'

13.5.2 Prohibition against torture and inhuman and degrading treatment

In the landmark case of *Soering v UK*,[162] the ECHR was of the opinion that to surrender a person to another State where there were substantial grounds for believing that he would be in danger of being subjected to torture, inhuman or degrading treatment would be a violation of Art 3 of the European Convention on Human Rights. In this case, the UK sought to extradite a German national from the UK to the US under the terms of an extradition treaty that had been incorporated into the law of the UK.[163] The applicant was accused of committing a murder in Virginia, in the US, and argued that his extradition would amount to a violation of Art 3 of the Convention. In capital murder cases, the State of Virginia could impose the death penalty which generally involved a prisoner spending long periods of time on 'death row'. The applicant accepted that the death penalty was not *per se* contrary to the Convention as Art 2(1) permits capital punishment under certain conditions. However, he argued that exposure to the death row phenomenon would amount to inhuman and degrading treatment and infringe Art 3. The UK Government submitted that the Convention should not be interpreted so as to impose responsibility on a contracting State for acts which occur outside its jurisdiction. The basis for this argument was that such an interpretation would interfere with international treaty rights and lead to a conflict with the norms of the international judicial process. Further, it would involve adjudication on the internal affairs of a foreign State and its domestic criminal justice system. In support of this argument, the UK Government relied upon traditional principles of extradition which respect the rule of non-inquiry. In rejecting this argument, the ECHR accepted that liability is incurred by the extraditing contracting State by reason of its having taken action which has as a direct consequence the exposure of an individual to proscribed ill-treatment.[164] Furthermore, it was noted that:

> . . . Art 3 enshrines one of the fundamental values of the democratic societies making up the Council of Europe. It is also to be found in similar terms in other international instruments such as the 1966 International Covenant on Civil and Political Rights and the 1969 American Convention on Human Rights and is generally recognised as an internationally accepted standard.[165]

---

162 (1989) 11 EHRR 439.
163 By Orders in Council, namely, the USA (Extradition) Order 1976 SI 1976/2144 and the USA (Extradition Amendment) Order 1986, SI 1986/2020.
164 (1989) 11 EHRR 439, para 91.
165 Ibid, para 88.

Since *Soering*, the ECHR has consistently reiterated its position regarding Art 3, which it accepts encapsulates the most fundamental right of an individual. Despite acknowledging the risk of establishing safe havens for fugitive offenders which could undermine the foundations of extradition, the ECHR has steadfastly maintained that there was no room for balancing the risk of ill-treatment against the reasons for expulsion in determining whether a State's responsibility under Art 3 is engaged.[166] Indeed, in *Hilal v UK*[167] the ECHR observed that, notwithstanding the State's right to control entry, Art 3 implies an obligation not to expel if there is a real risk of torture. In *Jabari v Turkey*[168] the ECHR observed that, having regard to the absolute nature of Art 3, States must undertake a rigorous scrutiny[169] of claims that expulsion to a third country will expose that individual to treatment prohibited by Art 3. The applicant, an Iranian national, alleged that she would face a real risk of ill-treatment and death by stoning if expelled by Turkey and returned to Iran. Finding for the applicant, the ECHR held that the Turkish authorities had failed to engage in any meaningful assessment of the application. Following the terrorist attacks in the US in September 2001, concerns have been expressed regarding the problems which may result if Council of Europe States are reluctant to extradite to the US on the basis of the death row phenomenon. However, the ECHR has generally indicated its willingness to accept undertakings from the US as evidence that extradition will not give rise to a breach of Art 3.

The *Soering* principle requires that applicants show that there are 'substantial grounds' for their argument that they would be exposed to inhuman and degrading treatment. In the absence of convincing evidence to this effect, extradition to States with poor human rights records will not necessarily be contrary to the Convention. In *Mamatkulov and Abdurasulovic v Turkey*,[170] for example, the applicants complained that following their extradition from Turkey to Uzbekistan their lives were at risk and they were in danger of being subjected to torture. The complaint also related to the unfairness of Turkish extradition proceedings and criminal proceedings in Uzbekistan. The ECHR reiterated that while contracting States have the right to control the entry, residence and expulsion of aliens, States may incur responsibility where substantial grounds exist for believing that a person would face a real risk of being subjected to treatment which is contrary to Art 3. Noting that the applicants in this case had already been expelled, the ECHR held that Turkey failed to comply with procedures designed to assist the ECHR to carry out an effective examination of the application. However, while the evidence in

---

166 (1989) 11 EHRR 439, para 81.
167 (2001) 33 EHRR 2.
168 (2000) 9 BHRC 1.
169 Ibid, para 39.
170 Application Nos 46827/99 and 46951/99.

this case indicated concern relating to the general situation in Uzbekistan, it did not confirm the specific allegations. In addition, allegations that the applicants had been subjected to torture were not corroborated by medical examinations conducted by prison doctors. Accordingly, the ECHR found that there was insufficient evidence to warrant a finding of a violation of Art 3. Referring to the complaint regarding the fairness of proceedings, the ECHR emphasised that proceedings relating to the entry and expulsion of aliens do not invoke fair trial rights under Art 6.

13.5.3 The *Soering* principle and deportation

Subsequent developments illustrate that the ECHR is prepared, within the context of Art 3, to extend the *Soering* principle to other forms of expulsion. In *Chahal v UK*,[171] the ECHR observed that the prohibition against expulsion in Art 3 cases was absolutely irrespective of the applicant's conduct and applied to deportation. The applicant, a leading figure in the Sikh community in the UK, was detained in 1985 under the Prevention of Terrorism (Temporary Provisions) Act 1984 in respect of a conspiracy to assassinate the Indian Prime Minister.[172] The Secretary of State ordered his deportation to India on the grounds that his continued presence in the UK was not conducive to the public good for reasons of national security.[173] The applicant sought asylum on the basis that he could establish the well founded fear of persecution test as required under the terms of the 1951 UN Convention on the Status of Refugees.[174] His application was rejected. Following Chahal's successful application for judicial review, the Secretary of State was required to re-examine the case. Again asylum was refused and the deportation order confirmed. The applicant complained that his deportation would result in a violation of Art 3 of the European Convention on Human Rights. The majority of the ECHR was satisfied that the order for the applicant's deportation would, if executed, give rise to a violation of Art 3, and where there are substantial grounds for believing that expulsion would result in ill-treatment, the national interests of the State could not be invoked to override the interests of the individual. The European Court observed that it was entitled to conduct its own examination of the existence of a real risk of ill-treatment, and considered reports supplied by Amnesty International and the UN's special rapporteur on torture. Notwithstanding the efforts of the Indian authorities to bring about reform, the European Court was sufficiently

---

171 (1996) 23 EHRR 413.
172 He was eventually released without charge. In 1986, he was convicted of assault and affray, and served concurrent sentences of six and nine months; however, these convictions were eventually quashed by the Court of Appeal.
173 See Immigration Act 1971, s 3(5)(b).
174 189 UNTS 150.

satisfied that the violation of human rights by certain members of the security forces in Punjab and elsewhere in India is a recalcitrant and enduring problem[175] and it was accepted that the applicant's return would amount to a violation of Art 3.

While the guarantees provided by Art 3 have generally been held to apply to risks created by public authorities in the receiving State, in *D v UK*[176] the ECHR was prepared to assess the risk resulting from the State's inability to prevent a violation of Art 3. On his arrival in the UK, the applicant was found in possession of a large quantity of a proscribed drug and sentenced to six years' imprisonment. He was discovered to be suffering from an AIDS-related condition and by mid-1996 his prognosis was poor. Shortly before his release from prison, the immigration authorities ordered his removal from the UK. The applicant complained that the receiving State could not provide the medical care needed to treat his condition and his health would deteriorate. While the ECHR accepted that the expulsion of alien drug couriers was a justified response to drug-trafficking, it must be balanced against the absolute prohibition on torture and inhuman or degrading treatment. Where there was a real risk that the applicant's deportation would result in a violation of Art 3, the balance must be in favour of non-expulsion. Persons can be lawfully detained pending a deportation hearing. In *Ex p Saadi*[177] the House of Lords held that detention for a short period in order to bring about a speedy decision-making process was not necessarily unlawful where the power is exercised to prevent unauthorised entry. However, the House of Lords has been critical of legislation which effectively permitted indefinite detention pending deportation because removal from the UK was unlikely due to the risk of torture or ill treatment if the detainees were returned to their country of origin.[178]

The *Soering* principle was further extended in *HLR v France*,[179] when the ECHR was called upon to consider whether the inability of the receiving State to protect the applicant from the acts of a third party would infringe Art 3. Having been found in possession of cocaine, the applicant was sentenced to imprisonment by a French court and permanently excluded from French territory. During the criminal proceedings, he gave evidence against members of a Colombian drug cartel and as a consequence feared for his safety. He claimed that his deportation to Colombia would give rise to a

175 (1996) 23 EHRR 413, para 105.
176 (1997) 24 EHRR 423.
177 [2002] UKHL 41.
178 See *A and others v Secretary of State for the Home Department* [2004] UK HL 56. The Anti-Terrorism, Crime and Security Act 2001 included provision for the detention of foreign nationals pending deportation. These provisions were eventually repealed by s 16(2) of the Prevention of Terrorism Act 2005.
179 (1998) 26 EHRR 29.

violation of Art 3 on the grounds that the Colombian authorities were incapable of giving him adequate protection from reprisals by members of the drug cartel. Whilst the Commission found for the applicant, the European Court was not satisfied that there were substantial grounds for believing his deportation would expose him to a real risk of the treatment prohibited by Art 3. Furthermore, this claim must be assessed against the background of the general situation regarding the protection of human rights in Colombia, and the applicant failed to show that his personal situation would be worse than that of other Colombians were he to be deported.

Notwithstanding the outcome of this case, the European Court acknowledges that Art 3 of the European Convention on Human Rights absolutely prohibits torture or inhuman or degrading treatment, irrespective of the victim's conduct or the source of the ill-treatment and, if extradition treaties fail to protect the person adequately, a minimum level of protection is provided by the Convention.[180] However, many of the other substantive clauses in the Convention and its protocols make provision for exceptions and derogations in the event of a public emergency.[181] The Convention does not in principle prohibit contracting States from regulating the length of stay of aliens and, in some circumstances, an expulsion motivated by concern to regulate the labour market will be justified.[182] Accordingly, the ECHR is not always willing to accept that Convention rights provide a bar to extradition.

13.5.4 1966 International Covenant on Civil and Political Rights

The *travaux préparatoires* reveal that during the drafting of the Covenant a proposal to include a provision addressing extradition was expressly rejected. However, while the Covenant may not specifically provide for a right not to be extradited, the effects of extradition can give rise to issues under other provisions of the Covenant. The surrender of a person to another State in circumstances in which it was foreseeable that torture would take place, for example, would place the contracting party in violation of its obligation under Art 7 of the Covenant. The foreseeability of a prohibited consequence would mean that there was a present violation of the Covenant, even though the consequence did not occur until later. The Covenant contains a provision acknowledging the principle of *ne bis in idem*, or double jeopardy. Thus, Art 14(7) of the Covenant provides that no one shall be liable to be tried or

---

180 It is now well established in the jurisprudence of the ECtHR that Art 3 of the Convention implies an obligation not to expel people to a country if there are substantial grounds for believing that they face a real risk of being subjected to torture or ill treatment. See *Ahmed v Austria* (1996) 24 EHRR 278; *Hilal v United Kingdom* (2001) 33 EHRR 2.
181 See *Ireland v UK*, Ser A, No 25, para 65.
182 *Berrehab v The Netherlands* (1988) 11 EHRR 322.

punished again for an offence for which they have already been finally convicted or acquitted in accordance with the law of another State. Communications alleging violations of the International Covenant on Civil and Political Rights are considered by the Human Rights Committee, which was established under Art 28. Whilst the Committee will consider whether the author of the communication was granted the necessary procedural safeguards provided in the Covenant, it has consistently maintained that it is not competent to reassess the facts and evidence considered by national courts. The Committee can request that a contracting party does not deport to States which carry out the death penalty.[183]

In *Kindler v Canada*[184] the author complained that the decision to extradite him under the Extradition Treaty of 1976 between the US and Canada violated several articles of the Covenant. Following his conviction for murder in the US, the jury recommended the imposition of the death penalty. However, prior to sentence he fled to Canada where he was arrested and eventually extradited to the US. The issue in this case was whether extradition exposed the author to a real risk of a violation of his rights under the Covenant. The Committee decided that the communication was admissible with respect to Art 6, which addresses capital punishment, and Art 7, which prohibits torture and cruel, inhuman and degrading treatment, and found that the material submitted by the parties did not support a complaint based on the absence of procedural guarantees during the course of the extradition process. The Committee did not find that the terms of Art 6 necessarily require Canada to refuse to extradite to death penalty States. Furthermore, on previous occasions the Committee found that 'prolonged periods' of detention under a severe custodial regime on death row cannot generally be considered to constitute cruel, inhuman or degrading treatment.[185] Accordingly, the facts of this case did not reveal a violation of either Arts 6 or 7 of the Covenant.

In *T v Australia*[186] the author claimed that her husband's deportation to Malaysia, where she alleged there was a real risk that he would face the death penalty, was a violation of Australia's obligation to protect his right to life. He had been convicted in Australia of importing heroin from Malaysia. Although the Australian Government sought his deportation on the grounds that he had no entitlement to remain in Australia, Malaysia had not requested his return. It was noted that deportation differs from extradition in that 'the purpose of extradition is to return a person for prosecution or to serve a sentence, whereas no such necessary connection exists between expulsion and possible prosecution'.[187] The Committee acknowledged that

183 International Criminal Tribunal for the Former Yugoslavia (ICTY) Rules, r 86.
184 Case No 470/1991.
185 See *Howard Martin v Jamaica*, Application No 317/1988, para 12.2.
186 Case No 706/1996.
187 Ibid, para 5.6.

deportation to a State where there is a real risk that a person's rights under the Covenant will be violated may result in a violation of the Convention. Whilst a real risk can be deducted from the intent of the receiving State, as well as from a general pattern in similar cases, in this case, the author failed to substantiate the claim that there was a real risk that, on his return to Malaysia, her husband would be charged, prosecuted and sentenced to death. Accordingly, the facts of this case did not reveal a violation by Australia of any of the provisions of the Covenant.

13.5.5 1984 UN Convention Against Torture and Other Cruel, Inhuman or Degrading Treatment or Punishment

This Convention was drafted by the UN Commission on Human Rights and adopted by the UN General Assembly in 1984.[188] Contracting parties are under an obligation to take steps to prevent acts of torture 'in any territory under its jurisdiction'.[189] Article 3 of the Convention requires that Member States undertake not to expel, return or extradite persons to States if there are substantial grounds for believing they would be at risk of being subjected to torture. In determining whether there are such grounds, the requested States may take account of a consistent pattern of human rights violations. Allegations of violations are considered by the Committee Against Torture, which is established under Art 17 of the Convention. The Committee can request that a State party refrain from expelling or extraditing a person whilst a communication is being considered.[190] Compliance with this provision is considered to be essential in order to protect a person from serious harm. In *Nunez Chipana v Venezuela*[191] the author of the communication claimed that her extradition to Peru placed her in danger of being subjected to torture by the Peruvian authorities and was in violation of Art 3 of the Convention. It was relevant to her claim that she was wanted in connection with terrorist offences. She also maintained that proceedings in Peru for offences in connection with terrorism did not comply with fundamental fair trial principles. The Committee observed that it had received many allegations from reliable sources detailing the use of torture by Peruvian authorities in relation to the investigation of terrorism. The Committee Against Torture considered that in view of the nature of the accusations set out in the extradition request, the author was indeed in a situation where her return to Peru placed her in

---

188 GA Res 29/46.
189 UN Convention Against Torture and Other Cruel, Inhuman or Degrading Treatment or Punishment, Art 1.
190 ICTY Rules, r 108, para 3.
191 Case No 110/1998; CAT/C/21/D/110/1998.

danger of being subjected to torture. The Committee found that in surrendering the author to the Peruvian authorities, Venezuela failed to fulfil its obligation under Art 3 of the Convention. In *Agiza v Sweden*[192] the Committee found a violation of Art 3 of the Convention based on a consistent and widespread use of torture against detainees. It was noted that this risk was particularly high in the case of detainees held for political and security reasons. Agiza, who had been convicted *in absentia* for offences relating to terrorism, was denied asylum in Sweden. He claimed that his removal from Sweden to Egypt exposed him to the likelihood of persecution and torture. Following guarantees from the Egyptian government that Agiza would not be subjected to ill treatment, the Swedish authorities aided by the US authorities arranged for his deportation. The Committee was critical of the asylum process and found that the Swedish authorities withheld sensitive information from the Committee in breach of Art 22 of the Convention. It was suggested that the Swedish authorities should have raised the issue of confidentiality with the Committee and sought exemption from a duty to disclose.

13.6 EXTRADITION AND THE CASE OF SENATOR PINOCHET[193]

In refusing to afford immunity to Senator Pinochet, a former Chilean Head of State, on the ground that there could be no immunity from prosecution for certain international crimes, the House of Lords aroused considerable public curiosity and created renewed interest in the law of extradition. These proceedings demonstrated the linkage between the judicial and political elements of the extradition process. The arrest of Pinochet for conduct amounting to gross abuse of human rights was heralded worldwide as a triumph for international law and human rights. It was argued on behalf of the Government of Spain that, first, the crimes alleged against Pinochet were so horrific that an exception must be made to the international law principle of State immunity and, secondly, that the crimes with which he was charged are crimes against international law, in respect of which State immunity is not available. The House of Lords was also called on to consider problems arising in relation to the principle of double criminality. This case illustrates the problems

---

192 233/03, CAT/C/34/D/233/2003 (2005) For further discussion of this case see S Joseph, 'Rendering Terrorists and the Convention against Torture' *Human Rights Law Review* 5:2 (2005), 339–46.

193 *R v Bow Street Metropolitan Stipendiary Magistrate and Others ex p Pinochet Ugarte (Amnesty International and Others intervening) (No 3)* [1999] 2 All ER 97.

facing domestic courts when dealing with serious human rights abuses and raises several important issues relating to international criminal law.

13.6.1 The facts

On 11 September 1973, a right wing coup removed the left wing regime of President Salvador Allende, who was arrested and subsequently murdered. A military junta led by General Pinochet, who later became Head of State, was responsible for organising and carrying out the coup. It is without doubt that during this regime thousands of people were arrested, tortured and murdered. Although it is not suggested that Pinochet personally carried out any acts of torture, it is alleged that they were done at his instigation and with his knowledge. None of the conduct alleged was committed by or against UK nationals or in the UK. Human rights violations continued throughout the period of military rule until the late 1980s. The Pinochet regime ended in March 1990. In October 1998, Senator Pinochet visited a London hospital to receive medical treatment. Spanish judicial authorities sought to extradite him in order to stand trial on a number of charges. Following a complaint filed on 15 October 1998 by the Human Rights Secretariat of Izquierda Unida, the second largest left wing political party in Spain, the investigating court of the Audiencia Nacional Espanola, the National Criminal Court, filed a petition in the UK requesting Pinochet's arrest. An international arrest warrant was issued in Spain. Although most of the charges had no connection with Spain, the Spanish court held that they have jurisdiction to try crimes of genocide, torture and hostage taking committed abroad by virtue of the principle of universal jurisdiction and not merely in respect of Spanish victims. Spain also sought to exercise jurisdiction under the nationality principle in respect of the offences committed against Spanish nationals.

A magistrate in London issued two provisional arrest warrants under s 8 of the EA 1989. Following his arrest, Pinochet started proceedings for *habeas corpus* and for leave to move for judicial review of the warrants. The Divisional Court quashed both warrants on the ground that, as former Head of State, Pinochet was entitled to State immunity in respect of the offences with which he was charged. The Divisional Court also considered whether the crimes alleged in the second warrant, which were not crimes under UK law at the date they were committed, were 'extradition crimes' within the meaning of the EA 1989. Torture committed outside the UK could not be prosecuted before UK courts until 29 September 1988, the date s 134 of the Criminal Justice Act (CJA) 1988 entered into force. This provision, which reflects Art 1 of the 1984 UN Convention Against Torture and Other Cruel, Inhuman or Degrading Treatment or Punishment 1984, provides that:

> A public official or person acting in an official capacity, whatever his nationality, commits the offence of torture if in the UK or elsewhere he

intentionally inflicts severe pain or suffering on another in the performance or purported performance of his official duties.

Lord Bingham CJ was satisfied that provided the fugitive's conduct amounted to a crime in the UK at the date of the request for extradition, the offences amounted to 'extradition crimes' for the purposes of the EA 1989. Leave was given to the Crown Prosecution Service to appeal to the House of Lords.

13.6.2 Pinochet (No 1) [194]

Their Lordships were asked to consider, as a preliminary issue, the proper interpretation and scope of the immunity enjoyed by a former Head of State from arrest and extradition proceedings in the UK in respect of acts committed while he was Head of State. Prior to this hearing, the Spanish Government added genocide, murder, and hostage taking to the second warrant. In addition to the Crown Prosecution Service and counsel for Pinochet, their Lordships agreed to hear submissions from Amnesty International as interveners and an independent *amicus curiae*, and considered written submissions from Human Rights Watch. The prosecution's appeal was allowed by a majority of 3:2 on the grounds that Pinochet was not entitled to claim immunity in relation to crimes under international law. Any argument surrounding the double criminality issue was minimal. Indeed, there is some suggestion in the judgments that their Lordships accepted that all charges constituted extradition crimes. This judgment was set aside on the ground that the committee was not properly constituted. It was thought that the links between Lord Hoffmann, a member of the appeal committee, and Amnesty International Charity Ltd, of whom he was a director and chairperson, were such as to give the appearance of bias. Although there was no suggestion that he was in fact biased, it was considered that in any case where the impartiality of a judge is in question, the appearance of the bias is as important as the reality. This was the first time the House of Lords had set aside one of its own decisions.

13.6.3 Pinochet (No 3) [195]

Before the second hearing, leave was granted to the Republic of Chile to intervene and the ambit of the charges against Pinochet widened. The House of Lords was now asked to consider the following charges: conspiracy to torture committed between 1 January 1972 and 20 September 1973 and

194 [1998] 3 WLR 1456.
195 [1999] 2 WLR 827.

between 1 August 1973 and 1 January 1990; conspiracy to take hostages between 1 August 1973 and 1 January 1990; conspiracy to torture in further-ance of which murder was committed in various countries including Italy, France, Spain and Portugal, between 1 January 1972 and 1 January 1990; torture between 1 August 1973 and 8 August 1973 and on 11 September 1973; conspiracy to murder in Spain between 1 January and 31 December 1976 and in Italy on 6 October 1975; attempted murder in Italy on 6 October 1975; torture on various occasions between 11 September 1973 and May 1977; and torture on 24 June 1989. The addition of charges relating to conduct occur-ring before Pinochet assumed power required the House of Lords to turn their attention to the double criminality rule.[196] Arguably, the issue of double criminality is in any event preliminary to questions relating to immunity *ratione personae*. Unless the charges specified in the warrants constitute extradition crimes, their Lordships would not be required to consider claims of immunity.

In considering whether it was necessary for the fugitive's conduct to consti-tute an offence in the UK at the date of the request for extradition, or the actual date the conduct occurred, Lord Browne-Wilkinson examined Sched 1 to the EA 1870, a precursor to the current legislation, which adopted the 'list' approach to extradition crimes, and observed that the preamble required the list to be interpreted at the date of the alleged crime. In construing the EA 1989, which repealed the 1870 Act and introduced an extradition scheme based on conduct, he noted references to the conduct date. Whilst acknow-ledging that there was an anomaly with respect to the relevant date when criminality is assessed, Lord Browne-Wilkinson considered that for the pur-poses of the double criminality rule, the relevant date was the 'conduct date' and not the 'request date'. He considered that 'it would be extraordinary if the same Act required criminality under English law to be shown at one date for one form of extradition and at another date for another'.[197] Interestingly, the *travaux préparatoires* relating to the 1957 European Convention on Extradition and the departmental papers relating to the EA 1989 are silent on the relevant date. The decision that criminality was to be assessed at the conduct date and not at the request date excluded from consideration the majority of the charges preferred against Pinochet.

In respect of the crime of torture, Lord Browne-Wilkinson observed that the international law prohibiting torture had the character of *jus cogens*, from which there can be no derogation. Nevertheless, in the absence of an inter-national tribunal to punish torture and no general jurisdiction to permit prosecution in domestic courts, he doubted whether this was sufficient to

---

196 For further discussion of this point, see M Birnbaum, 'Pinochet and Double Criminality', *Crim LR* [2000], 127.
197 [1999] 2 All ER 97, p 107.

justify the conclusion that torture ranked as 'a fully constituted international crime'.[198] However, in providing a universal jurisdiction for the crime of torture, the UN Torture Convention supplied the missing link and made State torture 'an international crime in the highest sense'.[199] As a consequence, there could be no safe haven for torturers. In enacting s 134 of the CJA 1988, Parliament recognised the international obligation of States in respect of the crime of torture, and that acts of torture and conspiracy to torture committed after the enforcement of this legislation were extraditable crimes. As a consequence of requiring conduct to be a crime under UK law at the date it was committed, acts of torture occurring before 29 September 1988, the date of enforcement of the CJA 1988, could not be classed as extraditable crimes.

Lord Hope noted that prior to the enforcement of the Suppression of Terrorism Act (STA) 1978, the presumption against the extra-territorial application of criminal law would have precluded a prosecution for murder and conspiracy to murder. The STA 1978 provides for the prosecution of specified offences committed in States which are party to the European Convention on the Suppression of Terrorism, provided the conduct would amount to an offence under UK law.[200] Murder is a specified offence. However, the charges against Pinochet related to murders committed in France, Portugal and the US. These could not be 'extradition crimes' on the ground that the conduct took place prior to the enforcement of the STA 1978. Hostage taking was also excluded from the extradition proceedings on the ground that the only charge relating to this offence did not disclose any offence under the Taking of Hostages Act 1982.

It is a basic principle of international law that one sovereign State does not adjudicate on the conduct of another and, as a consequence, the Head of a Foreign State is entitled to personal immunity in respect of criminal and civil liability. This immunity is said to be granted *ratione personae*. Lord Browne-Wilkinson observed that no other domestic court had refused to afford immunity to a Head of State on the grounds that there can be no immunity against prosecution for certain international crimes. He was of the opinion that whilst the State Immunity Act 1978 made some modifications to the complete immunity afforded by the common law, a former Head of State remained immune from prosecution in relation to acts performed in his capacity as Head of State. However, he believed there to be strong ground for concluding that State torture, which is an international crime against humanity, could not be considered to be an act done in an official capacity. Observing that the Torture Convention requires all Member States to ban torture, he considered that it could not be an official function to do something which

198 [1999] 2 All ER 97, p 114.
199 Ibid, p 109.
200 STA 1978, s 4.

international law prohibits. Accordingly, if Pinochet authorised acts of torture he was acting contrary to international law and his actions did not give rise to immunity *ratione personae*.

Their Lordships' decision with respect to the double criminality principle required Pinochet to claim immunity only in relation to charges of torture and conspiracy to torture committed after 29 September 1988 and conspiracy to murder in Spain and murder in Spain. Immunity was raised successfully with respect to the charges of murder and conspiracy to murder. Accordingly, extradition proceedings were allowed to proceed solely in respect of the allegation that Pinochet organised and authorised torture after 8 December 1988, the date at which the House of Lords held that he was not acting in any capacity which gave rise to immunity because his actions were contrary to international law. This decision illustrates some of the problems that arise when domestic courts are called upon to deal with matters involving serious human rights violations, and demonstrates the advantages of having recourse to the International Criminal Court.[201]

---

201 Following the decision of the House of Lords, the Home Secretary took the view that extradition should be refused on grounds of ill-health. Pinochet was permitted to return to Chile to be tried before a national court. In 2004, the Supreme Court ruled that he was fit to stand trial. In Nov 2006 he made a statement admitting responsibility for human rights abuses and was placed under house arrest. He died in December 2006.

Chapter 14

Abduction

14.1 INTRODUCTION

Extradition procedures are often so cumbersome and time consuming that frequently they are either ignored or intentionally circumvented by the authorities. The legality of the procedures used to secure the presence of the suspect is generally not the concern of the receiving State. An examination of the differing approaches taken by the courts to the irregular return of suspects by unlawful methods demonstrates little uniformity in principle and practice. Traditionally, national criminal courts have adhered to the *male captus, bene detentus* rule and have been prepared to hear criminal proceedings without regard to the circumstances by which the defendant was produced for prosecution. Any irregularities occurring outside the jurisdiction were considered irrelevant to the power of the court to try an offender lawfully arrested within the jurisdiction. Recently, courts in several jurisdictions have questioned whether adherence to the traditional rule may result in an abuse of the court process. Judges have been particularly critical of the involvement of their own national authorities in the blatant and extremely serious failure to adhere to the rule of law[1] with regard to extradition arrangements and have declined to exercise jurisdiction.

14.2 THE *MALE CAPTUS, BENE DETENTUS* RULE

Reluctant to inquire into circumstances occurring outside the jurisdiction, courts in England, Scotland and the US chose for many years to follow an early English authority. In *Ex p Scott*,[2] Lord Tenterden CJ granted a warrant for the arrest of Susannah Scott on a charge of perjury. Following the applicant's arrest in Brussels, she applied to the British ambassador for assistance,

---

1 *Mullen* [1999] 2 Cr App R 143, p 157.
2 (1829) 9B&C 446.

but he refused to interfere. The arresting officer brought her to England. On an application for *habeas corpus*, the court was called upon to consider whether, in the circumstances, account could be taken of the manner in which the accused was brought within the jurisdiction. The Lord Chief Justice held that, in considering whether to try the accused, the court should not concern itself with acts that occurred in a foreign country. In *Sinclair v HM Advocate*,[3] the High Court in Scotland adopted a similar approach to the same problem. It held that when a fugitive is brought before a court in Scotland on a valid warrant, the magistrate has jurisdiction, and is bound to exercise it without any consideration of the means which have been used to bring him from the foreign country into the jurisdiction.[4] Courts in the UK continued to support the traditional rule and in *O/C Depot Battalion, RASC, Colchester ex p Elliott*,[5] Lord Goddard CJ observed that Lord McLaren's speech in *Sinclair*:

> ... is a perfectly clear and unambiguous statement of the law administered in Scotland. It shows that the law of both countries is exactly the same on this point and that we have no power to go into the question, once a prisoner is in lawful custody in this country, of the circumstances in which he may be brought here.

However, in an apparent *volte face*, the court, in *Ex p Mackeson*[6] and in *Ex p Healy*[7] considered it did have the power to inquire into the manner in which the accused had been brought within the jurisdiction and could, at its discretion, stay proceedings. After some consideration of the authorities, Stephen Brown LJ held in *Ex p Driver*[8] that *Ex p Mackeson* had been decided *per curiam* and the court reverted to its policy of non-inquiry into pre-trial irregularity.

In *AG of the Government of Israel v Eichmann*[9] the District Court of Jerusalem noted that courts in both the UK and the US did not take account of violations of customary international law when deciding whether to try an accused. In this case, Eichmann had been abducted from Argentina and brought to Israel for trial for crimes committed during the Second World War. The District Court found very little authority to support the proposition that the prosecution should be dismissed on the ground of unlawful arrest.

---

3 (1890) 17 R(J) 38.
4 Ibid, p 43.
5 [1949] 1 All ER 138.
6 (1982) 75 Cr App R 24.
7 [1983] 1 WLR 108.
8 [1986] QB 95.
9 (1961) 36 ILR 5; 36 ILR 277.

However, reference was made to the Harvard Research project[10] which states in Art 16:

> In exercising jurisdiction under the Convention, no State shall prosecute or punish a person who has been brought within its territory or a place subject to its authority by recourse to measures in violation of international law or international convention without first obtaining the consent of the State or States whose rights have been violated by such measures.

The court held that, despite being satisfied that Eichmann had been abducted, it had jurisdiction to try him for crimes against humanity, a decision that was subsequently confirmed by the Supreme Court.

14.3 APPROACH TAKEN BY COURTS IN THE US

The US Supreme Court has adopted an approach which is substantially in line with the doctrine established by the early English authorities. Consistently refusing to regard forcible abduction from a foreign State as a violation of the right to a fair trial, which is guaranteed by the 14th Amendment to the Constitution, courts in the US have been content to permit the trial of fugitives despite a clear indication that their presence within the jurisdiction was achieved by kidnapping. In *Ker v Illinois*[11] the appellant, who was wanted in the US on charges of larceny, was kidnapped in Peru by a US envoy. Contrary to the President's instructions, the envoy failed to present the request for extradition to the Peruvian authorities and put the accused on a ship bound for the US. In holding that the US courts had jurisdiction to try the accused, the Supreme Court was satisfied that there had been no violation of the extradition treaty between Peru and the US. Any unlawful activity took place outside the jurisdiction and did not concern the trial court. A similar view has been taken in relation to interstate abduction. In *Frisbie v Collins*[12] the Supreme Court considered that the accused's constitutional right to due process had not been violated by his forcible abduction from Illinois by Michigan agents and, thus, there was nothing to prevent the court from exercising jurisdiction. In this case, there was no international extradition treaty to consider.

However, this position was challenged in *USA v Toscanino*.[13] The defendant alleged that he was brought into the US from Uruguay by abduction. He appealed to the US Court of Appeals for the Second Circuit from a decision

---

10 Supplement: Research in International Law, 29 *AJIL* (1935), 623–32.
11 119 US 436 (1886).
12 342 US 519 (1952); L Ed 541.
13 500 F 2d 267 (1974).

of the lower court that provided he was physically present at the time, allegations of torture and kidnap were immaterial to the exercise of its jurisdiction. The court held:

> ... that federal district court's criminal process would be abused or degraded if it was executed against the defendant Italian citizen, who alleged that he was brought into the USA from Uruguay after being kidnapped, and such abuse could not be tolerated without debasing the processes of justice, so that defendant was entitled to a hearing on his allegation ... Government should be denied the right to exploit its own illegal conduct, and when an accused is kidnapped and forcibly brought within the jurisdiction, court's acquisition of power over his person represents the fruits of the Government's exploitation of its own misconduct.

In *USA v Verdugo-Urquidez* [14] the US Court of Appeals for the Ninth Circuit adopted the same approach. A Mexican citizen was kidnapped in Mexico by US agents and taken to the US. The Mexican authorities were not party to the abduction, which was in violation of the 1978 US–Mexico Extradition Treaty, and argued that the fugitive should be returned to Mexico. When the fugitive was produced before the Court of Appeals, the indictment was dismissed on the ground that the court lacked jurisdiction to try the accused because he had been brought within the jurisdiction in violation of an international treaty. However, in *USA v Alvarez-Machain* [15] the Supreme Court refused to follow this principle and held that, in the absence of a specific term in the extradition treaty prohibiting abduction, the fugitive's forcible abduction by State agents did not prevent courts in the US from exercising jurisdiction in respect of a criminal offence. This case concerned a Mexican citizen wanted for the murder of a Drug Enforcement Administration agent. The District Court was satisfied that other agents were responsible for his kidnap and abduction, which was in violation of the extradition treaty between Mexico and the US, and that the defendant should be discharged and returned to Mexico. This decision was affirmed by the Court of Appeals but reversed by the Supreme Court by a majority of 6:3. Rejecting the suggestion that abduction was prohibited by international customary law, the court held that to 'imply from the terms of the Treaty that it prohibits obtaining the presence of an individual by means outside the procedures of the Treaty requires a much larger inferential leap, with only the most general of international principles to support it'. Although the English court has been referred to these decisions on several occasions, it considers that they are not

14 939 F 2d 1341 (1990).
15 112 S Ct 2188 (1992).

helpful on the ground that 'they deal with the issue of whether or not an accused acquires a constitutional defence to the jurisdiction of the US courts and not to the question whether, assuming the court has jurisdiction, it has a discretion to refuse to try the accused'.[16]

14.4 APPROACH TAKEN BY THE EUROPEAN COURT OF HUMAN RIGHTS

The ECHR contains no provisions concerning the circumstances in which extradition may be granted or the procedures to be followed. However, the applicant in *Öcalan v Turkey*[17] relied on authorities from the UK, the US, New Zealand and South Africa to support his argument before the ECHR that arrest pending his removal from Kenya for trial in Turkey for terrorist-related offences amounted to an abduction which rendered his detention contrary to Art 5(1)(c) of the Convention, and his trial null and void. The applicant maintained that there was *prima facie* evidence that the Turkish authorities, operating overseas and beyond their jurisdiction, had acted in collusion with their Kenyan counterparts, many of whom had been bribed, to deprive him of the substantive and procedural protections provided by the extradition process. Thus, he argued, failure by the authorities to follow formal extradition procedures resulted in his unlawful detention which was contrary to Art 5 of the European Convention on Human Rights. The Turkish Government submitted that the applicant's arrest and detention arose as a result of co-operation between the Turkish and Kenyan authorities. The Government denied that this case involved a disguised extradition and pointed out that no extradition treaty was in force between Kenya and Turkey. Further, prior to his arrest, the Turkish court had issued seven warrants for his arrest and Interpol had circulated a Red 'wanted' notice.[18] The applicant, who was an illegal immigrant in Kenya, had been handed over to the Turkish authorities under arrangements for co-operation between the two States for the prevention of terrorism. The ECHR observed that the Convention does not prevent States co-operating to obtain the extradition or deportation of fugitive offenders, provided that the co-operative procedures do not infringe any specific rights protected by the Convention.[19] The Court also noted that, provided there was a legal basis for the applicant's arrest, even deportation in the disguise of extradition would not necessarily be contrary to the Convention. Noting that inherent in the Convention is a search for a fair balance

16 *Bennett v Horseferry Road Magistrates' Court* [1993] 3 All ER 138.
17 Application No 46221/99.
18 See Chapter 17.
19 *Stocke v Germany*, Ser A, No 199, opinion of the Commission.

between the public interest and the protection of an individual's fundamental rights, the Court reiterated its observations in the *Soering* case that as crime:

> ... takes on a larger international dimension, it is increasingly in the interest of all nations that suspected offenders who flee abroad should be brought to justice. Conversely, the establishment of safe havens for fugitives would not only result in danger for the States obliged to harbour the protected persons but also tend to undermine the foundations of extradition.[20]

Thus the rules established in an extradition treaty, or, in the absence of a treaty, the level of co-operation between States are relevant to a complaint regarding unlawful arrest. However, handing a fugitive over as a result of informal co-operation between States does not necessarily make an arrest unlawful. The Court considered that it must decide on the basis of the evidence whether the acts of the Turkish and Kenyan officials had violated Kenyan sovereignty and international law or had resulted from co-operation between the respective authorities. Finding for the Turkish Government the Court considered that it had not been established beyond reasonable doubt that the activities of the Turkish and Kenyan Governments were in violation of international law; the Court held that the applicant's arrest and detention were in accordance with the law for the purposes of Art 5(1)(c).

14.5 THE DOCTRINE OF ABUSE OF PROCESS[21]

In recent years, English and Australian judges have expressed concern that the abduction of persons in disregard of specific international agreements may contaminate any subsequent proceedings. The need to discourage such conduct by law enforcement agencies has been perceived as an issue of public policy. In *Connelly v Director of Public Prosecutions*[22] the House of Lords held that the court has a residual, discretionary jurisdiction to stay criminal proceedings. This has become known as the doctrine of abuse of process and has been used in England to stay criminal proceedings in cases where the court considers the actions of prosecuting authorities threaten the moral integrity of the criminal process itself. In *Bennett v Horseferry Road*

---

20 Application No 46221/99, para 90.
21 For a discussion of abuse of process, see A Choo, *Abuse of Process and Judicial Stays of Criminal Proceedings*, 1993, Oxford: OUP, and A Choo, 'Halting Criminal Proceedings: The Abuse of Process Revisited', *Crim LR* [1995], 846–74. This aspect of abduction is discussed further in C Gane and S Nash, 'Illegal Extradition: The Irregular Return of Fugitive Offenders', 1 *Scottish Law & Practice Quarterly* (1996), 277, p 291.
22 [1964] AC 1254.

Magistrates' Court[23] the House of Lords held that the doctrine could also apply to the issue of the unlawful return of fugitive offenders. In the exercise of its inherent power to prevent an abuse of process, the court could inquire into how the accused had been brought before the court and, if satisfied that the procedures adopted in bringing the accused before the court involved a serious abuse of power, the court could express its disapproval by refusing to act upon it.[24] However, the court considers applications based on abuse of process very carefully and in *Lodhi v Governor of Brixton Prison; Government of the UAE*[25] held that it would be very rare that a second extradition request would trigger proceedings that would amount to an abuse of process. The application of the doctrine of abuse of process to the problem of abduction appears to have originated in the New Zealand case of *Hartley*,[26] and has subsequently been accepted by the Supreme Court of New South Wales in *Levinge v Director of Custodial Services, Department of Corrective Services and Others*.[27] In this case, an Australian court decided that it had jurisdiction to prevent an abuse of process by staying proceedings where it was established that an existing extradition treaty had knowingly been circumvented to secure the presence of the defendant within the jurisdiction. The appellant had been unlawfully taken from Mexico to the US by US law enforcement officers and extradited to Australia. There was no evidence connecting the Australian authorities with any unlawful activity. The Australian court acknowledged that, whilst it had jurisdiction to deal with the fugitive, it also had a discretionary power not to do so. The power of the court to grant this type of relief was, in the view of the court, based on, '. . . [a] conception of the necessary purity of the "temples of justice" and the undesirability that the administration of justice itself should become contaminated by involvement (or the perception of involvement) in unlawful or wrongful activities on the part of the authorities'.[28]

14.6 COLLUSION BY LAW ENFORCEMENT AGENCIES

Following a similar line of argument, the House of Lords, in *Bennett v Horseferry Road Magistrates' Court*,[29] decided as a matter of principle that

23 [1993] 3 All ER 138.
24 Ibid, p 150.
25 [2002] EWHC 2029.
26 [1978] 2 NZLR 199.
27 (1987) 9 NSWLR 546.
28 Ibid, p 557.
29 [1993] 3 All ER 138.

maintenance of the rule of law in these matters ought to prevail over the public interest in the prosecution of crime. If it could be shown that the defendant had been forcibly abducted and brought to the UK to face trial in disregard of the extradition laws, the court was prepared to stay proceedings as an abuse of process. Lord Griffiths observed that this power was predicated on the judiciary accepting responsibility for maintaining the rule of law:

> In the present case, there is no suggestion that the appellant cannot have a fair trial, nor could it be suggested that it would have been unfair to try him if he had been returned to this country through extradition procedures. If the court is to have the power to interfere with the prosecution in the present circumstances it must be because the judiciary accept responsibility for the maintenance of the rule of law that embraces a willingness to oversee executive action and to refuse to countenance behaviour that threatens either basic human rights or the rule of law.[30]

Lord Bridge, in agreeing with Lord Griffiths, considered executive lawlessness to be a critical factor:

> There is, I think, no principle more basic to any proper system of law than the maintenance of the rule of law itself. When it is shown that the law enforcement agency responsible for bringing a prosecution has only been enabled to do so by participating in violations of international law and of the laws of another State . . . I think that respect for the rule of law demands that the court take cognisance of that circumstance. To hold that the court may turn a blind eye to executive lawlessness beyond the frontiers of its own jurisdiction is, to my mind, an insular and unacceptable view. Since the prosecution could never have been brought if the defendant had not been illegally abducted, the whole proceeding is tainted.[31]

Lord Lowry's concerns were directed to the involvement of British authorities:

> If British officialdom at any level has participated in or encouraged the kidnapping, it seems to represent a grave contravention of international law, the comity of nations and the rule of law generally if our courts allow themselves to be used by the executive to try an offence which the courts would not be dealing with if the rule of law prevailed.[32]

---

30 [1993] 3 All ER 150.
31 Ibid, p 155.
32 Ibid, p 163.

Having been discharged by the English court, Bennett was immediately arrested on a warrant issued by the sheriff of Aberdeen. In *Bennett, Petitioner*,[33] a suspension of the Scottish arrest warrant was sought on the ground that the case of *Sinclair v HM Advocate*[34] should be reviewed in the light of *Bennett v Horseferry Road Magistrates' Court*.[35] The Lord Justice General held that, whilst in an appropriate case the Scottish court would reconsider its position, he was satisfied that in this case there was no collusion between the British and South African authorities. Furthermore, the Lord Advocate, as Public Prosecutor in Scotland, had had no involvement in Bennett's return to the UK. When considering the question 'whether to enforce the warrant would be an abuse of the processes of the Scottish court',[36] in the absence of evidence of collusion with foreign authorities to flout extradition procedures, the court answered in the negative.[37] However, it is arguably not inconsistent with the principles of Scots law to hold that it would be oppressive to allow a case to proceed if the production of the accused involved breaches of international law and human rights abuses.[38]

14.7 SERIOUSNESS OF THE CRIME

Mindful of its obligation to uphold the rule of law in the face of gross violations of international law and human rights standards, the English court continues to endorse a wide view of the scope of the doctrine of abuse of process in extradition cases. In *Mullen*[39] British authorities initiated the appellant's deportation by unlawful means in disregard of extradition arrangements, and, in order to prevent Mullen from contesting his deportation, denied him access to legal advice. In exercising its discretionary powers, the court was prepared to balance the seriousness of the crime against the 'need to discourage such conduct on the part of those who are responsible for criminal prosecutions'.[40] Following the enforcement of the Human Rights Act (HRA) 1998, the denial of rights guaranteed by the Convention assumes even greater importance in respect to the exercise of the court's discretionary powers to stay proceedings. There is some support for the argument that

33 [1994] SCCR 902.
34 (1890) 17 R(J) 38.
35 [1993] 3 All ER 138.
36 [1994] SCCR 902, p 923.
37 Whilst 'abuse of process' is not a term generally used by the Scottish courts, many of the matters regarded by the English court as an abuse of process are addressed in Scotland by use of the term 'oppression'. See op cit, Gane and Nash, note 21, p 292.
38 Ibid, p 304.
39 [1999] 2 Cr App R 143.
40 Ibid, p 157.

compliance with the HRA 1998 prevents courts from relying upon evidence obtained in violation of fair trial rights.[41] However, misconduct with regard to the production of the accused may not warrant a mandatory stay of proceedings. Whilst the ECHR has focused on the impugned pre-trial conduct of prosecuting authorities to determine whether a trial was fair,[42] it is still uncertain whether fair trial guarantees provide the right not to stand trial.

14.8 EXTRAORDINARY RENDITION

Extraordinary rendition is the process used to transport prisoners to various locations for interrogation and imprisonment. It usually involves the illegal abduction of persons suspected of terrorist offences by members of the security services to States with very low levels of human rights protection. The process of rendition frequently appears to involve the CIA, and the destination for many suspects is Guantanamo Bay in Cuba. It is suggested that transporting suspects to secret detention centres in third States is done to avoid US due process rules and the prohibition against torture. The interrogation techniques used in third States usually do not satisfy the requirements of international human rights instruments. The seizing and transfer of suspects does not involve the use of lawful arrest and detention provisions or extradition procedures. Suspects may be transported across the territories of several States without recourse to lawful surrender procedures before reaching detention centres. Many of the States allegedly allowing their airports and airspace to be used for transfer of suspects have signed and ratified the 1984 UN Convention Against Torture and Other Cruel, Inhuman or Degrading Treatment or Punishment which provides that no signatory state shall expel, return or extradite a person to another State where there are substantial grounds for believing that he or she will be subjected to torture. The treatment of detainees in this centre has been the subject of strong criticism by many States and international organisations.[43] In April 2005, the Parliamentary Assembly of the Council of Europe adopted a resolution and recommendation in which it urged the US Government to ensure that its

---

41 See *Allan v UK*, Application No 48539/99, judgment of 5 Nov 2002, in which the ECtHR considered that the use of evidence obtained in breach of the privilege against self-incrimination violated Art 6 of the European Convention on Human Rights,

42 See discussion of *Saunders v UK* (1997) 23 EHRR 313, and *Teixeira v Portugal* (1998) 28 EHRR 101 and in AL-T Choo and S Nash, 'What's the matter with s 78?' *Crim LR* [1999], 929, p 939.

43 See for example, 'Below the radar: Secret flights to torture and disappearance', Amnesty International Report, AMR 51/051/2006, 5 April 2006, available at <http://www.amnesty.org>; and the press release 19 May 2006, *CAT Concludes Thirty-Sixth Session*.

practices in respect to the transfer and treatment of detainees conformed to the rule of law. The UN Human Rights Committee has been highly critical of the US and called for the closure of Guantanamo following:

'. . . allegations that the State party had established secret detention facilities, which were not accessible to the International Committee of the Red Cross. The Committee recommended that the United States cease to detain any person at Guantanamo Bay and that it close that detention facility, permit access by the detainees to judicial process or release them as soon as possible, ensuring that they were not returned to any state where they could face a real risk of being tortured'.[44]

Acting under powers provided by Art 52 of the European Convention on Human Rights, the Secretary General of the Council of Europe commenced an inquiry in November 2005 into alleged secret detention centres in Member States. States were required to report whether their territories had been used in connection with the illegal transfer of detainees in violation of international human rights law. The report provides sound evidence that the US has been involved in transporting suspects from the US to third States without using lawful extradition procedures. Many Member States commenced judicial investigations into the alleged abduction of persons from their territories to the US detention centre in Guantanamo. German judicial authorities investigated the illegal abduction of Khaled El-Masri, a German citizen, to Kabul for interrogation following his arrest in Macedonia. He was arrested at the Serbian border and detained prior to being handed over to the CIA and flown to Afghanistan The Polish and Romanian authorities commenced investigations into the existence of secret detention centres which were allegedly used by the US authorities for interrogating suspects.[45] Several other Member States are investigating allegations that their airspace or airports were used by CIA-chartered aircraft for the purposes of transporting detainees to detention centres. In 2005, the Italian authorities issued arrest warrants against persons alleged to be CIA agents following the abduction of Hassan Mustafa Osama Nasr in Milan. He had been transferred to Egypt for interrogation without informing the Italian judicial or police authorities. At the time, the Italian authorities were conducting an investigation into allegations against him in connection with terrorist-related activities. His abduction by the CIA effectively sabotaged the Italian anti-terrorist operation. An

---

44 See Human Rights Committee, Consideration of Reports submitted by States Parties under Art 40 of the Covenant, United States of America (87th session, July 2006) and the press release 19 May 2006, *CAT Concludes Thirty-Sixth Session*.
45 See Human Rights Watch press release, 7 Nov 2005.

information memorandum published by the Parliamentary Assembly of the Council of Europe, noted that:

> This 'rendition' is a glaring illustration of the fact that such actions, which infringe the principles of the rule of law, are not only unacceptable from the legal and ethical point of view but also ineffective, or indeed damaging to the fight against terrorism. This lack of co-operation with and confidence in the authorities officially mandated to fight crime is bound to have very serious consequences, challenging the very functioning of the law-based state and its democratic foundation.[46]

Evidence is emerging which supports suggestions that States which have signed the 1984 UN Convention are involved in the process of illegal transfer of persons. In September 2006, a report was released by a Canadian Commission investigating the case of Maher Arar, a Canadian citizen detained while travelling through the US and transported to Syria for interrogation. The Commission concluded that there was no evidence to indicate that Maher Arar had committed any offence or that his activities constituted a threat to the security of Canada. The Commissioner also found that Canadian agencies had relied on information from Syria which was likely to have been obtained by torture.[47] In November 2006, the European Parliament's Temporary Committee on the alleged use of European countries by the CIA for the transport and illegal detention of prisoners produced a working document which examined 10 cases of extraordinary rendition.[48] The cases considered involved either the abduction of citizens or residents of Member States or the use of airspace of a Member State by flights chartered by the CIA. There were also allegations that officials of Member States were involved in providing support to the secret services. The rapporteur compared allegations received by the committee with the data supplied to the European Parliament by Eurocontrol, the EU's air traffic and control agency, and EUSC, the EU satellite centre. The committee held meetings with interested parties including the victims and their lawyers, heads of national judicial or parliamentary bodies, representatives of international organisations, journalists, NGO's and experts in the field. The committee found that where the victims were able to provide reliable details, the allegations corresponded with Eurocontrol data with regard to the existence and characteristics of the flights used. One of the cases examined by the committee involved Hadj Boumediene and five others

---

46 AS/Jur (2006) 03 rev. Available at <http://assembly.coe.int/committeeDocs/2006/20060124_Jdoc032006_E.htm> (accessed 1 Dec 2006).
47 Commission of Inquiry into the Actions of Canadian Officials in Relation to Maher Arar. See <http://www.ararcommission.ca>.
48 European Parliament working document No 7 on 'extraordinary renditions', 16 Nov 2006. DT/641309EN.doc.

who are Bosnian nationals of Algerian decent. In 2001, the Supreme Court of the Federation of Bosnia-Herzegovina issued arrest warrants in connection with terrorist offences. They were released by the court in 2002 and placed in the custody of the Federation police. Despite there being no formal extradition request from the US, they were immediately transferred to the control of the US authorities stationed in Bosnia and transported via Incirlik, the US Air Force base in Turkey, to Guantanamo Bay. Having considered all the material, the committee found that there was evidence of a 'widespread, methodical practice of "extraordinary rendition" following precise rules, and carried out by certain US secret services'.[49] The rapporteur concluded by reminding Member States that:

> Any suspect is entitled to a process affording all the judicial guarantees which are recognised by international conventions and by the principles common to all countries which are (or wish to become) Member States of the European Union. The mechanism of 'extraordinary rendition' is wholly illegal; it is a criminal act which cannot be justified in any circumstances. In addition, 'extraordinary renditions' have had the effect, in some cases, of hampering perfectly legal investigations by local security forces, and this has had substantial negative consequences for the security of the Member State concerned.'

49 Ibid, at para 3.

Chapter 15

Mutual Legal Assistance

15.1 INTRODUCTION

International judicial and police co-operation in criminal matters through formal mutual legal assistance arrangements is a fairly recent phenomenon.[1] Realising that participation in formal arrangements would provide prosecuting authorities with increased access to suspects and evidence located abroad, States have become increasingly willing to negotiate mutual legal assistance treaties (MLAT).[2] Whilst most forms of assistance can proceed on the basis of the principle of international comity, mutual assistance increasingly takes place by way of bilateral or multilateral treaty. Many States have demonstrated a preference to enter into bilateral agreements which allow for greater specificity.[3] Generally, MLATs require contracting parties to undertake to provide assistance in: taking written testimony; conducting searches for and seizing material for use as evidence; serving summonses; and tracing

---

1 For a discussion of the development of mutual legal assistance in criminal matters, see A Ellis and R Pisani, 'The United States Treaties on Mutual Assistance: A Comparative Analysis', *The International Lawyer*, (1985), 189; W Gilmore (ed), *Mutual Assistance in Criminal and Business Regulatory Matters*, 1995, Cambridge: CUP; A Jones, *Jones & Doobay on Extradition and Mutual Legal Assistance*, 2004, London: Sweet & Maxwell; C Murray and L Harris, *Mutual Assistance in Criminal Matters*, 2000, London: Sweet & Maxwell; E Nadelmann, 'Negotiations in Criminal Law Assistance Treaties', 33 *AJCL* (1985), 467; E Nadelmann, *Cops Across Borders: The Internationalisation of US Criminal Law Enforcement*, 1993, Pennsylvania: Pennsylvania State UP.
2 The UK, eg, has ratified the 1959 European Convention on Mutual Assistance in Criminal Matters and its Protocol, ETS 30; the 1990 European Convention on Laundering, Search, Seizure and Confiscation of the Proceeds of Crime, 30 ILM (1991), 148; the 1988 United Nations (UN) Convention Against Illicit Traffic in Narcotic and Psychotropic Substances, 28 ILM (1989), 493; and has adopted the Commonwealth Scheme Relating to Mutual Assistance in Criminal Matters.
3 The 1973 USA–Switzerland Treaty, 12 ILM (1973), 916, eg, addresses the specific problem relating to the depositing of 'dirty' money into Swiss bank accounts.

witnesses and suspects.[4] Conventionally, mutual assistance arrangements abide by the *locus regit actum* rule, which permits the requested party to execute letters rogatory in accordance with its national law and practice. While some MLATs encourage requesting States to indicate their preferred method of conducting the inquiry,[5] in practice, they exert little control over the manner in which requests are executed. To increase the effectiveness of MLATs and to combat admissibility problems, assistance mechanisms are placing increasing emphasis on compliance with the procedural requirements of the requesting State.[6]

Requests are subject to judicial authorisation in the requested State. In the UK, the Home Office Mutual Legal Assistance Section checks all letters rogatory and submits them for endorsement to the relevant judicial authority.[7] This is to ensure that the requests for assistance comply with both UK and international law. The process of administrative and judicial supervision can be cumbersome and time consuming. However, judicial input undoubtedly assists in maintaining a balance between competing interests and safeguards against an abuse of the mutual legal assistance process by governments.[8] While most MLATs do not contain specific human rights provisions, many have traditionally provided reservations and safeguards designed to protect the accused. These provisions are similar to those found in extradition treaties. Thus, Art 1(2) of the 1959 European Convention on Mutual Assistance in Criminal Matters, for example, provides that assistance may be refused, if the offence is of a political nature, or if the execution of a request will prejudice the sovereignty of the requested State. However, in contrast with extradition treaties, there is usually no specific double criminality requirement. Requests may also be refused if evidence would need to be taken under compulsion or from a witness who would be non-compellable in the requested State.[9]

---

4 See, eg, the 1990 UN Model Treaty on Mutual Assistance which was adopted by GA Res 45/117 (1990).

5 See, eg, 1973 USA–Switzerland Treaty.

6 See, eg, 1990 European Convention on Laundering, Search, Seizure and Confiscation of the Proceeds of Crime.

7 Under Art 53 of the 1990 Convention Implementing the Schengen Agreement (Schengen Implementing Convention), 30 ILM (1991), 68, the central authority can be bypassed and requests for assistance made directly between judicial authorities.

8 See, eg, *R v Secretary of State for the Home Department ex p (1) Mohammed Sani Abacha (2) Abubakar Baguda & Federal Republic of Nigeria* [2001] EWHC 787.

9 In *Re Request from L Kasper-Ansermet* 132 FRD 622 (1990), US Dist, the US District Court was called upon to consider the validity of a request from the Swiss authorities who sought assistance in taking testimony from two suspects in order to 'pronounce indictment' on behalf of the Swiss magistrate. The suspects objected on the ground that the Swiss proceedings would not conform with principles of due process because of the possibility of trial *in absentia*, and the Swiss provision which allowed silence under questioning to be inferred as guilt was contrary to their rights under US law. Adopting a purposive approach to the Swiss request, the court found that the treaty permitted the use of a civil subpoena to compel the

States may also refuse requests if the evidence is protected by the rules of privilege. While some treaties state that the requesting State shall not, without the consent of the requested State, use information or evidence provided by the requested State for investigations other than those stated in the request,[10] others allow evidence to be used in the prosecution of non-treaty offences.[11] Despite moves to introduce measures designed to offer the defence some procedural protection, criticism has been directed towards the lack of corresponding mechanisms for the accused needing to seek assistance from foreign authorities.[12] Concerns have also been raised regarding the potential for misusing mutual assistance provisions to obtain evidence from abroad which would be unobtainable under national law.[13]

15.2 UN INITIATIVES

15.2.1 UN Model Treaty on Mutual Assistance in Criminal Matters

Using features common to existing agreements, the 1990 UN Model Treaty on Mutual Assistance in Criminal Matters (1990 Model Treaty) creates a simple framework which can be used as a guide for States negotiating bilateral or multilateral agreements.[14] Each party is required to establish a 'competent authority' through which assistance should be directed[15] and the parties undertake to provide 'the widest possible measure of mutual assistance' with regard to taking evidence from witnesses, carrying out searches and seizures, serving documents and supplying documents and records'.[16] While areas of judicial co-operation such as the transfer of prisoners, proceedings

---

suspects' presence in court. The court adhered to the rule of non-enquiry in respect of the trial *in absentia* and considered that the argument based on inferences drawn from silence was, at the moment, hypothetical. However, compelling suspects to appear before the court in order to 'pronounce indictment' amounted to a Swiss judicial function which exceeded the ambit of the treaty.

10 See, eg, UN Model Treaty, Art 7; USA–Switzerland Treaty, Art 5; UK–USA Treaty, Art 7; Mexico–USA Treaty, Art 6.

11 See, eg, *USA v Johnpoll*, 739 F 2d 702 (1984). US prosecuting authorities had used evidence obtained under the USA–Switzerland Treaty, in relation to a conspiracy to transport stolen securities, to convict him of additional customs offences, offences which were not covered under the Treaty.

12 C Gane and M Mackarel, 'The Admissibility of Evidence Obtained from Abroad into Criminal Proceedings – The Interpretation of Mutual Legal Assistance Treaties and Use of Evidence Irregularly Obtained', 4 *Eur J Crime Cr L Cr J* (1996), 98.

13 For further discussion, see op cit, Murray and Harris, note 1.

14 1990 UN Model Treaty on Mutual Assistance in Criminal Matters, 30 ILM (1991), 1419.

15 Ibid, Art 3.

16 Ibid, Art 1.

and the execution of judgments are outside the remit of the 1990 Model Treaty, it includes a provision relating to co-operation in fiscal cases.[17] States may refuse to comply with a request for assistance on grounds similar to those found in extradition treaties.[18] Thus, a request may be refused in respect of investigations into political offences and offences arising out of discrimination on grounds of race, sex, religion, nationality or political opinions, or if the request offends against the principle of double jeopardy.[19] Although there is no double criminality requirement in the 1990 Model Treaty, it does contain a specialty provision. Thus, evidence may only be used in connection with matters for which the request was made, and documents and original records must be returned to the requested State as soon as possible, unless the requested State waives the right to have the material returned.[20] The requested State can be asked to provide assistance to enable a witness to travel to the requesting State to assist in a criminal investigation or to testify in criminal proceedings.[21] However, the requesting State must undertake to provide the witness with 'safe conduct'.[22] The 1990 Model Treaty complies with standard MLAT practice in that evidence must be obtained in accordance with the law of the requested State. Provided the requested State concurs, parties to the proceedings, their representatives and representatives of the requesting State may, subject to the law and procedure of the requested State, be present during the taking of statements.[23] The requested State can, in so far as national law and procedure allows, carry out requests for search and seizure of material for use as evidence in proceedings in the requested State. However, any procedures used during the search for and seizure of evidence should not violate third party rights.[24] The cost of executing a request is generally borne by the requested State.[25]

15.3 1959 EUROPEAN CONVENTION ON MUTUAL ASSISTANCE IN CRIMINAL MATTERS

The 1959 Council of Europe Convention on Mutual Legal Assistance in Criminal Matters, which entered into force in 1962, is one of the first multi-

---

17 1990 Model Treaty, Art 1(2)(g).
18 See Art 4, generally.
19 See, eg, the corresponding limitations included within the UK Extradition Act (EA) 1989, s 6.
20 1990 Model Treaty, Art 7.
21 Ibid, Arts 13 and 14.
22 Ibid, Art 15. A witness should not be detained, prosecuted or punished in respect of any offence committed on an earlier occasion, and must be free to leave the requesting State when no longer needed.
23 Ibid, Art 11.
24 Ibid, Art 17.
25 Ibid, Art 19.

lateral mutual legal assistance treaties and is acknowledged as an important development in international judicial co-operation.[26] This initiative complements the 1957 European Convention on Extradition.[27] However, matters relating to the transfer of prisoners and the transfer of proceedings are dealt with in different Conventions. The Committee of Experts which was responsible for drafting the 1959 Convention sought to distinguish between judicial assistance and collaborative police operations. Accordingly, policing and law enforcement are outside the scope of this instrument. All EU States are now parties to the 1959 Convention, which was ratified by the UK on 29 August 1991.[28] Parties undertake to provide each other with 'the widest measure of mutual assistance in proceedings' for offences which fall within the jurisdiction of the judicial authorities of the requesting State. Requests for assistance must be received from a 'judicial authority' and not an administrative authority. Thus requests may not be received from administrative bodies such as HM Customs & Excise. Assistance can be refused if the requesting State considers the offence to be either political or fiscal in nature. Thus States may refuse assistance if the request relates to a tax offence. Further, the requested State may refuse to respond to a request if it considers that the 'execution of the request is likely to prejudice the sovereignty, security, *ordre public* or other essential interests of its country'.[29] The 1959 Convention has been supplemented by two additional protocols. The first, which was signed in 1978 and entered into force in 1982[30] widens the scope of the 1959 Convention by including fiscal offences and relaxing the double criminality rule. Article 1 of the Additional Protocol provides that States shall not refuse assistance solely on the ground that the request relates to a tax offence. The second Protocol, which was signed in 2001 and entered into force in 2004, provides for the setting up of joint investigation teams.[31]

The mechanism for requesting assistance is through the exchange of letters rogatory, which are written requests sent by judicial authorities in the requesting State to the relevant authorities in the foreign State.[32] While

26 ETS, No 30.
27 See Chapter 13.
28 Bilateral conventions on the implementation of the 1959 Convention have also been concluded between EU States. Other conventions which impact on mutual legal assistance within the EU include the 1962 Benelux Treaty on Extradition and Mutual Assistance in Criminal Matters, the 1990 Schengen Implementing Convention and the 2000 EU Convention on Mutual Assistance in Criminal Matters.
29 1959 European Convention on Mutual Assistance in Criminal Matters, Art 2.
30 ETS, No 99.
31 ETS, No 182.
32 1959 European Convention on Mutual Assistance in Criminal Matters, Arts 2, 3 and 6. For a discussion of the problems of obtaining evidence by this means, see op cit, Nadelmann (1993), note 1, pp 318–24.

requests are normally sent between the relevant Ministries of Justice, in urgent cases they can be sent and received by judicial authorities. In addition to the summoning of witnesses,[33] provision is made in the Convention for the transfer of documentary and real evidence on the understanding it will be returned as soon as possible.[34] A request can also be made for assistance in serving writs and records of judicial verdicts.[35] Included in the list of reservations is a provision enabling the requested State to reserve the right to refuse to undertake searches for and seizure of evidence unless specific conditions are satisfied.[36] This provision, which introduces an element of double criminality into the Convention, provides that requests for search and seizure of property can be refused unless the offence in question is punishable under the law of both States and is extraditable. Requests for assistance are generally executed in accordance with the national law and practice in the requested State.[37] This is known as the *locus regit actum* principle. Although obtaining evidence in this manner can cause admissibility problems in criminal proceedings in the requesting State, the Convention does not address the issue of admissibility of evidence. Arguably, this problem may serve to frustrate some of the aims of the Convention.[38] In order to encourage certainty and reduce fishing expeditions, the requesting State is required to indicate, in some detail, the nature of the investigation and the assistance sought.[39] Requesting States are required to guarantee witnesses immunity from prosecution for offences committed before they return to give evidence.[40] Similarly, witnesses must not be detained in respect of any outstanding convictions.

15.4 EU INITIATIVES

15.4.1 Introduction

Although national law enforcement agencies acknowledge that the fight against cross-border crime requires collaborative action, Member States of the EU have consistently demonstrated a reluctance to relinquish sovereignty in matters relating to crime and public order.[41] Thus, unlike the common

---

33 Ibid, Art 8 states that the summons is not binding and Art 9 provides for the witness to claim expenses.
34 Ibid, Art 6.
35 Ibid, Art 7.
36 Ibid, Art 5.
37 Ibid, Art 3.
38 See below.
39 1959 European Convention on Mutual Assistance in Criminal Matters, Art 14.
40 Ibid, Art 12.
41 For a general discussion of EU law see D Chalmers, Ch Hadjiemmanuil, G Monti, A Tomkins, *European Union Law: Text and Materials*, 1st edn, 2006, Cambridge: Cambridge University Press.

agricultural policy and regional policies, matters related to justice and home affairs (JHA) have traditionally remained outside the Community legal order and have been dealt with under the Third Pillar.[42] Thus JHA matters have been dealt with at an intergovernmental level involving justice ministers and their departments Although under the Treaty of Amsterdam, which came into force in May 1999, issues relating to common foreign and security policy such as asylum and immigration became Community matters, police and judicial co-operation in criminal matters remain within the Third Pillar. Decision making in this area is still dominated by the Member States. However, the Third Pillar was reorganised and provisions relating to police and judicial co-operation in criminal matters are now contained in Title VI of the Treaty on European Union (TEU).[43] The provisions included within Title VI aim to create:

> ... an area of freedom, security and justice by developing common action among Member States in the fields of police and judicial co-operation in criminal matters and by preventing and combating racism and xenophobia.[44]

This objective is to be achieved through closer co-operation between police forces, customs authorities and judicial authorities in Member States. Common action in the field of police co-operation will include the collection and exchange of relevant information, joint initiatives in training, and the use of equipment and the common evaluation of investigative techniques.[45] Judicial co-operation will involve facilitating the enforcement of decisions and the process of extradition, preventing conflicts of jurisdiction and the approximation of laws on organised crime, drug trafficking and terrorism.[46]

Under Art 34, which was previously known as Art K4, the Council of the EU[47] is required to undertake a range of initiatives including adopting framework decisions for the purpose of approximation of the laws and regulations of the Member States. Although framework decisions are binding on

---

42 For a general discussion on the Third Pillar, see D O'Keeffe, 'Recasting the Third Pillar', *CML Rev* (1995), 893, and for consideration of its impact, see M Furse and S Nash, 'Free Movement, Criminal Law and Fundamental Rights in the European Community', 3 *Juridical Review* (1997), 148.

43 Detailed discussion of the debate relating to the criminal law competence of the European Community and Constitutional considerations are beyond the scope of this book. For further discussion see generally, op cit, Chalmers *et al*, note 41 above.

44 TEU, Art 29.

45 Ibid, Art 30.

46 Ibid, Art 31.

47 This body is comprised of ministers from each Member State. The Minister for Justice or the Minister of the Interior usually deals with JHA matters.

Member States with respect to the result to be achieved, the choice of method is left to national authorities.[48] The European Council has also organised special programmes which have played a decisive role in developing judicial co-operation initiatives. At a special meeting of the European Council,[49] which focused on JHA, it was agreed that the mutual recognition of judicial decisions should form the cornerstone of the future development of judicial co-operation. The 1999 Tampere proposals also included the setting up of joint investigative teams to combat trafficking in drugs and people and terrorism. Additionally, in order to reinforce the fight against serious organised crime, a Eurojust unit was proposed which would be comprised of national prosecutors and magistrates from all Member States. This body has been given the task of facilitating co-ordination of national prosecuting authorities and works with the European Judicial Network in order to simplify the execution of requests for assistance. The Tampere European Council invited the Commission to compile a 'scoreboard' to keep the implementation of policies on freedom, security and justice under review. The scoreboard kept track of progress made with implementation of the measures and compliance with the deadlines set in the Amsterdam Treaty, the Vienna Action Plan and the Tampere programme. The first scoreboard was produced in March 2000 and updated every six months taking into account objectives set in Laeken in 2001, Seville in 2002 and in Thessalonika in 2003. Following the presentation of the final scoreboard in June 2004, which marked the end of the five-year Tampere programme, the Commission issued a Communication assessing its implementation and setting down guidelines for a new Justice and Home Affairs agenda. The evaluation of the Tampere programme highlighted the need to ensure effective implementation by Member States.

The new programme adopted under the Dutch Presidency, which was endorsed by the European Council in November 2004, is known as the Hague programme. The Action Plan implementing this programme sets out a policy framework for EU activities on freedom, security and justice for the period

---

48 Framework Decisions were introduced by the 1997 Amsterdam Treaty. Article 34(2)(b) of the TEU provides that Framework Decisions have 'the purpose of approximation of the laws and regulations of the Member States. Framework Decisions shall be binding upon Member States as to the result to be achieved, but shall leave the national authorities the choice of the form and methods'. In C–105/03 *Criminal Proceedings against Maria Pupino*, ECR [2005] I–5285 the ECJ held that the principle of indirect effect applies to framework decisions, ie, domestic judges must interpret national law, as far as is possible, in the light of framework decisions. See further B Kurcz, A Lazowski, 'Two Sides of the Same Coin? Framework Decisions and Directives Compared' 26 YEL (2007).

49 This body is comprised of the Heads of State of the Member States and the President of the European Commission. The Council meets every six months.

2005 to 2010.[50] Priorities include immigration, asylum, border control and the prevention of terrorism. Other objectives include increasing civil and criminal cross-border co-operation, realising the full potential of Europol and Eurojust and the full application of the principle of mutual recognition of judicial decisions in criminal matters. Mutual recognition initiatives have embraced the gathering and admissibility of evidence, conflicts of jurisdiction and the *ne bis in idem* principle and the execution of final judgments. Some of these initiatives have been highly controversial and require Member States to balance loss of sovereignty against the need to have in place effective co-operative mechanisms to fight cross-border crime. The Commission is required to produce a yearly evaluation report to be submitted to the Council on the implementation of the Hague programme. This 'scoreboard' is similar to the six-monthly report produced under the Tampere programme and sets out to evaluate both the level of implementation and the effects of any JHA measures. In a Communication to the Council with regard to an evaluation of EU policies in this area, the Commission noted the need for a comprehensive mechanism to monitor implementation and evaluate results of the measures taken which should inform political decision making in the future. The Commission also noted that implementation of the Hague programme is hindered by the requirement of unanimity amongst Member States for decision making in some Third Pillar areas. In order to address this problem, the European Council in June 2006 called upon the Finnish Presidency to explore the possibility of improving decision making in the area of freedom, security and justice on the basis of existing treaties. This issue has been discussed by EU Ministers at an informal Council on Justice and Home Affairs in September 2006 and at a joint parliamentary meeting in October 2006. On 27 November 2006, the Council Presidency, in its review of the Hague programme, noted that, as many JHA polices were still in their infancy, evaluation and monitoring implementation by Member States was often premature. The review identified both qualitative and quantitative deficiencies as regards the rate of transposition of instruments under Title VI of the EU Treaty. Thus, agreement on the evidence warrant, for example, was only reached after lengthy negotiations and no agreement has yet been reached on common minimum standards for procedural rights.

50 The Hague Programme identified 10 priorities for the period 2005–2010. These can be summarised as fundamental rights and citizenship; the fight against terrorism; migration management; internal borders, external borders and visas; a common asylum area; integration; privacy and security in sharing information; the fight against organised crime; civil and criminal justice and freedom, security and justice.

15.4.2 1990 Schengen Implementing Convention[51]

The primary purpose of the 1990 Schengen Implementing Convention is to facilitate the free movement of persons between Member States of the EU by removing internal border controls. This initiative provides for the introduction of a common policy on free movement and contains provisions relating to the issuing of visas and residence permits,[52] the movement of aliens[53] and the processing of applications for asylum.[54] Subsequently, several measures have been introduced under the Schengen initiative, which focus on police, customs and judicial co-operation including measures which allow police officers to engage in the 'hot pursuit' of a suspect.[55] These measures were introduced, in part, to address concerns relating to crime and public security arising from the relaxation of border controls. In addition to police co-operation, the 1990 Convention also contains provisions on mutual assistance in criminal matters, the *ne bis in idem principle*, extradition, the transfer of enforcement of criminal judgments and the Schengen Information System. In 1997, the Treaty of Amsterdam formally integrated the Schengen *acquis* into the EU framework. Some of the judicial co-operation initiatives in the original Schengen Convention have now been replaced by secondary legislation, including Council Framework Decisions. Although not a party to the 1990 Convention, in May 1999 the UK formally applied to participate in parts of the Schengen *acquis* that deal with police and judicial co-operation, including customs co-operation, and the Schengen Information System (SIS).[56] The SIS is a database that stores criminal information from participating Member States and is considered to be the most prominent instrument of police co-operation devised under Schengen. The SIS database was set up to improve police and judicial cooperation by allowing police and custom officials to exchange information on specific individuals or stolen vehicles or objects. The data protection provisions of this system have been subjected to some severe criticism.[57] The current SIS lacks the capacity to function effectively in all States of the enlarged EU. This problem will be addressed by

---

51 Convention of 19 June 1990 implementing the Schengen Agreement of 14 June 1985 on the gradual abolition of checks at the common borders, OJ L 239.
52 Ibid, Arts 9–18.
53 Ibid, Arts 19–24.
54 Ibid, Arts 28–38.
55 Ibid, Arts 40 and 41.
56 Under Art 4 of the Schengen Protocol to the TEU, which incorporates the Schengen *acquis*, the UK is not bound by the Schengen *acquis* but can request to take part in some of the provisions. Before the JHA Council agrees to the UK's participation in Schengen, the other Schengen States are required to formally evaluate the UK's implementation procedures. A Council Decision approving the UK's request was delayed until 29 May 2000 due to the dispute between the UK and Spain. OJ L 131.
57 See 'Report on the Schengen Information System', JUSTICE, Autumn 2000.

the Council's proposal for a second generation Schengen information system, referred to as SIS II which should be operational in 2007.[58]

15.4.3 2000 EU Convention on Mutual Assistance in Criminal Matters[59]

In order to facilitate the operation of the 1959 Council of Europe Convention within Member States of the EU, and to address some of the problems caused by the complexity of existing procedures,[60] a draft convention was proposed in accordance with Art 34 of the TEU.[61] The primary purpose of the EU Convention on Mutual Assistance in Criminal Matters Between Member States of the European Union is to improve co-operation between judicial, police and customs authorities by modernising existing mutual legal assistance provisions. Following more than four years of negotiations the text of the simplified Convention was finally agreed in May 2000 and embraces both conventional forms of assistance and some controversial cross-border investigation methods. Although some relief was expressed that the EU Convention was finally approved, it has been the subject of much criticism.[62] While the new Convention was originally concerned with judicial co-operation, provisions on police co-operation were added later. Although the preamble and the first Article of the Convention indicate that the new arrangements supplement rather than extend the scope of existing conventions, including arrangements under the Benelux Treaty and the 1990 Schengen Implementing Convention,[63] some provisions represent a fundamental shift in traditional arrangements. This instrument, breaking with the Council of Europe's tradition of allowing contracting parties to enter reservations against any provision, stipulates which provisions contain opt-out clauses. Critical comment has been made regarding the failure to include a provision allowing States to refuse to execute a request on the ground that it would present a threat to sovereignty, security and public order. There has also been criticism regarding resistance to include data protection provisions

---

58 The Schengen *acquis* is considered in more detail in Chapter 17.
59 Convention of 29 May 2000 on Mutual Assistance in Criminal Matters between the Member States of the European Union, OJ C 197/01.
60 Evidence presented to a House of Lords Select Committee suggested that the system for the exchange of requests established under the 1959 Convention was at the point of collapse: *Select Committee on the European Communities on the Draft Convention for Europol: Memorandum from Fair Trials International*, Session 1994/95, 10th Report.
61 31 ILM (1992), 247.
62 See G Vermeulen, *Mutual Legal Assistance in Criminal Matters Within the European Union: Towards a Full Mutual Assistance Area Specific to the Member States?*, 1999, unpublished PhD thesis, University of Ghent.
63 The Convention on Mutual Assistance in Criminal Matters repeals Arts 49(a), 52, 53 and 73 of the 1990 Schengen Implementing Convention.

similar to those found in other Third Pillar conventions.[64] Whilst the new powers were introduced primarily as a response to governmental concerns about the growth in cross-border serious and organised crime, this Convention has been drafted to cover any crime. Although the preamble points out that States will act in a manner which is compatible with the European Convention on Human Rights, the body of the Convention does not allow assistance to be refused on the ground that fundamental rights will be compromised. Speed and efficiency may be achieved by reducing to an unacceptable level the procedural guarantees that provide the accused in transnational cases with protection from over-zealous States. This instrument has subsequently been supplemented by the 2001 Protocol which extends mutual assistance provision to matters related to money laundering and financial crime.[65]

The Convention imposes an obligation on contracting parties to execute requests for assistance from another EU State as soon as possible. The requested State has a duty to inform the requesting State if it cannot meet the deadline set for execution in order that they can agree on any further action. To aid the process of mutual assistance, contracting parties must identify the competent administrative authorities, the central authority, the police and customs authorities and the authority with the power to order the interception of communications. In order to expedite the process of mutual assistance, procedural documents can be posted directly to the person or body who can provide the necessary information, or can be sent via the competent authority.[66] Included with the documents should be a translated summary and a report indicating where the addressee can seek information about his rights and obligations concerning the document. Normally, requests for assistance are processed through judicial authorities, but in some cases a request may, and in some circumstances must, be sent via a central authority.[67] For example, requests for the temporary transfer or transit of prisoners and the sending of information from judicial records must be sent through the central authority. Urgent requests for assistance can be sent directly to Interpol or Europol. The police or customs authority in the requested State can be contacted directly by either the central or the judicial authority in the requesting State. Contracting parties can opt out of this clause.[68] Mutual assistance can be sought in relation to 'proceedings brought by administrative authorities' and for criminal proceedings relating to a 'legal person'. Thus requests can relate to administrative offences and criminal acts committed by corporate bodies. In respect to these

---

64 See UK Select Committee on the European Union in the House of Lords, July 1998.

65 The Protocol to the Convention on Mutual Assistance in Criminal Matters Between Member States of the European Union, 2001 OJ C326/01.

66 Convention on Mutual Assistance in Criminal Matters Between Member States of the European Union, Art 5.

67 Ibid, Art 6.

68 Ibid, Art 6(7).

proceedings, a request for assistance can be made directly to the administrative body in the requested State.[69] In appropriate circumstances States can exchange information about criminal or administrative offences without the need to resort to the formalities set out in the Convention.[70] To address the problem of incompatibility of evidence-gathering rules in Member States, evidence is gathered according to the law of the requesting State, the *forum regit actum* principle, rather than in accordance with the *locus regit actum* principle established in the 1957 Convention.[71] This is subject to the proviso that evidence-gathering activities do not involve a breach of fundamental principles of law in the requested State. There is a duty to inform the requesting State if the request cannot, or cannot fully, be executed in accordance with the procedural requirements set by the requesting State. However, the automatic reception of evidence gathered lawfully in another State was considered, and rejected, during negotiations.[72] The departure from the traditional principle is intended to prevent an admissibility problem arising when evidence obtained abroad is adduced at trial in the requesting State.

The Convention makes provision for requests for specific forms of mutual assistance. Thus, requests can be received for stolen property to be placed at the disposal of a requesting State with a view to it being returned to the owner.[73] Further in appropriate circumstances, prisoners can be temporarily transferred to the territory of a requesting State;[74] witnesses and experts can give evidence by telephone and video conference,[75] and controlled deliveries are permitted provided the criminal investigation involves an extraditable offence.[76] By mutual agreement, the competent authorities can set up a joint investigation team for a specific purpose and for a limited period of time.[77] Although the composition of the team may include personnel from more than one State, the team's activities must be co-ordinated by a person from the State in which the investigation is being conducted. States can also provide each other with assistance in conducting covert investigations provided the investigation is conducted according to the national law and practice of the State where the investigation is taking place.[78] Matters relating to the interception

---

69 Ibid, Art 3.
70 Ibid, Art 7.
71 Ibid, Art 4.
72 In January 1997, Steering Group III asked the Working Party on Mutual Assistance to consider this question and considered the free movement of evidence an unworkable concept. See op cit, Vermeulen, note 62.
73 Convention on Mutual Assistance in Criminal Matters Between Member States of the European Union, Art 7.
74 Ibid, Art 9.
75 Ibid, Arts 10 and 11.
76 Ibid, Art 12.
77 Ibid, Art 13.
78 Ibid, Art 14.

of communications held up the Convention's progress for several years.[79] Some States expressed concern in respect of the adequacy of the data protection provisions. However, it was eventually agreed that in appropriate circumstances communications can be intercepted and may be transmitted directly to a Member State, or recorded for subsequent transmission. A request for this form of assistance must be made through the competent authority, which is either a judicial authority or an administrative authority designated for this purpose. Due to the nature of modern telecommunications systems, interception frequently does not require technical assistance from other States. However, Member States are urged to inform each other in respect of activities relating to the interception of communications. The Convention contains provisions which restrict the use of data communicated under the Convention to specific purposes. Thus data may only be used for judicial and administrative proceedings and to prevent an immediate and serious threat to public security. However, data obtained under the Convention can also be used 'for any other purpose' if consent is obtained from either the State communicating the data or the individual concerned.[80] Parties to this Convention may only enter reservations in respect of specific articles which make express provision. As a result of concerns raised by some Member States the Council of the EU adopted a Protocol to the Convention with a view to improving mutual assistance provision in the area of money laundering and financial crime. Thus, under the Protocol States are required to provide information relating to both individual and company bank accounts and are prohibited from using bank secrecy rules as a reason for refusing a request for assistance.[81] Further, a request may not be refused in respect of fiscal offences and a refusal to provide assistance on the ground of the political offence exception is significantly restricted.[82] The 2000 Convention requires ratification by at least eight States before it enters into force, and the 2001 Protocol cannot enter into force before the Convention. However, prior to enforcement, a Member State can declare that it will apply the Convention in its relations with States that have made the same declaration. The 2000 Convention has now been ratified by sufficient States and entered into force on 23 August 2005.[83]

15.4.4 *Corpus Juris*

In addition to the Third Pillar initiatives, the European Commission financed a group of experts to consider the problem of prosecuting fraud on the

---

79 Convention on Mutual Assistance in Criminal Matters Between Member States of the European Union, Arts 15–18. See, eg, the *Memorandum by JUSTICE*, House of Lords Select Committee on the European Communities, October 1997.
80 Council Decision 2000/820/JHA, 22 Dec 2000, Art 6.
81 For further discussion, see Chapter 11.
82 See UK Select Committee on the European Union in the House of Lords, July 1998.
83 Council Act of 29 May 2005, OJ C 197 of 12 July 2005.

Community's finances. The *Corpus Juris* project proposed the creation of a 'European Judicial Space' within which financial crime against the EC would be prosecuted according to a set of common rules of procedure and evidence. The study proposed a standard set of rules on admissibility and a common set of powers for evidence gathering. Thus, under Art 33 of the European Rules:

> (1) Evidence must be excluded if it was obtained by community or national agents either in violation of the fundamental rights enshrined in the European Convention on Human Rights, or in violation of the European rules set out in this code or in violation of applicable national law without being justified by the European rules previously set out.

The national law applicable to determine whether the evidence has been obtained legally or illegally must be the law of the country where the evidence was obtained. When evidence has been obtained legally in this sense, it should not be possible to oppose the use of this evidence because it was obtained in a way that would have been illegal in the country of use. But it should always be possible to object to the use of such evidence, even where it was obtained in accordance with the law of the country where it was obtained, if it was obtained in a manner which violated the rights enshrined in the European Convention on Human Rights.

15.4.5 The European Judicial Network

The European Judicial Network (EJN) is a Third Pillar initiative established by a Joint Action adopted by the Council in June 1998.[84] Its primary aim is to improve standards of co-operation between judicial authorities in criminal matters. The Action Plan formalised the practice of exchanging legal personnel with expertise in judicial co-operation procedures. The EJN is a decentralised unit of lawyers and judges with contact points in all Member States.[85] The primary task of the EJN, which was inaugurated in September 1998, is to facilitate contacts and improve co-operation between judicial authorities with direct local jurisdiction. In order to achieve this aim, the EJN meets regularly and assists in disseminating information on the law and practice relevant to transnational investigations. Thus it is available to provide practitioners working in the field of judicial co-operation with practical information on mutual legal assistance. The EJN is particularly effective in co-ordinating judicial co-operation when there are numerous requests arising from the same case. Responsibility for the administration of the EJN lies

---

84 Joint Action 98/428 JHA of 29 June 1998.
85 The EJN website address is <http://ec.europa.eu/civiljustice/>.

with the General Secretariat of the Council. The EJN comprises the central authorities responsible for international judicial co-operation and other competent authorities with specific responsibilities related to international co-operation. Member States have a responsibility to ensure that personnel used as the national contact point have an adequate knowledge of at least two European languages. The personnel staffing the contact point must have: access to the contact points in each Member State; a simplified list of the judicial authorities and a directory of the local authorities in each Member State; concise legal and practical information concerning the judicial and procedural systems in all Member States; and the texts of the relevant legal instruments and conventions, including up to date information regarding declarations and reservations. The Council assesses the operation of the EJN every three years.

15.4.6 The European Public Prosecutor

Although an outline proposal to establish a European Public Prosecutor (EPP) was presented at the Nice intergovernmental conference in 2000, the European Council did not act on it until its meeting in Laeken in 2001. The Commission's proposal stemmed from concerns relating to fraud against the Community's finances and to remedy the fragmentation of law enforcement. The EPP would be a Community body with prosecuting powers specifically relating to the financial interests of the Community. The European Commission gave a presentation of its proposals to the Justice and Home Affairs Council and, although the Council identified several practical and constitutional difficulties, in December 2001 the Commission published a Green Paper on criminal law protection of the financial interests of the Community and the establishment of an EPP. The Green Paper explored the legal status and internal organisation of the EPP and substantive and procedural issues including the law of evidence and penalties. It also addressed the conduct of investigations, the choice of Member State and the right to review by national courts and the European Court of Justice (ECJ). The EPP will be an independent judicial authority with the power to conduct investigations and prosecutions into offences against the Community's financial interests, such as fraud and corruption, anywhere within the EU. The tasks allocated to the EPP would include the gathering of evidence for and against the accused. Although the trial would be held in national courts, the EPP would direct and co-ordinate prosecutions. However, the actions of the EPP would be subject to review by national courts. The Commission considered it essential that trials are held in national courts and did not foresee the creation of a Community court. It was proposed that in appropriate cases the EPP would co-operate with Eurojust and would exchange information in accordance with the rules on data protection and would be able to execute the European arrest warrant (EAW). The Commission considered that the activities of Eurojust and the EPP would be complementary to each other. Thus, the EPP would centralise the direction of prosecutions in relation to a limited number of offences, whereas Eurojust would work within the bounds of traditional mutual legal assistance mechanisms in relation to a wider range of serious crime. In its response to the Green Paper the UK Select Committee on European Scrutiny considered that:

> . . . this proposal is impractical and that it raises serious issues of principle. We see no reason for creating an institution at EU level, which will have the effect, on the one hand, of diluting the responsibility of Member States to deal with fraud and, on the other, of putting the function of criminal prosecutions beyond the reach of democratic accountability.[86]

In March 2003 the Commission adopted a follow-up report on the public consultation conducted during 2002 on the establishment of an EPP. There has been some resistance to this initiative. The UK government and the legal profession remain unconvinced of the need for an EPP which could encourage 'forum shopping', and continue to resist strenuously plans to establish such a body.

15.4.7 Eurojust[87]

A European Judicial Co-operation Unit (Eurojust), which was established in February 2002 under the Third Pillar, is given the task of facilitating co-operation between the judicial authorities of the Member States, supporting criminal investigations and assisting with the co-ordination of prosecutions for serious cross-border crime including terrorism, drug trafficking, money-laundering, and organised criminal activity, particularly when two or more Member States are involved. Eurojust can also assist in the prosecution of other crimes at the request of the competent authority in a Member State. The authority for establishing Eurojust can be found in the Conclusions of the Tampere European Council and in the Nice Treaty. It is an independent body with legal personality and its own budget, and is not subject to orders from the European institutions. Having legal personality means that Eurojust can negotiate and sign co-operation agreements with third States and organisations. Its funding comes from the EU budget which is administered by the European Commission. Eurojust provides immediate legal advice and assistance on cross-border cases to the criminal investigation team and can provide assistance with the formalities of mutual assistance procedures, such as letters rogatory. It receives information from Europol and is able to

---

86 House of Commons Select Committee on European Scrutiny, Thirty-Fourth Report, para 14.12.
87 Established by Council Decision 2002/187/JHA OJ L 63.

co-operate closely with the European Judicial Network and the European Anti-Fraud Office (OLAF). Although Eurojust has no authority to commence or conduct criminal investigations itself, it has the power to make formal requests to national authorities for an investigation or prosecution to be initiated. National authorities are required to provide reasons for refusing to comply with a request. A provisional Eurojust Unit, Pro-Eurojust, was set up in December 2000 and started work in March 2001 but was unable to fulfil the requirements of a permanent unit. Eurojust became an operational unit in May 2002 and began its preparatory work. Unlike the EJN, Eurojust is a centralised unit with offices in The Hague. It operates with a management team of prosecutors, magistrates and police officers drafted in from Member States, and each participant can seek information from their relevant national authorities and have access to the SIS. In order to meet Europol's objectives team members are expected to understand the legal systems of their respective States and to establish good contact with their national authorities. They should have access to national criminal records and other crime data, and the authority to exchange information with each other and with their national authority.[88] There are some restrictions on the processing of personal data and a requirement that a Data Protection Officer be appointed.[89] Some criticism has been levelled at the lack of effective data protection measures. A supervisory body has recently been established to monitor data processing and to ensure compliance with data protection rules. Each Member State must clarify the nature and extent of the powers granted to its national member within its own territory, and is required to define the right to act in respect to foreign judicial authorities.[90] Eurojust can also perform its tasks as a College which is comprised of all Member States. The competences of the College are set out in special rules of procedure.[91] In appropriate circumstances, Eurojust is permitted to exchange information with international organisations and law enforcement authorities in non-EU States.[92] Formal co-operation arrangements have recently been concluded with Romania and Iceland. Once ratified, the agreement signed in November 2006 between the EU Council of Ministers and the US will permit Eurojust and US prosecutors to exchange information on cross-border crime beyond that permitted in other co-operation agreements.

The President of Eurojust is required to present regular reports on activities to the Justice and Home Affairs Council.[93] In the 2005 report, he states that in 2004 the number of cases referred to Eurojust rose by 54 per cent

---

88 Art 13 of the Council Decision 2002/187/JHA, OJ L 63 of 06 March 2002.
89 Ibid, Arts 15 and 17.
90 Ibid, Art 9.
91 Rules of Procedure of Eurojust, OJ C 286/1.
92 Art 27 of the Council Decision 2002/187/JHA, OJ L 63 of 06 March 2002.
93 Ibid, Art 32.

to 588, and the proportion of cases involving only two Member States rose to 78 per cent. Several examples of successful cross-border co-operation co-ordinated by Eurojust were reported, including a case involving people-trafficking from Turkey to the UK, which resulted in a series of arrests co-ordinated between the UK and Belgium. The UK Parliamentary Select Committee on European Scrutiny acknowledged that while the Eurojust report provided a useful insight into the practicalities of judicial co-operation in the EU, it indicated that many States fail to give effect to the measures agreed in Council. This committee questioned the utility of introducing more initiatives until current measures are enforced and implemented. While Eurojust may improve cross-border prosecution rates, it has given rise to concerns about public accountability. In November 2003, Eurojust adopted a set of guidelines for deciding which authority should prosecute in cases where there is a conflict of jurisdiction. These guidelines, which are not binding on Member States, were intended to bring consistency to the problem of con-flicts by listing the factors to be taken into consideration. However, some Member States, including the UK, expressed concern that Eurojust appeared to be exceeding its mandate by assuming the role of directing national prosecuting authorities.[94]

15.4.8 Joint investigation teams

While joint investigation teams (JIT) have operated informally for some time, the legal framework is provided for by Art 13 of the EU Convention on Mutual Assistance in Criminal Matters and its Protocols and the Council Framework on JITs.[95] This initiative is aimed at facilitating judicial rather than police co-operation. Joint investigation teams aim to speed up criminal investigations in cross-border cases by improving the functioning of mutual recognition instruments and increasing the level of trust between judicial authorities.[96] A JIT is established by the competent authorities in at least two Member States entering into an agreement which sets out the composition of the team and the procedures to be adopted during an investigation. A JIT must be set up for a specific purpose and have a limited duration that can be extended by agreement. Representatives of Europol, OLAF and members of non-EU States can take part in JIT activities. Members of the team carry out

---

94 The UK House of Commons Select Committee on European Scrutiny, Thirty-Second Report.

95 Due to problems with ratification, a framework decision was adopted (Council Framework Decision 2002/465/JHA of 13 June 2002 on joint investigation teams, OJ 2002 L 162/1) which lapsed in 2005 when the Convention entered into force.

96 For further discussion on the aims and objectives of JITs, see C Rijken and G Vermeulen (eds) *Joint Investigation Teams in the European Union: From Theory to Practice*, 2006, The Hague, Netherlands: Asser Press.

their investigation in accordance with the law of the Member State in which the team is operating. Differences in national criminal justice systems can have a negative impact on the success of a joint investigation. Practical and legal obstacles to co-operation are particularly acute when cross-border investigations involve Member States from different legal traditions. Problems arose with respect to the admissibility of evidence, for example, in a drugs investigation conducted by a JIT established between the UK and the Netherlands in November 2004. In this case, difference in the rules on disclosure, the admissibility of telephone intercepts as evidence in criminal proceedings and the use of informers were identified as a potential threat to the success of the project. Doubts were expressed as to whether the JIT added value to the investigation compared with bi-lateral agreements using traditional forms of mutual legal assistance such as parallel investigations and letters of request.[97] The additional cost of a JIT needs to be balanced against improvement in information exchange and the eventual outcome of the proceedings. Similar 'added value' concerns have been expressed with respect to the involvement of Europol and Eurojust, organisations created specifically to support cross-border co-operation in criminal matters. Although Europol officers can support a JIT, particularly in facilitating information exchange, they do not actively participate in an investigation. Similarly, Eurojust staff can offer support to JIT participants, chairing meetings and drafting documents, rather than actively engaging in the investigation. It is predicted that Eurojust will have a greater impact on investigations involving more than two States. However, as with other mutual legal assistance measures, the success of the JIT initiative is dependant upon the willingness of Member States to co-operate and the level of mutual trust between participants.

15.5 MUTUAL RECOGNITION PROGRAMME

The 1999 Tampere European Council came to the conclusion that the principle of mutual recognition is essential to the process of establishing a European judicial area. However, mutual recognition is dependent upon mutual trust in the criminal justice system operating in other Member States, and a common approach to fundamental rights. Despite the success of the EAW, Member States remain resistant to the principle of mutual recognition. Problems have arisen, for example, with respect to Framework Decisions on racism and xenophobia, procedural rights and the European evidence warrant. In order to encourage trust between States, the Action Plan implementing the Hague Programme called for an evaluation of the implementation of EU policies in the field of justice, and in 2005, the Commission issued

---

97 See C Rijken and G Vermeulen (eds) *Joint Investigation Teams in the European Union: From Theory to Practice*, 2006, The Hague, Netherlands: Asser Press, pp 146–58.

a Communication focusing on aspects of mutual recognition.[98] Priority areas for the future included the mutual recognition of evidence, bail, the recognition of final judgments and, in order to reinforce mutual trust, legislative action to ensure the protection of suspect's rights. As part of the mutual recognition programme, the Commission has produced a Green Paper on conflicts in jurisdiction and double jeopardy,[99] and has plans for further Green Papers on the presumption of innocence, *in absentia* judgments, and the mutual recognition of a range of investigative measures including the questioning of suspects and witnesses, and telephone interception orders.[100] Other proposals include the application of mutual recognition to confiscation orders and a Framework Decision, the European Enforcement Order and the transfer of sentenced prisoners between Member States. Although these initiatives demonstrate a high level of commitment by the Council and the Commission, it is becoming clear that effective implementation requires greater commitment to the mutual recognition principle by Member States.

15.5.1 European arrest warrant

Since 1 January 2004 the EAW has replaced the formal process of extradition between Member States.[101] This development, which is based on the principle of mutual recognition of judicial decisions, has been contentious and was only implemented in all States in April 2005. This initiative is designed to improve and simplify judicial surrender procedures for the purposes of conducting a criminal prosecution or executing a sentence of imprisonment. Under this scheme, Member States can no longer refuse to surrender their own nationals. The EAW scheme provides for the direct transmission of European warrants. To facilitate transmission and execution of warrants, the authorities issuing a warrant make contact with the EJN. The EAW creates a list of 32 serious offences which require surrender under the warrant 'without verification of the double criminality of the act'.[102] Thus if a judge in the requesting State certifies that the offence is included in the European Framework list of offences, the authorities in the requested State is not

---

98 Communication on the mutual recognition of judicial decisions in criminal matters and the strengthening of mutual trust between Member States COM (2005) 195.

99 Green Paper on conflicts of jurisdiction and the principle of *ne bis in idem.* COM (2005) 696. The Commission considers that a mechanism that allows for the allocation of cases to an appropriate jurisdiction would reduce the risk of multiple prosecutions for the same offence and complement the principle of mutual recognition.

100 Communication on the mutual recognition of judicial decisions in criminal matters and the strengthening of mutual trust between Member States COM (2005) 195 final.

101 Council Framework Decision on the European Arrest Warrant (2002/584/JHA) OJ L 190.

102 Art 2(2) of the Framework Decision. The double criminality rule requires that the conduct alleged to constitute the extraditable offence be classified as a criminal offence in both States.

required to consider whether the alleged conduct amounts to an offence in national law. The EAW only applies within the EU; re-extradition to a third State requires agreement with the Member State which authorised the initial surrender. Refusal to execute the warrant is only permitted in very limited circumstances. The EAW is discussed in greater detail in Chapter 13.

15.5.2 European evidence warrant

Disappointed at the length of time taken for Member States to ratify the 2000 Convention on Mutual Assistance, in 2003 the Commission proposed a Framework Decision on the European evidence warrant (EEW), which is expected to eventually replace international and EU Conventions dealing with cross-border evidence gathering.[103] These include the 1959 Council of Europe Convention on mutual assistance[104] and its additional protocol of 1978,[105] and 2001,[106] the 2000 EU Mutual Assistance Convention and its Protocol,[107] and the 1990 Schengen Convention.[108] The proposal for an EAW, which supplements the Framework Decision on orders freezing property or evidence,[109] applies the principle of mutual recognition to a European warrant for the purposes of obtaining objects, documents and data for use in criminal proceedings.[110] The proposal to create an EEW, which will speed up and simplify the process of transferring evidence from one State to another, met with some resistance from Member States concerned about sovereignty issues. Germany was keen to establish a transitional opt-out clause which would allow national authorities to check whether offences mentioned in the warrant were offences under German law; and the Netherlands expressed concern that its approach to drugs enforcement may cause problems. Several human rights organisations were concerned that the draft proposal provided insufficient procedural safeguards for suspects and failed to achieve a satisfactory balance between

---

103 Council Framework Decision on the European Evidence Warrant (EEW) for obtaining objects, documents and data for use in proceedings in criminal matters COM (2003) 688 final, 14 Nov 2003.

104 ETS, No 30.

105 ETS, No 99.

106 ETS, No 182.

107 Convention of 29 May 2000 on Mutual Assistance in Criminal Matters between the Member States of the European Union, OJ C 197/01.

108 Convention of 19 June 1990 implementing the Schengen Agreement of 14 June 1985 on the gradual abolition of checks at the common boarders, OJ L 239.

109 OJ 2003 L 196/45.

110 For a discussion of EU initiatives in respect to obtaining evidence see J Spencer 'An Academic Critique of the EU Acquis in Relation to Trans-Border Evidence-Gathering' paper delivered at the ERA conference in Trier 18–20 Nov 2004 available at <http://www.era.int>.

the need to ensure effective criminal investigations and civil liberties.[111] However, the proposal for a Framework Decision on the EEW was eventually adopted in June 2006.

An EEW is an order issued by a judicial authority in one Member State, the issuing State, which is recognised in another Member State, the executing State, requiring the authorities to search and seize objects, documents or data and transfer them to the issuing State for use in criminal proceedings. Member States comply with the EEW on the basis of the principle of mutual recognition, therefore grounds for non-execution will be very limited. The warrant is executed in the same way as a domestic search warrant. Although an EEW will only be issued for evidence that is already in existence, it can cover any other relevant evidence discovered during its execution.[112] Authorities in the executing State cannot be asked to conduct interviews or take statements from suspects or witnesses, take DNA samples or fingerprints, intercept communications or conduct surveillance operations, monitor bank accounts or electronic communications data.[113] However, the EEW can cover relevant statements made by persons present during a search. Exchange of information on criminal convictions extracted from the criminal record will continue to be carried out in accordance with the Council Decision on this matter.[114] The warrant will be translated by the issuing State into an official language of the executing State.[115] The issuing State must be satisfied that the evidence is necessary and proportionate for the purposes of the proceedings, and that it could be obtained under the law of the issuing State if it had been located in the jurisdiction.[116] The executing State decides how to obtain the evidence, which will be in accordance with its domestic evidence-gathering rules. Requests can be refused if the rule against double jeopardy would be infringed, or if an immunity or privilege under the law of the executing State makes it impossible to execute the warrant. Requests can also be refused where the EEW relates to offences which were committed wholly or 'for a major or essential part' within the territory of the executing State. It can also be refused if offences were committed outside the territory of the issuing State, and the law of the executing State does not permit legal proceedings

---

111 See the responses of LIBERTY to the Home Office consultation on the EEW, 24 July; at <http://www.liberty-human-rights.org.uk/resources/policypapers/index.shtml> (accessed on 21 Dec 2006) and the Statewatch briefing on the EEW to the European Parliament at <http:/www.statewatch.org/analyses/no–25-swatch-evid-warrant.pdf> (accessed on 21 Dec 2006).

112 Council Framework Decision on the European Evidence Warrant, Art 3(4a).

113 Ibid, Art 3(2).

114 Council Decision 2005/876/JHA of 21 Nov 2005 on the exchange of information extracted from the criminal record. This decision provides for the setting up of central authorities with responsibility for sending requests to and receiving requests from Member States.

115 Council Framework Decision on the European Evidence Warrant, Art 5.

116 Ibid, Art 6.

to be taken in respect of these offences. If a State is considering refusing to execute a warrant for this reason, Eurojust should be consulted. National security interests are also valid grounds for refusal. The double criminality rule does not apply if the offence is on a list of 32 specified offences. Thus for these offences the executing State will not check whether the offence mentioned in the warrant is also an offence in national law. In order to ensure fast, effective co-operation, the Framework Decision sets out strict deadlines for the recognition and execution of the EEW.

In the explanatory memorandum to the Framework Decision, the Commission states that the EEW initiative is just a first step towards a single mutual recognition instrument, which could eventually replace the existing mutual assistance regime. Calling for a strengthening of mutual trust, the Commission is of the opinion that:

> ... the ultimate objective is to adopt a single administrative instrument that will facilitate the gathering of evidence of all kinds in criminal cases throughout the Union. In the Commission's view, the effect of applying the mutual recognition principle to the gathering of evidence should be to leave the investigations to be run by the issuing State (the State requesting another Member State to gather evidence). The executing State (the one providing the evidence) cannot question the decision to seek this or that piece of evidence.[117]

While this approach to mutual recognition of decisions in criminal matters may be attractive to prosecuting authorities and will undoubtedly speed up the transfer of evidence, it raises some fundamental fair trial concerns. These concerns are particularly acute with regard to the admissibility of evidence. Executing States are obliged to search and seize evidence listed in the warrant, but gather it according to the law and procedure of the executing State. It was suggested during the consultation stage that the Framework Decision should be altered to require the executing State to comply with a warrant only if the law and practice of the executing State permitted the instructions to be carried out.[118] Whether the evidence listed in the warrant is gathered lawfully is assessed according to the rules of the executing State. However, the issuing State will assess its admissibility during criminal proceedings according to the law and procedure of the issuing State. The obvious example for common law States relates to the admissibility of hearsay evidence. This evidence would not become admissible in the issuing State merely because it was gathered according to the rules of an executing State where hearsay evidence is admis-

---

117 COM (2005) 195.
118 Statewatch briefing on the EEW to the European Parliament at <http:/www.statewatch.org/analyses/no–25-swatch-evid-warrant.pdf> (accessed on 21 Dec 2006).

sible. Thus, at the moment, the issuing State could decline to use evidence if it would be inadmissible in their system. However, discussions have already taken place on the question of mutual admissibility of evidence.[119] It should be remembered that gathering evidence by one set of rules and assessing by it by another risks missing out the procedural safeguards that ensure fairness and guard against abuse.

15.5.3 Preventing conflicts of jurisdiction in criminal proceedings

While Art 54 of the Convention Implementing the Schengen Agreement provides that a person may not be prosecuted in another Member State if a final decision on whether to acquit or convict has been reached, there is no equivalent rule to prevent parallel prosecutions taking place for offences arising out of the same conduct. Currently there is no mechanism to determine which is the most appropriate jurisdiction to commence proceedings. Similarly, there is no mechanism to facilitate the satisfactory resolution of problems arising from conflicts of jurisdiction in Member States. The principle of mutual recognition provides that judicial decisions taken in a Member State are recognised and enforced by other Members States. Thus parallel prosecutions are unnecessary and increase the complexity and the costs of legal representation, create an administrative burden for the prosecuting authorities and are harmful to defence rights. In order to respond to this problem, the European Commission aims to introduce a mechanism for allocating cases to the appropriate jurisdiction. In December 2005, the Commission presented a Green Paper that identifies the current problems and suggests possible solutions.[120] Currently there is no accurate data on the extent and complexity of this problem in all Member States. The findings of an empirical study which is due to report in 2007 will facilitate the work of the Commission in preparing a Proposal for a Framework Decision on conflicts of jurisdiction and the principle of *ne bis in idem* in criminal proceedings. The Commission will use the information and data to assess the necessity and the impact of this initiative.

15.5.4 European supervision orders

Concerned at significant differences in the rate and length of pre-trial detention in Member States, and lack of uniformity in bail conditions for

---

119 Report on the Green Paper on the establishment of a European Prosecutor, COM (2003) 128.
120 Green Paper on conflicts of jurisdiction and the principle of *ne bis in idem* (COM (2005) 696 final).

non-resident and resident suspects, the European Parliament called for the Commission to take action. In the European Parliament's 2002 resolution, Member States were requested to examine pre-trial detention periods to ensure compatibility with human rights standards. In 2003 a Council of Europe report noted that prison overcrowding was particularly acute in remand prisons and called for a review of the law and practice relating to pre-trial detention.[121] In August 2004, the Commission issued a Green Paper to promote further discussion on the issue. The Framework Decision on the European Supervision Order proposed by the Council aims to ensure a common level of human rights protection and equal treatment.[122] A non-resident suspect will be treated the same as a suspect who is resident in the trial State. This initiative should be considered alongside the Commission proposal setting out common minimum standards for defendants, which contains provisions on the right to legal advice and the right to an interpreter. The European supervision order is a decision issued by a judicial authority in a Member State in respect of a non-resident suspect, which is recognised in other Member States. The Council is required to issue a list of authorities with competence to issue and execute an order.[123] The order imposes obligations on suspects to ensure that they do not abscond or interfere with the course of justice. Thus suspects may be required to surrender a passport; reside at a specific address which may include a bail hostel; report to the authorities at a specific time and place; and undergo specified medical treatment.[124] The State issuing the order transmits it to the State where it will be executed. If necessary, the EJN can provide assistance in locating the competent authorities. The executing authority is required to recognise the European supervision order and take the necessary measures to execute it. However, the Framework Decision provides grounds for non-recognition and non-execution. Thus an order will not be recognised 'if it is clear that criminal proceedings for the offence in respect of which that order has been issued would infringe the *ne bis in idem* principle'.[125] Grounds for non-execution include claims of immunity or privilege, or if the offence to which the order relates is covered by an amnesty.[126] Provision is made for a review of the order, which can take place by video or telephone link. If a suspect breaches an

---

121 The European Committee for the Prevention of Torture and Inhuman and Degrading Treatment or Punishment 2003.
122 Proposal for a Council Framework Decision on the European Supervision order in pre-trial procedures between Member States of the European Union COM(2006) 468 final.
123 Ibid, Art 4.
124 Ibid, Art 6.
125 Ibid, Art 10(1). This principle provides that no one should be tried or punished twice for the same criminal offence. The ECJ examined the scope of this principle in the context of Art 54 of the Schengen Convention. See C–187/01 and C–385/01 *Gozutok* and *Brugge* and C–469/03 *Miraglia* which concerned issues related to the definition of 'final decision'.
126 Ibid, Art 10(2).

order it can be revoked or amended. If the issuing State decides that the suspect should be returned, the State on whose territory the suspect is arrested can only refuse transfer on limited grounds.[127] The aim of this initiative is to allow non-resident suspects to be remanded on bail in their home environment. However, provided account has been taken of the right to liberty, the principle of proportionality and the presumption of innocence, judicial authorities are not required to make use of the European pre-trial supervision order. Non-resident suspects can request it, but there is no right to it. Given the resistance of some Member States to other mutual recognition measures, it is questionable whether this initiative will be implemented in the near future.

15.5.5 Common minimum standards for the rights of suspects and defendants[128]

Although defence rights were mentioned in the Tampere conclusions,[129] and the Hague programme provides for approximation of standards relating to procedural rights, the volume of judicial and police co-operation initiatives has not been matched by initiatives to protect defence rights.[130] However, in February 2003, the Commission presented a Green Paper on Procedural Safeguards for Suspects and Defendants in Criminal Proceedings.[131] This initiative aimed to establish European 'best practice' guidelines but did not create any new rights for suspects. The starting point for the Green Paper was the minimum standards established by the European Convention on Human Rights and the jurisprudence of the European Court of Human Rights. The areas proposed in the Green Paper are access to legal representation; access to free interpreters and translation; informing suspects of their rights; and protection for vulnerable suspects and defendants. The Commission considered that this would be the first step towards establishing a set of common minimum standards that would facilitate the application of the principle of mutual recognition. While the response to this paper was generally positive, some non-governmental organisations and legal practitioners considered that the proposals did not address some important rights, notably the right to bail, double jeopardy and trial *in absentia*. Member States opposed to the idea were concerned about technical difficulties and cost, and that imposing

---

127 Ibid, Art 18.
128 See generally, M Leaf (ed), *Cross Border Crime: Defence rights in a new era of international judicial co-operation*, 2006, London: JUSTICE.
129 Eg, Tampere Conclusion 30 refers to an adequate level of legal aid in cross-border cases, Conclusion 31 refers to the need for multilingual forms of documents and Conclusion 40 refers to the need to protect freedoms and legal rights of individuals.
130 See generally, op cit, Leaf, note 128.
131 Com (2003) 75 final, 19 Feb 2003.

obligations which would apply internally in each State could breach the principle of subsidiarity. Several States had misgivings about the legal basis for the proposal.[132] Further, setting minimum common standards could result in lowering standards in States where current provisions exceeded the basic EU requirements. The Commission considered that, notwithstanding Member States' obligations under the European Convention on Human Rights, action at EU level was necessary to avoid discrepancies in the level of procedural safeguards.

In May 2004, the Commission submitted a proposal for a Framework Decision on certain procedural rights in criminal proceedings throughout the EU which was due to be implemented in January 2006.[133] It is intended that these procedural guarantees will apply to all suspects arrested or detained in connection with a criminal charge, regardless of nationality. Suspects should have the right to effective legal advice as soon as possible, and before being required to answer questions, which in appropriate circumstances should be provided free of charge. If the suspect does not understand the language of the proceedings, or has a hearing or speech impediment, an interpreter or a translator should be provided free of charge. The standard of translation must be sufficient to allow the suspect to follow and participate in proceedings. Vulnerable suspects and defendants should be given special consideration, which could amount to allowing a third party to be present during police questioning.[134] Foreign suspects should be able to communicate with consular authorities or an international humanitarian organisation. All suspects remanded in custody should be given a Letter of Rights in a language that they understand informing them of basic rights as soon as possible after arrest. The inclusion of a regression clause was aimed at making sure States did not use the Framework Decision to lower national procedural safeguards. It provides that nothing 'shall be construed as limiting or derogating from any of the rights and procedural safeguards that may be ensured under the laws of any Member State and which provides a higher level of protection'.[135] The Framework Decision requires the collection of data for the purpose of evaluation and monitoring. This data should include the number of persons charged, whether legal advice was provided and whether it was free of charge, and the number of Letters of Rights issued. This information will form the basis of the Commission's report, which will be used to assess

---

132 However, the Commission considers that Art 31(1) of the TEU, as amended by the Treaty of Nice, which covers action of judicial co-operation in criminal matters, provides an appropriate legal basis for this initiative.

133 Framework Decision on certain procedural rights in criminal proceedings throughout the EU, COM(2004) 328.

134 Ibid, Art 10. Suspects may be classed as vulnerable due to their age, or their mental, physical or emotional condition.

135 Ibid, Art 17.

implementation. The draft proposal was discussed in the criminal law work-ing group, which is attended by representatives from the Ministries of Justice. A progress report made to the Council in December 2005 noted that several Member States continued to question the legal basis for this initiative.[136] Some States could see no added value in relation to the European Convention on Human Rights, and some expressed concern about risks arising from a dual protection system. The UK proposed a draft resolution that recom-mended a range of practical measures which would enhance compliance with European Convention on Human Rights standards. Although the proposal received support from legal practitioners, the European Criminal Bar Associ-ation and non-governmental organisations, in November 2006 the Council Presidency in its review of the Hague programme noted that no agreement on the proposed Framework Decision had been reached.

136 These States argue that Arts 29 and 31 of the TEU, which confer powers in the field of judicial co-operation in criminal matters, do not extend to mutual recognition initiatives.

Chapter 16

Mutual legal assistance: national perspectives

16.1 CRIME (INTERNATIONAL CO-OPERATION) ACT 2003

In 1986, the Home Secretary set up an interdepartmental working group to review the law and practice in the UK in relation to mutual legal assistance in criminal matters. This group recommended legislative reform in order to facilitate closer international co-operation in the rapid expansion in extra-territorial crime and to provide the UK with easier access to foreign evidence. Four areas where changes were necessary were identified: service of process; the taking of evidence; the transfer of prisoners; and the search and seizure of evidence for use in other jurisdictions. It was noted that the bulk of material generated under mutual legal assistance treaties (MLATs) is in documentary form. Reliance on oral testimony at trial can preclude the admission of witness statements taken abroad and is a disincentive to co-operation. Thus, in addition to reform of UK mutual legal assistance law, reform of the domestic rules on the reception of hearsay evidence was also required.[1] The Criminal Justice (International Co-operation) Act 1990 (the 1990 Act), which was enacted to enable the UK to request and provide assistance to other countries, established a procedure for the service of overseas procedural documents in the UK. The Secretary of State was given the task of directing letters requesting assistance to the appropriate central authority which had been authorised to receive requests for mutual legal assistance. However, within a decade this legislation required updating to improve mutual assistance procedures generally, and to implement several European Union (EU) initiatives designed to improve judicial and police co-operation. These included the mutual assistance provisions of the 1990 Schengen Implementing Convention,[2] the

---

1 The Criminal Justice Act 2003, ss 114–31 and 133–36 has removed the old common law exclusionary rule against hearsay. Hearsay evidence is now *prima facie* admissible, subject to certain safeguards.
2 Convention of 19 June 1990 implementing the Schengen Agreement of 14 June 1985 on the gradual abolition of checks at the common borders, OJ L 239.

2000 Convention on Mutual Assistance in Criminal Matters[3] and the 2001 protocol[4], and the evidence freezing provisions of the 2003 Council Framework Decision on the execution in the EU of orders freezing property or evidence.[5]

The Crime (International Co-operation) Act 2003 (the 2003 Act), which received Royal Assent on 30 October 2003, re-enacts many of the provisions in the 1990 Act and widens the scope of cases in which the UK can make requests and offer mutual assistance, and provides for the direct transmission of requests. Part 1 addresses mutual legal assistance generally, and introduces the mutual recognition of freezing orders on evidence as provided for in the 2003 Framework Decision. Chapter 4 of Part 1 implements the 2001 protocol to the 2000 Convention on Mutual Assistance which creates obligations for 'participating countries' to respond to requests for assistance with locating banking accounts and to provide banking information relating to criminal investigations. All Member States are participating countries for the purposes of these new provisions. In Part 2, which implements the 2002 Framework Decision on combating terrorism,[6] the UK is required to take extra-territorial jurisdiction over a range of terrorist offences. The 2003 Act gives effect to Art 9 of the 2002 Framework Decision by allowing the UK to have extra-territorial jurisdiction over terrorist offences committed by UK residents and nationals outside the UK, and over attacks on UK residents, nationals and diplomatic premises anywhere in the world. Part 3 introduces the mutual recognition of driving disqualifications, and also introduces new measures to prevent drivers banned from driving in Northern Ireland from obtaining a British driving licence. Part 4 implements measures set out in the 1990 Schengen Implementing Convention, which deal with police co-operation, extradition and data protection. Section 81 of the 2003 Act, for example, provides for a UK official to inspect the European information systems which will be used in the UK; s 82 provides for driver licensing information to be disclosed for the purpose of the Schengen Information System; ss 83 to 85 implement the Schengen Convention requirement that, in exceptional circumstances, law enforcement agencies from one Member State must be permitted to conduct unaccompanied surveillance in another Member State. Thus s 83 of the 2003 Act implements Art 40(2) of the Schengen Convention by amending s 76 of the Regulation of Investigatory Powers Act 2000 (RIPA). Accordingly, s 76A of RIPA permits law enforcement agencies from other Member States to continue surveillance operations on UK territory for a limited period.

---

3 Convention of 29 May 2000 on Mutual Assistance in Criminal Matters between the Member States of the European Union, OJ C 197/01.
4 The Protocol to the Convention on Mutual Assistance in Criminal Matters Between Member States of the European Union 2001, OJ C326/01.
5 Council Framework Decision 2003/577/JHA of 22 July 2003, OJ 2003 L 196/45.
6 Council Framework Decision 2002/475/JHA of 22 June 2002, OJ L 164.

Requests to obtain evidence located outside the UK for use in criminal proceedings or investigations must be made by a judge or a magistrate, or, in Scotland, a sheriff. In some circumstances, a designated prosecuting authority is also authorised to request assistance.[7] Requests for information about banking transactions, which is provided for by the 2001 protocol to the 2000 Convention on Mutual Assistance, must state the relevance of the evidence to the investigation and will be sent via the Secretary of State. Under the 2003 Act, requests for assistance from the UK to overseas authorities will usually be transmitted directly from the requesting authority to the relevant overseas authority, rather than via the central authorities. Direct transmission is a new development and is intended to speed up the process.[8] Urgent requests can be sent via Interpol or Eurojust.[9] Incoming letters of request for assistance in obtaining evidence located in the UK should be made by a 'competent authority', which will generally be a judge, an examining magistrate, a prosecutor, Interpol or Eurojust. In response to an overseas request, a police constable in England and Wales, or a sheriff in Scotland, can apply for and execute a search warrant or a production order in the same circumstances as in a domestic investigation. If a police constable is a member of a joint investigation team, a warrant can be applied for without an overseas request.[10] Warrants issued in response to an overseas request are still subject to legal privilege, excluded material or special procedure material as defined in the Police and Criminal Evidence Act 1984, s 28(3). The 2003 Act provides that once evidence is seized, it will be held by the police until it is sent directly to the court or authority requesting it. This is a new measure designed to speed up the proceedings by removing the need to send the evidence to a central authority.[11] The 2003 Framework Decision on freezing property or evidence, which is based on the principle of mutual recognition, requires the UK to recognise the validity of an overseas freezing order rather than consider it as a request for mutual legal assistance. Thus the UK is obliged to execute orders relating to the offences listed in the 2003 Framework Decision. Overseas authorities can request the transfer of a prisoner from the UK to assist with an investigation in the requesting State. Similarly, a prisoner can be transferred to the UK to assist with a domestic investigation. The prisoner's consent is required. The 2003 Act permits the hearing of witnesses by video link where a witness cannot travel to the UK to give evidence.[12] Courts in the UK can also take video evidence for transmission abroad, and in some circumstances evidence can be given by telephone.

7 Crime (International Co-operation) Act 2003, s 7.
8 Ibid, s 8.
9 Ibid, s 8(3).
10 Ibid, s 16.
11 Ibid, s 19.
12 Ibid, s 29.

16.2 THE USE OF EVIDENCE OBTAINED ABROAD

Under the terms of the Crime (International Co-operation) Act 2003, evidence obtained from a foreign authority may only be used for the purposes for which it was requested, unless the consent of the requested State has been obtained, and is subject to the same admissibility rules as evidence obtained under normal domestic arrangements.[13] Evidence obtained abroad for use in domestic criminal proceedings can raise difficult admissibility issues for national courts. The principle of mutual recognition, which lies at the heart of recent EU developments in mutual legal assistance, lends support to the notion that evidence gathered according to the law and procedure of one Member State should be admissible in criminal proceedings in another Member State. The European Commission in its Green Paper on the European Public Prosecutor considered the issue of mutual admissibility of evidence and came to the conclusion that:

> ... the prior condition for any mutual admissibility of evidence is that the evidence must have been obtained lawfully in the Member State where it is found. The law that must be respected if evidence is not to be excluded is first and foremost the national law of the place where the evidence is situated.[14]

However, it was decided that further work on this matter was needed as the principle of mutual admissibility has yet to be accepted by Member States. While the 2000 Convention on Mutual Assistance in Criminal Matters and the EU programme on mutual recognition may eventually arrive at a solution to this problem of admissibility for Member States, at the moment national courts need to consider the admissibility of evidence obtained without reference to formal assistance procedures. Whether evidence is obtained through formal or more informal methods of international co-operation, the admissibility dilemma remains a problem. Undoubtedly, traditional common law admissibility rules exacerbate the problem and create a potential disincentive to international co-operation in the investigation of serious crime. National courts have approached the admissibility problem in a variety of ways.

16.2.1 Evidence obtained in breach of foreign law

In *Governor of Pentonville Prison ex p Chinoy*,[15] the English Divisional Court was asked to consider the admissibility of evidence obtained in France in

---

13 Crime (International Co-operation) Act 2003, s 9.
14 Report on the Green Paper on the establishment of a European Prosecutor, COM (2003) 128.
15 [1992] 1 All ER 317.

breach of French law and sovereignty and the European Convention on Human Rights. The court was of the opinion that the admissibility of foreign evidence was primarily a matter of relevance and reliability.[16] The applicant in this case was the manager of the BCCI bank in Paris. Following his arrest in the UK, he had been committed to prison to await extradition to the USA on the basis of evidence obtained by US agents operating in France. The magistrate allowed the US Government to adduce as evidence transcripts of telephone conversations recorded in France without the knowledge of the French authorities, in breach of French sovereignty, in breach of Art 8 of the European Convention on Human Rights and without recourse to the available mutual legal assistance provisions. Counsel for Chinoy argued that the transcripts should have been excluded on the ground that US authorities had engineered the applicant's presence in the UK in order to avoid French proceedings, which amounted to an abuse of process of the English court, and, in the alternative, the trial judge should have exercised his exclusionary discretion under s 78(1) of the Police and Criminal Evidence Act 1984 (PACE).

In dismissing this application, Nolan J noted that 'crucial evidence against the applicant has been obtained by means which are criminal in France and, at any rate according to French law, are in breach of the European Convention on Human Rights'.[17] He proceeded to ask: 'If (subject to s 78 of PACE) evidence unlawfully obtained in England is admissible, as Sang declares, then why should a different rule apply with regard to evidence obtained unlawfully in another country?'[18] Holding that evidence obtained abroad in breach of foreign law or international law 'formed part of the circumstances in which the evidence was obtained',[19] Nolan J considered it relevant that 'all the misconduct of which complaint is made took place before the matter came within the jurisdiction of the magistrates' court, and involved no abuse of process before that court'.[20] The fact that the court may find the manner in which the evidence was obtained objectionable is relevant to, but not determinative of, the judge's discretion to admit or exclude such evidence.[21] Accordingly, the magistrate was entitled to take the view that these

---

16 PACE, s 78, applies to extradition proceedings. Whilst the Criminal Procedure and Investigations Act (CPIA) 1996, para 26, Sched 1, removed committal proceedings from the scope of PACE, s 78 by inserting s 78(3), it is arguable that in extradition proceedings the magistrate is not sitting in the same capacity as an examining magistrate in criminal proceedings.

17 [1992] 1 All ER 317, p 330.

18 Ibid.

19 Ibid, p 332.

20 Ibid, p 330.

21 Interestingly, in *Chinoy v UK*, Application No 15199/89, the European Commission for Human Rights dismissed the application that the committal to prison was in breach of Art 5 on the ground that the domestic court's decision to allow the prosecution to rely on unlawfully obtained evidence complied with national rules and could not, therefore, be considered arbitrary.

breaches carried 'no more weight than breaches of English law and therefore did not constitute sufficient reason for excluding the evidence'.[22] The court chose to adopt a policy of non-inquiry into the manner in which evidence was obtained outside the UK by foreign law enforcement agencies and has been criticised for engaging in the laundering of evidence.[23] In presenting evidence obtained in breach of foreign law for use in the criminal process in another jurisdiction, the manner in which the evidence was obtained can be more easily overlooked than if it was obtained within the jurisdiction. Gane and Mackarel argue that, in *Chinoy*, evidence obtained unlawfully by US agents was effectively 'laundered' through local admissibility rules.

In *Chinoy*,[24] the impugned conduct was attributable to US agents; there was no suggestion that English prosecuting authorities were party to the illegal acts of the foreign law enforcement officers. However, in *USA v Verdugo-Urquidez*,[25] the US Supreme Court was prepared to admit evidence obtained from outside the jurisdiction by US agents acting in deliberate breach of the law of a foreign State. Following the arrest of a Mexican citizen for drug offences, US Drug Enforcement Agency (DEA) agents, working with Mexican police officers, conducted a search of the respondent's premises in Mexico. A Federal District Court held that the evidence seized during the search should be excluded on the ground that the search was unlawful under the Fourth Amendment to the Constitution. The DEA failed to obtain a warrant and did not have sufficient grounds for conducting a search without a warrant. On appeal, the Supreme Court held that the Fourth Amendment, which provided citizens with protection against unlawful search and seizure, did not apply to searches of property that was owned by non-resident foreigners located in a foreign State and, thus, the evidence was admissible.

In a powerful dissenting opinion, Brennan J warned that 'the behaviour of our law enforcement agents abroad sends a powerful message about the rule of law to individuals everywhere – when US agents conduct unreasonable searches, whether at home or abroad, they disregard our nation's values'.[26] In holding that the respondent was entitled to the protections of the Fourth Amendment, he reminded the court that a judicial warrant was intended to protect suspects from the 'unbridled discretion of investigating officers' which was 'no less important abroad than at home'.[27] He considered that, in sanctioning the unlawful actions of the DEA, there was a danger that the

---

22 [1992] 1 All ER 317.
23 See C Gane and M Mackarel, 'The Admissibility of Evidence Obtained from Abroad into Criminal Proceedings – The Interpretation of Mutual Legal Assistance Treaties and the Use of Evidence Irregularly Obtained', 4 *Eur J Crime Cr L Cr J* (1996), 98, p 116.
24 [1992] 1 All ER 317.
25 108 L Ed 2d 222 (1990).
26 Ibid, p 246.
27 Ibid, p 252.

court was lending support to the argument that in the administration of criminal law the end justifies the means. It is arguable that, by failing to exclude this evidence, the Supreme Court missed an opportunity to discourage future illegal investigations by US agents.

Whilst the majority of the court in *Verdugo-Urquidez*[28] sought to justify not only misconduct by law enforcement agencies engaged in investigating criminal offences abroad but also the illegal activity of US personnel involved in 'other foreign policy operations which might result in "searches or seizures" ',[29] the same criticism cannot be made against the Divisional Court in *Chinoy*. Domestic prosecuting authorities were beyond reproach and it is doubtful whether an English court can exert any influence over the activities of foreign agents. However, the failure to reject evidence, which was obtained not merely in breach of foreign law, but also in violation of international human rights standards, on the ground that the misconduct took place outside the jurisdiction of the English court, is lamentable and demonstrates a lack of sensitivity and understanding of the rules operating in other legal systems. Whilst the court may decide to disregard a breach of local rules when considering the admissibility of evidence obtained within the jurisdiction, to take the same approach to a blatant disregard for the rules applicable in another State is an entirely different matter. In effectively disregarding the infringement of the sovereign rights of French law and the violation of rights guaranteed by the European Convention on Human Rights, the court failed to take account of generally recognised principles and rules of international law and international comity.[30]

16.2.2 Evidence obtained in compliance with foreign law but which is irregular under national law

Although acknowledging that its exclusionary discretion extends to foreign evidence, English courts have been reluctant to lay down guidelines as to when it would be appropriate to refuse to admit such evidence. In *Quinn*,[31] the Court of Appeal held that identification evidence obtained abroad as a result of arrangements made by a foreign police force was admissible. Several weeks after the shooting of a police officer in London, Quinn stood trial in Dublin for offences committed in the Republic of Ireland. A witness to the shooting went to Dublin and identified the appellant. The fact that this identification

---

28 108 L Ed 2d 222 (1990).

29 Ibid, p 238.

30 In 1975, over 30 Member States of the Council of Europe signed the Helsinki Declaration and agreed to abide by their obligations under international law including those 'arising from the generally recognised principles and rules of international law . . . In exercising their sovereign rights, including the right to determine their laws and regulations'.

31 Crim LR [1990], 581.

was carried out in a manner which did not correspond with PACE and the codes of practice, should not be 'disregarded in so far as it affects the intrinsic fairness of the identification procedure adopted'.[32] Noting that 'English courts cannot expect English procedural requirements to be complied with by police forces operating abroad, even if, as in the present case, they have similar procedural requirements',[33] Lord Lane considered that for the purposes of s 78(1) the critical factor was the fairness of the subsequent English proceedings. In dismissing this appeal, he was satisfied that when exercising his discretion the trial judge had taken into account relevant factors such as the lack of an opportunity to cross-examine the witness and the fact that the disputed evidence was not the sole evidence in the case. Interestingly, the court noted that 'the present case was not one where the procedural departures . . . were the responsibility of the British authorities'.[34]

The possibility of at least some control over evidence obtained as a result of serious extra-territorial irregularity is raised by the Scottish case of *HM Advocate v McKay*.[35] The court was required to consider the admissibility of evidence that had been obtained in Eire under an Irish search warrant. In accordance with the practice in Eire, documents were seized which were not in the name of the accused. At the subsequent trial in Scotland, objection was taken to the admissibility of the documents. It was submitted that it would be improper to admit the evidence because the search offended against the principles governing the search of premises in Scotland. Lord Wheatley took the view that:

> The procedure followed was regular according to the law of the land where it took place [and that] does not in itself necessarily constitute a sufficient justification for the admission of the evidence. I can visualise circumstances where the practice followed by the law and procedure of the local country was so offensive to our own fundamental principles of justice and fair play that the admissibility of such evidence would not be tolerated. It seems to me, therefore, to be a question of facts and circumstances in each case.[36]

The court held that, as far as Scottish procedure was concerned, the search was irregular. However, the irregularity was not necessarily fatal to the admissibility of the evidence. In this case the court was satisfied that in the circumstances the irregularity could be excused and the evidence admitted. The submission regarding the admissibility of evidence was not based on the

32 Crim LR [1990], 581.
33 Ibid, p 582.
34 Ibid.
35 1961 SLT 176.
36 Ibid, p 179.

premise that foreign police officers behaved improperly or that the evidence was gathered in breach of foreign procedures.

Unlike the court in *McKay*, the English court has so far failed to contemplate what would happen if foreign evidence-gathering rules did offend English sensibilities. Citing *Quinn* with approval, the English court, in *Konscol*,[37] was prepared to admit evidence obtained outside the UK in accordance with local law, notwithstanding that it was obtained in a manner which did not correspond with English practice. Konscol was arrested in Belgium and subsequently convicted of conspiracy to import drugs into the UK. At his trial, he objected to the prosecution adducing in evidence a note of an interview obtained in Belgium by a customs officer, acting under the instruction of a Belgian magistrate. In accordance with local procedures, the Belgian authorities did not offer the suspect the services of a lawyer and did not administer a caution. In refusing to exclude this evidence, the trial judge considered it relevant that there was no dishonesty or bullying behaviour by the Belgian authorities and at no time did the appellant deny that he said what was recorded. On appeal, the appellant submitted that as the interview was not conducted in accordance with the provisions of PACE and would have been excluded had it been taken in England, the judge was wrong to permit the prosecution to adduce it. In dismissing the appeal, the Court of Appeal assumed that the interview was conducted lawfully in accordance with Belgian procedures. It is of note that in both *Quinn* and *Konscol* the issue before the court was the application of its discretionary exclusionary power under s 78 of PACE. It is questionable whether the court's reasoning would be sustainable if the evidence had been a confession obtained by oppression and the submission was based on the exercise of the mandatory exclusionary power under s 76 of PACE.

On occasion prosecuting authorities have been able to use evidence obtained outside the UK in accordance with foreign law, notwithstanding a prohibition on the use of evidence obtained in the same manner within the jurisdiction. The Court of Appeal has ruled that the provisions of domestic legislation which rendered telephone intercepts effected within the UK inadmissible at trial did not apply to foreign telephone intercepts. Relying on evidence consisting of telephone calls intercepted in the US, the US Government, in *Governor of Belmarsh Prison ex p Martin*,[38] sought the applicant's extradition to stand trial for conspiracy to cause explosions. Having considered the intercepts, the magistrate found that there was a *prima facie* case against him and committed him to await the directions of the Secretary of State. The applicant applied for a writ of *habeas corpus* on the grounds that telephone intercepts were, by virtue of the Intercept of Communication Act (ICA)

37 Crim LR [1993], 950.
38 [1995] 1 WLR 412.

1985, inadmissible in proceedings in the UK. In this case, the Divisional Court did not concern itself with the question whether the intercept was obtained in accordance with foreign law. It was satisfied that a foreign telephone intercept obtained in the US, by US Government agents, could be adduced in evidence in England because the relevant domestic legislation had no extra-territorial jurisdiction.[39] Relevant to the court's decision was the fact that no offence had been committed by any person concerned in the operation of the public communications system in the UK.

Similarly, in *Aujla*,[40] the Court of Appeal held that evidence of an intercept obtained outside the UK in accordance with local law was admissible in an English trial. The applicants were charged with conspiracy to facilitate the illegal entry of persons into the UK. During the course of a preparatory hearing,[41] the trial judge ruled that an intercept obtained in the Netherlands in accordance with Dutch law and procedure was admissible as evidence. Having obtained the appropriate judicial authority to intercept telephone calls, Dutch police officers recorded conversations made between Dutch residents and the appellants. These transcripts were eventually used as evidence in criminal proceedings in the Netherlands. Following the conviction of the Dutch residents, the transcripts were made available to the English police for use in the prosecution of the appellants in England. There was no challenge to the authenticity of the transcripts or the accuracy of the translations.

In dismissing this interlocutory appeal, the Court of Appeal held that the operation of domestic legislation did not bar the use of material obtained by foreign phone tapping as evidence in proceedings in England. Furthermore, the court was satisfied that this evidence was obtained without violating the appellants' right to privacy, which is guaranteed by Art 8 of the Convention. Relevant to the court's decision was the fact that the evidence had been obtained in accordance with Dutch law and Dutch procedure which was presumed to meet the requirements of the Convention; the transcripts were part of a record of proceedings before a Dutch court and, thus, open to public scrutiny, and no issue was taken as to the relevance or the reliability of the transcripts which had been obtained in a manner which did not conflict with English law.

This issue has also been addressed by the Belgian *Cour de Cassation* in relation to telephone intercepts obtained outside the jurisdiction, but made available for use in criminal proceedings in Belgium. The court was asked

---

39 For further discussion of the ICA 1985, see S Nash, 'Interception of Communications in the European Union', 5 *Juridical Review* (1996), 321.
40 [1998] 2 Cr App R 16.
41 CPIA 1996, s 31(3), provides that a trial judge may make a ruling as to the admissibility of evidence and under s 35(1) of that Act, the accused can apply for leave to appeal to the Court of Appeal against this ruling. If leave is granted, the Court of Appeal has the power to confirm, reverse or vary the judge's ruling.

to consider whether a transcript of a telephone intercept obtained in the Netherlands at the request of the Belgian authorities was correctly admitted at trial, notwithstanding the prohibition on the interception of telephones in Belgium.[42] In upholding the conviction, the court ruled that an intercept obtained in the Netherlands in accordance with Dutch law and procedure was compatible with the European Convention on Human Rights.[43] Similarly, no objection was taken to the admissibility of transcripts obtained by French police in connection with a French criminal investigation which were made available to Belgian authorities for use in Belgium. Whilst the court was not prepared to determine the legality of foreign procedures, providing the transcript was obtained lawfully according to French law and did not conflict with rights guaranteed by the Convention, the evidence could be received by a Belgian court.

The courts in the US have consistently reaffirmed the principle that the actions of foreign law enforcement officials and evidence obtained outside the US by those actions are not subject to the usual constitutional protections afforded by the Bill of Rights. In *Brulay v USA*,[44] for example, the defendant was arrested in Mexico for the possession of drugs and subsequently convicted in the US for conspiracy to smuggle narcotics into the US. On appeal, he claimed that statements taken from him by Mexican police and searches and seizures made by them did not conform to standards set out by the constitution, that such evidence was therefore irregularly obtained and should be excluded. The court disagreed, maintaining that applying exclusionary rules to the actions of Mexican police would not alter their search policies and that the exclusionary rules relating to evidence improperly obtained were intended to require US police officers to obey US law. Notwithstanding a breach of Mexican law, the Fourth and 14th Amendments to the US Constitution did not apply to evidence obtained by Mexican police officers, or indeed to foreign law enforcement officials in general.

Providing the actions of foreign officials did not 'shock the conscience' of the court[45] or involve the participation of US officials so as to represent a joint venture, this principle has been acknowledged by the US courts on many occasions.[46] Arguably, the court has taken a rather disingenuous view

---

42 Loi du 13 Octobre 1930, Art 17.

43 Cour de Cassation (2ème ch, sect Néel) 26 January 1993 (en cause de Co D) Revue de droit penal, 1993.

44 383 F 2d 345 (1967), 9th Cir, Ct of Appeals.

45 No express guidance has been set down as to what constitutes malpractice severe enough to shock the conscience of the court; however, in *USA v Toscanino*, 500 F 2d 267 (1974), the court was 'shocked' by the torture of the respondent by US officials, but was not shocked by his forcible abduction.

46 See *Stonehill v USA*, 405 F 2d 738 (1968), 9th Cir Ct of Appeals; *USA v Marzano*, 537 F 2d 257 (1975), 7th Cir Ct of Appeals; *USA v Cotroni*, 527 F 2d (1975), 2nd Cir Court of Appeals; *USA v Busic*, 587 F 2d 577 (1978), 3rd Cir Ct of Appeals.

of the concept of 'joint venture'. In *USA v Marzano*,[47] a suspect wanted for substantial bank thefts in the US fled to the Cayman Islands. A police officer in Grand Cayman allowed two FBI agents to accompany him during the investigation, in the course of which the suspect was arrested and searches of a legally dubious nature carried out. He was then put on a plane destined for Miami. Thus, without any recourse to the formal procedures required under extradition or mutual assistance arrangements, prosecuting authorities in the US were in possession of the fugitive and the incriminating evidence. The FBI agents claimed that their role in the operation had been completely passive and this was supported by the Cayman police officer involved. The Court of Appeals, Seventh Circuit, accepted that the role of the US agents was entirely passive and found no evidence to support the view that the investigation involved a joint venture with the foreign agents. Accordingly, the evidence was properly admitted at trial.

16.3 ADMISSIBILITY OF FOREIGN EVIDENCE: FAIR TRIAL ISSUES

While mutual legal assistance mechanisms which simplify the transfer of evidence increase co-operation between prosecuting authorities, they also raise concerns about public accountability and arguably fail to take sufficient account of the human rights dimension of the transfer of evidence between jurisdictions. Despite divergent procedural mechanisms, criminal procedural systems aim to achieve a fair balance between conflicting public interest requirements. Whether confidence is placed in State institutions to exert control over the investigation or in the discretionary power of the trial judge to reject evidence, each system weighs the interests of the community in bringing to conviction the wrongdoer against the need to protect the rights and liberties of the individual.[48] In order to understand the function of procedural rules and safeguards, which operate in fundamentally different ways in each system, each component should be seen in the context of social and political structures and not in isolation. Transplanting procedural rules is fraught with danger. Safeguards which work well in the host system may be rejected by the donor due to procedural incompatibility. Misunderstanding or ignoring the complex interplay between procedural rules and safeguards designed to promote truth finding, and evidentiary rules devised to ensure fairness and balance at the proof stage of proceedings risks disturbing the coherence that exists within each system. In liberal democracies, the

---

47 537 F 2d 257 (1975), 7th Cir Ct of Appeals.
48 See S Nash 'Tipping the Scales: The Reduction of Procedural Protection for the Accused in Inter-jurisdictional Cases' 2000 PhD thesis, University of Aberdeen.

use of coercive police power is counterbalanced by the provision of procedural safeguards which operate at different points within each system. Gathering evidence by one set of rules and assessing by it by another risks missing out the procedural safeguards which are designed to ensure fairness and guard against abuse. Procedural protections found in human rights instruments offer minimal protection and are not intended to replace safeguards operating within national systems. The recent wave of enthusiasm to increase international co-operation to combat the rise in cross-border crime must not be allowed to reduce, to an unacceptable level, procedural guarantees designed to protect the accused from over-zealous prosecuting authorities.

16.4 EVIDENCE OBTAINED IN BREACH OF INTERNATIONAL HUMAN RIGHTS STANDARDS

In addition to the minimum standards of procedural fairness which are set out in Art 14 of the International Covenant on Civil and Political Rights (ICCPR)[49] and Art 6 of the European Convention on Human Rights,[50] the privilege against self-incrimination,[51] the right to remain silent[52] and the principle of equality of arms[53] are internationally recognised standards which are implicit in the right to a fair trial. Similarly, Statutes of both the International Criminal Tribunal for the Former Yugoslavia (ICTY) and the International Criminal Tribunal for Rwanda (ICTR) contain fair trial guarantees.[54] However, international human rights instruments do not set out formal rules of evidence and international tribunals have resisted any moves to be bound by

---

49 999 UNTS 171.
50 Rome, 4 November; TS71 (1953); Cmnd 8969.
51 *Funke v France* (1993) 16 EHRR 297.
52 The right to remain silent when questioned by law enforcement agencies and the freedom from self-incrimination is closely linked to the presumption of innocence. Although *Funke v France* (1993) 16 EHRR 297 and *Saunders v UK* (1994) 18 EHRR CD 23 establish that compelling the accused to provide incriminating evidence which is later adduced in evidence against him will infringe the freedom from self-incrimination, in *Murray v UK* (1996) 22 EHRR 29, the court held that drawing inferences from the accused's silence will not automatically result in breach of the Convention.
53 In *Dombo Beheer BV v The Netherlands* (1993) 18 EHRR 213, the court considered that the concept of equality of arms requires that 'each party must be afforded a reasonable opportunity to present his case, including his evidence, under conditions that do not place him at a substantial disadvantage vis-à-vis his opponent'.
54 SC Res 955 (8 Nov 1994). For further discussion, see Chapter 5.

strict exclusionary rules.[55] The case law of the European Court of Human Rights unequivocally establishes that the admissibility of evidence is a matter for regulation by national law and the assessment of evidence is a matter for national courts and any attempt to introduce exclusionary rules into Convention jurisprudence has been actively resisted.[56] Similarly, the Human Rights Committee[57] when considering alleged violations of the ICCPR considers itself free to assess all the evidence presented before it in order to establish the facts. Whilst the Statute of the ICTY does have specific rules of procedure and evidence, r 89 provides that the Trial Chamber shall apply rules of evidence 'which will best favour a fair determination of the matter before it', but can exclude evidence if its probative value is substantially outweighed by the need to ensure a fair trial.[58]

Notwithstanding the lack of formal exclusionary rules, implicit in the right to a fair trial is the rejection of evidence obtained in breach of fundamental human rights standards. Thus, although human rights jurisprudence has only limited impact on admissibility, the prohibition on torture, which is generally recognised as an internationally accepted standard and enshrines one of the fundamental values of democratic societies,[59] guarantees that evidence obtained in this manner will be excluded from a criminal trial regardless of its reliability.[60] In *Burgos v Uruguay*,[61] the Human Rights Committee found that the use at trial of evidence obtained under torture infringed the right to a fair trial.[62]

---

55 Although having no formal status, Art 33 of the European rules proposed by the *Corpus Juris* project, a discussion paper prepared by a group of experts asked by the European Commission to consider the problem of budgetary fraud sets out conditions for the exclusion of illegally obtained evidence.

56 *Schenk v Switzerland* (1988) 13 EHRR 242.

57 Under the ICCPR, Optional Protocol 1, contracting States may declare that they recognise the competence of the Human Rights Committee to receive complaints from individuals claiming to be victims of violations of the rights set out in the covenant. See generally D McGoldrick, *The Human Rights Committee*, 1994, Oxford: Clarendon.

58 Rules of Procedure and Evidence for the International Tribunal for the Former Yugoslavia, s 3, r 89(B), UN Doc IT/32 (14 March 1994).

59 See, eg, European Convention on Human Rights, Art 3; ICCPR, Art 7; and American Convention on Human Rights, Art 5. See also *A and Others v Secretary of State for the Home Department* [2005] UKHL 71, [2005] 3 WLR 1249 in which the House of Lords considers the admissibility of foreign evidence obtained by torture.

60 See discussion in *Soering v UK* (1989) 11 EHRR 439, para 88.

61 (1981) 1 Selected Decisions Human Rights Committee 88, p 90.

62 See also *Johnson v Jamaica* (1997) 4 IHRR 21 and *Zelaya Blanco v Nicaragua* (1995) 2 IHRR 123.

16.5 FAILURE TO USE MUTUAL LEGAL ASSISTANCE PROVISIONS [63]

In the absence of a specific treaty provision,[64] there is no mechanism whereby parties can be obliged to use formal mutual legal assistance provisions to obtain evidence abroad. In *Re Sealed Case*,[65] the US Court of Appeals rejected the argument that US law enforcement agencies were limited to obtaining evidence in accordance with the provisions set out in a mutual legal assistance treaty signed by the Swiss and US Governments.[66] The appellant refused to comply with a subpoena to appear before a US court to produce documents relating to Swiss companies. Rejecting the argument that compliance with the request would be contrary to Swiss secrecy laws and in breach of international comity, the court held that it could 'order any party within its jurisdiction to testify or produce documents regardless of a foreign sovereign's view to the contrary'.[67] Support for the court's decision can be found in Art 38(1), which states that the treaty would not prevent or restrict the use of procedures available under municipal law.

A similar approach towards international comity was adopted by the Court of Appeals in *Re Grand Jury Proceedings; Marsoner v USA*,[68] where, in the absence of any formal legal assistance arrangements with Austria, the District Court ordered the appellant to sign a disclosure directive to act as consent under Austrian law for obtaining documents from bank accounts. The appellant refused to sign and was fined and imprisoned for contempt. On appeal, the appellant argued that the disclosure order violated his rights under the fourth and fifth Amendments of the US Constitution, and Austrian law. After dismissing these claims, the Court of Appeals held that, despite the order of the District Court compelling the appellant to sign the disclosure directive breaching Austrian law and Arts 3, 6 and 8 of the European Convention on Human Rights, international comity did not preclude its enforcement. The Court balanced the interests of the US in collecting its taxes against the purported illegality of the order under Austrian law and considerations of bank secrecy and upheld the interests of the US in compelling the appellant's signature, leaving Austrian courts to decide what effect to

---

63 For further discussion of this topic, see op cit, Gane and Mackarel, note 23.
64 See, eg, the USA–UK Treaty concerning the Cayman Islands and Mutual Legal Assistance in Criminal Matters, Art 17, 26 ILM (1987), 536, which forbids US courts to use compulsory measures to obtain documents located outside the jurisdiction. Worthy of note is UN Model Treaty on Mutual Assistance in Criminal Matters, Art 8, which provides limitations on the use and transfer of evidence. Unless consent is obtained from the requested State, the evidence may only be used in connection with investigations set out in the request.
65 832 F 2d 1268 (1987), US Ct of Appeals for the District of Columbia.
66 1973 USA–Switzerland Treaty on Mutual Assistance in Criminal Matters.
67 Ibid, p 1283.
68 40 F 3d 959 (1994), 9th Cir, US Ct of Appeals.

give the disclosure directive with respect to Austrian bank records. The decision of the Court of Appeals shows little concern for international comity. Some disquiet has been expressed with respect to the extra-territoriality approach taken by the US courts. Following attempts by the US Court of Appeals to use coercive measures against a bank to obtain confidential documents in the Cayman Islands, the UK insisted on the inclusion of a specific provision forbidding the use of extra-territorial coercive measures by US courts. In this case, a fine was imposed on the bank for failure to comply with an order from the US court, despite the fact that compliance with the request would have been in breach of local law.[69] The UK reacted by insisting that an agreement to combat narcotics in 1984,[70] and subsequently the MLAT, signed two years later,[71] contained a variety of restrictions on assistance, including provisions designed to prevent 'fishing expeditions' for information.[72]

The reluctance of national courts to insist that the exchange of evidence takes place under formal arrangements has encouraged prosecuting authorities to engage in more informal methods of evidence gathering.[73] However, in *Radak*,[74] the Court of Appeal refused to sanction the prosecution's failure to make use of available mutual legal assistance procedures intended to safeguard defence rights. In this case, the prosecution could have issued a letter requesting assistance in obtaining the witness's written testimony for use in criminal proceedings in the UK. On receipt of a formal letter of request, the US authorities provide assistance in accordance with the provisions of the treaty between the Government of the UK of Great Britain and Northern Ireland and the Government of the US on mutual legal assistance in criminal matters. Article 8(4) provides that a requested party shall allow persons specified in the letter of request to ask questions of the person whose testimony

---

69 *USA v Bank of Nova Scotia*, 740 F 2d 817.
70 *Exchange of Letters of 26 July 1984 Between the USA and UK Concerning the Cayman Islands and Matters Connected with, Arising From, Related to, or Resulting from any Narcotics Activity Referred to in the Single Convention on Narcotic Drugs, 1961*, as amended by the Protocol Amending the Single Convention on Narcotic Drugs, 1961, Art 6, Cmnd 9344, 1984.
71 1986 US–UK Treaty Relating to the Cayman Islands, Art 17(3).
72 For a good summary to the background to and content of the Cayman Islands agreements see W Gilmore (ed) *Mutual Assistance in Criminal and Business Regulatory Matters*, 1995 Cambridge: CUP, pp xx–xxiii.
73 See, eg, *USA v Verdugo-Urquidez*, 110 S Ct 1056 (1990), in which no mention was made of the existence of a mutual legal assistance treaty between Mexico and the US which contained a provision for searches and seizure. In *USA v Alvarez-Machain*, 112 S Ct 2188 (1992) the Supreme Court held that unless a procedure was expressly prohibited by the treaty, the court would not prevent prosecuting authorities from acting in a manner which was arguably in breach of international law. In this case, the court refused to return a fugitive who had been abducted by US authorities. In the absence of an express provision in the extradition treaty prohibiting abduction, the court refused to pronounce the activities unlawful.
74 [1999] 1 Cr App R 187. See S Nash, 'The Admissibility of Witness Statements Obtained Abroad; *R v Radak*', 3 E&P (1999), 195.

is being taken. The examination of the witness is conducted through a legal representative qualified to appear before the courts of the requested State. Under this procedure the parties are provided with the opportunity to test the evidence of a witness living overseas by cross-examination. The court held that the failure to obtain evidence in accordance with s 3 of the Criminal Justice (International Co-operation) Act 1990 was relevant to the exercise of the judge's discretion to grant leave to admit a written statement. Although the prosecution had known from the outset that a crucial witness was reluctant to leave the US, they 'let slip the opportunity of obtaining cross-examined evidence on commission in time for the date fixed for the trial'.[75] The issue for the court was whether the lack of opportunity to cross-examine this witness was sufficiently unfair to the defence that it was not in the interests of justice to admit the evidence. In seeking leave to admit the statement, the prosecution were 'seeking leave to cover their culpability'[76] for failing to use treaty provisions designed to provide the prosecution and defence with an equal opportunity to summon and examine witnesses which would safeguard defence rights and minimise any unfairness. The court was satisfied that had this evidence been obtained on commission by a court in the US, it would have satisfied the requirements of Art 6(3)(d) of the European Convention on Human Rights.[77] In allowing this appeal, the court considered that, on balance, the degree of unfairness resulting from the failure to use available mutual legal assistance provisions was sufficient to exclude the statement. What is encouraging in the case is the willingness of the court to exclude evidence in order to ensure equality between the defence and the prosecution as regards the examination of witnesses.

16.6 MUTUAL LEGAL ASSISTANCE TREATIES AND INDIVIDUAL RIGHTS

While some States seek to provide the accused with a mechanism to obtain evidence located abroad, the US favours MLATs which expressly exclude the defence from obtaining access to evidence under the agreement. It has been suggested that any requirements for strict controls on the use of evidence can be met in the case of defence requests by providing for transmission through domestic courts; and where it was suspected that the means of carrying out requests would breach the requesting State's own obligations under human rights instruments, it should be incumbent on the requesting

---

75 [1999] 1 Cr App R 187, p 203.
76 Ibid.
77 European Convention on Human Rights, Art 6(3) provides that the accused shall have the right to 'examine or have examined witnesses against him and to obtain the attendance and examination of witnesses on his behalf under the same conditions as witnesses against him'.

State to particularise its requirements in the request.[78] Although the UK has attempted to ensure that evidence gathered under mutual legal assistance arrangements is used according to domestic rules of evidence,[79] the US continues to exclude individuals from taking any action to exclude evidence obtained under an MLAT.[80] Thus, treaty arrangements with the US, generally, contain a specific provision excluding the rights of any person to exclude evidence or to seek judicial relief in connection with requests under an MLAT.[81] In *USA v Garcia*,[82] the Court of Appeals confirmed that a defendant had no standing to challenge the erroneous use of Swiss banking records obtained under the Treaty. In *USA v George D Davis*,[83] the defendant claimed that his rights of confrontation under the sixth Amendment of the US Constitution had been violated on the grounds that he had not been informed of proceedings taking place in Switzerland which he or his counsel were entitled under the terms of the Treaty to attend.[84] Whilst acknowledging the defendant's predicament, the Court of Appeals observed that, notwithstanding his right to attend the hearing in Switzerland, he lacked any standing under the Treaty. Thus, his attendance was an academic point without practical merit. Under this type of treaty, the interests of the individual rest with the respective central authorities. However, whilst the authorities can make a claim to exclude evidence or require explanation for failure to comply with the treaty provisions,[85] it is not usually in their interest to pursue such a claim. Frequently, the admissibility of the evidence will enhance the chances of a successful prosecution, thus exclusion of the evidence will be counterproductive to the authorities' interests. Following their conviction for tax offences, the appellants in *USA v Sturman and Others*[86] claimed that the US Government had requested information and bank records from the Swiss authorities to investigate tax offences, which was expressly excluded under the Treaty.[87]

78 The Working Group on Mutual Legal Assistance in Criminal Matters, 1998 Oxford Conference on International Co-operation in Criminal Matters, 'Balancing the Protection of Human Rights With the Needs of Law Enforcement', 24–28 August 1998, Oxford: Christ Church.

79 Crime (International Co-operation) Act 2003 s 9.

80 See, eg, the Netherlands–USA Treaty, Art 18(2); Canada–USA Treaty, Art 2(4); USA–UK Treaty on the Cayman Islands, Art 1(3); Mexico–USA Treaty, Art 1(5).

81 See, eg, the USA–Switzerland MLAT, Art 37(1), which purports 'to suppress or exclude any evidence or to obtain other judicial relief in connection with requests under this treaty'. Under this provision, anyone the subject of information obtained by the US under an MLAT is unable to move that any of that evidence should not be admitted, leaving the court to act *ex officio* in excluding evidence containing some irregularity.

82 37 F 3d 1359 (1994), 9th Cir, US Ct of Appeals.

83 767 F 2d 1025 (1985); 18 Fed R Evid Serv (Callaghan) 53.

84 See USA–Switzerland MLAT, Art 18(5).

85 Ibid, Art 37(3).

86 *USA v D Sturman; R Levine; R Sturman; and M Kaminsky*, 951 F 2d 1466 (1991), 6th Cir, US Ct of Appeals.

87 USA–Switzerland MLAT, Art 2(1)(a) and (5).

The appellants claimed that the Government had misrepresented the facts, informing the Swiss authorities that the investigation was in relation to organised crime.[88] Disallowing the appeal, the Court of Appeals observed that Art 37 of the Treaty with Switzerland excluded the right of individuals to suppress evidence.[89] The court was satisfied that the requests for assistance 'contain no serious misrepresentations' and for a violation to warrant a reversal of a conviction it must constitute 'serious governmental misconduct'.[90]

16.7 INFORMAL METHODS OF MUTUAL ASSISTANCE

Despite the increased willingness of States to engage in formal methods of mutual legal assistance, there are many other less formal methods of evidence gathering which permit law enforcement agencies to exchange information and material relevant to transnational investigations. The *Explanatory Report on the European Convention on Mutual Legal Assistance in Criminal Matters*[91] indicates that the Convention was designed to supplement rather than replace existing co-operative arrangements. Informal methods of co-operation include: Memoranda of Understanding, which are non-legally binding written agreements setting out an undertaking to provide the assistance requested, indicating the procedures to be followed and the grounds for refusing a request for assistance; and mutual administrative assistance which allows for the delivery of information between investigating agencies on a voluntary basis. This procedure requires the consent of the person holding the information. The methods by which requests for information are transmitted through the international police networks of Interpol and Europol are discussed in some detail in the next chapter.

---

88 *US v D Sturman; R Levine; R Sturman; and M Kaminsky*, 951 F 2d 1466 (1991), 6th Cir, US
    Ct of Appeals, p 1482.
89 Ibid, p 1483.
90 Ibid, p 1484.
91 1969 report, Council of Europe.

Chapter 17

International police co-operation

17.1 INTRODUCTION

The increase in transnational organised crime and the mobility of suspects and witnesses generally has resulted in the increased willingness of States to develop co-operative procedures to facilitate the gathering and transmission of evidence for use in criminal prosecutions in other jurisdictions. International crime is an increasing phenomenon in terms of its frequency, scale and diversity. While the relaxation of border controls, ease of access to air travel and the dramatic advancement in the development of communications systems have combined to assist transnational criminal activity and has arguably facilitated the recent growth in terrorist-related crime, police investigative powers do not generally transcend national borders. Prosecuting authorities requiring access to suspects or material located outside the jurisdiction are required to seek assistance from their foreign counterparts through operational police co-operation and other mutual legal assistance procedures. Accordingly, the growth in cross-border crime and terrorism has resulted in the need for law enforcement agencies to modernise and increase their capability to investigate criminal activity taking place beyond national borders. However, some of the recent initiatives introduced to improve police and judicial co-operation in criminal matters have arguably reduced the traditional procedural protections for suspects to an unacceptable level. Thus, improving co-operation between policing agencies is a task beset with seemingly insurmountable hurdles. Even within Member States of the European Union (EU), which have close geographical and cultural ties, divergent legal systems, different law enforcement strategies and the increasing diversity of transnational criminal activity combine to hamper effective police co-operation.

17.2 INTERPOL

The International Criminal Police Commission (ICPC), known as Interpol, is an intergovernmental organisation which facilitates co-operation between national law enforcement agencies. It provides a secure police communication service, offers a range of operational databases for police and provides other operational police services. It operates in four official languages: English, French, Arabic and Spanish. The ICPC was formed in 1923 and in 2005 had a membership of 186 States including Afghanistan, Bhutan, Turkmenistan and East Timor. Its primary purpose is to facilitate cross-border police co-operation in the fight against transnational organised crime including drug-trafficking, terrorism and Internet-based child pornography. One of its most important functions is to assist police forces disseminate crime-related information to each other through the use of the Interpol communication system. The origins of this international police network can be traced back to 1914. At the First International Police Congress held in Monaco, representatives from 14 countries considered establishing an international criminal records office and discussed methods for improving extradition procedures. Although further progress was prevented by the outbreak of the First World War, in 1923 the Second International Police Congress met in Vienna and set up the ICPC, which was to be based in Vienna. The Commission, which focused on providing assistance to prosecuting authorities throughout Europe, suffered a severe setback with the outbreak of the Second World War and the Nazi occupation of Austria. It has been suggested that the information and records kept by Interpol assisted the Nazi regime in their persecution of minorities.[1] After the war, the ICPC moved to Paris and the process of rebuilding its reputation and membership commenced. It was during this period that the organisation took its telegraphic address, 'Interpol', which has since become the name by which the organisation is known. In 1956, the General Assembly, the governing body of the ICPC, agreed to draft new statutes which changed the name of the organisation to the International Criminal Police Organisation. Its membership has grown rapidly since the Second World War.

Interpol's modern constitution dates from 1956. Article 2 of this provides that its role is:

(I) To ensure and promote the widest possible mutual assistance between all criminal police authorities within the limits of the laws existing in different countries and in the spirit of the Universal Declaration of Human Rights.

(II) To establish and develop all institutions likely to contribute effectively to the prevention and suppression of ordinary law crimes.

---

1 M Andersen, *Policing the World: Interpol and the Politics of International Police Co-operation*, 1989, Oxford: OUP, pp 41–42.

Interpol's main function is to process inquiries and disseminate information by way of its international communications system. Consequently, it is not an operational agency in the same manner as a conventional domestic police force. Article 3 of its constitution, which strictly forbids the organisation to undertake any intervention or activities of a political, military, religious or racial character, has the effect of limiting its role. The interpretation of Art 3 rekindled some pre-war perceptions of the organisation and, for a time, it refused to assist investigations connected to the prosecution of Nazi war criminals. However, this changed with the issuing of a request for the arrest of Joseph Mengele in 1985. Article 3 caused further problems when some States refused to co-operate in undertaking investigations into terrorist activities on the basis that this category of offences was politically motivated. These problems threatened to jeopardise the general work of Interpol and it became clear that some regenerative action was required. In 1984, the General Assembly of Interpol met to draft revised guidelines with the intention of bringing about a change in focus to the problematic interpretation of Art 3. As a consequence of these discussions, the General Assembly agreed that the motive put forward by the terrorist would not in itself be sufficient to make the offence 'political' in nature. Each case must be considered separately on its merits and all the elements involved are to be considered.[2] Whilst Art 3 was not amended, the revised guidelines provided Interpol with a more pragmatic basis for distinguishing between ordinary criminal offences and 'politically motivated offences'.

17.2.1 Organisation of Interpol

Interpol is a non-political, independent policing organisation which has been recognised by the United Nations (UN) Economic and Social Council Resolution as an intergovernmental organisation,[3] and is independent from other international bodies such as the UN or the Council of Europe. The General Assembly and the Executive Committee are the two senior decision-making bodies and the General Secretariat, which is comprised of a number of departments, is responsible for implementing the decisions of the assembly and executive. The Secretariat and the Interpol National Central Bureau (NCB) are responsible for co-ordinating with law enforcement agencies in each Member State to facilitate the everyday work of police co-operation. The General Assembly is composed of delegates from all 181 Member States. Meeting annually, the General Assembly makes major decisions which affect general policy, operational priorities, resources and finances and elects the

---

2 A Bossard, 'Interpol and Law Enforcement: Response to Transnational Crime', 11 *Police Studies* (1988), 177, p 179.
3 E/RES/1579 (L).

organisation's officers. The Executive Committee is comprised of members elected from the General Assembly and aims to implement the decisions of the General Assembly, and works closely with the Secretary General. The General Secretariat, the permanent administrative body through which Interpol operates, co-ordinates investigations and information via both national and international authorities and implements policy set down by the General Assembly and the Executive Committee. Based in Lyon, France, the General Secretariat is headed by the General Secretary, who is elected every five years and is answerable to the General Assembly and the Executive Committee. The Secretariat operates with a staff of approximately 500 personnel from 78 Member States, consisting of about 100 police officers seconded from national authorities. The remainder are civilian support staff.

The NCBs have been described as 'the vital cogs upon which the organisation turns'.[4] Each Member State has an NCB, normally based with a central domestic policing agency. In the case of the UK, the NCB is attached to the Serious Organised Crime Agency (SOCA) which is based in London. The NCBs are charged with the responsibility of sending requests for assistance and receiving enquiries. National police officers or government officials staff the NCBs and are required to operate in accordance with national law. The function of NCBs is to carry out the following tasks:

(a) collecting criminal intelligence related to offences and offenders which have international elements. This intelligence is disseminated to other NCBs and the General Secretariat;
(b) ensuring that police operations requested by other States' NCBs are carried out;
(c) receiving requests from other NCBs for information and replying to those requests;
(d) transmitting requests for international co-operation from domestic police and courts to foreign NCBs;
(e) forming part of the national delegations which attend the annual meeting of the General Assembly.

Whilst NCBs communicate with each other, it is their responsibility to inform the General Secretariat of their work in order to ensure information and operations can be centralised and co-ordinated efficiently.

Interpol's historical origins lie within Europe and its early work was concerned primarily with improving police co-operation between the European States that made up the membership of the organisation. Priority was given to the policing concerns of the European and US members, who were the

4 J Benyon *et al*, *Police Co-operation in Europe: An Investigation*, 1993, Leicester: University of Leicester Centre for the Study of Public Order, 125.

heaviest users of Interpol. As a consequence of the organisation's expansion, Interpol's activities became concerned with criminal activity throughout the world. Towards the end of the 1980s, it was acknowledged that 'police collaboration in EU countries is constrained by the fact that it is the international police organisation of the world'.[5] Undoubtedly, the globalisation of criminal activity has tested the organisation's capacity to respond, and the increasingly transnational nature of crime has had repercussions on policy.[6] A fraudulent offence against a European bank will affect the bank's interests globally and any criminal investigation may involve activity in several geographically and culturally diverse regions. Similarly, possession and supply of proscribed drugs in Europe and the US cannot be viewed in isolation from the producer countries in South America and the Far East. Whilst Interpol continues to take measures to provide for the needs of its European members, there is a general shift towards regionalisation. In 1999, a Regional Co-ordination and Development Directorate was set up within the General Secretariat to increase the range of regional initiatives. In 1986, the European dimension of Interpol's work was given a sharper focus with the establishment of a European Secretariat and a European Liaison Bureau within the General Secretariat. This body has the task of overseeing criminal matters with a European dimension. The organisation's budget for 1999 was $US 27.2 million. In October 2002, the member countries agreed to a 23.4 per cent increase in contributions to ensure that Interpol can continue to respond effectively to current challenges. In 2005, its gross income was approximately $US 35 million. While all Member States of Interpol make financial contributions to the running of the organisation, individual contributions vary depending upon the size of the country and use made of the resources. States are required to indicate to the Executive Committee their intended contribution and the Secretary General is charged with implementing the budget. The accounts are externally audited under the direction of the General Assembly and Executive Committee.

17.2.2 Interpol operational activities

Although its primary role is to act as a conduit for information exchange between the Member States, in reality the breadth of tasks undertaken by Interpol is more extensive. Interpol's policy initiatives grew significantly during the 1990s as a consequence of rapid developments in communications, information and data storage and analysis. Undoubtedly, the success of the organisation depends to a large extent upon the efficient use of its extensive

---

5   Ibid, p 130.
6   'Memoranda of evidence, minutes of evidence and appendices', in Home Affairs Committee, *Seventh Report: Practical Police Co-operation in the European Community*, House of Commons, Session 1989–90, Vol II, p 37.

criminal databases. However, the efficient exchange of sensitive information relies not only on Interpol's sophisticated computer system but also on the national police communications network in the 186 Member States. Thus the telecommunications network operates on three tiers and involves the NCBs, the regional stations and the central station in Lyon.

Throughout the 1990s, the network system was upgraded to ensure that message exchange became efficient and has been designed for flexibility, providing for the interaction between the central system and a variety of equipment designed by different manufacturers. This technology allows for the exchange of other information such as data and images. Further improvement was attained when the capacity for messages to be encrypted was achieved, thereby rendering messages indecipherable to anyone except the intended recipient. Improvements in technology and the introduction of the Interpol Criminal Intelligence System have extended the amount of material that can be stored by the organisation, and have substantially reduced the time needed to answer enquiries received from NCBs. Interpol has also developed the automated search facility (ASF), which allows Interpol NCBs and other official agencies to consult databases at the General Secretariat. Searches can now be carried out for information relating to international fugitives; the database holds information on fugitives, missing persons, stolen works of art and stolen vehicles. It also has an international child abuse image database. In addition to fingerprint and DNA profile databases, Interpol has recently introduced an automated database known as the International DNA Gateway. Using its criminal information system database and intelligence from Member States, Interpol maintains a list of suspected terrorists, including known aliases, fingerprints, photos, passport data and relevant Interpol notices. These lists are made available to national police authorities.

Arguably, one of the most publicised aspects of Interpol's work is its circulation of international notices which provide information relating to photographs and fingerprints. There are several different categories of notice which are colour coded. A 'wanted notice' is a request for the arrest of a person with a view to extradition and is known as a red notice. An enquiry notice is published to collect information about individuals and is known as a 'blue' notice. A warning notice is given to provide information about known offenders operating internationally and is known as a 'green' notice. A request for information relating to the tracing of an individual, a missing person notice, is known as a 'yellow' notice and an unidentified body notice which provides a description of a corpse is known as a 'black' notice. An orange notice is used to warn police and other international organisations of possible threats from hidden weapons and parcel bombs. The Interpol–UN Special Security Council Notice is used to identify terrorist suspects who are banned from using international travel or from using financial institutions. The legal basis for issuing a red notice is a valid arrest warrant issued by judicial authorities in the requested State, and a commitment to seek the fugitive's extradition following arrest. Thus the issuing of a red notice is dependent upon the existence of an extradition treaty between the relevant States. In 2005, 2,200 red notices were issued. Following a request from the International Criminal Tribunal for the Former Yugoslavia (ICTY), a red notice was issued in respect of Milan Likic who was wanted in connection with war crimes in the former Yugoslavia. Interpol was involved in co-ordinating an exchange of information between NCBs in Chile and Argentina that eventually led to his arrest. While a red notice contains identifying information such as fingerprints and photographs, in urgent cases Member States can issue 'Diffusions' which are emails containing limited identifying information. In 2005, Interpol issued 12,831 diffusions which amounted to an increase of 31 per cent on the previous year. Interpol also provides notices relating to specific *modus operandi* used in the commission of certain offences. Improvements in telecommunications have assisted in the effectiveness of the notice system. The improved computer systems at the General Secretariat have given rise to the development of the Analytical Criminal Intelligence Unit (ACIU), which reviews information and intelligence received by Interpol and searches for patterns and links in criminal activity. These analyses are shared with relevant NCBs who may be working on separate elements of the same criminal activity.

In addition to supporting police co-operation in fighting cross-border crime, Interpol also sends incident response teams (IRT) to the scene of natural disasters and terrorist attacks. These teams provide urgent assistance to national agencies. The teams are comprised of specialised police officers from the General Secretariat, NCB's, forensic scientists and criminal analysts. IRT's have been deployed to the earthquake in Pakistan where national agencies were helped to devise child protection measures for children separated from family members. Following the Asian Tsunami in December 2004, IRT's were able to offer the affected States communications and forensic support. Within 24 hours Interpol had alerted its network of international victim identification teams who organised a crisis support group at the General Secretariat which co-ordinated the resources for staffing the Thai Tsunami Victim Identification Information Management Centre. Other new ventures have included an information-sharing agreement between Interpol and the International Criminal Court relating to genocide and war crimes. This initiative has resulted in the appointment of specialist officers to act as contact persons. A new Drugs Intelligence Unit formed in 2005 is now operational which has been given the task of organising operational meetings with law enforcement agencies in Africa and Europe and co-ordinating drug intelligence alerts and drafting reports. Another initiative aims to combat Internet-related drug trafficking in prescription drugs and anabolic steroids and to develop a global network of investigators.

During the period between 1970 and 1990, Interpol was criticised for its inefficiency and lack of rigour in matters of internal security and doubt was cast upon its ability to counteract the rapidly developing problem of organised crime. During this period, there was evidence that information relating to serious crimes had been inappropriately disclosed. There were suggestions that representatives of States allegedly sympathetic to terrorist activity were passing information to terrorist organisations.[7] Several States allegedly harbouring international terrorists were members of Interpol. Following events after 11 September 2001, the Secretary General of Interpol reiterated that its constitution prohibits involvement in political, ethnic or religious disputes. As an institution it is committed to neutrality, its mission being to assist all States to share police information under any lawful circumstances. Undoubtedly, improvements in telecommunication security and encryption techniques have combined to reduce the problem. Further criticism has been levelled at the inefficient system for the exchange of information, which is bureaucratic and laborious. Again, recent improvements in technology accompanied by efficient leadership have produced results. Following Interpol's relocation to headquarters in Lyon in 1989, the response to inquiries has improved. Thus, in 1986, Interpol was reported to take on average 14 days to respond to an inquiry, whereas in 1989 the delay was reduced to two hours.[8] In 1990, the Home Affairs Committee in its *Seventh Report on Practical Police Co-operation in the European Community* urged that '[m]istrust of Interpol should not be perpetuated on the basis of past failings'.[9] In an internal appraisal of the work of the British NCB, Interpol was described as having a 'pivotal and essential role in dealing with international criminal enquiries': for example, in 1998, the British NCB handled 157,345 messages.[10] In addressing criticisms made in the 1980s, Interpol has succeeded in developing its global role while operating in conjunction with collaborative policing initiatives taking place within Europe.[11]

17.3 EU INITIATIVES

The Amsterdam Treaty, which came into force in May 1999, provides the legal basis for cross-border police co-operation within the EU.[12] However,

---

7 Op cit, Benyon *el al*, note 4, p 129.
8 G Mason, 'Kendall's Kingdom', 14 *Police Studies* (1991), 19.
9 *Report Together with the Proceedings of the Committee*, House of Commons, Session 1989–90, Vol I.
10 NCIS, *Annual Report*, 1998–99, p 31.
11 For further information about Interpol, see <http://www.interpol.int>.
12 The Treaty establishing the European Community (EC Treaty) did not give legislative competence in the field of criminal law. Competence in this area was limited to the Third Pillar of the Treaty on European Unity (TEU). See generally, D Chalmers, Ch Hadjiemmanuil, G Monti, A Tomkins, *European Union Law: Text and Materials*, 1st edn, 2006, Cambridge: CUP.

although matters relating to common foreign and security policy became Community matters, police and judicial co-operation in criminal matters remain within the Third Pillar which has been subjected to some reorganisation.[13] Provisions relating to police and judicial co-operation in criminal matters are contained in Title VI of the Treaty of European Union (TEU). Initiatives in the field of police co-operation include the collection and exchange of relevant information, joint initiatives in training and the use of equipment and the common evaluation of investigative techniques.[14] In October 1999, the European Council held a special meeting to discuss making full use of the possibilities offered by the Amsterdam Treaty to create an area of freedom, security and justice in the EU. To counter the threat to freedom posed by serious crime, the Council considered that a common effort was needed to prevent and fight crime and criminal organisations throughout the EU. In order to achieve this objective it was considered necessary to facilitate the joint mobilisation of police and judicial resources. In its conclusions the Tampere European Council called for an increase in all forms of co-operation between law enforcement agencies in Member States. Measures should be taken to set up joint investigative teams to combat trafficking in drugs and people and terrorism. Additionally, in order to reinforce the fight against serious organised crime, a Eurojust unit was proposed which would be comprised of national prosecutors and magistrates from all Member States. This body would be given the task of facilitating co-ordination of national prosecuting authorities and working with the European judicial network (EJN) in order to simplify the execution of requests for assistance.[15] In November 2004, the Brussels European Council adopted the Hague programme, which set the agenda for EU activities on freedom, security and justice over the next five years. This programme not only reinforces judicial and police co-operation initiatives but also called for an evaluation of the implementation and the effects of these measures. The Council considered evaluation was essential to ensure the effectiveness of EU action in this area. The Action Plan implementing this programme sets out a policy framework and provides for the Commission to develop an evaluation mechanism. Priorities include increasing criminal cross-border co-operation, realising the

13 The EU is founded on three pillars: the European Communities, Common Foreign and Security Policy, and co-operation in the fields of justice and home affairs. Activities under the Third Pillar address the area of police and judicial co-operation in criminal matters. It is relevant whether mutual legal assistance measures come under the Third Pillar of the TEU or the First Pillar of the Treaty Establishing the European Communities (TEC), Third Pillar bodies being subject to less stringent control than Community bodies. Concerns have been raised regarding the adequacy of the democratic and judicial controls in the area of justice and home affairs. It is of note that Europol and Eurodac, bodies holding sensitive data, come under the Third Pillar and are not subject to the same protection regime as First Pillar bodies.
14 TEU, Art 30.
15 For further discussion of Eurojust and the EJN see Chapter 15.

full potential of Europol and Eurojust and the full application of the principle of mutual recognition of judicial decisions in criminal matters. Member States are required to prepare reports on the level of progress made towards implementing the measures set out in the action plan.[16]

The mechanism by which many of these EU initiatives are implemented has been the subject of some criticism. The UK parliamentary European Scrutiny Committee,[17] for example, noted in its report on amendments to the framework proposal to replace extradition between Member States with a European arrest warrant that:

> The presentation of radically changed texts in the last days of a Presidency, with calls for their immediate adoption, does not appear to us to be an appropriate way of determining changes at EU level to the criminal law. This is compounded by rules which prevent public and open discussion of what takes place in the Council, so that it may become possible for responsible Ministers to explain why particular changes were made. The legislative process should be open and transparent and not one of secret bargaining. We intend to return to this subject as part of our inquiry into democracy and accountability in the EU and the role of national parliaments.[18]

The rapid expansion in the field of police and judicial co-operation in criminal matters raises questions related to the protection of the fundamental rights traditionally enjoyed in modern democracies. In drafting mutual assistance initiatives care must be taken to maintain sufficient procedural safeguards to protect individual rights. Increasingly, police co-operation initiatives involve the creation of extensive computer networks and databases to facilitate the exchange of information and provide the basis for analysis and intelligence. Proliferation of these databases brings with it problems relating to data protection and efficiency. Member States have access to information provided by Interpol, Europol, the Schengen Information System (SIS), the Customs Information System and Eurodac, a DNA database. Thus, large amounts of data and intelligence are being circulated between countries, which raises concern about control and accuracy. The development of police co-operation is not solely concerned with information exchange. Measures to increase operational cooperation can be found in the redefined role of Europol in investigations and in the practical measures established under the 1990

16 For further discussion of the implementation of the Hague programme initiatives see Chapter 15.
17 UK Ministers cannot normally agree to EU legislative or other proposals until the parliamentary scrutiny process is completed.
18 UK parliamentary European Scrutiny Committee, Seventeenth Report of Session 2001–02, HC 152–xvii.

Convention Implementing the Schengen Agreement (Schengen Implementing Convention). Arguably, these initiatives blur the distinction between operational police co-operation and the traditional form of judicial assistance envisaged under mutual assistance arrangements. Both the 1990 Schengen Implementing Convention and the 1959 European Convention on Mutual Assistance in Criminal Matters, for example, provide for cross-border covert surveillance and controlled delivery arrangements.[19] Incorporating the Schengen *Acquis* into the EU has increased accountability in respect of the SIS; however, Third Pillar bodies remain subject to less rigorous scrutiny than Community bodies.[20] Most proposals for judicial and police co-operation measures originate not from the European Parliament but from either the Commission or the Council of Ministers. Accordingly, the role of Parliament in this area is limited. Lack of involvement by EU institutions, such as the European Court of Justice (ECJ) and the European Parliament, in Third Pillar activities has given rise to questions in respect to the level of democratic accountability. JUSTICE, the British section of the International Commission of Jurists, considers that it is increasingly anachronistic and unjustified to have different data protection standards at EU level, particularly when the lower Pillar standards of the Third Pillar cover areas that involve highly sensitive data.[21] It is unfortunate that an area which has ramifications for several aspects of Community policy and raises human rights issues has been removed from the community architecture and, in particular, from judicial clarification by the ECJ.

However, recent developments relating to the competence of the Community in relation to criminal law and procedure may result in increased democratic accountability in this area. Traditionally, Member States have demonstrated a reluctance to transfer competence to the Community in relation to police and judicial co-operation in criminal law matters, which is still dealt with under the Third Pillar. Third Pillar decisions do not benefit from the principle of direct effect, still require unanimous voting in the Council of Ministers, and are not subject to review by the ECJ. The principle of direct effect is based on the principle that EU law in some areas overrides national law. This principle has not been applied to criminal law matters. However, following the judgment of the ECJ in *Pupino*,[22] when applying domestic law

---

19 The problems of accountability with these operations can be illustrated by the inquiry of the Dutch Van Traa Committee in 1996 which considered the background to the apparent loss of control by the Dutch police over its controlled delivery system.

20 Activities taking place under the First Pillar are subject to scrutiny by EU institutions such as the European Parliament and the European Court of Justice (ECJ). For further discussion, see P Mathijsen, *A Guide to European Union Law*, 2000, London: Sweet & Maxwell.

21 M Colvin, *The Schengen Information System: A Human Rights Audit*, 2000, London: JUSTICE.

22 Case C 105/03.

national courts are required to interpret domestic law, as far as possible, in accordance with the relevant Framework Decision. Further, in September 2005 the ECJ held that while as a general rule criminal law matters did not fall within the scope of the EC Treaty, in limited circumstances the Community legislature could use the criminal law to achieve Community objectives.[23] Finally, in May 2006, the Commission suggested that the *passerelle* provision provided by Art 42 of the TEU could be used to enable judicial and police co-operation to be dealt with under the EC Treaty.[24] Moving criminal law and policing into the EC Treaty would automatically increase the role of the ECJ. The European Council is also in favour of exploring the possibility that existing treaties could be used to implement initiatives in the areas of freedom, security and justice. While this development would increase the role of the Commission, the European Parliament and the ECJ in this area, thereby increasing democratic legitimacy, it would replace unanimity with qualified majority voting in the Council. Removing the national veto in criminal law matters raises difficult constitutional and political issues for many Member States and their governments.[25] While accepting the need for co-operation in police and judicial co-operation matters, most Member States have criticised the Commission's fast-track scheme of transferring Third Pillar instruments into the First Pillar. Consequently, Member States are faced with the choice between protecting national sovereignty and facilitating effective EU action in the fight against cross-border crime.

17.3.1 The European Court of Justice

The extent of the involvement of the European Community with criminal justice matters is therefore, at present, rather limited.[26] Any move towards increasing Community competence in the area of police and judicial co-operation has caused some Member States to express concern over possible loss of national sovereignty. However, in some procedural areas a level of harmonisation has been achieved through the operation of the European Convention on Human Rights, which has been embraced by the ECJ, the judicial body responsible for ensuring Member States comply with Community law. While the ECJ traditionally has exercised no jurisdiction over Third Pillar activities the Amsterdam Treaty extended the power of the ECJ to a

---

23 Case C–176/03 *Commission v Council* ECR I–7879, discussed below.
24 The *passerelle* means 'bridge' and was introduced by the Amsterdam Treaty to enable the Council to transfer matters in Art 29 of the TEU into Title IV of the EC Treaty.
25 For a discussion of these issues from the UK standpoint see the Report by the House of Lords European Union Committee, *The Criminal Law Competence of the European Community*, 42nd Report of Session 2005–06, HL Paper 227, published 28 July 2006.
26 For further discussion, see M Furse and S Nash, 'Free Movement, Criminal Law and Fundamental Rights in the European Community', 3 *Juridical Review* (1997), 148.

limited extent. National courts can, for example, ask the ECJ for clarification of the meaning of terms or concepts in the Convention Implementing the Schengen Agreement (CISA). In February 2003, the ECJ gave its first ruling on the interpretation of Art 54 of the (CISA).[27] This provision states that:

A person whose trial has been finally disposed of in one Contracting Party may not be prosecuted in another Contracting Party for the same acts provided that, if a penalty has been imposed, it has been enforced, is actually in the process of being enforced or can no longer be enforced under the laws of the sentencing Contracting Party.

In *Huseyin Gozutok*[28] and *Klaus Brugge*,[29] the ECJ held that once a prosecutor makes a decision to discontinue criminal proceedings on the basis of an agreed settlement with the accused, without involving the court, a subsequent prosecution in another Member State based on the same set of facts would be contrary to this provision which enshrines the rule against double jeopardy. Decisions which under national law definitively bar further proceedings or discontinue prosecutions were to be considered as decisions which 'finally disposed of' a trial for the purposes of Art 54 of the CISA. The ECJ's decision in this case implies that it is for the domestic legal order of the sentencing state to determine whether a judgment bars further criminal proceedings for the same acts under national law, and is a decision that 'finally disposes' of a trial.

In *Staatsanwaltschaft Augsburg v Jurgen Kretzinger*[30] the ECJ was again asked to clarify the meaning of 'the same acts' in Art 54, and to consider whether the definition of enforcement was affected by implementation into national law of the Council Framework Decision on the European Arrest Warrant. The ECJ was also required to consider whether a judgment after a trial *in absentia* could be considered as a decision 'finally disposing' of a trial for the purposes of Art 54. The defendant had transported a shipment of cigarettes, which had been smuggled into Greece by a third party, through Italy and Germany intending to enter the UK without declaring them to customs authorities. He was found guilty *in absentia* by an Italian court on two occasions and received a custodial sentence. Aware that the Italian penalties had not been enforced, and noting that the Italian authorities had taken no steps under the Framework Decision to obtain a European arrest warrant (EAW), the German court found the defendant guilty of the initial importation from

---

27 The CISA is only applicable to those EU Member States which have implemented the Schengen *acquis*, and Norway and Iceland. Articles 54–58 of the CISA are also applicable in the UK and Ireland.
28 Case No C–187/01.
29 Case No C–385/01.
30 Case C–288/05.

Greece. The court took the view that although the same cigarette shipments formed the factual basis of the two Italian convictions and the German conviction, Art 54 of the CISA did not apply. The ECJ held that 'the same acts' in Art 54 refers to material facts that are 'inextricably linked' in time, in space and by their subject matter. In this case the defendant intended to smuggle the cigarettes from the point of entry to a final destination in the Community in a single operation. Any successive crossings of internal borders in the course of this operation could be regarded as acts, which are 'inextricably linked' for the purposes of Art 54. The concept of enforcement for the purposes of Art 54 is not affected by the fact that a Member State has not automatically issued an EAW. Further, a decision reached following a trial *in absentia* bars further criminal proceedings providing the trial satisfied the fair trial provisions of the European Convention on Human Rights.

The ECJ has also been asked to consider the relationship between Community law and the criminal law of Member States. On occasion, the ECJ has found that Community law overrides domestic criminal law where national law is incompatible with the EC Treaty, or rules made under the Treaty. Thus in *Criminal proceedings against Donatella Calfa* the ECJ found that national rules relating to expulsion for life following a criminal conviction were incompatible with EC rules on free movement of persons and freedom to provide services.[31] As a consequence of a recent ECJ judgment, the extent of the Community's competence in the area of criminal law and procedure is somewhat uncertain. It is questionable, for example, whether the Community can require Member States to impose criminal law and criminal sanctions in order to ensure compliance with Community actions and objectives. Notwithstanding the general rule that the Community's competence does not extend to criminal law and procedure, in September 2005 the ECJ held in *Commission v Council* that this rule did not:

> . . . prevent the Community legislature, when the application of effective, proportionate and dissuasive criminal penalties by the competent national authorities is an essential measure for combating serious environmental offences, from taking measures which relate to the criminal law of the Member States which it considers necessary in order to ensure that the rules which it lays down on environmental protection are fully effective.[32]

This controversial case concerned the legality of a Council Framework Decision on the protection of the environment through the criminal law of

---

31 Case C–348/96 [1999] ECR I–11.
32 C–176/03 Judgment, at para 48.

Member States.[33] The Framework Decision provided that conduct detrimental to the environment was to be criminalised by Member States. The Framework Decision listed a number of offences which were based on existing Community environmental measures and required Member States to impose effective criminal sanctions. The Commission sought to annul the Framework Decision on the ground that there was Community competence under the EC Treaty to address the problem.[34] The Council argued that the EC Treaty did not contain powers in relation to criminal sanctions and could find no grounds for accepting that the power had been implicitly transferred to the Community. The Council also noted the reluctance of Member States to relinquish sovereignty in the area of criminal law and procedure. Noting that environmental protection measures could have been adopted under the EC Treaty, the ECJ found for the Commission and struck down the Framework Decision.[35] In giving evidence to the UK House of Lords Select Committee on the European Union, Professor Steve Peers noted that although the ECJ's decision was unexpected, it was not:

> . . . so outrageous to reach the view that the Community has criminal competence. Given that Member States argued that this was not what they wanted to give to the Community as competence, it is surprising that the Court felt that it was. Nevertheless, from a purely legal point of view, there are reasonable grounds to support the Court's conclusion that the Community has some form of criminal competence'.[36]

The majority of Member States expressed concerns about the wide interpretation of Community competence relied on by the Commission in this case.[37] It has been argued that the scope of Community competence in criminal matters should be limited to those areas of policy that are fundamental to Community aims and objectives such as the environment. Although acknowledging that this matter can only be resolved by the ECJ, the UK Government has expressed disquiet at this development.[38] The arguments relating to

---

33 Council Framework Decision 2003/80/JHA of Jan 2003.

34 The Commission had originally proposed a similarly worded draft Directive, which had been rejected by Member States. It argued that the aim and content of the Framework Decision were within the scope of the EC Treaty.

35 For further discussion see S White 'Harmonisation of criminal law under the first pillar' (2006) 31 EL Rev 81.

36 See Report by the House of Lords European Union Committee, *The Criminal Law Competence of the European Community*, 42nd Report of Session 2005–06, HL Paper 227, published 28 July 2006. Minutes of Evidence taken before the Select Committee on the European Union: 3 May 2006, Question 47, page 28.

37 See Dossier 8866/06 Com (2006) 168.

38 Ibid, p 57.

Community competence in criminal matters will be considered by the ECJ again in the ship source pollution case.[39] The UK government is intending to intervene in this case and will be arguing in favour of limiting Community competence in criminal law. There remains considerable reluctance among many Member States to relinquish control to a supranational body in matters affecting public order and crime. Despite significant recent achievements in this area, full integration of justice and home affairs will be a slow process.

17.3.2 Europol

The European Police Agency (Europol) was set up under the Third Pillar by the 1995 Europol Convention and became operational in 1999. Europol's primary purpose is to facilitate operational police co-operation in respect to combating serious and organised criminal activity within Member States of the EU. Its primary role is the exchange and analysis of information. Thus, Europol maintains an extensive computerised database to store personal data for use in the prevention and investigation of serious crime, which can be accessed by national units and liaison officers. Amendments to the 1990 Schengen Implementing Convention allows Europol access to a limited number of categories of data stored in the Schengen Information System.[40] Each Member State is required to establish a national body which liaises between Europol and the competent national authorities. The liaison body in the UK is located in the Serious Organised Crime Agency (SOCA). From October 2005, the Europol Information System was made available to authorised law enforcement staff in all 25 Member States. An independent joint supervisory body is responsible for monitoring Europol's activities. The budget is financed by contributions from Member States who have agreed to allocate EUR 334 million for Europol between 2010 and 2013. Its budget for 2007 is set at EUR 68 million. From the outset, it was anticipated that Europol's operational role would increase and that it would be equipped with increased coercive powers. In October 2000, for example, the Council of the EU expressed concern that the definition of computer crime in the Annex to the Europol Convention[41] was insufficiently precise. Accordingly, it was proposed to add a specific definition of 'computer crime' to this instrument, which would include all forms of attack on automated data processing systems, and to extend Europol's mandate to cover these offences. In November 2002, a Protocol amending the Europol Convention was

---

39 *Commission v Council*, Case C 444/05.
40 Council Decision 2005/211/JHA of Feb 2005 concerning the introduction of some new functions for the Schengen information system, in particular in the fight against terrorism.
41 See the Convention based on Art K3 of the TEU establishing a European Police Office (Europol Convention) (CM 3050, 1995).

introduced which enables Europol to participate in joint investigation teams (JIT).[42] Further, in March 2003 the European Commissioner for Justice and Home Affairs and the Director of Europol signed a co-operation agreement that allows for the exchange of strategic information such as threat assessments but will not include the exchange of personal data. Extending Europol's mandate to cover not only a wider range of criminal activity but also to permit greater participation in criminal investigations increases concerns relating to accountability.[43] The need for national parliamentary scrutiny of Third Pillar proposals is seen as essential since under Title VI of the TEU there is still no effective role for the European Parliament. However, this will change if the Commission's proposal that Europol become part of the EU Framework is adopted. This proposal would also extend Europol's mandate to deal with a greater range of crimes.

The proposal to set up a European police office was first considered in 1970 and resulted from ministerial discussions considering measures to counter the growth in terrorism. These meetings, which took place outside the formal EC structure, produced some interesting initiatives in the area of European police co-operation.[44] In an effort to rationalise these efforts, and prompted by the view that Interpol was not serving the interests of European countries as well as it should, Germany proposed the creation of a specific policing agency for Member States of the EC. At the time of the signing of the TEU in 1992, it was agreed that the Third Pillar of the Treaty would include a commitment to the creation of a Central European Criminal Investigation Office.[45] Prior to the Europol Convention being ratified, an interim agency, the Europol Drugs Unit (EDU) was established by ministerial agreement and began operating from temporary premises in The Hague.[46] The role of the EDU was to begin work on the task of police co-operation by way of information exchange on a limited basis. At this stage, it was agreed that enquires would be restricted to investigations into drug-trafficking. While there has been a rapid growth in the workload of Europol, its activities have developed entirely under the auspices of the Council of Ministers and, thus, have not been subject to any significant scrutiny by the European Parliament. Although the Council of Ministers must provide an annual report on the activities of Europol,[47] and consult the European Parliament with respect to

---

42 2002 OJ C312 16/12.
43 See JUSTICE, *Report on the Rules and Regulations Governing Europol*, Submission to the House of Lords European Communities Committee, May 1997. See also Select Committee on European Legislation, *The Scrutiny of European Business*, 27th Report, July 1996.
44 T Bunyan, 'Trevi, Europol and the New European State', in T Bunyan (ed), *Statewatching the New Europe: A Handbook on the European State*, 1993, Nottingham: Russell.
45 1992 TEU, Title VI, Provisions on Co-operation in the Fields of Justice and Home Affairs, Art K1.
46 Joint Action on Europol Drugs Unit (10 March 1995).
47 1995 Europol Convention, Art 34(1).

any amendment to the Europol Convention, the Ministers are under no obligation to act upon comments or recommendations.

Article 2(1) of the 1995 Europol Convention provides that:

> The objective of Europol shall be . . . to improve . . . the effectiveness and co-operation of the competent authorities in the Member States in preventing and combating terrorism, unlawful drug-trafficking and other serious forms of international crime where there are factual indications that an organised criminal structure is involved and two or more Member States are affected . . .

Under Art 2(2) of this Convention, Europol was empowered to deal initially with drug-trafficking, the movement of illegal nuclear materials, illegal immigrant smuggling, trade in human beings and motor vehicle crime. The Convention allows further expansion of the agency's role by listing other forms of crime in an annex to the treaty. Thus, the Council of Ministers, acting unanimously, may decide to invest Europol with the power to investigate any offence in the list, which covers an extensive and diverse range of criminal activity. The annex itself may be expanded by the Council of Ministers.[48] The tasks for Europol in relation to the objective in Art 2 of the Convention are set out in Art 3 of the Convention. They include:

(a) facilitating the exchange of information between States;
(b) obtaining, collating and analysing information and intelligence;
(c) notifying Member States about information concerning them and any connections identified between criminal offences;
(d) aiding investigations in Member States by forwarding all relevant information to the national units;
(e) maintaining a computerised system of collected information containing data.

From the outset, it was evident that Europol was not simply concerned with collecting 'hard' information, but would also be proactive and undertake the analysis of any material it held in order to facilitate criminal investigations undertaken by national police forces. Initially, Europol aimed to engage in the analysis and exchange of information relating to a specific range of criminal activity which was listed in Art 3 of the Convention. These are defined as 'offences committed in order to procure the means for perpetrating acts [or] to facilitate or carry out acts [or] to ensure the impunity of acts', which covers a wide range of offences, from conspiracy to extortion. These two terms are not defined with any precision in the Convention. Further, allowing Europol

---

48 1995 Europol Convention, Art 43(3).

to hold information on 'related criminal offences' has resulted in a blurring of aims.[49] Problems have arisen, for example, in relation to the expression 'related criminal offences'. There is no consistency in the definition of criminal offences in Member States. The offence of conspiracy, for example, is defined very narrowly in Dutch law, whereas it is given a more expansive definition in English law. Thus, whilst authorities in the UK would be required to provide information on conduct which was defined as conspiracy in English law, and would, therefore, be classed as a 'related criminal offence', the same activity may not constitute a conspiracy in the Netherlands and the Dutch authorities would not incur liability.

Article 8 of the 1995 Europol Convention allows the information system 'to store, modify and utilise only the data necessary for the performance of Europol's tasks'. This includes not only a wide range of factual information, but also some categories of 'soft' intelligence including vague terms, such as 'belief', 'suspicion' and 'hearsay'. The use of soft information raises a number of civil liberty concerns. Soft information can include 'persons suspected of having committed . . . a criminal offence', details of 'alleged' crimes, 'suspected membership of a criminal organisation' and 'other characteristics likely to assist in identification'. These are subjective and imprecise categories of information. The 'other characteristics' category has given rise to a well-founded fear that data on race, sexuality and politics may be held on the information system. These fears were exacerbated by the approval of the Council of Ministers which confirmed such information as being suitable for being held on file.[50] Under Art 10 of the Convention, information may be held on witnesses, victims, 'contacts and associates' and informers. Thus, the Convention provides Europol with the power to obtain and hold a wide range of information. Whilst such information may be useful for national prosecuting authorities during a criminal investigation, concern has been raised regarding lack of scrutiny and accountability. The 1995 Europol Convention was ratified by all Member States on 1 October 1998 and was operational on 1 July 1999. Since the Convention was signed, Europol's remit has been extended to include offences ranging from forgery of money and credit cards, terrorism and money laundering. Priority areas now include counter terrorism, illegal immigration, drug trafficking, financial crime including money laundering and euro counterfeiting.[51] These areas are based on dominant trends in organised crime which come within Europol's mandate according to the Europol Convention.

During negotiations surrounding the drafting of the Europol Convention, Member States disagreed about the extent to which the European Parliament

---

49 Ibid, Art 2(3).
50 *Statewatch Bulletin*, No 6, Nov–Dec 1995, Vol 5, p 5.
51 Europol has been designated the Central Office for combating euro counterfeiting in accordance with Art 12 of the Geneva Convention.

and the ECJ would be permitted to scrutinise the agency's activities. The role of the European Parliament in decision making in respect of Europol was removed during the drafts of the Convention, and decisions about the operation of the agency became the responsibility of the Ministers of Justice and Home Affairs. The role allocated to the ECJ was also limited. Whilst the majority of States suggested that the ECJ should be a forum for resolving disputes concerning the interpretation of the Convention and should settle any disagreements between Member States and Europol staff, the UK opposed any involvement. Whilst the ECJ, generally, has no jurisdiction over Third Pillar activities, it is not unreasonable to assume that Europol, which has responsibility for policing within the EU, should be subject to scrutiny by the ECJ. Support for this view was expressed, even within the UK.[52] The role of the ECJ has been revisited with a Protocol to the Europol Convention, which allowed Member States to 'accept the jurisdiction of the Court of Justice of the European Communities to give preliminary rulings on the interpretation of the Europol Convention'.[53]

While it was agreed that the main function of Europol is to collect, exchange and analyse information, Member States disagreed over rights of access by the public to personal information and the necessary standards of data protection. Thus, access to information is subject to national guidelines and currently Member States are also responsible for data protection under national guidelines.[54] This is an example of so called 'Variable geometry' within the EU. Problems have arisen when international agreements are applied in accordance with national law. Alleged corruption in the data collection office is a sensitive issue and, in June 2001, an investigation was begun by Dutch criminal authorities into allegations of fraud and money laundering by police officers working in the computer and data section in The Hague.

Under Art 30 of the Amsterdam Treaty, the Council of Ministers was given a mandate to widen the operational scope of Europol, thereby extending the remit of Europol. The Council has recently adopted a recommendation that Member States give 'due consideration' to requests from Europol to initiate, conduct or co-ordinate investigations in specific cases.[55] It has also given Europol authority to enter into agreements for the exchange of data with countries outside the EU. The States listed for early co-operation agreements include Canada, Iceland, Norway, the Russian Federation, Switzerland,

52 Select Committee on the European Communities on the Draft Convention for Europol: Recommendations of the Committee on 'Jurisdiction over Disputes', 10th Report, House of Lords Papers, 1994–95, pp 30–31.
53 Protocol drawn up on the basis of the TEU, Art K3, on the interpretation, by way of preliminary rulings, by the ECJ on the Convention on the Establishment of a European Police Office (Europol Convention), 24 July 1996.
54 1995 Europol Convention, Art 14.
55 Justice and Home Affairs Press Release, 28 Sept 2000,11705/00 (Presse 341-G).

Turkey and the US. Agreements facilitating the exchange of information with several South American States were also contemplated. These initiatives would also involve Interpol. The agreement on the exchange of personal data between the US and Europol has given rise to concerns relating to data protection.[56] Concern is also increasing over Europol's lack of accountability. It is unclear, for example, whether restrictions exist on the transmission of evidence or information obtained in violation of international human rights standards or in breach of national law, and whether a distinction will be made between hard facts and 'soft intelligence'.[57] Europol has undertaken a major strategic analysis on specific crimes such as drug trafficking, carried out operational analysis looking at information transmitted during inquiries to the agency and maintained a directory of 'Centres of Excellence' giving details to Member States of specialised agencies and experts in particular fields such as DNA analysis.[58] The Director of Europol is required to produce an annual organised crime report that provides a review and assessment of threats posed by transnational organised crime in the EU. The report, which focuses on cross-border activities, is based on contributions from Member States, Interpol and official EU documentation. In addition to identifying risks, it includes recommendations based on the findings of strategic and tactical assessments. These recommendations cover policy, legislation and operational matters. While the report is available to the public, access to the closed version is restricted to law enforcement agencies.

The Europol initiative is an acknowledgment that Member States share common problems in respect of criminality. Offences such as drug-trafficking and illegal immigration are cross-border by nature and, following the relaxation of internal border controls, cause similar problems for all law enforcement agencies of the Member States. While initiatives to fight the 'euro-criminal' are popular with the public, critics argue that the political policy behind Europol is the product of a 'mutual internal security ideology'.[59] This 'fortress Europe' mentality is criticised for placing security and policing arrangements to the fore, and in giving public accountability and civil liberties insufficient attention. Two of the major criticisms levelled at Europol relate to its 'legal deficit' arising from the exemption prohibiting the ECJ from reviewing cases involving matters of law and order, and its lack of

---

56 For a detailed discussion see V Mitsilegas, 'The new EU–US co-operation on extradition, mutual legal assistance and the exchange of police data', 8/4 *European Foreign Affairs Review* (2003) 515.

57 Council Decision authorising the Director of Europol to enter into negotiating agreements with third States and non-EU related bodies, 27 March 2000. See also *Statewatch*, No 2, 2000, Vol 10, pp 23–24.

58 Available at <http://www.europol.eu.int>.

59 M Den Boer and N Walker, 'European Policing After 1992', 31 *Journal of Common Market Studies* (1995), 3.

accountability before the European Parliament, which has been described as the 'democratic deficit'. Problems arising from this lack of accountability have given rise to concern amongst national police forces that shared data may be misused. Recent proposals that could improve this lack of democratic legitimacy and accountability have yet to be approved by Member States. In November 2004, the European Council agreed a programme, known as the Hague programme, which set the agenda for EU activities on police and judicial co-operation in criminal matters over the next five years. Priorities included increasing criminal cross-border co-operation and realising the full potential of Europol. In its assessment of this programme in 2006, the Commission considered a proposal to replace the existing Europol Convention and to improve parliamentary scrutiny and control over Europol's activities. Similarly, in its report in November 2006, the Council Presidency considered that Europol needed a more flexibly legal basis to ensure that political decisions taken to improve its functioning could be implemented more effectively. However, three protocols amending the original Convention, which would improve its operational capabilities, are still awaiting ratification by Member States and are not yet in force. Europol is not part of the EU framework. Consequently, its activities are still not subject to supervision by the European Parliament or judicial review by the European Court of Justice.[60]

17.3.3 The Schengen *acquis*[61]

On the 14 June 1985 France, Germany, Belgium, the Netherlands and Luxembourg reached an agreement with respect to the gradual abolition of checks at their common borders. This agreement, which was signed in the Luxembourg village of Schengen,[62] was designed to encourage free movement of goods and services within Member States of the European Economic Community. The territory created by this agreement became known as the 'Schengen area'. From its inception, the EC has been committed to facilitating the free movement, within its common borders, of goods,[63] services,[64] capital[65] and workers[66] (the four freedoms). In its Resolution adopting the Declaration of Fundamental Rights and Freedoms, the European Parliament[67] considers

---

60 See further, *The Activities and Development of Europol – Towards an unaccountable 'FBI' in Europe* available from Statewatch, PO Box 1516 London, N16 0FW.
61 This term encompasses all the initiatives arising from the 1985 Agreement and the 1990 Schengen Implementing Convention.
62 Schengen Agreement on the Gradual Abolition of Checks at Common Borders and the Convention Applying the Agreement, 30 ILM (1991), 68.
63 EC Treaty, Arts 30–37.
64 Ibid, Arts 59–66.
65 Ibid, Arts 67–73h.
66 Ibid, Arts 48–51.
67 1989 OJ C120/51.

it 'fundamental' that 'Community citizens shall have the right to move freely and the right to choose their residence within Community territory'.[68] In an attempt to address some of the less desirable consequences flowing from the removal of restrictions on free movement across borders, the initial Schengen Agreement made some provision for the establishment of policing and security measures. In June 1990, the Schengen Implementing Convention was introduced which provided for the abolition of internal border controls between signatory States. This initiative has been described as a 'landmark in the history of the regulation of international police co-operation in Western Europe'.[69] It introduced a system of compensatory measures centred on policing and immigration which were designed to tackle the increase in cross-border crime. These measures included the intensification of external border checks,[70] harmonisation of policies on the issuing of visas and residence permits,[71] a common policy on asylum applications,[72] and harmonisation of rules relating to illicit drugs and arms.[73] Signatories to the 1990 Schengen Implementing Convention undertake that national police authorities will assist each other 'for the purpose of preventing and detecting crime' within the limits of their national law.[74] Whilst the Convention lays down regulations for cross-border observation and allows police officers from the Member States to maintain their observation of persons suspected of having committed cross-border criminal offences, permission from other States should generally be sought before beginning the cross-border observation. However, the Convention lists several serious offences for which observation may be maintained without prior permission. Police carrying out cross-border observation are obliged to comply with the law of the host State and to submit a report to the relevant authorities. The Convention also provides for 'hot pursuit', that is, the pursuit by 'foreign' police officers of fugitives who escape across borders, providing the fugitive was observed committing an offence or had escaped from lawful custody. This provision allows Member States to set down rules governing the duration of the pursuit and the limitation on the powers of the pursuing officers. Under the Convention, police officers involved in cross-border operations acquire the same powers as indigenous police officers. Liability for damages rests with the originating State in respect of the activities of pursuing officers. The Convention also contains provisions

---

68 Declaration, Art 8(1); see K Lenaerts, 'Fundamental Rights to be Included in a Community Catalogue' [1991] ECR 366.
69 C Fijnaut, 'The Schengen Treaties and European Police Co-operation', 1 *Eur J Crime Cr L Cr J* (1993), 37.
70 1990 Schengen Implementing Convention, Arts 3–8.
71 Ibid, Arts 9–27.
72 Ibid, Arts 28–38.
73 Ibid, Arts 77–91.
74 1990 Schengen Implementing Convention, Art 39.

designed to improve technical aspects of police co-operation, including agreements to exchange communication equipment, broaden radio frequency bands in border areas and the harmonisation of communication links. Thus, police forces may send unsolicited information which might be of assistance in investigations to other police forces, and there is provision for the exchange of liaison officers between the parties. Although not contained within the general framework for police co-operation, the Convention also provides for the use of controlled deliveries in order to counter drug trafficking. Although in recent years, the use of controlled deliveries by law enforcement agencies has become more widespread, this provision was considered to be innovative at the time.

Since 1985, the Schengen area has gradually extended to include all Member States. It grew steadily after the 1990 Schengen Implementing Convention came into operation with Austria, Denmark, Finland, Greece, Italy, Portugal, Spain and Sweden all agreeing to join. Notwithstanding the continued reluctance on the part of the UK and Ireland to sign this Convention, by the time it was integrated into the EU, all other Member States of the EU had signed. Incorporating the Schengen Agreement into the framework of the EU was brought about in May 1999 by a Protocol annexed to the Amsterdam Treaty. The Schengen area is now within the legal and institutional framework of the EU and comes under Parliamentary and judicial scrutiny. The Schengen Agreement of 1985, subsequent measures taken by Schengen group members which include harmonising rules regarding visas and improving co-ordination between police and customs, decisions and declarations adopted by the Executive Committee of the 1990 Schengen Implementing Convention, and subsequent protocols and accession agreements are known as the 'Schengen *acquis*'. Both the *acquis* and the Schengen Information System are now integrated into the EU Framework. Initiatives taken under the Schengen *acquis* have encouraged EU collaboration in police and judicial co-operation in criminal law matters. It was anticipated that the UK would seek to be included in some of these initiatives and, indeed, the UK's application to participate in part of the Schengen *acquis* relating to policing was accepted[75] and, in June 2000, Ireland applied to participate on a similar basis.[76] Having evaluated the conditions that must precede implementation of the provisions governing police and judicial co-operation, the Council decided in December 2004 that this part of the Schengen *acquis* could be implemented by the UK.[77] Issuing opinions on these two applications, the Commission emphasised that the partial participation of the UK and Ireland should not have the effect of

75 OJ L 131 of 01 June 2000.
76 OJ L 64 of 07 March 2002. Participation by the UK and Ireland must be proposed and adopted in compliance with Art 5 of the Protocol integrating the Schengen *acquis* into the Framework of the EU annexed to the EU Treaty.
77 OJ L 395 of 21 Dec 2004.

reducing the consistency of the *acquis* as a whole. States joining the EU after 1 May 2004 are bound by all elements of the Schengen *acquis* and must apply all the provisions relating to police and judicial co-operation.

17.3.4 The Schengen Information System

The 1990 Schengen Implementing Convention provides for the establishment of an information system, which is a database used by policing agencies and immigration authorities in the Schengen Convention States.[78] Article 93 of the 1990 Convention states that the purpose of the Schengen Information System (SIS) is to maintain public policy and public security, including national security, in the Member States and to apply the provisions of the 1990 Convention relating to the movement of persons, by using information communicated via the SIS in accordance with the provisions of that Convention. The SIS came into operation in 1995 and collapsed within 90 minutes due to overuse. It is a series of national databases connected to a central system which holds information on suspected criminals, missing persons, unwanted aliens and stolen vehicles and documents. The information held on the SIS can be used for judicial and police co-operation in criminal matters as well as for controlling entry at external borders. Police officers, immigration officials and staff responsible for issuing visas can access this system. Member States supply the network through national networks (N-SIS) which are connected to a central system (C-SIS) The SIS is supplemented by a network known as the Supplementary Information Requests at the National Entry (SIRENE), a database which allows for research for further information held on the SIS and facilitates the 'spontaneous' exchanges of information between police forces.[79] Statistics reveal that the majority of entries on the SIS relate to immigration concerns rather than other criminal concerns. It has been suggested that the SIS is not primarily a tool for tackling serious crime, but is a basis for preventing illegal immigration and for tracing lost or stolen property. Nevertheless, amendments to the 1990 Schengen Convention will add new functions to the SIS to address concerns related not only to illegal immigration but also to terrorism.[80] The successful 'hit' rate of the system is generally low and it is questionable whether the information held on the SIS is accurate.[81] The data protection provisions of this system, which holds approximately 9.7 million files, have been subjected to some severe criticism.[82] The UK has made a successful application to participate in parts of the

---

78 1990 Schengen Implementing Convention,, Arts 92–119.
79 Ibid, Arts 39 and 46.
80 Council Decision 2005/211/JHA of Feb 2005 concerning the introduction of some new functions for the Schengen information system, in particular in the fight against terrorism.
81 See generally op cit, Colvin, note 21, p 8.
82 Ibid.

Schengen *acquis*, which deals with policing and criminal and customs matters and which will include use of the SIS.[83] The decision to allow the UK to participate is made by the other Schengen States and requires unanimity voting in favour within the Council.

While the SIS is considered to be the most prominent instrument of police co-operation devised under Schengen, the original network lacked the capacity to operate in more than 15 States. Accordingly, EU expansion resulted in the need to design a new information system, which is known as the SIS II, the second generation Schengen Information System.[84] In December 2001, the Council adopted two instruments, which gave the responsibility for developing the SIS II to the Commission and allocated the necessary financial resources from the EU budget. The new system has two distinct purposes. The first is to improve police and judicial co-operation in criminal matters, which is covered by Title VI of the TEU. The second deals with the policy on visas, immigration and the free movement of persons contained in the EC Treaty. In May 2005, the Commission adopted a series of proposals for legislative instruments to replace provisions of the 1990 Schengen Implementing Convention relating to SIS.[85] These proposals have now been adopted.[86] The legal basis for the SIS II is in Title VI of the EU Treaty and amounts to a development of the Schengen *acquis*. Consequently, the UK and Ireland will need to apply to use the SIS II in the usual manner.[87] In addition to alerts on missing persons, the SIS II will contain alerts on objects for seizure or use as

---

83 Under the 1992 TEU, Schengen Protocol, Art 4, which incorporates the Schengen *acquis*, the UK is not bound by the Schengen *acquis* but can request to take part in some of the provisions. The decision is made by the other 13 Schengen States and requires unanimity.

84 Council Regulation (EC) No 2424/2001 on the development of the second-generation Schengen Information System (SIS II) based on Art 66 of the Treaty establishing the European Community, and Council Decision 2001/866/JHA on the development of the second-generation Schengen Information System (SIS II) based on Arts 30(1), 31 and 34 of the Treaty on European Union.

85 Proposal for a Regulation of the European Parliament and of the Council on the establishment, operation and use of the second-generation Schengen Information System (SIS II) [COM(2005) 236]; Proposal for a Council Decision on the establishment, operation and use of the second-generation Schengen Information System (SIS II) (COM(2005) 230 final); Proposal for a Regulation of the European Parliament and of the Council regarding access to the second-generation Schengen Information System (SIS II) by the services in the Member States responsible for issuing vehicle registration certificates (COM(2005) 237) final.

86 Regulation (EC) No 1987/2006 of the European Parliament and of the Council of 20 December 2006 on the establishment, operation and use of the second generation Schengen Information System; Regulation (EC) No 1986/2006 of the European Parliament and of the Council of 20 Dec 2006 regarding access to the second generation Schengen Information System (SIS II) by the services in the Member States responsible for issuing vehicle registration certificates.

87 Participation by the UK and Ireland must be proposed and adopted in compliance with Art 5 of the Protocol integrating the Schengen *acquis* into the Framework of the EU annexed to the EU Treaty.

evidence in criminal proceedings, and alerts on persons wanted for arrest and surrender or extradition. The new system will provide for the processing of biometric data, including fingerprints and photographs, to allow for reliable identification of individuals. Subject to safeguards, information can be shared with non-EU States and organisations. The development of the SIS II, like many other police and judicial co-operation initiatives, has been criticised for failing to take sufficient account of the views of democratically elected bodies.[88] The Commission is required to produce a report on activities every two years with an overall evaluation every four years. The operational phase of the new system is anticipated to be in 2007.

17.3.5 The European arrest warrant

Initiatives to reform the surrender mechanisms within Member States have been expedited by the events that took place in the US in September 2001. At an Extraordinary European Council meeting held on 21 September 2001, the Heads of State of the EU, the President of the European Parliament and the President of the European Commission called for the creation of a European warrant for arrest and extradition in accordance with the conclusions reached at the Tampere meeting. Consequently, the European Commission presented a proposal for a Council Framework Decision on the European arrest warrant (EAW) and the surrender procedures between the Member States.[89] In its report on this proposal, the UK Parliamentary European Scrutiny Committee expressed some concern at the speed with which this initiative was processed through the EU legislative machinery. The Committee noted that 'judicial authority' was not defined in the proposal and sought assurances that only arrest warrants issued by a court would be enforced in the UK. Further, the Committee considered that there should be a right to refuse to surrender suspects to Member States which failed to meet the standards required by Art 6 of the European Convention on Human Rights in respect to fair trials. Concern was also voiced at the lack of a double criminality requirement and the absence of a guarantee for retrial for persons convicted *in absentia*. This initiative required implementing legislation before it became operative in the UK. The EAW replaces formal extradition within the EU with a system of surrender on the basis of mutual recognition of the warrant. This system, which sets out to facilitate law enforcement in the EU, only applies to Member States. The European Commission has given its assurance that persons detained under an EU warrant will not be surrendered to a third

---

88 For further discussion see 'SIS II: *fait accompli.* Construction of the EU's Big Brother database underway' at <http://www.statewatch.org/news/2005/may/sisII-analysis-may05.pdf> (accessed 29 Dec 2006).
89 67 COM (2001) 0522.

State.[90] The EAW operates on the mutual recognition of court judgments and is the enforced transfer of a person from one Member State to another. A warrant will be issued in respect to the prosecution of all offences carrying a sentence of imprisonment of at least 12 months, or for persons already sentenced to a custodial or detention order exceeding four months. Having received a request from a judicial authority for the surrender of a convicted person or a person wanted for prosecution, Member States must arrange transfer. Grounds for refusal to execute a warrant are very limited. The whole process is judicial with no executive or administrative discretion to refuse surrender, and there is no exception for nationals. Persons arrested under a warrant cannot rely on either the double criminality rule or the specialty rule. However, provision has been made for States to create a list of offences for which they will refuse to execute an arrest warrant. The mechanism of the EAW, which assumes a high level of trust between both judicial and law enforcement authorities of Member States, replaces many of the instruments authorising extradition within the EU, including provisions of the 1990 Schengen Implementing Convention.[91]

17.3.6 Framework Decision on simplifying the exchange of information and intelligence [92]

This initiative arose from concerns that the absence of a common legal framework for the effective and fast exchange of intelligence between law enforcement agencies hampered the fight against serious cross-border crime. It aims to simplify the mechanisms used to exchange information and intelligence between law enforcement agencies in the Member States. In proposing this Framework Decision, the Commission was concerned that current arrangements are slow and cumbersome. Law enforcement agencies complain that the success of criminal investigations is affected by the need to use formal procedures which take too much time. This Framework Decision establishes the rules to be applied by law enforcement agencies requesting information or intelligence. A request is made to a 'competent authority'. The authority in the requested State acts in accordance with the national law governing criminal investigations. Information can be requested for the purpose of detention, prevention or investigation of an offence provided there are reasonable grounds to believe the relevant information is available in another Member State. The Framework Decision requires Member States to implement measures to ensure requests can be dealt with expeditiously. The Framework Decision contains the usual requirement that Member States ensure that data protection

---

90 69 E–3359/01EN. Answer given by Mr Vitorino on behalf of the Commission.
91 For more detailed discussion of the EAW see Chapter 13.
92 Council Framework Decision on simplifying the exchange of information and intelligence between law enforcement authorities of the EU 2006/960/JHA 18 Dec 2006.

mechanisms comply with human rights obligations. Requests may be refused if they appear disproportionate and irrelevant, or if it would interfere with an on-going domestic investigation, or on grounds of national security.

17.3.7 The European Police College

The European Police College (CEPOL) was established to train senior police officers of the Member States.[93] Its base is in Bramshill in the UK. The aim of the original Council initiative was to develop a European approach to the problems facing Member States in the fight against crime, particularly the cross-border dimension of the problem. CEPOL was given the following objectives:

(a) to increase knowledge of the national police systems and structures of other Member States, of Europol and of cross-border police co-operation within the European Union;
(b) to strengthen knowledge of international instruments, in particular those which already exist at EU level in the field of co-operation on combating crime;
(c) to provide appropriate training with regard to respect for democratic safeguards with particular reference to the rights of the defence.

The Council Decision establishing CEPOL was to be reviewed after a three-year period in order to decide whether to extend CEPOL's tasks. It was agreed that in order to improve CEPOL's functioning it should be financed from the general EU budget. Several technical changes were necessary to bring the structure of CEPOL in line with the procedure to be followed in the framework of the general budget of the EU. Regulations regarding staffing also needed changing. Thus while the objectives of this initiative remain basically unchanged, in order to implement the amendments it was necessary to repeal the original Council Decision. The new Council Decision incorporates amendments to the provisions dealing with relationships with third States and access to documents and data.[94]

17.3.8 1959 European Convention on Mutual Assistance in Criminal Matters[95]

The drafting of this Convention and its Protocol took place under the Third Pillar of the EU, the area relating to justice and home affairs. While the

---

93 Council Decision 2000/820/JHA.
94 Council Decision 2005/681/JHA.
95 For further discussion see Chapter 15.

Convention was originally concerned with judicial co-operation, provisions on police co-operation were added later. The Convention provides for: controlled deliveries; the examination of witnesses and experts by telephone and video conference; the direct transmission of requests for assistance; the spontaneous exchange of information between competent authorities; the setting up of joint investigative teams; and the provision of assistance during covert investigations. It also sets out arrangements for the interception of communications. Critical comment has been made regarding resistance to the inclusion of data protection provisions similar to those found in other Third Pillar conventions.[96]

96 See UK Select Committee on the European Union in the House of Lords, July 1998.

Chapter 18

Evidence before the
ad hoc tribunals

18.1 INTRODUCTION

By virtue of Art 15 of the International Criminal Tribunal for the Former Yugoslavia (ICTY) Statute and Art 14 of the International Criminal Tribunal for Rwanda (ICTR) Statute the Rules of Procedure and Evidence were adopted on 11 February 1994 and 29 June 1995 respectively. The principal drafters of the Rules of Procedure and Evidence of the ICTY were the Trial Chamber judges and Appeals Chamber judges, in co-operation with States and organisations. Proposals were submitted by Argentina, Australia, Canada, France, Norway, Sweden, the UK and the US as well as the American Bar Association, Helsinki Watch, the Lawyers Committee for Human Rights and the International Women's Human Rights Law Clinic, as well as the judges themselves.[1] The purpose of this inclusionary approach was to ensure that different domestic legal systems would be considered and incorporated.[2] Particularly common law and civil law systems, the leading systems in the world and therefore the most influential systems in the development of international criminal law and procedure, differ significantly and have far-remote historical roots.

In civil law systems, which are predominantly inquisitorial, judges play an active role. Most civil law systems have incorporated the concept of an investigative judge, who has the task to ensure that the investigation is fair and efficient. In discharging this task the investigative judge will review the actions of the investigators. In addition, the investigative judge may hear witnesses and predetermine their reliability. Although most civil law systems apply the principle of orality, meaning that witnesses should be heard at trial in the presence of the accused, it is not always perceived to be necessary to hear witnesses again if they have been heard by an investigative judge. Trial

---

1 V Morris and MP Scharf, *The International Criminal Tribunal for Rwanda*, 1998, Irvington-on Hudson, NY: Transnational, 414.
2 Ibid, pp 413–14.

judges lead and control the trial and rely heavily on the 'Dossier' drafted by a police officer or other investigator, containing detailed information about the pre-trial stage. Hence, the core stage of a criminal proceeding in a civil law system is the pre-trial stage, rather than the trial stage. Since the finding of guilt is a task of the judges, with or without the assistance of lay members who are trained and experienced in assessing the weight of evidence, evidence is more likely than not admitted at trial.

Common law systems are party-based systems. The judges have a more passive role to play. They respond to the submissions of the parties, but will rarely take their own initiatives. Generally, the onus to object to the admission of evidence is on counsel. Contrary to civil law jurisdictions, the judge does not intervene in support of the accused unless counsel for defence raises an issue to which the judge has to respond. In principle, all evidence has to be presented at trial. The determination of guilt is a task of jury members, who merely rely on the evidence that is produced by the parties at trial. Judges, being responsible for the legal aspects of the trial, need to ensure that the evidence presented to the jury is relevant and reliable. If evidence does not meet these criteria, judges will exclude it.[3] From these brief and simplified descriptions of common law and civil law systems, it appears that they are fundamentally different, which explains the difficulties in finding consensus on the core issues of procedure and evidence.[4]

Representatives of common law systems, particularly the US, played a more influential role in the drafting process of the ICTY Rules. Consequently, the Rules of Procedure and Evidence are predominantly common law rooted. This is particularly the case with regard to the procedure, which is based on the adversarial approach of common law. Thus, the leading role is played by the parties, and the role of the judges is, with exceptions, to monitor the proceedings. A body similar to an investigative judge has not been incorporated into the Rules of Procedure and Evidence. The Rules on Evidence are nonetheless more civil law influenced. As Antonio Cassese J, President of the ICTY at the time, pointed out:

---

3 For further reading about the differences of domestic systems, see M Damaška, *The Faces of Justice and State Authority*, 1991, Yale University Press: New Haven/London; JF Nijboer, *Proof and Criminal Justice Systems*; P Lang, *Criminalia*, 2nd edn, 1997; Roelof Haveman *et al* (eds), *Supranational Criminal Law: a System Sui Generis*, Intersentia, 2003; A West, Y Desdevises, A Fenet, D Gaurier, MC Heussaff, B Lévy, *The French Legal System*, 2nd edn, 1998, UK: Butterworths; M Delmas-Marty and JR Spencer, *European Criminal Procedures*, Cambridge Studies in International & Comparative Law, 2002, Cambridge: Cambridge University Press; M Delmas-Marty, *Procédure Pénale d'Europe*, 1995, France: Presses Universitaires de France; G Stefani, G Levasseur, B Bouloc, *Procédure Pénale*, 18th edn, 2001, Dalloz.

4 For similar arguments see C Buisman, 'Defence and Fair Trial', in op cit, R Haveman *et al*, note 3, Ch VI.

. . . there are two important adaptations to that general adversarial system. The first is that, as at Nuremberg and Tokyo, we have not laid down technical rules for the admissibility of evidence . . . [T]his Tribunal does not need to shackle itself to restrictive rules which have developed out of the ancient trial by jury system. All relevant evidence may be admitted to this Tribunal unless its probative value is substantially outweighed by the need to ensure a fair and expeditious trial. An example of this would be where the evidence was obtained by a serious violation of human rights. Secondly, the Tribunal may order the production of additional or new evidence *proprio motu*. This will enable us to ensure that we are fully satisfied with the evidence on which we base our final decisions and to ensure that the charge has been proved beyond reasonable doubt. It will also minimise the possibility of a charge being dismissed on technical grounds for lack of evidence. We feel that, in the international sphere, the interests of justice are best served by such a provision and that the diminution, if any, of the accused's rights is minimal by comparison.[5]

These arguments, particularly that trials are conducted by professional judges, rather than juries, have often been repeated in the ad hoc tribunals.[6]

The ICTY Rules of Procedure and Evidence served as a model for the ICTR Rules of Procedure and Evidence.[7] This was the intention of the Security Council as similar rules of procedure in the two tribunals would ensure consistency in the development of international criminal procedural matters. This also ensured a quick adoption of the Rules of Procedure and Evidence at the ICTR without having to elaborate on issues that were already discussed in detail in relation to the ICTY Rules. As a result, the Rules on Evidence

---

5 Statement by the President of the International Tribunal, UN Doc IT/29 (1994), reprinted in op cit, Morris and Scharf, note 1, pp 649, 651.

6 See, *inter alia, Prosecutor v Tadic*, Decision on Defence Motion on Hearsay (*Tadic* decision on hearsay) (5 August 1996), Case No IT–94–1-T, paras 14 and 17. In this case, the Trial Chamber held that one of the reasons the drafters of the Rules have opted for a civil law approach towards the admission of evidence is that 'the trials are conducted by judges who are able, by virtue of their training and experience, to hear the evidence in the context in which it was obtained and accord it appropriate weight. Thereafter, they may make a determination as to the relevancy and the probative value of the evidence'. See also *Prosecutor v Brdanin and Talk*, Order on the Standards governing the admission of evidence (*Brdanin and Talk* Admission of Evidence Order) (15 Feb 2002), Case No IT–99–36-T, para 14; and *Prosecutor v Delalic and Others*, Decision on the Motion of the Prosecution for the Admissibility of Evidence (19 Jan 1998), Case No IT–96–21-T, para 20.

7 This is in compliance with ICTR Statute, Art 14, which provides that '[t]he judges shall adopt . . . the Rules of Procedure and Evidence . . . of the International Criminal Tribunal for the Former Yugoslavia with such changes as they deem necessary'.

of the ICTY and ICTR, were identical, save for minor differences.[8] Over the years the Rules have, however, evolved, resulting in a great number of amendments.[9] These amendments have widened the gaps between the Rules of Evidence of the two ad hoc tribunals. The fundamentals of the ICTR and ICTY Rules of Evidence nevertheless remained similar, though not identical.

In this chapter an analysis is given of the prime rules and principles of evidence as developed and applied by the ad hoc tribunals. The focus is on principles of admissibility and weight assessment of evidence. Where necessary, attention will be paid to the differences between the Rules of the two tribunals and the amendments made. In addition, this chapter will examine to what degree common law and civil law systems have influenced the Rules of Evidence and their application.

18.2 GENERAL EVIDENTIARY PRINCIPLES

Rules and principles of evidence applied in the international system have not been regulated in any rigid format as in certain domestic systems. The

8 Rule 89 was and still is different in the sense that the ICTY Rules include sub-r 89(D), providing that '[a] Chamber may exclude evidence if its probative value is substantially outweighed by the need to ensure a fair trial'. The ICTR never incorporated a similar Rule. Another difference was that r 95 of the ICTY Rules originally stated that evidence obtained directly or indirectly by means that constitute a violation of internationally protected human rights shall be inadmissible. The title of this Rule was 'evidence obtained by means contrary to internationally protected human rights'. Rule 95 of the ICTR Rules, entitled 'exclusion of evidence on the grounds of the means by which it was obtained', on the other hand, provided (and still provides) that 'no evidence shall be admitted if obtained by methods which cast substantial doubt on its reliability or if its admission is antithetical to, and would seriously damage, the integrity of the proceedings'. By subsequent amendments in 1995 and 1997, ICTY, r 95 is now identical to its ICTR counterpart. The amendments are said to have been introduced in order to give a wider interpretation to the rights of the defendant. A final difference was that r 96(i) of the ICTR Rules, r 96(i) of the ICTY Rules, begins with '[notwithstanding r 90(C) . . .'.

9 The main purpose of these amendments was to better guarantee fairness and efficiency. It should be noted that amendments are introduced by the judges after consulting the Prosecutor's and the Registrar's proposals for amendments (ICTY and ICTR Rules, r 6). Initially, defence counsel were excluded from this process, but could submit their proposals to the Registrar, who would consider whether or not they are relevant for discussion in the Plenary Session. Recently, more participation of defence counsel is permitted; they are also invited to the discussion table of the Plenary Session. The reason to opt for a system where the Rules can be easily amended by the judges, who also apply and interpret the Rules, is to ensure a flexible system which is adaptable to emerging international criminal law exigencies. Although there may have been good reasons to choose a system where the legislative and legal tasks are carried out by the same body, this is incompatible with the principle of separation of powers. See ST Johnson, 'On the Road to Disaster: The Rights of the Accused and the International Criminal Tribunal for the Former Yugoslavia', 10 *International Legal Perspective* (1998), 111, pp 116–17, and 166–71.

evidentiary rules and principles that have been incorporated are to be found throughout the Rules of Procedure and Evidence but primarily in s 3 of those Rules. As aforementioned, the lack of a rigid system is no coincidence but a choice. Given that the concept of an international system was new and it was supposed to reflect a great variety of different legal cultures, it was believed that the Trial Chambers 'should not be hindered by technical rules in its search for the truth, apart from those listed in Section 3 of the Rules'.[10] It was further pointed out that '[t]he purpose of the Rules is to promote a fair and expeditious trial, and Trial Chambers must have the flexibility to achieve this goal'.[11]

Thus, flexible rules have been adopted that need to be in compliance with overriding due process principles set out in the Statutes of the ad hoc Tribunals. Article 21 of the Statute of the ICTY, similar to Art 20 of the Statute of the ICTR, embodying fair trial rights, provides:

1   All persons shall be equal before the International Tribunal.
2   In the determination of charges against him, the accused shall be entitled to a fair and public hearing, subject to article 22 of the Statute.
3   The accused shall be presumed innocent until proved guilty according to the provisions of the present Statute.
4   In the determination of any charge against the accused pursuant to the present Statute, the accused shall be entitled to the following minimum guarantees, in full equality:

   (a) to be informed promptly and in detail in a language which he understands of the nature and cause of the charge against him;
   (b) to have adequate time and facilities for the preparation of his defence and to communicate with counsel of his own choosing;
   (c) to be tried without undue delay;
   (d) to be tried in his presence, and to defend himself in person or through legal assistance of his own choosing; to be informed, if he does not have legal assistance, of this right; and to have legal assistance assigned to him, in any case where the interests of justice so require, and without payment by him in any such case if he does not have sufficient means to pay for it;
   (e) to examine, or have examined, the witnesses against him and to

---

10 *Brdanin and Talic*, Admission of Evidence Order (15 Feb 2002), para 10.
11 *Prosecutor v Aleksovski*, Appeals Decision on Prosecutor's Appeal on Admissibility of Evidence (*Aleksovski* appeals decision on admissibility) (16 Feb 1999), Case No IT–95–14/1-AR73, para 19. As quoted in *Prosecutor v Kordic and Cerkez*, Decision on the Prosecution Application to Admit the Tulica Report and Dossier into Evidence (*Kordic and Cerkez* decision on the Tulica Report) (29 July 1999), Case No IT–95–14/2-T, para 11.

obtain the attendance and examination of witnesses on his behalf under the same conditions as witnesses against him;

(f) to have the free assistance of an interpreter if he cannot understand or speak the language used in the International Tribunal;

(g) not to be compelled to testify against himself or to confess guilt.

The rights set out in Art 21(4) ICTY Statute and Art 20(4) ICTR Statute are minimum guarantees that cannot be ignored in any proceeding. A dissenting ICTR judge held that '[t]he minimal guarantees under Article 21(4) are "non-negotiable" and cannot be balanced against other interests. The use of the word "minimum" demonstrates that these enumerated rights are an essential component of every trial'.[12]

The right 'to examine, or have examined, the witness against him', laid out in Art 21(4)(e) ICTY Statute and Art 20(4)(e) ICTR Statute, is particularly relevant to the application of the evidentiary principles. Pursuant to Art 21(2) in conjunction with Art 21(4)(e), an accused is entitled to have an adversarial process where his accusers appear in court for testimony and cross-examination. This right to an adversarial process is a common law principle. It also exists in civil law systems, although as a right which is to be balanced with other interests, particularly witness protection. In civil law systems this right is referred to as the principle of orality. The increasing use of indirect evidence in the ad hoc tribunals (see below), amounting to a curtailment of the principle of orality, is at odds with the statutory right to a fair trial.

Also of relevance to the application of evidentiary principles is Art 20 of the ICTY Statute, identical to Art 19 of the ICTR Statute, stating that '[t]he Trial Chambers shall ensure that a trial is fair and expeditious and that proceedings are conducted in accordance with the rules of procedure and evidence, with full respect for the rights of the accused and due regard for the protection of victims and witnesses'. Thus, in addition to the rights of the accused, the interests of witnesses have to be duly considered in applying evidentiary rules. Some Trial Chambers have held that the rights of the accused on the one hand and victims and witnesses on the other, need to be balanced;[13] while at least one Trial Chamber held that 'the need to carry any balancing exercise which limits the rights of the accused necessarily results in a less than perfect trial'.[14]

---

12 *Prosecutor v Bagosora et al*, 98–41-T, Separate and Dissenting Opinion of Judge Pavel Dolenc on the Decision and Scheduling Order on the Prosecution Motion for Harmonisation and Modification of Protective Measures for Witnesses (5 Dec, 2001), paras 11 and 14.

13 *Prosecutor v Musema*, Case No ICTR-96-13-A, Judgment (AC) (16 Nov 2001), paras 68–69; *Prosecutor v Haradinaj et al*, Decision on Prosecution's Application for Pre-Trial Protective Measures for Witnesses (20 May 2005), p 4

14 *Prosecutor v Brdanin and Talic*, IT–99–36-PT, Decision on Motion by Prosecution for Protected Measures (3 July 2000), para 31.

In compliance with the presumption of innocence, as set out in Art 21(3) of the ICTY Statute and Art 20(3) of the ICTR Statute, the burden of proof beyond reasonable doubt lies with the prosecutor.[15] If the prosecutor does not succeed in discharging this burden in respect of every element of a crime and form of liability, the judges have to acquit the accused by virtue of r 87 of the Rules of both ad hoc tribunals.[16] The accused is thereby entitled to the benefit of the doubt in accordance with the principle of *in dubio pro reo*.[17] Consequently, 'the evidence of the witnesses upon which the prosecution relied should be accepted as establishing beyond reasonable doubt the facts alleged, notwithstanding the evidence given by the Accused and the witnesses upon which the Defence relied'.[18]

15 This principle has been confirmed by case law. See *Prosecutor v Delalic and Others*, Judgment (*Delalic* judgment) (16 Nov 1998), Case No IT–96–21-T, paras 599, 601, where the Trial Chamber held that the onus of proof on the prosecutor was a general principle of law. See also *Prosecutor v Kayishema and Ruzindana*, Judgment (*Kayishema and Ruzindana* judgment) (21 May 1999), Case No ICTR–95–1-T, para 84. There is a shift of burden where the defence 'makes an allegation, or when the allegation made by the Prosecutor is not an essential element of the charges of the indictment'. See *Delalic* judgment, para 602. In such situations, the defence is required to prove its allegations on the balance of probabilities, ibid, para 603. See also *Prosecutor v Krnojelac*, Judgment (15 March 2002), Case No IT–97–25-T, para 3; *Prosecutor v Kunarac, Kovac and Vukovic*, Judgment (22 Feb 2001), Case Nos IT–96–23-T and IT–96–23/1-T, para 559.

16 Rule 87(A) of the ICTY Rules provides: 'When both parties have completed their presentations of the case, the Presiding Judge shall declare the hearing closed, and the Trial Chamber shall deliberate in private. A finding of guilt may be reached only when a majority of the Trial Chamber is satisfied that guilt has been proved beyond reasonable doubt.' Rule 87(A) of the ICTR Rules is similar but for the first phrase. Rule 87(A) begins with: 'After presentation of closing arguments, . . .' This is a difference in language, not a difference in substance. The principle that Trial Chambers can convict only when satisfied that the guilt of the accused has been proved beyond reasonable doubt has been confirmed, eg, in *Prosecutor v Tadic*, Appeals Judgment on Allegations of Contempt against Prior Counsel, Milan Vujin (*Tadic* judgment on allegations of contempt) (31 Jan 2000), Case No IT–94–1-A-R77, para 131; *Prosecutor v Limaj et al*, No. IT–03–66-T, Judgment (30 Nov 2005), para 10.

17 *Delalic* judgment (16 Nov 1998), paras 601, 603; *Krnojelac* judgment (15 March 2002), para 5; *Kunarac* judgment (22 Feb 2001), para 560; *Prosecutor v Blagojevic & Jokic*, No IT–02–60-T, Judgment (17 Jan 2005) para 18; *Prosecutor v Halilovic*, No. IT–01–48-T, Judgment (16 November 2005) para 12. See also *Blagojevic & Jokic* Judgment, para 21; and *Halilovic* Judgment, para 15; *Limaj* Judgment, para 10; *Strugar* Judgment, para 5, stating that, if there is any inference reasonably open from the evidence inconsistent with the guilt of the accused, the accused must be acquitted.

18 *Prosecutor v Akayesu*, Judgment (2 Sept 1998), Case No ICTR–96–4-T, para 136. See also Limaj Judgment, para 22.

18.3 ADMISSIBILITY

18.3.1 Rules and principles of admissibility

Rule 89 is the core provision dealing with admissibility of the evidence. Rule 89 of the ICTY and ICTR Rules cover distinct but overlapping principles. Rule 89 of the ICTY provides:

(A) A Chamber shall apply the rules of evidence set forth in this Section, and shall not be bound by national rules of evidence.
(B) In cases not otherwise provided for in this Section, a Chamber shall apply rules of evidence which will best favour a fair determination of the matter before it and are consonant with the spirit of the Statute and the general principles of law.
(C) A Chamber may admit any relevant evidence which it deems to have probative value.
(D) A Chamber may exclude evidence if its probative value is substantially outweighed by the need to ensure a fair trial.
(E) A Chamber may request verification of the authenticity of evidence obtained out of court.
(F) A Chamber may receive the evidence of a witness orally or, where the interests of justice allow, in written form.

Rule 89 of the ICTR Rules provides:

(A) The rules of evidence set forth in this Section shall govern the proceedings before the Chambers. The Chambers shall not be bound by national rules of evidence.
(B) In cases not otherwise provided for in this Section, a Chamber shall apply rules of evidence which will best favour a fair determination of the matter before it and are consonant with the spirit of the Statute and the general principles of law.
(C) A Chamber may admit any relevant evidence which it deems to have probative value.
(D) A Chamber may request verification of the authenticity of evidence obtained out of court.

Rule 89 of the ICTY Rules and r 89 of the ICTR Rules are not identical. Contrary to the ICTY (r 89(D)), the ICTR does not provide an exclusionary rule to safeguard the fairness of the trial. This does not mean, however, that the ICTR does not take account of the necessity to ensure a fair trial. *Inter alia* in the case of *Akayesu*, the Trial Chamber made clear that it 'can freely assess the probative value of all relevant evidence'. The Chamber had thus determined that in accordance with r 89, any relevant evidence having probative value may be admitted into evidence, provided that it is in accordance with the requirements of a fair trial'.[19] That r 89(C) of the ICTR Rules gives power to a Trial Chamber to exclude evidence to safeguard fair trial principles is also apparent from r 70(F) of the ICTR Rules stating: 'Nothing in Sub-Rule (C) or (D) above shall affect a Trial Chamber's power under Rule 89(C) to exclude evidence if its probative value is substantially outweighed by the need to ensure a fair trial'.

The ICTR Rules have not incorporated r 89(F) of the ICTY Rules. Rule 90(A) of the ICTR Rules nevertheless sets out a similar, though more stringent principle in favour of oral testimony.[20] There are further various amendments made to the ICTY Rules (see below), facilitating the admission of indirect evidence, which have not been adopted by the ICTR. The gap between the two ad hoc Tribunals is therefore widening.

A number of core principles, common to both tribunals, can be deduced from r 89 and other rules of admission. One such principle is that national rules of evidence have no binding effect (r 89(A)).[21] The ICTY and ICTR Rules of Procedure and Evidence are nevertheless influenced by domestic legal systems, and so are their interpretations.[22] The civil law influence can be traced back to r 89(C) by virtue of which all relevant evidence with probative value may be admitted.

Determinations of admissibility pursuant to r 89(C) fall squarely within the discretion of the Trial Chamber. In exercising its discretion pursuant to r 89(C), the Trial Chamber is guided by r 89(B) according to which the rules and principles of evidence applied by the Trial Chambers 'must be those which best favour a fair determination of the matter before the Chamber and

---

19 *Prosecutor v Akayesu*, Judgment (2 Sep 1998), Case No ICTR–96–4–T, para 136.

20 ICTR Rules, r 90(A), provides: 'Witnesses shall, in principle, be heard directly by the Chambers unless a Chamber has ordered that the witness be heard by means of a deposition as provided for in r 71.' Thus, unless r 71 applies, witnesses should appear at trial to give their testimony. Note that the same rule applied at the ICTY until it was first amended on 25 July 1997 to include the possibility of receiving a testimony via video-conference link in exceptional circumstances and in the interests of justice. By amendments of 1 and 13 December 2000, ICTY r 90(A) became what is now r 89(F). The amendments aimed to facilitate the admission of written evidence.

21 This has been confirmed by the case law of both ad hoc tribunals. See, eg, *Tadic* decision on hearsay (5 August 1996), para 7; *Akayesu* judgment (2 Sept 1998), para 131, where the Chamber noted that 'it is not restricted under the Statute of the Tribunal to apply any particular legal system and is not bound by any national rules of evidence. In accordance with r 89 of its Rules of Procedure and Evidence, the Chamber has applied the rules of evidence which in its view best favour a fair determination of the matter before it and are consonant with the spirit of the Statute and general principles of law. Further confirmed, in *Prosecutor v Rutaganda*, Judgment (6 Dec 1999), Case No ICTR–96–3–T, paras 16–17, and *Prosecutor v Musema*, Judgment (27 Jan 2000), Case No ICTR–96–13–T, para 33; *Brdanin and Talic*, Admission of Evidence Order (15 Feb 2002), para 5.

22 Although less so now than initially, the Chambers examine domestic systems, mainly civil and common law systems, when there is a need for their examination in determining an issue. See *Tadic* decision on hearsay (5 Aug 1996), para 7.

which are consonant with the Tribunal's Statute and the general principles of law; the exercise of discretion under Rule 89(C) ought therefore to be in harmony with the Statute and the other Rules to the greatest extent possible.'[23]

Rule 89(B) has not prevented Trial Chambers from adopting a flexible policy of admission. Although r 89(C) is supposed to 'provide a preliminary threshold for the exclusion of irrelevant, unreliable or otherwise improper information',[24] the general practice is to admit, rather than exclude evidence pursuant to r 89(C).[25]

Rule 92*bis*, adopted on 13 December 2002 by the ICTY (as amended on 15 September 2006, see below) and on 6 July 2002 by the ICTR, can be used as a basis for admission of evidence in written form in lieu of oral testimony only if it 'goes to the proof of a matter other than the acts and conduct of the accused as charged in the indictment'. In order for such evidence to be admissible, it has to be supplemented by a declaration of the person producing the written statement, stating that the contents are true and correct to the best of his or her knowledge and belief. This declaration must be witnessed by a person authorised to do so on the basis of domestic law and procedure ((B)(i)(a)), or 'a Presiding Officer appointed by the Registrar of the Tribunal for that purpose' ((B)(i)(b)). The witness attaches a dated note, mentioning the place of the declaration ((B)(ii)(d)), identifying the person making the declaration as the person in the written statement ((B)(ii)(a)), verifying that the person in question indeed stated that the contents are true and correct to the best of his knowledge and belief ((B)(ii)(b)), and stating that the person knew that he may be prosecuted for false testimony if the content of the written statement is not true ((B)(ii)(c)).

If the formal requirements under r 92*bis*(B) have been met, and the evidence does not directly address the conduct of the accused as charged in the indictment without loosing its relevance and probative value to the case pursuant to r 89(C),[26] it is within the Trial Chamber's discretion to admit such

---

23 *Prosecutor v Milosevic*, Decision on Admissibility of Prosecution Investigator's Evidence, (30 Sept, 2002), para 18.

24 *Prosecutor v Bagosora et al*, 98–41-T, Decision on Admission of Statements of Deceased Witnesses (19 January 2005) para 17.

25 Indeed, as confirmed in *Prosecutor v Aleksovski*, Appeal Judgment (24 March 2000), Case No IT–95–14/1-A, para 60, '[u]nless the Rules or general international law provides otherwise, Trial Chambers are free to admit various types of evidence to determine whether or not a particular fact has been established beyond reasonable doubt'.

26 *Prosecutor v André Ntagerura and Others*, Decision on the Defence Motion for Leave to Present Evidence in the Form of a Written Statement under r 92*bis* (13 March 2003), Case No ICTR99–46-T, para 14, where it was held that the evidence 'needs to bear some evidentiary value related to the issues at stake'; and *Prosecutor v Ntagerura et al*, No ICTR–98–46-T, *Decision on the Defence Motion for Leave to Present Evidence in the Form of a Written Statement Pursuant to Rule 92bis* (13 March 2003) para 16, where the Trial Chamber stated that statements cannot be admitted pursuant to r 92*bis* if they have not passed the relevance test under r 89(C).

evidence, giving due consideration to the factors in favour and against admission of evidence under r 92*bis*(A).[27]

ICTY r 89(F) provides that a chamber may receive witness testimony orally or, where the interests of justice allow, in written form. Compared to the initial position, set out in former r 90(A) ICTY and current r 90(A) ICTR, that 'witnesses shall, in principle, be heard directly by the Chambers', the text of r 89(F) allows interpretations further encroaching the principle of orality, which lies at the heart of adversarial proceedings.

Rule 89(F) of the ICTY Rules permits the admission of evidence in written form, provided that its admission is in the interests of justice, in compliance with r 89(C) and not in contravention of r 92*bis*.[28] In which circumstances the receipt of written evidence is in the 'interests of justice' pursuant to r 89(F) is a case-by-case determination, depending, *inter alia*, on the nature of the evidence,[29] and the extent to which the right to assess the credibility of the witness has been infringed.[30]

The ICTR practice is to have witnesses testify orally in court or, where the interests so require, via video link. Attempts to introduce evidence pursuant to r 89(F) ICTY applied by analogy to ICTR cases were unsuccessful.[31] The ICTR Chambers made clear that r 92*bis* in conjunction with r 90(A) only allows the admission of written evidence by following the procedure set out in r 92*bis*.[32] A written statement can further not be admitted pursuant to r 89(C)

---

27 Factors in favour of admitting such evidence include: its cumulative nature ((A)(i)(a)); its relationship with relevant historical, political or military background ((A)(i)(b)); whether the evidence consists of a general or statistical analysis of the ethnic composition of the population in the places to which the indictment relates ((A)(i)(c)); whether it concerns the impact of crimes upon victims ((A)(i)(d)); its relationship with issues of the character of the accused ((A)(i)(e)); or its relationship with factors to be taken into account in determining sentence ((A)(i)(f)). Factors against admitting such evidence include: an overriding public interest in the evidence in question being heard orally ((A)(ii)(a)); a demonstration of an objecting party that its nature and source renders the evidence unreliable, or that its prejudicial effect outweighs its probative value ((A)(ii)(b)); any other factors which make it preferable that the witness gives evidence in court ((A)(ii)(c)).

28 Unless the opposing party consents to the admission or the written evidence has become admissible on another ground. See *Prosecutor v Milosevic*, Decision on Admissibility of Prosecution Investigator's Evidence (30 Sept 2002), para 18.

29 In *Prosecutor v Martic*, No IT–95–11-T, Decision on Prosecution's Motion for Admission of Statement of Witness Milan Babic Pursuant to Rule 89(F) (10 Feb 2006), a written statement and related exhibits were admitted pursuant to Rule 89(F) where witness's statement did not directly relate to the accused, but contained information on the political developments in the territory.

30 *Prosecutor v Milosevic*, Decision on Interlocutory Appeal on the Admissibility of Evidence-in-Chief in the Form of Written Statements (30 Sept, 2003), paras 20–21.

31 *Prosecutor v Bagosora*, 98–41-T, Decision on Certification of Appeal concerning Admission of Written Statement of Witness XXO (11 Dec, 2003), para 2.

32 *Prosecutor v Bagosora et al*, Decision on Admission of Statements of Deceased Witnesses (19 Jan 2005), para 15; *Prosecutor v Muhimana*, Decision on Prosecution Motion for Admission

thereby bypassing the formal requirements of r 92*bis*, since 'the general requirement under r 89 that admissible evidence be relevant and probative applies in addition to, and not in lieu of, the more specific provisions of r 92*bis*'.[33] Thus, the ICTR applies a stricter approach to the admission of written statements in lieu of oral testimony than the ICTY.

There are further options for a party who is seeking to introduce evidence other than through live testimony of a witness present before the Trial Chamber in accordance with the principle of orality. One such option is testimony via video conference by which the witness testifies from a different location via a direct video link to the court room. Such procedure is considered not to be incompatible with the '[d]irect observation of the witness's demeanor'.[34] Indeed, notwithstanding the absence of a witness from the court room, the parties can directly communicate with the witness by a video link and, thus, their right to cross-examination has not been infringed. The ICTY introduced r 71*bis*, explicitly allowing testimony via video link if in the 'interests of justice'. The ICTR did not follow this example but nevertheless applies the 'interests of justice' standard.[35] Rule 54 of the ICTR Rules, permitting the Trial Chamber to 'issue such orders, summonses, subpoenas, warrants and transfer orders as may be necessary for the purposes of an investigation or for the preparation or conduct of the trial', has served as a basis for authorising testimony via video conference where 'the testimony of a witness is shown to be sufficiently important to make it unfair to proceed without it and that the witness is unable or unwilling to come to the International Tribunal'.[36] There

of Witness Statements (rr 89(C) and 92*bis*) (20 May 2004), paras 23–28; *Prosecutor v Nyiramasuhuko et al*, Decision on Prosecutor's Motion to Remove from Her Witness List Five Deceased Witnesses, and to Admit into Evidence the Witness Statements of Four of the Said Witnesses (22 Jan, 2003), para 20.

33 See *Prosecutor v Ndayambaje, Kanyabashi and Others*, Decision on the Prosecutor's Motion to Remove from her Witness List Five Deceased Witnesses and to Admit into Evidence the Witness Statements of Four of Said Witnesses (22 Jan 2003), Case No ICTR–98–42-T, para 20, thereby following the approach adopted in *Prosecutor v Galic*, Appeal Judgment (7 June 2002), Case No IT–98–29-AR73 2, para 31; see also *Prosecutor v Nyiramasuhuko et al*, No ICTR–98–42-T, Decision on Prosecution Motion for Verification of the Authenticity of Evidence Obtained Out of Court, Namely the Alleged Diary of Pauline Nyiramasuhuko (1 Oct 2004) para 26.

34 *Prosecutor v Bagosora*, ICTR–98–41-T, Decision on Prosecution Request for Testimony of Witness BT via Video-Link, 8 Oct 2004, para 12.

35 The first decision where the 'interests of justice' criteria were explicitly recognized was: *Prosecutor v Nahimana et al*, Decision on the Prosecutor's Application to Add Witness X to Its List of Witnesses and for Protective Measures, 14 Sept 2001, para 35.

36 *Prosecutor v Tadic*, Decision on the Defence Motions to Summon and Protect Defence Witnesses, and on the Giving the Evidence by Video-Link, 25 June 1996, para 19. Additional factors to be considered include the persuasion of the reasons adduced for the inability or unwillingness to attend, and whether there is a fair opportunity to confront the witness and for the judges to assess the demeanour and credibility of the witness. See *Prosecutor v Simba*,

is also the r 71 procedure, allowing for the production of deposition evidence on request of one of the parties if in 'the interests of justice'. At the ICTR such production must further be justified by 'exceptional circumstances'.[37]

Thus, at least on paper, any form of indirect evidence is allowed only in certain conditions and where its admission does not violate the due process rights of the accused. However, through the adoption of new Rules and the amendment of old Rules, the system increasingly permits the admission of paper or other forms of evidence that have not passed the test of cross-examination before the fact finders or whose probative value is outweighed by its prejudicial effect. This is in line with a civil law approach.

Moreover, r 93, which allows for the admission of evidence of a 'consistent pattern of conduct relevant to serious violations of international humanitarian law', is in line with a typical civil law approach. Whilst civil law systems generally allow the admission of evidence of previous misconduct of the alleged perpetrator, such is prohibited in common law jurisdictions.

Rule 95 describes the only exclusionary rule that has been incorporated in the Rules of the ICTY and ICTR, allowing for the exclusion of evidence that has been obtained irregularly where this has had an impact on its reliability or the integrity of the proceedings.[38] In addition, a privilege of communications

No ICTR–01–76-T, Decision Authorizing the Taking of the Evidence of Witnesses IMG, ISG, and BJK1 by Video-Link, 4 Feb 2005; *Prosecutor v Bagosora et al*, No ICTR–98–41-T, Decision on Testimony by Video Conference, 20 Dec 2004; *Prosecutor v Zigiranyirazo*, No ICTR–2001–73-T, Decision on Defence and Prosecution Motions Related to Witness ADE, 31 Jan 2006, at para 31; *Prosecutor v Muvunyi*, No ICTR–2000–55A-T, Decision on Muvunyi's Amended Motion to Have Defence Witnesses M005, M015, M036, M046, and M073 Testify by Closed Video-Link Pursuant to Rules 54 and 71(D)of the Rules of Procedure and Evidence, 7 Feb 2006, at para 18; *Prosecutor v Muvunyi*, No ICTR–2000–55A-T, Decision on Muvunyi's Supplemental Motion to Have Defence Witness MO72 Testify by Closed Video-Link Pursuant to Rules 54 and 71(D) of the Rules of Procedure and Evidence, 21 Feb 2006, at para 6; *Prosecutor v Muvunyi*, No ICTR–2000–55A-T, Decision on Prosecution Motion to Have Prosecution's Witnesses QCM and NN Testify by Closed Video Link Pursuant to rr 54 and 71(D) of the Rules of Procedure and Evidence, 23 May 2005, at para 20; *Prosecutor v Rwamakuba*, No ICTR–98–44C-T, Decision on Confidential Motion for the Testimony of Defence Witness 1.15 to be Taken by Video Link, 8 Dec 2005, at para 3; *Prosecutor v Karemera et al*, No ICTR–98–44-T, Decision on Prosecutor's Confidential Motion for Special Protective Measures for Witness ADE, 3 May 2006, at paras 4 and 5.

37 By amendment of 7 Dec 1999, the ICTY deleted the requirement of 'exceptional circumstances'; thus, the party seeking to produce deposition evidence only needs to demonstrate that such is required in the interests of justice. This example was not followed by the ICTR.

38 *Delalic and Others*, Decision on Motion by the Defendants on the Production of Evidence by the Prosecution (8 Sept 1997), para 9; this ground of exclusion exists also in most civil law systems under influence of regional human rights bodies. See, eg, for the case of France, G Stefani, G Levasseur and B Bouloc, *Procédure Pénale*, 1867, 18th edn, 2001, France: Dalloz, pp 222–24. The German system incorporated a number of '*Beweisverbote*' (prohibitions of evidence non-admissibility of evidence) in paras 52–55 and 136(a) of the 1987/2001 Strafprozess Ordnung (Code of Criminal Procedure). See *Procédure Pénale d'Europe*, ibid, p 105. The

between lawyer and client is provided for in r 97, which has been recognised in most domestic systems, whether civil law or common law.

In conclusion, the procedure of the admission of the evidence at the tribunals as reflected in the rules described above, constitutes a free system of proof, which is inherent to most civil law jurisdictions.[39] As pointed out in the *Tadic* case: 'In the civil law system, the judge is responsible for determining the evidence that may be presented during trial, guided primarily by its relevance and its revelation of truth.'[40] Common law systems, on the other hand, are familiar with exclusionary rules, such as rules that exclude irrelevant evidence in general,[41] and more specifically hearsay evidence, similar fact or character evidence, opinion evidence, evidence protected by public immunity interest, evidence protected by legal privilege, and improperly obtained evidence, in particular confessions that are made under pressure. Thus, the assessment of the reliability of evidence takes place at a different point in time. In common law systems the assessment occurs prior to trial, at the stage of the admission of evidence, while the assessment in civil law systems occurs after trial when judges deliberate on the basis of the totality of evidence presented at trial. The main reason for this difference in approach is, as briefly pointed out in the introduction, that common law systems rely on juries to render their judgments. Dubious evidence should be kept away from them, as such may influence the minds of the jury members. Civil law countries often have judges on the bench who determine the case with or without lay members. Judges are trained to give appropriate weight to the evidence that is

---

Dutch system created a discretion for judges to exclude evidence if principles of fair administration of justice have been violated, depending on the gravity of the violation and the consequences thereof, in accordance with Art 359(a) of the Wet van Strafvordering (Code of Criminal Procedure).

39 In the French system this principle is referred to as '*le principe de la liberté des preuves*', meaning that, apart from the cases where the law provides otherwise, offences may be proven by any means of evidence, and it is for the judge to decide according to his 'intime conviction' (ie, inner conviction) (Art 427, Code de Procedure Pénale). Op cit, Stefani *et al*, note 38, p 108, paras 131, 132 and pp 117–18, para 150. In Belgium the same principle of 'intime conviction' is applied (Code d'Instruction Criminelle, Art 342). In Germany, the system of proof is one of '*Freibeweis*' (ie, free proof), which means that judges are free in assessing the weight of evidence. They are nonetheless bound by means of proof incorporated in statutory law. See M Delmas-Marty, *Procédure Pénale d'Europe*, 1995, France: Dalloz, pp 65, 103, 105–06. The Dutch system of proof is similar to the German system. The judges are free to assess the evidence on the basis of their '*rechterlijke overtuiging*' (judicial conviction), but have to base their judgment on those means of proof that are enumerated in the statutory law, in Wetboek van Strafrechtsvordering (Code of Criminal Procedure), Art 339(1).

40 *Tadic* decision on hearsay (5 Aug 1996), para 13.

41 See, eg, r 402 of the US Federal Rules of Evidence applied, which provides: 'All relevant evidence is admissible, except as otherwise provided . . . evidence which is not relevant is not admissible.'

presented before them. Another reason is that common law jurisdictions are reluctant to rely on indirect evidence. It is at the heart of adversarial proceedings to have witnesses testify to matters within their own knowledge rather than to rely on out-of-court statements. Although contemporary civil law systems tend to rely more on court proceedings than in previous years, restrictions on the admission of evidence are still rare.

18.3.2 Amendments to ICTY Rules

On 15 September 2006, a number of significant amendments were introduced to the ICTY Rules. The purpose of the amendments was to facilitate the admission of written evidence. The amendments were considered necessary in order to comply with the completion strategy. With the trials coming to an end, the Tribunals need to be very efficient without undermining the right to a fair trial. However, with the new amendments the right to cross-examination and to confront the accusers is seriously undermined. The ICTR did not consider it necessary to adopt the amendments, even though the ICTR has the same closing date (official date: 2008, unofficial date: 2010) and have to still complete a fair amount of trials. The new Rules are not subject to discussion in this chapter given that it is unclear how the case law on these rules is going to evolve. They provide as follows:

Rule 92*bis*

Admission of Written Statements and Transcripts in Lieu of Oral Testimony

~~Proof of Facts other than by Oral Evidence~~

A.   A Trial Chamber may **dispense with the attendance of a witness in person, and instead** admit, in whole or in part, the evidence of a witness in the form of a written statement **or a transcript of evidence, which was given by a witness in proceedings before the Tribunal,** in lieu of oral testimony which goes to proof of a matter other than the acts and conduct of the accused as charged in the indictment.

   i.   Factors in favour of admitting evidence in the form of a written statement **or transcript** include but are not limited to circumstances in which the evidence in question:

   a.   is of a cumulative nature, in that other witnesses will give or have given oral testimony of similar facts;
   b.   relates to relevant historical, political or military background;
   c.   consists of a general or statistical analysis of the ethnic

composition of the population in the places to which the indictment relates;

   d.   concerns the impact of crimes upon victims;

   e.   relates to issues of the character of the accused; or

   f.   relates to factors to be taken into account in determining sentence.

ii.   Factors against admitting evidence in the form of a written statement **or transcript** include **but are not limited to** whether:

   a.   there is an overriding public interest in the evidence in question being presented orally;

   b.   a party objecting can demonstrate that its nature and source renders it unreliable, or that its prejudicial effect outweighs its probative value; or

   c.   there are any other factors which make it appropriate for the witness to attend for cross-examination.

B.   **If the Trial Chamber decides to dispense with the attendance of a witness, a** A̶ written statement under this Rule shall be admissible if it attaches a declaration by the person making the written statement that the contents of the statement are true and correct to the best of that person's knowledge and belief and

i.   the declaration is witnessed by:

   a.   a person authorised to witness such a declaration in accordance with the law and procedure of a State; or

   b.   a Presiding Officer appointed by the Registrar of the Tribunal for that purpose; and

ii.   the person witnessing the declaration verifies in writing:

   a.   that the person making the statement is the person identified in the said statement;

   b.   that the person making the statement stated that the contents of the written statement are, to the best of that person's knowledge and belief, true and correct;

   c.   that the person making the statement was informed that if the content of the written statement is not true then he or she may be subject to proceedings for giving false testimony; and

   d.   the date and place of the declaration.

The declaration shall be attached to the written statement presented to the Trial Chamber.

(C) The Trial Chamber shall decide, after hearing the parties, whether to require the witness to appear for cross-examination; if it does so decide, the provisions of Rule 92*ter* shall apply.

A.   ~~A written statement not in the form prescribed by paragraph (B) may nevertheless be admissible if made by a person who has subsequently died, or by a person who can no longer with reasonable diligence be traced, or by a person who is by reason of bodily or mental condition unable to testify orally, if the Trial Chamber:~~

   i.   ~~s so satisfied on a balance of probabilities; and~~
   ii. ~~finds from the circumstances in which the statement was made and recorded that there are satisfactory indicia of its reliability.~~

A.   ~~A Chamber may admit a transcript of evidence given by a witness in proceedings before the Tribunal which goes to proof of a matter other than the acts and conduct of the accused.~~

B.   ~~Subject to Rule 127 or any order to the contrary, a party seeking to adduce a written statement or transcript shall give fourteen days notice to the opposing party, who may within seven days object. The Trial Chamber shall decide, after hearing the parties, whether to admit the statement or transcript in whole or in part and whether to require the witness to appear for cross-examination.~~

Rule 92*ter*

Other Admission of Written Statements and Transcripts

(A) A Trial Chamber may admit, in whole or in part, the evidence of a witness in the form of a written statement or transcript of evidence given by a witness in proceedings before the Tribunal, under the following conditions:

   (i)   the witness is present in court;
   (ii)   the witness is available for cross-examination and any questioning by the Judges; and
   (iii) the witness attests that the written statement or transcript accurately reflects that witness' declaration and what the witness would say if examined.

(B) Evidence admitted under paragraph (A) may include evidence that goes to proof of the acts and conduct of the accused as charged in the indictment.

Rule 92*quater*

Unavailable Persons

(A) The evidence of a person in the form of a written statement or transcript who has subsequently died, or who can no longer with reasonable diligence be traced, or who is by reason of bodily or mental condition unable to testify orally may be admitted, whether or not the written statement is in the form prescribed by Rule 92 *bis*, if the Trial Chamber:

> **(i)   is satisfied of the person's unavailability as set out above; and**
> **(ii) finds from the circumstances in which the statement was made and recorded that it is reliable.**

(B) If the evidence goes to proof of acts and conduct of an accused as charged in the indictment, this may be a factor against the admission of such evidence, or that part of it.

18.3.3 Application of Rule 89(C)

In relation to admissibility of evidence, r 89 is particularly relevant. As already mentioned, this Rule has a wide scope for evidence to be admitted.[42] In the *Brdanin and Talic* case,[43] the ICTY Trial Chamber set out some general principles relating to the admission and weight of evidence. In brief, these principles are as follows:

1   A distinction should be made between legal admissibility of documentary evidence and the weight given to it.[44]
2   Judges are entitled to reverse a decision to exclude evidence if at a later stage 'further evidence emerges that is relevant, has persuasive value and hence justifies the admission of the evidence in question'.[45]
3   The 'mere' admission of a document into evidence does not indicate that the contents will be considered to be 'an accurate portrayal of the facts'. *Inter alia*, authenticity and proof of authorship are important factors, not so much in relation to the admission of documents, but rather in relation to the assessment of the weight of a particular piece of evidence.[46] As already mentioned, 'the threshold standard for the admission of evidence . . . should not be set excessively high, as often documents are

---

42 See, eg, *Rutaganda* judgment (6 Dec 1999), para 18.
43 *Brdanin and Talk*, Admission of Evidence Order (15 Feb 2002).
44 Ibid, para 16.
45 Ibid, para 17.
46 Ibid, para 18.

sought to be admitted into evidence, not as ultimate proof of guilt or innocence, but to provide a context and complete the picture presented by the evidence in general'.[47] At the stage of admission of evidence, 'the implicit requirement of reliability means no more than that there must be sufficient indicia of reliability to make out a *prima facie* case for the admission of that document'.[48]

4   Authenticity is a matter of weight, rather than admissibility.[49]

5   There is 'no blanket prohibition on the admission of documents simply on the grounds that their purported author has not been called to testify'. Also, absence of a signature or a stamp does not necessarily mean it lacks authenticity.[50]

6   Hearsay evidence is admissible if relevant and has probative value.[51]

7   The Tribunal applies the 'best evidence rule', a common law concept.[52] In determining what is the best evidence, whilst exercising its discretion, the Tribunal will take account of the 'particular circumstances attached to each document and to the complexity of [the case in question] and the investigations that preceded it'.[53]

8   Statements that were made involuntary as a result of oppression will be excluded on the basis of r 95. The Trial Chamber held that it is up to the prosecutor to 'prove beyond reasonable doubt that the statement was voluntary and not made under oppression'.[54]

9   'Reliability is an inherent and implicit component of each element of admissibility . . . However, in respect to other documentary evidence, the Trial Chamber does not agree that the determination of the issue of reliability, when it arises, should be seen as a separate, first step in assessing a piece of evidence offered for admission'.[55]

10   The Trial Chamber imposes on itself 'an inherent right and duty' to secure the admission of each piece of evidence that so qualifies. At the same time, the Trial Chamber will go out of its way, *ex officio* where

---

47 Ibid. See also *Tadic* judgment on allegations of contempt (31 Jan 2000), para 94, where the Appeals Chamber held that a document may be admitted, not so much to prove the guilt of the accused, but to 'demonstrate a particular course of conduct or to explain the events in issue which took place within that period'.

48 *Brdanin and Talic*, Admission of Evidence Order (15 February 2002), para 18.

49 Ibid, para 19.

50 Ibid, para 20.

51 Ibid, para 21.

52 For an analysis of the common law concept of the 'best evidence rule' as applied in the UK, see C Allen, *Practical Guide to Evidence*, 2nd edn, 2001, London: Cavendish Publishing, p 22.

53 *Brdanin and Talic*, Admission of Evidence Order (15 February 2002), para 22.

54 Ibid, para 23.

55 Ibid, para 24.

needed, to ensure that pieces of evidence that do not so qualify on the basis of the Rules are not admitted.[56]

From these principles it follows that, indeed, the preferable approach is to admit evidence, provided it is relevant and has probative value pursuant to r 89(C), and to assess the appropriate weight 'when all the evidence is being considered by the Trial Chamber in reaching its judgment'.[57]

18.3.4 Relevant definitions of Rule 89(C) terminology

18.3.4.1 Relevance

The ICTY defined relevance as requiring that in relation to two facts there needs to be 'a connection or nexus between the two which makes it possible to infer the existence of one from the other',[58] thereby referring to the *Cloutier* case, determined by the Canadian Supreme Court.[59] Facts which are not related, directly or indirectly, to the criminal responsibility of the accused are not relevant to the issues to be adjudicated at trial.[60]

18.3.4.2 Probative value

Dissenting Stephen J in the *Tadic* case defined probative value as a 'quality of necessarily very variable content and much will depend on the character of the evidence in question'.[61] Probative value is interwoven with the credibility and reliability of the evidence and its relevance to the charges.[62]

Even if evidence is both relevant and probative, a Trial Chamber may still exclude it, in accordance with its statutory obligation to safeguard the

---

56 *Brdanin and Talic*, Admission of Evidence Order, para 25.
57 Ibid, para 13.
58 *Delalic and Others*, Case No IT–96–21-T, Decision on the Prosecutor's Oral Request for the Admission of Exhibit 155 into Evidence and for an order to Compel the Accused, Zdravko Mucic, To Provide a Handwriting Sample (*Delalic* Decision on Admission of Evidence) (19 Jan 1998), para 29.
59 *R v Cloutier* [1979] 2 SCR 709; 99 DLR (3d) 577, *per* Pratte J.
60 *Prosecutor v Karemera et al*, No ICTR–98–44-AR73(C), Decision on Prosecutor's Interlocutory Appeal of Decision on Judicial Notice (16 June 2006), para 48.
61 *Tadic* decision on hearsay (5 Aug 1996), Separate Opinion of Judge Stephen, p 3. See also *Aleksovski* appeals decision on admissibility (16 Feb 1999), para 15, where reference is made to the content and character of the evidence in question in connection to relevance.
62 *Musema* judgment (27 Jan 2000), paras 39–40.

fairness and expeditiousness of the trial, 'where its prejudicial effect will adversely affect the fairness or expeditiousness of the proceedings'.[63]

18.3.4.3 Reliability

Reliability is not a separate condition for admission,[64] but an inherent and implicit component of relevance and probative value under r 89.[65] Reliability is the invisible golden thread that runs through all components of admissibility.[66] Complete lack of reliability, such that it is not probative, should therefore result in exclusion of the evidence.[67] Further, '[e]vidence whose reliability cannot adequately be tested by the Defence cannot have probative value'.[68]

18.4 DOCUMENTARY EVIDENCE

Documentary evidence has been construed as follows:

> Documentary evidence consists of documents, produced as evidence for evaluation by the Tribunal. For the purposes of this case, the term 'document' is interpreted broadly, being understood to mean anything in which information of any description is recorded. This interpretation is

---

63 In the ICTY this can be done on the basis of r 89(D) and in the ICTR this notion has been developed in case law. See *Prosecutor v Bagosora et al*, 98–41-T, Decision on Prosecutor's Interlocutory Appeals regarding Exclusion of Evidence (19 Dec, 2003, para 16). See also *Prosecutor v Nahimana et al*, Decision on the Interlocutory Appeals, Separate Opinion of Judge Shahabuddeen, 15 Sept, 2003, para 90; *Prosecutor v Muvunyi*, No ICTR–00–55A-T, Decision on the Prosecutor's Motion Pursuant to Trial Chamber's Directives of 7 December 2005 for the Verification of the Authenticity of Evidence Obtained Out of Court Pursuant to Rules 89(C) and (D) (26 April 2006), para 15, *Prosecutor v Karemera et al*, No ICTR–98–44-T, Decision on Defence Oral Motions for Exclusion of Witness XBM's Testimony, for Sanctions Against the Prosecution, and for Exclusion of Evidence Outside the Scope of the Indictment (20 Oct 2006) at para 20.
64 *Musema* judgment (27 Jan 2000), para 38.
65 *Tadic* decision on hearsay (5 August 1996), para 15; confirmed in the *Musema* judgment (27 Jan 2000), paras 35–36.
66 *Delalic* decision on admission of evidence (19 Jan 1998), para 32; *Musema* judgment (27 Jan 2000), para 37.
67 *Tadic* decision on hearsay (5 Aug 1996), para 15; *Nyiramasuhuko v Prosecutor*, No ICTR–98–42-AR73.2, Decision on Pauline Nyiramasuhuko's Appeal on the Admissibility of Evidence (4 Oct 2004), para 7; *Prosecutor v Simba*, No ICTR–01–76-T, Decision on the Admission of Prosecution Exhibits 27 and 28 (31 Jan 2005), para 10; Rutaganda v Prosecutor, No ICTR–96–3-A, Judgment (26 May 2003), para 33; *Prosecutor v Muvunyi*, No ICTR–2000–55A-T, Decision on the Prosecutor's Motion to Admit Documents Tendered During the Cross-Examination of Defence Witness Augustin Ndindliyimana (28 Feb 2006), para 12.
68 *Prosecutor v Bagosora et al*, ICTR–98–41-T, Decision on Admissibility of Evidence of Witness DBQ, 18 Nov, 2003, para 8.

wide enough to cover not only documents in writing, but also maps, sketches, plans, calendars, graphs, drawings, computerised records, mechanical records, photographs, slides and negatives.[69]

The party which seeks the admission of a document needs to prove that it meets the criteria necessary for admission, namely relevance and probative value linked with reliability.[70] The standard of proof is on the balance of probabilities. This means that the party who seeks to tender a document has to show some relevance, some probative value, and some reliability.[71] Authenticity of the document in question mainly goes to its weight, not its admission.[72] The fact that the author is unknown, the signature illegible, and the seizure disputed are matters which will affect the weight to be given to the evidence so long as there is a minimum showing of *indicia* of reliability.[73] *Indicia* of reliability need be demonstrated by giving some explanation of what the document is and its authenticity. In the *Bagosora* case, the Trial Chamber held: 'Authenticity and reliability are overlapping concepts: the fact that the document is what it purports to be enhances the likely truth of the contents thereof'.[74]

Indicia of reliability include:

1   the place where the document was seized;
2   the chain of custody after seizure of the document;

---

69 *Musema* judgment (27 Jan 2000), para 53.
70 Ibid, para 55. On appeal, Musema claimed that it was not fair to place a burden of proof on the defence to show that the documents the defendant wished to tender were reliable. Musema alleged that the only burden that was placed upon the defence was the burden to cast reasonable doubt on the prosecution case. His arguments were rejected. See *Prosecutor v Musema*, Appeal Judgment (16 Nov 2001), Case No ICTR–96–13-A, para 39.
71 *Musema* judgment (27 January 2000), para 56; see also Principle 3 enunciated in *Brdanin and Talic*, Admission of Evidence Order (15 February 2002), para 18; *Prosecutor v Bagosora et al*, 98–41-T, Decision on Admission of Tab 19 of Binder Produced in Connection with the Appearance of Witnesses Maxwell and Nkole, (13 September, 2004), para 7; *Prosecutor v Hadzihasanovic & Kubura*, No. IT–01–47-T, Decision on the Admissibility of Documents of the Defence of Enver Hadzihasanovic (22 June 2005), para 21.
72 *Prosecutor v Blagojevic & Jokic*, No. IT–02–60-T, Judgment (17 Jan 2005), para 29; *Prosecutor v Blaskic*, Judgment (3 March 2000), Case No IT–94–14-T, para 36; see Principle 4 enunciated in *Brdanin and Talic*, Admission of Evidence Order (15 Feb 2002), para 19. At common law, authenticity, which needs to be proven through direct or circumstantial evidence, is a requirement for the admission of a document.
73 *Prosecutor v Simba*, No ICTR–01–76-T, *Decision on the Admission of Prosecution Exhibits 27 and 28* (31 Jan 2005), para 10.
74 *Prosecutor v Bagosora et al*, Decision on Admission of Tab 19 of Binder Produced in Connection with the Appearance of Witness Maxwell and Nkole (13 Sept, 2004), para 8. In this case, the Trial Chamber excluded 22 handwritten documents, attached to an FBI report because the prosecution, who sought their admission, failed to provide any explanation as to where those documents came from, thus undermining their reliability and authenticity (para 10).

3   corroboration of the contents of the document with other evidence;
4   the nature of the document itself such as signature, stamps, handwriting.[75]

If a copy of a document is sought to be admitted, there should be some explanation about the non-availability of the original, or some confirmation that the copy sought to be tendered genuinely emanates from the original.[76]

When these *indicia* of relevance, probative value and reliability have been established the document can be admitted pursuant to r 89(C). Unless the admission is reconsidered at a later stage upon showing that these *indicia* were based on a false premise,[77] the question whether the relevance, probative value and reliability are sufficient for judges to rely on the document is a question of weight, not of admissibility. Credibility is not yet an issue at the admission stage.[78] When the rights of the accused are at stake, it may be more appropriate to apply the burden of proof beyond reasonable doubt.[79]

It should be noted that Chambers are inclined to admit a document without any further debate where the opposite party does not dispute the relevance, probative value and reliability of the document. Documents in general are mostly admitted as evidence, even if their source is dubious, the justification being that documents usually do not directly address the issue of guilt,

---

75 *Prosecutor v Bagosora et al*, No. ICTR–98–41-T, *Decision on Request to Admit United Nations Documents Into Evidence Under Rule 89(C)* (25 May 2006) para 4; *Prosecutor v Bagosora et al*, No. ICTR–98–41-T, *Decision on the Prosecutor's Motion for the Admission of Certain Materials Under Rule 89(C)* (14 October 2004), para 22; *Prosecutor v Bagosora et al*, No. ICTR–98–41-T, *Decision on Admission of Tab 19 of Binder Produced in Connection With Appearance of Witness Maxwell Nkole* (13 September 2004), para 8; *Prosecutor v Delalic et al*, Appeals Chamber Decision on Application of Defendant Zejnil Delalic for Leave to Appeal Against the Decision of the Trial Chamber of 19 January 1998 for the Admissibility of Evidence (4 March 1998), para 18; *Prosecutor v Kordic and Cerkez*, Decision on Prosecutor's Submissions Concerning 'Zagreb Exhibits' and Presidential Transcripts (1 December, 2000), paras 43–44.

76 *Prosecutor v Muvunyi*, No ICTR–2000–55A-T, Decision on the Prosecutor's Motion to Admit Documents Tendered During the Cross-Examination of Defence Witness Augustin Ndindliyimana (28 Feb 2006), para 13.

77 *Prosecutor v Muvunyi*, No ICTR–2000–55A-T, Decision on Motion to Strike or Exclude Portions of Prosecutor's Exhibit #34, Alternatively Defence Objections to Prosecutor's Exhibit #34 (30 May 2006).

78 *Musema* judgment, ibid, para 57; *Delalic and Others*, Decision on the Motion of the Prosecution for the Admissibility of Evidence (*Delalic* decision on admissibility) (21 June 1998); *Prosecutor v Rutaganda*, Appeals Chamber Judgment, May 26, 2004, para 216: reliability and credibility are not synonymous.

79 *Musema* judgment, ibid, para 58, thereby relying on the arguments in *Delalic and Others*, Decision on Zdravko Mucic's Motion for the Exclusion of Evidence (*Delalic* decision on exclusion of evidence) (2 Sept 1997).

but are of a more general nature.[80] Unlike common law jurisdictions, these documents do not necessarily need to be presented by a witness.[81]

18.5 HEARSAY EVIDENCE

Hearsay has been described as 'the statement of a person made otherwise than in the proceedings in which it is being tendered, but nevertheless being tendered in those proceedings in order to establish the truth of what that person says'.[82] On the basis of this definition, hearsay evidence may cover 'any written document, including expert reports and official documents, which is not adduced by its author while testifying, as well as any behaviour carried out and words uttered by a person other than the witness who reports them in court to establish the truth of the matter'.[83] Common law and civil law positions are remote, almost opposite in relation to hearsay evidence although traditionally more so than now. While the civil law traditions have no specific ground on which to exclude hearsay evidence,[84] at common law hearsay evidence is inadmissible save a number of limited exceptions.[85]

The ad hoc tribunals do not give the same consideration to hearsay evidence as common law courts. On the basis of arguments already presented, namely, that the trials are conducted by professional judges and judges seek to avoid being hampered by technicalities, hearsay evidence is more often than not admitted. In principle, witnesses must give oral testimony in the

---

80 *Delalic and Others*, Decision on Admissibility (21 June 1998).
81 *Blaskic* judgment, ibid, para 35.
82 *Aleksovski* appeals decision on admissibility (16 Feb 1999), para 14.
83 A Rodrigues and C Tounaye, 'Hearsay Evidence', in R May *et al, Essays on* ICTY *Procedure and Evidence in Honour of Gabrielle Kirk McDonald*, 2001, The Hague: Kluwer, p 291.
84 The European Convention on Human Rights, of which a large number of European civil law jurisdictions are members, may constitute a possible ground to exclude hearsay evidence. Although the European Court of Human Rights does not prohibit the use of hearsay evidence *per se*, it has imposed restrictions on States in its application. Assessing evidence is primarily a matter for domestic courts. See, eg, *Delta v France*, ECHR Judgment (19 Dec 1990), para 35, and *Van Mechelen and Others v The Netherlands*, ECHR Judgment (23 April 1997), p 691, para 50. However, where the right to a fair trial is affected, it will nevertheless intervene, such as in *Lüdi v Switzerland*, ECHR Judgment (15 June 1992), p 21, para 49. Hearsay evidence should not be the most substantial evidence (*Unterpertinger v Austria*, Judgment (24 Nov 1986), para 33), otherwise, its admission violates the right to question the witness (Art 6(3)(d)). Reading out statements rather than hearing the witness is itself not inconsistent with Art 6, 'but the use made of the statements as evidence must nevertheless comply with the rights of the defence' (*Unterpertinger v Austria*, para 31).
85 The necessity for the exclusionary rule of hearsay evidence is explained in the case of *Teper v R* [1952] AC 480: The truthfulness and accuracy of the person whose words are spoken by another witness cannot be tested by cross-examination and the light which his demeanour would throw on his testimony is lost.

presence of the accused (r 89(F) of the ICTY Rules and r 90(A) of the ICTR Rules in combination with Art 21(4)(e) of the ICTY Statute and Art 20(4)(e) of the ICTR Statute).[86] However, the tribunals underscored that the principle set out in r 90(A) of the ICTR Rules, which is currently set out in different terms in r 89(F) of the ICTY Rules, does not necessarily indicate that priority is given to direct and oral evidence. Instead, it deals with technicalities in relation to the reception of testimony. So, irrespective of the availability of the actual witness, both parties can produce hearsay evidence instead.[87] To avoid a violation of the Trial Chamber's statutory obligation to safeguard the fairness of the trial, of which an element is the right to cross-examination pursuant to Art 21(4)(e) ICTY Statute and Art 20(4)(e) ICTR Statute, the Chambers have given a wide interpretation to this right, in that it applies to 'the witness testifying before the Trial Chamber and not to the initial declarant whose statement has been transmitted to this Trial Chamber by the witness'.[88] Cross-examination is the only tool available to the defence to test the reliability and credibility of the actual witness. This is gravely undermined by admitting hearsay evidence.

The issue of hearsay arose for the first time in the *Tadic* case.[89] In that case the Trial Chamber held that there was no 'blanket prohibition on the admission of hearsay evidence',[90] but that its admission depends on its relevance and probative value, focusing on its reliability.[91] Many subsequent cases followed this example.[92] In the *Kordic* and *Cerkez* case, approximately 40 transcripts from other trials were admitted. Only those which repeated already heard testimonies were excluded, due to lack of relevance. The Chamber also determined that the witnesses should be called when the transcripts concerned the determination of the guilt of the accused directly.[93] In the

86 European Convention on Human Rights, Art 6(3)(d); International Covenant on Civil and Political Rights, Art 14(4)(e), upon which ICTY and ICTR Statutes, Arts 21 and 20 are based. As the European Court of Human Rights pointed out, *inter alia*, in *Kostovski v The Netherlands*, Judgment (20 Nov 1989), para 41, '[i]n principle all the evidence has to be produced in the presence of the accused at a public hearing with a view to cross-examination, although statements obtained at a pre-trial stage could be used as evidence, provided the rights of the defence were respected'. Although human rights treaties generally apply to Member States only, and not to international institutions, the ICTY and ICTR have confirmed that the decisions of the ECHR are 'authoritative and applicable'. See *Prosecutor v Delalic and Others*, Decision on the Motion by the Prosecutor for Protective Measures for the Prosecution Witnesses Pseudonymed 'B' through 'M', Preliminary Judgment (28 April 1997), para 27.
87 *Aleksovski* appeals decision on admissibility (16 Feb 1999).
88 *Elastic* hearsay decision (21 Jan 1998), para 29.
89 *Tadic* decision on hearsay (5 Aug 1996).
90 Ibid, para 7.
91 Ibid, para 19.
92 See *Aleksovski* appeals decision on admissibility (16 February 1999).
93 *Kordic and Cerkez* decision on the Tulica Report (29 July 1999).

Aleksovski case[94] the Trial Chamber did not accept that the admission of a transcript from another case violated the fundamental right of the accused to confrontation and cross-examination guaranteed by the ICTY Statute.[95] However, the Trial Chamber added that 'this ruling will not preclude the application by the Defence to cross-examine the witnesses on the ground that there are significant relevant matters not covered by cross-examination in *Blaskic* which ought to be raised in this case'.[96] The ICTR adopted a similar approach; ICTR Trial Chambers have the discretion to admit hearsay evidence, even when it cannot be examined at its source and when it is not corroborated by direct evidence.[97]

The same approach is applied to the admission of hearsay evidence as to other forms of evidence. The core issues are again relevance and probative value in connection with reliability.[98] To evaluate the relevance, probative value and reliability of the hearsay evidence:

> the Trial Chamber will hear both the circumstances under which the evidence arose as well as the content of the statement. The Trial Chamber may be guided by, but not bound to, hearsay exceptions generally recognised by some national legal systems, as well as the truthfulness, voluntariness, and trustworthiness of the evidence, as appropriate. In bench trials before the International Tribunal, this is the most efficient and fair method to determine the admissibility of out-of-court statements.[99]

In sum, from the case law it appears that hearsay evidence is admitted as a rule, even where a statement constitutes multiple hearsay. This fact on its own gravely undermines the right to cross-examination, which is inherent in a fair trial. This disadvantage to the defence can be partly compensated if judges take it sufficiently into account when weighing the evidence.

---

94 *Aleksovski* appeals decision on admissibility (16 Feb 1999).
95 Ibid, para 25.
96 Ibid, para 28.
97 *Prosecutor v Rwamakuba*, No. ICTR–98–44C-T, *Judgment* (20 Sept 2006) at para 34. See further, *Musema* judgment (27 Jan 2000), para 51, where the Trial Chamber noted that 'hearsay evidence is not inadmissible *per se*, even when it cannot be examined at its source or when it is not corroborated by direct evidence. Rather, the Chamber has considered such hearsay evidence, with caution, in accordance with Rule 89'; see also *Prosecutor v Ntahobali and Others*, Decision on Ntahobali's Motion to Rule Inadmissible the Evidence of Prosecution Witness 'TN' (1 July 2002), Case No ICTR–98–42-T, para 21, where the Trial Chamber held that 'hearsay evidence is permissible at the Chamber's discretion'.
98 *Prosecutor v Natelic & Martinovic*, No IT–98–34-A, *Judgment* (3 May 2006) para 217; *Prosecutor v Milosevic*, No IT–01–54-T, *Decision on Testimony of Defence Witness Dragan Jasovic* (15 April 2005) p 4.
99 *Tadic* decision on hearsay (5 Aug 1996), para 19.

18.6 DEPOSITION EVIDENCE

Deposition evidence is out-of-court evidence given by a witness. Thus, the deposition replaces the witness's appearance in court, and is generally conditional upon the unavailability of the witness.[100] The deposition will normally be taken by a court official in the presence of the defence who has the right to cross-examine the witness. The trial judges or jury members will not hear the witness directly but will rely on the record made of the deposition. Notwithstanding the maintenance of the defendant's right to cross-examine the witness, this is a form of hearsay by common law standards. Its use at the *ad hoc* Tribunals is explicitly allowed on the basis of r 71 of the ICTY and ICTR Rules. The use of deposition evidence is another exception to the general rule that witnesses should testify orally in court, which follows from r 90(A) of the ICTR Rules and r 89(F) of the ICTY Rules.

In its original form, r 71 could only be invoked in exceptional circumstances and in the interests of justice. The onus is on the party seeking to admit deposition evidence to demonstrate exceptional circumstances and interests of justice. Over time, the use of deposition evidence became standard, and exceptional circumstances were easily accepted.[101] In Kupreskic,[102] the Appeals Chamber gave a restrictive interpretation of r 71 and held that it should be invoked only as intended, namely as an exception to the general rule that witnesses should be heard directly by the Trial Chamber. An exception applies where both parties agree.[103] The witness's age, poor mental or physical condition may amount to exceptional circumstances.[104] Also, the refusal of the government of the country where the witness is residing to

100 See JW Strong (ed), *McCormick on Evidence*, 1999, St Paul, Minnesota: West, pp 391–92.

101 Even the unavailability of one of the Trial Chamber judges amounted to exceptional circumstances. See *Kordic and Cerkez*, Decision on the Prosecutor's Request to Proceed by Deposition (13 April 1999); *Prosecutor v Kupreskic and Others*, Decision on Prosecutor's Request to Proceed by Deposition (25 Feb 1999), Case No IT–95–16-T.

102 *Kupreskic and Others*, Appeals Decision on Appeal by Dragan Papic against Ruling to Proceed by Deposition (15 July 1999), Case No IT–95–16-AR73, p 3.

103 *Prosecutor v Kvocka and Others*, Decision to Proceed by Way of Deposition Pursuant to Rule 71 (15 November 1999), Case No IT–98–30-PT.

104 *Prosecutor v Bagosora and Others*, Decision on Prosecutor's Motion for Deposition of Witness OW (5 Dec 2001), Case No ICTR–98–41-I, para 12; *Prosecutor v Muvunyi*, No ICTR–2000–55-I, *Decision on Prosecutor's Extremely Urgent Motion for the Deposition of Witness QX* (11 Nov 2003); *Prosecutor v Simba*, No ICTR–2001–76-I, *Decision on the Defence's Extremely Urgent Motion for a Deposition* (11 March 2004) at para 7. The fact that a witness is protected, indigent or fearful does not amount to an exceptional circumstance justifying deposition. These are issues that can be dealt with by the Tribunal's Witness and Victim Support Section, and hence, deposition is not necessary. See *Prosecutor v Semanza*, Decision on Semanza's Motion for Subpoenas, Depositions, and Disclosure (20 Oct 2000), Case No ICTR–97–20-I, para 27.

allow the transfer of the witness to the Tribunal may constitute an exceptional circumstance.[105]

Trial Chambers are more reluctant to accept that deposition is in the interests of justice. The ICTY Trial Chambers established the following criteria on the basis of which to evaluate whether a deposition is in the interests of justice:

1   the testimony must have sufficient importance in the sense that it would be unfair to run the trial without its admission;
2   the witness is unwilling or unavailable to testify orally;
3   the deposition will not prejudice the right of the accused to confront the witness.[106]

These criteria are equally accepted by the ICTR Trial Chambers, but one ICTR Chamber added an additional ground: 'the practical considerations (including logistical difficulty, expense, and security risks) of holding a deposition in the proposed location [should] not outweigh the potential benefits to be gained by doing so.'[107]

At the ICTR, applications for depositions based exclusively on a witness's security concerns have been consistently denied.[108] Deposition requests where testimony by video-link was feasible, which allows the Trial Chamber to observe the witness's demeanour, have likewise been rejected.[109] Thus, ICTR Trial Chambers treat deposition as a last resource. Important witnesses should appear in person for testimony to allow Trial Chambers to directly observe the witness's demeanour and to test his or her credibility.

In *Naletilic*, the ICTY Trial Chamber stated that deposition evidence would be admitted where 'the witness proposed for deposition will not present eyewitness evidence directly implicating the accused in the crimes charged, or alternatively, their evidence will be of a repetitive nature in the

---

105   This is only so if the prosecutor has made all efforts to secure the attendance of the witness. See *Prosecutor v Niyitegeka*, Decision on the Prosecutor's Amended Extremely Urgent Motion for the Deposition of a Detained Witness Pursuant to Rule 71 (4 Oct 2002), Case No ICTR–96–14-T, para 5.

106   *Delalic and Others*, Decision on the Motion to Allow Witnesses K, L, and M to Give Their Testimony by Means of Video-Link Conference (28 May 1997).

107   *Bagosora*, Decision on Deposition of Witness OW (5 Dec 2001), paras 13–14. All four criteria were confirmed in subsequent case law. See *Prosecutor v Bagosora et al*, No ICTR–98–41-T, *Decision on Prosecutor's Motion to Allow Witness DBO to Give Testimony by Means of Deposition* (25 Aug 2004) at para 8.

108   *Prosecutor v Bagosora et al*, No ICTR–98–41-T, Decision on Prosecution Request for Deposition of Witness BT (4 Oct 2004).

109   *Prosecutor v Simba*, No ICTR–01–76-T, Decision on the Defence Request for Taking the Evidence of Witness FMP1 by Deposition (9 Feb 2005), para 4.

sense that many witnesses will give evidence of similar facts'.[110] It should be noted that the tribunals do not make a distinction between requests for deposition of evidence from the defence and those from the prosecution; notwithstanding the fact that the main problem of taking deposition is that it may undermine the position of the defence.

The ICTY amended r 71. The term 'exceptional circumstances' has been deleted to make its use more flexible. It still needs to be in the interests of justice, which relates to the importance and the disputable nature of the evidence. The ICTR Rules still require the presence of both exceptional circumstances and the interests of justice. The ICTY amendment has not made a significant difference, as most requests strand on the requirement of the interests of justice, rather than exceptional circumstances.

18.7 CHARACTER EVIDENCE

A rule of common law provides that evidence, which tends to prove the bad character of the accused or his previous misconduct, is excluded as such, being only prejudicial while it does not indicate anything about the accused's guilt in the matter at issue.[111] An exception applies where the probative value of evidence outweighs its prejudicial effect.[112] This will only be the case where the facts shown by the evidence are strikingly similar to the facts alleged by the prosecutor. Another exception applies where the accused produces evidence of his 'good' character, which may be rebutted by the prosecutor by bringing evidence of his 'bad' character. A final exception applies where the evidence does not tend to demonstrate the accused's guilt, but rather his

---

110 *Prosecutor v Naletilic and Martinovic*, Decision on Prosecutor's Motion to Take Depositions for Use at Trial (Rule 71) (10 Nov 2000), Case No IT–98–34-PT, p 4; *Niyitegeka* decision on deposition (4 Oct 2002), para 3.

111 See, eg, *Makin v AG for New South Wales* [1894] AC 57, determined by the Privy Council (UK): The prosecution is not competent 'to adduce evidence tending to show that the accused has been guilty of criminal acts other than those covered by the indictment for the purpose of leading to the conclusion that the person is likely from his criminal conduct or character to have committed the offence for which he is being tried' (*per* Lord Herschell, p 65); see also US Federal and Revised Uniform Rules of Evidence, r 404(a) which provides that, subject to a number of exceptions, '[e]vidence of a person's character or, a trait of his character is not admissible for the purpose of proving that he acted in conformity therewith on a particular occasion'.

112 See *DPP v P* [1991] 2 AC 447, decided by the British Court of Appeal: It was not appropriate to single out striking similarity as an essential feature of every case involving the admission of evidence of one victim on a charge relating to another victim. The principle was whether the probative force of the evidence was sufficiently great to make it just to admit the evidence, notwithstanding its prejudicial effect in showing the defendant's guilt of another crime' (*per* Lord Mackay).

motive, intent, plan or similar issues.[113] Civil law jurisdictions are unfamiliar with such a rule. Since the assessment of evidence is in the hands of professionally trained judges, who are responsible for the factual and legal findings, the prosecutor is free to adduce evidence showing the alleged perpetrator's tendency to commit a crime.

The Tribunals have not incorporated an exclusionary rule in relation to character evidence. To the contrary, r 93 specifically allows for the admission of evidence of a consistent pattern of conduct relevant to serious violations of international humanitarian law. The term 'consistent pattern of conduct' seems to be broader than the common law term 'striking similarities'. Under certain conditions, this Rule allows admission of evidence that relates to events outside the temporal jurisdiction of the Tribunals or the scope of the indictment if the evidence constitutes 'similar fact evidence' that demonstrates a consistent pattern of conduct.[114] The Tribunal judges have qualified such evidence as circumstantial evidence, but they apply this Rule with caution.[115]

The following factors must be considered in determining whether the evidence qualifies as 'similar fact evidence' and is admissible under r 93:

1 proximity in time of the similar acts;
2 extent to which the other acts are similar in detail to the charged conduct;
3 number of occurrences of the similar acts;
4 any distinctive feature(s) unifying the incidents;
5 intervening events; and

---

113 See Federal and Revised Uniform Rules of Evidence, r 404(b) which provides: 'Evidence of other crimes, wrongs, or acts is not admissible to prove the character of a person in order to show that he acted in conformity therewith. It may, however, be admissible for other purposes, such as proof of motive, opportunity, intent, preparation, plan, knowledge, identity or absence of mistake or accident.' Rule 405(a), furthermore, allows opinion testimony as well as reputation testimony to prove character whenever any form of character evidence is appropriate. In addition, when character is 'in issue', it may also be proved by testimony about specific acts.

114 *Prosecutor v Ndlindliyimana et al*, No ICTR–00–56-T, Decision on Nzuwonemeye's Motion to Exclude Parts of Witness AOG's Testimony (30 March 2006), para 22.

115 *Krnojelac* judgment (15 March 2002), para 4: 'Evidence of a consistent pattern of conduct relevant to serious violations of international humanitarian law under the Statute was admitted pursuant to r 93(A) in the interests of justice. Such evidence is similar to circumstantial evidence. A circumstantial case consists of evidence of a number of different circumstances which, taken in combination, point to the existence of a particular fact upon which the guilt of the accused person depends because they would usually exist in combination only because a particular fact did exist. Such a conclusion must be established beyond a reasonable doubt. It is not sufficient that it is a reasonable conclusion available from that evidence. It must be the only reasonable conclusion available. If there is another conclusion which is also reasonably open from that evidence, and which is consistent with the non-existence of that fact, the conclusion cannot be drawn.'

6   any other factor which would tend to support or rebut the underlying unity of the similar acts.[116]

Similar fact evidence can further be used to undermine the credibility of the accused as a witness.[117] It may even be taken into account in relation to the guilt or innocence of the accused if relevant to prove identity or to disprove innocent associations,[118] or 'it bears on the questions as to whether the conduct alleged ... was deliberate or accidental, and whether it is likely that a person of good character would have acted in the way alleged'.[119] Where evidence fails to pass the test of r 93(C), its prejudice outweighs its probative value or its admission is not in the interests of justice, such evidence must be excluded.[120]

On a similar reasoning, evidence of past crimes, introduced merely to blacken the character of the accused and to demonstrate that the accused is 'capable of committing the offence, is inclined to commit the offence, or on some prior occasion actually did have the intent to commit the criminal offence', is inadmissible under r 93.[121] This is so because such evidence is 'prejudicial' in a manner that compels exclusion, outweighing its probative value, because it 'so severely blacken[s] the reputation of the accused as to make acquittal virtually impossible, even though the direct evidence of the commission of the offence is weak'.[122]

Although often acknowledged that professional judges may be less susceptible to distraction or prejudice by the admission of irrelevant or prejudicial evidence than juries, 'dealing with evidence of past conduct may be unduly

---

116 *Prosecutor v Bagosora et al*, No. ICTR–98–41-T, Decision on Admissibility of Proposed Testimony of Witness DBY (18 September 2003) at para 38.

117 *Tadic*, Appeals Judgment on Allegations of Contempt (31 Jan 2000), para 128.

118 *Prosecutor v Bagosora et al*, No ICTR–98–41-T, Decision on Admissibility of Proposed Testimony of Witness DBY (18 Sept 2003) paras 9–14; *Prosecutor v Simba*, No ICTR–2001–76-I, Decision on the Defence Motion for Preclusion of Prosecution Evidence (31 Aug 2004), para 3.

119 Ibid; *Tadic*, Appeals Judgment on Allegations of Contempt (31 January 2000), para 130.

120 *Prosecutor v Bagosora et al*, No ICTR–98–41-T, Decision on Admissibility of Proposed Testimony of Witness DBY (18 Sept 2003), paras 9–14; *Prosecutor v Simba*, No ICTR–2001–76-I, Decision on the Defence Motion for Preclusion of Prosecution Evidence (31 Aug 2004), para 3. These arguments have further been confirmed by the Appeals Chamber in: *Prosecutor v Bagosora et al*, Decision on Prosecutor's Interlocutory Appeals regarding Exclusion of Evidence, 19 December 2003, para 13.

121 *Prosecutor v Kupreskic*, Decision on Evidence of Good Character of the Accused and the Defence of *Tu Quoque* (17 Feb, 1999), para 31; *Prosecutor v Bagosora et al*, Decision on Admissibility of Proposed Testimony of Witness DBY (18 Sept 2003), para 12.

122 *Prosecutor v Bagosora et al*, No ICTR–98–41-T, Decision on Admissibility of Proposed Testimony of Witness DBY (18 Sept 2003), paras 12 and 17.

distracting and time consuming, leading to an unfocused trial that undermines the truth-finding function'.[123]

18.8 INVESTIGATOR'S REPORT

In civil law systems it is common for police investigators to file a dossier containing the results of their investigations. This may include witness statements, scientific reports, psychoanalysis reports and others. It is often considered unnecessary to call for testimony the witnesses whose statements are duly reported in the Dossier. Judges rely on the accuracy of the police investigator's report.[124] This approach gravely undermines the right to cross-examine and is, in specific circumstances, severely criticised by the European Court of Human Rights.[125] The Prosecutor attempted to pursue this controversial practice common in some civil law countries, such as Belgium, France and the Netherlands.

In the *Kordic and Cerkez* case,[126] the prosecutor proposed to submit into evidence[127] a dossier of evidence relating to the attack on Tulica in June 1993. The dossier itself contains seven categories of documents:

(i)   five maps relevant to the presentation;
(ii) one video containing footage relevant to the presentation;
(iii) eight witness statements;
(iv) four court transcripts;
(v)   exhumation documents, including on-site reports, photographs and death certificates;

---

123 *Prosecutor v Bagosora et al*, No ICTR–98–41-T, Decision on Admissibility of Proposed Testimony of Witness DBY (18 Sept 2003), paras 12 and 28.

124 In France, great importance is attached to a '*process-verbal*', the contents of which, in relation to 'contraventions' (ie, misdemeanours) are held to be true unless the contrary is proved (Code de Procédure Pénale, Art 537). Thus, it results in shifting the burden of proof. In relation to crimes, the judges are able to assess the weight of the information contained in such '*procès-verbal*' in accordance with their inner conviction (Code de Procédure Pénale, Art 430); op cit, West *et al*, note 3, pp 221–22. In the Dutch system, an accused can be convicted on the contents of a '*process-verbal*' only (Wetboek van Strafvordering, Art 344(2)), which is an exception to the rule that evidence needs to be corroborated (Wetboek van Strafvordering, Arts 341(4) and 342(3)).

125 In particular, the European Court of Human Rights has condemned this approach where witnesses are not called to testify without taking proper action to safeguard the right 'to examine or have examined witnesses against him' (Art 6(3)(d)). See, eg, *Van Mechelen*, ECHR Judgment (23 April 1997), p 691; *Visser v The Netherlands*, ECHR Judgment (14 Feb 2002), Application No 00026668/95.

126 *Kordic and Cerkez* decision on the Tulica Report (29 July 1999).

127 Ibid, para 7.

(vi)   photographs, a schematic diagram and a map relating to destruction of property;

(vii) 13 photographic 'stills' taken from the video footage.

The prosecutor suggested calling the investigator for cross-examination by the defence on the materials in his report, including the statements of persons who were not to be called as witnesses.[128] The defence objected on the basis that the inclusion of the Tulica report would amount to a violation of the fundamental right of the accused to 'examine, or have examined, the witnesses against him' (Art 21(4)(e) of the ICTY Statute). The defence underlined the fact that the report contained second- or third-hand hearsay evidence.[129] While confirming that relevant hearsay evidence may be admitted under r 89(C),[130] the Tribunal determined that not all categories of the proposed evidence should be held admissible. The report itself was not admitted into evidence, as the investigator could not be qualified as a factual witness, nor as an expert witness. He gathered materials long after the events took place and was thus not in a position to say anything more than which materials were in the dossier.[131] Instead, the Tribunal looked at the materials independently, rather than the report as a whole. As for the witness statements (iii), the Tribunal held that 'this is not an appropriate case for the exercise of the discretion under that provision [r 89(C)], as it would amount to the wholesale admission of hearsay untested by cross-examination, namely the attack on Tulica, and would be of no probative value'.[132] As for the transcripts (iv), the Trial Chamber held that there was no justification for admitting the transcript of a witness testimony given earlier in the same trial. The inclusion of this testimony would therefore be 'unnecessarily repetitious'.[133] The transcripts of three other witnesses were found admissible, as the witnesses had been cross-examined in the *Blaskic* case, the defence of which the Trial Chamber considered to have a common interest with the defence in the case in question. The right to cross-examine the witnesses on matters which were not raised in the *Blaskic* case was nonetheless reserved for the defence.[134] The Trial Chamber admitted into evidence the exhumation documents (v), consisting of an 'on-site report' carried out by an Investigating Judge for the Sarajevo Cantonal Court, photograph documentation concerning exhumation autopsy and identification, and death certificates. With regard to the on-site report, the Trial Chamber, however, held that '[a]ny assumptions or conclusions which

128 Ibid, para 8.
129 Ibid, para 9.
130 Ibid, para 19.
131 Ibid, para 20.
132 Ibid, para 23.
133 Ibid, para 26.
134 Ibid, para 28.

are expressed in this material will be disregarded by the Trial Chamber and will not form part of the record of evidence which it will consider in determining the innocence or guilt of the accused'.[135] Thus, the Chamber refused to admit a 'dossier' as a whole without examining the materials independently.

In the *Milosevic* case, the Trial Chamber refused to admit into evidence, a summary of various written statements put together by a prosecution investigator, because the investigator's conclusions constituted hearsay evidence of little or no probative value and would not assist the Trial Chamber in performing its task of assessing the weight of the written statements whereupon the investigator drew his conclusions. That assessment did not require expertise beyond that which was within any capacity of a tribunal of fact; and the investigator's summary would not, in the eye of the public, appear to be an independent evaluation of the evidence. The investigator was further not allowed to testify to the witness statements because they were not admissible pursuant to r 92*bis*; and the infringement of the right to cross-examine the accusers would not be remedied by allowing the defence to cross-examine the prosecution investigator.[136] All these grounds in support of the Trial Chamber's decision to exclude the evidence were confirmed by the Appeals Chamber.[137]

In *Kordic and Cerkez*, the Defence sought to introduce a report of an assistant Professor at the University of Zagreb, teaching phonetics and allied subjects. The proposed evidence provided interpretations of the words spoken by one of the Accused in a conversation. The Prosecution objected because the assistant Professor was not present during the conversation. The Trial Chamber refused to admit the proposed evidence on the ground that 'it is for the Trial Chamber to assess the credibility and the truthfulness of witnesses and, therefore, if this witness were to give evidence upon this topic, he would do so either as an expert in which case he would be trespassing on the Trial Chamber's province or if he were doing it as a non-expert, he would be offering an opinion which would not be allowed. There is a general matter of principle which is this: How much of such evidence should be permitted? There is a danger if, in a case of this sort, evidence were permitted, why then on every issue of which credibility of witnesses arose, it may be said that experts of various sorts or witnesses should be called and that cannot be in the interests of fair and expeditious trials.'[138]

---

135 Ibid, para 32. The Trial Chamber repeated this reasoning in relation to the remaining categories of evidence (i, ii, vi, vii) (paras 34 and 36).

136 *Prosecutor v Milosevic*, English transcript of 20 February 2002, pp 672–73 and 30 May 2002, pp 5931–33, 5936, 5940–44.

137 *Prosecutor v Milosevic*, No IT–01–54-AR73.2, Decision on Admissibility of Prosecution Investigator's Evidence (30 Sept 2002), paras 17 and 21–24).

138 *Prosecutor v Kordic and Cerkez*, IT-95-14/2, English Transcript of 6 October 2000, pp 26093–26100, at p 26100.

18.9 EXPERT EVIDENCE

At common law a witness cannot make a value judgment or express an opinion. The reason for this prohibition of value judgments or opinions is that the fact finder is to draw his own conclusions on the facts brought before him; the witness should not replace this function of the fact finder.[139] An exception applies with regard to experts who can give their opinion within the limits of their expertise. If a person qualifies as an expert on the basis of his professional qualifications or expertise, which requires special skills and knowledge, and the expert's opinion is likely to be outside the experience and knowledge of a judge or jury, the opinion may be admitted into evidence.[140] If judges or jury members can form their own conclusions on the facts without the assistance of an expert opinion, such opinion is irrelevant and therefore not admitted into evidence.

An important rule is the 'ultimate issue rule': the expert cannot testify as to the guilt of the alleged perpetrator.[141] Another important rule is that an expert cannot express the opinion of another expert or assistant-expert (primary facts). It is, however, permitted to rely on the opinions of other experts to make up one's own opinion (expert's facts). It is very difficult not to rely to some extent on hearsay evidence, as the expertise is normally based on someone else's expertise.[142]

In civil law systems generally, there is little that binds the court in relation to expert opinion evidence. It is entirely within the discretion of the court to determine who can be qualified as an expert and on what basis. In practice, civil law courts tend to accept expert evidence without any further

---

139 *R v Robb* (1991) 93 Cr App R 161; C Allen, *Practical Guide to Evidence*, 2nd edn, 2001, London: Cavendish Publishing, pp 307–16.
140 In *R v Silver Lock* [1894] 2 QB 766, handwriting was considered to be an expertise on the basis that it required special skills and knowledge. See also *R v Turner* [1975] QB 834, *per* Lawton LJ, and *R v Robb*, ibid.
141 See however the English case *R v Stockwell* (1993) 97 Cr App R 260, where it was found acceptable for an expert witness to give his opinion on an ultimate issue, such as identification, provided the judge directed the jury that they were not bound to accept the opinion. See also US Federal Rules of Evidence, r 704(a), which states: 'Except as provided in subdivision (b), testimony in the form of opinion or inference otherwise admissible is not objectionable because it embraces an ultimate issue to be decided by the trier of fact.' Rule 704(b) provides that when an accused's mental state or condition is in issue (such as premeditation in homicide, lack of predisposition in entrapment, or the true affirmative defence of insanity), an expert witness may not testify that the defendant did or did not have the mental state or condition constituting an element of the crime charged or of the defence.
142 Under US Federal Rules on Evidence, rr 703 and 705, an expert may give a direct opinion upon facts and data, including technically inadmissible reports, provided the reports or other data are 'of a type reasonably relied upon by experts in the particular field in forming opinions or inferences upon the subject'. JW Strong (ed), *McCormick on Evidence*, 1999, St Paul, Minnesota: West, pp 28–29.

scrutiny.[143] There is no equivalent to the common law ultimate issue rule, although, implicitly, there is, as the expert witness can only testify according to his expertise. The ultimate matter of guilt of the alleged perpetrator would not fall within the ambit of his expertise.

In principle, the Tribunals follow the common law approach. Testimony qualifies as expert testimony where 'intended to enlighten the judges on specific issues of a technical nature, requiring special knowledge in a specific field'.[144]

The evidence given by the expert needs to be relevant and useful in assisting the Chamber in deliberating.[145] If the evidence relates merely to legal issues, rather than issues of a technical nature, it will not be admitted, as the judges are well capable of drawing their own conclusions on legal matters.[146] In the *Military I* case, the ICTR Trial Chamber held that:

> . . . [i]t is widely accepted and the parties in this case do not dispute that the role of an expert is to provide opinions or inferences to assist the finders of fact in understanding factual issues. In addition, there is no dispute that before being permitted to submit opinion testimony, the Chamber must find that the expert is competent in her proposed field or fields of expertise. The expert must possess some specialised knowledge acquired through education, experience, or training in a field that may assist the fact finders to understand the evidence or to assess a fact at issue.[147]

---

143 Some argue that one needs to be careful in qualifying a witness as an 'expert' as judges are inclined to attach great importance to an expert opinion, sometimes too much. See op cit, West *et al*, note 3, p 221.

144 *Prosecutor v Akayesu*, Decision on a Defence Motion for the appearance of an Accused as an Expert Witness (9 March 1998); reiterated in *Prosecutor v Nahimana, Barayagwiza, Ngeze*, Case No ICTR–99–52-T, Decision on the Expert Witnesses for the Defence (24 Jan 2003), para 2.

145 Ibid, *Nahimana*, paras 6 and 11; *Prosecutor v Bizimungu et al*, No ICTR–99–50-T, Decision on Casimir Bizimungu's Urgent Motion for the Exclusion of the Report and Testimony of Deo Sebahire Mbonyinkebe (2 Sept 2005), para 12; *Prosecutor v Nyiramasuhuko et al*, No ICTR–98–42-T, Oral Decision on the Qualification of Mr Edmond Babin as Defence Expert Witness (13 April 2005), para 5.

146 Ibid, paras 16 and 22; *Nahimana and Others*, Decision to Reconsider the Trial Chamber's Decision of 24 January 2003 on the Defence Expert Witnesses (25 Feb 2003), para 4; *Prosecutor v Stakic*, No IT–97–24-A, Judgment (22 March 2006), para 164.

147 *Prosecutor v Bagosora and Others*, Oral Decisions on Defence Objections and Motions to Exclude the Testimony and Report of the Prosecution's proposed Expert Witness, Dr Alison DesForges, or to Postpone her Testimony at Trial (4 September 2002), Case No ICTR–41–98-T, para 5; see also *Prosecutor v Bagosora et al*, No. ICTR–98–41-T, Decision on Motion for Exclusion of Expert Witness Statement of Filip Reyntjens (28 September 2004), para 8; *Nahimana* oral decision (20 May 2002), pp 122–26; *Prosecutor v Martic*, No. IT–95–11-T, Decision on Prosecution's Motions for Admission of Transcripts Pursuant to Rule 92 *bis* and of Expert Reports Pursuant to Rule 94 *bis* (13 January 2006), para 22; *Prosecutor*

An ICTY Trial Chamber held that expert reports can only be used to prove general events, not for the determination of the guilt of a specific alleged perpetrator.[148] Thus, it respects the ultimate issue rule of common law. In the ICTR, however, a different approach was adopted in respect of expert reports, which were admitted although the report discussed the culpability of the four accused in great detail.[149] The Trial Chamber held:

> With respect to the sceptre raised by the defence that Dr DesForges should not be permitted to opine upon the ultimate issue, lest the parties forget, this matter is being tried by a panel of seasoned Judges who will not permit the opinion of an expert to usurp their exclusive domain as fact finders. Rules disallowing an expert to provide opinions and inferences on the ultimate issue are ordinarily directed at protecting against lay jurors from substituting the opinion of the expert for their independent assessment of the facts. There is no such danger here.[150]

In other cases in respect of other experts, Trial Chamber mostly admitted expert testimony relating to general matters only, not the speculations on the behaviour of the accused on the ground that the Trial Chamber is the only competent body to make determinations on the ultimate issues of fact in the case.[151] An expert witness is further only permitted to give testimony which falls within the scope of the witness's expertise.[152]

Moreover, different Trial Chambers have different levels of tolerance to the use of hearsay evidence and anonymous sources in expert testimony. In the *Kovacevic* case,[153] the defence made an objection against inclusion of prosecution Exhibit 10 on the ground that it contained multiple hearsay and otherwise inadmissible evidence.[154] The document constituted a report of an

v Bizimungu et al, No. ICTR–99–50-T, Oral Decision on Qualification of Prosecution Expert Sebahire Deo Mbonyikebe (2 May 2005); *Prosecutor v Nyiramasuhuko et al*, No. ICTR–98–42-T, Oral Decision on the Qualification of Mr. Edmond Babin as Defence Expert Witness (13 April 2005), para 5.

148 See, eg, *Prosecutor v Kovacevic*, Official Transcript (6 July 1998), Case No IT–97–24-T, p 71; *Kordic and Cerkez*, Official Transcript (28 Jan 2000), pp 13,268–306.

149 *Bagosora and Others*, Oral Decisions on Objections to Exclude Testimony (4 Sept 2002), para 8.

150 Ibid, pp 13,305–07.

151 *Semanza v Prosecutor*, No ICTR–97–20-A, Judgment (20 May 2005) para 304; *Prosecutor v Bizimungu et al*, No ICTR–99–50-T, Decision on the Admissibility of the Expert Testimony of Dr Binaifer Norwojee (8 July 2005), para 12; *Prosecutor v Bizimungu et al*, No ICTR–99–50-T, Decision on Casimir Bizimungu's Urgent Motion for the Exclusion of the Report and Testimony of Deo Sebahire Mbonyinkebe (2 Sept 2005), para 13.

152 *Prosecutor v Bizimungu et al*, No. ICTR–99–50-T, *Decision on the Admissibility of the Expert Testimony of Dr. Binaifer Norwojee* (8 July 2005), para 11.

153 *Kovacevic*, Official Transcript (6 July 1998).

154 Ibid, pp 69–71.

expert, namely a judge, who summarised, analysed and collated information from 400 witnesses. Thus, the defence argued that it was denied the fundamental right to cross-examination, and the right to confront witnesses, as the judge, the only witness available for cross-examination, was not a direct witness herself. The defence made the correct observation that '[t]hey cannot merely summarise evidence and introduce it under the guise of being an expert.'[155] The defence further argued:

> We're not talking about simply hearsay that an expert may use to fortify their expert opinion. We're talking about being denied the right to cross-examine a paper witness.[156]

May J responded:

> It is our view that the witness should be treated as an expert in this sense, an expert who has made a study of material and is therefore qualified to give evidence about it. The position being analogous to that of the historian. We take entirely the point made by the defence, that they cannot cross-examine the 400 witnesses on whose statements this evidence will be based. We understand that. But in this Tribunal we admit all types of evidence. The hearsay rule does not apply, but the issue of how much weight is given to this evidence is very much a matter for the Tribunal. And, in that connection, we shall, of course, bear in mind that it is hearsay. And, as I said earlier, sometimes hearsay upon hearsay. With those considerations in mind, we shall admit the report. But, I should make it quite plain, there is no question of this defendant being convicted on any count on the basis of this evidence. And we shall require other evidence before we consider taking any such course.[157]

In the above case, it is highly questionable why the person in question qualified as an expert, and, if yes, an expert in what? Is gathering materials an expertise? The dangers of qualifying a witness as an expert are well known. Often, their opinions are blindly followed. Experts in the Tribunals tend to rely on materials of others. They may have collected the materials but base their findings entirely on what others have said. The dangers of relying mainly on hearsay evidence are nevertheless recognised, and Judge May rightly stated that someone should not be convicted on the basis of such report only.

In the *Kordic and Cerkez* case, the defence raised an objection with regard to the expertise of a professor, the author of a book on ethnic cleansing in 1995.[158] The prosecution argued that the controversy surrounding his expert-

---

155 Ibid, p 71.
156 Ibid, p 74.
157 Ibid, p 75.
158 *Kordic and Cerkez*, Official Transcript (28 Jan 2000).

ise should not be a ground for exclusion, but should rather be addressed during cross-examination.[159] May J raised concerns as regards the ultimate issue rule, as well as the relevance of the allegations.[160] The prosecutor responded that the document included conclusions:

> . . . which are the principal matters that are outside the experience of the Chamber and upon which expertise is vital and helpful. And in his survey of and marshalling of the material and then, applying his analysis to reach the conclusions that precede the final conclusions, he is doing the work of an expert and not expressing final conclusions.[161]

The prosecutor moreover argued that:

> He gathers together the material with expertise that is not available to us. This is a recognised and respected area of expertise to which he's devoted some part of his life, entirely neutrally gathering materials that aren't available to us in their broad range and knowing where to look, and that marks him out and it gives him a particular insight and a particular value.[162]

Counsel for the defence objected, arguing that the professor was neither neutral nor an expert, and had no expertise to offer something which the court did not already have.[163] He stated about the professor:

> He has instead looked at a variety of newspaper documents, things supplied to him by the Tribunal from witnesses, some of whom have appeared and some of whom have not, and he has made his conclusion . . . [H]e has made his conclusion having decided the credibility and reliability of witness statements, reports in news journals, accepted some and rejected others . . . Cigar's report contains not only news articles but a number of, 'open sources which have been analysed with due regard to their reliability' . . . Judge Cigar has decided who is reliable and who isn't, taking that entirely from your hands, and presents to you his analysis of the shadow case which I suggest.[164]

After the Trial Chamber deliberated on the matter, May J held:

> Much of the complaint made by the defence about this witness is a matter which is susceptible to cross-examination and is a question of

159 Ibid, pp 13,267–68.
160 Ibid, pp 13,269–71.
161 Ibid, pp 13,271–72.
162 Ibid, p 13,275.
163 Ibid, p 13,289.
164 Ibid, pp 13,292–93.

weight. However, they raise a fundamental point, which is that what this witness effectively is doing is to provide evidence or provide opinion, more accurately, upon the very matters upon which this Trial Chamber is going to have to rule, and that, as they correctly point out, invades the right, power, and duty of the Trial Chamber to rule upon this issue . . . It is littered, if I may say, with examples of conclusions, drawing inferences, drawing conclusions, which it is the duty of this Trial Chamber to consider and to draw if appropriate or to reject. It's correctly pointed out that the witness hasn't heard the evidence. We have, and we have to decide the case. It's not a matter for him to decide . . . We also don't think, and this is a matter where Rule 89(C) comes into play, that his evidence is going to assist us very much. 89(C) says we may admit any relevant material which it deems to have probative value. Because it's dealing with the matters which we have to deal with ultimately, drawing the conclusions and inferences which we have to draw, we think that it does not assist and is, therefore, not of probative value . . . Accordingly, we shall exclude the evidence.[165]

In the ICTR, many historians who conducted research into the Rwandan genocide have been qualified as experts. Their opinions are generally formulated upon the narratives of others. This may be totally acceptable within the context of research into human rights abuses and should therefore not be read as criticism of their work. However, in a court of law, this causes problems, given that the credibility of the witnesses whose stories are being told, have not been tested in cross-examination.

Objections have been raised in relation to non-disclosure of the identity of persons or sources that form the basis of the expert opinion. In one such case, the Trial Chamber stated that there was no danger of a deprivation of the right to know the expert's sources, as the defence teams had ample opportunity to ask questions relating to the sources during cross-examination.[166]

Thus, one may conclude that, in comparison with the rules of common law on expert evidence, expert reports, particularly at the ICTR, are being accepted far too lightly.

18.10 EXCLUSION OF IMPROPERLY OBTAINED EVIDENCE

A rule excluding improperly obtained evidence exists in practically all systems, civil and common law systems alike. Civil law systems tend to focus on

---

165 Ibid, pp 13,305–07.
166 *Bagosora and Others*, Oral Decisions on Objections to Exclude Testimony (4 Sept 2002), para 11.

procedural matters, which means that evidence will be excluded if obtained in violation of procedural fairness irrespective of the relevance of the evidence. Common law systems focus more on issues of reliability: if the prejudicial effect exceeds probative value the evidence will not be admitted. To a more limited degree, evidence, the admission of which would affect fairness, may also be excluded at common law.[167]

The scope of r 95 is wide. In the *Delalic* case, the ICTY held that for 'evidence to be reliable, it must be . . . obtained under circumstances which cast no doubt on its nature and character'. Thus, r 95 creates an additional element to reliability, namely the source.[168] Another element of r 95 is the integrity, which refers to a fair trial. On the basis of r 95, certain pieces of evidence, such as those obtained in an armed search,[169] in irregular investigation procedures,[170] or by a mere breach of the Rules of Procedure and Evidence, will be found inadmissible.[171] Thus, irregularities in the procedure

---

167 See *Sang* [1980] AC 402, where Lord Diplock, p 437, held that judges have no discretion 'to refuse to admit relevant admissible evidence on the ground that it was obtained by improper or unfair means. The Court is not concerned with how it was obtained'. Even though s 78 of the Police and Criminal Evidence Act 1984 (PACE) incorporates the judicial discretion to exclude evidence if improperly obtained, *Chalkley* [1998] 2 Cr App R 79, *per* Lord Auld, pp 105–06, confirms the common law position set out in *Sang*. This approach may, however, have become invalidated in light of the incorporation of the European Convention on Human Rights through the adoption of the Human Rights Act 1998. In Canada, the position is similar. See *R v Wray* [1971] SCR 272; *R v Harrer* [1995] 3 SCR 562. However, the Canadian Charter provides for a remedy itself: if the manner with which the evidence was obtained is in violation of the Canadian Charter, the evidence may be excluded under Art 24(2) of the Charter if its admission would bring the administration of justice into disrepute. The US has shown considerable concern with the fairness in which evidence was obtained, even where the reliability of the evidence is not directly affected. This appears, *inter alia*, from *State v Brown*, 543A 2d 750, 763 (1988); and *USA v Leon*, 468 US 897 (1984). See also Federal and Revised Uniform Evidence Rules, r 403, which codifies the common law power of the judge to exclude relevant evidence, 'if its probative value is substantially outweighed by the danger of unfair prejudice, confusion of the issues, or misleading the jury or by considerations of undue delay, waste of time, or needless presentation of cumulative evidence'.

168 *Delalic*, Decision on Exclusion of Evidence (2 September 1997), para 41.

169 *Kordic and Cerkez*, Decision Stating Reasons for Trial Chamber's Ruling of 1 June 1999 Rejecting Defence Motion to Suppress Evidence (25 June 1999), pp 3–5.

170 *Delalic and Others*, Decision on the Motion for the Exclusion of Evidence and Restitution of Evidence by the Accused Zejnil Delalic (25 Sept 1997), para 45; *Delalic* judgment (16 Nov 1998), para 65.

171 *Delalic and Others*, Decision on the Tendering of Prosecution Exhibits 104–08 (9 Feb 1998), para 20. The 'mere' breach was the breach of the right to counsel. Although this restriction of the right to be represented while being questioned by Austrian police and prosecution investigators during a criminal investigation was in accordance with Austrian law and was allowed under the European Convention on Human Rights, Art 6(3) of which Austria is a member, the Trial Chamber nevertheless considered it to be 'inconsistent with the unfettered right to counsel in Art 18(3) [of the Statute] and sub-Rule 42(A)(i) [of the Rules]'. On that

suffice to exclude the evidence obtained therein. It is not necessary that the quality of evidence is thereby affected. It appears that r 95 is wide enough to properly sanction misconduct of investigators, regardless of whether or not the Tribunal is responsible for its actions.

Particular care needs to be taken when it concerns admissions of the accused. To admit evidence of the accused's statement under r 95, the prosecution needs to prove 'convincingly and beyond reasonable doubt' that the statement was made voluntarily.[172]

A suspect or an accused who is subjected to an interview by someone working for the prosecution is entitled to be represented by counsel and should be so informed. Failure to do so will lead to exclusion of the interview as evidence in the case against him or her. However, where a statement is taken after the accused was properly advised of his rights and voluntarily waived them, such interview can be used to impeach the accused during his or her testimony and, if the requirements of r 89(C) are met, admitted as evidence.[173] If, on the other hand, the waiver of the right to be represented by counsel was not voluntary, explicit, unequivocal and informed, such interview may be excluded under r 95 because this right is considered to be fundamental, particularly during preliminary questioning, to ensure that the other rights of the accused are being respected.[174] The voluntariness of the waiver of the right to representation must, as the voluntariness of the interview, be established by the prosecution 'convincingly and beyond reasonable doubt'.[175] To meet this burden, the Prosecution must establish that the suspect or accused was informed of his right to 'the *prompt* assistance of counsel, prior to and during *any* questioning. *Any implication that the right is conditional, or that the presence of counsel may be delayed until after the questioning, renders any waiver defective* . . . Once the detainee has been fully

ground, it excluded the statements made by the accused to the Austrian police as evidence under r 95. The Trial Chamber nonetheless admitted statements made in Munich notwithstanding the defence's allegation that irregularities occurred in recording the interview. *Delalic* judgment (16 Nov 1998), para 64; *Akayesu* judgment (2 Sept 1998), para 95.

172 *Prosecutor v Delalic et al*, Decision on Zdravko Mucic's Motion For the Exclusion of Evidence, (2 Sept 1997), para 42.

173 *Prosecutor v Nyiramasuhuko et al*, No. ICTR–98–42-T, Decision on Kanyabashi's Oral Motion to Cross-Examine Ntahobali Using Ntahobali's Statements to Prosecution Investigators in July 1997 (15 May 2006), para 80.

174 *Prosecutor v Bagosora et al*, Decision on the Prosecutor's Motion for the Admission of Certain Materials Under Rule 89(C), (14 Oct 2004), para 21.

175 *Prosecutor v Delalic et al*, Decision on Zdravko Mucic's Motion For the Exclusion of Evidence, (2 Sept 1997), para 42; *Prosecutor v Bagosora et al*, Decision on the Prosecutor's Motion for the Admission of Certain Materials Under Rule 89(C), (14 Oct 2004), paras 16–18.

apprised of his right to the assistance of counsel, he or she is in a position to voluntarily waive the right.'[176]

18.11 DETERMINATION OF WEIGHT OF EVIDENCE

18.11.1 General principles

The Trial Chambers need to accord appropriate weight, if any, to evidence which has been admitted pursuant to r 89(C). The mere admission of evidence during trial 'has no bearing on the weight which the Chamber subsequently attaches to it'.[177] A tribunal of fact must never look at the evidence of each witness separately, as if it existed in a hermetically sealed compartment; it is the accumulation of all the evidence in the case which must be considered. The evidence of one witness, when considered by itself, may appear at first to be of poor quality, but it may gain strength from other evidence in the case. The converse also holds true.[178] One unfortunate consequence of this reasoning may be that a person will be convicted on the basis of evidence that, independently, lacks relevance, probative value and reliability, but because of other factors supporting a finding of guilt, the evidence becomes sufficiently reliable to secure a conviction. This reasoning, however, does not suggest that the Chambers do not consider the weight of evidence individually. In the *Akayesu* case, the Chamber held that the evidence, whether testimony or documentary evidence, has to be assessed individually on its probative value 'according to its credibility and relevance to the allegations at issue'.[179] The Chamber thereby relies on the evidence produced by the parties. In addition, it may consider and rely on 'indisputable facts and on other elements relevant to the case, such as constitutive documents pertaining to the establishment and jurisdiction of the Tribunal, even if these were not specifically tendered in evidence by the parties during trial'.[180]

On occasions defendants have complained that the Chambers have not established sufficiently clear criteria in order to assess the weight of evidence.[181] In response, the Appeals Chamber pointed out that 'it is neither possible nor proper to draw up an exhaustive list of criteria for the assessment of evidence, given the specific circumstances of each case and the duty of the judge to rule on each case in an impartial and independent manner'.[182]

---

176 *Bagosora* Decision, ibid paras 17–18.
177 *Limaj* Judgment, para 12.
178 *Tadic*, Judgment on Allegations of Contempt (31 Jan 2000), para 92.
179 *Akayesu* judgment (2 Sept 1998), para 131.
180 Ibid.
181 See, *inter alia, Prosecutor v Kayishema and Ruzindana*, Appeal Judgment (1 June 2001), Case No ICTR–95–1-A, paras 307–11.
182 Ibid, para 319.

In essence, the evidence needs to be 'reasonable' and 'reliable'.[183] Reliability has to be assessed in the context of the facts of each particular case, and requires a consideration of the circumstances under which the evidence arose, the content of the evidence, whether and how the evidence is corroborated, as well as the truthfulness, voluntariness, and trustworthiness of the evidence.[184]

18.11.2 Corroboration

The Rules of Procedure and Evidence prescribe one situation where corroboration of the evidence is required and one situation where corroboration is not required. Corroboration is required where a child who is 'sufficiently mature to be able to report the facts of which the child had knowledge and understands the duty to tell the truth' testifies without taking the oath pursuant to r 90(B) of the ICTY Rules and r 90(C) of the ICTR Rules. In cases of sexual assault r 96 of the ICTY/ICTR Rules make it explicit that no corroboration of the victim's testimony shall be required. Other than these two Rules, the Statutes and Rules are silent on corroboration. Case law has, however, established that corroboration is not a requirement.

Here, the Tribunals differ from civil law jurisdictions. As regards the application of the civil law principle *unus testis, nullus testis* (one witness is no witness), implying that corroboration of evidence is required before any weight can be attached to it, the Trial Chamber has held that such does not apply: 'the Chamber can rule on the basis of a single testimony provided such testimony is, in its opinion, relevant and credible.'[185]

However, although corroboration may not be required in order to accept evidence as sufficiently credible, the Chambers are 'nevertheless aware of the importance of corroboration'.[186] Where the evidence does not corroborate, the Chambers scrutinise the evidence against the accused 'with great care before accepting it as sufficient to make a finding of guilt against the accused'.[187] The Trial Chamber may in such situations, as it has done in some

183 *The Prosecutor v Kayishema & Ruzindana*, Case No ICTR–95–1-A, Appeal Judgment, Appeals Chamber (1 June 2001), paras 320 and 322.

184 *Prosecutor v Tadic*, Decision on Defence Motion on Hearsay (5 Aug 1996), para 19; *Prosecutor v Kajelijeli*, Decision on Motion to Limit the Admissibility of Evidence (2 June 2001).

185 *Akayesu* judgment (2 Sept 1998), para 135; *Rutaganda* judgment (6 Dec 1999), para 18; *Musema* judgment (27 Jan 2000), para 43; *Semanza* Appeal Judgment, para 153; *Gacumbitsi* Appeal Judgment, para 72.

186 *Kayishema and Ruzindana* judgment (21 May 1999), para 80; *Musema* judgment (27 Jan 2000), paras 42 and 75: '[a]ny evidence which is supported by other evidence logically possesses a greater probative value than evidence which stands alone, unless both pieces of evidence are not credible.'

187 *Prosecutor v Krnojelac*, Case No IT–97–25-T, Judgment, Trial Chamber, 15 March 2002, para 8.

instances, decide not to rely on the evidence at all.[188] Alternatively, 'the corroboration of testimonies, even by many witnesses, does not establish the credibility of those testimonies'.[189]

18.11.3 Documentary evidence

As highlighted in the *Brdanin and Talic* case, the standard of proof for admission of documents is lower than the standard which is applied when assessing the weight of the evidence.[190] In order to accord appropriate weight to a document, its authenticity and its source or authorship need to be considered.[191] The admission into evidence of a document does not have any bearing on the determination as to the authenticity or trustworthiness of the document. These are matters of weight to be assessed by the Trial Chamber at a later stage.[192] The absence of a signature or a stamp does not necessarily mean a document lacks authenticity.[193] In order to determine the authenticity of a document, the form, contents and purported use of the document, as well as the position of the parties on the matter, are important factors for consideration.[194]

As regards the form of documentary evidence, the Tribunals consider elements such as: whether it is an original copy; whether it is registered or enrolled with an institutional authority; whether it contains a signature; whether it is sealed, certified or stamped; whether it is officially authorised by an authority or organisation; and whether it is duly executed.[195] Regarding the content of a document, the Chamber will consider all circumstances of the case, 'including its relation to oral testimony given before the Chamber pertaining to the content of the document'.[196] These factors are not conclusive. In addition, it should be noted that '[a]s a general rule, it is insufficient to rely on any one factor alone as proof or disproof of the authenticity of the

---

188 *Krnojelac*, Judgment, para 71; *Prosecutor v Brdjanin*, Case No IT–99–36-T, Judgment (1 Sept 2004), para 27.

189 *Musema* judgment (27 Jan 2000), para 46; *Prosecutor v Tadic*, Judgment on Allegation on Contempt Against Prior Counsel Milan Vujin (31 Jan 2000), para 92.

190 *Brdanin and Talic*, Admission of Evidence Order (15 Feb 2002), para 18.

191 *The Prosecutor v Brdanin & Talic*, Case No IT–99–36-T, Order on the Standards governing the admission of evidence (15 Feb 2002), paras 18 and 19, referring to *The Prosecutor v Delalic et al*, Case No IT–96–21-T, Decision on the Motion of the Prosecution for the Admissibility of Evidence (19 March 1998), para 20.

192 *Prosecutor v Bizimungu et al*, No ICTR–99–50-T, Decision on Bicamumpaka's Request for Certification to Appeal a Decision on 6 October 2004 on Bicamumpaka's Motion Opposing the Admissibility of Testimony of Witnesses GFA, GKB, and GAP (17 Nov 2004), para 14.

193 *Brdanin and Talic*, Admission of Evidence Order (15 Feb 2002), para 20.

194 *Musema* judgment (27 Jan 2000), para 66.

195 Ibid, para 67.

196 Ibid, para 70.

document. Authenticity must be established through reference to all relevant factors'.[197]

Documents should not be considered in isolation. The Trial Chamber must review all the evidence and be satisfied that the prosecution proved the authenticity, reliability and completeness of the documents it is relying on beyond a reasonable doubt.[198] The Trial Chamber cannot, *à priori*, accept that the contents of the documents are true, accurate and a complete portrayal of the facts.[199] The reliability, relevance and probative value of the documents in the overall context of the evidence must be established before any significant weight can be accorded to it.

It has further been made clear that the reliability and credibility of the source may have an impact on the reliability and credibility of the document in question.[200] Although the fact that the source is the party which itself adduces the document does not necessarily render the document unreliable,[201] evidence which aims to support a defence of alibi is normally held to be more reliable when the source is not the accused himself.[202]

18.11.4 Weight of hearsay evidence

As already explained, the ICTY and ICTR rejected the common law approach in relation to the admission of hearsay evidence. Trial Chambers are nonetheless, generally, more cautious in assessing the weight of hearsay evidence. On the one hand, hearsay evidence is treated as 'indirect evidence with the understanding that such evidence is as much evidence as direct evidence'.[203] In order to accord any weight to hearsay evidence, such evidence must be reliable, and credible, just like any other evidence. As the Trial Chamber in the *Akayesu* case held, 'evidence which appears to be 'second-hand' is not, in and of itself, inadmissible; rather it is assessed, like all other evidence, on the basis of its credibility and relevance.'[204] The Appeals Chamber in Milosevic, on the other hand, confirmed that 'although it depends upon infinitely variable circumstances of the particular case, the weight or

197 Ibid, para 72.
198 *Prosecutor v Brdjanin*, Case No IT–99–36–T, Judgment (1 Sept 2004), para 32.
199 Guidelines Standards Governing the Admission of Evidence, (23 April 2003), para 4.
200 Ibid, para 63.
201 Ibid, para 61.
202 Ibid, para 63. On appeal Musema complained about this reasoning. It was held on his behalf that 'since all persons are entitled to equal treatment before the Tribunal, documents produced by him cannot be accorded a lesser status than documents produced by others' (*Musema*, Appeals Judgment (16 Nov 2001), para 40). The Trial Chamber disagreed, but stated that 'it is correct to state that the sole fact that evidence is proffered by the accused is no reason to find it, *ipso facto*, less reliable', para 50.
203 *Prosecutor v Brdjanin*, Case No IT–99–36–T, Judgment (1 Sept 2004), para 20.
204 *Prosecutor v Akayesu*, Case No ICTR–96–4–T, Judgment (2 Sept 1998) (ICTR), para 103.

probative value to be afforded to hearsay evidence will usually be less than that given to the testimony of a witness who has given it under a form of oath and who has been cross-examined.'[205] The reason for this caution is that the reliability of the hearsay evidence 'may be affected by a potential compounding of errors of perception and memory'.[206]

Particular emphasis has been given to the reliability of hearsay evidence.[207] In order to test the reliability of hearsay evidence, 'the content of the evidence and the circumstances under which it arose',[208] as well as the voluntariness, truthfulness and trustworthiness of the evidence are factors to be considered.[209]

Although there is no requirement of corroboration, most Trial Chambers are reluctant to rely on uncorroborated hearsay evidence even if it is reliable and credible. One ICTY Trial Chamber has affirmed that hearsay evidence has no weight unless substantiated by other evidence and it is shown to be reliable.[210] In another context, the same Trial Chamber held: 'It will be important, however, to evaluate with care the reliability of any hearsay evidence which has been admitted before reliance is placed on it for the purpose of establishing guilt'.[211] An ICTR Trial Chamber held that hearsay evidence, standing alone, has limited probative value; and that '[t]he reliability of the testimony and its probative value are likely to depend primarily on corroborative or contradictory evidence to be presented later by the Defence

205 *Prosecutor v Milosevic*, Decision on Admissibility of Prosecution Investigator's Evidence (30 Sept 2002), para 18; see also *Prosecutor v Kordic & Cerkez*, No IT–65–14/2-A, Judgment (17 Dec 2004), para 787, *Prosecutor v Tadic*, Case No IT–94–1, Separate of Judge Stephen on the Prosecutor's Motion Requesting Protective Measures for Victims and Witnesses (10 Aug 1995), pp 2–3; *Prosecutor v Simba*, No ICTR–2001–76-T, Judgment (13 Dec 2005), para 209.

206 *Prosecutor v Kamuhanda*, Decision on Kamuhanda's Motion to Admit Evidence Pursuant to Rule 89 of the Rules of Procedure and Evidence (10 Feb 2003), Case No ICTR–99–54A-T, para 10; *Prosecutor v Simic*, Judgment, para 23; *Naletilic*, Judgment, para 11 and *Krnojelac*, Judgment, para 70.

207 *Prosecutor v Natelic & Martinovic*, No IT–98–34-A, Judgment (3 May 2006), para 217.

208 *Prosecutor v Aleksovski*, Decision on the Prosecutor's Appeal on Admissibility of Evidence, Case No IT–95–14/1-AR73 (16 Feb 1999), para 15; *Prosecutor v Limaj et al*, Decision on the Prosecution's Motion to Admit Prior Statements as Substantive Evidence (25 April 2005), para 17.

209 *Prosecutor v Aleksovski*, Decision on the Prosecutor's Appeal on Admissibility of Evidence, Case No IT–95–14/1-AR73, (16 Feb 1999), para 15.

210 *Prosecutor v Limaj et al*, Oral Ruling of 18 November 2004, pp 447–49.

211 *Prosecutor v Limaj et al*, Decision on the Prosecution's Motions to Admit Prior Statements as Substantive Evidence (25 April 2005), para 27.

or Prosecution'.[212] It has further regularly been held that hearsay evidence is not inadmissible *per se*, it but it is considered with caution.[213]

Double hearsay raises greater concerns of reliability, because the truthfulness of that information depends not only on the credibility of the witness and the accuracy of his observation, but also on the credibility and reliability of the declarant.[214]

18.11.5 Credibility of witnesses

In order to determine the credibility of *viva voce* witnesses the Trial Chamber must consider 'their demeanor, conduct and character', as well as 'the probability, consistency and other features of their evidence, including the corroboration which may be forthcoming from other evidence and circumstances of the case', as well as 'the knowledge of the facts upon which they give evidence, their disinterestedness, their integrity, their veracity'.[215]

The Appeals Chamber has confirmed the Trial Chamber's practice of considering 'inconsistencies in the light of its evaluation of the overall credibility of each particular witness'.[216] Trial Chambers further assess the credibility of witnesses 'on the basis of the circumstances surrounding the testimony as a whole, and in light of the testimony of the earlier witnesses',[217] as well as the exhibits admitted.[218]

Whether or not a witness was honest in giving evidence is not the decisive factor in assessing the reliability of the witness's testimony. Where a witness is considered credible, the Trial Chamber must still make a determination on the reliability of the witness's testimony. The objective reliability of the evidence constitutes the primary basis for accepting the evidence.[219]

---

212 *Prosecutor v Bagosora et al*, Decision on Admissibility of Evidence of Witness DP (18 Nov 2003), para 8.

213 *Prosecutor v Nahimana et al*, No ICTR–99–52-T, Judgment and Sentence (3 Dec 2003), para 97.

214 *Prosecutor v Ntakirutimana*, No. ICTR–96–10-A, Judgment (13 Dec 2004), para 211. See also *Prosecutor v Aleksovski*, No IT- 95–14/1-AR73, Decision on Prosecutor's Appeal on Admission of Evidence (16 Feb 1999), para 15; *Prosecutor v Blaskic*, Decision on the Standing Objection of the Defence to the Admission of Hearsay with no Inquiry as to its Reliability, para 12.

215 *Prosecutor v Brdjanin*, Case No IT–99–36-T, Judgment, (1 Sept 2004), para 25. See also *The Prosecutor v Akayesu*, Case No ICTR–96–4-A, Appeals Chamber Decision, (1 June 2001), para 128.

216 Ibid, para 136.

217 *Simic*, Judgment, para 26.

218 *Ntagerura* Appeal Judgment, paras 172–74.

219 *Celibici* Appeal Judgment, paras 491 and 506.

18.11.6 Lapse of time

An expert for the defence in the *Kayishema and Ruzindana* case pointed out the dangers of relying on eyewitnesses, who were, in his opinion, often not a reliable source of information.[220] He contended that witnesses have often not paid attention to what they have seen, but will nevertheless give a firm answer to a question they do not know the answer to. He also emphasised the accuracy of recollection, which is undermined by the lapse of time, and mixed up with 'other external factors such as media reports or numerous conversations about the events'.[221]

The Trial Chamber agreed on certain matters and pointed out that these general observations are not in dispute. It agreed that the 'corroboration of events, even by many witnesses, does not necessarily make the event and/or its details correct'.[222] In the opinion of the Trial Chamber this does not, however, mean that the reflections of eyewitnesses have no value *per se*:

> [I]t is for the Trial Chamber to decide upon the reliability of the witness' testimony in light of its presentation in court and after its subjection to cross-examination. Thus, whilst corroboration of such testimony is not a guarantee of its accuracy, it is a factor that the Trial Chamber has taken into account when considering the testimonies.[223]

The fact that a witness is not specific about the dates of the event does not on its own render the witness unreliable.[224] As the ICTY Chamber held in the *Delalic* case, 'inconsistencies or inaccuracies between the prior statements and oral testimony of a witness, or between different witnesses, are relevant factors in judging weight but need not be, of themselves, a basis to find the whole of a witness' testimony unreliable'.[225] In the ICTY case of *Limaj*, the Chamber held that a time lapse of seven years between the events charged in the indictment and the witnesses' testimonies thereon, 'in all likelihood, affected the accuracy and reliability of the memories of witnesses, understandably so'.[226] The Trial Chamber held that this matter, nonetheless 'called for careful scrutiny when determining the weight to be given to any such evidence'.[227]

220 *Kayishema and Ruzindana* judgment (21 May 1999), para 68.
221 Ibid, para 69.
222 Ibid, para 70.
223 Ibid, para 70.
224 *Kayishema and Ruzindana*, Appeal Judgment (1 June 2001), para 325; *Krnojelac* judgment (15 March 2002), para 6.
225 *Delalic* Judgment (16 Nov 1998), para 596.
226 *Limaj* Judgment, para 12.
227 Ibid.

18.11.7 Traumas

An expert for the defence in the *Kayishema and Ruzindana* case addressed the fact that 'strong emotions experienced at the time of the events have a negative effect upon the quality of recollection'. In his opinion, traumatised witnesses tend to have buried their memories 'so deep that they are not easily, if at all, accessible'.[228] Not all experts agree on this issue. To the contrary, as the prosecutor pointed out, there are plenty of 'experts' who support the opposite.[229] It is also important to recognise the limits of an expert. The Trial Chamber held that 'different witnesses, like different academics, think differently'.[230] It stated:

> The Chamber is aware of the impact of trauma on the testimony of witnesses. However, the testimonies cannot be simply disregarded because they describe traumatic and horrific realities. Some inconsistencies and imprecision in the testimonies are expected and were carefully considered in light of the circumstances faced by the witnesses.[231]

This reasoning is consistent with other cases at the ICTY and ICTR. In the *Akayesu* case, for example, the Chamber worked on the basis of the assumption that all the witnesses suffered from post-traumatic or extreme stress disorders and '[i]nconsistencies or imprecisions in the testimonies, accordingly, have been assessed in the light of this assumption, personal background and the atrocities they have experienced or have been subjected to'.[232] Moreover, 'there is no recognised rule of evidence that traumatic circumstances necessarily render a witness's evidence unreliable. It must be demonstrated *in concrete* why "the traumatic context" renders a given witness unreliable'.[233]

Thus, it seems that implicitly the Trial Chamber agrees with the findings of Dr Pouget, that traumatic experiences affect the witness's ability to accurately

---

228 *Kayishema and Ruzindana* judgment (21 May 1999), para 73.
229 Ibid, para 74.
230 Ibid.
231 Ibid, para 75, where the Trial Chamber also stated that '[t]he possible traumatism of these witnesses caused by their painful experience of violence during the conflict in Rwanda is a matter of particular concern to the Chamber. The recounting of traumatic experience is likely to evoke memories of the fear and the pain once inflicted on the witness and thereby affect his or her ability fully or adequately to recount the sequence of events in a judicial context. The Chamber has considered the testimony of those witnesses in this light'; see *Akayesu* judgment (2 Sept 1998), para 142; *Rutaganda* judgment (6 Dec 1999), para 22.
232 *Akayesu* judgment, ibid, para 143.
233 *Prosecutor v Kunarac*, Appeal Judgment (12 June 2002), Case No IT–96–23-A, para 12; *Prosecutor v Furundzija*, Appeal Judgment (21 July 2000), Case No IT–95–17/1-A, para 109, where the Trial Chamber held that '[t]here is no reason why a person with [post-traumatic stress disorder] cannot be a perfectly reliable witness'.

reflect on the matter, but rather than being more cautious as a consequence, the Trial Chamber believes such witness and explains any inconsistency in this light.[234]

Although Trial Chambers generally excuse witnesses who narrate 'repetitive, continuous or traumatic' events in court in front of the accused for memory gaps regarding exact dates or time and/or sequence of these events,[235] discrepancies in relation to matters peripheral to the charges in the indictment in general weaken the credibility of the witness in question.[236] Indeed, although it seems to have become the general practice, particularly at the ICTR, to give traumatised witnesses a greater benefit of the doubt than witnesses who do not suffer from trauma, there are Trial Chambers who have taken a different course. In the ICTY case of *Limaj*, in which members of the Kosovar Liberation Army were standing accused, the Trial Chamber adopted a reverse approach. In evaluating the reliability of the testimonies given by traumatised witnesses, the Trial Chamber took into consideration 'that any observation they made at the time may have been affected by stress and fear; this has called for particular scrutiny on the part of the Chamber'.[237] The Trial Chamber further took account of the possibility that cultural factors of loyalty and honour, the witnesses being so inter-connected, may have affected the reliability of the evidence given by traumatised witnesses.[238]

Trauma should not be perceived as a mitigating factor explaining inconsistencies, even if that leads to the undesired result of an acquittal. It is submitted that the judges in *Limaj* correctly interpreted the principles of evaluation. Moreover, the defence in the *Musema* case was correct in stating that 'the testimony of a Prosecution witness is either credible or not credible and that if the credibility of such testimony is vitiated, the testimony must be regarded as not credible, notwithstanding the origin of the factors affecting its credibility'.[239]

---

234 *Akayesu* judgment (2 Sept 1998), paras 142–56; *Kunarac, Vukovic and Kovac* judgment (22 Feb 2001), para 564.
235 *Prosecutor v Kunarac*, Case No IT–96–23, Appeal Judgment (12 June 2002), para 267; see also Celibici Appeal Judgment, para 497 and *Kunarac* Appeal Judgment, para 254.
236 *Prosecutor v Simic*, Judgment, para 22; *Prosecutor v Krnojelac*, Judgment, para 69.
237 *Limaj* Judgment, para 15.
238 Ibid.
239 *Musema*, Appeal Judgment (16 Nov 2001), para 58. The Appeals Chamber disagreed. It held that the fact that 'the Trial Chamber should take into account the impact of trauma on a witness's memory implies the Trial Chamber's awareness of such factors (as in the case of the passage of time) and of their possible effect on the ability of the witness to recount events impartially and accurately'.

18.11.8 Prior statements

A distinction should be made between: (1) witness statements and other non-judicial testimonies; (2) testimonies before this Tribunal; and (3) statements before other judicial bodies.[240]

As regards discrepancies between witnesses' written statements and their oral statements in court, the Trial Chamber held that the written statements of witnesses are not evidence *per se*, but may be so admitted, in part or in whole, to undermine a witness's credentials.[241] The Chamber will compare the written statements with the oral testimony and consider the discrepancies between the two. In doing so, the Chamber will take account of the significant lapses of time between the events, the written and oral statements,[242] language and translation problems, and whether or not the witness had read the written statement.[243] It has further been recognised that 'it lies in the nature of criminal proceedings that a witness may be asked different questions at trial than he was asked in prior interviews and that he may remember additional details when specifically asked in court'.[244] Thus, a lot depends on the 'conditions under which the prior statement was provided, as well as on other factors relevant to, or indicia of, the prior statement's reliability or credibility, or both'.[245] Given the fact that the written statements were not made under solemn declaration and not taken by judicial officers, 'the probative value attached to the statements is, in the Chamber's view, considerably less than direct sworn testimony before the Chamber, the truth of which has been subjected to the test of cross-examination'.[246]

The Trial Chamber in *Limaj* was faced with prior inconsistent statements of witnesses who had completely reversed their stories and declared hostile to the prosecution. The Trial Chamber accepted that 'as a matter of principle, prior inconsistent statements may possibly have some positive probative force, at least if they corroborate other apparently credible evidence adduced from other witnesses during trial'. In the instant proceedings, the Chamber was not persuaded that the prior inconsistent statements of two witnesses could be safely relied upon 'as the sole or principal basis for proof of a material fact. In the case of these two witnesses, this is especially so because

---

240 *Musema* judgment (27 Jan 2000), para 83.
241 *Kayishema and Ruzindana* judgment (21 May 1999), para 77.
242 Ibid, para 77; *Akayesu* judgment (2 Sept 1998), para 140, where the Chamber held that memory over time naturally degenerates.
243 *Akayesu* judgment, ibid, para 137; *Rutaganda* judgment (6 Dec 1999), para 19; *Musema* judgment (27 Jan 2000), para 85.
244 *Limaj* Judgment, para 13; *Naletilic* Trial Judgement, para 10; *Vasiljevic* Trial Judgment, para 21.
245 *Musema* judgment, para 83.
246 *Akayesu* judgment (2 Sept 1998), para 137; *Musema* judgment, ibid, para 86.

each witness, in oral evidence, disavowed, in very material respects, what previously had been stated in the interview.'[247]

Trial Chambers will consider the prior statement in so far as the inconsistencies between the prior statement and the oral testimony 'raise doubt in relation to the particular piece of evidence in question or, where such inconsistencies are found to be material to the witnesses' evidence as a whole'.[248] The Trial Chamber will listen to the explanation of the witnesses[249] for the inconsistencies that may occur and will, in light of all circumstances of the case, determine whether this explanation removes the doubt. In order to remove the doubt, the explanation needs to be of substance; an explanation of mere procedure does not suffice.[250] The Trial Chamber in the ICTR case of *Kayishema and Ruzindana* also held that a doubt can be removed with the corroboration of other evidence, even though corroboration is not necessary.[251]

As far as point (2) is concerned, inconsistency between two testimonies of the same witness, both given under solemn declaration, affects the credibility and reliability of the later testimony.[252] The Chamber only assesses the credibility and reliability in the later test, as the earlier one has been assessed by a Chamber.[253]

In assessing the probative value of statements made before other judicial bodies, the Chamber relies on the general principles, 'taking into account the circumstances and conditions in which the documents were produced'.[254] However, 'judicial testimonies (and other testimonies made under oath or solemn declaration) tend, as a general rule, to demonstrate greater reliability than non-judicial testimonies'.[255]

247 *Limaj* judgment, para 14.
248 *Kayishema and Ruzindana* judgment (21 May 1999), para 77.
249 *Musema* judgment (27 Jan 2000), para 88.
250 An explanation commonly given is that the interviewer did not correctly transcribe what the witness said. In absence of evidence supporting that allegation, such explanation does normally not remove the doubt raised. *Kayishema and Ruzindana* judgment (21 May 1999), para 78. An explanation relating to the contents of the interview may, however, suffice to remove the doubt, ibid, para 79; *Prosecutor v Ignace Bagilishema*, Judgment (7 June 2001), Case No ICTR–95–1A-T, para 24, where it was held that issues, such as traumas, lapse of time, language problems and related issues, may provide an adequate explanation for inconsistencies. However, where the inconsistencies cannot be so explained to the satisfaction of the Chamber, the reliability of witness testimony may be questioned.
251 *Kayishema and Ruzindana* judgment, ibid, para 80.
252 *Musema* judgment (27 Jan 2000), para 89.
253 Ibid, para 90.
254 Ibid, para 92.
255 Ibid, para 94.

18.11.9 Language problems

Language problems do not only occur in relation to prior written statements, but also in court. In the ICTR, most witnesses testify in Kinyarwanda, which then has to be translated into English and French. In the ICTY, most witnesses testify in Serb-Croat, thus similar problems occur. In the ICTR, judges have relied on a language expert to explain how to interpret Kinyarwandan terminology. The expert stated that 'in ascertaining the specific meaning of certain words and expressions in Kinyarwanda, it is necessary to place them contextually, both in time and in space'.[256] Language difficulties 'have been taken into consideration by the Chamber in its assessment of all evidence presented to it, including evidence for which the source was not available for examination by the Chamber'.[257]

18.11.10 Cultural aspects

Cultural aspects may be the cause for inconsistencies. Cultural aspects may include language problems, such as the intonation of the language.[258] An expert pointed out that it is inherent to Rwandan culture to spread the word of someone else as if it were your own. This is an important aspect in relation to eyewitnesses who come to testify at the ICTR. Witnesses have sometimes testified to an event, which they themselves did not experience, but someone else in the community did. Thus, eyewitness accounts may have been reported as first-hand accounts, although they were in fact second-hand accounts. The Tribunal has taken this cultural phenomenon into consideration in its assessment of a witness's credibility without failing to recognise that Rwandan witnesses could, like anyone else, distinguish between what they had heard and what they had seen.[259]

Cultural aspects may also include lack of familiarity with the manner in which the trials are conducted at the ad hoc tribunals, or equipment used, such as 'spatiotemporal identification mechanisms and techniques (dates, times, distances, locations, use of maps, films, photographs and other graphic representations)'.[260] Also, cultural restraints may explain why the witness is reluctant to give a direct answer to questions which he perceived as delicate.[261] These are a few examples in which the witness's appearance of credibility may be affected. The Tribunals have determined that one should be sensitive as regards the cultural identity of the witness. Equipment a witness is not

---

256 *Akayesu* judgment (2 Sept 1998), para 146.
257 *Musema* judgment (27 Jan 2000), para 102.
258 *Rutaganda* judgment (6 Dec 1999), para 23.
259 *Prosecutor v Akayesu*, Appeal Judgment (1 June 2001), Case No ICTR–96–4-A, para 155.
260 Ibid, para 156.
261 Ibid.

familiar with should not be used.[262] Moreover, the Chambers held that no adverse inference should be drawn from inconsistencies caused by cultural restraints.[263]

Cultural aspects may indeed explain why a witness, for example, gives evasive answers or behaves in another manner which generates a perception of unreliability even where the testimony is, in fact, reliable. However, in some situations, cultural differences negatively impact on the reliability of the testimony. There may, for example, be cultural reasons why a testimony should be treated with caution. A clear example is the oath. The Trial Chambers attach great importance to the witness's solemn declaration. However, the oath may not have the same significance in the cultures to which the accused and witnesses for and against him belong.

Moreover, ethnic loyalty and solidarity may be a reason for a witness to give false testimony against an accused. In *Limaj*, some former Kosovo Liberation Army (KLA) members who testified for the prosecution against their former KLA fellow:

> left the Chamber with a distinct impression that it was materially influenced by a strong sense of association with the KLA in general, and one or more of the Accused in particular. It appeared that overriding loyalties had a bearing upon the willingness of some witnesses to speak the truth in court about some issues. It is not disputed that notions of honour and other group values have a particular relevance to the cultural background of witnesses with Albanian roots in Kosovo.

In assessing the credibility of the witnesses, the judges carefully considered their cultural background, thereby relying on an expert who explained the Kosovar culture.[264]

18.11.11 Expert evidence

The Trial Chamber will rely on expert evidence to the extent the subject matter is within the expertise of the expert. The expert evidence further has to be reliable. In weighing expert testimony, the Trial Chamber will take into consideration the basis upon which the expert formed an opinion, and the expert's explanation on that, corroboration with other evidence, and the extent to which the accused has had the opportunity to test the accuracy of the information given by the expert.[265] The competence of the experts, the

---

262 Ibid.
263 Ibid.
264 *Limaj* judgment, para 13.
265 *Prosecutor v Bizimungu et al*, No ICTR–99–50-T, Decision on Defence Motion for Exclusion of Portions of Testimony of Expert Witness Dr Alison Des Forges (2 Sept 2005), para 21.

methodologies used by the expert and the credibility of the findings by the expert are also important considerations in evaluating expert evidence.[266] Alleged bias of the expert witness and his relationship to the accused are also matters that may be weighed in assessing the expert's credibility.[267]

An expert's refusal to disclose the sources upon which he or she has based his or her information may be a factor undermining the weight to be given to the testimony, depending on the other sources the expert has used in forming his or her opinion.[268] An expert who is more experienced than another is not necessarily accorded more weight.[269]

18.11.12 Standard on appeal

The task of assessing the evidence and giving it its appropriate weight, which includes the determination of the credibility of witness statements, lies with the Trial Chamber. Therefore, 'the Appeals Chamber must give a margin of deference to a finding of fact reached by a Trial Chamber'.[270] Only where no reasonable tribunal of fact could have reached the conclusion of guilty beyond reasonable doubt will the Appeals Chamber intervene.[271] This is understandable in light of the fact that an appeal 'is not an opportunity for a party to have a *de novo* review of their case'.[272] Thus, the Trial Chamber, having seen and heard the witnesses is in a much better position to determine their credibility.[273]

The Trial Chambers have nonetheless a duty to provide a 'reasoned opinion in writing' (Art 22(2) of the ICTY Statute; Art 21(2) of the ICTR Statute and r 88(C) of the Rules) explaining how they reached their conclusions.[274] They are thereby not required to give reasoning for each step they took in the

266 *Prosecutor v Blagojevic & Jokic*, No IT–02–60-T, Judgment (17 Jan 2005), para 27.

267 *Prosecutor v Milosevic*, No IT–02–54-T, Decision on Admissibility of Expert Report of Vasilije Krestic (7 Dec 2005), para 5.

268 *Prosecutor v Bizimungu et al*, No ICTR–99–50-T, Decision on Defence Motion for Exclusion of Portions of Testimony of Expert Witness Dr Alison Des Forges (2 Sept 2005), paras 17 and 25.

269 *Prosecutor v Kunarac*, Appeal Judgment (12 June 2002), Case No IT–96–23-A, para 21.

270 *Musema*, Appeal Judgment (16 Nov 2001), para 18; *Akayesu*, Appeal Judgment (1 June 2001), para 232; *Prosecutor v Tadic*, Appeal Judgment (15 July 1999), Case No IT–94–1-A, para 64; *Furundzija*, Appeal Judgment (21 July 2000), paras 37, 63.

271 *Musema*, Appeal Judgment (16 Nov 2001), para 17.

272 Ibid.

273 *Aleksovski*, Appeal Judgment (24 March 2000), para 63; *Kayishema and Ruzindana*, Appeal Judgment (1 June 2001), para 319.

274 ICTY Rules, r 98*ter* (C). In *Furundzija*, Appeals Judgment (21 July 2000), para 69, the ICTY relied on ECHR jurisprudence, stating that the right to a reasoned opinion is an aspect of the fair trial requirement embodied in Arts 20 and 21 of the Statute.

process of weighing and assessing the evidence.[275] There is no guiding principle on the extent to which Trial Chambers have to be specific about their reasons to reject or accept a witness testimony as reliable and credible. The reliability and credibility of witness testimony has to be determined on a case-by-case basis.[276]

In addition, the Appeals Chamber of the ICTY has stated that although the evidence produced may not have been referred to by a Trial Chamber, based on the particular circumstances of a given case, it may nevertheless be reasonable to assume that the Trial Chamber had taken it into account.[277] This is particularly so in the evaluation of witness testimony, including inconsistencies and the overall credibility of a witness. A Trial Chamber is not required to set out in detail why it accepted or rejected a particular testimony.[278] In the *Celebici* case, the Appeals Chamber stated that:

> [t]he Trial Chamber is not obliged in its Judgment to recount and justify its findings in relation to every submission made during trial. It was within its discretion to evaluate the inconsistencies highlighted and to consider whether the witness, when the testimony is taken as a whole, was reliable and whether the evidence was credible. Small inconsistencies cannot suffice to render the whole testimony unreliable.[279]

In conclusion, although Trial Chambers occasionally exclude evidence for lack of probative value, relevance or reliability, the general policy is to admit evidence, the weight to be determined at the deliberation stage. This also applies to indirect evidence, such as hearsay and paper evidence. Over the years, particularly at the ICTY, there has been an increasing tendency to facilitate the admission of indirect and paper evidence, thereby undermining the principle of orality. This is not a problem *per se*, given that the trials are conducted by professional judges, as in civil law systems. If the judges give the admitted evidence the weight it deserves, no more no less, this is not a problem at all. As indicated above, judges review indirect and paper evidence with caution. However, corroboration is not required, which allows trial judges to establish guilt on uncorroborated indirect evidence. Most Trial Chambers are reluctant to rely on uncorroborated indirect evidence, but there is no

275 *Prosecutor v Delalic*, Appeal Judgment, Appeals Chamber (20 Feb 2001), Case No IT–96–21-A, para 481.
276 *Ruiz Torija v Spain*, ECHR Judgment (9 Dec 1994), para 29, cited in *Furundzija*, Appeal Judgment (21 July 2000), para 69.
277 *Musema*, Appeal Judgment (16 Nov 2001), para 19; *Akayesu*, Appeal Judgment (1 June 2001), para 306.
278 *Musema*, Appeal Judgment, ibid, para 20; *Akayesu*, Appeal Judgment, ibid, para 306.
279 *Prosecutor v Delalic and Others*, Appeal Judgment, Appeals Chamber (20 Feb 2001), Case No IT–96–21-A, para 498.

uniform practice to disregard such evidence. Moreover, factors, such as traumas, time lapse, language problems, cultural barriers and similar factors, which are normally perceived as undermining a witness statement, in the tribunals, are used to explain inconsistencies and tend to be perceived as increasing, rather than decreasing, the reliability and credibility of the testimony.

Chapter 19

Nuremberg, Tokyo and the birth of modern international criminal law

19.1 INTRODUCTION

Following their victory in the Second World War, the allied powers established International Military Tribunals (IMT) in Nuremberg and Tokyo to try war criminals from the German and Japanese forces respectively. These trials were not limited to military personnel, but encompassed a variety of civilian officials. The creation of these tribunals was without precedent, and the law and procedure of the tribunals represented the first proper expression of international criminal law and procedure. This chapter will examine and appraise the law of the tribunals, as well as the development of international criminal law in the post-Second World War era.

19.2 EFFORTS TO TRY INTERNATIONAL CRIMES PRIOR TO THE SECOND WORLD WAR

Previous to the Nuremberg and Tokyo tribunals there had been sporadic instances in history where efforts had been made to bring individuals to account for what would be regarded today as international crimes. In Naples in 1268, Conradin von Hohenstafen, Duke of Suabia, was tried, convicted and executed for initiating an unjust war. In 1474, Peter von Hagenbach was convicted of crimes against 'the laws of God and man', including murder and rape, by an international tribunal comprising of judges from Alsace, Austria, Germany and Switzerland in respect of offences committed during his occupation of Breisach on behalf of Charles, the Duke of Burgundy.[1] Although there were calls for the King of England to be called to account for 'war against the natural rights of all mankind' following the US revolutionary

---

1 G Schwarzenberger, *International Law As Applied by Courts and Tribunals*, 1968, London: Stevens, pp 462–66.

war,[2] another 400 years elapsed before a proposal was tabled for the creation of an international criminal court to hear cases relating to atrocities committed during the Franco–Prussian war in 1870. Lack of interest by European governments saw the proposal eventually losing interest and was not pursued further.[3]

Following the end of the First World War, the Commission on the Responsibility of the Authors of the War and on the Enforcement of Penalties for Violations of the Laws and Customs of War, established by the Paris Peace Conference in 1919, proposed that an ad hoc tribunal be set up to try those responsible for war crimes and violations of the laws of humanity. As in the past, the proposal did not come to fruition but was set aside in favour of trying the Kaiser before an international tribunal under the terms of the 1919 Peace Treaty of Versailles (Versailles Treaty). Other cases were to be tried by Allied military courts. In the event, the Kaiser fled to the Netherlands. His extradition was requested by the Allied powers; however, the Netherlands refused the request on the grounds that Dutch law only provided for extradition to a sovereign State, not a coalition of States as was the case with the Allies. Moreover, he was deemed by the Dutch Government at the time to be a political fugitive. No further serious attempts were made to secure his presence for trial and the Kaiser remained in the Netherlands until his death. Also, under the terms of the Versailles Treaty, Germany had agreed to surrender suspected war criminals to the Allies for trial by specially established tribunals. However, since German capitulation was not unconditional the German Government in essence possessed an effective veto vis-à-vis the demands of the Allies. As a result, when the Allies demanded during the Paris Peace Conference in 1920, the extradition of 896 Germans that were accused of violating the laws of war, Germany refused to comply. As a compromise, the Allies agreed that some individuals would be tried before the Criminal senate of the Imperial Court of Justice in Leipzig. Only 12 accused were actually brought to trial and the Leipzig trials were hugely unpopular with the German press and public. The trials that took place dealt mainly with the treatment of survivors of torpedoed ships and prisoners of war and not with the actual conduct of hostilities.[4] The hearings fizzled out after a small number of cases had been considered. Some of these cases do, however, remain of value for the law set down.[5]

---

2 JJ Paust, 'Aggression Against Authority: The Crime of Oppression, Politicide and Other Crimes Against Human Rights', 18 *Case W Res J Int'l L* (1986), 283, pp 283–84.

3 P Boissier, *From Solferino to Tsushima: History of the International Committee of the Red Cross*, 1985, Geneva: Henri Durant Institute, pp 283–84.

4 See IF Willis, *Prologue to Nuremberg: The Politics and Diplomacy of Punishing War Criminals of the First World War*, 1982, Westport, Conn: Greenwood.

5 *Dover Castle* case, 16 *AJIL* (1922), 704; *Llandovery Castle* case, 16 *AJIL* (1922), 708; *Trial of Emil Mueller*, 16 *AJIL* (1922), 684.

19.3 THE BACKGROUND TO THE ESTABLISHMENT OF THE INTERNATIONAL MILITARY TRIBUNALS

Even early during the Second World War, news reached Western Europe of the atrocities committed by German forces and their allies against the Jews, other minority civilian groups and against prisoners of war. As early in the war as 1941, Churchill and Roosevelt made statements expressing their intention to seek 'retribution' for these offences. Subsequent discussions amongst the allied powers and governments-in-exile developed the policy that war criminals would face prosecution after the war. In a note sent by the British Government to the other allied governments on 6 August 1942, it was suggested that agreement should be reached as to how trials should proceed so as to ensure rapid justice, prevent individuals and groups exacting their own revenge, and so that Europe could return to a peaceful atmosphere. Significantly, the note also proposed that:

> In dealing with war criminals, whatever the court, it should apply the existing laws of war and no specific *ad hoc* law should be enacted.

This was not the end of the matter and views had changed by the time that Roosevelt, Stalin and Churchill came to sign the Moscow declaration on 30 October 1943. The declaration stated that German war criminals would be returned to the countries in which their offences had taken place, and 'that they [would] be brought back to the scene of their crimes and judged on the spot by the peoples whom they have outraged'. Shortly after this, Churchill proposed that the major war criminals should be declared as 'world outlaws' and be shot without trial.

The IMT was formally established by the London Agreement of 8 August 1945 between the Governments of Great Britain, the US, France and the Union of Soviet Socialist Republics.[6] The Charter of the IMT was annexed to the London Agreement. The Charter provided for the trials of 'major war criminals of the European Axis'.[7] Other war criminals were to be tried by individual allied powers responsible for the administration of occupied Germany in accordance with Allied Control Council Law No 10, while other countries were permitted to prosecute individuals on the basis of the territorial principle of jurisdiction, that is, with regard to offences perpetrated on their respective territories. Moreover, in 1946 the International Military Tribunal for the Far East (IMTFE) sitting in Tokyo was established by order of the Allied Supreme Commander of the Pacific Theatre of Operations,

---

6 See generally T Taylor, *The Anatomy of the Nuremberg Trials: A Personal Memoire*, 1993, London: Bloomsbury; A Tusa and J Tusa, *The Nuremberg Trial*, 1983, London: Macmillan.

7 Charter of the International Military Tribunal at Nuremberg (IMT Charter), Art 1.

General Douglas McArthur, whose purpose was to try the major Japanese war criminals. It is obvious, therefore, that the legal bases of the two tribunals are different; whereas the IMT was premised on a treaty, the IMTFE was the result of a domestic statute adopted by an occupying force.

19.3.1 The law and jurisdiction of the International Military Tribunal (IMT) at Nuremberg

The London Charter for the Nuremberg IMT (Nuremberg Charter)[8] is brief but is of enormous significance for the development of international criminal law. The Charter defines offences and sets out the parameters for individual criminal responsibility with regard to these offences. Both the Charter and the judgment of the IMT have been extremely influential on the evolution of the law and procedure of more contemporary institutions, namely, the International Tribunals for the Former Yugoslavia and Rwanda (ICTY and ICTR, respectively), as well as the newly established International Criminal Court (ICC).

The subject matter jurisdiction of the IMT was set out under Art 6 of the Tribunal's Charter, which provided:

> The tribunal established by the agreement referred to in Art 1 hereof for the trial and punishment of the major war criminals of the European Axis countries shall have the power to try and punish persons who, acting in the interests of the European Axis countries, whether as individuals or as members of organisations, committed any of the following crimes.
>
> The following acts, or any of them, are crimes coming within the jurisdiction of the tribunal for which there shall be individual responsibility:
>
> (a) Crimes Against Peace: namely, planning, preparation, initiation or waging of a war of aggression, or a war in violation of international treaties, agreements, or assurances, or participation in a common plan or conspiracy for the accomplishment of any of the foregoing.
>
> (b) War Crimes: namely, violations of the laws or customs of war. Such violations shall include, but not be limited to, murder, ill treatment or deportation to slave labour or for any other purpose of civilian population of or in occupied territory, murder or ill treatment of prisoners of war or persons on the seas, killing of hostages, plunder of public or private property, wanton destruction of cities, towns or villages, or devastation not justified by military necessity.
>
> (c) Crimes Against Humanity: namely, murder, extermination, enslavement, deportation, and other inhumane acts committed against any

---

8 UKTS 4 (1945), Cmnd 6671; 5 UNTS 251.

civilian population, before or during the war, or persecutions on political, racial, or religious grounds in execution of or in connection with any crime within the jurisdiction of the tribunal whether or not in violation of the domestic law of the country where perpetrated. Leaders, organisers, instigators, and accomplices, participating in the formulation or execution of a common plan or conspiracy to commit any of the foregoing crimes are responsible for all acts performed by any persons in execution of such plan.

Mindful that these offences had not been set out in this manner before, the IMT in its judgment set out the legal basis behind the offences. The Tribunal approached its explanation in a bullish way, stating that:

The Charter makes the planning or waging of a war of aggression or a war in violation of international treaties a crime; and it is therefore not strictly necessary to consider whether and to what extent aggressive war was a crime before the execution of the London Agreement. But in view of the great importance of the questions of law involved, the tribunal has heard full argument from the prosecution and the defence, and will express its view on the matter.[9]

The IMT rejected the argument presented by the defence that the Charter breached the principle that there can be no punishment without law, *nullum crimen sine lege, nulla poena sine lege*, by arguing that this maxim was a principle of justice and not a limitation of sovereignty. Its rationale was that if a war of aggression is illegal in international law, then it necessarily follows that those who plan and wage such a war are committing a crime.[10]

The IMT found that:

Occupying the positions they did in the Government of Germany, the defendants or at least some of them must have known of the treaties signed by Germany, outlawing recourse to war for the settlement of international disputes, they must have known that they were acting in defiance of all international law when in complete deliberation they carried out their designs of invasion and aggression. On this view of the case alone, it would appear that the maxim has no application to the present facts.[11]

The inherent problem with formulating the offence of crimes against peace lies with the fact that even if aggression could be deemed to have been illegal

---

9 IMT judgment, reprinted in 41 *AJIL* (1947), 172, p 217.
10 Ibid, p 218.
11 Ibid, p 217.

by 1939, this would at best be considered an act entailing State responsibility rather than personal criminal responsibility. The League of Nations Covenant had by no means prohibited recourse to armed force for the settlement of international disputes, although it had established a complex conciliatory mechanism that was aimed at delaying recourse to violence rather than prohibiting it altogether.[12] New attempts to define aggression as an international crime took place with the 1923 Draft Treaty on Mutual Assistance and the 1924 Protocol for the Pacific Settlement of International Disputes. Article I of the 1923 Draft Treaty declared that aggressive war was an international crime, as did the 1924 Protocol. Although the Protocol did not enter into force, 48 States recommended its ratification in the League Assembly, thereby indicating a willingness to outlaw such behaviour.[13] Where prior attempts to prohibit war had formally failed, the 1928 General Treaty for the Renunciation of War as an Instrument of National Policy, also known as the Kellog-Briand Treaty or Pact of Paris,[14] outlawed recourse to war entirely. However, not even the Pact of Paris specifically penalised aggression and, hence, it can hardly be asserted that as a matter of positive international law the perpetration of aggression entailed with certainty the personal liability of the culprit. The IMT in its judgment made reference to the aforementioned instruments to which Germany was a party, the result of which was to denounce the waging of aggressive war as well as certain methods of warfare, and nonetheless found that the crime of aggression had been established under customary law. Interestingly, the Tribunal attempted an analogy with the 1907 Hague Conventions and its annexed Regulations, stating that neither the Hague Regulations expressly penalised the breaches contained therein – that is, much like the Pact of Paris – but went on to say that despite non-explicit criminalisation breaches of this nature had long been prosecuted by national courts.[15] This analogy hardly supports the Tribunal's argument, since it is an example of a legal instrument having attained the status of customary law through consistent and continuous State practice, whereas the same cannot be said of the crime of aggression. A number of scholars, such as Finch, rejected the argument that the crime of aggression could have been established by reference to unratified treaties and resolutions of international conferences that were not sanctioned by subsequent national or international action. He argued, moreover, that if aggressive war in violation of international treaties was a crime entailing individual responsibility, then such responsibility should also encompass those in the UK and France that

---

12 See I Brownlie, *International Law and the Use of Force by States*, 1963, Oxford: OUP, 62.
13 On 24 Sept 1927, the Assembly of the League of Nations unanimously adopted a resolution regarding wars of aggression, the preamble of which expressly stated that such wars constituted international crimes. See IMT judgment, reprinted in 41 *AJIL* (1947), 172, p 220.
14 94 LNTS 57.
15 Op cit, IMT judgment, note 9, p 218.

compelled Czechoslovakia to consent to German aggression, as well as those Soviet officials that were responsible for the invasion of Poland in violation of their non-aggression pact with Germany of 23 August 1939 – although Germany had herself invaded Poland 16 days earlier.[16] Other jurists, nonetheless, were of the view that the waging of an aggressive war was an international crime.[17]

Since a war of aggression could only be committed by persons in the highest echelons of authority and after formulating a plan to that effect, the Tribunal set out the parameters of criminal participation in crimes against peace. First, it held that the conspiracy charge could only apply to the crime of aggressive war, although the indictment had applied it to all the offences in the Charter. It rejected the prosecution's argument that any significant participation in the workings of the Nazi Party since its inception in 1919 was evidence of involvement in a conspiracy to commit the offences that were within the Tribunal's jurisdiction, holding that the conspiracy must not have been too far removed from the time of decision and of action.[18] The IMT found that plans to wage aggressive war had been revealed as early as 5 November 1937, if not earlier, but this involved many separate plans rather than a single conspiracy embracing them all. The Tribunal was of the opinion that a crime against peace required not mere participation in the Nazi conspiracy, but also an intention to commit aggressive war. Thus, Schacht was acquitted of this charge because he terminated his financial and armament building activity in 1937, after discovering Hitler's intention to invade other nations.[19] The IMT held that, even though the plan or conspiracy may have been conceived by only one person, its status as a conspiracy remains unaltered where other persons participate in its execution. Indeed, as the Tribunal pointed out, since Hitler could not have waged aggressive war on his own, it was evident that those executing the plan did not avoid responsibility 'by showing that they acted under the directions of the man who conceived it'.[20] The unsatisfactory, from a legal point of view, formulation of the crime against peace in Art 6(a) of the IMT Charter did not readily evolve as a principle of either treaty or customary law in the post-Nuremberg era. It was not until the 1998 ICC Statute that it was included, albeit without any force until an appropriate definition is agreed upon in the future by participating States. For a more comprehensive analysis of developments on the crime of aggression in the post-Nuremberg era see Chapter 21, section 21.3.1.

The IMT was more vague when it came to justifying the existence of crimes against humanity. It had been common knowledge that atrocities against

16   G Finch, 'The Nuremberg Trial and International Law', 41 *AJIL* (1947), 20, pp 26–28.
17   S Glueck, 'The Nuremberg Trial and Aggressive War', 59 *Harv L Rev* (1946), 396; Lord Wright, 'War Crimes Under International Law', 62 *LQR* (1946), 40.
18   Op cit, IMT judgment, note 9, p 222.
19   Q Wright, 'The Law of the Nuremberg Trial', 41 *AJIL* (1947), 38, p 67.
20   Op cit, IMT judgment, note 9, p 223.

German Jews and minority groups had been carried out by the Nazi regime, as well as similar offences against other civilians of other countries occupied by Germany. Whilst the brutality against civilians of other countries during the course of fighting or occupation might have been covered by 'established' international law on war crimes and aggression, atrocities against a State's own citizens were not. Article 6(c) of the Charter, concerning crimes against humanity, was drafted so as to encompass these acts, which had occurred on such a massive scale that they could not be ignored. Article 6(c) of the Charter covered acts against 'any' civilian population.[21] However, the IMT sidestepped any discussion of precedents for crimes against humanity in international law. Instead, it took the approach of delineating its own jurisdiction over such offences:

> The tribunal is of the opinion that revolting and horrible as many of these crimes were, it has not been satisfactorily proved that they were done in execution of, or in connection with, any such crime.[22]

Although it had found that the Jewish minority in Germany, as well as other minority groups, had been subjected to acute discrimination and extermination policies long before the outbreak of the Second World War, in order to describe these pre-war acts as crimes against humanity it had to establish that they were committed in 'execution of, or in connection with, any crime within the jurisdiction of the tribunal'. Evidently, the Tribunal was not prepared to go that far, possibly because of the evidentiary difficulties this exercise would entail, taking account of the limited resources and time it was allocated in carrying out its task. Alternatively, it could be said that because there was more than ample evidence of large scale atrocities perpetrated against civilians and other minority groups in the course of the war there was no need to indulge, at least for the purposes of that particular prosecution, in other events that were harder to establish in legal terms. The Tribunal did not, however, exclude the possibility that crimes against humanity might be committed also before a war.

Although Art 6(c) required a link between crimes against humanity and crimes against peace or war crimes, it was not entirely clear whether international law required an additional nexus between crimes against humanity and the existence of an armed conflict. Control Council Law No 10 later provided for the prosecution of crimes against humanity, without requiring a nexus to other crimes in the IMT Charter, or other crimes in general. In fact, prosecutions under this law by US military courts resulted in the conviction

---

21 Art 6(b) dealt with acts committed against the 'civilian population of, or in, occupied territory'.
22 Op cit, IMT judgment, note 9, p 249.

of hundreds of Nazi soldiers and officers and, significantly, these courts were not limited to the examination of post-1939 events, but looked into crimes perpetrated before the outbreak of the war. Article 6(c) of the Charter distinguished between two categories of punishable acts: first, murder, extermination, enslavement, deportation and other inhuman acts committed against any civilian population, before or during the war; and second, persecution on political, racial or religious grounds.[23] For a more comprehensive analysis of the contemporary formulation of crimes against humanity, see Chapter 6.

The legality of the concept of 'war crimes' was unquestionable, although the defence argued that the Tribunal did not enjoy jurisdiction for violation of the laws or customs of war. This argument was correctly rejected on the basis that war crimes prosecutions against aliens had a long history in the law of nations.[24] Since any nation could initiate criminal proceedings, it was therefore possible for a group of nations, in this case the Allies, to do so in concert. As far as the law of nations was concerned, the concept of war crimes was precisely delineated under treaty and customary law. Efforts to codify and enforce this law had begun as early as 1864 with the adoption of the Geneva Convention for the Amelioration of the Condition of the Wounded in Armies in the Field.[25] The most significant codification of the *jus in bello* principles was that undertaken in the context of the 1899 and 1907 Hague Peace Conferences where a number of conventions regulating conduct in warfare were adopted. Most important among these was, undoubtedly, the 1907 Hague Convention IV on Respecting the Laws and Customs of War on Land and the regulations annexed thereto. The IMT found that the evidence furnished by the prosecution demonstrated beyond doubt the perpetration of pre-planned war crimes that were to be committed whenever the Fuhrer and his close associates thought them to be advantageous. This was done, for example, in relation to the plunder and ill-treatment of Soviet civilians and their property, the exploitation of slave labour of other occupied territories, as well as the murder of captured enemy commandos and Soviet Commissars.[26] The existence of these policies was revealed by reference to orders that were issued and circulated by some of the accused, such as the 1941 'Night and Fog Decree' that was issued by Hitler and signed by Keitel, under which persons who committed offences against the Reich or the German forces in occupied territories, except where the death sentence was certain, were to be taken secretly to Germany and handed over to criminal

---

23 See E Schwelb, 'Crimes against Humanity', 23 *BYIL* (1946), 178.
24 *Ex p Quirin*, 317 US 27 (1942) and *Re Yamashita*, 327 US 1 (1946).
25 18 Martens Nouveau Recueil General de Traites, p 607. The 1868 Additional Articles Relating to the Condition of the Wounded in War extended the humanitarian principles enunciated in the 1864 Convention to Warfare at Sea.
26 Op cit, IMT judgment, note 9, p 224.

organisations for trial or punishment.[27] As is evident, the IMT dealt with war crimes as far as this concept encompassed a policy. Subsequent military tribunals had ample opportunity to prosecute individuals who had willingly implemented and executed such policies during the war.

Significantly, the Charter provided for the determination by the Tribunal of the criminal character of indicted German organisations whose purpose was to serve as a precedent in cases before other military tribunals. The Tribunal declared that the SS (Hitler's bodyguards) and its subsidiary the SD, the Gestapo and the Leadership Corps of the Nazi Party were criminal. The SA (stormtroopers), the Reich Cabinet and the High Command were acquitted without prejudice to the individual liability of their members. In exercising its power to declare organisations criminal, the Tribunal pointed out that membership of such organisations did not necessarily entail the liability of each member. Rather:

> A criminal organisation is analogous to a criminal conspiracy in that the essence of both is co-operation for criminal purposes. There must be a group bound together and organised for a common purpose. The group must be formed or used in connection with the commission of crimes denounced by the Charter. Since the declaration with respect to the organisations and groups will, as has been pointed out, fix the criminality of its members, that definition should exclude persons who had no knowledge of the criminal purposes or acts of the organisation and those who were drafted by the State for membership, unless they were personally implicated in the commission of acts declared criminal by Art 6 of the Charter as members of the organisation. Membership alone is not enough to come within the scope of these declarations.[28]

The Charter went on to develop the extent of individual criminal responsibility for the offences set out in Art 6 by specifically excluding their official position or the fact that the accused were acting under orders as a defence.[29] The IMT did not deal in any great detail with the defence of superior orders for two reasons. First, as it was dealing with the most senior Axis officials it had already found that the majority of them were co-conspirators in the waging of aggressive wars and each according to his position had planned the commission of offences against the occupied civilian populations. Secondly, the orders circulated to the respective High Commands and Hitlerite groups were either issued by Hitler, but in the acquiescence and prompting of

27 Op cit, IMT judgment, note 9, p 229. Similarly, Keitel was found to have issued the 'Commissar Order' in 1941 and the 'Commando Order' in 1942.
28 Op cit, IMT judgment, note 9, p 251.
29 IMT Charter, Arts 7–8.

the accused, or were alternatively authored by them. The Tribunal held that the defence of superior orders could be urged in mitigation of punishment in cases where 'moral choice was in fact possible'. Hence, even in the extreme event that any one of the accused was under a direct order from Hitler, his position in the Reich structure would, in fact, be so high that a moral choice should have been possible. The same is not always true of the soldier on the battlefield, where the order and its consequences are not directly or immediately clear and the threat of punishment for disobedience is certain.[30]

The judgment of the IMT at Nuremberg was delivered on 30 September 1946 and sentences were pronounced on 1 October 1946. Of the 22 indicted – the accused Bormann was not found, while Goering had succeeded in committing suicide before the judgment was rendered – three were acquitted. The remainder were convicted of one or more of the crimes set down in Art 6 of the IMT Charter. Twelve of the accused were sentenced to death, while seven were sentenced to imprisonment for terms ranging from 10 years to life (three were actually sentenced to life imprisonment). As already observed, of the six accused organisations only three were found to be criminal. The Soviet judge dissented from all the aforementioned acquittals. The details of punishment, which in the case of the death penalty was hanging, as well as any appeals against the sentences passed upon the accused were handled by the Allied Control Council.

19.3.2 The legal basis and criticism of the International Military Tribunal

The IMT is commonly regarded as the first 'international' criminal tribunal of its type. However, it can be argued that the Tribunal was not so much an international tribunal but rather an Allied Forces tribunal. In outlining the legal basis under which the Allied powers had established the Tribunal, the judgment of the IMT held that:

> The making of the Charter was the exercise of the sovereign legislative power by countries to which the German Reich unconditionally surrendered; and the undoubted right of these countries to legislate for the occupied territories has been recognised by the civilised world.[31]

This suggests that the nature of the IMT was more akin to that of a municipal court established by the Allied Governments exercising sovereign power in Germany after the war. This conclusion is also borne out from the fact that

---

30 See ICC Statute, Art 33; see also MJ Osiel, 'Obeying Orders: Atrocity, Military Discipline, and the Law of War', 86 *Cal L Rev* (1998), 939. See also Chapter 3.
31 Op cit, IMT judgment, note 9, p 216.

the Allies had effectively occupied Germany, without however intending its annexation. As for the recognition of the IMT by the international community, although no State objected to its establishment, the Allied powers received only 22 statements of support.

Although the IMT Charter should be regarded as a landmark in international criminal law, the rules relating to evidence and procedure during trial seem simplistic in the light of modern day developments. Conduct of the trials at Nuremberg operated under the rules set out in Arts 17 to 25 of the IMT Charter. The rules of evidence and procedure seem hopelessly inadequate when one considers the complexity of the rules and procedure that apply in respect of the ICTY and ICTR. Whilst Art 16(d) of the Nuremberg Charter gave the accused the right to legal representation, the accused did not actually meet their counsel until immediately before, or even on the first day of the trials. All this suggests that the IMT is an easy target for criticism. Allegations that the law of the IMT was *ex post facto*, that there were insufficient procedural safeguards for the accused, that the trials were victor's justice have all been levelled at the Tribunal. A number of commentators criticised the way in which the IMT supported the law of the Charter, especially with regard to the crimes contained in Art 6.[32] Further criticisms were made regarding the delineation of crimes against humanity, which it has been suggested, because of the IMT's decision to restrict its jurisdiction to events occurring only during the war, effectively rendered the offence almost synonymous with war crimes.[33] On the other hand, had the principal Axis officials not been held accountable for their atrocious deeds, justice would have been sacrificed and their impunity would have adversely affected future generations. Prosecution under the terms of German law was inappropriate because the Reich Government had decriminalised all the crimes committed in Germany and abroad. It was exactly for this reason that Art 6(c) upheld liability for crimes against humanity, even if the said offence did not violate the domestic law of the country where it was perpetrated. Perhaps, therefore, the creation of the IMT with the jurisdictional competence granted to it under Art 6 represented the most appropriate solution as far as the meting out of justice was concerned, regardless of the legal sensitivities this exercise necessarily entailed.

If one considers the consequences for the development of international law, and more particularly the concept of individual criminal responsibility, had Churchill's option of summary execution been followed, the proceedings of the IMT may have taken on a rosier hue. Whilst they may have been imperfect, they no doubt formed the starting point for the 1948 Convention on the Prevention and Punishment of the Crime of Genocide, the 1949 Geneva

---

32 Op cit, Finch, note 16, p 334.
33 F Biddle, 'The Nuremberg Trial', 33 *Va L Rev* (1947), 679.

Conventions and the development of domestic legislation amongst States prescribing the offences against international law as set at Nuremberg.[34]

19.4 THE INTERNATIONAL MILITARY TRIBUNAL FOR THE FAR EAST

Imperial Japan had waged wars of aggression in the vicinity of South East Asia since 1928 in an effort to subjugate and control that part of the world. However, Japanese aggression entered the greater theatre of the Second World War from the moment its forces attacked the US naval forces at Pearl Harbor, Hawaii, on 8 December 1941, although the Japanese army had previously attacked and occupied territories in China, Thailand and others, some of which formed part of the British Commonwealth. Therefore, the Pacific theatre of operations during the Second World War encompasses merely one phase of the war and the parties involved. Since the invasion of China in 1933, Chinese nationalist forces were engaged in a brutal war with the Japanese army, which culminated in large scale atrocities against Chinese civilians, the most notorious being the so called 'Rape of Nanking'.

On 1 December 1943 the Cairo Declaration on World War II was proclaimed by the Presidents of the US and Nationalist China and the Prime Minister of Great Britain. It read, in relevant part, that:

> The Three Great Allies are fighting this war to restrain and punish the aggression of Japan. They covet no gain for themselves and have no thought of territorial expansion.

Prior to the signing of the Instrument of Japanese Surrender on 2 September 1945, the Allied Forces adopted the Declaration of Potsdam on 26 July 1945. They reiterated what was said in the Cairo Declaration, but added that:

> We do not intend that the Japanese people shall be enslaved as a race or destroyed as a nation, but stern justice shall be meted out to all war criminals including those who have visited cruelties upon our prisoners.

Unlike the Nuremberg Tribunal, the IMTFE[35] was established not by treaty but on the basis of a Special Proclamation adopted on 19 January 1946 by the Supreme Commander for the Allied Forces in the Pacific Theatre, General

---

34 CM Bassiouni, 'Nuremberg Forty Years After: An Introduction', 18 *Case W Res J Intl L* (1986), 261.
35 4 Bevans 20 (as amended on 26 April 1946).

Douglas McArthur.[36] His authority to establish the IMTFE and promulgate its Charter was exacted from his mandate through which he possessed the competence to create military commissions and tribunals. Many such commissions were subsequently established by all the Allied Forces involved in the war. In fact, the conviction of General Yamashita, Governor and Supreme Military Commander of the Japanese Army in the Philippines prior to the emancipation of the islands by the Allies, emanated from such a commission. The indictment included 55 counts, charging 28 accused with crimes against peace, war crimes and crimes against humanity during the period from 1 January 1928 to 2 September 1945. Of the 28 accused, three were acquitted. Although the IMTFE was established with the aim of prosecuting the most senior Japanese officials holding both political as well as military positions, this did not affect Emperor Hirohito who was not arraigned.

From a legal point of view, both the substantive and procedural law of the IMTFE were essentially similar to that of the Nuremberg Tribunal. Once again, the same criticisms levelled against the IMT and concerning the retroactive character of crimes against peace and against humanity were directed at the IMTFE. Its response to these and other arguments was the same as that given by the Nuremberg Tribunal. This was not, however, a unanimous decision, as the Indian judge, Justice Pal, strongly dissented from the majority's opinion on the illegality of aggressive war and the establishment of personal liability for acts of State.[37] Unlike the IMT, however, the IMTFE addressed the issue of superior responsibility in count 55 of the indictment, holding, especially as this relates to the maintenance of prisoner of war camps, that all those involved with captured enemy personnel, from the incumbent Minister to the last camp commander, have a duty to initiate a system of protection and thereafter to ensure its effective functioning. This served as an important precedent in subsequent cases both in Europe and Asia. It has been suggested that because McArthur exerted substantial influence on the trials so as not to allow the proceedings to threaten the success of the occupation, the IMTFE never enjoyed the attention and precedential authority of the IMT.[38]

---

36 See generally RH Minear, *Victor's Justice: The Tokyo War Crimes Trial*, 1971, Princeton: Princeton UP.

37 ES Kopelman, 'Ideology and International Law: The Dissent of the Indian Justice at the Tokyo War Crimes Trial', 23 *NYUJ Intl L & Pol* (1991), 373.

38 M Ratner and J Abrams, *Accountability for Human Rights Atrocities in International Law*, 1997, Oxford: OUP, p 164.

19.5 THE INTERNATIONAL LAW COMMISSION'S ROLE IN THE POST-NUREMBERG ERA

Perhaps the crucial point which has given the judgment of the IMT its place as the starting point for contemporary international criminal law was the fact that one of the first acts of the newly created United Nations was the General Assembly's affirmation of 'the principles of international law recognised by the Charter of the Nuremberg Tribunal and the judgment of the Tribunal'.[39] In the following year, the Assembly requested the International Law Commission (ILC) to formulate the Nuremberg judgment and Charter provisions into a set of principles.[40] The ILC considered this request during its first session in 1949 and concluded that, since these principles had already been affirmed by the General Assembly, its task should not be to express its appreciation on their content, but rather to formulate them as substantive principles of international law.[41] The report of special rapporteur Spiropoulos was adopted by the Commission, which subsequently forwarded its formulation of the seven principles,[42] together with their commentaries, to the General Assembly.[43] The Assembly asked Member States for their comments and requested the ILC to prepare a Draft Code of Offences Against the Peace and Security of Mankind.[44]

The Commission's work in preparing the Draft Code of Offences was undertaken in two distinct phases, from 1947 to 1954, and the second from 1982 to 1996. Although it was successful in formulating and convincing

---

39 GA Res 95(1), GAOR Resolutions, First Session, Pt II, p 188. Significantly, in 1963, the Lord Chancellor told the UK Parliament that the Nuremberg Principles were 'generally accepted among States and [had] the status of customary international law'. Hansard, HL, Vol 253, col 831, 2 Dec 1963; BPIL 1963, p 212.

40 GA Res 95(I) (11 Dec 1946).

41 YBILC (First Session, 1949), p 282.

42 Principle I, Any person who commits an act which constitutes a crime under international law is responsible therefore and liable to punishment; Principle II, The fact that internal law does not impose a penalty for an act which constitutes a crime under international law does not relieve the person who committed the act from responsibility under international law; Principle III, The fact that a person who committed an act which constitutes a crime under international law acted as a Head of State or responsible government official does not relieve him from responsibility under international law; Principle IV, The fact that a person acted pursuant to an order of his government or of a superior does not relieve him from responsibility under international law, provided a moral choice was in fact possible to him; Principle V, Any person charged with a crime under international law has the right to a fair trial on the facts and law; Principle VI, Crimes against Peace, War Crimes and Crimes against Humanity are punishable as crimes under international law; Principle VII, Complicity in the commission of a crime against peace, a war crime, or a crime against humanity as set forth in Principle VI is a crime under international law.

43 YBILC (Second Session, 1950), Vol II, p 374.

44 GA Res 488(V) (12 Dec 1950).

States to adopt the ICC Statute in 1998, completion of the Draft Code was never achieved. The ILC had made such progress by 1951 that it submitted the Draft Code to the General Assembly, but in light of the comments received it resubmitted its final version in 1954.[45] The Assembly felt, however, that the definition of aggression raised unsurpassed problems and decided to postpone consideration of the Code until further work was done on the question of aggression.[46] A definition on aggression was adopted with consensus some 20 years later in 1974,[47] and the Commission once again suggested that it might resume examination of the Code. This was done in 1981 when the Assembly invited the Commission to examine the Code as a matter of priority, taking into account 'the results achieved by the process of the progressive development of international law'.[48] The Commission resumed its work in 1982 and by 1996 it had adopted a final set of 20 draft Articles constituting the Code of Crimes Against the Peace and Security of Mankind,[49] a number which constituted a substantial reduction from the initial proposals and drafts that had been presented since 1982. The Commission, however, made it clear that the inclusion of certain crimes in the Code did not affect the status of other crimes under international law, nor did the adoption of the Code preclude the further development of this area of law. As to the implementation of the statute, the Assembly was presented with two options: adoption of an international convention, or incorporation into the statute of an international criminal court. Since the Preparatory Committee for the establishment of the ICC had already commenced its work, the Assembly drew the attention of the participating States to the relevance of the Draft Code.[50]

On 17 July 1998 the Statute of the ICC was adopted without the Code having ever entered into force. It is more than evident, however, that one of the significant catalysts for the adoption of the ICC Statute as well as the establishment of the ad hoc tribunals for Yugoslavia and Rwanda was the work of the ILC on the Draft Code. From a legal point of view, the possible adoption of the Code in light of the ICC would be relevant only for those countries that had not ratified the ICC Statute, while it would also reaffirm the substantive law of that statute and other international conventions. Its application might even instigate the extension of the ICC's jurisdiction to encompass other international crimes, or bind those States that are not parties to particular multilateral criminal conventions. Overall, the Draft Code represents an example of the variety of processes that exist within the

---

45 YBILC (Sixth Session, 1954), Vol II, p 149.
46 GA Res 897(IX) (4 Dec 1954).
47 GA Res 3314(XXIX) (14 Dec 1974).
48 GA Res 36/106 (10 Dec 1981).
49 See ILC Draft Code Commentary, UN Doc A/51/10 (1996); 18 HRLJ (1997), 96.
50 GA Res 51/160 (16 Dec 1996).

science of international law. The ILC worked diligently on a 'difficult' set of rules on the basis of State consent, waiting patiently for the time they would mature into solid concepts, but did not insist on their adoption in the form contemplated in its reports. Instead, it proposed that they be accepted in any form the international community could reach agreement on. This turned out to be the ICC, but it could very well have been the Code itself.

Chapter 20

The international crimina
tribunals for Yugoslavia
and Rwanda

20.1 INTRODUCTION

Reports since 1991 of widespread and gross human rights violations as a result of the armed conflicts raging between rival ethnic groups in the territory of the former Yugoslavia prompted the Security Council to express its deep concern and describe the situation as a threat to international peace and security.[1] This determination was premised in large part on a series of detailed interim reports that were submitted to the Council by a United Nations (UN) Commission of Experts established under Security Council Resolution 780 in 1992. Security Council Resolution 808 instructed the Secretary General to examine whether the establishment of a criminal tribunal would have a basis in law, and if so, formulate an appropriate statute. The Secretary General promptly replied in the affirmative and duly formulated a statute on the basis that it would apply only those portions of international law which were beyond any doubt part of customary international law.[2] Based on the Secretary General's report, to which a statute was annexed, the Security Council adopted Resolution 827 on 25 May 1993 and established the International Tribunal for the Prosecution of Persons Responsible for Serious Violations of International Humanitarian Law Committed in the Territory of the Former Yugoslavia (ICTY).[3]

Both the establishment of the Commission of Experts and, more so, the ICTY itself, constitute a historic breakthrough for the UN and the role of the Security Council. The Commission was created as an international fact-finding body as envisaged under Art 90 of the 1977 Protocol I Additional to the 1949 Geneva Conventions (Protocol I).[4] Although such commissions

---

1 SC Res 808 (22 Feb 1993).
2 *Report of the Secretary General pursuant to Security Council Resolution 808* (1993), UN Doc S/25704 (1993), para 2, reprinted in 32 ILM (1993), 1159.
3 See JC O'Brien, 'The International Tribunal for Violations of International Humanitarian Law in the Former Yugoslavia', 87 *AJIL* (1993), 639.
4 1125 UNTS 3.

ure the explicit consent of the States involved, the Council departed from this rule in Resolution 780.[5] The establishment of the ICTY on the basis of a Security Council Resolution under Chapter VII of the UN Charter merits closer consideration. It was preferred to a treaty because it was speedier and did not require the consent of the, by then, crumbling Yugoslavia. Obviously, the reinvigoration of the Council after the end of the Cold War meant that it could reach consensus far more easily than in the past and take concerted action with regard to situations jeopardising international peace and security. The establishment of the ICTY under Chapter VII was a measure not involving the use of force and, thus, fell squarely within the ambit of Art 41 of the 1945 UN Charter, despite the fact that the indicative list of measures envisaged in that provision make no reference to judicial bodies. Its relation to the Security Council is that of a subsidiary organ under Art 29 of the UN Charter.[6] As the product of a Security Council resolution, the Statute of the ICTY is binding upon every member of the UN in accordance with Art 25 of the UN Charter. There is no doubt that such a result would never have been achieved through the negotiation of a treaty, as few States would have seen any benefit in partaking of an enterprise of this magnitude, especially since the protagonist countries would, themselves, have refused to participate. From its very nature, therefore, the ICTY could not take the form of a permanent judicial institution but an ad hoc one, whose jurisdiction is limited in time, place and subject matter and whose mandate may theoretically be terminated by its creator at any time.

In 1994, atrocities of a scale many times greater than those perpetrated in the former Yugoslavia were reported taking place in Rwanda in the form of genocide against the Tutsi minority by extremist Hutu elements. The estimated number of dead as a result of this genocide is estimated to be anywhere between 500,000 and one million. The Security Council instructed a Commission of Experts to investigate the situation in Rwanda in the same manner it had acted in the case of Yugoslavia and, on the basis of the Commission's reports, it determined that there was a threat to international peace and security. It subsequently ordered the establishment of an International Criminal Tribunal for the Prosecution of Persons Responsible for Genocide and Other Serious Violations of International Humanitarian Law Committed in the Territory of Rwanda and Rwandan Citizens Responsible for Genocide and Other Such Violations Committed in the Territory of Neighbouring States between 1 January 1994 and 31 December 1994 (ICTR).[7] By

5 See CM Bassiouni, 'The United Nations Commission of Experts Pursuant to Security Council Resolution 780 (1992)', 88 *AJIL* (1994), 784.
6 See D Sarooshi, 'The Legal Framework Governing United Nations Subsidiary Organs', 67 *BYIL* (1996), 413, pp 428–31.
7 SC Res 955 (8 Nov 1994).

Resolution 977 the Security Council decided that the seat of the Tribunal would be located in Arusha, United Republic of Tanzania.[8] Initial suggestions for expanding ICTY jurisdiction to incorporate Rwandan crimes failed because a number of States feared this would lead to a permanent international criminal court. Instead, the Council expedited matters further by establishing the ICTR without demanding a prior report from the Secretary General as in the case of the ICTY.[9] Both institutions are, nonetheless, inter-related not only because they are subsidiary organs of the Security Council, but also because they share a common Appeals Chamber[10] and prosecutor.[11] The intention behind these common institutions was the development of a balanced and coherent jurisprudence, which has evidently been achieved. It should be noted that although the ruling Rwandan Government that over-threw the Hutu extremists responsible for the genocide in that country had, itself, proposed the creation of the ICTR, it finally voted against Resolution 955 because, *inter alia*, it had envisaged both control over the Tribunal as well as wide temporal jurisdiction, well before the January 1994 boundary fixed by the Security Council.[12]

In 1995 the Appeals Chamber of the ICTY was seized by an appeal against a Trial Chamber decision regarding, amongst other issues, the legality of its establishment by the Security Council and its authority, as a subsidiary organ thereto, vis-à-vis the Council to determine the legality of its mandate. The Appeals Chamber, presided over by Antonio Cassese, in a cornerstone decision for the development of international law, ruled that in the case of the ICTY the Security Council intended to establish not just any subsidiary organ, but a special organ with judicial functions; a tribunal.[13] It further affirmed that international law at the time – as indeed now – dictated that each tribunal be set up as a self-contained system whose jurisdictional powers may be limited by its constitutive instrument, although this does not mean that the judicial character of these tribunals may be jeopardised.[14] More importantly, the Appeals Chamber expressly confirmed the inherent or incidental juris-diction of any judicial body to determine its own competence, whether this is provided for in its constitutive instrument or not (that is, the so-called doctrine of 'Kompetenz-Kompetenz').[15]

8 SC Res 977 (22 Feb 1995).
9 P Akhavan, 'The International Criminal Tribunal for Rwanda: The Politics and Pragmatics of Punishment', 90 *AJIL* (1996), 501, p 502.
10 ICTR Statute, Art 12(2).
11 Ibid, Art 15(3).
12 Op cit, Akhavan, note 9, pp 504–05.
13 *Prosecutor v Tadic*, Appeals Chamber Decision on the Defence Motion for Interlocutory Appeal on Jurisdiction (*Tadic* Appeals Jurisdiction Decision) (2 Oct 1995), para 15.
14 Ibid, para 11.
15 Ibid, para 18. Reference was made to Cordova J's dissenting opinion in the International Court of Justice (ICJ)'s *Advisory Opinion on Judgments of the Administrative Tribunal of the ILO* (1956) ICJ Reports 77, p 163 (dissenting opinion of Judge Cordova).

Before we proceed to examine the substantive provisions and rich juris-prudence that has emanated from both Tribunals, it is useful to investigate the possible interpretative means by which to construe their Statutes. Although these are not *stricto sensu* international agreements, it is reasonable to subject them to the rules of interpretation available for treaties,[16] since they constitute legal instruments with the attributes of international agreements as defined by Art 2(a) of the 1969 Vienna Convention on the Law of Treaties (Vienna Convention).[17] The applicability of the interpretative rules of the Vienna Convention is further supported by the status of the ICTY and ICTR as subsidiary organs of the Security Council and, thus, directly linked to the constituent instrument of the UN, its Charter. Therefore, since Art 5 of the 1969 Vienna Convention applies to treaties which are the constituent instruments of an international organisation and treaties adopted within an international organisation, it would seem appropriate that, by extension of the powers vested in the Security Council by the UN Charter, the rules of treaty interpretation apply also to the ICTY and ICTR Statutes.

Thus, the ICTY Chambers' primary reliance on a 'literal' construction of their Statute, followed by 'teleological', logical' and 'systematic' methods of interpretation as secondary means,[18] is consonant with Art 31(1) of the 1969 Vienna Convention, according to which treaties are to be interpreted in accordance with their ordinary meaning and in the light of their object and purpose, as well as Art 32 which allows for supplementary means when literal interpretation does not clarify the meaning of a provision. It should be stated that although humanitarian and human rights instruments warrant an interpretation which ensures their widest possible effectiveness in accordance with their object and purpose,[19] the so-called 'evolutionary' method of interpretation,[20] according to which contemporary developments in international law are to be incorporated into the relevant provisions of humanitarian treaties, should not generally apply to the ICTY or ICTR because of their ad hoc character, their specific mandate to apply customary law and the possible

---

16 *Prosecutor v Tadic*, Decision on Protective Measures for Victims and Witnesses (10 Aug 1995) (1997) 105 ILR 599, para 18.
17 1155 UNTS 331. Article 2(a) provides that the term 'treaty' means 'an international agreement concluded between States in written form and governed by international law, whether embodied in a single instrument or in two or more related instruments and whatever its particular designation'; the Chinese representative to the Security Council made a statement to this effect during the deliberations of Resolution 808 (1993). See UN Doc S/PV3217 (1993), p 33.
18 *Tadic* Appeals Jurisdiction decision (2 Oct 1995), paras 71–72, 79.
19 Advisory Opinion Concerning Reservations to the Genocide Convention (1951) ICJ Reports 23; *Ireland v UK* (1978) EuCtHR, Ser A, No 25, para 239.
20 Advisory Opinion Concerning Legal Consequences for States of the Continued Presence of South Africa in Namibia (1971) ICJ Reports 3, para 53; *Tyrer* case, Judgment (1978) EurCtHR, Ser A, No 26, para 31.

violation of the principle of certainty belying criminal proceedings. The only possible exception could perhaps lie in those rules of procedure that are more favourable to the accused. Finally, although the issue of intra-ICTY precedent has been a problematic one, especially as regards the classification of armed conflicts by the various Chambers, it now seems settled that decisions of the Appeals Chambers should be followed, except where cogent reasons in the interests of justice require a departure. Such a departure is justified where the previous decision was decided on the basis of a wrong legal principle or wrongly decided on account of the judges' misconstruction of the relevant law.[21]

20.2 FORMATIVE YEARS OF THE AD HOC TRIBUNALS

Unlike the ICTR, where a large number of accused were already apprehended by the new government, the ICTY did not in its early years enjoy the co-operation of States on whose territory the alleged offenders had taken refuge. This was due to a large degree to the fact that the various conflicts in the Republic of Bosnia and Herzegovina officially terminated as late as 14 December 1995 with the conclusion of the General Framework Agreement for Peace (GFAP, otherwise known as Dayton Peace Agreement).[22] Although the signatory former Yugoslav Republics undertook an obligation after 1995 in accordance with the Dayton Agreement to co-operate with the Tribunal, such co-operation was not forthcoming, especially from Croatia[23] and more so from the Federal Republic of Yugoslavia (now Serbia).[24] Another complicating factor was the division of the Republic of Bosnia and Herzegovina into two autonomous entities, an ethnic Serbian (Republika Srpska) and a Moslem one (Federation of Bosnia and Herzegovina), governed, however, by a common presidency.[25] Republika Srpska has refused to render much assistance to the Tribunal on account of its leaders' alliance to a number of those indicted by the ICTY.

21 *Prosecutor v Aleksovski*, Appeals Chamber Judgment (24 March 2000), paras 101–15; *Prosecutor v Kordic and Cerkez*, Trial Chamber Judgment (26 Feb 2001) (*Kordic and Cerkez* judgment), para 148.
22 35 ILM (1996), 75. Although the GFAP was signed in Paris, the Agreement itself was concluded in a US Air Force base in Dayton, Ohio, on 21 Nov 1995.
23 Request by the Prosecutor under r 7*bis* (B) that the President Notify the Security Council of the Failure of the Republic of Croatia to Comply with its Obligations under Art 29 (28 July 1999).
24 'President Cassese reports to the Security Council on the continuing violation of the FRY of its obligation to co-operate with ICTY', ICTY Doc CC/PIO/075-E (23 May 1996).
25 GFAP, Art 3.

With an empty docket, the ICTY faced an imminent danger of redundancy and oblivion by the very international community that created it, since it was no secret that by early 1995 a substantial number of States were growing weary of funding a judicial institution which had no accused to try.[26] During this time the prosecutor was busy establishing liaisons and investigative teams in order to collect evidence and identify potential witnesses, not only in the former Yugoslavia but across the globe, since a large number of witnesses and victims had subsequently sought refuge abroad. Endowed with the authority to formulate their own Rules of Procedure,[27] the ICTY judges adopted the first ever comprehensive code of international criminal procedure, adapted to the special needs of the Tribunal and based on a combination of both common law and civil law elements. For example, as regards examination of individuals, the adversarial system was preferred, while the almost unlimited admission of evidence, including hearsay, as long as it was deemed to have probative value,[28] reflects, rather, civil law criminal practice.

Rule 61 is of particular relevance to the present discussion. This rule permits the prosecutor to submit his or her evidence against an accused to a Trial Chamber in order for the latter to review the indictment in cases where a warrant of arrest has not been executed and personal service of the indictment has not been effected despite sincere efforts by the prosecutor. If, thereafter, the Trial Chamber ascertains there are reasonable grounds for believing that the accused committed any or all of the crimes charged, it is empowered to make a formal declaration to that effect[29] and issue an international arrest warrant, which is then transmitted to all UN Member States.[30] If any State fails to execute the contents of the warrant, the ICTY President may notify the Security Council.[31] Five cases were brought before a Trial Chamber by the Prosecutor under r 61 proceedings, the most prominent of which was that against the political leader of the Bosnian Serbs, Radovan Karadzic and the Chief of Staff of the Bosnian Serb Army, Radko Mladic,[32] where an abundance of testimony and other documentation evinced the existence of a policy of 'ethnic cleansing' against non-Serbs and whose planning, at least, was attributed to the two accused. In each of these cases, the judgment stressed that r 61 proceedings were intended to serve as public reviews of indictments and did not constitute trials *in absentia*, a guarantee

---

26 'The judges of the ICTY express their concern regarding the substance of their programme of judicial work for 1995', ICTY Doc CC/PIO/OO3-E (1 Feb 1995).
27 ICTY Statute, Art 15. The first version of the rules is reprinted in 33 ILM (1994), 484.
28 ICTY Rules, r 89(C).
29 Ibid, r 61(C).
30 Ibid, r 61(D).
31 Ibid, r 61(E)
32 *Prosecutor v Karadzic and Mladic* (*Karadzic and Mladic* decision) r 61 Decision (11 July 1996), 108 ILR 86.

prescribed under Art 21(d) of the ICTY Statute. They did not culminate in a verdict, nor deprive the accused of their right to contest the charges in person. Furthermore, it was pointed out that such proceedings provided an opportunity for victims to be heard in a public hearing and become part of history.[33] Indeed, the publicity that followed these proceedings, and especially the detailing of the horrific crimes that were found to have been perpetrated, sustained the impetus for international justice and instigated efforts for effective enforcement.

Despite the clear obligation under Art 29(2) of the ICTY Statute to arrest, detain or surrender accused persons to the Tribunal, Trial Chamber orders or requests to this effect were largely disobeyed by the independent former Yugoslav Republics and all the prosecutor and judges could do was inform the Security Council on an *ad hoc* basis, as well as through the ICTY President's Annual Report to the Council. This stalemate was ultimately resolved on account of two factors: international pressure on recalcitrant States[34] and amelioration of the Tribunal's image which led to the voluntary surrender of a significant number of accused; and increased willingness on the part of the North Atlantic Treaty Organisation (NATO)-led Stabilisation Force (SFOR) – legal successor to IFOR under Security Council mandate – to co-operate in the arrest of accused persons residing in the territory of Bosnia. Likewise, some central European States had begun exercising universal criminal jurisdiction over persons accused of having violated the laws or customs of war in the course of the Yugoslav armed conflicts.[35] One such criminal proceeding initiated in the Federal Republic of Germany, against Dusan Tadic, was deferred to the jurisdiction of the ICTY after an official request, despite the accused's pleas to the contrary.[36] Tadic, although only a guard at the Bosnian Serb Omarska prisoner and detention facility, was the first person physically brought before the jurisdiction of the ICTY and was utilised as a vehicle for initiating prosecutions and developing a coherent jurisprudence, upon which both the ICTY and ICTR relied and further elaborated in future cases.

The obligation to co-operate with the Tribunal under Art 29 of its Statute is addressed only to States, not to international organisations or peace-keeping

---

33 See *Prosecutor v Nikolic* (*Nikolic* decision) r 61 Decision (20 Oct 1995), 108 ILR 21.
34 It is instructive that one of the most significant reasons for Croatia's failed attempts thus far to enter the European Union (EU) has been its slack and failed cooperation with the ICTY.
35 *Prosecutor v Saric* (1995) unreported (Denmark); *Public Prosecutor v Djajic*, reported in 92 *AJIL* (1998), 528, FRG; *Public Prosecutor v Grabec* (*Re* G) (Swiss), reported in 92 *AJIL* (1998), 78.
36 Decision of the Trial Chamber on the Application of the Prosecutor for a Formal Request for Deferral to the Competence of the International Criminal Tribunal for the Former Yugoslavia in the Matter of Dusko *Tadic* (8 Nov 1994); see C Warbrick, 'International Criminal Law', 44 *ICLQ* (1995), 465, p 471.

or peace enforcement entities. Accordingly, the ICTY, having no enforcement mechanisms of its own, was forced to rely on the co-operation of individual States and the goodwill of peace-keeping forces. In a meeting on 19 January 1996 between the ICTY President and the Secretary General of NATO, it was agreed that, within the limits of its resources and mandate, SFOR would not only assist in ICTY investigations, but would also detain any indicted persons whom it came across in the ordinary conduct of its duties.[37] Although it was initially doubted that NATO forces entertained the political or military will to make any arrests, such clouds soon disappeared as SFOR has since proceeded to detain a substantial number of accused in Bosnia.[38] This task has been considerably facilitated by the fact that since 1997 the prosecutor has pursued only high-ranking officials and has applied a sealed indictment policy, thereby allowing for the element of surprise and relative safety of NATO operations in their pursuit of indicted persons.

There has also been much speculation over the existence, during the ICTY's early years, of a secret bargain between the leaders of the warring factions and the third party instigators of the Dayton Agreement to the effect that the former would be excluded from the prosecutorial ambit of the ICTY. It is alleged that this was the price for achieving peace and ending the war.[39] Even if this allegation contains some truth vis-à-vis the drafters and sponsors of the Dayton Agreement, it certainly carries no weight as far as the Office of the Prosecutor is concerned. In fact, not only has the prosecutor carried out a meticulous investigation against former Bosnian Serb leaders Karadzic and Mladic, which culminated in a detailed indictment, an r 61 review and an international arrest warrant, but also the Office of the Prosecutor went as far as charging an acting Head of State, President Slobodan Milosevic of the Federal Republic of Yugoslavia (FRY) for a number of offences allegedly ordered or tolerated by him during the civil unrest in Kosovo in 1999.[40] At the same time that the indictment against Milosevic was confirmed by a Trial Chamber, the prosecutor requested the freezing of all assets of the accused, upon which a subsequent order to all UN Members was duly issued by the Tribunal.[41] The accused was later transferred to the jurisdiction of the ICTY and the indictment was amended to encompass crimes committed during the civil war in Bosnia and Croatia. However, Milosevic passed away before the

37 See 'The Parties, IFOR and ICTY' (1996) *ICTY Bulletin*, No 2, 22 Jan.
38 See ICTY Doc JL/PIS/475-e (6 March 2000) and JL/PIS/513-e (26 June 2000), regarding the arrest by SFOR of accused Prcac and Sikirica, respectively. From July 1997 until July 2000, SFOR has detained and transferred to the ICTY 15 suspected war criminals.
39 A D'Amato, 'Peace vs Accountability in Bosnia', 88 *AJIL* (1994), 500.
40 See 'President Milosevic and Four Other Senior FRY Officials Indicted for Murder, Persecution and Deportation in Kosovo', ICTY Doc JL/PIU/403-E (27 May 1999).
41 *Prosecutor v Milosevic and Others*, Decision on Review of Indictment and Application for Consequential Orders (24 May 1999), para 29.

tribunal had the chance to deliver its final judgment. As for the prosecutorial discretionary practice of 'plea bargaining', which is common to many legal systems, it generally should not be applied to the ad hoc tribunals where immunity is specifically prohibited. However, neither of the two Statutes nor the Rules of Procedure deny the authority to engage in plea-bargaining, which as an implied power may be 'necessary for completing the investigation and the preparation and conduct of the prosecution'.[42] In order to balance, on the one hand the interests of justice by avoiding impunity, and on the other, the enhancement of its resources, the Office of the Prosecutor has restricted its plea negotiations to lower level officials.[43]

The Rwanda Tribunal, as already explained, was not seriously plagued by problems relating to the absence of accused or lack of State co-operation, since most of the accused were already in Rwanda and, in any event, with the exception of the Republics of Congo and Burundi, no other States had/have any national or other substantial interest in shielding persons in their territory or withholding evidentiary material. Nonetheless, lack of support by the Rwandan Government as well as the Organisation for African Unity (OAU),[44] serious delays in prosecution and poor trial management, coupled with financial and administrative mismanagement, resulted in the resignation of the first ICTR deputy, Prosecutor Honore Rakotomanana, and plunged the by-then beleaguered Tribunal into chaos and uncertainty. The ICTR, however, was faced with overcoming a further obstacle, directly related to its previously elaborated misfortunes. Although its judicial focus was on the highest ranking Hutu officials who had allegedly planned, instigated, incited and executed genocide, more than 75,000 accused were detained since the change of rule in July 1994 under extremely poor conditions in Rwandan prisons, the vast majority without having been formally indicted. The devastated infrastructure of the country and the absence of a criminal justice system as a result of the genocide and the subsequent departure abroad of many educated Hutus, including lawyers, meant that not only were there insufficient local trial chambers to guarantee speedy trials for the multitudes of accused, but there did not exist a single Rwandan lawyer who would be willing to defend them.[45]

---

42 ICTY Rules, r 39(ii).
43 JE Alvarez, 'Crimes of States, Crimes of Hate: Lessons from Rwanda', 24 *Yale J Int'l L* (1999), 365, pp 377–78.
44 The OAU initially criticised the establishment of the ICTR under a Chapter VII resolution instead of through a treaty, but by 1997 its prior hesitation had given way to full co-operation. See D Wembou, 'The International Criminal Tribunal for Rwanda: Its Role in the African Context', 321 *IRRC* (1997), 685.
45 Op cit, Akhavan, note 9, p 49. This problem has been resolved to a large degree by the Ministry of Justice's authorisation to foreign lawyers working for Lawyers Without Borders to plead on behalf of accused persons. O Dubois, 'Rwanda's National Criminal Courts and the International Tribunal', 321 *IRRC* (1997), 717.

Moreover, the retention of the death penalty under Rwandan law, in contrast to its rejection in the ICTR, led to an absurd result whereby the planners and instigators of genocide would, at most, receive life imprisonment sentences by the ICTR, whereas minor executioners were to suffer capital punishment under Rwandan criminal law.[46] The Rwanda Tribunal could do nothing regarding the discrepancy in sentencing, but it has played a seminal role in raising awareness over the need to enhance the Rwandan criminal justice system through international financing and training, so that at least accused persons would not suffer lengthy detention periods. The ICTR seems to have overcome its initial problems and has since concluded a significant number of cases, including one against the former Prime Minister of the Interim Rwandan Government, Jean Kambanda.[47] It has, moreover, made a substantial contribution to the development of international humanitarian law and restoration of peace in Rwanda.

20.2.1 Jurisdiction of the ICTY and ICTR

Although both the ICTY and ICTR enjoy concurrent jurisdiction with other national courts, they are endowed with primacy over all national courts in relation to offences falling within the ambit of their respective Statutes.[48] However, since the ad hoc tribunals were established with the aim of prosecuting the most serious offences, it is natural that a large number of prosecutions dealing with minor offenders be undertaken by national authorities, especially from the countries in the former Yugoslavia. In order to better monitor these prosecutions and assess their relevance to ICTY proceedings, a clause was inserted in an agreement signed in Rome on 18 February 1996 between the presidents of FRY, Croatia and the Republic of Bosnia and Herzegovina. Paragraph 5 of the Rome Agreement requires review by the ICTY before the national authorities of the aforementioned States can arrest individuals suspected of having committed any offences related to the Yugoslav wars. To this end, a set of Procedures and Guidelines for Parties for the Submission of Cases to the ICTY under the Agreed Measures of 18 February 1996 was developed.[49] This procedure simply facilitates the ICTY's work and promotes justice and is in no way a substitute for the international Tribunal's primacy over any national proceedings.

---

46 From July 1996 until April 2000 more than 2,500 persons have been sentenced by Rwandan courts, 300 of them to death. The first executions took place on 24 April 1998, when 22 people were put to death publicly. There have been no executions since, although the Government has not ruled them out; 'Rwanda Court Sentences Eight to Death' (2000) *Associated Press*, 2 April.

47 *Prosecutor v Kambanda*, Judgment (4 Sept 1998).

48 ICTY Statute, Art 9; ICTR Statute, Art 8.

49 These procedures have become known as the 'Rules of the Road'.

The subject matter jurisdiction of the Yugoslav Tribunal consists of four core offences: grave breaches of the 1949 Geneva Conventions,[50] violations of the laws or customs of war,[51] genocide[52] and crimes against humanity.[53] A detailed analysis of these offences, as well as the significance of the ICTY/ICTR jurisprudence in their development is given in Chapters 5 to 7 of this book. Although the majority of crimes charged took place in Bosnia, the Tribunal enjoys, under Art 1 of its Statute, jurisdiction over offences falling within Arts 2 to 5, as long as these were perpetrated anywhere on the territory of the former Yugoslavia since 1991. This wide jurisdiction both in time and place has enabled the prosecutor to investigate and indict persons for offences committed in Kosovo by FRY forces and Kosovo Liberation Army (KLA) members in 1999, as well as Croat military and police personnel for crimes committed during, and in the aftermath of, operations 'Flash and Storm' in the retaking of Serb-held Krajina. Equally, the ICTY has expanded its jurisdiction to cover events that took place in the Former Yugoslav Republic of Macedonia (FYROM).

In the case of the ICTR, the Security Council was conscious, on the one hand, that there were no international elements to the armed conflict between the Hutu Government and the Rwandan Patriotic Front (RPF) and, on the other, it wished it to be recognised that a well planned campaign of genocide had taken place. This intention is clearly reflected in the Rwanda Tribunal's Statute, whose jurisdiction consists of the crimes of genocide,[54] crimes against humanity[55] and violations of Art 3 common to the 1949 Geneva Conventions and the 1977 Additional Protocol II to these Conventions.[56] Although one may presume that the temporal jurisdiction of the ICTR, spanning from 1 January until 31 December 1994, is wider than the actual duration of hostilities, since the mass killings commenced on 14 June 1994 and lasted approximately three months, evidence shows that plans to commit genocide existed at least as far back as 1992.

Both statutes penalise participation in the preparatory and execution

---

50 Convention for the Amelioration of the Condition of the Wounded and Sick in Armed Forces in the Field (No I), 75 UNTS 31; Convention for the Amelioration of the Condition of the Wounded, Sick, and Ship-wrecked Members of Armed Forces at Sea (No II), 75 UNTS 85; Convention Relative to the Treatment of Prisoners of War (No III), 75 UNTS 135; Convention Relative to the Protection of Civilian Persons in Time of War (No IV), 75 UNTS 287, Art 2.
51 ICTY Statute, Art 3.
52 Ibid, Art 4.
53 Ibid, Art 5.
54 ICTR Statute, Art 2.
55 Ibid, Art 3.
56 Ibid, Art 4. Geneva Protocol II Additional to the Geneva Conventions of 12 August 1949, and Relating to the Protection of Victims of Non-International Armed Conflicts, 1125 UNTS 609.

stages of prescribed offences, that is, planning, instigation, ordering, or aiding and abetting in the planning, preparation or execution.[57] However, an accused can only be found guilty if the offence charged was actually completed. This rule does not apply with regard to genocide which, taken verbatim from the 1948 Convention on the Prevention and Punishment of the Crime of Genocide (Genocide Convention), does not require the commission of acts of genocide in order to hold the accused liable. Furthermore, following established principles of customary law, persons incur criminal liability where they fail to either prevent or punish crimes committed by their subordinates in cases they know or had reason to know that subordinates were about to commit such acts or had already done so.[58] This latter form of criminal participation, initially borne for the exigencies of military authorities, is known as the doctrine of command or superior responsibility. The various forms of participation in crime and the different types of liability recognised by the ad hoc tribunals and generally in international law are examined in Chapter 2.

20.2.2 Rape and sexual violence as international offences

Although in the past rape had been explicitly[59] or implicitly[60] prohibited under international humanitarian law, until the establishment of the ICTY it had never been defined in any of the instruments in which it was contained. It was not elucidated even when prosecuted as a war crime at the International Military Tribunal for the Far East or its Charter.[61] Lack of specificity was not a pressing issue to the post-war tribunals because not only did rape not play a significant role in prosecutorial agendas that were then working under severe time constraints, but where reference to rape was made in the Tokyo Trials its elements must have seemed to all parties as self-proven and in no need of further elaboration.[62] There is no doubt that Nazi and Japanese licence to commit rapes and forced prostitution (the so-called practice of 'comfort women') was intended to both encourage soldiers and serve as an instrument of policy.[63] In any event, neither the relevant provisions of the 1949 Geneva Conventions nor of the 1977 Additional Protocols listed rape amongst their grave breaches provisions.

The practice and variety of rape in the conflicts occurring in the former

---

57 ICTY Statute, Art 7(1); ICTR Statute, Art 6(1).
58 ICTY Statute, Art 7(3); ICTR Statute, Art 6(3).
59 Geneva IV, Art 27; Protocol I, Art 76(1); Protocol II, Art 4(2)(c).
60 Hague Regulations, Art 46; Geneva Conventions, Art 3; Geneva IV, Art 147; Protocol I, Art 85(4)(c); Protocol II, Art 4(1) and (2)(a).
61 4 Bevans 20.
62 Control Council Law No 10, Art II(1)(c) included rape as a crime against humanity.
63 T Meron, 'Rape as a Crime Under International Law', 87 *AJIL* (1993), 424, p 425.

Yugoslavia was both widespread and deliberate.[64] The special rapporteur of the UN Commission on Human Rights clearly pointed out the purpose of rape therein as constituting an individual attack and a method of ethnic cleansing designed to degrade and terrify the entire ethnic group.[65] Indiscriminate and widespread rape was also practised in the Rwandan genocide. Any assessment of rape must be viewed particularly in the context of gender-based crimes, that is, whereas 'sex' refers to biological differences, 'gender' refers to socially constructed differences, such as power imbalances, socio-economic disparities and culturally reinforced stereotypes.[66]

Rape is a particular offence contained in the list of crimes encompassing crimes against humanity in both the ICTY[67] and ICTR Statutes[68] and as a war crime of internal conflicts under the ICTR.[69] Notwithstanding the absence of explicit reference to rape in the definition of other offences within the jurisdiction of the Tribunals, this egregious violation may also be prosecuted as a war crime or grave breach under 'inhuman treatment' or 'torture', as well as under genocide.[70] Although the two ad hoc tribunals basically agree on the definition of rape as a physical invasion of a sexual nature committed on a person under coercive circumstances,[71] there has been a substantial difference of opinion as to the sources of this definition and its scope. The *Akayesu* judgment viewed rape as a form of aggression and a violation of personal dignity whose central elements could not be captured in a mechanical description of objects and body parts.[72] Variations of rape, the Rwanda Tribunal held, may include acts involving the insertion of objects and/or the use of bodily orifices not considered to be intrinsically sexual. This conceptual and flexible definition of rape, having subsequently been followed by other ICTR Chambers,[73] is in contrast with the *Furundzija* judgment which, in fact, relied on a detailed description of objects and body parts.[74]

---

64 C Niarchos, 'Women, War and Rape: Challenges Facing the International Tribunal for the Former Yugoslavia', 17 *HRQ* (1995), 649.

65 *Report on the Situation of Human Rights in the Territory of the Former Yugoslavia*, UN Doc A/48/92-S/ 25341, Annex (1993), pp 20, 57; *Kamdzic* decision (11 July 1996), para 64.

66 K D Askin, 'Sexual Violence and Indictments of the Yugoslav and Rwandan Tribunals: Current Status', 93 *AJIL* (1999), 97, p 107.

67 ICTY Statute, Art 5(g).

68 ICTR Statute, Art 3(g).

69 Ibid, Art 4(e).

70 The use of rape as a process of 'slow death' was recognised as a means of deliberately inflicting on a group conditions of life calculated to bring about its physical destruction, thus, constituting genocide. *Kayishema* judgment (21 May 1999), para 116.

71 *Akayesu* judgment (2 Sept 1998), para 598; *Prosecutor v Furundzija*, Trial Chamber Judgment (10 Dec 1998), para 181.

72 *Akayesu* Trial Chamber judgment (2 Sept 1998), paras 596–98.

73 *Musema* judgment (27 Jan 2000), para 228.

74 *Furundzija* Trial Chamber judgment (10 Dec 1998), paras 175–84.

In inquiring into the precise ambit encompassed by the term 'rape' and, specifically, whether this included 'forced oral penetration', the Trial Chamber in the *Furundzija* case highlighted the lack of a definition in international law, but found that the various relevant international instruments distinguished between 'rape' and 'indecent assault'. Unable to discover any relevant customary law or other definition based on general principles of public international or international criminal law, the judges turned their attention to general principles of criminal law common to the major legal systems. Although they ascertained that the forcible sexual penetration by the penis or similar insertion of any other object into either the vagina or anus is considered as constituting rape in all the examined legal systems, there was still some discrepancy concerning 'oral penetration', as in some countries it was classified as 'rape' while in others as 'sexual assault'.[75] The court ruled, nonetheless, that the principle of respect for human dignity dictated that extremely serious sexual outrage such as forced oral penetration could be classified as rape, amply outweighing any concerns the perpetrator might have of being stigmatised as a rapist rather than as a sexual assailant.[76] Although the *Furundzija* approach purports to be specifically oriented, in reality it does not seem to differ much from the conceptual position adopted in *Akayesu*, especially since it is obliged to employ a non-specific principle to categorise forced oral penetration. The *Furundzija* judgment adopted, therefore, the following definition of the *actus reus* of rape under international law:

(i) the sexual penetration, however slight:

    (a) of the vagina or anus of the victim by the penis of the perpetrator or any other object used by the perpetrator; or

    (b) of the mouth of the victim by the penis of the perpetrator;

(ii) by coercion or force or threat of force against the victim or a third person.[77]

The *Kunarac* judgment, although agreeing with this definition, argued that element (ii) of the definition is narrower than what is required under international law, since it omits any reference to factors that do not involve some form of coercion or force, especially factors that 'would render an act of sexual penetration non-consensual or non-voluntary on the part of the victim'.[78] Finding that the common denominator underlying general principles of law with regard to the criminalisation of rape is the violation of 'sexual

---

75 *Furundzija* Trial Chamber judgment (10 Dec 1998), paras 175–82.
76 Ibid, paras 183–84.
77 Ibid, para 185.
78 *Kunarac* Trial Chamber judgment (22 Feb 2001), para 438.

autonomy', it added two further components to the *Furundzija* definition. These are that:

    (a) the sexual activity be accompanied by force or a variety of other speci-
fied circumstances which made the victim particularly vulnerable or
negated her ability to make an informed refusal, or:

    (b) the sexual activity occurs without the consent of the victim.[79]

These specified circumstances, explained the Chamber, may include situations where the victim is put in a state of being unable to resist, particular vulnerability, or incapacity of resisting because of physical or mental incapacity, or was induced into the act by surprise or misrepresentation. These factors clearly rob the victim of the opportunity for an informed or reasoned refusal.[80]

To the extent that an act of rape carries the attributes of the crime of torture – that is, infliction of severe physical or mental suffering by a State official whether for ascertaining a confession, rendering of punishment, intimidation, coercion or discrimination – it may be characterised as torture.[81] 'Outrages upon personal dignity' as a species of 'inhuman treatment' under Art 2 of the ICTY Statute, comprising acts animated by contempt for another person's dignity and whose aim is to cause serious humiliation or degradation to the victim, can also include rape.[82] Physical harm in this case is not necessary as long as the humiliation has caused 'real and lasting' suffering, whose effect is based on that of a reasonable person whom the perpetrator intended to humiliate, or at least perceived this result as foreseeable.[83]

The inherently personal and sensitive object which rape violates should not allow for the use of regular principles of evidence pertaining to other offences. This notion was reflected in the Tribunals' Statutes, which provide guarantees for the protection of victims and witnesses,[84] further implemented by the Rules of Procedure, which do not require corroboration in cases of sexual assault.[85] This influence is evident in the ICC context, where r 70 of its Rules of Procedure and Evidence provides that consent cannot be inferred by

---

79 Ibid, para 442.
80 Ibid, paras 446–60; see concurring decisions, adopted in *Prosecutor v Kvocka and Others*, Trial Chamber Judgment (2 Nov 2001), para 177, and *Prosecutor v Kunarac and Others*, Appeals Chamber Judgment (12 June 2002).
81 *Furundzija* judgment (10 Dec 1998), para 163.
82 *Prosecutor v Aleksovski*, Trial Chamber Judgment (25 June 1999), paras 54–56. The application of this particular ruling was unrelated to acts of rape.
83 Ibid.
84 ICTY Statute, Art 22; ICTR Statute, Art 21. Such measures include, but are not limited to, the conduct of *in camera* proceedings and the protection of the victim's identity. M Leigh, 'The Yugoslav Tribunal: Use of Unnamed Witnesses against Accused', 90 *AJIL* (1996), 235; C Chinkin, 'Due Process and Witness Anonymity', 91 *AJIL* (1997), 75.
85 ICTY Rules, r 96(1); see *Prosecutor v Tadic*, Trial Chamber Opinion and Judgment (7 May 1997), para 536.

words or conduct under situations that undermined the victim's ability to give voluntary and genuine consent, nor by silence or lack of resistance. Moreover, the victim's prior sexual life or character will not be admitted as evidence. Nonetheless, in the ICTY Rules of Procedure (r 96) the description of 'consent' as a defence is used in a non-technical sense. Thus, the burden of proof is not shifted to the accused.[86] Finally, the establishment of a Victims and Witnesses Unit with authority to recommend protective measures and provide counselling and support has had a significant impact in cases of rape and sexual assault.[87]

20.3 ENFORCEMENT CAPACITY OF THE TRIBUNALS

Article 29 of the ICTY Statute obliges Member States of the UN to co-operate and offer judicial assistance to the Yugoslav Tribunal without undue delay. Such calls for co-operation are to be addressed in the form of binding orders or requests, including, but not limited to:

(a) the identification and location of persons;
(b) the taking of testimony and the production of evidence;
(c) the service of documents;
(d) the arrest or detention of persons;
(e) the surrender or the transfer of the accused to the International Tribunal.

Since the ICTY Statute constitutes a Security Council enforcement measure, any order or request by a Trial Chamber for the surrender and transfer of documents or persons is *ipso facto* binding.[88] A large number of States have enacted implementing legislation in order to harmonise their obligations under Art 29 and prepare national mechanisms to cope with the legal intricacies of possible future requests.[89] Some of these domestic Acts have been criticised for not offering adequate safeguards and of permitting for extradition of offences under the ICTY Statute that are not contained in the criminal law of the extraditing State.[90] These criticisms have no legal basis since, as Warbrick correctly points out, the obligation of States to surrender

86 *Kunarac* Trial Chamber judgment (22 Feb 2001), para 463.
87 ICTY Rules, r 34(A)(i) and (ii).
88 *Report of the Secretary General pursuant to Security Council Resolution 808* (1993), UN Doc S/25704 (1993), paras 125–26.
89 UK UN ICTY Order 1996 SI 1996/716; Australian International War Crimes Tribunals Act No 18 (1995).
90 H Fox, 'The Objections to Transfer of Criminal Jurisdiction to the UN Tribunal', 46 *ICLQ* (1997), 434, regarding the UK's 1996 SI.

accused persons found on their territory does not amount to extradition[91] it is simply an act of surrender founded on a unilateral obligation.

In response to an ICTY subpoena for the production of documents addressed to Croatia, the latter challenged the Tribunal's authority to order sovereign States, and argued that, in any event, requests of this nature must adhere to national channels of communication and should not jeopardise national security. On appeal, the Appeals Chamber in the *Blaskic* case admitted that the ICTY possesses enforcement powers neither under its Statute, nor inherently by its nature as a judicial institution.[92] It pointed out that, as a general rule, States cannot be 'ordered' by other States or international organisations. The power to 'order' under Art 29 of the ICTY Statute, however, derives its binding force from Chapter VII and Art 25 of the UN Charter, laying down an *erga omnes* obligation which every Member of the UN has a legal interest in fulfilling.[93]

After deciding on the legitimacy of addressing binding orders, the Appeals Chamber next examined the requirements[94] which such subpoena *duces tecum* orders (that is, for the production of documentary evidence) must satisfy. These were held to be:

(a) the identification of specific documents, rather than categories;
(b) justification of the relevance of requested documents to each trial;
(c) avoidance of unduly onerous requests; and
(d) allowance of sufficient time for compliance.

Where a State persists to defy compliance, the Tribunal is endowed under its inherent power to make a judicial determination regarding a State's failure to observe the Court's Statute or Rules. This power also includes formal notification to the Security Council.[95] The fact that Art 29 constitutes an *erga omnes* obligation empowers all UN Members to request termination of the breach once a relevant judicial determination has been made.[96]

---

91 C Warbrick, 'Co-operation with the International Criminal Tribunal for Yugoslavia', 45 *ICLQ* (1996), 945, p 950; see R Kushen and KJ Harris, 'Surrender of Fugitives by the United States to the War Crimes Tribunals for Yugoslavia and Rwanda', 90 *AJIL* (1996), 510.

92 *Prosecutor v Blaskic*, Appeals Judgment on the Request of the Republic of Croatia for Review of the Decision of Trial Chamber I of 11 July 1997 (*Blaskic* appeals subpoena decision) (29 Oct 1997), para 25.

93 Ibid, para 26; the ad hoc tribunals have at times found it necessary to go beyond the indicative list of orders and requests identified in their respective Statutes, such as in the case of ordering all UN members to freeze former FRY President Milosevic and co-accuseds' assets abroad. *Prosecutor v Milosevic and others*, Decision on Review of Indictment and Application for Consequential Orders (24 May 1999).

94 *Blaskic* appeals subpoena decision (29 Oct 1997), para 32.

95 Ibid, para 33.

96 Ibid, para 36.

Binding orders in the form of subpoenas cannot be addressed to State officials acting in their official capacity. It is the prerogative of each State to determine the internal organs competent to receive and carry out the order.[97] The Appeals Chamber found that it possessed unlimited authority, on the basis of its incidental jurisdiction, to issue orders to private individuals within the framework of domestic channelling procedures, unless otherwise permitted by national law or when State authorities refuse to comply by hindering this process.[98] The concept of private individuals for the purposes of Art 29 also includes State agents possessing information or material obtained before they accepted office, members of peace-keeping forces, because their mandate stems from the same source as the Tribunal, and State agents who refuse to obey national authorities.[99] As for possible national security concerns, although every possible protective measure should be observed, the Appeals Chamber emphasised the exceptional departure from Art 2(7) of the UN Charter relating to the Security Council's authority acting under Chapter VII to interfere in the domestic affairs of States, the establishment of the ICTY being one such specific application.[100]

In a related case in 1999, the ICTY was seized with a request by the prosecutor to order the International Committee of the Red Cross (ICRC) to disclose information that its employees had collected in the course of their duty. The Chamber held that admissibility of evidence may be limited not only by the ICTY Statute and Rules, but also by customary international law.[101] The ICRC was found to be an independent humanitarian organisation organised under Swiss law, generally acknowledged as enjoying international legal personality and whose functions and tasks were directly derived from international law, that is, the 1949 Geneva Conventions and subsequent Protocols thereto.[102] Based on the object and purpose of the Geneva Conventions, the ICRC is recognised by States parties as enjoying impartiality, neutrality and confidentiality, all of which are necessary in order to carry out its mandate. The ICTY noted that widespread ratification of these treaties, taken together with relevant State acceptance, reflected a customary international law right to non-disclosure by the ICRC.[103] In any event, the Trial Chamber held that Art 29 of the ICTY Statute does not apply vis-à-vis international organisations.[104]

---

97 Ibid, paras 38, 43.

98 Ibid, para 55.

99 Ibid, paras 49–51.

100 Ibid, para 64.

101 *Prosecutor v Simic and Others*, Decision on the Prosecution Motion under r 73 for a Ruling Concerning the Testimony of a Witness (27 July 1999), paras 41–42.

102 Ibid, para 46.

103 Ibid, paras 72–74.

104 Ibid, para 78. See S Jeannet, 'Recognition of the ICRC's Long Standing Rule of Confidentiality', 838 *IRRC* (2000), 403.

20.4 RIGHTS OF THE ACCUSED

The drafters of the ad hoc tribunals have paid heed to accusations of unfair proceedings that have in the past been levelled against the framers of the Nuremberg Tribunal, ensuring that not only customary international law would constitute applicable law,[105] but that fair trial guarantees would permeate trial and pre-trial proceedings. Articles 20 and 21 of the ICTY Statute guarantee such fair and expeditious proceedings to all accused. Established in accordance with appropriate procedures under the UN Charter, providing further all necessary safeguards for a fair trial, both ad hoc tribunals are properly considered as being established by law.[106] Their creation, the ICTY itself claims, does not violate the right to be tried by one's national courts (known also as *jus de non evocando*), since transfer to the jurisdiction of the ICTY does not infringe or threaten the rights of the accused.[107]

Although the principle of 'equality of arms' underlies ICTY judicial proceedings,[108] it is also true that the accused cannot compete with the prosecutor's resources, despite being entitled to receive both legal and financial assistance to defend oneself.[109] In the later stages of the *Tadic* case, the accused claimed violation of the principle of equality of arms on account of the Republika Srpska's failure to co-operate with the ICTY, thus depriving Tadic of adequate facilities for the preparation of his defence. The Appeals Chamber interpreted the principle of equality of arms as obligating a judicial body to ensure that neither party is put at a disadvantage when presenting its case, so far as this applies to situations which are within the control of the court.[110] Several safeguards exist in order to protect an accused from prosecutorial abuse of authority and to remedy the imbalance in resources. Most importantly, the 'presumption of innocence' principle constitutes a fundamental right under Art 21(2) of the ICTY Statute, as does also the right against self-incrimination.[111] The Trial Chambers ensure that these rights are observed, even in cases where the accused seems to have waived them. The Appeals Chamber in the *Erdemovic* case did not hesitate to overturn a Trial

---

105 In this regard, cautious use of domestic legal concepts and precedent has been made. The *Aleksovski* appeals judgment (25 June 1999), paras 107–08, categorically stated that ICTY Chambers should observe precedent 'in the interests of certainty and predictability, but be free to depart from previous decisions for cogent reasons in the interests of justice, such as in the case of a legally incorrect decision.

106 *Tadic* appeals jurisdiction decision (2 Oct 1995), para 47.

107 Ibid, para 62.

108 ICTY Statute, Art 21(1). This principle is also satisfied through the right to adequate time and facilities for preparation of one's defence, as well as to examine witnesses under the same conditions as the prosecutor, in accordance with Art 21(4)(b) and (e) respectively.

109 Ibid, Art 21(4)(d).

110 *Tadic* appeals judgment (15 July 1999), paras 44, 48–52.

111 ICTY Statute, Art 21(4)(g).

judgment which accepted a guilty plea that did not, however, satisfy the criteria for its admission. The accused was a soldier in the Bosnian Serb Army who took part in the execution of civilians during the Srebrenica massacres, albeit under severe duress. Although he pleaded guilty to crimes against humanity he also invoked the said duress as a defence. The majority of the Appeals Chamber held that duress does not afford a complete defence and consequently found the appellant's guilty plea to have been equivocal.[112] In his dissenting opinion Judge Cassese correctly argued that a guilty plea must satisfy the following requirements under international law: it must be voluntary, that is, not obtained by threats, inducements or promises; the accused must be in good mental health; the plea must be entered knowingly, that is, the accused must be fully aware of its legal implications; and the plea must not be ambiguous or equivocal, that is to say the accused cannot be allowed on the one hand to admit his or her guilt and at the same time claim to be acting under some exculpatory reason.[113] The criteria established by Cassese J's dissenting opinion have subsequently been upheld by ICTY and ICTR Chambers.[114]

The *Barayagwiza* case is perhaps highly instructive of the prosecutor's strict duty to adhere to all aspects of the 'fair trial' principle, or face dismissal of the charges. The accused was detained in Cameroon for 19 months at the request of the prosecutor without an indictment drawn against him before being transferred to the ICTR. He endured three further months of detention from the moment of transfer until his initial appearance before an ICTR Trial Chamber. On the basis of this lengthy delay the Tribunal held that, although the prosecution may request other countries in cases of urgency to arrest and detain suspects,[115] it certainly does not enjoy unlimited power to keep a suspect under provisional detention.[116] The remedy for failure to issue a prompt indictment is the release of the suspect.[117] Likewise, the Appeals Chamber held that when one State applies to another for a 'detainer', that is, a special type of warrant filed against a person already in custody so as to ensure his or her availability upon completion of present confinement, the accused is in 'constructive custody' of the requesting State, while the detaining State acts as an agent of the requesting State for all purposes

---

112 *Prosecutor v Erdemovic*, Appeals Judgment (7 Oct 1997), para 19.

113 *Erdemovic* appeals judgment (7 Oct 1997). Separate and dissenting opinion of Judge Cassese, para 10. Cassese J convincingly argued that in exceptional circumstances duress can be urged in defence to crimes against humanity or war crimes, paras 11–49.

114 *Prosecutor v Serushago*, Judgment (5 Feb 1999), para 1.

115 ICTY Rules, r 40.

116 *Barayagwiza v Prosecutor*, Appeals Decision (3 Nov 1999), para 46.

117 Ibid.

related to *habeas corpus* challenges.[118] Thus, despite lack of physical control, the appellant was in ICTR custody because his detention in Cameroon was instigated upon request of the prosecutor. Even if not deemed to be in custody on the behest of the ICTR, the appellant's detention was impermissibly lengthy.[119] The right to be tried without undue delay was found to have been violated by the 96-day interval between the accused's transfer and his initial appearance before a Trial Chamber.[120]

The Appeals Chamber classified this case of prosecutorial incompetence, resulting in a lengthy detention and delay in trial, as 'abuse of process'. This concept comprises proceedings which although lawfully initiated are thereafter continued improperly or illegally in pursuance of an otherwise lawful process, such as resort to kidnapping. Under such circumstances, courts or tribunals enjoy judicial discretion to terminate proceedings where it is felt that further exercise of jurisdiction in light of serious violations of the accused's rights would prove detrimental to the court's integrity.[121] Such discretion, the Tribunal remarked, may be relied upon where the delay has made a fair trial impossible, or in the particular circumstances of a case, where proceeding to the merits would contravene the court's sense of justice due to pre-trial impropriety.[122] Barayagwiza's release understandably sparked vehement Rwandan condemnation, but it must be acknowledged that it was fully justified, reflecting an international tribunal that respects fundamental rights and the rule of law. The Appeals Chamber reconvened in order to examine the prosecutor's request for reconsideration of the release order on the basis of new information that could not have been submitted in 1999. In its Decision of 31 March 2000, the Appeals Chamber admitted the prosecutor's evidence as 'new' and held that these new facts diminished the role played by the failings of the prosecutor, as well as the intensity of the violation of the accused's rights. It thus revoked its earlier release and reparation order on the basis that this was disproportionate in relation to the prosecutor's role in the continued detention of the accused. Understandably, the independence of the tribunals and that of the judges was called into question and three of the judges entered Separate Opinions denying that their independence had been impaired as a result of coercion.

---

118 Ibid, paras 56–57; lack of an arrest warrant or evidence demonstrating the accused's responsibility over an offence is not required at the pre-trial stage of requesting States to detain a suspect, since the prosecutor's request will be determined in accordance with the requested State's domestic law. *Prosecutor v Kajelijeli*, Decision on the Defence Motion Concerning the Arbitrary Arrest and Illegal Detention of the Accused and on the Defence Notice of Urgent Motion to Expand and Supplement the Record (8 May 2000), para 34.
119 *Barayagwiza* decision (3 Nov 1999), paras 58, 61, 67, 100.
120 Ibid, para 71.
121 Ibid, para 74.
122 Ibid, paras 77, 101.

In the *Todorovic* case the accused challenged his arrest by SFOR and requested to see certain SFOR documents and question SFOR officials. The ICTY agreed with this motion and issued a relevant subpoena,[123] deeming it consistent with fair trial guarantees, but it was unlikely that its Security Council mandate stretched as far as enforcing an order of that nature on SFOR. The US government, NATO and individual Member States intervened and filed motions for judicial review against the subpoena issued by the Trial Chamber. Perhaps on account of these interventions Todorovic eventually entered into a plea bargain and withdrew his motion, but as a result of admitting his motion for subpoena a decline in arrests by SFOR was thereafter apparent.

The protection of the rights of the accused has not caused neglect for safeguarding victims and witnesses. This has been made possible by a variety of measures, such as the non-disclosure of identities,[124] assignment of pseudonyms,[125] ordering of closed sessions,[126] or the giving of testimony through image or voice altering devices and closed circuit television,[127] or through video conference link.[128] Furthermore, a Code of Professional Conduct for Defence Counsel was adopted by the ICTY Registrar on 12 June 1997, in an attempt to limit harassment and intimidation of victims and witnesses.[129] A more detailed exposition of ICTY/ICTR procedural law and the rights of victims and witnesses is provided in Chapter 18.

---

123 *ICTY Prosecutor v Todorovic*, Trial Chamber Decision (18 Oct 2000) on the Motion for Judicial Assistance.
124 ICTY Rules, rr 69(A) and 75(B)(i)(a) and (b).
125 Ibid, r 75(B)(i)(d).
126 Ibid, rr 75(B)(ii) and 79.
127 Ibid, r 75(B)(i)(c). This is not a novel conception, as some States in the US allow it. The US Supreme Court held in *Maryland v Craig*, 497 US 836 (1990) that closed circuit television depositions do not violate the sixth amendment right to confrontation where a court finds it necessary to protect a child witness from psychological harm.
128 Ibid, r 71(D).
129 See I Bantekas, 'Study on the Minimum Rules of Conduct in Cross-Examination to be Applied by the International Criminal Tribunal for the Former Yugoslavia', 50 *Rev Hel* (1997), 205.

Chapter 21

The permanent international criminal court

21.1 THE HISTORICAL ORIGINS OF THE INTERNATIONAL CRIMINAL COURT

Following the adoption of the 1948 United Nations (UN) Convention on the Prevention and Punishment of the Crime of Genocide (Genocide Convention)[1] the General Assembly also invited the International Law Commission (ILC) 'to study the desirability and possibility of establishing an international judicial organ for the trial of persons charged with genocide'.[2] The ILC studied this question at its 1949 and 1950 sessions and concluded that a court of that nature was both desirable and possible.[3] Subsequent to the ILC's report the General Assembly established a committee to prepare proposals relating to the establishment of such a court. The committee first prepared a draft statute in 1951[4] and a revised draft statute in 1953,[5] but the Assembly decided to postpone consideration of the matter pending the adoption of a definition on aggression. Despite periodical consideration of the issue since 1953, it was in December 1989, in response to a letter addressed to the UN Secretary General by Trinidad and Tobago regarding the establishment of an international court with jurisdiction over the illicit trafficking in drugs, that the General Assembly once more requested the ILC to resume work on the creation of an international criminal court.[6] Following the shocking first reports from the armed conflicts in the former Yugoslavia and the establishment of the International Criminal Tribunal for the Former

---

1 GA Res 260(II) (9 Dec 1948).
2 This was in accordance with the 1948 Convention on the Prevention and Punishment of the Crime of Genocide, Art VI, 78 UNTS 277, which provided for the establishment of an international penal tribunal with jurisdiction over acts of genocide.
3 *Report of the ILC on the Work of its Second Session* (5 June–29 July 1950) UN GAOR, Fifth Session, Supp No 12, UN Doc A/1316 (1950), para 140.
4 UN GAOR, Seventh Session, Supp No 11, UN Doc A/2136 (1952).
5 UN GAOR, Ninth Session, Supp No 12, UN Doc A/2625 (1954).
6 GA Res 44/39 (4 Dec 1989).

Yugoslavia (ICTY), the General Assembly urged the ILC to elaborate a viable statute as a matter of priority. This culminated in the production of a draft statute in 1994.[7] In order to consider major substantive issues arising from the draft statute the General Assembly created an Ad Hoc Committee on the Establishment of an International Criminal Court, which met twice in 1995.[8] After consideration of the Ad Hoc Committee's work the General Assembly established the Preparatory Committee (Prep Com) on the Establishment of an International Criminal Court.[9] The task of the Prep Com, unlike its predecessor, was to formulate a generally acceptable instrument and not simply to assess the viability and preliminary concerns regarding such a project, for eventual submission to a diplomatic conference. Upon concluding its work the Prep Com, having met six times since 1996, asked the General Assembly to convene a diplomatic conference for the purposes of finalising the statute in treaty form and adoption by the international community. A heavily bracketed draft treaty – the brackets indicating unresolved issues and details – was laid before a conference of plenipotentiaries for negotiation in July 1998 in Rome, where after extremely intense negotiations and compromises on all sides, the International Criminal Court (ICC) Statute was signed on 17 July 1998.[10] One hundred and twenty States voted in favour of the treaty, seven voted against (US, China, Libya, Iraq, Israel, Qatar, Yemen) and 21 abstained. Following the Rome Conference in the summer of 1998, the US proclaimed that it would not sign the Statute. However, after fears that the country would isolate itself from the proceedings of the ICC Preparatory Commission and create a negative international image,[11] the US finally signed the text of the Statute on 31 December 2000, but then withdrew its signature on 6 May 2002, making it clear that it had no intention of ratifying this instrument. This was not a symbolic act, since it connoted that the US was no longer bound to respect the object and purpose of the treaty and as will become clear below in this chapter, from that moment onwards it openly adopted a hostile attitude towards it. Following the required sixtieth ratification, the ICC Statute finally entered into force on 1 July 2002.

Unlike the two *ad hoc* Tribunals for Yugoslavia and Rwanda, the ICC is a permanent international criminal court established by its founding treaty.[12] It

---

7 J Crawford, 'The ILC Adopts a Statute for an International Criminal Court', 89 *AJIL* (1995), 404.

8 See *Report of the Ad Hoc Committee on the Establishment of an International Criminal Court*, UN GAOR, 50th Session, Supp No 22, UN Doc A/50/22 (1995); see V Morris and CM Bourloyannis-Vrailas, 'The Work of the Sixth Committee at the Fiftieth Session of the UN General Assembly', 90 *AJIL* (1996), 491.

9 GA Res 50/46 (11 Dec 1995).

10 37 ILM (1998), 999.

11 DJ Scheffer, 'Staying the Course with the International Criminal Court', 35 *Cornell ILJ* (2002), 47.

12 ICC Statute, Art 1.

has been endowed with international legal personality[13] and, although it is an independent judicial institution, the drafters of the ICC Statute wished it to be related through an agreement with the UN.[14] This is desirable because the Security Council plays a significant role in referring cases to the Court and there is, further, a need to assert the Council's absolute authority over issues concerned with international peace and security, and thus maintain coherency in that field. There is no financial relationship between the ICC and the UN, except in cases where the Court's expenses have been incurred as a result of Security Council referrals.[15] All other expenses are to be borne from assessed contributions made by States parties, or voluntary contributions.[16] The Preparatory Commission, established as a result of the 1998 Rome Conference, worked, *inter alia*, on a relationship agreement between the ICC and the UN. This provides for mutual respect and recognition by the UN of the ICC's international legal personality, and accordingly respect by the ICC of the UN's role in the maintenance of international peace and security, envisaging close co-operation between the two institutions. Thus, the Negotiated Relationship Agreement between the ICC and the UN was approved and came into being in 2004 in the form of a treaty between two international organisations.

The Court consists of a judicial, prosecutorial and administrative (registry) branch. The judicial section comprises 18 full-time judges, which are to be elected for a non-renewable nine-year term by the Assembly of State Parties (ASP).[17] Unlike the ad hoc tribunals, there is a requirement that at least nine judges possess competency in criminal proceedings while a minimum of five judges must be experts in relevant areas of international law, such as international humanitarian law and human rights. Moreover, both the pre-trial and trial chambers are to be composed predominantly of judges with criminal law experience.[18] Under Art 43(4) the judges are also empowered to elect the registrar for a five-year term, whose office is open to re-election only once. As will be shown below, the prosecutor is an independent organ of the Court. He or she may designate appropriate deputy prosecutors whose candidacy must be approved by the ASP. Prosecutors shall serve on a full-time basis.[19]

13 Ibid, Art 4(1).
14 Ibid, Art 2.
15 Ibid, Art 115(b). Nonetheless, in its referral to the ICC of the Darfur (Sudan) situation, the Security Council made it clear in Resolution 1593 (2005) that all expenses associated to the referral, including investigations and prosecution, were to be borne by ICC-State parties, as well as by voluntary contributions, if any.
16 ICC Statute, Arts 115(a) and 116.
17 Ibid, Art 35. If the workload of the Court, however, does not justify the full-time engagement of all 18 judges, the Presidency of the Court may decide from time to time to what extent the remaining judges shall be required to serve on a full-time basis.
18 Ibid, Art 36.
19 Ibid, Art 42.

The ICC enjoys subject matter jurisdiction over four core offences: geno-cide, crimes against humanity, war crimes and aggression.[20] No consensus was reached during the Rome diplomatic conference on a definition for the crime of aggression, which will remain dormant until such time as the ASP approves a definition that is consistent with the Charter of the UN. Before we proceed to examine these offences in detail, the regulation of the Court's jurisdiction and admissibility procedures will be first analysed.

21.2 JURISDICTION AND ADMISSIBILITY

In accordance with Art 34 of the 1969 Vienna Convention on the Law of Treaties,[21] international agreements are capable of binding only contracting parties. They do not bind third States without their consent. Practice sug-gests, however, that multilateral treaty arrangements may on the basis of political or legal reality impose certain constraints on the behaviour of third States. These constraints do not result from legal obligations, but accrue instead from the formation of a broad international consensus stemming from multilateral agreements that possess a 'constitutional' nature.[22] Although this is true in the case of the UN, if this is also true with regard to the ICC this would mean that the ICC, as an international legal entity, has the cap-acity through its Statute to affect States parties as well as non-parties, albeit in expressly defined and specifically limited circumstances. That this possibil-ity in fact exists in international law was confirmed by the International Court of Justice (ICJ) in its Advisory Opinion in the *Reparations* case, where it held that universal intergovernmental organisations possess 'objective inter-national legal personality and not merely personality recognised by [their members] alone'.[23]

Under Art 12 of its Statute, the ICC's jurisdiction over a case or 'situation' may be triggered in any of the following cases; either where a situation or offence takes place in the territory of, or by a national of a State party;[24] where the territorial State or the State of the nationality of the accused are parties to the Statute;[25] or where the Security Council acting under Chapter VII of the UN Charter refers a situation to the ICC prosecutor.[26] Whereas, under Art 12(1), a party to the Statute is subject to the automatic

---

20 ICC Statute, Art 5.
21 1155 UNTS 331.
22 GM Danilenko, 'The Statute of the International Criminal Court and Third States', 21 *Mich J Int'l L* (2000), 444, p 448.
23 Reparation for Injuries Suffered in the Service of the UN (1949) ICJ Reports 174, p 185.
24 ICC Statute, Arts 12(1) and 14(1).
25 Ibid, Art 12(2).
26 Ibid, Art 13(b).

jurisdiction of the Court, non-parties under para 2 (that is, the territorial State or the State of the accused's nationality as the case may be) can accept ICC jurisdiction with regard to a specific case or situation by lodging a declaration to that effect.[27] The US vehemently opposed the type of jurisdiction envisaged under Art 12(2) because, in the opinion of its delegates, this provision violates the rule that treaties can only bind contracting parties.[28] This is a valid legal argument, since Art 12(2) establishes ICC jurisdiction if either the territorial State or the State of nationality of the accused is a party to the Court's Statute or has made a declaration under Art 12(3), despite the fact that one of these States may not be a party and be, thus, adversely affected. A relevant example would be where a US national – the US not being a party to the Court's Statute – is accused of having committed an offence in State B, which is either a party to the Statute or has lodged a declaration, and by succumbing to the ICC's authority, thus gives the ICC jurisdiction over the accused. In this case, the US, although not a party to the ICC Statute, is nonetheless directly affected by its application through the surrender to the ICC of one of its nationals. Justification for this provision cannot be substantiated with regard to the principles of territorial or active personality jurisdiction, because these are principles pertaining solely to the judicial competence of individual States and find no application vis-à-vis an international tribunal whose competence is only delineated by its statute. Rather, jurisdiction under Art 12(2) can only be justified on the basis of the Court's character as a universal institution whose legal personality necessarily affects the interests of third States. Moreover, the Court's jurisdiction is curtailed by a plethora of procedural and substantive safeguards against possible abuse.

Article 12(2) is clearly inconsistent with treaty law, but it is not entirely clear whether it is also inconsistent with contemporary developments in international criminal justice which have eroded the right of States to freely invoke the principle of 'domestic jurisdiction' in order to shield their nationals from serious human rights violations. Moreover, in contemporary international relations and particularly in the context of global multilateral treaties, it is inevitable that the nationals of third States will be affected where they have undertaken action outside their home State. This result is not tantamount to a treaty producing effects for a third party for action undertaken solely on its territory or in its relations with other third parties.

After the adoption of the ICC Statute, the US concluded a number of bilateral treaties with other States, with the aim of precluding investigation and prosecution of US nationals accused of offences falling within the jurisdiction of the ICC. These so-called 'impunity agreements' (or Art 98

---

27 Ibid, Art 12(3).
28 DJ Scheffer, 'The United States and the International Criminal Court', 93 *AJIL* (1999), 12, p 18.

Agreements) were signed, among others, by Romania, Tajikistan and Israel.[29] As far as ICC-Member States are concerned, these agreements violate their obligations under Art 86 of the Statute to co-operate with the Court in the investigation and prosecution of alleged offenders. These States have argued that Art 98(2) of the ICC Statute does not oblige them to adhere to ICC surrender requests that violate existing treaty obligations, thus legitimising the 'impunity agreements'. This is fallacious, since Art 98(2) seems to relate more to Status of Forces Agreements (SOFAs), ensuring that they will not be nullified – that is, that the sending State will retain criminal jurisdiction over offences committed by its personnel on the territory of the host State – but does in no way grant a licence for impunity, as this would violate the object and purpose of the ICC Statute. Moreover, although no legal consequences arise for those States non-parties to the ICC Statute that have signed the bilateral agreements with the USA, the same is not true with regard to ICC Member States. The latter will incur State responsibility because the obligations assumed under the bilateral treaty are subsequent in time to their commitments under the ICC Statute. A State is not permitted to absolve its existing obligations by entering into a new conflicting treaty without the prior treaty having been terminated by the express consent of all relevant parties.

Of even further limitation to the ICC prosecutor's competence, and a sign of strong US opposition to the Court's aim and purpose, was the adoption of Security Council Resolution 1422, on 12 July 2002. The short history of this Resolution can be traced to 19 June 2002 when the US threatened to veto the continuation of the mandate of the UN Mission in Bosnia and Herzegovina (UNMIBH) under the pretence that US troops could potentially be prosecuted by the ICC in accordance with Art 12(2) of its Statute.[30] Following several Council meetings concerning the future of UNMIBH, the Council decided to adopt Resolution 1422 under Chapter VII of the UN Charter, para 1 of which requested that in accordance with Art 16 of the ICC Statute:

> If a case arises involving current or former officials or personnel from a contributing State not a party to the Rome Statute over acts or omissions relating to a United Nations established or authorized operation, [then the ICC] shall for a twelve-month period starting 1 July 2002 not commence or proceed with investigation or prosecution of any such case, unless the Security Council decides otherwise.

29 Amnesty International (AI), *International Criminal Court: US Efforts to Obtain Impunity for Genocide, Crimes Against Humanity and War Crimes*, AI Doc IOR/40/025/2002 (2 Sept 2002). By mid-2005 the US had concluded 100 such Agreements with both ICC and non-ICC Member States. See <http://www.state.gov/r/pa/prs/ps/2005/45573.htm>.
30 UN Press Release SC/7430 (21 June 2002).

The Resolution went on to say that such a deferral may be extended by subsequent 12-month periods by the Council and that UN Member States must take no action inconsistent with para 1 and their international obligations. This Resolution is worrying in the sense that, besides the impunity it grants, it implies that the application of justice constituted under the Rome Statute represents a threat to international peace and security![31]

One of the safeguards that should alleviate some of the mistrust and apprehension is the principle of complementarity, which is found in the Statute's preamble and its Arts 1 and 17, which establish that the Court may assume jurisdiction only when national legal systems are genuinely unable or unwilling to do so, or where an accused has already been tried for the same offence.[32] In determining unwillingness in a particular case, the Court shall consider whether national proceedings are intended to shield the accused or avoid impartial prosecution.[33] The establishment of truth commissions whose purpose is to avoid criminal proceedings would generally be incompatible with a party's obligation to diligently prosecute under the ICC Statute. Equally, the granting of amnesties in accordance with national law does not release a person from criminal responsibility under international law. A determination by the Court of either shielding or lack of impartiality can be challenged by the accused, the State which has commenced or completed investigation of the case, as well as the State from which acceptance of jurisdiction is required under Art 12(2).[34] Thus, unlike the primary jurisdiction enjoyed by the ICTY and the International Criminal Tribunal for Rwanda (ICTR), national courts enjoy primacy in cases of concurrent jurisdiction with the ICC, but, clearly, this is neither unlimited nor without challenge from the prosecutor and other States with concurrent jurisdiction or custody of the accused. In fact, there is no requirement that the custodial State should even consent to the jurisdiction of the ICC where an order for the accused's surrender has been issued.[35]

Another safeguard is contained in Art 98, which recognises that compliance with an ICC order for surrender should not violate the custodial State's obligations under international law. Article 98(1) requires the third State's express waiver of State or diplomatic immunity over persons and

---

31 The mandate of SC Res 1422 was renewed once under SC Res 1487 (12 June 2003). Equally, SC 1497 (1 Aug 2003) and relating to the deployment of a multinational stabilisation force to Liberia, at the insistence of the USA, exempted non-ICC Member State nationals from the Court's jurisdiction.

32 ICC Statute, Art 17(1).

33 Ibid, Art 17(2).

34 Ibid, Art 19(2).

35 D McGoldrick, 'The Permanent International Criminal Court: An End to the Culture of Impunity?', *Crim LR* [1999], 627, p 642.

property situated in a country that has accepted the Court's jurisdiction.[36] Similarly, para 2 requires the consent of the sending State in all cases of ICC surrender orders with regard to accused persons forming part of status-of-forces agreement contingents and stationed at the time of the order in the receiving State. The principle of complementarity therefore covers not only the exercise of actual prosecution, but also the possibility of jurisdiction itself under a particular legal system, such as the applicability of immunities and the possibility of surrender.

Although the concept of 'universal' jurisdiction in this treatise is reserved for national judiciaries, it is worth mentioning a German proposal that the ICC be entitled to try anyone surrendered to it, irrespective of whether that person is a national of a State party or, if a national of a non-party, whether that State made a relevant declaration accepting the jurisdiction of the Court. This approach, Germany contended, was consonant with the practice of national courts under customary law.[37] Indeed, if the ICC were to exercise the universal jurisdiction normally enjoyed by States, it would mean that the ICC is competent to exercise also the pre-existing jurisdiction of States parties which they have delegated to the ICC. As a result, the ICC's jurisdiction could also be derived from sources outside the ICC Statute. Although Art 12 of the Statute refutes such universal jurisdiction, it recognises a single exception where the Security Council itself refers a situation under Chapter VII of the UN Charter. Concerns have been raised as to whether complementarity is applicable where a situation has been referred to the ICC by the Security Council, as was the case with Sudan under Resolution 1593 of 31 March 2005. Since the Council's mandatory powers extend only against UN Member States and not international organisations, such as the ICC, the Council cannot generally exclude the application of complementarity even when it is referring a situation under Chapter VII of the UN Charter. In order to be able to do so, this power must be provided for in the ICC Statute itself. Article 13 of the ICC Statute suggests that referrals by a State party, the Council or the prosecutor (acting under Art 15) reserve primacy of jurisdiction for the Court. That the ICC assumes primacy upon Security Council referral is equally evident from the wording of Art 12(2), which specifically excludes Security Council referrals from the general requirement of consent to which the territorial State or the State of nationality of the accused is entitled.[38] In any event, if the Security Council were to adopt a resolution referring a case to the Court in which it expressly or impliedly excluded the

---

36 Presumably, State officials who cannot claim immunity *ratione personae* must try to prove that they enjoy immunity *ratione materiae* under customary international law. Op cit, Danilenko, note 22, p 472.

37 UN Doc A/AC 249/1998/DP2 (1998).

38 For a contrary argument, see M Arsanjani, 'The Rome Statute of the International Criminal Court', 93 *AJIL* (1999), 22, p 28.

exercise of jurisdiction by national courts, the ICC would enjoy primacy in accordance with Art 103 of the UN Charter vis-à-vis UN Member States.

We have already alluded to the fact that the Court's jurisdiction can be triggered by referral from a State party[39] or the Security Council[40] and, also, *proprio motu*, by the prosecutor.[41] To alleviate the concerns of many States regarding possible abuse of the prosecutor's independent right of referral, a variety of mechanisms serve to counterbalance his or her authority. Article 15(1) demands that the prosecutor submit a case to a pre-Trial Chamber for authorisation of an investigation only if there exists a 'reasonable basis' to proceed with the investigation. The pursuance of an investigation may be refused not only where a reasonable basis is lacking, but also where a situation is considered inadmissible under Arts 17–19 (that is, breach of lawful complementarity, *non bis in idem*, and where it is not of sufficient gravity to justify action by the Court). Nonetheless, irrespective of whether a case is deferred to national authorities or is pending a ruling by the pre-Trial Chamber on the Court's jurisdiction, the prosecutor is not prevented from seeking authority to take necessary measures for preserving both material and oral evidence which could subsequently be impaired or lost.[42] In the event that a situation is deferred to the jurisdiction of a national court, the prosecutor retains authority to request periodical progress reports of investigations and judicial proceedings, as well as review national investigations at any time a significant change of circumstances has occurred, indicating a State's unwillingness or inability to proceed.[43] The Security Council acting under Chapter VII of the UN Charter may also defer investigation or prosecution of a situation for a period of 12 months, which is renewable under the same procedure.[44] Indeed, Art 16 could work against Chinese and US desire to dominate ICC referrals,[45] as the other permanent members of the Security Council can effectively use their veto power against such resolutions.

21.2.1 The first referrals

Three situations have until early 2007 been investigated by the ICC Prosecutor. Of these, two were referred by Member States, ie, the Democratic Republic of the Congo (DRC) and Uganda, while the other concerned the situation in Sudan's Darfur region, which was referred to the ICC by the UN Security Council through resolution 1593 (2005). During the same time the

---

39 ICC Statute, Arts 13(a) and 14(1).
40 Ibid, Art 13(b).
41 Ibid, Art 15(1).
42 Ibid, Arts 17(6) and 19(8).
43 Ibid, Art 18(5) and (3).
44 Ibid, Art 16.
45 Op cit, Scheffer, note 28, p 13.

prosecutor has declined to investigate further referrals by the Central African Republic, Iraq[46] and Venezuela.[47] The prosecutor has not had a chance to exercise his *proprio motu* powers, despite the fact that until mid-2006 he had already received more than 1,700 communications.[48]

21.3 SUBJECT MATTER JURISDICTION

As already explained, the ICC enjoys subject matter jurisdiction over genocide, crimes against humanity, war crimes and the crime of aggression. Although the inclusion of other treaty crimes, especially drug-trafficking, terrorism and offences against UN and associated personnel, was contemplated, both before and during the Rome conference, they were finally excluded since it was felt that investigation of drug-trafficking and terrorism involved sensitive and long term planning operations, best suited for domestic authorities, while there does not yet exist an international definition of terrorism.[49] Similarly, the Convention on the Safety of United Nations and Associated Personnel[50] came into force in early 1999. Therefore, in order to salvage the Statute and avoid time-consuming revisions detracting from more serious issues, only the four aforementioned core crimes were included. There is provision in Arts 121 and 123 for a future review of the list of crimes contained in Art 5, which may encompass possible amendment to the existing offences or the addition of new ones.

The Statute is applicable only to natural persons and then only if they were 18 years of age at the time of the alleged offence.[51] The gravity of the four offences has further necessitated their exclusion from any statute of limitations.[52]

21.3.1 The crime of aggression

The absence of an acceptable binding definition of 'crimes against peace' since that offence first appeared as Art 6(a) of the Nuremberg Charter, coupled with resistance from the permanent members of the Security Council

---

46 <http://www.icc-cpi.int/library/organs/otp/OTP_letter_to_senders_re_Iraq_9_February_2006.pdf>.
47 <http://www.icc-cpi.int/library/organs/otp/OTP_letter_to_senders_re_Venezuela_9_February_2006.pdf>.
48 <http://www.icc-cpi.int/library/organs/otp/OTP_Update_on_Communications_10_February_2006.pdf>.
49 Op cit, Arsanjani, note 38, p 29.
50 34 ILM (1995), 482.
51 ICC Statute, Art 26.
52 Ibid, Art 29. This is in accordance with the 1968 Convention on Non-Applicability of Statutory Limitations to War Crimes and Crimes Against Humanity, Art 1, 754 UNTS 73.

over its definition and identification by another body, meant that the definition of aggression for the purposes of the Statute had become too cumbersome to negotiate in time. Clearly, an appropriate definition under Art 5(2) of
the Statute would need, as is clearly required for reasons of coherency, to take
cognisance of the UN Charter, but it is less clear whether this obligation
extends beyond Arts 2(4) and 51 of the Charter to encompass also Security
Council determination of an act of aggression under Art 39 of the Charter.
Whilst it would be prohibited to implicitly or explicitly amend the UN Charter
when defining any aspects of the crime of aggression, the referral of acts of
aggression as international offences by a concerned State or the prosecutor,
especially in cases where the Security Council is blocked by veto, does not
necessarily amend the UN Charter, nor does it usurp Security Council
powers. Let us consider these issues in light of developments a little prior to
and subsequent to the Nuremberg process.

A century apart, both Napoleon and Kaiser William II of Germany were
arraigned for international offences akin to crimes against peace. In the case
of the Kaiser, Art 227 of the 1919 Peace Treaty of Versailles contemplated
his arraignment on the basis of initiating war in violation of international
morality and the sanctity of treaties. Whereas Napoleon was exiled twice, the
Kaiser fled prosecution. As already explained in Chapter 19, no international
instrument between 1919 and 1939 contained provision to the effect that
individuals would incur liability for acts of aggression. Thus, the inclusion of
crimes against peace in the Nuremberg Charter, and later in the International
Military Tribunal for the Far East (IMTFE) Charter, was criticised as violating the principle *nullum crimen sine lege*. Article 6(a) of the Nuremberg
Charter stipulated individual criminal responsibility for crimes against peace,
constituted of the following elements:

> Planning, preparation, initiation, or waging of a war of aggression, or a
> war in violation of international treaties, agreements, or assurances, or
> participation in a common plan or conspiracy for the accomplishment of
> any of the foregoing.

The Nuremberg Tribunal held that Germany had violated a number of
bilateral anti-aggression pacts, as well as other multilateral agreements prohibiting the use of armed force, especially the 1928 Kellogg-Briand Pact.[53]
From a legal point of view, however, neither the bilateral agreements nor
the Kellogg-Briand Pact stipulated individual criminal responsibility, merely
State responsibility. Therefore, and in accordance with the *nullum crimen
sine lege* rule, no one could have been tried for crimes against peace since
they had not been recognised as offences in international law prior to the

---

53 94 LNTS 57.

enactment of the Nuremberg Charter. The Tribunal brushed aside the *nullum crimen sine lege* objections to the charge by relying on the unlawfulness of the force used by Nazi Germany and by making an analogy with the 1907 Hague Convention IV, which it found to stipulate personal responsibility despite the absence of an express provision to that effect. Nonetheless, the allocation of responsibility to individual defendants reflected the precise and actual function of each accused in the commission of the ingredients of crimes against peace under the Charter.[54] The inclusion of the crime of aggression sparked two dissenting opinions by judges Pal and Roling in the IMTFE judgment.

Despite the inclusion of crimes against peace in the set of the Nuremberg Principles, adopted by the General Assembly in 1946,[55] the crime of aggression has not featured in any legally binding instrument since. The explanation is simple. Unlike war crimes, crimes against humanity and genocide which require that the perpetrator commit the *actus reus* of the offence, crimes against peace require that an act typically associated with the functions of a State must first occur; namely, an act of aggression in violation of the rules of international law dealing with the use of force.[56] If this is so, then the criminality of aggression depends to a large extent on the legal definition of armed force under international law, which itself is a controversial matter. In brief, Art 2(4) of the UN Charter prohibits all instances of armed force by one State against another, save for two express exceptions. The first concerns force as a means of self-defence, in accordance with Art 51 of the Charter, whereas the second relates to authorisation by the Security Council to use force under Art 42 of the Charter. Article 51 permits the use of armed force only in cases where a State is under an 'armed attack', clearly suggesting that an armed attack constitutes a significant amount of force against the defending State. Controversies arise from the various interpretations of the concept of self-defence, as enshrined in Art 51, and specifically the precise meaning of the word 'inherent', describing the right of self-defence. Some States argue in favour of the validity of pre-Charter use of force law, such as anticipatory self-defence, humanitarian intervention, and others, whereas the majority of States adhere to a restricted interpretation of Art 51, as allowing for no other exceptions. This controversy in the scope of and the precise definition of the permissible exceptions to the use of force by States has necessarily imposed a stalemate in the construction of an internationally agreed definition of aggression as a crime. This ambiguity, both in terms of permissible uses of force as well as the contours of the crime of aggression, was not fully resolved even by the General Assembly's Definition of Aggression of 1974, despite the

---

54 C Antonopoulos, 'Whatever Happened to Crimes Against Peace?', 6 *Journal of Conflict & Security Law* (2001), 33, p 38.
55 GA Res 95(1) (11 Dec 1946).
56 Op cit, Antonopoulos, note 54, p 37.

fact that it called a 'war of aggression' an international crime.[57] Antonopoulos correctly argues that the 1974 Definition was intended to serve as a guide for the Security Council in determining acts of aggression and therefore did not precisely elaborate who and under what particular circumstances an individual would incur personal liability as a result. It did, however, strongly suggest that the criminality of aggression is to be sought at the level of State action.[58] It is true to say that the 1974 Definition gave a satisfactory construction as regards the term 'aggression', but not one that satisfies the needs of criminal law in assessing criminal responsibility.[59]

The assessment of culpability regarding the crime of aggression necessitates, as already stated, determination of aggression undertaken on behalf of a State. It is not entirely obvious that this task befalls the ICC. Rather, the ICC Preparatory Commission has put forward a proposal whereby the ICC will defer the task of determining the existence of aggression to the UN system for a certain period of time, after the lapse of which the ICC would be seized of the matter.[60] It is clear that the allocation of responsibility for the crime of aggression incorporates the following elements: (a) the unlawfulness of a specific resort to force of some magnitude; and (b) only those persons that played a direct, actual and influential role in the aggression and the decision making behind it, in accordance with the Nuremberg principles and judgment. Thus, the mere fact that someone was a member of the government or a high-ranking official in the armed forces would not *ipso facto* render that person culpable of the offence.

21.3.2 Genocide, crimes against humanity and war crimes

Article 6 of the Statute relating to genocide was taken *verbatim* from Art II of the 1948 Genocide Convention, receiving a quick and unanimous consensus. Some variations with regard to the Statutes of the ICTY/ICTR exist with regard to crimes against humanity and war crimes. These are analysed in detail in Chapters 5, 6 and 7.

21.4 GENERAL PRINCIPLES OF CRIMINAL LAW

Part 3 of the Statute sets out the bases for both incurring and excluding individual criminal responsibility. Unlike the ad hoc Tribunals, the ICC

---

57 GA Res 3314(XXIX) (14 Dec 1974).
58 Op cit, Antonopoulos, note 54, p 39.
59 GA Res 2625(XXV) (24 Oct 1970), confirmed simply in Principle I that a war of aggression is a crime against peace entailing individual responsibility.
60 ICC Doc PCNICC/2000/L 3/Rev 1 (12–30 June 2000), pp 10–12.

enjoys jurisdiction over natural persons, even if the alleged offence is not completed, but is at least attempted.[61] The Statute penalises four forms of participation in criminal acts: principal participation, ordering, aiding or abetting, and acting with a common purpose. Incitement to commit an offence within the jurisdiction of the Court is limited only to the crime of genocide, which under customary law does not require that genocide actually take place. The Court does not have jurisdiction over persons that were below the age of 18 when the alleged offence was perpetrated.[62] An additional form of responsibility confirmed in the Statute is that attaching to military or civilian persons in positions of authority who fail to prevent or punish criminal acts committed by their subordinates. Article 28(a)(i) requires either actual knowledge of the offences or the 'should have known standard', which, being similar to Art 86(2) of Protocol I 1977, stipulates the liability of the superior where, 'owing to the circumstances at the time', he or she should have known that the forces under his or her command were committing or about to commit such crimes. Although the Yugoslav Tribunal's jurisprudence has been consistent in denying a rebuttable presumption of knowledge in similar circumstances,[63] Art 28(a)(i) of the ICC Statute may be construed, albeit cautiously, as accepting such presumption.

Criminal liability may be excluded on several grounds. Persons suffering from a mental disease or involuntary intoxication which renders them unable to control or appreciate the nature of their conduct, as well as persons acting reasonably under self-defence are completely exculpated from liability.[64] Similarly, the invocation of duress may serve to relieve one from liability if the criminal conduct caused by duress resulted from:

> . . . a threat of imminent death or of continuing or imminent serious bodily harm against that person or another person, and the person acts necessarily and reasonably to avoid this threat, provided that the person does not intend to cause a greater harm than the one sought to be avoided.[65]

The characterisation of duress as a full defence that is capable of excluding liability has clearly been influenced by the dissenting opinion of Cassese J in the *Erdemovic* case before the ICTY.[66]

---

61 ICC Statute, Art 25(3).
62 Ibid, Art 26.
63 *Prosecutor v Delalic and Others*, Trial Chamber Judgment (*Celebici* judgment) (16 Nov 1998), para 384; subsequently followed in *Prosecutor v Blaskic*, Trial Chamber Judgment (3 March 2000), paras 307, 408, and *Prosecutor v Aleksovski*, Trial Chamber Judgment (25 June 1999), para 80.
64 ICC Statute, Art 31(1)(a)–(c).
65 Ibid, Art 31(1)(d).
66 *Prosecutor v Erdemovic*, Appeals Chamber Judgment (7 Oct 1997), dissenting opinion of Cassese J, paras 11–49.

Another possible defence is the invocation of a mistake of fact or of law. While none of these constitute general grounds for excluding criminal responsibility, exceptionally they will do so if the perpetrator's mistake as to fact or law actually negates the mental element required for the particular crime.[67] Similarly, the fact that an offence within the jurisdiction of the Court was committed pursuant to orders received from a superior does not as a rule relieve the recipient perpetrator from liability. The ICC Statute, carefully following customary law,[68] excludes the recipient's liability where: (a) that person was under a legal obligation to obey the orders; (b) he or she did not know that the order was unlawful; and (c) the order was not manifestly unlawful.[69] Although two schools of thought have emerged on whether the plea of superior orders offers a complete defence, the jurisprudence of the post-Second World War military tribunals, as well as subsequent military legislation, suggests that the plea of superior orders has excluded liability where a 'moral choice was in fact available' to the accused, and where the order was not 'manifestly unlawful'. On this basis, para (2) expressly points out that orders to commit genocide or crimes against humanity are, in every case, considered to be manifestly unlawful.[70]

21.5 INTERNATIONAL COOPERATION AND JUDICIAL ASSISTANCE

Parties to the Statute are under a general obligation to co-operate with the Court in accordance with Art 86. The Court enjoys broad authority to make requests of a varying nature where these are relevant to the investigation and prosecution of crimes within its jurisdiction, including surrender of accused persons as well as a plethora of material that has evidentiary value. In the execution of any requests States are permitted to comply with their national procedural law.[71] Non-parties to the Statute are not obliged to co-operate with the Court, but may choose to do so on the basis of an *ad hoc* arrangement.[72] Under Art 87(4) binding requests of any kind may demand that measures be taken for the protection of evidence or for the physical and psychological well being of victims, witnesses and their families. The Court may also ask any intergovernmental organisation to provide information or documents, in accordance with Art 87(4), but, since such entities are not parties to

---

67 ICC Statute, Art 32.
68 C Garraway, 'Superior Orders and the International Criminal Court: Justice Delivered or Justice Denied?', 836 *IRRC* (1999), 785.
69 ICC Statute, Art 33(1).
70 For a detailed analysis of defences, see Chapter 3.
71 ICC Statute, Art 88.
72 Ibid, Art 87(5).

the Rome Statute, they are not bound to adhere.[73] In relation to the Congo investigation we are faced with conflicting statements. On the one hand, para 5(g) of Security Council Resolution 1565 of 1 October 2004 authorises the UN Mission in Congo (MONUC) to 'continue to cooperate with efforts to ensure that those responsible for serious violations of human rights and international humanitarian law are brought to justice, while working closely with the relevant agencies of the United Nations'. This could suggest an authorisation to cooperate with the ICC in the arrest of indicted persons, as was the conviction of the UN Secretary-General.[74] Such an authorisation, however, must be rejected because of a statement by the UN Ambassador to the UN, according to which the US supports Resolution 1565 with the 'understanding that it does not direct MONUC to cooperate with the ICC'.[75]

Equally, the ICC cannot direct binding orders and requests to non-governmental organisations (NGOs) and the International Committee of the Red Cross. In practice, however, NGOs will provide substantial assistance, as has been the case with assistance rendered to the ICTY, where organisations of this kind actively supported many crucial areas of the Tribunal's work, such as the taking of depositions, affidavits and the collection of other forms of evidence.[76] Unlike the ad hoc Tribunals, Art 15(2) of the ICC Statute actually empowers the prosecutor to seek additional information from a variety of sources, including NGOs. With regard to its investigations in Uganda, Darfur and the Congo, the ICC has directly requested the surrender of persons, evidentiary material and permission to conduct investigations from the referring States, but with regard to non-parties it has entered into cooperation agreements.[77]

Besides material evidence, the Court has the authority to request the arrest and surrender of persons from the custodial State.[78] While this process would normally be defined as 'extradition' in the context of interstate criminal co-operation, the terminology applied in the Statute, as indeed in the context of the ICTY and ICTR, refers to it as 'surrender' of persons. The accused may challenge the ICC request as being contrary to the principle *non bis in idem* and, once surrendered, the Court must respect the principle of specialty,

---

73 For example, in order to receive logistical assistance and judicial support from the UN Mission in the Congo (MONUC), the ICC concluded a Memorandum of Understanding on 8 Nov 2005 with MONUC. See Report of the ICC, UN Doc A/61/217 (3 Aug 2006), para 47.
74 Cited in Status of Cooperation with the ICC, Doc ICC–02/04–01/05 (6 Oct 2006), para 19.
75 Available at: <http://www.usunnewyork.usmission.gov/04_173.htm>.
76 'The ICTY and NGOs' (1996) 4 *ICTY Bulletin*, 15 March, p 4.
77 Cooperation Agreement of 2 October 2005 with Sudan, in relation to the investigation in Uganda. Equally, a General Framework Cooperation was concluded between the ICC and Chad on 18 August 2005 for the purposes of investigation and interviewing witnesses on the territory of the latter through an exchange of letters. See ICC Report, supra note 74, paras 22, 24.
78 ICC Statute, Art 59.

unless the requested State waives it.[79] In cases of competing requests between the ICC and other countries for the surrender of a person, and where both requests relate to the same offence, the custodial State shall give priority to the Court's request if it has already determined that the case is admissible. The same applies where the competing requests are for the same person, but not for the same crime. In all other cases, the custodial State is free to decide which request it shall give primacy to.[80]

A party may deny a request for assistance, in whole or in part, only where the request concerns the production of any documents or disclosure of evidence that relates to its national security.[81] In such cases, Art 72(5) envisages a co-operative procedure whereby conciliatory attempts are to be made to modify the request, determine the relevance of the contested evidence, or seek an alternative source, or convince that State to provide the information in terms that do not prejudice its national security, particularly through *in camera* or *ex parte* proceedings.[82] If, after this procedure, the dispute has not been resolved and the Court determines that the evidence is relevant and necessary for the establishment of the guilt or innocence of the accused, it may either request further consultations, inform the Assembly of States Parties or the Security Council of that State's refusal to comply, or make an inference as to the existence or not of a fact at trial.[83] The right to confidentiality afforded to States parties under Art 93(4) is not absolute, as sub-para (7)(b)(i) of Art 72 empowers the Court to order the disclosure of evidence in all other circumstances. Sub-paragraph (b)(i) seems to adhere to the ICTY Appeals Chamber decision in the *Blaskic* appeals subpoena case, where it was held that, although all possible modalities accommodating national security concerns must be provided, States cannot invoke such concerns where a binding obligation for disclosure has been issued.[84]

In practical terms, however, refusal to comply with an order for disclosure of sensitive national information will be dealt with in the same way as all other instances of failure to comply with the Court's binding requests. In general, the Court will make a finding of non-compliance and thereafter refer the matter to the Assembly of States Parties, or, where the Security Council

79 Ibid, Art 101.
80 Ibid, Art 90.
81 Ibid, Art 93(4).
82 The ICTY made use of *in camera* proceedings in relation to sensitive information, such as satellite photographs of the Srebrenica mass grave sites, which were utilised to compare the ground before and after its excavation. While this type of evidence may be excluded following official requests, States may allow for it to be made available. See 'Special: exhumations' (1996) *ICTY Bulletin*, 19 July, p 8.
83 ICC Statute, Art 72(7)(a)(i)–(iii).
84 *Prosecutor v Blaskic*, Appeals Judgment on the Request of the Republic of Croatia for Review of the Decision of Trial Chamber I of 11 July 1997 (29 Oct 1997) (1997) 110 ILR 607, paras 61–69.

referred the matter to the Court, to the Security Council.[85] The experience of the Yugoslav Tribunal demonstrates that State co-operation and Security Council support are inextricably linked issues, and are themselves dependent on the Court's image as a powerful institution. If the ICC manages to attain this status, as did the ICTY after 1996, it, too, will receive obeisance not only from parties to its Statute, who are under an express obligation to do so, but also from intergovernmental organisations, especially in the form of arrests and detention of suspects by peace-keeping missions, an aspect which has proved seminal to the ICTY's judicial function.

21.6 RESERVATIONS AND AMENDMENTS TO THE STATUTE

Article 120 does not permit reservations to the Statute. This prohibition must also include all interpretative declarations whose effect is that of reservations, except in cases where parties are expressly afforded discretion under the Statute. An example of an acceptable interpretative declaration would be one that describes those national procedures required for co-operation with the Court, under Art 88. The prohibition of reservations follows similar practice adopted with regard to human rights and humanitarian law treaties, even though such practice eventually results in a smaller participation of States to the treaty.[86] Although less so in the case of the ICC, most provisions contained in human rights and humanitarian law treaties constitute miniature treaties in their own right, rendering, thus, any possible reservations, by and large, contrary to the purpose and object of these instruments. While it is true that the obligations incorporated in the ICC Statute are not reciprocal, in practice, States find that to accept the unconditionality of such obligations impairs their strategic or other interests. The adoption of the ICC Statute is no less of a bargain than is, say, the negotiation of other permanent international judicial organs, such as the International Tribunal for the Law of the Sea (ITLOS). This *erga omnes* nature of the Statute, even against non-parties,

---

85 ICC Statute, Art 87(5)(b) and (7).
86 1993 Chemical Weapons Convention, Art 22; 1997 Convention on the Prohibition of the Use, Stockpiling, Production and Transfer of Anti-Personnel Mines and on Their Destruction, Art 19, 320 IRRC (1997), 563; the Human Rights Committee stated in its General Comment No 24, entitled 'General Comment on issues relating to reservations made upon ratification or accession to the Covenant or the Optional Protocols thereto, or in relation to declarations under Art 41 of the Covenant', that because human rights treaties are not a web of interstate exchanges of mutual State obligations, reservations should not lead to 'a perpetual non-attainment of international human rights standards', UN Doc CCPR/C/21/Rev 1/Add 6 (2 Nov 1994), paras 17, 19, reprinted in 107 ILR 64. This *erga omnes* character of human rights and humanitarian treaties was early recognised by the ICJ in its *Advisory Opinion in the Genocide* case (1951) ICJ Reports 15.

is recognised in Arts 12(2) and 13(b), which permit the Court to exercise jurisdiction irrespective of a non-party's consent.

Despite the impossibility of reservations, Art 124 of the ICC Statute provides States parties with a possible opt-out clause with regard to war crimes contained in Art 8 of the Statute for a period of seven years after the entry into force of the Statute. France and Colombia have already declared the applicability as to themselves of this opt-out clause.

The body responsible for the functioning of the Court and the highest authority regarding all its substantive and procedural aspects is the ASP, established under Art 112 of the Statute. The ASP is composed of all parties to the Statute, every one of which is represented by one official, accompanied by alternatives and advisers, holding a single vote. Decisions in the Assembly should be reached by consensus. If this proves untenable, decisions on matters of substance must be approved by a two-thirds majority of those present and voting, provided that an absolute majority of States parties constitutes the quorum for voting. Decisions on matters of procedure will be taken by a simple majority of States parties present and voting.[87] The Assembly shall have a bureau consisting of a president, two vice presidents and 18 members elected by the Assembly for three-year terms, and its purpose is to assist the Assembly in the discharge of its responsibilities.[88]

Amendments to the Statute can be proposed and considered only seven years after the Statute has entered into force. If the States parties cannot reach consensus on the amendment, a two-thirds majority is required to adopt it. This amendment would enter into force for all parties after its ratification by seven-eighths of them. This amendment procedure applies also with respect to a proposed amendment to Arts 5–8, which contain the four core crimes comprising the jurisdiction of the ICC. In this case, however, the Court cannot exercise its jurisdiction regarding a crime covered by the amendment where the party on whose territory or whose national committed the offence has not accepted the said amendment.[89] A practical implication of this latter procedure could arise with regard to a possible future prohibition of nuclear weapons, in which case nuclear powers would remain parties to the Statute but be excluded from the application of the nuclear weapons prohibition.[90] A Review Conference is to be convened seven years after the entry into force of the Statute, under Art 123(1). This shall consider possible amendments to the Statute, which may include expanding upon the list of crimes that are currently contained in Art 5. It is not unlikely that, by that time, parties will have agreed on the inclusion of new offences to be added

---

87 ICC Statute, Art 112(7).
88 Ibid, Art 112(3).
89 Ibid, Art 121.
90 Op cit, McGoldrick, note 35, p 631.

to the existing list. During its first session, the ASP adopted a number of instruments and established a number of bodies in order to implement and execute its administrative functions. First, it adopted its own Rules of Procedure, which allow the presence of non-party observer States to attend its meetings. It further appointed a Credentials Committee. It then agreed to a set of basic principles governing a Headquarters Agreement and an Agreement on the Privileges and Immunities of the ICC.

The Court is to be funded not from the regular budget of the UN, as was proposed by some States, but from assessed contributions of States parties, adjusted in accordance with the principles on which the scale adopted by the UN for its regular budget rests.[91] In cases where a situation is referred to the Court by the Security Council the UN will cover any expenses incurred,[92] although as we explained earlier, the Security Council ordered otherwise in its referral of the Darfur situation to the Court. During the first meeting of the ASP in September 2002, a set of financial regulations and rules was adopted. It was decided that assessments would be determined based on membership of the ASP at the date of the adoption of that decision (that is, 3 September 2002), and that assessments after this date would be treated as miscellaneous income.[93] Article 116 permits the Court to receive and utilise voluntary contributions from governments, international organisations, individuals and other entities, in accordance with criteria to be established by the ASP.[94]

21.7 REPARATION TO VICTIMS

Unlike the ICTY and ICTR, the Permanent International Court has been empowered to offer reparation to the victims of crimes, including restitution, compensation and rehabilitation.[95] Although a substantial number of arbitral tribunals have adjudicated tort claims in the past, this is the first time an international judicial organ whose mandate is to render criminal justice faces this dual task. Hence, the Court is legally required to establish principles relating to reparations. This is a particularly sensitive issue, since there are no clear guidelines on whether monetary reparation need be made from the property, assets or instrumentalities of crimes as suggested by Arts 75(4) and 93(1)(k), or whether every asset belonging to the convicted person's estate is

---

91 ICC Statute, Arts 115(1) and 117.
92 Ibid, Art 115(2).
93 ICC Doc ICC-ASP/1/3 (3–10 Sept 2002), Resolution 14.
94 Ibid, Resolution 6.
95 ICC Statute, Art 75; in their plenary meeting in July 2000 the judges of the ICTY considered the issue of the right of victims to seek compensation. Upon completion of a report containing compensatory methods and practical recommendations in September of that year they invited the UN to consider its application. ICTY Doc JL/PIS/528-e (14 Sept 2000).

liable to forfeiture. The Statute merely subjects any measures which the Court might order to possible rights of *bona fide* third parties.[96] Consistent with their obligations under the Statute, States parties must comply with any such order made by the Court. In order to facilitate the purpose of such reparations, Art 79 provides for the creation of a trust fund for the benefit of victims and their families. The fund will be managed by a Board of Trustees whose members participate in an individual capacity and serve on a *pro bono* basis. The fund will not accept those voluntary contributions that create a manifest inequality between the recipient victims.[97] Finally, the right to compensation is also granted to victims of unlawful arrest, detention, or wrongful conviction entailing a miscarriage of justice under Art 85.

96 Ibid, Art 93(1)(k).
97 ICC Doc ICC-ASP/1/3 (3–10 Sept 2002), Resolution 6.

Chapter 22

Internationalised domestic criminal tribunals

22.1 INTRODUCTION

In previous chapters we examined two types of tribunals: those established under Security Council resolutions as ad hoc tribunals, such as the International Criminal Tribunal for the Former Yugoslavia (ICTY) and International Criminal Tribunal for Rwanda (ICTR) and a permanent institution that was created through a treaty, the International Criminal Court (ICC). The Nuremberg Tribunal before these was premised on a treaty between the victorious allies of the Second World War. The judicial institutions examined in this chapter have all been established on different legal bases. Their common feature is that they are domestic tribunals, albeit with international elements. In that sense they can be considered as mixed, or internationalised domestic criminal tribunals. The Sierra Leone Special Court, for example, is an extension of the Sierra Leonean judicial system, established by treaty between the government of that country and the United Nations (UN); the East Timor Special Panels are similarly an extension of the local judiciary, established by law under UN Transitional Administration in East Timor (UNTAET)'s mandate, as is the case with the jurisdiction of Kosovo courts under the UN Interim Administration Mission in Kosovo (UNMIK). The Extraordinary Chambers of Cambodia are premised *in toto* on Cambodian law, although the relevant law envisages the participation of international judges from a list proposed by the UN Secretary General.[1] Finally, the Lockerbie Tribunal is a Scottish court that operated on neutral territory, in the Netherlands, applying Scottish law. Such internationalised domestic tribunals attempt to balance their obligations between domestic and international law and this is not always easy. Moreover, in the majority of the cases, the

---

1 Although the War Crimes Chamber (WCC) in Bosnia and Herzegovina is also a hybrid internationalised criminal tribunal, it is not examined in this book. For more information on the WCC, see Human Rights Watch, Looking for Justice: The War Crimes Chamber in Bosnia and Herzegovina, available at <http://hrw.org/reports/2006/ij0206/>.

countries in which they operate have recently surfaced from devastation. These courts must, furthermore, function in a legal environment where amnesties have been granted and while they may not always be valid under international law, especially where they serve to preserve impunity for serious violations, they may well be deemed to be valid under domestic law.

22.2 THE SIERRA LEONE SPECIAL COURT

Since 23 March 1991, the West African country of Sierra Leone had been the battleground of fierce fighting, initially between the Revolutionary United Front (RUF) led by Foday Sankoh and the one party military regime of the All People's Congress (APC).[2] Hostilities have continued relentlessly since then but ceased for a short interlude with the signing of the Abidjan Peace Agreement on 30 November 1996 between a newly elected democratic government and the RUF. No sooner had the ink dried on the Peace Agreement, than fighting on an even larger scale broke out again. The new circle of violence culminated in a *coup d'état* orchestrated by the Armed Forces Revolutionary Council (AFRC), an ally of the RUF, which seized power over the greater part of Sierra Leone on 25 May 1997.[3] In an attempt to take control of the capital Freetown a combined force of AFRC/RUF forces launched a military operation which was marked by widespread atrocities against the civilian population, although serious violations of international humanitarian law had ensued since the 1997 coup, especially mass rape and abduction of women, forced recruitment of children, mutilations and summary executions.[4] Likewise, during its retreat in February 1999, RUF forces abducted hundreds of people, particularly young women who they then proceeded to use as forced labourers, fighting forces, human shields and sexual slaves.[5] The Lome Peace Agreement, signed on 7 July 1999 by the democratically elected government of President Ahmed Kabbah, the RUF and the Special Representative of the UN Secretary General, granted amnesty to RUF members – although the UN Special Representative expressly rejected the validity of any amnesties to

---

2 Soon after Sankoh's arrest on 27 May 2000 by Sierra Leonean (SR) forces, his wife applied for *habeas corpus* before the High Court in London, on the grounds that at the request of SR forces, British troops provided assistance in transporting Sankoh, and as a result he was under British custody and control. Both the High Court and Court of Appeal rejected these arguments. *In the Matter of Sankoh* (2000) 119 ILR 386.
3 Acting under the UN Charter, Chapter VII, the Security Council adopted Resolution 1132 on 8 Oct 1997, demanding that the RUF relinquish power and cease acts of violence, further imposing a general embargo.
4 See SC Res 1181 (13 July 1998).
5 Report of the Secretary General on the Establishment of a Special Court for Sierra Leone, UN Doc S/2000/915 (4 Oct 2000), paras 25–26.

international crimes – and set up a Truth Commission to investigate and document violations in lieu of prosecutions. In further disregard of its commitments and the rule of law, the RUF resumed attacks against government troops and the civilian population and, despite being quickly defeated and its leader captured, RUF forces had found time to commit yet more widespread atrocities against civilians.[6]

The Government of Sierra Leone subsequently asked the UN to establish an international tribunal to prosecute those responsible for violations of international humanitarian law during the civil war. On 14 August 2000, the Security Council adopted Resolution 1315 wherein it instructed the Secretary General to negotiate with Sierra Leone on the establishment of an independent special court, recommending that its subject matter jurisdiction include crimes against humanity, war crimes and other serious violations of international law, as well as crimes under Sierra Leonian law committed by 'persons who bear the greatest responsibility for [these] crimes'. The resolution requested the production of a detailed statute. After two rounds of successful negotiations the Secretary General presented the Security Council with a report on the creation of a Special Court, to which both the Agreement[7] and the Statute were annexed.

Unlike the ICTY and ICTR the Special Court was established through a bilateral treaty between the UN and the Government of Sierra Leone on 16 January 2002, and not on the basis of a Security Council resolution. This means that the Special Court lacks primacy over other national courts and public authorities of third countries, whether this involves requests for surrender of evidence or of accused persons. In examining measures to enhance the deterrent powers of the Court, the Secretary General invited the Security Council to consider endowing it with Chapter VII powers for the specific purpose of requesting the surrender of an accused from outside the jurisdiction of the Court.[8] The Security Council never responded to that request. The Agreement and the Statute should be read together as a single instrument, rather than two separate ones, in light of the fact that there is considerable overlap between them.[9] Under Art 8 of its Statute, the Special Court has concurrent jurisdiction with Sierra Leone courts but enjoys primacy over them. The Special Court is composed of two Trial Chambers, each consisting of three judges, and an Appeals Chamber consisting of five judges. Sierra

---

6 Following international concern at the role played by the illicit diamond trade in fuelling the conflict in Sierra Leone, the Security Council adopted Resolution 1306 (5 July 2000) imposing a ban on the direct or indirect import of rough diamonds from areas not controlled by the government through the establishment of a certificate of origin regime.

7 2002 Agreement between the UN and the Government of Sierra Leone on the Establishment of a Special Court for Sierra Leone.

8 Op cit, Report of the Secretary General, note 5, para 10.

9 A McDonald, 'Sierra Leone's Shoestring Special Court', 84 *IRRC* (2002), 121, p 126.

Leone was to appoint one of the three trial judges in each chamber, as well as two of the judges that will serve in the Appeals Chamber, with the remaining judicial vacancies to be filled by the UN.[10] Similarly, the Secretary General was to appoint the Special Court's Registrar[11] and prosecutor, who is assisted by a Sierra Leonian deputy prosecutor.[12] In accordance with Art 2 of the 2002 Agreement, from the three judges serving in the Trial Chamber, one is appointed by Sierra Leone, whereas the remaining two by the Secretary General, upon nominations forwarded by Member States of the Economic Community of West African States (ECOWAS) and the Commonwealth. Under Art 3 of the 2002 Agreement, the prosecutor is appointed on the basis of a consultation between the Government of Sierra Leone and the Secretary General.

The subject matter jurisdiction of the Special Court comprises crimes under international humanitarian law and Sierra Leonian law. The first category includes crimes against humanity,[13] violations of common Art 3 to the Geneva Conventions and of Additional Protocol II,[14] as well as 'other violations of international humanitarian law'.[15] Article 4 includes the intentional targeting of civilians, *hors de combat* and personnel/material of peace-keeping missions, as well as abduction and forced recruitment of children under the age of 15 for the purpose of using them to participate actively in hostilities. Despite the Secretary General's comment that the Special Court's list of crimes against humanity follows the enumeration included in the ICTY and ICTR Statutes, one readily observes that Art 2(g) contains 'sexual slavery, enforced prostitution, forced pregnancy and any other form of sexual violence', whereas the two *ad hoc* Tribunals make reference only to 'rape'. It must be presumed, however, that in every other respect Art 4 of the Statute of the Special Court for Sierra Leone follows the ICTY Statute and not that of the International Criminal Court (ICC). Recourse to SR law has been provided in cases where a specific situation was considered to be either unregulated or inadequately regulated under international law.[16] The crimes considered to be relevant for this purpose and included in the Statute[17] are: offences relating to the abuse of girls under the SR 1926 Prevention of Cruelty to Children Act (ss 6, 7 and 12) and offences relative to wanton destruction of property and in particular arson, under the SR 1861 Malicious Damage Act (ss 2, 5 and 6). Genocide was not included because the Security

---

10 SLSC Statute, Art 12(1).
11 Ibid, Art 16.
12 Ibid, Art 15(3) and (4).
13 Ibid, Art 2.
14 Ibid, Art 3.
15 Ibid, Art 4.
16 Op cit, Report of the Secretary General, note 5, para 19.
17 SLSC Statute, Art 5.

Council was not furnished with evidence of intent to annihilate an identified group as such.

Finally, the Special Court has no legal links with the ICTR and ICTY, except in so far as it is bound to apply the Rwanda Tribunal's Rules of Procedure[18] and its Appeals Chamber is to be guided by the decisions of the ad hoc Tribunals' common Appeals Chamber,[19] in order to produce a coherent body of jurisprudence. The Special Court has made it clear that it is not bound by the jurisprudence of the ad hoc tribunals and will only follow it where it finds it appropriate.[20] As to its financing, the Secretary General had initially suggested this should take place through assessed contributions, rather than by voluntary emoluments.[21] Finally, Art 6 of the 2002 Agreement provided that the Court's expenses be borne by voluntary contributions from the international community, the Court becoming operational when sufficient funds had been gathered. Article 6 further provides that should voluntary contributions prove insufficient for the Court to implement its mandate, the Secretary General and the Security Council will explore alternate means of financing. After agreement with the Sierra Leone Government, it was decided that the temporal jurisdiction of the Special Court would commence from 30 November 1996.

22.2.1 Amnesties and immunities

Two important issues arise in connection to the existence of the Special Court; whether amnesties granted prior to its establishment continue to have binding force and whether the immunities generally afforded to foreign dignitaries constitute a bar to prosecution before the Special Court. As regards the non-applicability of immunities, this will depend on whether the Special Court possesses international jurisdiction, much in the same way as the ICTY, ICTR and ICC. Although there is no reason why international jurisdiction cannot be conferred by a bilateral treaty, the effect of such an agreement will be to limit that court's international jurisdiction to the two particular parties alone. It is nonsense to assume that a bilateral treaty can produce legal effects on third countries, particularly where a customary rule to the contrary is in operation (that is, immunity), absent moreover any Security Council authorisation. It is to be noted once again that the Security Council has given no authority to the Special Court whatsoever and where it discusses the Special Court's jurisdiction, it simply 'recommends' the boundaries of

---

18 Ibid, Art 14(1). In accordance with Art 14(2) the judges may amend or adopt additional rules where the applicable rules do not adequately provide for a specific situation.

19 Ibid, Art 20(3).

20 *SLSC Prosecutor v Norman et al*, Decision on Interlocutory Appeals against Trial Chamber Decision Refusing to Subpoena the President of Sierra Leone (11 Sept 2006), para 13.

21 Op cit, Report of the Secretary General, note 5, para 71.

its jurisdiction, but in no way normatively defines it or imposes it on third States. In a decision defeating legal reasoning, the Special Court astonishingly emphasised that:

> The Agreement between the United Nations and Sierra Leone is thus an agreement between all members of the United Nations and Sierra Leone. This fact makes the Agreement an expression of the will of the international community. The Special Court established in such circumstances is truly international.[22]

On the basis of this remarkable legal conclusion the Special Court arbitrarily equated its jurisdiction and powers with those of the ad hoc tribunals and the ICC, and thus held that the former Head of State of Liberia, Charles Taylor, did not enjoy even immunity *ratione personae* when indicted while still an acting Head of State.[23] Presumably, the Special Court believes that by implication it possesses jurisdiction over every Head of State!

With regard to the normative value of pre-existing amnesties the Special Court has done a much better job. Article 10 of the Statute does not consider amnesties granted with respect to offences included in Arts 2–4 of the Statute of the Special Court for Sierra Leone as posing a bar to prosecution. This provision necessarily refers to, and essentially purports to invalidate, Art IX of the 1999 Lome Peace Agreement which indeed granted amnesties to all combatants as long as the terms of that Agreement were adhered to, but to which the Special Representative of the UN Secretary General appended a reservation to the effect that amnesties under Art IX would not apply to international crimes.[24] The Special Court did not hold that local amnesties are always invalid under international law, but that under the particular circumstances the terms of the Lome Agreement had been breached. Robertson J correctly observed that although it may seem harsh to deprive combatants of an amnesty because their leaders reneged on the agreement, this is an inevitable occurrence for what is ultimately an enormous indulgence to persons that have committed serious offences.[25] Another reason for rejecting the Lome amnesties was due to the status of the Special Court's Statute as an international agreement. Equally, it was held that a rule had emerged under customary international law that 'nullifies amnesties

---

22 *SLSC Prosecutor v Taylor*, Appeals Chamber Decision on Immunity from Jurisdiction (31 May 2004), para 38.
23 Ibid, paras 53–54.
24 Op cit, Report of the Secretary General, note 5, para 22. This UN understanding on the status of the particular amnesties was reiterated in the preamble to SC Res 1315.
25 *SLSC Prosecutor v Kondewa*, Appeals Chamber Decision on Lack of Jurisdiction/Abuse of Process: Amnesty Provided by the Lome Accord (25 May 2004), Separate Opinion of Robertson J, para 28.

given to persons accused of bearing great responsibility for serious breaches of international law'.[26]

22.2.2 Child recruitment as an international crime and prosecution of children

The Security Council had since 30 August 1996 condemned the recruitment, deployment and training of children for combat in Resolution 1071 in connection with the civil conflict in Liberia. It was only in 1999 that the Council not only took up the matter annually on its agenda, but condemned all forms of recruiting and deployment of children in armed conflict as a war crime.[27] Although children are protected persons under the Geneva Convention IV (1949), it was not clear until the late 1990s whether it was also a war crime to recruit them into active military service. Article 4(3)(c) of Additional Protocol II (1977) states that:

> Children who have not attained the age of fifteen years shall neither be recruited in the armed forces or groups allowed to take part in hostilities.

A similar provision was also inserted in Art 77(2) of Additional Protocol I (1977) and Art 38(3) of the 1989 Convention on the Rights of the Child (CRC).[28] By the time of the adoption of the ICC Statute in 1998, the Sierra Leone Special Court was of the opinion that the particular behaviour had culminated in a war crime under customary international law, on account particularly of the almost universal ratification of the CRC and the adoption of national laws criminalising child recruitment.[29] The Secretary General pointed out in his 2000 Report on Art 4, and in relation to the criminality of child recruitment, that although the prohibition on child recruitment had acquired customary international law status, it was not clear at the time to what extent it was recognised as a war crime entailing individual criminal responsibility.[30] Eventually, Art 8(2)(b)(xxvi) of the ICC Statute and Art 4 of

---

26 Ibid, para 57; see also, *SLSC Prosecutor v Kallon et al*, Appeals Chamber Decision on Challenge to Jurisdiction: Lome Amnesty Accord (13 March 2004).

27 SC 1261 (30 Aug 1999).

28 1577 UNTS 3.

29 *SLSC Prosecutor v Norman*, Appeals Chamber Decision on Preliminary Motion based on Lack of Jurisdiction (Child Recruitment) (31 May 2004), paras 34, 53. On the basis of its findings of State practice, the SLSC asserted that 'child recruitment was criminalised before it was explicitly set out as a criminal prohibition in treaty law and certainly by November 1996'.

30 The Secretary General had initially proposed the more precise and restrictive offence of 'conscripting or enlisting children', being unsure as to whether the ICC Statute formulation was consistent with customary international law. Op cit, Report of the Secretary General, note 5, para 18.

the SLSC Statute are identical. This new crime of child recruitment is defined as follows:

> Conscripting or enlisting children under the age of 15 years into armed forces or groups using them to participate actively in hostilities.

The Special Court went a step further, arguing that by the time of the adoption of the 2000 CRC Optional Protocol on the Involvement of Children in Armed Conflict, the discussion of criminalisation of child recruitment below the age of 15 had been settled and the matter had shifted to raising the standard to include all children below the age of 18.[31] This is a plausible argument. There is no contention of course that the recruitment of all persons above the age of 15 is an international offence under customary law, since a significant number of countries enlist persons who are at least 17, although admittedly they are not always deployed to combat zones.[32]

The prosecution of children for war crimes and crimes against humanity has presented a 'difficult moral dilemma' for a number of reasons.[33] Although they were feared for their brutality, the Secretary General noted that these children have been subjected to a process of psychological and physical abuse and duress that has transformed them from victims into perpetrators.[34] In a balancing act catering on the one hand for the concerns of humanitarian organisations responsible for rehabilitation programmes, who objected to any kind of judicial accountability for children below 18 years of age, and on the other adhering to vociferous popular feeling demanding punishment of offenders, the Secretary General decided in favour of prosecuting juveniles above 15 years of age, but instructed the prosecutor in cases of juvenile offenders to:

> . . . ensure that the child rehabilitation programme is not placed at risk and that, where appropriate, resort should be had to alternative truth and reconciliation mechanisms, to the extent of their availability.[35]

22.3 THE EAST TIMOR SPECIAL PANELS

East Timor had been a Portuguese colony. During the post-Second World War decolonisation period Portugal was unwilling to forgo its power completely

---

31 *Norman* Decision on Child Recruitment, supra note 29, para 34.
32 See generally, M Happold, *Child Soldiers in International Law*, 2005, Manchester: Manchester University Press.
33 Op cit, Report of the Secretary General, note 5, para 32.
34 Op cit, Report of the Secretary General, note 5, para 32.
35 SLSC Statute, Art 15(5).

on the half-island entity. In 1960 the UN General Assembly declared East Timor to be a non-self-governing territory, administered by Portugal[36] and this was generally the case as East Timor was looking towards complete independence. This process was abruptly interrupted, however, when on 7 December 1975 the territory was invaded and subsequently occupied by Indonesian armed forces. During the 24-year occupation of the half-island, there were frequent reports of extreme brutality and genocide, but the Indonesian Government remained in power essentially because its purchase of military material from western States helped to silence its critics before international fora. After conclusion of a 'General Agreement' between Indonesia and Portugal on 5 May 1999 on the question of East Timor, a referendum was held on 30 August 1999.[37] This, although supervised by a UN body, UNAMET, was conducted in the midst of intimidation and violence by East Timorese militias with the full support of the Indonesian Armed Forces, and 78.5 per cent of the population voted in favour of independence. The widespread violence sparked by the election result prompted the Security Council to adopt Resolution 1264 by which it mandated an international force (INTERFET) to restore peace and security in East Timor, facilitate humanitarian assistance and protect and support UNAMET in the fulfilment of its duties.[38] The presence of INTERFET secured significant stability on the island and paved the way for the Council to establish the UN Transitional Administration in East Timor (UNTAET) through Resolution 1272,[39] headed by a Special Representative of the Secretary General who acts as Transitional Administrator of the Territory until complete devolution to the people of East Timor is secured.

A significant function of UNTAET's mandate was the establishment of an effective judicial system, which includes the administration of criminal justice. This was no easy task, as prior to 1999 the East Timorese as a general rule were excluded from public office or the civil service. Further compounded by the fact that 500,000 civilians became internally displaced as a result of the 1999 events, there was no effective local judiciary on the island.[40] Moreover, under such circumstances, it would have been logistically impossible to prosecute offences that occurred during the 24-year Indonesian occupation, even if an ad hoc tribunal of the ICTY type was to be set up. A UN Commission of Inquiry, specifically established for this purpose, concluded that an international tribunal should be set up, comprising both Indonesian and East

36 GA Res 1542(XV) (15 Dec 1960).
37 UN DocS/1999/513, Annex I.
38 SC Res 1264 (15 Sept 1999), operative para 3.
39 SC Res 1272 (25 Oct 1999).
40 For an overview of the problems facing UNTAET, see H Strohmeyer, 'Collapse and Reconstruction of a Judicial System: The United Nations Missions in Kosovo and East Timor', 95 *AJIL* (2001), 46.

Timorese judges, but precluded the examination of cases referring to the period of Indonesian occupation.[41] UNTAET, however, urged in part by Indonesian promises that they would investigate and prosecute alleged offenders, decided to enhance the local judicial system, albeit augmented with an international presence. This development was not welcomed by the East Timorese, in part because they allege they were not sufficiently consulted on this issue.[42]

Finally, UNTAET established the Serious Crimes Project for the prosecution of serious criminal cases perpetrated in the period between 1 January and 25 October 1999, through the District Court of Dili. On the basis of its authority to adopt legislation, it promulgated Regulation 2000/11,[43] s 10.1 of which gave the District Court exclusive jurisdiction over the following offences: genocide, war crimes, crimes against humanity, murder, sexual offences, torture. Section 10.3 envisaged the creation of Special Panels composed of East Timorese and international judges. The final composition of the Panels was elaborated through Regulation 2000/15,[44] s 22.2 of which requires that the Panels be composed of two international and one East Timorese judge, whereas in cases of special gravity or importance it may be composed of three international and two local judges. The judgments of the Panels can be appealed to the Court of Appeal. Interestingly, s 10.4 of Regulation 2000/11 did not rule out the creation of a possible *ad hoc* or other tribunal with jurisdiction over the same offences.

Section 2.1 of Regulation 2000/15 endowed the Special Panels with a species of 'universal jurisdiction' over the listed offences (although that term was not expressly used), the correct interpretation of which would encompass any crimes irrespective of the nationality of the offender or the victim, as long as the relevant offence was either consummated or commenced on the territory of East Timor. In accordance with s 2.4, the Panels do have jurisdiction over offences that occurred in East Timor prior to 25 October 1999, which would cover the period during the Indonesian occupation, but the applicable law for that period would be whatever Indonesian criminal law existed during the relevant time. This is consistent with the principle of intertemporal law, which may demonstrate that the concept of grave breaches and the prohibition of genocide and crimes against humanity were binding upon Indonesia during relevant periods of its occupation of the island. The definition of the offences is almost identical to definitions encountered in

41 *Report of the International Commission of Inquiry on East Timor to the Secretary General*, UN Doc A/54/726, S/2000/59 (2000), para 153.

42 S Linton, 'New Approaches to International Justice in Cambodia and East Timor', 84 *IRRC* (2002), 93, p 106.

43 UNTAET/REG/2000/11 (6 March 2000), on the Organisation of Courts in East Timor.

44 UNTAET/REG/2000/15 (6 June 2000), on the Establishment of Panels with Exclusive Jurisdiction over Serious Criminal Offences.

other international legal texts. Hence, s 4 of Regulation 2000/15 adopts the customary definition of genocide codified by the 1948 Convention on the Prevention and Punishment of the Crime of Genocide (Genocide Convention) and the ICC Statute. Section 5.1 reproduces the definition of crimes against humanity found in the ICC Statute, with the sole difference that both the punishable act and the widespread and systematic attack must be directed against the civilian population. Section 6.1 on war crimes once again mirrors Art 8 of the ICC Statute. The fact that no distinction is made with regard to the international or non-international character of the conflict implies either that the matter was left to be decided by the Panels, or that the formulation of Art 8 of the ICC Statute represents generally accepted law on war crimes.[45] The definition of the crime of torture in s 7.1 is wider than that found in the 1984 UN Convention Against Torture and Other Cruel, Inhuman or Degrading Treatment or Punishment, since it does not limit the commission of the offence to public officials or other persons acting in an official capacity. This may be due to the fact that many of the offences charged were committed by militias whose links with the Indonesian State authorities were not sufficiently clear for the purposes of attributing them to the Jakarta regime.[46] As for murder[47] and sexual offences,[48] Regulation 2000/15 states that the 'provisions of the applicable Penal Code in East Timor' will apply.[49]

As expected, the functioning of the Panels has generated significant problems. First, despite the existence of a Memorandum of Understanding between UNTAET and Indonesia, signed on 5 April 2000, by which the latter agreed to provide, inter alia, transfer of accused to the Special Panels, it has not been adhered to. The second point of frustration relates to the perceived impartiality of the Panels. In one of the first judgments rendered by the Panels, the *Los Palos* case,[50] it was accepted that the existence of an extensive attack by 'pro-autonomy armed groups supported by Indonesian authorities targeting the civilian population in the area … had been proven beyond reasonable doubt'.[51] The Panel's reasoning was based on the report of the UN Commission of Inquiry, as well as certain witness testimonies and physical evidence supported by the Commission's findings. However, before

45 See D Turns, ' "Internationalised" or Ad Hoc Justice for International Criminal Law in a Time of Transition: The Cases of East Timor, Kosovo, Sierra Leone and Cambodia', 7 *ARIEL* (2002) 123.
46 Ibid.
47 S 8.
48 S 9.
49 UNTAET/REG/1999/1, s 3 provides that the applicable law in East Timor is that in force before 25 Oct 1999 (ie, Indonesian law), as long as such law does not conflict with international human rights law, the mandate or other UNTAET Regulations.
50 *Prosecutor v Joni Marques and Others* (*Los Palos* case), Judgment (11 Dec 2001), Case No 09/2000.
51 Ibid, para 686.

reaching this conclusion, the Panel examined the possible existence of an armed conflict in East Timor during 1999, wrongly assuming the requirement of a nexus between the crimes under consideration and an armed conflict.[52] No such nexus is required in Regulation 2000/15, or international law in general, except in the ICTY Statute, which in any event is irrelevant for the purposes of the Special Panels, because Regulation 2000/15 is premised on the ICC Statute. The judgment was flawed in some other respects, such as the omission of the fact that East Timor was occupied by Indonesia and that alone is enough under common Art 2 of the 1949 Geneva Conventions to substantiate the existence of an armed conflict. Moreover, in the *Leki* case, which did not involve crimes against humanity, the Panel made findings about Indonesia's role in the 1999 events, without any evidence submitted by the parties and without the issues being litigated, by relying on a test of 'what even the humblest and most candid man in the world can assess'.[53] If such mistakes can be forgiven the inexperienced East Timorese judiciary, it is difficult to do the same with regard to internationally appointed judges.

22.4 UNMIK AND THE KOSOVAR JUDICIAL SYSTEM

Until 21 March 1989 Kosovo was an autonomous region within the Socialist Federal Republic of Yugoslavia (SFRY). In order to appease Serbian nationalism, in part of his own making, the then President Milosevic removed Kosovar autonomy in violation of the SFRY Constitution. This was the starting point of mounting ethnic tension which culminated in the establishment of ethnic Albanian pro-independence military movements, particularly the Kosovo Liberation Army (KLA), which clashed with FRY – the SFRY had by then disintegrated – security and armed forces. Clashes of this sort, and mounting military activity from both sides, had been reported since 1997, with evidence suggesting that both sides were responsible for serious atrocities. By 1999, and with Milosevic having lost all international credibility, NATO commenced a bombing campaign of dubious legality – if not complete illegality – against FRY on 24 March 1999. By early summer of that year, with FRY having sustained severe blows to its infrastructure and economy, it concluded an agreement with NATO States on 9 June, whereby it agreed to remove its security forces from Kosovo, while retaining its sovereignty over the territory. This agreement is reflected in Security Council Resolution 1244 which was adopted on the following day. Operative para 10 of the Resolution authorised the Secretary General to establish an interim

---

52 Ibid, para 684.
53 *Prosecutor v Joseph Leki*, Judgment (11 June 2001), Case No 5/2000, reported in op cit, Linton, note 42, p 111.

administration in Kosovo,[54] including among its mandate, as provided in operative para 11, the maintenance of civil law and order. This task was part of the UN Interim Administration Mission in Kosovo's (UNMIK) mission.

Although not on top of UNMIK's agenda, it had to decide how to administer criminal justice in Kosovo; this concerned issues of applicable criminal law, organisation of courts and possible establishment of special panels for serious violations of humanitarian law. In its first Regulation, 1999/1,[55] s 3 provided that the laws applicable in the territory of Kosovo prior to 24 March 1999 were to apply again so long as they did not conflict with international law standards, UNMIK's mandate, or any subsequent UNMIK regulation. Since, however, pre–1999 law was FRY Milosevic-inflicted law, the Albanian judges either resigned from their posts or refused to enforce it, applying instead pre–1989 Kosovar criminal law, which in any event did not differ much from FRY criminal law.[56] As a result of this intransigence, and in the face of a judicial vacuum, Regulation 1999/1 was amended by Regulation 1999/24,[57] which held as applicable law all primary and secondary UNMIK instruments, as well as the law in force in Kosovo on 22 March 1989. In case of conflict between the two, the former takes precedence, and where a matter is not covered by the laws set out in a regulation but is instead covered by another law in force in Kosovo after 22 March 1989, which is not moreover discriminatory and complies with international legal standards, that law is, as an exceptional measure, applicable. Moreover, s 3 of Regulation 1999/24 rendered this amendment retroactive as of 10 June 1999. However, between 10 June and 12 December 1999, at which time the amendment was adopted, some Kosovar courts had already convicted a number of defendants on the basis of the pre–1989 Kosovar criminal law, which, as Turns correctly points out, 'had the highly objectionable effect of retrospectively validating convictions that had been handed down under a non-operative law'.[58] The saving grace in all this confusion, as far as the rights of the accused are concerned, is the fact that defendants are to benefit from the most favourable provision in the criminal laws which were in force in Kosovo between 22 March 1989 and 10 June 1999, in accordance with Regulation 1999/24.[59]

Unlike UNTAET, UNMIK did not introduce a regulation establishing special panels, nor international offences for adjudication before Kosovar courts. Nonetheless, on 13 December 1999 an UNMIK Commission recommended

---

54 R Wilde, 'From Danzig to East Timor and Beyond: The Role of International Territorial Administration', 95 *AJIL* (2001), 583.
55 UNMIK/REG/1999/1 (25 July 1999), on the Authority of the Interim Administration in Kosovo.
56 Op cit, Turns, note 45.
57 UNMIK/REG/1999/24 (12 Dec 1999), on the Law Applicable in Kosovo.
58 Op cit, Turns, note 45.
59 Regulation 1999/24, s 1.

the creation of the Kosovo War and Ethnic Crimes Court (KWECC), with jurisdiction over war crimes, crimes against humanity and other serious offences on the grounds of ethnicity and functioning within the Kosovo legal system, albeit staffed also by international judges. Although the project was endorsed, it was eventually abandoned.[60] Finally, Regulation 2000/64[61] should be mentioned. This allowed the prosecutors and defendants to petition the UNMIK Department of Judicial Affairs for the substitution of international judges where the impartiality of a local judge was in doubt; it also included petitions for the change of venue. The petition is of no avail once trial or appeal proceedings have commenced, hence the petitioner is required to institute proceedings in advance of such judicial proceedings.

22.5 THE CAMBODIAN EXTRAORDINARY CHAMBERS

The Khmer Rouge seized power in Cambodia on 17 April 1975. By all accounts, although during their reign information from the country was extremely difficult to obtain, the Khmer Rouge, led by Pol Pot, eliminated their so-called internal enemies, which included Buddhist monks, the Muslim Cham, Chinese and Vietnamese communities, as well as anyone who was or even resembled an intellectual. Those urban dwellers that survived the genocide which ensued were sent to rural camps as part of the regime's peasant revolution, purging the country of all foreign elements as well as of economic, scientific or cultural institutions.[62] Following an invasion by the Vietnamese armed forces on 6 January 1979, Cambodia was liberated from Pol Pot – who regrouped and launched a guerilla war – but the latter's legacy resulted in the extermination of at least 1.7 million people, amounting to 20 per cent of the entire population.

Despite the aforementioned atrocities, Cold War politics, which viewed the post-1979 Government of Heng Samrin as an instrumentality of the Vietnamese 'communists', were responsible for retaining for some time the Khmer seat at the UN. Following the Vietnamese withdrawal in 1989 and the subsequent Paris Conferences on Cambodia which resulted in the signing of a Comprehensive Settlement Agreement on 23 October 1991,

---

60 For an excellent overview of the post–1999 Kosovo legal system, see M Bohlander, 'Kosovo: The Legal Framework of the Prosecution and the Courts', in K Ambos and M Othman, *New Approaches in International Criminal Justice: Kosovo, East Timor, Sierra Leone and Cambodia*, 2003, Freiburg Br.

61 UNMIK/REG/2000/64 (15 Dec 2000), on Assignment of International Judges/Prosecutors and/or Change of Venue, as amended by UNMIK/REG/2001/34 (15 Dec 2001).

62 See B Kiernan, *The Pol Pot Regime: Race, Power and Genocide in Cambodia under the Khmer Rouge, 1975–79*, 2002, Boston, Mass: Yale University Press.

the UN installed an interim administration, the Transitional Authority in Cambodia (UNTAC).[63] It was only after the departure of UNTAC that any attempted prosecution of Khmer Rouge members could take place. In 1997 the Cambodian Government requested UN assistance. Thereafter, a Group of Experts was appointed with the task of evaluating the feasibility of trials, ascertaining an appropriate legal basis and court structure and assessing the viability of apprehensions.[64] Among five possible types of tribunals, the Group of Experts recommended the establishment of an ad hoc international tribunal under the aegis of the UN, partly due to well-documented and widespread corruption within the Cambodian judiciary.[65] By March 1999, however, when the report was circulated to the General Assembly and the Security Council, the Cambodian Government had rejected the option of an ad hoc tribunal and the UN eventually agreed on a compromise position whereby jurisdiction would be vested in a tribunal situated within the Cambodian legal system and composed of both national and international judges. The UN pledged its co-operation in the process only if the Cambodians agreed to incorporate in their implementing law the modalities set out in a draft Memorandum of Understanding. Their failure to do so was explained as the most serious reason for the UN's first withdrawal from the negotiations. The truth remains that the UN was not prepared to support a corrupt judicial system over which it had no effective control.

This UN withdrawal did not deter the Cambodian Government. Following a second approval by the Cambodian Senate on 23 July 2001, the Law on the Establishment of Extraordinary Chambers in the Courts of Cambodia for the Prosecution of Crimes Committed During the Period of Democratic Cambodia was adopted.[66] The 2001 Law establishes distinct chambers within the Cambodian legal system with a number of international elements. First, it includes international as well as domestic judges; secondly, all international judges and prosecutors, although appointed by Cambodia's Supreme Council of Magistracy, will be selected from a list prepared by the UN Secretary General.[67] Moreover, the UN will contribute to the funding of the Chambers through the creation of a special fund soliciting voluntary contributions.[68] Thirdly, some of the listed offences have drawn heavily on definitions found in international instruments. In a surprising move, the UN brokered an

---

63 R Ratner, 'The Cambodian Settlement Accords', 87 *AJIL* (1993), 1, pp 3–5; SC Res 717 (16 Oct 1991).
64 GA Res 52/135 (12 Dec 1997), para 16.
65 *Report of the Group of Experts for Cambodia*, UN Doc A/53/850-S/1999/231, para 129; see R Ratner, 'The United Nations Group of Experts for Cambodia', 93 *AJIL* (1999), 948.
66 Translation reprinted in 34 *Critical Asian Studies* (2002), 611.
67 2001 Law on the Establishment of Extraordinary Chambers, Art 11(2) and (3); op cit, Linton, note 42, p 99.
68 Op cit, Linton, note 42, p 103.

agreement with the Cambodian Government in mid-March 2003, allowing for UN participation in this project. This development was premised on earlier efforts to revive negotiations, especially General Assembly resolution 57/228, adopted in December 2002, which urged the Secretary General to make the UN an active participant in the trials. At the time of writing the details of the agreement remained unknown, but there was consensus on funding, retention of the 2001 Law, though agreeing to streamline the court to two levels from the previously planned three, thus eliminating a final appeal option.

The Extraordinary Chambers possess jurisdiction over offences under the 2001 Law, as well as under international law. As far as the former is concerned, Art 3 of the Law includes homicide, torture and religious persecution under the 1956 Cambodian Penal Code. Article 4, on the other hand, relating to genocide, is similar to that found in the 1948 Genocide Convention, while Art 5, on crimes against humanity, has been taken from the Statute of the ICTR – that is, including the requirement that they be committed on national, political, ethnical, racial or religious grounds – which does not conform with customary international law, where this particular requirement is absent. Article 6 gives jurisdiction over grave breaches of the 1949 Geneva Conventions, Art 7 over destruction of cultural property during armed conflict, in accordance with the 1954 Convention for the Protection of Cultural Property in the Event of Armed Conflict,[69] and Art 8 relates to crimes against internationally protected persons, in accordance with the 1973 Convention on the Prevention and Punishment of Crimes against Internationally Protected Persons, Including Diplomatic Agents[70] – although the relevant provision refers to the 1961 Vienna Convention on Diplomatic Relations.[71] An unsatisfactory aspect of the 2001 Law is the fact that it omits references to defences, except for superior orders,[72] which may constitute an excuse only if they came from a legitimate authority. Other than that, the accused will have to rely on the 1956 Penal Code and the 1992 UNTAC Supreme National Council Decree on Criminal Law and Procedure, because the status of the relevant international criminal defences – which themselves are ambiguous – is uncertain, as they are not mentioned in the 2001 Law.[73]

As we have already mentioned, the Chambers will also include international judges. The Chambers, based on the existing Cambodian court structure, will comprise a trial court, consisting of three Cambodian and two international judges and a Supreme Court composed of five Cambodian and four international judges. Decisions are to be reached by unanimity and where this is

---

69 249 UNTS 240.

70 13 ILM (1974), 41; see Chapter 10, section 10.3.2.

71 500 UNTS 95.

72 2001 Law on the Establishment of Extraordinary Chambers, Art 29(4).

73 Op cit, Turns, note 45; op cit, Linton, note 42, pp 100–02.

not possible, qualified majority voting will apply.[74] This formula, known as the 'Super-Majority' rule, represents a compromise between the UN and the Cambodian Government. Essentially, it requires that even if the Cambodian judges are unanimous among themselves they would still need the favourable vote of at least one international judge. Article 46 of the 2001 Law allows the Supreme Council of Magistracy to appoint judges, co-prosecutor and investigating judges, where the foreign candidates do not assume their posts. It is also difficult to assess the future of the Extraordinary Chambers in relation to the regime of amnesties, especially those granted to senior Khmer leaders, such as Ieng Sary, Pol Pot's second in command. In any event, Art 40 of the 2001 Law, rather confusingly, does not render amnesties a bar to prosecutions. The 2003 UN–Cambodia Agreement clearly states that the Agreement is the principal instrument for the trials. Hence, any conflicting provision in the 2001 Law would be devoid of legal force and the Chambers would be compelled to apply the law stipulated under the Agreement.

22.6 THE IRAQI SPECIAL TRIBUNAL FOR CRIMES AGAINST HUMANITY

The Special Tribunal must be examined in light of Iraq's occupation by the USA and coalition forces following an armed conflict in 2003.[75] The recognition of such de facto status was conferred on the Coalition Provisional Authority (CPA), in essence the occupying force's political wing in Iraq, by Security Council Resolution 1483, as well as by the CPA itself through the promulgation of CPA Regulation No. 1.[76] Both of these instruments acknowledged the exercise of temporary governmental powers by the CPA. The exercise of judicial criminal jurisdiction by the occupying power is within its prerogative, but Art 66 of the 1949 Geneva Convention IV requires that accused persons subject to post-occupation penal legislation be tried before military tribunals sitting in occupied territory.

Following the cessation of major military operations on 1 May 2003, the USA appointed 25 Iraqis to the so-called Iraq Governing Council (IGC) on 13 July 2003.[77] Although the IGC was proclaimed as assuming a transitional parliamentary role, the Coalition Provisional Authority was in fact the real bearer of authority in the country, having the power to veto all the decisions of the IGC, leaving it with practically no law-making

---

74 2001 Law on the Establishment of Extraordinary Chambers, Art 14.
75 See I Bantekas, 'The Iraqi Special Tribunal for Crimes against Humanity', 54 *ICLQ* (2005) 237, from which this section has been partly excerpted.
76 CPA/REG/16 May 2003/01.
77 CPA Regulation No. 6, CPA/REG/13 July 2003/06.

powers.[78] Exceptionally, however, the CPA granted temporary legislative authority to the IGC with the intent of formulating a law establishing a tribunal for the most serious crimes perpetrated by the regime of Saddam Hussein since its ascent to power in 1968.[79] By the time CPA Order No 48 was enacted in December 2003 the Statute had already been drafted and was annexed to Order No 48. Thus, approval by the IGC was in effect an act of administrative approval, particularly since under Order No 48 the promulgation of subsequent Elements of Crimes and Rules of Procedure by the IGC required the prior approval of the CPA.[80] Unsurprisingly, the Statute was approved by the IGC establishing the Iraqi Special Tribunal for Crimes against Humanity (Iraqi Special Tribunal) on 10 December 2003. Following the entry into force of the Iraqi Special Tribunal, the IGC adopted on 8 March 2004 the 'Transitional Administrative Law' (TAL),[81] which was hailed as an interim constitution with the aim of serving as an instrument for governing Iraq upon restoration of sovereignty on 30 June 2004 until a permanent constitution was adopted. A simple reading of the TAL clearly demonstrates that it was in conflict with the Special Tribunal Statute with regard to jurisdictional matters. For one thing, Art 48(A) of the TAL stated that: 'the [Iraqi Special] Statute exclusively defines its jurisdiction and procedures, notwithstanding the provisions of this Law'. Moreover, Art 15(I) of the TAL was unequivocal in that 'special or exceptional courts may not be established'. Despite the conflict between the TAL and the Special Statute, the latter retained primary jurisdiction over its subject matter. Nonetheless, Art 48(A) of the TAL contradicts its own Art 15(I) in as much as the Special Tribunal is not merely exceptional but outside the 'constitution'.

As regards the Tribunal's relationship with the national courts of Iraq, it is expressly stated in the Tribunal's Statute, and reiterated in the TAL, that jurisdiction is concurrent, albeit the Tribunal retains primacy in relation to war crimes, crimes against humanity and genocide.[82] However, in the case of offences lifted from Iraqi law and enumerated in Art 14 of the Tribunal's Statute, no primacy is afforded to the Tribunal under Art 29(a) of its Statute, with the matter left unresolved also in Art 48(B) of the TAL, which refers back to the Tribunal's Statute. When a newly elected government was formed in Iraq in 2005, it proceeded to re-promulgate the Statute, effectively bringing it into force on 18 October 2005 and renaming it the Iraqi High Criminal Court. This legislative action was meant to demonstrate that the Tribunal

---

78　See, eg, SC Res 1511 (16 Oct 2003) and 1500 (14 Aug 2003), which proclaim the IGC as being the principal body of Iraqi interim administration, but make no reference to the fact that it has practically no exclusive law or decision-making capacity.

79　CPA Order No 48, CPA/0RD/9 Dec 2003/48.

80　Arts 1 and 2, id.

81　Available at: <http://www.cpa-iraq.org/government/TAL.html>.

82　Art 29(b), Special Tribunal Statute.

was no longer the creation of an occupying authority, but rather the product of the sovereign State of Iraq and its people.

The Tribunal's temporal jurisdiction spans from 17 July 1968, the date of the coup that brought the Ba'athists to power, up until 1 May 2004, at which time an end to major hostilities was declared by US President Bush.[83] This expansive temporal jurisdiction aims to target crimes allegedly perpetrated in three significant military campaigns, ie, the 1980–88 Iran–Iraq conflict, the 1990–91 Gulf War and the occupation of Kuwait, and the 2003 Iraq–US/Coalition war, as well as all cases of internal campaigns of repression and extermination against the Kurds, Shi'ites and Marsh Arabs – without excluding crimes against Sunnis disloyal to the regime.

As regards the Tribunal's jurisdiction *ratione loci*, this is not confined only to Iraqi territory, but extends to all other territories where Iraqi nationals or residents committed crimes falling within the Tribunal's Statute, 'including crimes committed in connection with Iraq's wars against Iran and Kuwait'.[84]

The Special Tribunal possesses subject matter jurisdiction over genocide,[85] crimes against humanity,[86] war crimes[87] and violations of stipulated Iraqi laws.[88] The formulation of the crime of genocide has been taken verbatim from the 1948 Genocide Convention[89] – and Art 6 of the ICC Statute where appropriate – whereas crimes against humanity have similarly been lifted verbatim from Art 7 of the ICC Statute with the omission of enforced sterilisation and apartheid as acts constituting an attack. The situation is no different with regard to war crimes, with slight differences in wording and order of listed offences in comparison to Art 8 of the ICC Statute. In accordance with Art 17(b) of the Special Tribunal Statute, when interpreting these international offences 'the Trial and Appellate chambers may resort to the relevant decisions of international courts or tribunals as persuasive authority for their decisions'. The offences under Iraqi law comprise of the following:

(a) manipulation of the judiciary;
(b) wasting national resources or squandering of public assets and funds,[90] and;
(c) abuse of position and the pursuit of policies that may lead to the threat of war or the use of the armed forces of Iraq against an Arab country.[91]

---

83 Art 1(b), Special Tribunal Statute.
84 Ibid.
85 Art 11, Special Tribunal Statute.
86 Art 12, id.
87 Art 13, id.
88 Art 14, id.
89 Convention on the Prevention and Punishment of the Crime of Genocide, 78 UNTS 277.
90 In accordance with Art 2(g) of Law No 7 (1958), as amended.
91 In accordance with Art 1, id.

The incorporation of international offences taken verbatim from multilateral treaties or from the Statutes of other international tribunals is not necessarily a wise option in every instance. It is doubtful, for example, whether international criminal liability existed prior to 1993 for offences taking place in non-international armed conflicts.[92] Equally, there is a need for an exceptional Tribunal of this nature to adapt itself to its particular contextual exigencies. One of the major factors contributing to violent repression in all fields of society and government during the reign of Saddam Hussein was the Ba'athification of all aspects of Iraqi life. Efforts to rid post-war Iraq of such elements are evident in the TAL, as well as the Special Tribunal Statute.[93] One, therefore, would have expected a provision similar to Arts 9 and 10 of the Charter of the International Military Tribunal (IMT) at Nuremberg,[94] which criminalized participation in designated criminal organisations. The object of those provisions was not the criminalisation of the organisation as a legal entity, but personal participation and involvement in its activities. Most possibly, the drafters of the Special Tribunal Statute found no equivalent in Iraqi criminal law,[95] or justification in customary international law and decided to exclude this concept from its ambit. Although the use of analogies in criminal law is wholly undesirable and prohibited,[96] 'common plan' liability is identical to that described under Arts 9 and 10 of the Nuremberg Charter. Its construction for present purposes would have added a historical and symbolic element to the trials – and would have probably been a good supplement for a truth and reconciliation commission – without jeopardising procedural or substantive fairness.

On the whole, the Special Tribunal is an internal judicial institution with international elements. These are:

---

92 See, eg, a Letter dated 24 May 1994, addressed to the President of the Security Council by the UN Secretary-General, which reads in relevant part: 'It must be observed that the violations of the law or customs of war . . . are offences when committed in international, but not in internal, armed conflicts.' UN Doc S/1994/674, para 52. This was at pace with scholarly writings at the time.

93 See Art 33 of the Special Tribunal Statute, which states that none of the Tribunal's judicial or other personnel must have been a member of the Ba'ath party; Art 31, TAL, supra note 81, which provides the criteria for election to the National Assembly. Similarly, the CPA adopted Order No 1, which is entitled 'De-Ba'athification of Iraqi Society', CPA/0RD/16 May 2003/01.

94 London Agreement for the Prosecution and Punishment of the Major War Criminals of the European Axis, 82 UNTS 280.

95 Iraqi Law No 111 (15 Dec 1969, without regard to amendments made thereafter) [1969 Iraqi Criminal Code] and a limited source of law for the Special Tribunal contains in Arts 55–59 the offence/liability form of 'criminal conspiracy, where participation or membership in the conspiracy even without an attempt to commit an offence renders the person liable as a conspirator, available at: <https://www.jagcnet.army.mil/JAGCNETInternet/Homepages/AC/CLAMO-Public.nsf>.

96 Art 22(2), ICC Statute.

(a) occupation by foreign State entities;
(b) jurisdiction *ratione loci* extends beyond the borders of Iraq;[97]
(c) appointment of non-Iraqi judges[98] and advisors;[99]
(d) limited, yet direct application of international law[100] and;
(e) limited role for the UN, with potentially significant role for the Security Council.

Although these elements purport to equate the Iraqi Tribunal with the hybrid, internationalised tribunals of Sierra Leone and Cambodia, this could not be further from the truth. Whereas the authority of the Sierra Leone and Cambodia Tribunals, as well as the insertion therein of international elements is determined by their respective UN Agreements, the introduction of international elements in the Iraqi Special Tribunal is exclusively voluntary and may be removed at any point, subject to the rights of the accused. Saddam Hussein was the first accused to be executed, on 30 December 2006.

22.7 THE LOCKERBIE TRIAL

On 22 December 1988, Pan Am flight 103 exploded above the village of Lockerbie in Scotland, having taken off from London, killing all of its 259 passengers and crew as well as 11 Lockerbie residents killed by the debris. Investigations immediately commenced in the UK and US, also involving law enforcement authorities around the world. All relevant investigations implicated two Libyan agents, Al-Megrahi and Fhimah, as having concealed plastic explosives in a suitcase on an Air Malta flight KM180 to Frankfurt, re-routed from there to London and subsequently transferred onto the tragic 103 flight bound for JFK airport in New York city. The explosives were detonated by an electronic timer, with the then alleged perpetrators managing not to board flight 103 and the luggage being stored on the aircraft without being counted or x-rayed.[101]

While ongoing investigations had been conducted in secrecy, on 27 November 1991 the Lord Advocate obtained an arrest warrant for the two Libyans on charges of conspiracy to murder and breaches of the 1982 Aviation Security Act. Thereupon, the US and UK Governments demanded

---

97 Art 10, Special Tribunal Statute.
98 Art 4(d), id.
99 Arts 6(b), 7(n), 8(j), id.
100 Arts 17(b) and 24(e), id; see also, Art 2(1)–(2), CPA Order No 48, which states that the elements of crimes promulgated by the IGC should be consistent with international law and that the Tribunal must meet, at a minimum, international standards of justice.
101 See A Klip and M Mackarel, 'The Lockerbie Trial – A Scottish Court in The Netherlands', 70 *Revue Internationale de Droit Penale* (1999), 777.

through the Security Council that Libya surrender the accused so that they could stand trial in either of the two countries. At the behest of the two Governments, Resolution 731 was initially adopted,[102] requesting Libyan condemnation of terrorism and deploring its lack of co-operation. The Libyan Government protested that it was fulfilling its obligations under Art 7 of the 1971 Montreal Convention for the Suppression of Unlawful Acts Against the Safety of Civil Aviation, which imposes an obligation to either prosecute or extradite. The Libyans sued the US and UK before the International Court of Justice (ICJ), arguing that since they had submitted the case to a competent judicial authority they had fulfilled their obligations under the 1971 Montreal Convention. Before the ICJ could reach a judgment on its jurisdiction, the Security Council adopted Resolution 748,[103] under chapter VII of the UN Charter, demanding that within two weeks Libya establish its responsibility over the acts and essentially surrender the accused for trial, otherwise a range of sanctions would have to be imposed, as they were.[104] The ICJ, somewhat crippled by Resolution 748, held that on the basis of Art 103 of the UN Charter, according to which obligations under the Charter supersede all other obligations of Member States, the Council's authority to adopt binding resolutions prevailed over the terms of the 1971 Montreal Convention. The majority of the judges noted, however, that had it not been for Resolution 748, Libya would not have been at fault.[105] During this time, and until 1998, Libya maintained that not only was it precluded by constitutional constraints from surrendering its own nationals, but, because of the inevitable media coverage in the US and UK, the accused would not receive a fair trial. Nonetheless, Libya offered to surrender the accused for trial in a neutral country, but this proposal was resisted.

The impasse was finally resolved in 1998 when the UK agreed to a proposal envisaging the trial in a neutral country and heard by a Scottish court. The Netherlands concurred to host it on its territory and an agreement was signed between the two countries on 18 September 1998.[106] Subsequently, Council Resolution 1192 welcomed the end to the stalemate, asking all States to co-operate, further designating the Netherlands as the detaining power once the accused had been surrendered for trial.[107] The Agreement between the UK and the Netherlands entered into force on 8 January 1999. Unlike the

---

102　SC Res 731 (21 Jan 1992).
103　SC Res 748 (31 March 1992).
104　Further sanctions were imposed more than a year later through SC Res 883 (11 Nov 1993).
105　*Libya v UK, Libya v USA*, Questions of Interpretation and Application of the 1971 Montreal Convention Arising from the Aerial Incident at Lockerbie, Order of 14 April 1992 (1992) ICJ Reports 3.
106　Agreement between The Netherlands and UK Concerning a Scottish Trial in The Netherlands, 38 ILM (1999), 926.
107　SC Res 1192 (27 Aug 1998)

two ad hoc tribunals (that is, the ICTY and ICTR), and other internationalised domestic tribunals (that is, the Sierra Leone Special Court and East
Timor Special Panels), the court (the Scottish High Court of Justiciary)
specified in the 1998 Agreement did not have a Security Council mandate and
did not sit in the territory of the country exercising territorial jurisdiction. In
that sense, it is a unique creature, adapted to the particular exigencies of the
case, demonstrating a flexibility that is rare for international criminal justice.
Under the Agreement, Scots law was applicable only in relation to the
accused and the offences, whereas Dutch law was generally applicable in
every other respect. Thus the jurisdiction of the Scottish court was limited to
the trial, which included all investigative and pre-trial phases in accordance
with Scots law and practice.[108] Thus, the Agreement was ultimately an
instrument for delineating sensitive matters of sovereignty. Besides the
particular details agreed to between the parties, the Agreement fell in the
category of host country treaties and the international law applicable with
regard to official foreign premises. Under the terms of the Agreement, the
court was, *inter alia*, empowered to issue regulations concerning its day-to-
day affairs,[109] exchange Letters of Understanding with the Dutch Ministry of
Justice,[110] while the Netherlands was obliged to allow the entry and protection of witnesses[111] and international observers,[112] among others.

Although the matter of jurisdiction and the seat of the court were resolved
in terms of international law, this was not self-evident as a matter of UK
law. Council Resolution 1192, which had called on the UK to facilitate the
arrangements for establishing the court, would have had to be implemented
through the adoption of an Order in Council, approved by Parliament and
given royal assent by the Queen, in accordance with the requisite procedure
under the 1946 UN Act. Thus, the High Court of Justiciary (Proceedings in
The Netherlands) Order 1998 (1998 Order) was adopted,[113] giving authority
to the Scottish High Court to hear the case against the two accused, who were
specifically named in the 1998 Order.[114] Contrary to Scots criminal procedure
law, the case was not heard by a jury, although this need not have been so
had the accused consented to a trial by jury in Scotland.[115]

Finally, the two accused, apparently with their consent, were handed to a
UN official in Libya and were flown to the Netherlands to stand trial. The trial
began on 3 May 2000, and on 31 January 2001 the High Court handed down

---

108 1998 Agreement, Art 1(I).
109 Ibid, Art 6.
110 Ibid, Art 27.
111 Ibid, Art 17.
112 Ibid, Art 18.
113 SI 1998/2251 (16 Sept 1998), entering into force two days later.
114 1998 Order, s 3(1).
115 Ibid, Art 16(2)(a).

its judgment, finding only one of the accused, Al-Megrahi, guilty of murder in respect of the bombing of PanAm flight 103 and the ensuing deaths caused both in mid-air and on the ground at Lockerbie. The lengthy judgment did not analyse points of law in any great detail, but instead focused on the examination of evidence and fact. Although the evidence that was accumulated was circumstantial, it was such that it established Al-Megrahi's guilt beyond a reasonable doubt. He was sentenced to serve life imprisonment, which he appealed not on grounds of the sufficiency of evidence, but on the treatment by the trial court of the evidence presented and the submissions made to it by the defence. By its judgment of 14 March 2002, the Appeal Court of the High Court of Justiciary rejected the appeal and the case was officially closed.[116]

22.8 NATIONAL TRUTH COMMISSIONS AND AMNESTIES

While many view the processes of criminal accountability as the only viable and reliable mechanisms for reconstruction and reconciliation of devastated societies, some States have come to the conclusion that the same purpose may alternatively be served through Truth Commissions.[117] The purpose of these commissions is to administer restorative rather than retributive justice and their application may be complementary to judicial proceedings, as in the case of South Africa, or the sole mechanism of accountability, as was the case with El Salvador. Such commissions are mechanisms used to investigate and accurately record human rights violations in a particular country, but very often result in sweeping amnesties.[118] Investigatory commissions of this type have been established at transitional phases in the democratic process of various States, in which civilian governments had recently replaced repressive regimes, with the aim of either investigating human rights abuses of prior regimes, as was done with the panels created in Argentina and Chile, or as a means of resolving a civil war through a political agreement, as in El Salvador. In one instance, however, it was the Security Council that established an international commission of inquiry in order to investigate the violence that resulted from the 1993 coup in Burundi.[119]

---

116 *Al-Megrahi v HM Advocate*, Opinion in Appeal against Conviction, 14 March 2002 (Appeal No C104/01).
117 P Hayner, 'Fifteen Truth Commissions 1974 to 1994: A Comparative Study', 16 *HRQ* (1994), 597.
118 See M Scharf, 'The Case for a Permanent International Truth Commission', 8 *Duke J Intl & Comp L* (1997), 1; T Klosterman, 'The Feasibility and Propriety of a Truth Commission in Cambodia: Too Little? Too Late?', 15 *Ariz J Intl & Comp L* (1998), 2.
119 SC Res 1012 (25 Aug 1995).

Although most of these commissions were established and functioned at a purely domestic level, in every case it was evident that the involvement of international personnel would potentially lift suspicions of impartiality. Hence, the staff serving on the El Salvador commission were entirely foreign, as were those in Burundi, assigned and sponsored by the UN.[120] The purposes of investigative or Truth Commissions can vary, but in general their purpose is to create an authoritative record, provide redress for the victims, make recommendations for reform and establish accountability of perpetrators.[121] However, the primary purpose of most commissions is not to identify perpetrators, but to document repression and crime. This is best achieved only by permitting victims and culprits to come forward and recount their personal testimony as regards their participation in particular events. To secure such testimony, commissions are generally empowered, depending on their mandate, to grant amnesties to those who confess their prior crimes.

Let us examine the most significant Truth Commission of the last decade, the South African Truth and Reconciliation Commission (TRC).[122] It was set up in 1993 on the basis of the 1993 interim Constitution and the Promotion of National Unity and Reconciliation Act, No 34 of 1995, and comprised of three branches: a Committee on Human Rights Violations (HRV); a Committee on Amnesty; and a Committee on Reparation and Rehabilitation (R&R). The mandate of the HRV Committee has been to investigate human rights abuses that took place between 1960 and 1994, based on statements made to the TRC. Its aim is to establish the identity and fate of victims, the nature of the crimes suffered and whether the violations were the result of deliberate planning by the prior regimes or any other organisation, group or individual. Victims are then referred to the R&R Committee, which considers requests for reparation only in regard to those formally declared victims by the TRC or their relatives and dependants. The primary purpose of the Amnesty Committee is to ascertain whether or not applications for amnesty are in respect of human rights violations that were committed within the ambit prescribed by the 1995 Act, that is, whether they relate to omissions or offences associated with political objectives and committed between 1960 and 1994, in the course of the struggle for internal self-determination. An amnesty is granted only in those cases where the culprit makes a full disclosure of all the relevant facts. Therefore, in cases where an offence was committed for purely private motives, no amnesty will be granted.

The internationalised domestic tribunals examined in the present chapter,

---

120 See T Buergenthal, 'The United Nations Truth Commission for El-Salvador', 27 *Vand J Trans L* (1994), 498.

121 M Ratner and J Abrams, *Accountability for Human Rights Atrocities in International Law,* 1997, Oxford: OUP, 196.

122 See generally P Parker, 'The Politics of Indemnities: Truth Telling and Reconciliation in South Africa', 17 *HRLJ* (1996), 1.

except for the Lockerbie Tribunal, have been established alongside Truth Commissions. Their operation is problematic because: (a) the boundaries between the two institutions are not clearly delineated; (b) similarly problematic and ambiguous is the application of the rule *ne bis in idem* (that is, that one cannot be tried twice for the same offence) in both domestic and international law; and (c) where truth commissions grant blanket amnesties, or amnesties excusing serious international offences, neither the UN nor most individuals[123] will be inclined to recognise or respect them in their respective legal systems. Where the UN is involved in the interim administration of a war-torn nation, the Truth Commission does not supersede the jurisdiction of criminal tribunals, but supplements them.[124] The same is not true for Cambodia, however, where the status of amnesties granted prior to the creation of the Extraordinary Chambers remains uncertain. As even the most conciliatory commissions involve some kind of punitive judicial mechanisms, Truth Commissions are generally able to serve the purposes of both restorative and retributive criminal justice. To the extent they are not used as platforms for granting sweeping amnesties they are a welcome supplement to the international criminal justice system. It should be remembered that in every case, truth commissions are never a sufficient alternative to prosecution with regard to serious international offences.[125]

In the Sierra Leone context, a significant effort was made by the Special Court to accommodate the work of the Truth and Reconciliation Commission (TRC), although the Special Court is empowered with primacy. In 2003, a senior indictee, Chief Norman, after having heard other high-ranking officials provide public testimonies before the TRC, and while awaiting for his trial to commence, requested the Special Court along with the TRC itself to be given permission to hold a public hearing. The request was refused twice on the grounds that there was a grave danger that such a public hearing would prejudice the defendant's position and that of his co-defendants, as well as influence witness testimonies, at trial. The Special Court did, however, authorise the use of an affidavit instead 'on condition that it gives an undertaking not to bring or assist any other person or agency to bring a prosecution for perjury'.[126]

---

123 As far as subsequent claims in tort are concerned.
124 UNTAET/REG/2001/10 (13 July 2001), on the establishment of a Commission for Reception, Truth and Reconciliation in East Timor.
125 Inter-American Commission on Human Rights (IACHR), Report No 36/96, Case 10,843 (Chile), (15 Oct 1996), para 77; similarly, IACHR Report No 34/96, Cases 11,228, 11,229, 11,231 and 11,282 (Chile), (15 Oct 1996), para 76; Report No 25/98, Cases 11,505, 11,532, 11,541, 11,546, 11,549, 11,569, 11,572, 11,573, 11,583, 11,585, 11,595, 11,652, 11,657, 11,675 and 11,705 (Chile), (7 April 1998), para 50; IACHR Report No 136/99, Case 10,488 *Ignacio Ellacuria SJ and others* (El Salvador), (22 Dec 1999), para 230.
126 *SLSC Prosecutor v Norman*, Decision on Appeal by the TRC and Chief Norman against the Decision of Bankole J delivered on 30 Oct 2003 to Deny the TRC's Request to Hold a Public Hearing with Chief Norman (28 Nov 2003), para 41.

We have already examined the practice of the Sierra Leone Special Court, which did not rule out the normative validity of local amnesties. Rather, the Special Court emphasised generally that:

(a) the terms of an amnesty are automatically invalidated where its terms are breached, even if the breach arose out of action undertaken by the leaders of an amnestied group and not all of its members;
(b) amnesties are inapplicable before criminal tribunals exercising international jurisdiction;
(c) persons bearing great responsibility for serious international crimes are not exonerated by an amnesty; and
(d) a local amnesty can be invalidated by a subsequent treaty – apart from the conditions contemplated in (a)–(c) – is valid under international law but contrary to domestic law and would nonetheless create a bad precedent for the credibility of a particular government internally.

Both the UN[127] and various multilateral treaties have advocated the granting of general amnesties, such as Art 6(5) of the 1977 Protocol II to the 1949 Geneva Conventions (and relating to non-international armed conflicts), which requires the parties to grant 'the broadest possible amnesty to persons who have participated in the armed conflict'. However, none of these instruments and statements of support with regard to broad amnesties have ever been interpreted to encompass serious violations of international law, particularly grave breaches, crimes against humanity and genocide.[128] Given that these are international crimes carrying universal jurisdiction (at least under customary law for the latter two), it would be inconceivable that a domestic amnesty law could bar the exercise of jurisdiction by other courts or limit the liability of the perpetrators. Moreover, the granting of amnesties have been held by international human rights bodies to have violated many of the victim's (and that of family members) rights, particularly the right to life, access to justice, security of person and others.[129]

The granting of amnesties for serious international crimes thus comes into conflict with particular State obligations such as the duty to either prosecute or extradite persons accused of serious offences, or simply to prosecute those responsible for having committed serious international crimes. This has been

---

127 See Art 34 of the 2003 Accra Peace Agreement between the Government of Liberia and the Political Parties, LURD and MODEL, which drew UN support.
128 See specifically, IACHR Report No 1/99, Case 10,480, *Lucio Parada Cea and Others* (El Salvador) (27 Jan 1999), para 116; *ICTY Prosecutor v Furundzija*, Trial Chamber Judgment (10 Dec 1998), para 155.
129 IACHR Report No 28/92, Cases 10,147, 10,181, 10,240, 10,262, 10,309 and 10,311 (Argentina), (2 Oct 1992); UN Human Rights Committee (HRC) General Comment No 20 (44) on Art 7 of ICCPR, UN Doc A/47/40, Supp No 40, Appendix VI.A (1992).

the adamant position of the UN, so irrespective of the process utilised to grant amnesties for serious international offences, such amnesties cannot constitute a bar to subsequent prosecution by other national or international judicial bodies.[130] Criminal trials will generally be required where the offence is a serious one, otherwise international law would be taken to mean that all amnesties are null *ab initio*.[131] Even if this was a valid statement in law – which it is not – it would, as Robertson J has noted in his Separate Opinion in the *Lome Amnesty* case, create a significant logistical problem because the incumbent government would be pressed to hold tens of thousands of trials for all accused of war crimes following the termination of an internal armed conflict.[132] It will be recalled that the UN Special Representative to the signing of the 1999 Lome Agreement objected to immunity for the most serious offences, not all. Equally, it should not be forgotten that the Security Council approved the Governors' Island Agreement in Haiti, which provided a broad amnesty.[133]

---

130 D Orentlicher, 'Settling Accounts: The Duty to Prosecute Human Rights Violations of a Prior Regime', 100 Y*ale LJ(*1991), 2537; M Scharf, 'Swapping Amnesty for Peace: Was There a Duty to Prosecute International Crimes in Haiti?', 31 *Texas ILJ* (1996), 1; The South African Supreme Court in *Azanian Peoples Organisation v President of the Republic of South Africa* (1996) 4 SA 671, wrongly held that international human rights law does not compel domestic criminal prosecution of human rights abuses. Summarised in 91 *AJIL* (1997), 360.
131 J Gavron, 'Amnesties in the Light of Development in International Law and the Establishment of the International Criminal Court', 51 *ICLQ* (2002), 91, pp 94–99.
132 *Lome Amnesty* Decision, Separate Opinion, op cit note 25.
133 Gavron, op cit note 131.

Index

abduction 343; abuse of process and 348–9; collusion by law enforcement agencies 349–51; ECHR approach 347–8; extraordinary rendition 352–5; *male captus, bene detentus* rule 343–5; seriousness of crime and 351–2; US courts' approach 345–7
abuse of process 52; abduction and 348–9
accomplice liability 37
accused persons 19; *ad hoc* international tribunals 531–4; defences *see* defences; EU common minimum standards for rights of 383–5; presumption of innocence 52; terrorist offences 229–31
Achille Lauro incident 179–80
Act of State doctrine 102–3
active personality principle 79–81
admissibility of evidence 398–9, 444–57
adoption of children 156
Afghanistan 212, 219–20
aggression 499–501, 507, 510; International Criminal Court (ICC) and 544–7
aiding and abetting 21–3
airspace 78
Allende, Salvador 337
Al-Qaeda 212, 213, 214, 219–20, 224–5
amnesties 558–9, 561–3, 581, 583–4
Amnesty International 338
anti-personnel mines 119
Anti-Slavery International 151, 160
Antonopoulos, C 547
apartheid 11, 16, 18, 135–6, 166–8
appeals: evidence 492–4; ICTR and ICTY 515
approving spectators 23
archipelagic states 173

Argentina: Truth Commission 580
armed conflict *see* war (armed conflict)
arrest: European Arrest Warrant (EAW) 80–1, 299, 300, 304, 307, 308, 320–5, 327, 372, 377–8, 416, 433–4
asylum 230, 331
Australia: abduction and 349; cybercrime initiatives 278–9; extradition in 334–5
Austria: universal jurisdiction and 89–90
aut dedere aut judicare principle 91–2, 308
aviation *see* civil aviation

Baader Meinhof 222
bacteriological warfare 118
Bank for International Settlements (BIS) 16
banking system: self-regulation 15–16
Basle Committee 16, 248, 249
Bassiouni, Cherif M 7, 18, 126, 308
Belgium: evidence obtained in compliance with foreign law but irregular under national law 396–7; extradition in 324; protective principle and 84; universal jurisdiction and 87–8
belligerency *see* war (armed conflict)
boatjacking 179–80
Bolivia 239
bombings: terrorist 208–9
Bosnia and Herzegovina 13, 517; extraordinary rendition and 355
bribery 8, 239, 280–5
bride-price 155
bride-wealth 155
broadcasting: unauthorised broadcasting from the high seas 188–9
Brownlie, I 106
burden of proof 52

Burundi 140; Truth Commission 580,
    581

cables: offences against submarine cables
    5, 185–8
Cambodia 140; Extraordinary Chambers
    557, 570–3
Canada: extradition in 294, 334;
    extraordinary rendition and 354;
    superior orders defence and 60
capital punishment: extradition and
    305–6, 329
Cassese, Antonio 438–9, 515
Chad 104
character evidence 465–9
chemical warfare 118
children: adoption 156; child labour
    155–6; debt bondage 154–5;
    prosecution of 564; recruitment to
    armed forces 119, 563–4; sexual
    exploitation 156, 276, 279, 290–1
Chile 105, 337; Truth Commission 580
China 507
Churchill, R R 189
Churchill, Winston 497, 506
civil aviation: offences against 92–3,
    199–205
Clinton, Bill 220
Colombia 212, 239; extradition in 332–3
command/superior responsibility 37–47;
    duty to prevent or punish 46–7; mental
    element 42–6; nature of 37–9; superior
    orders defence 56–61, 504–5, 549;
    superior-subordinate relationship
    39–42
commission through another person
    36
conspiracy 26, 34–6
constructive presence doctrine 193–4
consular immunities 109
contiguous zone 174
continental shelf 174
continuing act doctrine 76–7
corporal punishment 137
corporations: corporate liability 47–9;
    jurisdiction over multinational
    corporations 77
Corpus Juris project 370–1
corroboration of evidence 480–1
corruption 8, 239, 280–5
Crawford, James 17
credibility of witnesses 484

Croatia 517
Crossman, Gareth 326
Cuba: Act of State doctrine and 102
cultural genocide 148
customary law 3–4; freedom from slavery
    and 152; international criminalisation
    process and 8; piracy in 176, 178
cybercrime 265–7, 291; Council of
    Europe initiatives 267–9; EU
    initiatives 269–76; national initiatives
    278–80; OECD Security Guidelines
    277
Cyprus: extradition in 324
Czechoslovakia 500

damages 17
death penalty see capital punishment
debt bondage 154–5
defences: domestic defences in ICC
    Statute 53–6; duress 59, 60, 61–5, 548;
    intoxication 67–8, 548; mental
    incapacity 69–70, 548; mistake of
    fact/mistake of law 68–9, 549;
    necessity 61–5; self-defence 65–7;
    superior orders 56–61, 504–5, 549;
    theoretical underpinnings 51–6
delicts: international 16–17
deportation 331–3, 334
deposition evidence 463–5
diminished responsibility 69–70
Dinstein, Y 6
diplomats: immunities 101, 108–10;
    terrorist attacks on 207–8
direct enforcement of international
    criminal law 10–11
disappeared persons 136, 168–71
dissident forces 123–4
documentary evidence 457–60, 481–2
double jeopardy: extradition and 306–7
drug trafficking 235, 239–46; as crime
    against international law 245–6;
    international measures against 240–5
duress defence 59, 60, 61–5, 548

East Timor Special Panels 557, 564–8
effects doctrine 75–6
El Salvador: Truth Commission 580, 581
enforced disappearances 136, 168–71
enforcement of international criminal
    law 10–15; ad hoc international
    tribunals 528–30; slavery 160–1
erga omnes obligations 11, 14, 17;

genocide prohibition as 139–40
espionage 83, 84
European Banking Federation (EFB) 15
European Court of Human Rights 14,
    164, 327–8, 347–8
European Union (EU) 5; anti-terrorism
    measures 217–18; common minimum
    standards for rights of accused
    persons 383–5; corporate liability in
    48–9; Corpus Juris project 370–1;
    cybercrime initiatives 269–76; drug
    trafficking measures 245; Eurojust
    373–5, 376, 416; European Arrest
    Warrant (EAW) 80–1, 299, 300, 304,
    307, 308, 320–5, 327, 372, 376–8, 416,
    433–4; European Court of Justice
    (ECJ) 4, 418–22; European Evidence
    Warrant (EEW) 378–81; European
    Judicial Network 371–2, 415;
    European Police Agency (Europol)
    375, 416, 422–8; European Police
    College 435; European Public
    Prosecutor 372–3; European
    Supervision Orders 381–3; joint
    investigation teams 375–6; jurisdiction
    issues and 76; money laundering and
    257, 258–61; mutual legal assistance
    and 361, 362–85; mutual recognition
    programme 376–85; police
    co-operation initiatives 414–36;
    prevention of jurisdiction conflicts
    381; Schengen *acquis* 428–31;
    Schengen Information System 431–3
evidence 389, 437–94; admissibility
    398–9, 444–57; appeals 492–4;
    character 465–9; communication of
    12; corroboration 480–1; credibility of
    witnesses 484; cultural aspects 490–1;
    depositions 463–5; determination of
    weight of 479–94; documentary
    457–60, 481–2; European Evidence
    Warrant (EEW) 378–81; exclusion of
    improperly obtained evidence 476–9;
    expert 470–6, 491–2; fair trial issues
    398–9; general evidentiary principles
    440–3; hearsay 460–2, 482–4;
    investigator's report 468–70; language
    problems 490; lapse of time and 485;
    obtained in breach of foreign law
    390–3; obtained in breach of
    international human rights standards
    399–400; obtained in compliance with
    foreign law but irregular under
    national law 393–8; prior statements
    and 488–9; traumatic events and 486–7
exclusion of criminal responsibility 53,
    54
exclusive economic zone (EEZ) 174
excuses 55
experiments: unlawful 119
expert evidence 471–6, 491–2
extradition 12, 80, 293–4; *aut dedere aut
    judicare* principle and 91–2, 308;
    capital punishment and 305–6, 329;
    double criminality rule 296–9; double
    jeopardy and 306–7; EU initiatives
    313–25; European Convention 1957
    312–13; fiscal offences and 306;
    general principles 294–5; human rights
    issues and 326–36; military law
    offences: and 306; non-inquiry rule
    309–10; Pinochet case 298, 336–41;
    political offences and 229, 302–5;
    re-extradition 301–2; specialty
    provisions 299–301; surrender of
    nationals 308–9; terrorist offences and
    229, 230; torture and 161, 298, 329–33,
    335–41; UN Model Treaty on 310–11;
    United Kingdom 294, 296–306,
    308–10, 318–19, 325–6, 329–32,
    336–41; universal jurisdiction and 89
extraordinary rendition 352–5

facts: mistake of 68–9, 549
fair trial right 229–30; admissibility of
    evidence and 398–9
feudalism 157
Financial Action Task Force (FATF)
    215–16, 248, 249–50, 251
financial system 5; money laundering *see*
    money laundering; self-regulation
    15–16, 248–51
financing of terrorism 15–16, 208,
    211–16
Finch, G. 501–2
firearms 238
fiscal offences: extradition and 306
forced labour 159
France: drug trafficking and 239;
    extradition in 301, 332–3; superior
    orders defence and 60; universal
    jurisdiction and 90–1
Franco-Prussian war (1870) 496
freedom of expression 289

Gane, C 392
gas warfare 118
general defences 52
general principles of law 4–5, 54–5
Geneva Conventions: grave breaches of 113–15
genocide 6, 11, 16, 535; acts constituting 147–9; definitions 140–3; historical origins and legal status of prohibition 139–40; incitement to commit 28, 29, 149–50; International Criminal Court (ICC) and 547; membership of targeted group 145–6; Rwanda 141–50, 514; specific intent required 143–5; Yugoslavia 141–9, 513
geopolitics 19
George III, King 495
Germany: deprivation of citizenship 98; extradition in 324; extraordinary rendition and 353; Leipzig war trials 496; succession of states and 78–9; superior orders defence and 57, 60, 61; universal jurisdiction and 90; see also Nuremberg Tribunal
Grotius, Hugo 12, 177
Guantanamo Bay detainees 224–5; extraordinary rendition 352–5
guerilla movements 18, 123–4, 177, 197, 198, 222–5, 227
Guevara, Ernesto 'Che' 222

Habre, Hissene 104
Halsbury, Lord 71
Harvard Draft Convention on Piracy 178
Heads of State 39–40, 207; extradition and 298, 336–41; human rights abuses committed by 103–6, 336–41; immunities 101, 103–6, 336, 337, 340
hearsay evidence 460–2, 482–4
hijacking 92–3, 199–203; boatjacking 179–80
Hirohito, Emperor 508
Hitler, Adolf 501, 503, 504
hostage taking 205–6
hot pursuit right 189–91; commencement and continuous nature of hot pursuit 192–3; constructive presence doctrine 193–4
human rights issues 3, 14, 18–19; abuses by Heads of State 103–6, 336–41; evidence obtained in breach of

international human rights standards 399–400; extradition and 326–36; extraordinary rendition 352–5; freedom of expression 289; individual legal personality 5; mutual legal assistance treaties and 403–5; terrorism and 229–32; see also fair trial right
human shields 119
human trafficking 7–8, 87, 157–9
humanitarian law 3, 9; individual legal personality 5; universal jurisdiction and 85, 87
humanity, crimes against 18, 34, 501–3, 506; fundamental elements of offence 127–34; ICC statute and 134–7; International Criminal Court (ICC) and 547; nature of targeted 'civilian population' 132–3; origins of concept 125–7; subjective element 133–4; universal jurisdiction and 85, 87; widespread or systematic element 130–2; see also apartheid; genocide; slavery

ideological offences 12
immunities 13, 16; Act of State doctrine 102–3; from criminal jurisdiction 100–2, 110–11; diplomats 101, 108–10; domestic law and jus cogens norms 103–6; general conception of immunity in international law 96–100; Heads of State 101, 103–6, 336, 337, 340; from international criminal jurisdiction 110–11; Sierra Leone Special Court 561–3
incapacity: mental see mental incapacity
incitement 28; to commit genocide 28, 29, 149–50
India: debt bondage in 154; extradition in 331–2
individuals: human rights violations by 18; as subjects of international law 5, 14
Indonesia 565
innocence: presumption of 52
innocent passage right 78, 173
instigation of criminal action 28–9
insurgency 177
intergovernmental organisations 5
internal conflicts: war crimes 120–4
internal waters 77–8

International Atomic Energy Agency (IAEA) 210
International Cable Protection Committee 13, 187–8
International Chamber of Commerce 183
International Committee of the Red Cross (ICRC) 13, 530
International Court of Justice (ICJ) 14, 139, 140
International Criminal Court (ICC) 11, 51, 94, 95, 96, 246, 341, 557; composition 537; crime of aggression and 544–7; first referrals 543–4; general principles of criminal law 547–9; genocide, crimes against humanity, war crimes and 547; international co-operation and judicial assistance 549–52; jurisdiction 538–47; origins 535–8; reparation to victims 554–5; reservations and amendments to statute 552–4
International Criminal Police Organisation (Interpol) 407–14; operational activities 411–14; organisation of 409–11
International Criminal Tribunal for Rwanda (ICTR) 5, 9, 11, 55, 60, 110, 114, 120, 122–3, 140, 141, 514–15, 516, 557; admissibility of evidence 444–57; appeals evidence 492–4; character evidence 465–9; corroboration of evidence 480–1; credibility of witnesses 484; crimes against humanity and 127–34; cultural aspects of evidence 490–1; depositions 463–5; determination of weight of evidence 479–94; documentary evidence 457–60, 481–2; exclusion of improperly obtained evidence 476–9; expert evidence 470–6, 491–2; formative years 517, 521–2; general evidentiary principles 440–3; hearsay evidence 460–2, 482–4; investigator's report 468–70; jurisdiction 94, 522, 523; language problems 490; lapse of time and 485; principles of liability 21, 35–6; prior statements and 488–9; rights of the accused 532–3, 534; sexual violence as international offences 525; traumatic events and 486–7

International Criminal Tribunal for the Former Yugoslavia (ICTY) 5, 9, 11, 55, 60, 62, 65, 69, 101, 110, 114–15, 116–17, 120–2, 140, 141, 163–4, 413, 513–14, 516–17, 535, 552, 557; admissibility of evidence 444–57; appeals evidence 492–4; character evidence 465–9; corroboration of evidence 480–1; credibility of witnesses 484; crimes against humanity and 127–34; cultural aspects of evidence 490–1; depositions 463–5; determination of weight of evidence 479–94; documentary evidence 457–60, 481–2; enforcement capacity 528–30; exclusion of improperly obtained evidence 476–9; expert evidence 470–6, 491–2; formative years 517–21; general evidentiary principles 440–3; hearsay evidence 460–2, 482–4; investigator's report 468–70; jurisdiction 94–6, 522–3; language problems 490; lapse of time and 485; principles of liability 21–33, 36–47; prior statements and 488–9; rights of the accused 531–2, 534; sexual violence as international offences 524–8; traumatic events and 486–7
international criminalisation process 6–10
International Labour Organisation (ILO) 159, 160
International Law Commission (ILC) 509–11, 535–6; articles on state responsibility 16–17; draft articles on jurisdictional immunities 99; draft code of crimes 35, 59, 110, 223, 246, 509–11; drug trafficking measures 245–6; Nuremberg Principles 59, 110, 509; piracy and 178
International Maritime Bureau (IMB) 183, 184
International Military Tribunals see Nuremberg Tribunal; Tokyo Tribunal
International Mobile Satellite Organisation (INMARSAT) 184
International Narcotics Control Board 241
International Opium Commission 240
International Tribunal for the Law of the Sea (ITLOS) 191

international tribunals 11, 94, 495–6; *see also* International Criminal Tribunal for Rwanda (ICTR); International Criminal Tribunal for the Former Yugoslavia (ICTY); Nuremberg Tribunal; Tokyo Tribunal

Internet: crime and *see* cybercrime; obscene publications and 290–1

Interpol *see* International Criminal Police Organisation (Interpol)

intoxication defence 67–8, 548

investigator's report 468–70

involuntary intoxication defence 67–8, 548

Iran 140; downing of Flight 655 203

Iraq: invasion of Kuwait 14; US-backed invasion of 19

Iraqi Special Tribunal for Crimes Against Humanity 573–7

Ireland 208; extradition in 304; Schengen *acquis* and 430

Israel 198, 219; *male captus, bene detentus* rule 344–5; protective principle and 84; self-defence and 66; superior orders defence and 59

Italy: extradition in 301; extraordinary rendition and 353

Jewish Holocaust 139

joint criminal enterprise (JCE) 23, 26, 27, 28, 29–34

jurisdiction issues 12, 71–2; active personality principle 79–81; *ad hoc* international tribunals 522–4; *aut dedere aut judicare* principle 91–2, 308; crimes against civil aviation 92–3; foreign and multinational armed forces abroad 106–8; immunity from jurisdiction *see* immunities; International Criminal Court (ICC) 538–47; international criminal jurisdiction 93–6; passive personality principle 81–2; prevention of jurisdiction conflicts in EU 381; protective principle 75, 83–5; territorial jurisdiction 73–9; universal jurisdiction 85–91

jus cogens 3, 14, 17; genocide prohibition as 139–40; immunities and 103–6; torture prohibition and 161; universal jurisdiction and 86, 87

JUSTICE 417

justifications 53, 55

Karadzic, Radovan 131

Kenya: abduction in 347

Korea (South): downing of airliner 1987 203–4

Korean War 59

Kosovo 523, 568–9; UNMIK courts 557, 569–70

Koufa, Kalliopi 231

Kurdish separatism 208, 224

Kuwait: Iraqi invasion of 14

Laos 239

laser weapons 119

law: mistake of 68–9, 549

League of Arab States: Anti-Terrorism Agreement 217

League of Nations 500

legality: principle of 5

Leipzig war trials 496

Lesotho 284–5

liability: accomplice liability 37; aiding and abetting 21–3; command/superior responsibility 37–47; commission through another person 36; conspiracy 26, 34–6; corporate 47–9; instigation 28–9; joint criminal enterprise (JCE) 23, 26, 27, 28, 29–34; ordering 24–6; planning/preparation 26–7; vicarious liability 37

Liberty 326

Libya: Lockerbie incident 1988 204–5, 220–1, 577

Likic, Milan 413

limitations 52

Lockerbie incident 1988 204–5, 220–1, 577

Lockerbie Tribunal 557, 577–80

Lowe, A V 189

McArthur, Douglas 498, 508

Macedonia 523

Mackarel, M 392

Malaysia: extradition in 334–5

male captus, bene detentus rule 343–5

manifest illegality principle 57–61

Maritime Safety Committee 184

marriage: bride-price 155; bride-wealth 155

Mengele, Joseph 409

mental incapacity: as defence 69–70, 548

migrants: smuggling of 237–8
military: children in 119, 563–4;
    command/superior responsibility
    37–47; duress defence 59, 60, 61–5;
    extradition and offences under
    military law 306; foreign and
    multinational armed forces abroad
    106–8; ordering of criminal actions
    24–6; superior orders defence 56–61,
    504–5, 549; tribunals 4
Milosevic, Slobodan 101, 568
mines: anti-personnel 119
missions: immunities of 109–10
mistake of fact/mistake of law defences
    68–9, 549
money laundering 15–16, 213, 237, 246,
    247–8; Council of Europe initiatives
    256–8; EU initiatives 257, 258–61;
    self-regulation 248–51; UN initiatives
    252–5; United Kingdom initiatives
    261–4
moral choice principle 57–9
mutiny and other violence against ships
    not amounting to piracy 179–80
mutual legal assistance 357–9; European
    Convention 1959 360–2; European
    Union (EU) and 361, 362–85; failure
    to use provisions 401–3; individual
    rights and 403–5; informal methods
    405; International Criminal Court
    (ICC) and 549–52; UN Model Treaty
    359–60; United Kingdom and 358,
    387–92; see also police co-operation
Myanmar (Burma): forced labour in
    159

Napoleon I Bonaparte 545
nation states: breach of international
    criminal law by 14; criminality 15–17;
    Heads of State 39–40; human rights
    violations 18–19; immunities 96–100;
    jurisdiction see jurisdiction issues;
    sanctions against 14–15, 19;
    sovereignty 83; state-sponsored
    terrorism 16, 197, 218–21; as subjects
    of international law 5; succession of
    78–9
national courts: enforcement of
    international criminal law and 11–12,
    12
national legislation: direct applicability
    55; international criminalisation

process and 8–9; as source of law for
    ICC 55
national liberation movements 18, 177,
    197, 198, 222–5, 227
nationality: active personality principle
    79–81; extradition and 308–9; grave
    breaches of Geneva Conventions and
    114–15; passive personality principle
    81–2
ne bis in idem 52
necessity defence 61–5
negligence 28
Netherlands: exile of German Kaiser
    495; universal jurisdiction and
    86
New Zealand: superior orders defence
    and 60
Nicaragua 239
Noriega, General 239
North Atlantic Treaty Organisation
    (NATO) 106–7, 519, 520, 568
nuclear weapons 119; terrorism and 208,
    209–11
nullem crimen nulla poena sine lege scripta
    52
Nuremberg Principles 59, 110, 509
Nuremberg Tribunal 11, 34, 35, 58, 96,
    495, 545–6, 557; background to
    establishment of 497–8; law and
    justification of 498–505; legal basis
    and criticisms 505–7

objective territoriality 75–7
obscene publications 288–91
oceans see sea and ocean
offences: international criminalisation
    process 6–10
offences against the person 151;
    apartheid 11, 16, 18, 135–6, 166–8;
    enforced disappearances 136, 168–71;
    see also slavery; torture
ordering of criminal actions 24–6
Organisation for African Unity (OAU)
    521
Organisation for Economic
    Co-operation and Development
    (OECD): Committee on International
    Investment and Multinational
    Enterprises (CIME) 281–2; cybercrime
    Security Guidelines 277; Financial
    Action Task Force (FATF) 215–16,
    248, 249–50, 251

Organisation of American States (OAS):
Inter-American Committee Against
Terrorism 216
organised crime 18, 233–8; terrorism and
211–12, 225–7
outer space 3

pacta sunt servanda principle 4
Palestine Liberation Organisation (PLO)
197, 223
Panama 239
Paraguay 140
Paris Peace Conference (1919) 496
passive personality principle 81–2
peremptory norms 3–4
persecution 136–7
Peru: extradition and 335–6
Pinochet Ugarte, General 298, 336–41
pipelines: offences against submarine
cables and pipelines 5, 185–8
piracy 1, 2, 5, 174–85; air piracy 201–2;
definition under international law
176–9; international maritime
terrorism 180–3; mutiny and other
violence against ships not amounting
to piracy 179–80; prevention and
eradication mechanisms 183–5;
universal jurisdiction and 86, 87,
88
Piracy Reporting Centre (PRC) 13,
183–4
pirate broadcasting 188–9
planning/preparation of criminal action
26–7
Pol Pot 140, 570
Poland: extradition in 324; invasion of
(1939) 501
police co-operation 407; EU initiatives
414–36; International Criminal Police
Organisation (Interpol) 407–14
police investigator's report 468–70
political offences 2, 12; extradition
and 229, 302–5; Interpol and 409;
see also terrorism
postal offences 5, 285–8
preparation/planning of criminal action
26–7
Princeton Principles of Universal
Jurisdiction 91
prisoners of war (POWs) 123
private organisations: avoidance of
criminal legislation 15–16; corporate

liability 47–9; enforcement of
international criminal law and 13
procedural defences 52
proof: burden of 52
property: self-defence and 66–7
proportionality principle 64, 67
prostitution 7–8, 157–9
protective principle 75, 83–5
public office: immunity from criminal
jurisdiction and 100–2

radio 185; unauthorised broadcasting
from the high seas 188–9
Rakotomanana, Honore 521
reconciliation process 13
Red Brigades 222
Red Cross 13, 530
re-extradition 301–2
rendition: extraordinary 352–5
reparation to victims 554–5
reprisals: belligerent 66
reservations to treaties 12
retroactivity 52; prohibition of 5
Roosevelt, Franklin D 497
Roosevelt, Theodore 240
Rwanda: genocide in 141–50, 514;
see also International Criminal
Tribunal for Rwanda (ICTR)

sanctions 14–15, 19, 214
Sankoh, Foday 558
Schwarzenberger, G 10
sea and ocean 173–4; hot pursuit right
see hot pursuit right; internal waters
77–8; natural resources under seabed
3; offences against submarine cables
and pipelines 5, 185–8; territorial
waters 77–8, 173–4; unauthorised
broadcasting from the high seas 188–9;
see also piracy
selectivity in international criminal law
19
self-defence 65–7
self-regulation 15–16; cybercrime 265;
money laundering and 248–51
Senegal 104
Serbia 517
serfdom 156–7
sexual offences 119, 137, 148, 524–8,
560; human trafficking for sexual
purposes 7–8, 157–9; prostitution
7–8, 157–9; sexual exploitation of

children 156, 276, 279, 290–1; sexual tourism 80
ships: jurisdiction and 77–8
Shubber, S 200
Sierra Leone: Truth and Reconciliation Commission 582
Sierra Leone Special Court 557, 558–64, 582–3; amnesties and immunities 558–9, 561–3, 583; child recruitment and prosecution of children 563–4
slavery 18, 151–61; remedies and international enforcement measures 160–1; slave trade and similar institutions 86–7, 153–60
smuggling of migrants 237–8
Somalia: UN peace-keeping forces 107
sources of international law 2–5, 54–5
South Africa: apartheid regime 11, 16, 18, 135–6, 166–8; Truth and Reconciliation Commission 581
South Asian Association for Regional Co-operation (SAARC): Terrorist Offences Monitoring Desk 216–17
special defences 52
Stalin, Josef 497
states see nation states
subjective territoriality 73–4
subjects of international law 5
substantive defences 52, 53
succession of states 78–9
Sudan 219–20
superior responsibility see command/superior responsibility
supervision: European Supervision Orders 381–3
Sweden: active personality principle in 80
Syria: extraordinary rendition and 354

Taliban 212, 214
territorial jurisdiction 73–9; ambit of national territory 77–9; objective territoriality 75–7; subjective territoriality 73–4
territorial waters 77–8, 173–4
terrorism 6, 18, 195–7; attacks on diplomats and other protected persons 207–8; boatjacking 179–80; bombings 208–9; financing 15–16, 208, 211–16; hostage taking 205–6; human rights issues and 229–32; international maritime terrorism 180–3; national liberation movements 18, 177, 197, 198, 222–5, 227; nuclear 208, 209–11; offences against civil aviation 92–3, 199–205; organised crime and 211–12, 225–7; regional mechanisms against 216–18; state-sponsored 16, 197, 218–21; terrorist acts as political offences 227–9; thematic approach in international law 197–8
theory of international criminal law 1–2; theoretical underpinnings of defences 51–6
Tokyo Tribunal 11, 495, 507–8, 545; background to establishment of 497–8
torture 18, 19, 85, 88, 137, 161–6; definition 162–4; extradition and 161, 298, 329–33, 335–41; 'public official' requirement 165–6
transferred intent 68–9
transit passage right 173
Transparency International 285
treason 79, 80, 83
treaties: international criminalisation process and 6–10; as sources of international law 2–3
trial: fair trial right 229–30
truce flags: improper use of 119
Truth Commissions 13, 559, 580–4
Turkey: abduction in 347; extradition in 330; Kurdish separatism in 208, 224; massacre of Armenians (1915) 125–6, 139
Turns, D 569

United Kingdom: abduction and 343–4, 348–9, 350–2; active personality principle in 79–80; drug trafficking and 239; evidence obtained in breach of foreign law 390–2, 393; evidence obtained in compliance with foreign law but irregular under national law 393–6; extradition in 294, 296–306, 308–10, 318–19, 325–6, 329–32, 336–41; jurisdictional issues and 76–7; Lockerbie incident 1988 204–5, 220–1, 577; Lockerbie Tribunal 557, 577–80; money laundering initiatives 261–4; mutual legal assistance and 358, 387–96, 404; piracy in 176; Schengen acquis and 430; state immunities 99–100, 104; superior orders defence and 60; terrorism in 208, 220–1, 228,

229–30; universal jurisdiction and 86, 88, 89
United Nations 12–13, 240; Commission on Narcotic Drugs 241; Economic and Social Council (ECOSOC) 160, 240, 241, 281; extradition Model Treaty 310–11; Fund for Drug Abuse Control 241; General Assembly 3, 281, 509, 510, 536, 546, 565; Human Rights Committee 14, 353; International Criminal Court (ICC) and 535–6, 537; money laundering initiatives 252–5; mutual legal assistance Model Treaty 359–60; Office for Drug Control and Crime Prevention (ODCCP) 248, 254; peace-keeping forces 107; Security Council 11, 14, 94, 214, 220, 513, 514, 515, 519, 547; terrorism and 197–8
United States of America: abduction and 345–7, 352–5; armed forces abroad 107–8; bribery initiatives 280–1; drug trafficking and 239; evidence obtained in breach of foreign law 392–3; evidence obtained in compliance with foreign law but irregular under national law 397–8; extradition in 229, 294, 296, 305, 309, 326, 330, 334; extraordinary rendition 352–5; Guantanamo Bay detainees 224–5, 352–5; International Criminal Court (ICC) and 536, 539, 540; jurisdictional issues and 75–6, 77; mutual legal assistance provisions and 401–2; piracy in 176–7; political offences exception to extradition 229; protective principle and 84; Revolutionary War 495; self-defence and 66; state immunities and 100, 105; superior orders defence and 59–60, 61; terrorism and 180–1, 197, 219–20; universal jurisdiction and 89
universal crimes 6, 11
universal jurisdiction 85–91

Universal Postal Union (UPU) 286–7
Uzbekistan: extradition in 330–1

Venezuela: Act of State doctrine and 102–3; extradition and 335–6
vicarious liability 37
victims: reparation to 554–5
Vienna Declaration and Programme of Action 1993 231
Vietnam: invasion of Cambodia 140
Vietnam War 59
voluntary intoxication defence 67–8, 548
von Hagenbach, Peter 495
von Hohenstafen, Conradin 495

Waldheim, Kurt 198
war (armed conflict) 177; aggression 499–501, 507, 510, 544–7; authorised by UN Security Council 14; classification of 115–17; non-international 9; self-defence 65–7
war crimes 5, 11, 18, 34, 86, 113–24, 495–6, 503–4, 506, 507; grave breaches of Geneva Conventions 113–15; internal conflicts 120–4; international armed conflict war crimes 117–20; International Criminal Court (ICC) and 547; superior orders defence 56–61, 504–5, 549; see also humanity, crimes against
War Crimes Commission 62
Warbrick, C 528–9
Wilhelm II, Kaiser 496, 545
Wolfsberg Principles 16
World Bank 284–5
World Conference on Human Rights 1993: Vienna Declaration and Programme of Action 231

Yugoslavia: genocide in 141–9, 513; Roma people 165; see also International Criminal Tribunal for the Former Yugoslavia (ICTY)

Learning Resources
Centre